EU Competition Law and Intellectual Property Rights

EU Competition Law and Intellectual Property Rights

The Regulation of Innovation

Second Edition

Steven Anderman
Hedvig Schmidt

OXFORD
UNIVERSITY PRESS

Great Clarendon Street, Oxford OX2 6DP

Oxford University Press is a department of the University of Oxford.
It furthers the University's objective of excellence in research, scholarship, and education by publishing worldwide in

Oxford New York

Auckland Cape Town Dar es Salaam Hong Kong Karachi Kuala Lumpur Madrid Melbourne Mexico City Nairobi New Delhi Shanghai Taipei Toronto

With offices in

Argentina Austria Brazil Chile Czech Republic France Greece Guatemala Hungary Italy Japan Poland Portugal Singapore South Korea Switzerland Thailand Turkey Ukraine Vietnam

Published in the United States
by Oxford University Press Inc., New York

First published 2011

British Library Cataloguing-in-Publication Data
Data available

Library of Congress Cataloging-in-Publication Data
Data available

Typeset by Glyph International, Bangalore, India
Printed in Great Britain
on acid-free paper by
CPI Antony Rowe, Chippenham, Wiltshire

ISBN 978–0–19–958996–8

1 3 5 7 9 10 8 6 4 2

Contents

TABLES OF CASES ix
TABLES OF LEGISLATION AND RELATED INSTRUMENTS xxiii
LIST OF ABBREVIATIONS xxix

PART I: INTRODUCTION

1. General Introduction 3
   1.1 EU Competition Law as a System of Regulation of Intellectual Property Rights 3
   1.2 Competition Policy and Intellectual Property Rights: The Innovation Policy Context 11
2. The Relationship Between Intellectual Property Rights and Competition Law under the Treaty 17
   2.1 Introduction 17
   2.2 Grant and 'Existence' 20
   2.3 Permitted and Prohibited Exercise of Intellectual Property Rights 21
   2.4 The Objectives of the Rules on Competition in the Treaty 25
   2.5 Effective Competition 25
   2.6 The Goal of Fair Competition 27
   2.7 The Goal of Integration 29

PART II: ARTICLE 102 AND INTELLECTUAL PROPERTY RIGHTS

3. Article 102 and Intellectual Property Rights 33
4. The Relevant Market and Intellectual Property Rights 37
   4.1 Introduction 37
   4.2 The Relevant Product Market 38
   4.3 The Relevant Geographic Market 53
5. The Concept of Dominance and Intellectual Property Rights 57
   5.1 Introduction 57
   5.2 Dominance and Intellectual Property Rights 58
   5.3 The Methods of Assessing Dominance 59
   5.4 Dominance, Intellectual Property Rights, and Barriers to Entry 63
   5.5 A Note on Ordinary and Special Dominance 64

6. THE CONCEPT OF ABUSE AND INTELLECTUAL PROPERTY RIGHTS 73

6.1 The Expansion of the Concept of Abuse under Article 102 from Exploitative to Exclusionary Conduct 75
6.2 The Expanded Concept of Abuse and Restrictions on Intellectual Property Rights 85

7. REFUSALS TO SUPPLY AND LICENSE AND INTELLECTUAL PROPERTY RIGHTS 93

7.1 Refusals to Supply: The Court of Justice and Commission 93
7.2 From Refusal to Supply to Refusal to License: The Commission Decisions 98
7.3 *Magill* and the 'Exceptional Circumstances' Test 102
7.4 Refusals to Continue to License or Supply Interface Information on an 'Aftermarket' 109
7.5 The *Microsoft* Case in Europe and 'Exceptional Circumstances' 111
7.6 Competition and IP Remedies 119
7.7 The Pricing of Compulsory Licensing 120

8. TYING 127

8.1 Introduction 127
8.2 The EU Courts' Approach to Tying in Case Law 130
8.3 Tying and Intellectual Property Rights 142

9. EXCESSIVE PRICING AND INTELLECTUAL PROPERTY RIGHTS 143

9.1 Introduction 143
9.2 Article 102(a) Generally 145
9.3 Article 102(a) and Intellectual Property Rights 150
9.4 Dual Markets, Intellectual Property Rights, and Unfair Pricing 154
9.5 Collecting Societies and Excessive Pricing 155
9.6 Conclusion 159

10. EXCLUSIONARY PRICING POLICIES: DISCRIMINATORY PRICING, REBATES, AND DISCOUNTS 161

10.1 Discriminatory Pricing 161
10.2 Conditional Rebates in a Single Market 174

11. EXCLUSIONARY PRICING: PREDATORY PRICING AND MARGIN SQUEEZE 189

11.1 Predatory Pricing 189
11.2 Margin Squeeze 194

PART III: ARTICLE 101 AND INTELLECTUAL PROPERTY LICENSING IN A MODERNIZED SETTING

12. Introduction: Intellectual Property Rights Licensing and Competition Policy Generally 201

12.1 Introduction 201
12.2 The Modernization of EU Law Applicable to IP Licensing Agreements 203
12.3 The New Analytical Tools Provided by the New *More* Economic Approach 207

13. The Structure of Article 101 TFEU and IP Licensing Agreements 213

13.1 Introduction 213
13.2 The Process of Exemption under Article 101(3) TFEU 215
13.3 Article 101(2) TFEU And Unenforceability 217
13.4 The Clearance of IP Licensing Agreements under Article 101(1) TFEU 218

14. The Judicial Concept of Restriction of Competition and IPR Licensing 233

14.1 Introduction 233
14.2 Judicial Authority before Modernization 234
14.3 The Scope of the Patent Doctrine and Restriction on Competition 235
14.4 The *Consten and Grundig* Judgment 236
14.5 The Commission's Change of Policy 238
14.6 The Court of Justice's Application of the Appreciability Test to Intellectual Property Rights 242

15. The Technology Transfer Block Exemption Regulation and Technology Transfer Agreement Guidelines 251

15.1 Introduction: The Evolution of EU Competition Policy towards IP Licensing Agreements 251
15.2 The Current Phase 255
15.3 The Main Features of the New Technology Transfer Regulation and Guidelines 257
15.4 The New Methods of Assessing Individual Restraints in Licensing Agreements outside the Safe Harbour of the TTBER 266

16. The Regulation of Territorial Restraints in Intellectual Property Right Licensing Agreements under Article 101 TFEU 273

16.1 Introduction 273
16.2 Exemptible Exclusive Territoriality 274
16.3 Field of Use Restrictions 278

17. The Regulation of Non-Territorial Restraints in Licensing Agreements 279
17.1 Introduction 279
17.2 Non-Territorial Restraints which are Non-Restrictive of Competition 280
18. Technology Pools, Industrial Standards, and TTBER 291
18.1 Introduction 291
18.2 Stage 1: The Product Formulation Stage 293
18.3 Stage 2: The Creation of the Standard and the Selection of Essential Patents 294
18.4 Stage 3: Licensing Out 296
18.5 The FRAND Commitments 297
18.6 The Legal Framework for Technology Pools and Standardization Agreements 298
18.7 Technology Pools, TTBER, and Guidelines 300
18.8 The Competition Concerns and the Creation of the Pool 300
18.9 The Assessment of Individual Restraints 302
18.10 The Institutional Framework Governing the Pool 303
18.11 Conclusions 304
19. Remedies 307
19.1 Introduction 307
19.2 Remedies Applied to Article 102 Cases 309
19.3 Article 101 Remedies 312
19.4 Commitment Decisions 315
19.5 Fines and Penalties 315
19.6 Conclusion 317
20. Conclusions 319
20.1 Introduction 319
20.2 Article 102 TFEU and IPRs 320
20.3 Article 101 TFEU and IPRs 324
20.4 Conclusion 326
Appendix 1: Excerpts from the Treaty on the Functioning of the European Union 329
Appendix 2: Commission Regulation (EC) No 772/2004 333
Bibliography 343
Index 351

Tables of Cases

European Union
Court of Justice

AB Volvo v Erik Veng (UK) Ltd (Case 238/87) [1988] ECR 6039; [1988] ECR 6211 .... 18, 20, 22–4, 44–6, 52–3, 61, 63, 65, 74, 78, 95–8, 102, 107, 109, 111, 122, 143, 151, 154

AEG Telefunken v Commission (Case 107/82) [1983] ECR 3151, [1983] 3 CMLR 325 220–1

Ahlström Oy v Commission (Wood pulp I—Wood Pulp Cartel) (Cases 89, 104, 114, 116, 117, and 125–9/85) [1988] ECR 5193; [1988] 4 CMLR 901 221

AKZO Chemie BV v Commission (Case 62/86) [1991] ECR I–3359, [1993] 5 CMLR 215 .... 26–8, 34, 60, 64, 74–5, 78–9, 90, 189–91, 193

Alsatel v Novasam (Case 247/86) [1988] ECR 5987 45

Basset v Société des auteurs, compositeurs et éditeurs de musique (SACEM) (Case 402/85) [1987] ECR 1747 .... 97, 172

Bayer AG & Machinenenfabrik Henneker v Heinz Süllhöfer, (Case 65/86) [1988] ECR 5249, [1990] 4 CMLR 182 289–90

BMW Belgium v Commission (Case 32/78) [1979] ECR 2435, [1980] 1 CMLR 370 220

Bodson v Pompes funèbres des régions libérées SA (Case 30/87) [1985] ECR 2479; [1989] 4 CMLR 984 219

British Airways plc v Commission (Case C-95/04P) [2007] ECR I–2331, [2007] 4 CMLR 22 .... 27, 75, 83, 85, 137, 162, 166, 178–80, 322

British Leyland plc v Commission (Case 226/84) [1986] ECR 3263, [1987] 1 CMLR 185 .... 145, 154

BRT v SABAM and Fonier (Case 127/73) [1974] ECR 313 .... 80, 156

Bundesverband der Arzneimittel-Importeure v Commission (Joined Cases C-2/01P and C-3/01) [2004] ECR I–23, [2004] 4 CMLR 653 221

Centrafarm BV and Adnaan De Peijper v Sterling Drug Inc (Case 15/74) [1974] ECR 1147, [1974] 2 CMLR 480 .... 21, 219

Centre Belge d'Etudes de Marché-Télémarketing (Case 311/84) [1985] ECR 3261, [1986] 2 CMLR 558 .... 50–1, 58, 66, 68, 80, 84, 89, 94, 101, 110, 113, 137

CICRA et Maxicar v Renault (Case 53/87) [1988] ECR 299, [1990] 4 CMLR 18, 44–5, 63, 74, 87, 122, 151, 154

Coditel v Ciné Vog Films (Coditel I) (Case 62/79) [1980] ECR 881, [1981] 2 CMLR 362 244–5
Coditel v Ciné Vog Films (Coditel II) (Case 262/81) [1982] ECR 3381, [1983] 1 CMLR 49 .... 6, 22, 214, 244–5, 320
Compagnie Maritime BelgeTransports SA v Commission (Cases C-395 and 396/ 96P) [2000] ECR I–1365, [2000] 4 CMLR 1076 .... 184, 193
Compagnie Royale Asturienne des Mines SA and Rheinzink GmbH v Commission (Cases 29 and 30/83) [1984] ECR 1679, [1985] 1 CMLR 688 .... 224, 229
Competition Authority v Beef Industry Development Society Ltd et al (Case C-209/07) [2008] ECR I–8637 .... 207, 225, 227, 231, 249, 325–6
Delimitis v Henninger Bräu AG (Case C-234/89) [1991] ECR I–935, [1992] 5 CMLR 210 .... 224, 229–30, 234
Deutsche Grammophon GmbH v Metro-SB-Grossmärkte GmbH (Case 78/70) [1971] ECR 487, [1971] CMLR 631 .... 21, 145, 214, 219
Erauw-Jacquéry Sprl v La Hesbognonne Société Coopérative (Case 27/87) [1988] ECR 1919 246–7
Establissements Consten SA & Grundig-Verkaufts-GmbH v Commission (Case 56 and 58/64) [1966] ECR 299, [1966] CMLR 418 .... 19–21, 24–5, 29–30, 214, 220, 224, 226–7, 234–8, 251, 268
Europemballage & Continental Can v Commission (Case 6/72) [1973] ECR 215, [1973] CMLR 199 .... 25, 34, 39, 59, 62, 74, 76, 78, 86, 89
Ford Werke AG & Ford of Europe Inc v Commission (Cases 228 and 229/82) [1985] ECR 2725, [1984] 1 CMLR 649 220
France Télécom SA v Commission, 2 April 2009, Case C-202/07 P 184, 191–4
GEMA (Gesellschaft für musikalische Aufführungs- und mechanische Vervielfältigungsrechte) v Commission (GEMA I) (Case 45/71) [1971] ECR 791 97
GEMA (Gesellschaft für musikalische Aufführungs- und mechanische Vervielfältigungsrechte) v Commission (GEMA II) (Case 125/78) [1979] ECR 3173 97
General Motors Continental NV v Commission (Case 26/75) [1976] ECR 1367, [1976] 1 CMLR 95 145–6
General Motors BV v Commission (Case C-551/03P) [2006] ECR I–3173 .... 224, 229
GlaxoSmithKline v Commission (Case C-501/06) [2009] ECR I–9291 .... 207, 216, 225, 231, 326
Gøttrup-Klim Grovvareforening v Dansk Landbrugs Grovvareselskab AmbA (Case C-250/92) [1994] ECR I–5641, [1996] 4 CMLR 191 229
Hilti AG v Commission (Case C-53/92P) [1994] ECR I–667, [1994] 4 CMLR 614 .... 3, 35–6, 41–3, 49, 52–3, 61–3, 73, 78–9, 128, 132–3, 135–7, 140, 142, 163, 166, 169, 181

Hoffmann-La Roche & Co AG v Commission (Case 102/77) [1978] ECR 1139 ... 6, 22, 24, 75, 79, 320
Hoffmann-La Roche & Co AG v Commission (Case 85/76) [1979] ECR 461, [1979] 3 CMLR 211 ... 33–5, 38–9, 57–9, 61–2, 76, 174–5
Hugin Kassaregister AB and Hugin Cash Registers Ltd v Commission (Case 22/78) [1979] ECR 1869, [1979] 3 CMLR 345 ... 35, 43, 52, 63
IBM v Commission (Case 60/81) [1981] ECR 2639, [1981] 3 CMLR 635 ... 66, 95
IHT Internationale Heiztechnik GmbH v Ideal-Standard GmbH (Case C-9/93) [1994] ECR I–2789 ... 214
IMS Health GmbH & Co OHG v NDC Health GmbH & Co KG (IMS) (Case C-418/01) [2004] ECR I–5039, [2004] 4 CMLR 1543 ... 3, 47, 52, 64, 73–4, 108–9, 114–18, 310
Istituto Chemioterapica Italiano SpA and Commercial Solvents Corp v Commission (Case 6 and 7/73) [1974] ECR 223, [1974] 1 CMLR 309 ... 34, 50, 58–9, 65–6, 76, 78, 80, 84, 89, 93–4, 97, 99–101, 104, 106, 110–11, 113, 118, 219, 308–9, 313
Italy v Commission (Case 13/63) [1963] ECR 165 ... 161
Kanal 5 Ltd, TV 4 AB v Föreningen Svenska Tonsättares Internationella Musikbyrå (STIM) upa (Case C-52/07) [2008] ECR I–9275 ... 158
Keurkoop v Nancy Kean Gifts (Case 144/81) [1982] ECR 2653, [1983] 2 CMLR 47 ... 20–1, 96
Langnese-Iglo v Commission (Case C-279/95P) [1998] ECR I–5609, [1998] 5 CMLR 933 ... 310, 313
Lucazeau v SACEM (Joined Cases 110, 241, and 242/88) [1989] ECR 2811, [1991] 4 CMLR 248 ... 97, 147, 156–8, 214
Masterfoods Ltd v HB Ice Cream Ltd (Case C-344/89) [2000] ECR I–11369, [2001] 4 CMLR 449 ... 140
Metro-SB Grossmärkte GmbH v Commission (no 1) (Case 26/76) [1977] ECR 1875, [1978] 2 CMLR 1 ... 26, 216
Miller v Commission (Case 19/77) [1978] ECR 131, [1978] 2 CMLR 334 ... 224
Ministère Public v Tournier (Case 395/87) [1989] ECR 2521, [1991] 4 CMLR 173 ... 80, 97, 147, 156–8
Musique Diffusion Française SA v Commission (Pioneer) (Cases 100–103/80) [1983] ECR 1825, [1983] 3 CMLR 221 ... 316
Nederlandsche Banden-Industrie Michelin v Commission (Michelin I) (Case 322/81) [1983] ECR 3461 ... 27, 33, 40, 54, 57, 60, 62, 69, 73, 75, 83, 174, 176, 179–80, 184
Nederlandse Federatieve Vereniging voor de Groothandel op Elektrotechnisch Gebied v Commission (Case C-105/04) [2006] ECR I–8725 ... 224
Nungesser v Commission (Case 258/78) [1982] ECR 2015, [1983] 1 CMLR 278 ... 229, 234, 242–3, 252, 268

Oscar Bronner GmbH & Co KG v Mediaprint Zeitungs-und-Zeitschriftenverlag GmbH & Co KG (Case C-7/97) [1998] ECR I–7791, [1999] 4 CMLR 112 .... 65, 107–8, 115
Oude Luttikhuis and Others v Verenigde Coöperatieve Melkindustrie (Case C-399/93) [1995] ECR I–4515 229
Parke Davis v Probel (Case 24/67) [1968] ECR 55, [1968] CMLR 47 .... 18–21, 25, 145, 150, 214
Portugal v EC Commission (Case C-163/99) [2001] ECR I–2613, [2002] 4 CMLR 1319 .... 164–5, 179
Pronuptia de Paris GmbH v Pronuptia de Paris Irmgard Schillgallis (Case 161/84) [1986] ECR 353, [1986] 1 CMLR 414 .... 221, 229, 234, 247–8
Radio Telefis Eireann (RTE) and Independent Television Publications Ltd (ITP) v Commission (Magill) (Case C-241 and 242/91P) [1995] ECR I–743, [1995] 4 CMLR 718 .... 18, 20, 24–5, 47, 49, 52–3, 58–9, 63, 65, 69–70, 77, 89, 93, 102–9, 113–14, 116–17, 119, 121, 308–10, 312
Remia BV and Verenigde Bedrijven Nutricia v Commission (Case 42/84) [1985] ECR 2545, [1987] 1 CMLR 1 .... 234, 248
SA Brasserie de Haecht v Consorts Wilkin Janssen (Case 23/67) [1967] ECR 407 .... 228, 230, 234
Sandoz (Case 227/87) [1990] ECR 145 220
Sirena Srl v Eda Srl (Case 40/70) [1971] ECR 3169, [1971] CMLR 260 .... 144, 153, 214
Société Technique Minière (STM) v Maschinenbau Ulm (Case 56/65) [1966] ECR 235; [1966] CMLR 357 .... 221–3, 225, 227–9, 242
Tetra Pak International SA v Commission (Tetra Pak II) (Case C-333/94P) [1996] ECR I–5951, [1997] 4 CMLR 662 .... 3, 55, 59, 73, 78, 90–1, 99, 128, 132, 135, 139–40, 142, 166, 190, 310
United Brands v Commission (Case 27/76) [1978] ECR 207, [1978] 1 CMLR 429 .... 27–8, 35, 37–40, 53, 57, 62, 64, 79–81, 100, 144, 146, 150, 156–7, 162–3, 165, 169–73, 316
Völk v Vervaecke (Case 5/69) [1969] ECR 295; [1969] CMLR 277 222–3
Walt Wilhelm v BundesKartelamnt (Case 14/68) [1969] ECR 1, [1969] CMLR 100 221
Windsurfing International Inc v Commission (Case 193/83) [1986] ECR 611, [1986] 3 CMLR 489 .... 235, 247, 288, 290
Zuiker Unie v Commission (Joined Cases 40 to 48, 50, 54 to 56, 111, 113, and 114/73) [1975] ECR 1663; [1976] 1 CMLR 295 .... 221, 226, 235

Court of Justice—Numerical table

Case 13/63 Italy v Commission [1963] ECR 165 161
Case 56 and 58/64 Establissements Consten SA & Grundig-Verkaufts-GmbH v Commission [1966] ECR 299, [1966] CMLR 418 .... 19–21, 24–5, 29–30, 214, 220, 224, 226–7, 234–8, 251, 268

Case 56/65 Société Technique Minière (STM) v Maschinenbau Ulm [1966] ECR 235; [1966] CMLR 357 ....221–3, 225, 227–9, 242
Case 23/67 SA Brasserie de Haecht v Consorts Wilkin Janssen [1967] ECR 407 .... 228, 230, 234
Case 24/67 Parke Davis v Probel [1968] ECR 55, [1968] CMLR 47 ....18–21, 25, 145, 150, 214
Case 14/68 Walt Wilhelm v BundesKartelamnt [1969] ECR 1, [1969] CMLR 100 221
Case 5/69 Völk v Vervaecke [1969] ECR 295; [1969] CMLR 277 222–3
Case 40/70 Sirena Srl v Eda Srl [1971] ECR 3169, [1971] CMLR 260 .... 144, 153, 214
Case 78/70 Deutsche Grammophon GmbH v Metro-SB-Grossmärkte GmbH [1971] ECR 487, [1971] CMLR 631 ....21, 145, 214, 219
Case 45/71 GEMA (Gesellschaft für musikalische Aufführungs- und mechanische Vervielfältigungsrechte) v Commission (GEMA I) [1971] ECR 791 97
Case 6/72 Europemballage & Continental Can v Commission [1973] ECR 215, [1973] CMLR 199....25, 34, 39, 59, 62, 74, 76, 78, 86, 89
Case 6 and 7/73 Istituto Chemioterapica Italiano SpA and Commercial Solvents Corp v Commission [1974] ECR 223, [1974] 1 CMLR 309....34, 50, 58–9, 65–6, 76, 78, 80, 84, 89, 93–4, 97, 99–101, 104, 106, 110–11, 113, 118, 219, 308–9, 313
Joined Cases 40 to 48, 50, 54 to 56, 111, 113, and 114/73 Zuiker Unie v Commission [1975] ECR 1663; [1976] 1 CMLR 295 .... 221, 226, 235
Case 127/73 BRT v SABAM and Fonier [1974] ECR 313 ....80, 156
Case 15/74 Centrafarm BV and Adnaan De Peijper v Sterling Drug Inc [1974] ECR 1147, [1974] 2 CMLR 480 ....21, 219
Case 26/75 General Motors Continental NV v Commission [1976] ECR 1367, [1976] 1 CMLR 95....145–6
Case 26/76 Metro-SB Grossmärkte GmbH v Commission (no 1) [1977] ECR 1875, [1978] 2 CMLR 1....26, 216
Case 27/76 United Brands v Commission [1978] ECR 207, [1978] 1 CMLR 429.... 27–8, 35, 37–40, 53, 57, 62, 64, 79–81, 100, 144, 146, 150, 156–7, 162–3, 165, 169–73, 316
Case 85/76 Hoffmann-La Roche & Co AG v Commission [1979] ECR 461, [1979] 3 CMLR 211....33–5, 38–9, 57–9, 61–2, 76, 174–5
Case 19/77 Miller v Commission [1978] ECR 131, [1978] 2 CMLR 334 224
Case 102/77 Hoffmann-La Roche & Co AG v Commission [1978] ECR 1139....6, 22, 24, 75, 79, 320
Case 22/78 Hugin Kassaregister AB and Hugin Cash Registers Ltd v Commission [1979] ECR 1869, [1979] 3 CMLR 345 ....35, 43, 52, 63
Case 32/78 BMW Belgium v Commission [1979] ECR 2435, [1980] 1 CMLR 370....220

Case 125/78 GEMA (Gesellschaft für musikalische Aufführungs- und mechanische Vervielfältigungsrechte) v Commission (GEMA II) [1979] ECR 3173 97
Case 258/78 Nungesser v Commission [1982] ECR 2015, [1983] 1 CMLR 278 .... 229, 234, 242–3, 252, 268
Case 62/79 Coditel v Ciné Vog Films (Coditel I) [1980] ECR 881, [1981] 2 CMLR 362 244–5
Cases 100–103/80 Musique Diffusion Française SA v Commission (Pioneer) [1983] ECR 1825, [1983] 3 CMLR 221 316
Case 60/81 IBM v Commission [1981] ECR 2639, [1981] 3 CMLR 635 .... 66, 95
Case 144/81 Keurkoop v Nancy Kean Gifts [1982] ECR 2653, [1983] 2 CMLR 47 .... 20–1, 96
Case 262/81 Coditel v Ciné Vog Films (Coditel II) [1982] ECR 3381, [1983] 1 CMLR 49 .... 6, 22, 214, 244–5, 320
Case 322/81 Nederlandsche Banden-Industrie Michelin v Commission (Michelin I) [1983] ECR 3461 .... 27, 33, 40, 54, 57, 60, 62, 69, 73, 75, 83, 174, 176, 179–80, 184
Case 107/82 AEG Telefunken v Commission [1983] ECR 3151, [1983] 3 CMLR 325 220–1
Cases 228 and 229/82 Ford Werke AG & Ford of Europe Inc v Commission [1985] ECR 2725, [1984] 1 CMLR 649 220
Cases 29 and 30/83 Compagnie Royale Asturienne des Mines SA and Rheinzink GmbH v Commission [1984] ECR 1679, [1985] 1 CMLR 688 .... 224, 229
Case 193/83 Windsurfing International Inc v Commission [1986] ECR 611, [1986] 3 CMLR 489 .... 235, 247, 288, 290
Case 42/84 Remia BV and Verenigde Bedrijven Nutricia v Commission [1985] ECR 2545, [1987] 1 CMLR 1 .... 234, 248
Case 161/84 Pronuptia de Paris GmbH v Pronuptia de Paris Irmgard Schillgallis [1986] ECR 353, [1986] 1 CMLR 414 .... 221, 229, 234, 247–8
Case 226/84 British Leyland plc v Commission [1986] ECR 3263, [1987] 1 CMLR 185 .... 145, 154
Case 311/84 Centre Belge d'Etudes de Marché-Télémarketing [1985] ECR 3261, [1986] 2 CMLR 558 .... 50–1, 58, 66, 68, 80, 84, 89, 94, 101, 110, 113, 137
Cases 89, 104, 114, 116, 117, and 125-9/85 A. Ahlström Oy v Commission (Wood pulp I—Wood Pulp Cartel) [1988] ECR 5193; [1988] 4 CMLR 901 221
Case 402/85 Basset v Société des auteurs, compositeurs et éditeurs de musique (SACEM) [1987] ECR 1747 .... 97, 172
Case 62/86 AKZO Chemie BV v Commission [1991] ECR I–3359, [1993] 5 CMLR 215 .... 26–8, 34, 60, 64, 74–5, 78–9, 90, 189–91, 193
Case 65/86 Bayer AG & Machinenenfabrik Henneker v Heinz Süllhöfer, [1988] ECR 5249, [1990] 4 CMLR 182 289–90

Case 247/86 Alsatel v Novasam [1988] ECR 5987 45
Case 27/87 Erauw-Jacquéry Sprl v La Hesbognonne Société Coopérative [1988] ECR 1919, ... 246–7
Case 30/87 Bodson v Pompes funèbres des régions libérées SA [1985] ECR 2479; [1989] 4 CMLR 984 219
Case 53/87 CICRA et Maxicar v Renault [1988] ECR 299, [1990] 4 CMLR 18, 44–5, 63, 74, 87, 122, 151, 154
Case 227/87 Sandoz [1990] ECR 145 220
Case 238/87 AB Volvo v Erik Veng (UK) Ltd [1988] ECR 6039; [1988] ECR 6211 .... 18, 20, 22–4, 44–6, 52–3, 61, 63, 65, 74, 78, 95–8, 102, 107, 109, 111, 122, 143, 151, 154
Case 395/87 Ministère Public v Tournier [1989] ECR 2521, [1991] 4 CMLR 173 .... 80, 97, 147, 156–8
Joined Cases 110, 241, and 242/88 Lucazeau v SACEM [1989] ECR 2811, [1991] 4 CMLR 248 .... 97, 147, 156–8, 214
Case C-234/89 Delimitis v Henninger Bräu AG [1991] ECR I–935, [1992] 5 CMLR 210 .... 224, 229–30, 234
Case C-344/89 Masterfoods Ltd v HB Ice Cream Ltd [2000] ECR I–11369, [2001] 4 CMLR 449 140
Case C-241 and 242/91P Radio Telefis Eireann (RTE) and Independent Television Publications Ltd (ITP)v Commission (Magill) [1995] ECR I–743, [1995] 4 CMLR 718 .... 18, 20, 24–5, 47, 49, 52–3, 58–9, 63, 65, 69–70, 77, 89, 93, 102–9, 113–14, 116–17, 119, 121, 308–10, 312
Case C-53/92P Hilti AG v Commission [1994] ECR I–667, [1994] 4 CMLR 614 .... 3, 35–6, 41–3, 49, 52–3, 61–3, 73, 78–9, 128, 132–3, 135–7, 140, 142, 163, 166, 169, 181
Case C-250/92 Gøttrup-Klim Grovvareforening v Dansk Landbrugs Grovvareselskab AmbA [1994] ECR I–5641, [1996] 4 CMLR 191 229
Case C-9/93 IHT Internationale Heiztechnik GmbH v Ideal-Standard GmbH [1994] ECR I–2789 214
Case C-399/93 Oude Luttikhuis and Others v Verenigde Coöperatieve Melkindustrie [1995] ECR I–4515 229
Case C-333/94P Tetra Pak International SA v Commission (Tetra Pak II) [1996] ECR I–5951, [1997] 4 CMLR 662 .... 3, 55, 59, 73, 78, 90–1, 99, 128, 132, 135, 139–40, 142, 166, 190, 310
Case C-279/95P Langnese-Iglo v Commission [1998] ECR I–5609, [1998] 5 CMLR 933 .... 310, 313
Cases C-395 and 396/96P Compagnie Maritime BelgeTransports SA v Commission [2000] ECR I–1365, [2000] 4 CMLR 1076 .... 184, 193
Case C-7/97 Oscar Bronner GmbH & Co KG v Mediaprint Zeitungs-und-Zeitschriftenverlag GmbH & Co KG [1998] ECR I–7791, [1999] 4 CMLR 112 .... 65, 107–8, 115

Case C-163/99 Portugal v EC Commission [2001] ECR I–2613, [2002] 4 CMLR 1319 .... 164–5, 179
Joined Cases C-2/01P and C-3/01 Bundesverband der Arzneimittel-Importeure v Commission [2004] ECR I–23, [2004] 4 CMLR 653 221
Case C-418/01 IMS Health GmbH & Co OHG v NDC Health GmbH & Co KG (IMS) [2004] ECR I–5039, [2004] 4 CMLR 1543 .... 3, 47, 52, 64, 73–4, 108–9, 114–18, 310
Case C-551/03P General Motors BV v Commission [2006] ECR I–3173 .... 224, 229
Case C-95/04P British Airways plc v Commission [2007] ECR I–2331, [2007] 4 CMLR 22 .... 27, 75, 83, 85, 137, 162, 166, 178–80, 322
Case C-105/04 Nederlandse Federatieve Vereniging voor de Groothandel op Elektrotechnisch Gebied v Commission [2006] ECR I–8725 224
Case C-501/06 GlaxoSmithKline v Commission [2009] ECR I–9291 .... 207, 216, 225, 231, 326
Case C-52/07 Kanal 5 Ltd, TV 4 AB v Föreningen Svenska Tonsättares Internationella Musikbyrå (STIM) upa [2008] ECR I–9275 158
Case C-202/07P France Télécom SA v Commission, 2 April 2009 .... 184, 191–4
Case C-209/07 Competition Authority v Beef Industry Development Society Ltd et al [2008] ECR I–8637 .... 207, 225, 227, 231, 249, 325–6

General Court/Court of First Instance

AstraZeneca v Commission, (Case T-321/05) (1 July 2010) 3, 8, 48, 60–1, 324
Atlantic Container Line AB v Commission (Case T-395/94) [2002] ECR II–875, [2002] 4 CMLR 1008 313–14
Automec Srl v Commission (Auromec II) (Case T-24/90) [1992] ECR II–2223, [1992] 5 CMLR 431 313
Bayer AG v Commission (Case T-41/96P) [2000] ECR II–3383, [2001] 4 CMLR 126 221
British Airways v Commission (Case 219/99) [2003] ECR II–5917, [2004] 4 CMLR 1008 .... 55, 64, 75, 137–8, 178–80
Clearstream v Commission (Case T-301/04) [2009] ECR II–3155 162
Compagnie Maritime Belge Transport (Joined Cases T-24/93, T-25/93, T-26/93, and T-28/93) [1996] ECR II–1201, [1997] 4 CMLR 273 184
Der Grüne Punkt-Duales System Deutschland GmbH (DSD) v Commission (Case T-151/01) [2007] ECR II–1607 .... 151–2, 181
Deutsche Telekom AG v Commission (Case T-271/03) [2008] ECR II–477 .... 82, 194, 196–8, 323
European Night Services (ENS) v Commission (Cases T-374, 375, 384, and 388/94) [1998] ECR II–3141, [1998] 5 CMLR 718 .... 55, 224, 229
France Telecom SA (formerly Wanadoo Interactive SA) v Commission (Case T-340/03) [2007] ECR II–107 .... 184, 191–4

Hilti AG v Commission (Case T-30/89)[1991] ECR II–1439, [1992] 4 CMLR 16 .... 3, 35–6, 41–3, 49, 52–3, 61–3, 73, 78–9, 128, 132–3, 135–7, 140, 142, 163, 166, 169, 181
Industrie des Poudres Spheriques (IPS) v Commission (Case T-5/97) [2000] ECR II–3755, [2001] 4 CMLR 1020 .... 149–50, 195–6
International Confederation of Societies of Authors and Composers (CISAC) v Commission (Case T-442/08) (Case pending) 158
Società Italiana Vetro SpA, Fabbrica Pisana SpA and PPG Vernante Pennitalia SpA v Commission (Italian Flat Glass) (Cases T-68, 77, and 78/89) [1992] ECR II–1403, [1992] 5 CMLR 302 33
Langnese-Iglo and Schöller Lebensmittel GmbH & Co. KG v Commission (Case T-7 and 9/93) [1995] ECR II–1533, [1995] 5 CMLR 602 .... 310, 313
Manufacture Française des Pneumatiques Michelin v Commission (Michelin II) (Case T-203/01) [2003] ECR II–4071, [2004] 4 CMLR 923 .... 54, 64, 83, 85, 174, 176–9, 184
Micro Leader Business v Commission (Case T-198/98) [1999] ECR II–3989, [2000] 4 CMLR 886 .... 148, 163
Microsoft v Commission (Microsoft I) (Case 201/04) [2007] ECR II–3601 .... 3, 8, 47, 49, 65, 70, 73, 77, 79, 81, 84–5, 111, 114, 116, 119, 127–9, 131–2, 134–5, 137–8, 141, 198, 308, 312, 321
O2 (Germany) GmbH & Co v Commission (Case T-328/03) ECR II–1231; [2006] 5 CMLR 5 .... 207, 225, 228, 231
RTE, ITP, BBC v Commission (Magill) (Cases T-69, 70, and 76/89) [1991] ECR II–485 .... 3–4, 18, 20–1, 24–5, 34–6, 45, 47, 49, 52–3, 58–9, 63, 65, 69–70, 73–4, 77, 86, 89, 93, 102, 105–9, 113–14, 116–19, 121, 308–10, 312
Soda Ash-Solvay et Cie v Commission (Case T-30/91) [1995] ECR II–1775 163
Tetra Pak Rausing SA v Commission (Tetra Pak I) (Case T-51/89) [1990] ECR II–309, [1991] 4 CMLR 334 .... 3, 33, 49, 62–3, 73–4, 78, 86, 98, 128, 190
Tetra Pak International SA v Commission (Tetra Pak II) (Case T-83/91) [1994] ECR II–755, [1997] 4 CMLR 726 .... 43, 55, 128, 133, 137, 139–40, 142, 166–7, 171, 190–1
Tiercé Ladbroke v Commission (Case T-504/93) [1997] ECR II–923, [1997] 5 CMLR 309 107
VGB and Others v Commission (Case T-77/94)[1997] ECR II–759 229
Viho Europe BV v Commission (Case T-102/92) [1995] ECR II–117, [1997] 4 CMLR 469 220

General Court/Court of First Instance—Numerical table

Case T-30/89 Hilti AG v Commission [1991] ECR II–1439, [1992] 4 CMLR 16 .... 3, 35–6, 41–3, 49, 52–3, 61–3, 73, 78–9, 128, 132–3, 135–7, 140, 142, 163, 166, 169, 181

Case T-51/89 Tetra Pak Rausing SA v Commission (Tetra Pak I) [1990] ECR II–309, [1991] 4 CMLR 334 .... 3, 33, 49, 62–3, 73–4, 78, 86, 98, 128, 190
Cases T-68, 77, and 78/89 Società Italiana Vetro SpA, Fabbrica Pisana SpA and PPG Vernante Pennitalia SpA v Commission (Italian Flat Glass) [1992] ECR II–1403, [1992] 5 CMLR 302 33
Cases T-69, 70, and 76/89 RTE, ITP, BBC v Commission (Magill) [1991] ECR II–485 .... 3–4, 18, 20–1, 24–5, 34–6, 45, 47, 49, 52–3, 58–9, 63, 65, 69–70, 73–4, 77, 86, 89, 93, 102, 105–9, 113–14, 116–19, 121, 308–10, 312
Case T-24/90 Automec Srl v Commission (Auromec II) [1992] ECR II–2223, [1992] 5 CMLR 431 313
Case T-30/91Soda Ash-Solvay et Cie v Commission [1995] ECR II–1775 163
Case T-83/91 Tetra Pak International SA v Commission (Tetra Pak II) [1994] ECR II–755, [1997] 4 CMLR 726 .... 43, 55, 128, 133, 137, 139–40, 142, 166–7, 171, 190–1
Case T-102/92 Viho Europe BV v Commission [1995] ECR II–117, [1997] 4 CMLR 469 220
Case T-7 and 9/93 Langnese-Iglo and Schöller Lebensmittel GmbH & Co. KG v Commission [1995] ECR II–1533, [1995] 5 CMLR 602 .... 310, 313
Joined Cases T-24/93, T-25/93, T-26/93, and T-28/93 Compagnie Maritime Belge Transport [1996] ECR II–1201, [1997] 4 CMLR 273 184
Case T-504/93 Tiercé Ladbroke v Commission [1997] ECR II–923, [1997] 5 CMLR 309 107
Case T-77/94 VGB and Others v Commission [1997] ECR II–759 229
Cases T-374, 375, 384, and 388/94 European Night Services (ENS) v Commission [1998] ECR II–3141, [1998] 5 CMLR 718 .... 55, 224, 229
Case T-395/94 Atlantic Container Line AB v Commission [2002] ECR II–875, [2002] 4 CMLR 1008 313–14
Case T-41/96P Bayer AG v Commission [2000] ECR II–3383, [2001] 4 CMLR 126 221
Case T-5/97 Industrie des Poudres Spheriques (IPS) v Commission [2000] ECR II–3755, [2001] 4 CMLR 1020 .... 149–50, 195–6
Case T-198/98 Micro Leader Business v Commission [1999] ECR II–3989, [2000] 4 CMLR 886 .... 148, 163
Case 219/99 British Airways v Commission [2003] ECR II–5917, [2004] 4 CMLR 1008 .... 55, 64, 75, 137–8, 178–80
Case T-151/01 Der Grüne Punkt-Duales System Deutschland GmbH (DSD) v Commission [2007] ECR II–1607 .... 151–2, 181
Case T-203/01 Manufacture Française des Pneumatiques Michelin v Commission (Michelin II) [2003] ECR II–4071, [2004] 4 CMLR 923 .... 54, 64, 83, 85, 174, 176–9, 184
Case T-271/03 Deutsche Telekom AG v Commission [2008] ECR II–477 .... 82, 194, 196–8, 323

Case T-328/03 O2 (Germany) GmbH & Co v Commission ECR II–1231; [2006] 5 CMLR 5 .... 207, 225, 228, 231
Case T-340/03 France Telecom SA (formerly Wanadoo Interactive SA) v Commission [2007] ECR II–107 .... 184, 191–4
Case 201/04 Microsoft v Commission (Microsoft I) [2007] ECR II–3601 .... 3, 8, 47, 49, 65, 70, 73, 77, 79, 81, 84–5, 111, 114, 116, 119, 127–9, 131–2, 134–5, 137–8, 141, 198, 308, 312, 321
Case T-301/04 Clearstream v Commission [2009] ECR II–3155 162
Case T-321/05 AstraZeneca v Commission, (1 July 2010) 3, 8, 48, 60–1, 324
Case T-442/08 International Confederation of Societies of Authors and Composers (CISAC) v Commission (Case pending) 158

Commission

Adalat-Bayer [1996] 5 CMLR 416 220
Alpha Flight Services/Aéroports de Paris OJ [1998] L 230/10, [2001] 4 CMLR 611 164
AstraZeneca Commission decision 15 June 2005, COMP/A.37.507/F3 .... 48, 61
BBI/Boosey & Hawkes: Interim Measures [1987] OJ L286/36, [1988] 4 CMLR 67 .... 95, 100
Bendix/Ancien Ets. Mertons & Strae 1 June 1964 5 OJ EC 1496 (1964) 226
Boussois/Interpane OJ [1987] L50/30 .... 281, 288
British Midland/Aer Lingus [1992] OJ L 96/34, [1993] 4 CMLR 596 99
Brussels National Airport (Zaventem) [1995] OJ L 216/8, [1996] 4 CMLR 232 164
BUMA and SAMBA [2005] OJ C200/5 315
Burroughs-Delplanque OJ EC L13/50 (1972); [1972] CMLR D 67 .... 239, 281
Burroughs-Geha-Werke OJ L13/53 (1972) 239
CISAC Commission decision, Case COMP/C2/38.698 [2008] OJ C 323/12 158
Clearstream Commission decision, Case COMP/38.096, [2005] 5 CMLR 1302, ... 162
Coca-Cola Undertaking [2005] OJ L253/21 and Commission decision COMP/A.39.116/B2-Coca-Cola 128–9
Commission v Solvay and La Porte [1985] 1 CMLR 481 219
Crehan v Courage [2001] 5 CMLR 1058 217
Decca Navigation Systems [1990] 4 CMLR 627 99
Delta Chemie/DDD [1989] 4 CMLR 535 .... 247, 281–2, 286
Deutsche Post AG Commission decision, COMP/35.141, [2001] OJ L125/27 191
Deutsche Post AG-Interception of cross-border mail Commission decision OJ [2001] L 331/40, [2002] 4 CMLR 598 .... 148, 165
Deutsche Telekom Commission decision of 21 May 2003, [2003] OJ L 263/9, [2004] 4 CMLR 790 194–6
Digital undertaking, XXVIIth Report on Competition Policy 1997, and Commission Press Release IP/97/868 .... 128, 136, 181, 315

Distillers Company Limited [1978] OJ 50/16 230
Duales System Deutschland AG (DSD) [2001] OJ L166/1, [2001] 5 CMLR 609 .... 151–2, 181
ECS/AKZO Commission decision [1985] OJ L 374/1, [1986] 3 CMLR 273 189–90
Eurofix-Bauco/Hilti, OJ (1988) L 65/19, Case IV/30.787 .... 128, 132, 135–7, 140, 181
Europort AIS v Denmark [1993] CMLR 457, Commission decision 101
IBM Personal Computer EC Comm. December 84/233 (1984) 51, 110
IBM Undertaking, 1984 OJ L 118/24 .... 110–12, 129, 311, 315
ICI v Solvay OJ L 152/21 [1991 .... 49, 175
Ilmailuaitos/Luftfartsverket (Finnish Airports) [1999] OJ L 69/24, [1999] 5 CMLR 90 164
Intel Commission decision of 13 May 2009 (D (2009) 3726 final), COMP/37.990 .... 8, 55, 59, 64, 70, 73, 88, 181–6, 316
Irish Continental Group v CCI Morlaix [1995] 5 CMLR 177 101
Johnson and Johnson [1981] 2 CMLR 287 219
London European/Sabena [1988] OJ L 317/47, [1989] 4 CMLR 662 99
Magill TV Guide/ITP, BBC, and RTE, Re (Commission decision 89/205) (1989) OJ L 78/43, [1989] 4 CMLR 757 308–9
Merck v Prime Crown [1997] 1 CMLR, 83 18
Michelin II [2001] OJ L143/1, [2002] 5 CMLR 388 .... 54, 64, 83, 85, 174, 176–9, 184
Microsoft 1999 Commission's XXIXth Report on Competition Policy (1999), points 55-6 314
Microsoft, Commission decision of 12 July 2006, [2008] OJ C 138/10 316
Microsoft, Commission decision of 27 February 2008 [2009] OJ C 166/20 317
Microsoft, Commission Press Release IP/94/653, [1994] 5 CMLR 143 315
Microsoft I [2005] 4 CMLR 965, COMP/C-3/37.792 .... 61, 73, 111, 127–9, 132–4, 136–8, 140, 308, 311–12
Microsoft IP (94) 643 [1994] 5 CMLR 143 110
Microsoft (tying) (COMP/C-3/39.530) [2009] OJ C242/20 .... 129, 315
Moosehead/Whitbread [1991] 4 CMLR 391 286
Napier Brown/British Sugar Commission decision 88/519/EEC, 1988 OJ L284 .... 137–8, 196
NDC Health/IMS Health: Interim measures, Case COMP D3/38.044 [2002] OJ L59/18, [2002] 4 CMLR 111 310
Nestle/Perrier [1993] 4 CMLR M17 33
Polypropylene [1986] OJ L230/1, [1988] 4 CMLR 34 219
Prokent-Tomra Commission decision, OJ C 219, 28 August 2008, COMP/E-1/38.113 181
Rambus Commission decision 9 December 2009, COMP/38.636 .... 8–9, 48, 61, 63, 291, 295

Reuter/BASF [1976] 2 CMLR D44 ... 248
Rich Products/Jus Rol [1988] 4 CMLR 527 ... 247, 286
Scandlines Sverige v Port of Helsingborg COMP/36.568 [2006] 4 CMLR 1298 ... 74, 143, 149–51
Sega and Nintendo, Commission's XXVIIth Report on Competition Policy (1997), point 80 ... 314
Spanish Airports [2000] OJ L 208/36 ... 164
Steel Beams Commission decision 94/215, OJ L116, 1994; [1994] 5 CMLR 353 ... 310
Tetra Pak II Commission decision 92/163, OJ L72, 18 March 1992, [1992] 4 CMLR 55 ... 128, 135, 190
Vaassen/Moris [1979] OJ L19/32, [1979] 1 CMLR 511 ... 131, 289
Vacuum Interrupters [1977] 1 CMLR D 67 ... 221
Velcro/Aplix [1989] 4 CMLR 157 ... 247
Virgin/British Airways Commission decision OJ L 30/1, [2000] 4 CMLR 999 ... 164, 178–9
Wanadoo Interactive Commission decision of 16 July 2003, COMP/38.233 ... 184, 191–4
Welded Steel Mesh [1989] OJ L260/1, [1990] 4 CMLR 13 ... 312–13

Other

New Zealand

Telecom Corporation of New Zealand v Clear Communication Ltd [1995] 1 NZLR 385 ... 123–4

United Kingdom

Catnic Components Ltd and another v Hill & Smith Ltd [1983] FSR 512 (Ch Patents Ct) ... 122
Napp Pharmaceutical Holdings Ltd v Director General of Fair Trading [2002] CAT 1, CompAR 13 ... 148
Nokia Corporation v Interdigital Technology Corporation [2007] EWHC 3077 ... 294

United States

Berkey Photo, Inc v Eastman Kodak Co. 603 F 2d 263, 274 n. 12 (2d Cir. 1979) ... 143
Brook Group Ltd v Brown and Williamson Tobacco Group 405 US 209 (1993) ... 190
Brunswick Corporation v Riegel Textile Corporation 752 F 2d 261 (7th Cir, 1984) ... 8
Dell Computer Corp, in re 121 FTC 616 (1996) ... 295
EBay Inc v MercExchange LLC, 126 S Ct 1837 (2006) ... 8
Handguards, Inc v Ethicon Inc 601 F 2d 986 (9th Cir, 1979) ... 8

Illinois Tool Work Inc v Independent Ink Inc 547 US 1 (2006) 136
International Salt Co v United States, 332 U.S. 392, (1947).................................... 136
Morton Salt Co v. G. S. Suppiger Co 314 US 488 (1941).. 240
Pacific Bell v linkLine Communications Inc, 555 U.S. (2009)................................ 196
Rambus Inc v FTC 522 F 3d 456 CADC 2008.. 295
United States v Loew's Inc 371 US 38, 83 S. Ct. 97, 9 L.Ed.2d 11 (1962) 46......... 136
United States v Microsoft Corp 147 F 3d 935 (D.C. Cir. 1998) (US Microsoft II)... 141
United States v Microsoft Corp 253 F 3d 34 (D.C. Cir. 2001) (US Microsoft III) 129, 131, 135
United States v United States Gypsum Co 333 US 364 (1947)................................ 240
Verizon Communications Inc v Law Offices of Curtis Trinko 540 U.S. 398 (2004) 143, 196
Walker Process Equipment Inc v Food Machinery & Chemical Corp 382 US 172... 8

Tables of Legislation and Related Instruments

European Union

Ordered by category of instrument (those with the greatest/most direct legal force first: Treaties, Regulations, Directives, Recommendations, Commission Notices). Regulations and Directives are ordered by date of adoption, the remainder alphabetically.

Treaties/Statutes, etc.

EC Treaty
- Art 2 17
- Art 3 17
- Art 3a 17
- Art 3(f) 89
- Art 3(g) 17–18, 26, 34

Statute of the Court of Justice,
- Art 51 42

Treaty on the Functioning of the European Union
- Art 2 18
- Art 34 19–22
- Arts 34–37 18
- Art 36 .... 18, 20, 23
- Art 101 .... 3–4, 6, 9–11, 15–22, 24–7, 29–30, 33, 35, 37–8, 50, 55, 80, 82–3, 89, 99, 101, 120, 127, 131, 138, 140, 158, 167, 199–327
- Art 101(1) 19–20, 29–30, 204, 212–31, 233–7, 239–49, 263–4, 266–8, 270–1, 274–6, 279–82, 285–90, 299, 301–2, 307
- Art 101(1)(a)–(e) 236
- Art 101(1)(e) 127
- Art 101(2) 217–18, 231, 248, 307
- Art 101(3) 29–30, 80, 82, 131, 203–6, 212, 215–18, 227, 231, 234, 237–8, 240–2, 247, 254–6, 263, 265, 268–9, 271, 275–7, 279, 283, 285, 287–90, 299, 301, 303–5, 307, 313, 323, 326
- Art 102 .... 4–5, 8–11, 15–29, 31–198, 204, 215, 219, 222, 253, 283, 292, 295–6, 298, 307–10, 313, 315–16, 319–24, 326–7
- Art 102(a) 23, 34, 97–8, 107, 121, 143–55, 159, 321
- Art 102(a)–(d) 97
- Art 102(b) 23–4, 27, 34, 77, 89, 95, 97, 104, 106, 109, 113, 116, 118, 120–1, 124
- Art 102(c) 23, 34, 88–9, 94, 107, 113, 155, 161–9, 171–3
- Art 102(d) 23, 34, 106–7, 127, 129, 133, 137–40, 142
- Art 345 19

Regulations

Regulation 17/62 .... 94, 254, 307, 309, 312
- Art 3 309
- Art 4(2) 264

Commission Regulation (EC) No 240/96 on technology transfer Agreements 206, 253–4
- Recital 6 252
- Recital 20 282
- Art 1(1) 252
- Art 2 314
- Art 2(1)(3) 282
- Art 5(1)(4) 252

Commission Regulation (EC) No 2790/1999 of 22 December 1999 on the application of Article 81(3) of the Treaty to categories of vertical agreements and concerted practices 254
Commission Regulation (EC) No 2658/2000 of 29 November 2000 on the application of Article 81(3) of the Treaty to categories of specialisation agreements 254
Commission Regulation (EC) No 2659/2000 on the application of Article 81(3) of the Treaty to categories of research and development..............254, 292, 298
Council Regulation (EC) No 1/2003 on the implementation of the rules on competition laid down in Articles 81 and 82 of the Treaty 82, 94, 205, 223, 254–5, 265, 307–8, 315
Recital 4....................................... 205
Recital 12..................................... 308
Recitals 1–3 307
Art 2... 82
Art 5... 205
Art 6... 205
Art 7(1) 308
Art 8... 308
Art 9.....................................308, 315
Art 9(2) 315
Art 17... 147
Art 23(2) 316
Art 24(1)(a).................................. 316
Council Regulation (EC) No 139/2004 of 20 January 2004 on the control of concentrations between undertakings (Merger Regulation).................. 10, 17–18, 37, 53, 202, 308, 323
Art 2... 26
Art 2(1)(b) 82
Commission Regulation (EC) No 772/2004 of 27 April 2004 on the application of Article 81(3) of the Treaty to categories of technology transfer agreements (Technology Transfer Block Exemption Regulation—TTBER) 6, 38, 40, 131, 203–6, 209–12, 217–18, 230–1, 233, 251, 255–66, 268–71, 275–7, 282–7, 289, 291, 293–308, 314, 325–6
Recital 12..................................... 207
Recitals 10–12 206
Art 1.......................................255, 259
Art 1(1)(b) 257–8
Art 1(1)(c) and (d)........................ 271
Art 1(1)(h) 257
Art 1(j)(i) 259
Art 1(j)(i) and (ii)......................... 209
Art 1(j)(ii) 210, 259–60
Art 2... 258
Art 2(1) 281
Art 2(1)(7)(a) 287
Art 3......................206, 208, 210, 260
Art 3(1) 263
Art 3(3) 261
Art 4......................212, 230, 260, 275
Art 4(1) 271
Art 4(1)(a)...........................263, 288
Art 4(1)(b) 263–4, 271, 278
Art 4(1)(c)............................264, 278
Art 4(1)(d) 264, 288
Art 4(2) 264, 268
Art 4(2)(b) 264, 276, 278
Art 4(3) 260, 262, 269
Art 4(d) 283
Art 5......................................231, 265
Art 5(1)(a).................................... 284
Art 5(2) 283
Art 6... 265
Art 6(1)(b) 266
Art 7... 266
Art 8... 206

Regulation (EC) No 717/2007 of the European Parliament and of the Council of 27 June 2007 on roaming on public mobile telephone networks within the Community 147
Commission Regulation (EU) No 330/2010 of 20 April 2010 on the application of Article 101(3) of the Treaty on the Functioning of the European Union to categories of vertical agreements and concerted practices (Vertical Block Exemption Regulation)......... 131, 204, 217, 283

Directives

Council Directive 91/250/EEC of 14 May 1991 on the legal protection of computer programs 120
Directive 2009/24/EC of the European Parliament and of the Council of 23 April 2009 on the legal protection of computer programs (Computer Programs Directive) 13, 106, 119–20
Recital 17...................................... 120
Art 1 120
Art 6......................................120, 324

Recommendation

Commission Recommendation 2003/361/EC concerning the definition of micro, small and medium sized enterprises 29

Commission Notices

Agreements of Minor Importance 29, 35, 223
Contractors and Subcontractors [1979] 1 CMLR 264 239
Definition of relevant market for the purposes of Community competition law..................38–9, 48
para 8 53
paras 28–30..................................... 53
paras 44–52..................................... 53
Guidance on the Commission's Enforcement Priorities in Applying Article 82 EC Treaty to Abusive Exclusionary Conduct by Dominant Undertakings (Brussels, 3 December 2008)................................127, 129, 134–5, 149, 161, 181, 183–4, 193–4
paras 5–6... 85
paras 19–20..............................83, 322
para 22 322
para 23 194
para 26 193
para 28 140
para 29 82
para 45 162
para 50 131
para 51 ....53, 132, 134
para 53 138
para 61 ....49, 82
para 62 ....135, 191
para 63 193
para 64 193
para 65 193
para 74 194
para 75 198
para 82 198
para 89 198
Guidelines on the application of Article 81 of the EC Treaty to technology transfer agreements (TTA Guidelines) 6, 40, 83, 131, 194, 203–6, 208, 212, 217–18, 230–1, 234, 249, 255–6, 258, 260–3, 266–71, 275–6, 278–80, 283–5, 290, 292, 297, 300–5

Guidelines on the application of Article 81 of the EC Treaty to technology transfer agreements (TTA Guidelines) (*Cont.*)
paras 3–6 206
para 8 256
para 9 .... 202, 205, 325
paras 11–12 266
paras 13–18 59
para 17 .... 202, 205, 325
paras 17–18 207
paras 19–25 208
para 20 208
para 21 208
para 22 47
para 24 .... 210, 259
para 25 .... 71, 208
para 27 209
para 28 261
para 29 .... 261, 267
para 31 .... 210, 259–60, 262–3, 269
para 32 .... 261, 271
para 33 262
para 37 207
para 41 258
para 42 258
para 44 258
para 51 258
para 53 258
paras 65–73 206
para 68 262
para 74 263
paras 79–80 263
paras 82–83 263
para 84 264
para 101 265
paras 107–116 265
para 109 283
para 111 284
para 131 271
para 132 266
para 155 .... 267, 280
para 156 .... 263, 287–8
para 158 288
para 159 287
para 160 289
para 163 275
paras 164–165 266
para 165 275
para 170 276
para 172 276
para 174 276
para 175 263
paras 175–177 277
para 179 278
para 193 286
para 195 286
para 204 214
paras 204–210 290
para 210 .... 214, 300
para 214 300
para 219 301
para 220 301–2
para 222 302
para 224 .... 302, 305
para 225 302
para 226 .... 303, 305
para 227 303
para 229 303
para 230 305
para 231 304
para 232 304
para 234 304
para 235 304
para 1040 289
Guidelines on the Application of EEC Competition Rules in the Telecommunications Sector, 91 121
Guidelines on the effect on trade concept, 2004 222
Guidelines on the method of setting fines imposed pursuant to Article 23(2)(a) of Regulation No 1/2003, 1 September 2006 316

Guidelines on Vertical Restraints, 19 May 2010 .... 131, 204, 217, 253, 260, 283
Guidelines to the Applicability of Article 81 of the EU Treaty to Horizontal Cooperation Agreements 292, 298–300, 304
para 19 322
para 64 299
para 67 299
para 163 299
Immunity from fines and reduction of fines in cartel cases, 2006 316

Germany

Act against Restraints of Competition
s 20(1) 235

United States

Antitrust Guidelines for the Licensing of Intellectual Property 46, 205, 252, 257, 262, 326
Fair Trade Act
s 5 295
National Cooperative Research (and Production) Act NCRPA 15 USCA S.4302 294
Sherman Act
s 2 .... 8, 71, 143, 147, 295

List of Abbreviations

AAC	Average avoidable cost
ATC	Average total cost
AVC	Average variable cost
BERs	Block Exemption Regulations
CAT	Competition Appeal Tribunal
CJEU/Court of Justice	Court of Justice of the European Union
Commission	European Commission
CMLR	Common Market Law Reports
CML Rev	Common Market Law Review
Court of Appeals DC Cir./CA DC Cir.	United States Court of Appeals for the District of Columbia Circuit
DoJ	US Department of Justice
DRAMS	Dynamic Random Access Memory Chips
EEC	European Economic Community
EC	European Community
EC Treaty	European Community Treaty
ECLR	European Competition Law Review
ECR	European Court Reports
EEC	European Economic Community
EIPR	European Intellectual Property Review
EL Rev	European Law Review
ETSI	European Telecommunications Standard Institute
EU	European Union
EU Courts	General Court and Court of Justice of the European Union
F 2d, F 3d	Federal Reporter (Federal Court of Appeals Cases)
F. Supp.	Federal Supplement (Federal District Court Cases)
Fordham Corp Law Inst	Fordham Corporate Law Institute
Fordham Int'l LJ	Fordham International Law Journal
FRAND	Fair, Reasonable, and Non-Discriminatory
FTC	US Federal Trade Commission
GC	General Court of the European Union
Harv Law Rev	Harvard Law Review
ICLQ	International and Comparative Law Quarterly
IIC	International Review of Industrial Property and Copyright Law
IP	Intellectual Property
IPR	Intellectual Property Right

J. Competition L. & Econ.	Journal of Competition Law and Economics
LRAIC	Long-Run Average Incremental Costs
MLR	Modern Law Review
Minn Law Rev	Minnesota Law Review
Notre Dame L Rev	Notre Dame Law Review
NZLR	New Zealand Law Reports
OECD	Organisation for Economic Co-operation and Development
OEM	Original Equipment Manufacturer
OFT	Office of Fair Trading
OFTEL	Office of Telecommunications–superseded by Ofcom (Office of Communications) in 2003
OJ	Official Journal of the European Union (Official Journal of the European Communities prior to 1 February 2003)
Ox Yrbk in Eur Law	Yearbook in European Law, Oxford University Press
R&D	Research and Development
SIEC	Significant Impediment of Effective Competition
SLC	Substantial Lessening of Competition
SSNIP	Small but significant non-transitory increase in price
SSO	Standard Setting Organization
TFEU	Treaty of the Functioning on the European Union/ Lisbon Treaty
TTA Guidelines	Guidelines on the application of Article 81 of the EC Treaty [now Article 101 of the TFEU] to technology transfer agreements
TTBER	Transfer of Technology Block Exemption Regulation
UKCLR	United Kingdom Competition Law Reports
UMTS	Universal Mobile Telecommunications Systems
US	United States, United States Report
USC	United States Code
US Licensing Guidelines	'Antitrust Guidelines for the Licensing of Intellectual Property' 6 April 1995. Issued by the US Dept of Justice and Federal Trade Commission, <http://www.justice.gov/atr/public/guidelines/0558.htm>

Part I

INTRODUCTION

1

GENERAL INTRODUCTION

1.1 EU Competition Law as a System of Regulation of Intellectual Property Rights 3
1.2 Competition Policy and Intellectual Property Rights: The Innovation Policy Context 11

1.1 EU COMPETITION LAW AS A SYSTEM OF REGULATION OF INTELLECTUAL PROPERTY RIGHTS

In recent years EU competition law has continued to demonstrate its capacity to regulate the exercise of IPRs. In *Magill*[1] and *IMS*[2] the Court of Justice (or CJEU) confirmed that in exceptional circumstances the European Commission has the power to end an abusive refusal to license by imposing a compulsory copyright licence. In *Microsoft*,[3] the General Court (GC) upheld the Commission's decision to order compulsory access of interface codes protected by IPRs on the basis that Microsoft's refusal impeded technological progress in the sector. These have added weight to the case law of the Court of Justice holding that the EU competition rules may be used as the basis to prevent IPR owners from acquiring competitor firms with similar technology,[4] using aggressive discounting and pricing schemes,[5] and engaging in tie-ins or 'product bundling'.[6]

The reach of the competition rules has been widened still further by recent cases in the pharmaceutical industry involving cases of misuse of the patent system as an abuse of

[1] C-241–2/91P *Radio Telefis Eireann v Commission (Magill)* [1995] ECR I–743, [1995] 4 CMLR 718.

[2] C-418/01 *IMS Health GmbH & Co. OHG v NDC Health GmbH & Co. KG* [2004] 4 CMLR 1543.

[3] Case T-201/04 *Microsoft Corp v Commission* [2007] ECR II–3061. Note that we use the term 'General Court' to describe decisions of the Court of First Instance (now the General Court).

[4] See eg Case T-51/89 *Tetra Pak Rausing SA v Commission* (*Tetra Pak I*) [1990] ECR II–309, [1991] 4 CMLR 334.

[5] See eg C-333/94 *Tetra Pak International SA v Commission* (*Tetra Pak* II) [1996] ECR I–5951, [1997] 4 CMLR 662; see also Case COMP/C-3/37.990—*Intel* Commission Decision of 13 May 2009, D (2009) 3726 final.

[6] Ibid. See also T-30/89 *Hilti v Commission* [1991] ECR II–1439, [1992] 4 CMLR 16; T-201/04 *Microsoft v Commission*.

dominance,[7] as well as suggesting a capacity to infringe Article 101 of the Treaty on the Functioning of the European Union (TFEU) with 'reverse' or 'delay' payment settlement agreements, both devices aiming to prevent the entrance of generics into existing markets.[8] The field of standard setting and technology pools has attracted the attention of the competition authorities not only because of cases of patent ambush[9] and FRAND (Fair, Reasonable and Non-Discriminatory) ambush[10] but also because of competition concerns with the selection and licensing of patented technologies in industrial standard setting activities. These forms of collaboration amongst competitors, as well as that of licensing collection societies, have been examined by the European Commission under Article 101 as well as Article 102 TFEU. Finally, the modernization of Article 101 TEU has produced new detailed guidelines and block exemptions for R&D and specialization agreements and IP licensing agreements in the form of technology transfers.

This pattern of competition law enforcement is a vivid reminder that the competition rules have evolved to create a 'second tier' of regulation of the exercise of IPRs, providing an 'external' system of regulation that applies to anti-competitive conduct not prevented by the 'internal' system of regulation offered by IP legislation.[11] IPR specialists have argued that IPR legislation and EU competition law should be viewed as of equal weight and status under EU law, or even that EU competition law should defer to IPR legislation in the interests of innovation.[12] The thinking behind such arguments was that IPRs offered a major contribution to innovation owing to the reward/incentives to inventors and creators provided by the grant of exclusive rights. Moreover, the system of protection of IPRs balances the exclusivity granted to 'pioneer' inventors and creators with the limits and exceptions in favour of 'follow on' innovators.

However, the limits of permitted exercise of IPRs are drawn not only by the laws of IP but also by reference to the rules of competition law. The case law suggests that when certain forms of exercise of IPRs are characterized as anti-competitive or restrictive of competition, they can be unlawful even if they are perfectly lawful under the IP laws. In that sense the exercise of the exclusivity rights of IPRs is subject to the competition rules as well as to the limits and exceptions created by the IP rules.

The reasons for this hierarchy are now fairly clear. The IP legislative system co-exists with other forms of legal regulation of markets such as competition law. At one

[7] Case T-321/05 *AstraZeneca v Commission*, 1 July 2010. See also the recent *Bohringer* case being investigated by the Commission to determine whether Bohringer misused patents to exclude competitors.

[8] European Commission, *Pharmaceutical Sector Inquiry Final Report* (8 July 2009) (*Sector Inquiry Report*), available at: <http://ec.europa.eu/competition/sectors/pharmaceuticals/inquiry/communication_en.pdf>.

[9] EC Notice on Acceptance of Commitments in *Rambus* case IP/09/1897 (9 December 2009).

[10] See 'Antitrust: Commission welcomes IPCom's public FRAND declaration MEMO/09/549' (10 December 2009) (IPCom's role in the UMTS pool after its belated acceptance that it was bound by its predecessor's commitment to a FRAND licence of its essential patents).

[11] See I. Rahnasto, *Intellectual Property Rights, External Effects and Antitrust Law* (Oxford: OUP, 2002).

[12] See eg I. Govaere, *The Use and Abuse of Intellectual Property Rights in EC Law* (London: Sweet & Maxwell, 1996). See also Advocate Gulman's argument in C-241–2/91P *Magill op cit* n 1; A. Reindl, 'Intellectual Property and Intra-Community Trade' [1996] *Fordham Corp Law Inst* 453.

point, the exercise of intellectual rights was thought to be subject to the competition law rules owing to the central role of competition law in the EU Treaty and the national character of IP laws. However, as IPRs have increasingly become Community-wide laws, it is clear that there is a more fundamental reason for this hierarchy between the two systems. Although the IP laws themselves are a public law system designed to regulate market behaviour, once an individual obtains the grant of an IPR, that right is a private property right. Its exercise is therefore subject to all the public law rules that regulate private property rights in markets including the competition rules.

Consequently, the outer limits of the exclusive rights of IPRs are determined by the prohibitions of the competition rules even when the conduct is allowed by the IP laws. The full extent to which IP owners can enjoy the exercise of their IPRs untrammelled by the competition rules can only be understood by a better appreciation of the internal logic of the competition rules.

A closer look at the EU competition rules makes it clear that, while they offer no general immunity to the exercise of IPRs, they do make significant concessions or accommodations in recognition of the unique nature of IPRs and their contribution to the process of innovation. The competition rules make some limited special concessions, requiring, for example, a showing of 'exceptional circumstances' before a remedy of compulsory licence of an IPR can be obtained, but perhaps as importantly, the design of their general rules seems almost customized to leave room for the 'normal' exercise of IPRs and to focus on the extreme cases where their exercise happens to coincide with abusive conduct or restrictions of competition.

The reasons for this are not far to seek. In the first place, there is a natural overlap in the aims of the two fields of law. The exclusive rights created by IP laws provide an incentive to inventors to create substitute products within markets and new products which establish new markets. Similarly, IP licensing is a vehicle to enlarge exploitation of protected technologies and thereby create a wider diffusion of the new technology which either creates new markets or brings substitutes to existing markets. Finally, the internal rules of IP legislation prevent copying but in fact encourage 'competition by substitution' between follow on innovators and pioneer innovators.[13] They do this both by offering exceptions to exclusive rights such as 'experimental use in patent law' and 'fair use' in copyright law during the period of protection and informational benefits to innovation during the period of protection as well as after the period of protection has expired. And of course, if there is weak market power associated with an IPR, its capacity to impose a restraint on competition or a barrier to entry is limited or non-existent.

Moreover, the legal framework of competition policy has become more economically sophisticated, creating a better basis for an accommodation to the exercise of IPRs within the competition rules. The modern approach to abuse of dominance under Article 102 involves a much more careful assessment of the actual market power of the

[13] A phrase originally coined by H. Ullrich and mentioned by J. Drexl in 'Is there a More Economic Approach to Intellectual Property and Competition Law?' in J. Drexl (ed), *Research Handbook on Intellectual Property and Competition Law* (Cheltenham, UK, Northampton, MA, USA: Edward Elgar, 2008).

legal monopolies conferred by patents and industrial copyright. These legal 'monopolies' are now assessed entirely on the basis of their *de facto* market power.

There were periods in the past, in both the USA and the EU, when the legal monopoly conferred by a patent in the form of a right to exclude anyone else from exploiting the patented invention was presumed to coincide with market power. This led to judicial and administrative competition rules which paid inadequate attention to the effects of IPRs upon investment in R&D and innovation. This historical presumption has finally been replaced by a more appropriate judicial and administrative understanding that the actual market power associated with an IPR must be assessed empirically in each case.

Moreover, a new and more realistic economic approach has been introduced into the block exemption regulations and guidelines under Article 101 TFEU, reducing much of the substantive burden of regulation on IP licensing agreements between non-competitors as well as R&D joint ventures and standardization agreements. The new Technology Transfer Block Exemption Regulation (TTBER) provides a 'safe harbour' and the Technology Transfer Agreements Guidelines (TTA Guidelines) offer *inter alia* a new methodology to apply Article 101 TFEU to IP licensing agreements outside the safe harbour of the TTBER. This focuses regulation more carefully upon agreements in which the IP owning parties have or achieve real market power, and upon agreements between competitors, thus significantly lessening the effect of the competition rules upon licensing agreements between non-competitors. In both areas the 'external tier' of regulation provided by the competition rules of the Treaty is actually designed to be less interventionist.

A final crucial factor is that the competition rules do not apply to the exercise of IPRs as such. They only apply when the IPR is used as an 'instrument of abuse'[14] or as a means of restricting competition.[15]

Nevertheless, in recent years IPRs have been associated with commercial strategies that have been used to block innovation by blocking competition and this conduct has infringed the competition rules. The actual number of confrontations between the owners of IPRs and the competition authorities has been on the increase. Why has this been so? What accounts for this increase in regulatory confrontations when the overall framework has become more nuanced? Not surprisingly, the answer can be found in both sides of the equation: the conduct of the regulated and the actions of the regulator. As corporations have developed a greater understanding of the book value of their IP assets, they have been finding more imaginative uses for their IPRs within their corporate strategies as well as adopting more rigorous enforcement policies. On the other hand, it can be seen that regulatory authorities have adapted their techniques for measuring market power and defining abuse in response to recent developments in commercial practice involving IPRs.

[14] Case 85/76 *Hoffman-La Roche v Commission* [1979] ECR 461, [1979] 3 CMLR 211, para 51.

[15] See eg Case 262/81 *Coditel SA v Cine-Vog Films (Coditell II)* [1982] ECR 3381 at para 14.

1.1.1 The new commercial strategies

As corporations have developed a greater understanding of the value of their corporate intangible assets and have given a more realistic book value to those assets, they have been finding more imaginative uses for IPRs within their overall commercial strategies as well as pursuing more rigorous enforcement policies. Many of these strategies have occurred in a form that is legitimate profit taking and a lawful adaptation of commercial practice to commercial realities. An example of this is the strategic decision of Qualcomm to concentrate on research-only IPRs and derive its income from royalties from licensing out of its CDMA wireless technology and other patents.[16] This breaks with the strategy of R&D and patenting for the purpose of manufacturing and distribution and causes demands for higher royalty rates but is a legitimate exercise of entrepreneurial imagination. Another strategy increasingly adopted by firms is to acquire wide patent portfolios. In the microprocessing sector, the emphasis on the acquisition of patent portfolios has been motivated by the defensive concern to have sufficient bargaining chips when negotiating cross-licences or pre-empting claims of infringement.[17] In other sectors, such as telecoms, patents proliferate as part of the process of creating new technology standards. Further, in pharmaceuticals, strategic patenting involves patent 'flooding' as part of a wider strategy of staving off competition from generic competitors during the period of patent protection as well as offering competition during the post-protection years. The aim of the portfolio is to create a defensive wall around the core protected technology. These strategies undoubtedly have the purpose and/or effect of 'raising rivals costs'.[18] For example . . . 'a firm may create an array of patents on marginal or even non-existent innovations, knowing that other firms will either have to invent around the patents or else litigate their validity'. [19] Further 'in a dynamically competitive market . . . the abuse of IP that reduces rivals' incentives to innovate may lessen innovation competition'.[20] Nevertheless, not all such activity by IP owners will be viewed as anti-competitive.

For example, some patent flooding may cause 'patent thickets' and thereby deter innovation but this practice will not itself attract the attention of the competition authorities unless it is allied with some form of bundling and tying conduct or mandatory package licensing. Similarly, some attempts to concentrate on research-only

[16] See 'Antitrust: Commission closes formal proceedings against Qualcomm', MEMO/09/516 (24 November 2009). <http://europa.eu/rapid/pressReleasesAction.do?reference=MEMO/09/516> (last accessed 5 July 2010).

[17] See Carl Shapiro, 'Navigating the Patent Thicket: Cross Licences, Patent Power and Standard Setting' in A. Jaffe, J. Lerner, and S. Stern (eds), *Innovation and the Economy* (National Bureau of Economics, 2001).

[18] D. Rubinfeld and R. Maness, 'The Strategic Use of Patents; Implications for Antitrust' in F. Leveque and H. Shelanski, *Antitrust, Patents and Copyright EU and US Perspectives* (Cheltenham, UK, Northampton, MA, USA: Edward Elgar, 2000).

[19] H. Hovenkamp, *Federal Antitrust Policy: The Law of Competition and its Practice* (St. Paul, Minnesota: West Publishing Co, 1994), p 286.

[20] D. Rubinfeld and R. Maness, n 18 above.

patenting may be designed to raise royalty rates both within and outside technology pools but this is normally not an offence under the competition rules unless some form of patent or FRAND ambush is involved. Further, the excesses of 'patent trolling' may have occasionally resulted in widespread condemnation and alterations to the IP rules.[21] However, they have not necessarily been viewed as prohibited conduct under the competition rules. Moreover, even when patent enforcement strategies move from enforcing valid patents to enforcing known invalid patents,[22] there may be a fraud on the Patent Office but the result may not necessarily involve a breach of competition law.[23] Overall, a considerable amount of aggressive and imaginative commercialization of IPRs has long proved to be essentially compatible with 'competition on the merits' under the competition rules.

On the other hand, a number of new commercial practices by IP owners have been caught as prohibited exclusionary or exploitative abuses under the competition rules. The *Microsoft*[24] case highlights the sensitivity of the competition authorities to vertical integration strategies aimed at capturing 'aftermarkets' by incumbent dominant firms in the information technology sector. The *Intel* case[25] reminds of the limits to dominant firms engaging in anti-competitive discounting designed to create exclusivity in primary markets. The *AstraZeneca* case[26] raises the issue of when a misuse of the patent process amounts to a violation of Article 102 TFEU. The emergence of strategic attempts to obtain greater than FRAND royalties through patent ambush[27] and FRAND ambush[28] in the context of patent pools and industrial standards has awakened the interest of the competition authorities to the possibility of anti-competitive aspects of those processes.

This competition interest has not only spread within the field of unilateral action but has been extended to various forms of bilateral and multilateral cooperation between competitors. The reverse payment settlements in the pharmaceutical sector have raised competition issues in the conduct of the pharmaceutical firms directed against competition by

[21] See eg *EBay Inc v MercExchange LLC*, 126 S Ct 1837 (2006).

[22] See *Walker Process Equipment Inc v Food Machinery & Chemical Corp* 382 US 172 (1965); see also *Handguards, Inc v Ethicon Inc* 601 F 2d 986, 996 (9th Cir, 1979) which gave rise to a series of similar cases.

[23] See eg *Brunswick Corporation v Riegel Textile Corporation* 752 F 2d 261 (7th Cir, 1984) in which Judge Richard Posner distinguished between a fraudulent procurement of an invalid patent in circumstances that create market power and the theft of a perfectly valid patent which only shifted the patent monopoly into different hands. He stated that the first type of fraud on the Patent Office, fraudulent procurement, could be a violation of s 2 Sherman Act until unmasked or cancelled, whereas the second, theft of a patent, '. . . has no antitrust significance or consumer interest because antitrust law is designed to protect the process of competition and not to promote the welfare of particular competitors.' Judge Posner specified three conditions for such a violation: (i) the patent must dominate a real market; (ii) the invention sought to be patentable must not be patentable; and (iii) the patent must have some colourable validity, conferred by the patentee's efforts to enforce it by bringing patent infringement suits.

[24] Case T-201/04 *Microsoft Corp v Commission* [2007] ECR II–3061.

[25] Case COMP/37.990 *Intel* Commission decision of 13 May 2009 (D (2009) 3726 final) ('*Intel*').

[26] Case T-321/05 *AstraZeneca v Commission* (Judgment of the General Court dated 1 July 2010).

[27] EC Notice on Acceptance of Commitments in Case IP/09/1897 *Rambus* (9 December 2009).

[28] See 'Antitrust: Commission welcomes IPCom's public FRAND declaration' MEMO/09/549 (10 December 2009).

generic producers. Even before the *Rambus* case, the competition authorities had shown an interest in regulating the process of standard setting and R&D joint ventures and that interest is currently intensifying. Finally there has been a renewed interest by the European Commission in collective licensing.[29]

The key feature of all these confrontations and investigations is the fact that the IP is used either as a component of market power or as a suspected instrument of the abuse in the chosen commercial strategy that leverages the dominance into abusive conduct or uses the IPR as an integral feature of a restrictive licensing agreement or a restrictive form of collaboration between competitors. In the event, the competition rules in most cases have not been applied to the exploitation of the IPR alone; they have more often applied to the IPR used as a means within a wider strategic effort. Hence, despite the accommodations and the appreciation of the real market power of IPRs, the competition authorities have been drawn into a wider range of cases of anti-competitive conduct by IP owners.

The first purpose of this book is to demonstrate how both under the Treaty and as a matter of competition *policy*, the general norms of EU competition law provide a set of outer limits to the exploitation and licensing of IPRs by IP owners which can override their entitlements under IPR legislation. It shows how in defining the borderline between permitted and prohibited conduct by IP owners, the case law of the EU Courts and the decisions of the Commission create a framework of rules which regulates the exercise of IPRs in the interests of existing effective competition which fosters innovation in its own way.

The book argues that the key to understanding the way this happens is to appreciate how the exercise of IPRs is viewed within the logic of EU competition law. Hence the book is designed to explain in a systematic way how each of the competition rules adapts its role to the exercise of IPRs. There is a dramatic variation in the way in which the individual prohibitions of the competition rules treat the strategic use of IPRs. Thus, the concept of abuse under Article 102 when applied to IPRs requires evidence of 'exceptional circumstances' for certain abuses, whereas at the stage of defining dominance there is little evidence of special treatment of IPRs. Indeed, the assessment of the contribution of the IPRs to market power can sometimes seem magnified. Under Article 101 we have a different story. The overall effect of modernization and a more economic approach generally has been to reduce the burden of regulation of IP licensing. Moreover, in some micro-rules of regulation of clauses in IP licences, there is evidence of special treatment of IPRs.

By identifying the existing ground rules in EU competition law which are relevant for its regulation of IPRs, and the basis upon which they are generated, the book can provide a useful template of the rules of EU competition law. Any true understanding of this template requires an appreciation of the differences between the case law that

[29] Commission Press Release, 'Antitrust: Commission prohibits practices which prevent European collecting societies offering choice to music authors and users' IP/08/1165.

forms the legal framework and the policy generated by the Commission within its own area of expertise. To what extent does Commission policy operate within the parameters established by the legal rules? The competition authorities have a margin of appreciation in which they make their decisions on a policy basis. This can be seen in the limited review of Commission decisions by the GC and the points of law decided in the judgments of the Court of Justice. Yet there are outer limits to the Commission's freedom of policy choice established by the legal rules. The Commission may propose its own priorities of enforcement but in any case that is appealed, these priorities will be tested against the constraints imposed by the judgments of the EU Courts. This dimension of competition policy—the interplay between competition policy and competition law—will be emphasized throughout this book.

An understanding of this template will also require some adaptation to the different types of IPR as well as to new technologies supported by IP protection not yet regulated by EU competition law in the form of block exemptions, such as computer programs[30] and telecommunications.[31] For example, it is striking that much of the case law regulating compulsory licences concerns industrial copyright. It will require a good understanding of patent law to work out how these rules apply to the exercise of patent rights.

The book has a second aim, to make some assessment of the 'interface' between EU competition law and IPRs in the light of the established criteria of modern competition policies relating to IPRs. It makes use, in particular, of the criterion that the rules of EU competition policy should be designed and applied to minimize its interference with the process of IPR exploitation and the incentives it offers to investment in innovation while effectively pursuing competition policy objectives. By assessing the role of competition policy in the light of this criterion, the book will provide a background to the conflicting views of line drawing by regulators.

This second edition of the book captures EU competition law in a state of change. The modernization of Article 101 and the introduction of a more economic approach to Article 101 and the Merger Regulation[32] have produced considerable improvements in regulation and this has led to calls for a more economic approach to Article 102 as well. In response, the Commission has produced a Discussion Paper,[33] an Economists' Report,[34] and a Guidance Paper to Enforcement Priorities, which in the Commission's own words, sets out 'an economic and effect-based approach to exclusionary abuse'

[30] See eg J. Derbyshire, 'Computer Programs, and Competition Policy' [1994] 9, *EIPR* 374; J. Hendricks, 'The Information Technology Revolution: The Next Phase' [1995] *Fordham Corp Law Inst* 549.

[31] See eg H. Ungerer, 'EU Competition Law in the Telecommunications, Media and Information Technology Area' [1995] *Fordham Corp Law Inst* 465; T. Ramsay, 'The EU Commission's Use of the Competition Rules in the Field of Telecommunications: A Delicate Balancing Act' [1995] *Fordham Corp Law Inst* 561.

[32] Council Regulation (EC) No 139/2004 of 20 January 2004 on the control of concentrations between undertakings, OJ L 24, 29 January 2004, pp 1–22.

[33] DG Competition, Commission 'DG Competition discussion paper on the application of Article 82 of the Treaty to exclusionary abuses' (Brussels, December 2005). (<http://ec.europa.eu/competition/antitrust/art82/discpaper2005.pdf>).

[34] EAGCP, 'An Economic Approach to Article 82', July 2005 (<http://ec.europa.eu/comm/competition/publications/studies/eagcp_july_21_05.pdf>).

under Article 102.[35] However, this book suggests that it may be a mistake to assume that the move to a more economic policy by the Commission generally will have as great an impact on Article 102's concept of abuse of a dominant position. By looking at the values that underpin the Treaty article as interpreted by the CJEU and GC it seems clear that there are serious obstacles to a reinterpretation of the normative thrust of that Article. The decision to shift interpretation of 'abuse' towards a more economic approach lies ultimately with the EU Courts and although the Commission may have applied an effect-based approach in its recent cases, such as *Microsoft*, the EU Courts have so far not indicated a strong interest in pursuing this approach.

This book does not attempt to cover the entire field of EU competition law and IPRs. Instead, it concentrates upon two main areas of interest: Article 102 and the regulation of the conduct of dominant firms in technology and product markets (Part II); and Article 101 and licensing agreements (Part III). Before looking at these two fields, it is necessary to examine in greater detail the relationship between competition policy and IPRs in two contexts: the innovation policy context (next section) and in the context of the EU Treaty (Chapter 2).

1.2 COMPETITION POLICY AND INTELLECTUAL PROPERTY RIGHTS: THE INNOVATION POLICY CONTEXT

Many, if not most, legal systems today monitor the exercise of IPRs within the framework of their competition policies.[36] Even though the exercise of IPRs is already extensively regulated by IP legislation,[37] as we have seen, an extra tier of regulation is added by competition law to ensure that the grant of exclusivity by IP legislation is not misused by being incorporated into cartels and market sharing arrangements or monopolistic practices which deny access to markets.

In this second tier of regulation, competition authorities attempt to balance the aim of preserving effective competition on markets with the aim of IPR legislation to reward investment in innovation. This is not a case of competition versus innovation. Some economists building on the reward/incentives theory of IPRs contend that IPRs are the primary drivers of innovation and that competition policy fails to give adequate recognition to the long-term benefits of IPR incentives to innovation. They argue that the competition rules may actually stand in the way of long-term innovation because they concentrate upon the current state of competition on markets.

[35] Commission website 'Article 82 Review' (<http://ec.europa.eu/competition/antitrust/art82/index.html>) (accessed 17 November 2010).

[36] See eg S. Anderman (ed), *The Interface between Intellectual Property and Competition Law* (Cambridge, UK: Cambridge University Press, 2007).

[37] See eg W. Cornish and D. Llewellyn, *Intellectual Property: Patents, Copyright, Trade Marks and Allied Rights* (7th edn, London: Sweet & Maxwell, 2010); L. Bently and B. Sherman, *Intellectual Property* (Oxford: OUP, 2008); H. MacQueen, C. Waelde, and G Laurie, *Contemporary Intellectual Property: Law and Policy* (Oxford: OUP, 2008).

However, this may misrepresent the type of innovation theory that is embodied both in the EU competition law rules *and* in the IP rules. The EU competition rules are actually designed to stimulate innovation but the means they favour is to foster existing effective competition in markets. Existing effective competition, it is thought, creates the pressures on firms that promotes innovation. It has sometimes been called the 'stick' approach to innovation. Yet the 'carrot' theory of innovation in the IP rules has also been subject to some misrepresentation. It is not purely an inducement to 'pioneer' inventors and creators[38]; it is also an inducement to 'follow on' innovation and the internal rules of IP law contain an elaborate balance between the rights of these two sources of innovation.

1.2.1 The internal balance in the IP rules

There is some evidence that the grant of an exclusive right for a limited period of time to the inventor to exploit the invention is a necessary incentive for investment in R&D and innovation in some important sectors of the economy.[39] Whilst not a guarantee, it offers the prospects of a reward to the inventor because it reduces the risk that free riders can devalue the investment in R&D and provides an opportunity for the IPR owner to recoup investments at a higher level than would have been the case in a fully competitive market. IPR licensing helps by offering an opportunity for exploitation in situations where the inventor has insufficient means to exploit the invention itself.[40]

Moreover, IPRs are now recognized as an asset to trade.[41] By encouraging investment in R&D and innovation,[42] they stimulate economic growth and increased competitiveness.[43] Over the years, many of the specific industries whose development is currently crucial to economic growth and competitiveness in world trade—information technology, telecommunications, biotechnology, and new materials—have been shown to be dependent on IPR protection for investment.[44]

However the role of the reward/incentive function of IPR exclusivity as the driver of innovation should not be exaggerated even within the IP rules. An analysis of IPRs that focuses solely upon this protective function of the IP rules presents an

[38] Of course almost all pioneer innovators are themselves following on from previous innovators.

[39] See eg C. Taylor and Z. Silberstone, *The Economic Impact of the Patent System* (Cambridge, 1984), p 198. There are other methods of protecting such investment (see eg F. M. Scherer, *Industrial Market Structure and Economic Performance* (2nd edn, 1980), pp 444–7, who points out that some firms rely on imitation lags, oligopolistic markets, and methods of differentiation to secure protection from rivals) but economists have found that IPRs are particularly useful for most firms in certain sectors of industry, such as pharmaceuticals and engineering (see eg Taylor and Silberstone above), and to small and medium-sized firms in most sectors of industry. (See Scherer above.)

[40] See eg F. J. Contractor, 'Technology Licensing Practices in U.S. Companies: Corporate and Public Policy Implications' [1983] *Col. Jnl Of World Business* 80.

[41] See eg I. Govaere, n 12 above, p 2.

[42] See eg J. Schmookler, *Invention and Economic Growth* (Cambridge, Mass.: Harvard University Press, 1996), p 206.

[43] Ibid.

[44] See eg *Competition Policy and Intellectual Property Rights* (OECD, 1989).

oversimplified picture. In fact the IP laws create a more elaborate self-regulating system. Not only do they provide a reward/incentive to pioneer inventors but they are also designed to encourage alternative sources of innovation by balancing protection for follow on innovators with that given to pioneer innovators.[45] The means they use to do this include specific exceptions to and limitations of exclusive rights during the period of protection and informational benefits to innovation both during and after the period of protection. It is this system as a whole which makes a contribution to innovation.

The grant of exclusivity is intended to apply protection only against copying. It is not meant to protect against competition by substitution of other products by other undertakings. Indeed, the internal rules of IPRs all provide support for such competition by substitution. In some cases this is built into the very design of the IPR. The patent for example ensures that the information contained in the patent claim and description is extracted from the trade secrets of the patentee and made public to all other inventors *during the period of protection* as well as placing the protected technology into the public domain for all to use at the end of the protected period. The scope of protection of copyright, even industrial copyright, is limited by the idea/expression dichotomy. Some IPRs offer specific exclusions from the scope of protection, again designed to encourage competition by substitution. For example, there is an experimental use exception to patents as well as the possibility of compulsory licences in case of non-use or blocking patents. Moreover, there is the possibility of a patent for the second medical use of a protected compound. Under copyright law, there are exceptions, such as fair use, educational use, and public interest use. In the Computer Program Directive[46] there is provision for interoperability and decompilation right for competitors. All these make it clear that the innovation policy of IPRs cannot be viewed in narrow terms as solely focused on the reward/incentive to the original inventor. The incentives are designed as well to provide a spur to follow on innovation and the innovation policy of IPRs actually consists of a balance struck between these two interests. The balance can and does vary from country to country but the fundamental design of IP legislation is to maintain a balance between the two sources of innovation.

1.2.2 The theory of innovation in the competition rules

Some economists contend that IPRs are the primary drivers of innovation and that competition policy fails to give adequate recognition to the long-term benefits of IPR incentives to innovation which they describe as dynamic efficiencies. They argue that the competition authorities may actually stand in the way of IP-driven innovation

[45] A phrase coined by J. Drexl in 'Is there a More Economic Approach to Intellectual Property and Competition Law?' in J. Drexl (ed), *Research Handbook on Intellectual Property and Competition Law* (Cheltenham, UK, Northampton, MA, USA: Edward Elgar, 2008).

[46] Directive 2009/24/EC of the European Parliament and of the Council of 23 April 2009 on the legal protection of computer programs, OJ (2009) L 111/16.

producing 'dynamic efficiencies' in the form of new and improved products in markets owing to their excessive concerns with short-term 'static efficiencies' ie creating pressures on companies to offer the best products at the lowest prices. One result of concentrating upon the current state of competition on markets, it is maintained, is to sacrifice dynamic efficiencies to obtain static efficiencies.

However, this contention undervalues the *innovation* theory that is embodied in the EU competition law rules and competition policy. The competition rules are designed to stimulate innovation but the means they use are aimed at fostering effective competition in markets. The competition authorities consider that effectively competitive markets produce not only 'allocative efficiencies' and 'productive efficiencies'; they also produce innovative and dynamic efficiencies.

'Allocative efficiencies' presupposes that the price mechanism will ensure that producers will produce the products that consumers want. This is an important feature of the 'invisible hand' of the market at work. It was the original premise of competition law dating back to the nineteenth century. Today there may be other non-price reasons for allocative efficiencies but the effect of a competitive market is to ensure that products are made that will sell to consumers and users. It is sometimes contrasted with the command and control economies of the former Soviet Union and China before its market reforms. This picture of allocative efficiency also needs to be adjusted to take in the role of advertising which can suggest that producers can have an active role in influencing consumer choices. This is a reminder that competitive markets must be regulated to protect consumers from misleading advertising. However, since in the end buyers pay with their own money, the effects of the allocative efficiencies of competitive markets are empirically verifiable.

Similarly, 'productive efficiencies' are a demonstrable characteristic of effectively competitive markets. This term was introduced by the Chicago School and presupposes that producers will produce at lower costs because the pressure of price competition from other producers will drive down prices closer to costs. There is enormous evidence that competition lowers production costs and indeed this can result in lower prices for the consumer. However, there is also enormous evidence that lower productive costs can be associated with the negative externalities of higher environmental risks and damage, health and safety risks, and damage to employees. This too is a reminder that effectively competitive markets require regulation in those spheres in addition to competition law.

The third and more controversial contention of EU competition policy is that effective competition will also produce 'innovative efficiencies'. The idea is that producers will respond to the pressures of competition by continuously seeking to innovate as well as to examine means of lowering productive costs using existing levels of technology.

On the one hand, the concept that fierce competition breeds innovation has been challenged by economists arguing the need for a more 'dynamic' view of competition. A more common distinction is that between the short-term and static model of micro-economic markets and the long-term, dynamic efficiency affects on innovation of IPRs.[47] Schumpeter,[48] for example has suggested that innovation is better achieved in conditions of monopoly because that condition provides the best profit incentive for investments in R&D and high rewards for innovation will encourage other competitors to attempt to match innovative efforts. His followers contend that by attacking monopoly and preventing market power from arising, competition policy may have positive effects on static efficiency but at the same time undermines dynamic efficiency and innovation.

Moreover, in recent years, the costs of research, particularly high tech research, seem to require a scale of capital that presupposes either a large enterprise or cooperation between enterprises rather than atomistic competition. Furthermore, the concept of scale of operation has also been suggested as an important element of competitiveness in global competition, leading to cries for 'Eurochampions' from several quarters.[49]

However, EU competition law has resisted weakening its concept of effective competition to embrace either Schumpeterian models of monopoly,[50] or the value of size for its own sake. It draws some support from the work of Kenneth Arrow and others who maintain that 'competition may provide more incentives for innovation than monopoly'. Arrow contends that in favouring monopolies Schumpeter underestimated the incentives for innovation that competition can offer, for example by not recognizing that firms under competitive pressure are less complacent and know that inventing a new product is their best strategy for taking over their competitors' market share. In a competitive market, new entrants know that innovation can help them to succeed in the market.[51]

The Commission retains a belief that effective competition will provide the breeding ground for innovation and competitiveness. As the Commission stated in its *XXVIth Report on Competition Policy*:

> The Commission does not believe that [globalization of competition] calls for less strict application of the competition rules. Its experience, through its decision making practice in all the areas covered by competition policy, shows that competition-mindedness and efficiency required to be an effective competitor internationally are acquired through competition between firms on domestic markets.[52]

[47] See eg *OECD Report*.

[48] See eg J. Schumpeter, *Capitalism, Socialism and Democracy* (USA: George Allen & Unwin, 1976).

[49] See eg Bulletin of the EC, *White Paper on Growth, Competitiveness, Employment* (1993), Supp.6/93.

[50] Insofar as EU competition law accepts that the normal exercise of IPRs under national legislation is acceptable under Arts 101 and 102, it might be said to be accepting a limited Schumpeterian view built into IPR legislation.

[51] See C. Madero, and T. Kramer, 'Intellectual Property Rights and Competition Rules, a Complex but Indispensable Coexistence' in S. Anderman and A. Ezrachi, *IP and Competition Policy: New Frontiers* (Oxford: OUP, 2011); see also R. J. Gilbert, 'Competition and Innovation' (27 January 2007) *Competition Policy Center, Institute of Business and Economic Research, UC Berkeley* <http://repositories.cdlib.org/iber/cpc/CPC07-069> (accessed 17 November 2010).

[52] *XXVIth Report on Competition Policy* (1996) Brussels 1997 SEC(97) 628 Final, p 5.

In a sense both theories are plausible explanations of innovation. The IPRs offer a carrot; the competition laws a stick. However, the rules of competition law are more focused on maintaining effective competition in the markets in the here and now than in accepting the argument that a short term decrease in effective competition will be justified by the speculative long-term contribution to innovation. There are built-in mechanisms within EU competition law that limit policy arguments based on long-term dynamic efficiencies as a justification for current anti-competitive activity. Unless there is insufficient evidence in the present of pro-innovative benefits, EU competition policy is resistant to sacrificing the innovative benefits of existing effective competition.

This policy choice of the competition authorities is strongly reinforced by the rules that the EU Courts have read into the interpretation of Articles 101 and 102 and in their reviews of Commission decisions on mergers. Built into EU competition law is an assumption that the competition rules must preserve existing competition in markets in the interests of consumers. Built into the competition rules is the requirement that they must also keep to the margins of business activity. They must intervene only where firms are acting abusively unilaterally, bilaterally, or collaboratively. This self-restricting ordinance presupposes that entrepreneurial freedom produces innovative activity induced by the incentives of the IP laws.

The task for competition policy today, therefore, is to ensure that it uses an appropriate balancing mechanism in drawing a line between the two interests. The rules of competition policy must not be designed so tightly in the effort to protect effective competition in markets, that they unnecessarily reduce the incentives to invest in R&D.[53] The optimum role of competition policy is to complement the IP system concentrating on the edges of this activity and giving it room to breathe.

[53] See eg *OECD Report* (n 44 above), p 13.

2

THE RELATIONSHIP BETWEEN INTELLECTUAL PROPERTY RIGHTS AND COMPETITION LAW UNDER THE TREATY

2.1	Introduction	17
2.2	Grant and 'Existence'	20
2.3	Permitted and Prohibited Exercise of Intellectual Property Rights	21
2.4	The Objectives of the Rules on Competition in the Treaty	25
2.5	Effective Competition	25
2.6	The Goal of Fair Competition	27
2.7	The Goal of Integration	29

2.1 INTRODUCTION

Under EU law, the way the balance is struck between competition law and IPRs has historically been shaped by the structure of the EU Treaty and the interpretation it has been given by the Community Courts and the European Commission. In the pre-Lisbon Treaties, the role of competition law was given a high 'constitutional' profile. Article 2 of the EC Treaty provided that: 'The Community shall have as its task, by establishing a Common market . . . and by implementing the Common policies or activities referred to in Articles 3 and 3a, to promote throughout the Community a harmonious and balanced development of economic activities.' Article 3(g) of the EC Treaty required the institution of a system to ensure that competition in the internal market is not distorted. Articles 101 and 102 (ex Articles 81 and 82) were then set out as the two main means of achieving this goal.[1] The Lisbon Treaty, TFEU, has removed Article 3(g) from the body of the Treaty and placed it in an accompanying Protocol.

[1] A merger control regulation was added to the armoury of competition policy measures in 1989. Council Regulation (EC) No 139/2004 of 20 January 2004 on the control of concentrations between undertakings, OJ L 24, 29 January 2004, pp 1–22.

However, in Article 2 TFEU, the Lisbon Treaty retains the creation of a single market as one of the main goals of the European Union. Hence the system of competition law consisting of Articles 101 and 102, the Merger Regulation, and State Aid rules continue to occupy a central role in the Treaty as the means to maintain effective competition within the European Union.

Article 101 regulates 'all agreements between undertakings which have the object or effect of preventing, restricting or distorting competition'. IP licensing agreements fall within its scope. Article 102 regulates unilateral action by undertakings, prohibiting abuses of a dominant position. This can apply to various forms of exercise of an IPR by its owner.

The Treaty ensures that the reconciliation between IP legislation, which is predominantly national legislation,[2] and EU competition law occurs within the framework of Articles 101 and 102. The Court of Justice has regularly reaffirmed that the exercise of IPRs must in principle be compatible with the rules of competition (Articles 101 and 102) as well as the rules of free movement of goods (Articles 34-37 (ex Articles 28-31)).[3] In the case of the rules concerning the free movement of goods, the Treaty offers a guide to the appropriate balancing mechanism in Article 36 which provides that 'the protection of industrial and commercial property' can justify a prohibition on imports or exports between Member States as long as they are not 'a means of arbitrary discrimination or a disguised restriction on trade'.[4]

In the case of Articles 101 and 102, the Treaty contains no comparable provision. Yet the Court of Justice has regularly given the reassurance to IP owners that the Treaty rules will not interfere with the 'normal exercise' of IPR rights.[5] Thus, in *Maxicar*, the CJEU stated that 'the mere fact of securing the benefit of an exclusive right granted by law, the effect of which is to enable the manufacture and sale of protected products by unauthorised third parties to be prevented, cannot be regarded as an abusive method of eliminating competition'.[6] In *Volvo*, the CJEU also pointed out that to be abusive some 'additional factor' was required in addition to the elimination of competition from  other manufacturers in respect of the protected product since that corresponds to the substance of the protected right.[7] Further, in *Magill*, the CJEU held that 'exceptional circumstances' must be found before the exercise of an IPR can be held to be contrary to the Articles of the Treaty.[8]

[2] IP legislation is still predominantly national, although Community legislation and the harmonization process is slowly building towards a Community legislative framework for IPRs.

[3] Case 24/67 *Parke Davis v Probel* [1968] ECR 55 [1968] CMLR 47; Case 78/70 *Deutsche Grammophon Gesellscharft mbH v Metro-S8-Grossmarketet GmbH & Co* [1971] ECR 487, [1971] CMLR 631.

[4] This in turn has led to a body of case law in which doctrines such as 'consent', 'exhaustion', and 'discrimination' provide ground rules drawn with reference to the specific functions of the IPRs as well as the board policy of Art 36. See eg C-267–68/95 *Merck v Prime Crown* [1996] ECR–6825, [1997] 1 CMLR, 83; see I. Govaere, *The Use and Abuse of Intellectual Property Rights in EC Law* (London: Sweet & Maxwell, 1996), Ch 4.

[5] Case 24/67 *Parke Davis v Probel* Case 78/70 *Deutsche Grammophon*.

[6] Case 53/87 *CICRA et Maxicar v Renault* [1988] ECR 6039, [1990] 4 CMLR 265.

[7] Case 238/87 *Volvo v Veng (UK) Ltd* [1988] ECR 6211at para 15.

[8] C-241-242/91P *Radio Telefis Eireann v Commission (Magill)* [1995] ECR I–743, [1995] 4 CMLR 718.

The argument has been made that because the CJEU has tended to decide these issues on a case by case basis, it is difficult to discern the framework the CJEU uses to distinguish between the permitted and prohibited exercise of IPRs.[9] Moreover, it is also claimed that the function of IPRs should figure prominently in the demarcation even to the point of requiring the competition rules to defer to the logic of reward and incentive built into the IP legislation.[10]

A close reading of the EU Court's decisions, however, suggests that neither assertion is tenable. The Court's judgments do suggest that the CJEU uses a framework to define the borderline between permitted and prohibited exercise of IPRs based on the competition rules of the Treaty and the CJEU has long maintained that the prohibitions in Articles 101 and102 are unyielding restrictions upon the exercise of IPRs.[11] The CJEU has regularly held that the exercise of IPRs must defer to the competition rules in cases where the two are in conflict.

The foundations for the current form of reconciliation between IPRs and the competition rules were established in the early case of *Consten and Grundig*.[12] In *Consten and Grundig*, a trade mark was used to reinforce a sole distribution agreement between a German manufacturer, Grundig, and a French distributor, Consten. As part of that agreement, Consten was allowed to register the Grundig trade mark, GINT, in France. When it was discovered that another French distributor, UNEF, had bought Grundig appliances in Germany and tried to sell them in France, Consten used its trade mark to stop the infringing exports. In response to UNEF's complaint, the Commission investigated and ordered Consten to stop its exercise of the trade mark licence. On appeal, the CJEU upheld the Commission's decision. To do otherwise, it said, would make the prohibition under Article 101 meaningless; the exercise of an IPR could not be used to frustrate the rules of competition law.[13] The CJEU found that neither Article 34 (ex Article 28) nor Article 345 (ex Article 295) could operate to exclude 'any influence whatever of Community law on the exercise of national intellectual property rights'.[14]

The CJEU was concerned to ensure that the enforcement of Article 101 would not interfere with the grant of the IPR by the Member State. It emphasized that 'the injunction . . . does not affect the grant of those rights but only limits their exercise to the extent necessary to give effect to the prohibition under Article [101(1)]'.[15]

The CJEU clearly indicated, however, that if an IPR was linked to an agreement which was contrary to Article 101 then the Commission could prohibit this form of exercise. As the CJEU pointed out, it was the agreement which enabled Consten to

[9] See eg I. Govaere (n 4 above), p 104.

[10] See Sources at n 12 in Ch 1. Govaere (n 4 above) alone argues for a redefinition of the function of IPRs to enable it to be reconciled with Arts 101 and 102 (p 69).

[11] Joined Cases 56 and 58/64 *Établissements Consten S.à.R.L. and Grundig-Verkaufs-GmbH v Commision* [1966] ECR 299, [1966] CMLR 418; Case 24/67 *Parke Davis v Probel.*

[12] Cases 56 and 58/64 *Consten and Grundig*.

[13] Ibid at p 346.

[14] Ibid at p 345.

[15] Ibid at p 345.

register the trade mark in the first place and 'the prohibition would be ineffective if Consten could continue to use the trade-mark to achieve the same object as that pursued by the [unlawful] agreement'.[16]

In *Parke Davis v Probel*,[17] this distinction between grant and exercise was reaffirmed. The issue in the case was whether Articles 101 and 102 would limit the use of a patent to prevent the importation of an antibiotic product into Holland from Italy where the product had been manufactured without the consent of the Dutch patentee. The CJEU ruled that under those Treaty provisions,[18] the patent could be used to block the import. Again it referred to the distinction between grant and exercise. The patent taken by itself was merely the expression of a legal status granted by a Member State to products under certain conditions. The CJEU used the expression the 'existence' of the grant of rights by a Member State to the holder of a patent and stated that this was not affected by the prohibitions contained in Articles 101(1) and 102 TFEU; it then went on to add that the 'exercise' of such rights cannot of itself fall either under Article 101(1), in the absence of any agreement, decision, or concerted practice prohibited by this provision, or under Article 102, in the absence of any abuse of a dominant position.[19]

At this stage, the CJEU could be seen to have marked out three legal categories in the interface between EU competition law and IPRs.[20] The first category, 'existence', was the authority of Member States to determine the conditions for granting IPRs. This was beyond the reach of Articles 101 and 102. The second category, 'permitted forms of exercise' of IPRs, was defined by a combination of the powers granted by IP legislation and the limits imposed by Articles 101 and 102 (and 36). The third category, 'prohibited forms of exercise' of IPRs, was defined by the prohibitions in Articles 101 and 102 (and 34). This book limits itself to the treatment of these categories under Articles 101 and 102.

2.2 GRANT AND 'EXISTENCE'

The early judgments of the CJEU clearly indicated that there was no competition law interest in regulating the conditions upon which the Member States conferred the legal status of IPRs. Nor did it have any role to play in the harmonization of IPRs in the common market. This position was steadily maintained by the CJEU over the years.[21]

[16] Ibid, at p 345.

[17] Case 24/E7 *Parke Davis v Probel*.

[18] The CJEU did not deal with the issue of Arts 34–6.

[19] Since the act was that of the patentee alone Art 101(1) was not applicable. Moreover, since the act was the normal use of the IPR it could not be treated as an abuse of a dominant position under Art 102. It was only if the use of the patent were for another purpose that it could be curbed by Art 102 as an abuse.

[20] See eg Govaere (n 4 above), p 65. See also Chs 4 and 6 re Art 36.

[21] See eg Case 144/81 *Keurkoop v Nancy Kean Gifts* [1982] ECR 2653; Case 238/87 *Volvo v Veng (UK) Ltd.*

By the time of *Magill*, the CJEU felt that it was so well established that the point could be stated without reference to earlier authority: 'in the absence of Community standardisation or harmonisation of laws, determination of the conditions and procedures for granting protection of an intellectual property right is a matter for national rules'.[22]

In later years assertions were made that the concept of the 'existence' of the IPR could be widened beyond the concept of the conditions which had to be fulfilled to qualify for the grant to extend to the exercise of the legal prerogatives which were the entitlement of the IPR owner. These included the claims that the 'existence' should be expanded to include the 'essential function' or 'specific subject matter' of the intellectual right.[23] These claims appeared to be unwarranted attempts to use the concepts of 'existence', which is effectively only the basis for the grant, and 'permitted exercise' interchangeably under Article 101, a confusion which appears to have also occurred in the context of Article 34.[24]

2.3 PERMITTED AND PROHIBITED EXERCISE OF INTELLECTUAL PROPERTY RIGHTS

The earlier competition law cases also established that the rules in Articles 101 and 102 created a set of outer limits to the lawful exercise of IPRs. In *Consten and Grundig*, the CJEU was unwilling to allow the exercise of the trade mark to frustrate the rules of competition law.[25] In *Parke Davis*, the CJEU upheld the entitlement to exercise the patent but only because it was not contrary to rules on competition law.[26]

2.3.1 Normal exercise

The CJEU's frequent statement that the 'normal exercise' of the IPR was not caught by either Article 101 or 102, hinted at a core of lawful exploitation rights for IPRs under the rules of competition law.[27] Thus, in *Parke Davis*, the CJEU stated that the exercise of the rights arising under the patent in accordance with the legislation of a Member State does not *of itself* constitute an infringement of the rules on competition laid down in the Treaty.[28] In *Deutsche Grammophon*,[29] the CJEU stated that, in principle, the owner of an IPR does not occupy a dominant position merely by exercising his

[22] C-241–242/91P *Magill*.

[23] See discussion by AG Gulman in *RTE v Commission* [1991] ECR II–485.

[24] Case 15/74 *Centrafarm v Sterling Drug* [1974] ECR 1147; see F.-K. Beier, 'Industrial Property and the Free Movement of Goods in the Internal Market' [1990] *IIC* 131.

[25] Cases 56 and 58/64 *Consten and Grundig* at 346.

[26] Case 24/67 *Parke Davis v Probel*.

[27] The CJEU prefaced that remark by saying that this was 'for similar reasons' to the effect of Art [34.] Article [34] in its first sentence presupposed that the normal exercise of IPRs could be justified.

[28] Case 24/67 *Parke Davis v Probel*. The CJEU has held this to be true of trade marks (Case 51/75 *EMI v CBS (UK) Ltd* [1976] ECR 811 at para 26) and design rights (Case 144/81 *Keurkoop* at para 27).

[29] Case 78/70 *Deutsche Grammophon*.

exclusive right to distribute the protected articles.[30] In *Volvo*[31] the Court of Justice went so far as to declare that a refusal to grant an IP licence cannot in itself constitute an abuse of a dominant position under Article 102.

These statements by the CJEU were meant in the first place to reassure that the exclusivity of an IPR and its exercise are not in themselves regarded as anti-competitive despite the prohibitions on restrictions and distortion of competition in Articles 101 and 102. They were designed to suggest a basis of accommodation between the statutory grant of exclusivity which is literally a restriction of competition in pursuit of a wider objective and the strictures of Article 101 which prohibits agreements which prevent, restrict, or distort competition, and Article 102 which prohibits dominant undertakings from weakening the competitive structure in markets. In themselves, they do not provide a springboard for asserting that the function of the IPR can offer protection against the prohibitions of Articles 101 and 102, or a basis for narrowing the scope of the Treaty provisions. They are essentially a statement of the residual area of exercise permitted under the rules of EU competition law.

The basis for the test of permitted exercise of IPRs under Article 102 was spelt out by the CJEU in *Hoffmann-La Roche*.[32] Assuming that it is in accordance with Article 34, 'the exercise of a trade mark right is . . . not contrary to [Article 102] on the sole ground that it is the act of an undertaking occupying a dominant position on the market if the trade mark right has not been used as an instrument for the abuse of such a position'.[33]

Hence, the mere exercise of the exclusive right is not automatically abusive. To be unlawful the exercise of the IPR must be linked in some way to a commercial practice which is itself unlawful under Articles 101 and 102. As the CJEU described it in *Hoffmann-La Roche*, an IPR must be used as an 'instrument of abuse' of a dominant position to be unlawful under Article 102.[34]

Similarly, under Article 101, before an IP licence, even an exclusive licence, is unlawful, it must 'serve to give effect to', or 'be the means of an agreement, decision or concerted practice which itself is prohibited as a restriction of competition under that Article 101'.[35]

It is thus only in unusual circumstances that the exercise of an IPR will be limited by Articles 101 and 102. However, if the exercise of the IPR is associated with a commercial practice which is unlawful under Articles 101 and 102, it cannot be saved by the fact that it is lawful under national law.[36]

[30] Ibid, at para 16.

[31] Case 238/87 *Volvo v Veng*.

[32] Case 85/76 *Hoffman-La Roche v Commission* [1979] ECR 461, [1979] 3 CMLR 211.

[33] Ibid, at para 16.

[34] Ibid. This also implicitly indicates that, even if an act is lawful under Art 34, it may nevertheless be unlawful under Art 102.

[35] Case 262/81 *Coditel SA v Cine-Vog Films (Coditel II)* [1982] ECR 3381 at para 14.

[36] See Case 85/76 *Hoffmann-La Roche*.

2.3.2 A functional test for permitted exercise?

It is true that certain statements made by the CJEU in competition cases have offered support for the view that the delineation between permitted and protected exercise should be made by reference to the specific function of the individual IPR.

Thus in *Volvo* the CJEU stated that: 'the right of the proprietor of a protected design to prevent third parties from manufacturing and selling and importing, without his consent, products incorporating the design constitutes the very subject-matter of his exclusive right.' It followed that an obligation imposed on the proprietor of an IPR, in this case a protected design, to grant a licence would constitute a deprivation of 'the substance of his exclusive right, and that a refusal to grant such a license cannot in itself constitute an abuse of a dominant position'.[37]

This statement, taken in isolation, might suggest that the CJEU accepts that there is a core of IPR exploitation rights defined by reference to the substance or specific subject matter which is protected from the rules of competition law. It is reminiscent of the assertions made about the protective scope of specific subject matter or essential function concepts under Article 34.[38] The difficulty with this interpretation is its selectivity; it does not give sufficient weight to the contradictory statements by the CJEU in the same judgments.[39]

For example in *Volvo*, whilst the above statement appeared on its own to suggest an unqualified test of permitted exercise, the CJEU went on to add in the very next paragraph, the following qualifications:

> It must however be noted that the exercise of an exclusive right by the proprietor of a registered design in respect of car body panels may be prohibited by [Article 102] if it involves ... certain abusive conduct such as the arbitrary refusal to supply spare parts to independent repairers, the fixing of prices for spare parts at an unfair level or a decision no longer to produce spare parts for a particular model even though many cars of that model are still in circulation ...[40]

The significance of these qualifications is that they refer to examples of specific abuse under Article 102[41] and imply limits to the scope of exclusive exploitation in secondary markets, such as maintenance markets. They also imply limits to the concept implicit in IPR legislation of charging what the market will bear for a product incorporating an exclusive IPR.

Unfortunately, at the time of the decision, these qualifications were not interpreted as qualifications of the rights of normal exercise of the IPR effectively curbing their

[37] Case 238/87 *Volvo v Veng* at para 8.

[38] The decision appeared consistent with the law under Art 36 which places great emphasis upon the right-holder's consent to the manufacture or marketing of the protected goods.

[39] See discussion by J. Kallaugher, 'Existence, Exercise and Exceptional Circumstances: The Limited Scope for a More Economic Approach to IP Issues under Article 102 TFEU' in S. Anderman and A. Ezrachi, *Intellectual Property and Competition Law: New Frontiers* (Oxford: OUP, 2011).

[40] Case 238/87 *Volvo v Veng* at para 9.

[41] The first is an abuse under Art 102(b) or (c); the second is an abuse under Art 102(a); the third is an abuse under Art 102(d).

specific subject matter or substance.[42] Instead, the general statements of principle in the previous paragraph were given excessive weight, particularly in the light of the decision of the CJEU that the IPR could be enforced in an infringement proceeding. The case was thought by many to signal recognition of the specific functions of IPR as protected against the prohibitions of the rules of competition law even in secondary markets.[43]

In *Magill*,[44] however, the CJEU made it clear that the exceptions mentioned in *Volvo* were to be given considerable weight. It acknowledged that a refusal to grant a licence, even by an undertaking in a dominant position, cannot in itself constitute an abuse, adding however that the exercise of the exclusive right by the proprietor may in exceptional circumstances involve abusive conduct.[45] It then went on to hold that where the refusal of the TV companies to license Magill prevented him from introducing a new product for which there was a potential demand and which was not provided by them, this was an abuse under Article 102(b) where no objective justification was offered by the TV companies.[46]

The *Magill* judgment confirmed that the CJEU regarded the specific abuses in Article 102 as outer limits to the exercise of IPRs in the sense that if an IPR was used as an instrument of such an abuse by a dominant firm,[47] then the fact that it was lawful under national law was not an obstacle to 'review in relation to [Article 102]'.[48] The ground rules established in the earlier case law were reiterated. The concept of normal exploitation of IPRs which was built into the legislative policy for each type of IPR could not be used to override the competition rules.

In *Consten and Grundig*,[49] Advocate General Roemer attempted to define the relationship between Article 102 and the trade mark in terms of whether or not the Commission's injunction 'interfered with the function of the trade mark', which he defined as guaranteeing the origin of the product to the consumer. The CJEU refused to accept that conceptual approach to the reconciliation between IPRs and the competition rules in the Treaty. It stated that the concept of specific function could not provide an immunity from unwarrantable interference when its exercise was contrary to Article 101.

[42] See eg Friden, 'It is submitted that one should not read too much into them . . . the court probably felt obliged, after having given an example of what was not abusive conduct, to give a few examples of what would be considered as abusive': 'Recent Developments in EEC Intellectual Property Law: The Distinction Between Existence and Exercise Revisited' [1989] *CML Rev* 193, p 210.

[43] See eg opinion of AG Gulman in Case 241–242 91P *Magill* at para 111.

[44] Case 241–242/91P *Magill.*

[45] Ibid, at paras 49–50.

[46] Ibid, at paras 54–5.

[47] In Case 85/76 *Hoffmann-La Roche*, the CJEU said that 'the exercise of an IPR could be a violation of [Article 102] when a dominant undertaking uses its IPR as an instrument for the abuse of such a position'.

[48] Case 241–242/91P *Magill* at para 48.

[49] Cases 56 and 58/64 *Consten and Grundig* at 366.

In *Magill*, Advocate General Gulman also attempted to define an irreducible minimum level of protection for IPRs against the strictures of competition law. He conceded that the specific subject matter was subject to regulation by Article 102, but he maintained that the 'essential function' of the IPR should be treated as equivalent to the 'existence' of the IPR and not subject to Article 102.[50] The Court of Justice, however, showed no interest in a test of the 'function' of the IPR as the decisive criterion for 'exceptional circumstances'. As in the earlier cases of *Consten and Grundig* and *Parke Davis*, it preferred the line to be drawn by the competition rules.[51]

2.4 THE OBJECTIVES OF THE RULES ON COMPETITION IN THE TREATY

Since Articles 101 and 102 provide a framework for the regulation of IPRs, a closer look at their objectives is necessary to understand how they can be used to generate rules limiting the exploitation of IPRs. EU competition policy differs from other competition law systems, such as the USA[52] and Japan,[53] largely because of the influence of the Treaty in infusing political economic objectives into EU competition policy.

The starting point for understanding the objectives of EU competition law is the position of the competition rules in the Treaty. This competition law 'system' has been interpreted to have three distinct objectives. The first is the maintenance of 'effective competition'. The second is the application of the principle of fair competition, most particularly in the form of special protections for small and medium-sized businesses. The third is the use of the rules of competition to help integrate the individual national markets of the Member States into a single market. Each objective has had an effect on the interpretation of Articles 101 and 102 which in turn has influenced the interface between EU competition law and IPRs.

2.5 EFFECTIVE COMPETITION

In referring to the goal of Articles 101 and 102 as 'the maintenance of effective competition within the common market' in *Continental Can*,[54] the CJEU had in mind two separate but related concepts. The first was the view that an effective level of competition should be maintained in markets by preserving market structures from inappropriate harm from powerful undertakings. Thus in *Continental Can*, the CJEU stated that the

[50] In this he drew some assistance from the General Court which had made reference to the essential function of the IPR as a desideratum, but the GC had qualified its remarks by defining the essential function as itself being subject to the rules in the Treaty.

[51] Case 241–242/91P *Magill* at para 48.

[52] See eg *Competition Policy and Intellectual Property Rights* (OECD, 1989), p 42.

[53] Ibid, p 36.

[54] Case 6/72 *Europemballage & Continental Can v Commission* [1973] ECR 215, [1973] CMLR 199.

Treaty (what was Article 3(g) of the EC Treaty) requires the limitation of practices which affect consumers 'through their impact on an effective competition structure'.[55]

The goal of an effective competitive structure entails acceptance of the economists' paradigm that if the structure of a market is competitive, this will affect the conduct of companies on that market as well as their economic performance.[56] Economists, particularly, those of the Chicago school,[57] have extensively criticized the structure/conduct/performance paradigm which maintains that structure will determine conduct and performance on a market, but these criticisms have not persuaded the EU Courts to abandon their acceptance of the structural goal for competition policy. The judicial view is that structure can influence competition. Examples, offered by cases before the CJEU, talk about high and persistent market shares can be taken as good evidence of dominance.[58] Moreover, the acceptance of the HHI index of concentration in merger assessments for coordinated effects is evidence of a structural starting point to investigate market conditions.

The maintenance of effective competition now goes beyond a purely structural analysis of competition; it also analyses elements in the process of competition. The existing structure of the market is now viewed more as the starting point for investigations of the actual process of competition on a market.

Since workable[59]or effective competition presupposes that the pricing mechanism must be in good working order, competition policy is aimed at preventing any pair or group of firms from controlling output and prices by coordinating their activities to establish cartels or other market sharing arrangements. Competition policy also attempts to maintain effective competition structures by preserving access to markets by preventing abuses of market power by firms in dominant or near-monopoly positions and by preventing mergers or joint ventures which will result in a market structure which is too concentrated to allow workable competition to exist.

The legal framework expresses this commitment to the preservation of existing competition markets in all three tools of competition policy. Thus agreements will not be enforceable under Article 101 if they are restrictive of existing competition or threaten to eliminate existing competition. Similarly under the Merger Regulation, Article 2 makes it plain that a merger should not be approved if it constitutes a substantial impediment to effective competition. Moreover, under Article 102, the concerns to protect existing effective competition and existing competitive market structures have led to a concept of abuse of power which has been widened to include conduct which threatens to eliminate competitors not only in the same market as the dominant

[55] Ibid, at p 245.

[56] See eg Scherer and Ross, *Industrial Market Structure and Economic Performance* (3rd edn, Boston, US: Houghton Mifflin Company, 1990), Chs 3 and 4.

[57] See eg Landes and Posner, 'Market Power in Antitrust Cases', 94 *Harv Law Rev* 937.

[58] Case 62/86 *AKZO-Chemie v Commision* [1991] ECR I–3359, [1993] 5 CMLR 215.

[59] The Court of Justice said in Case 26/76 *Mertro-SB-Grossmärkte GmbH v Commission*: [1977] ECR 1875: [t]he requirement contained in Article 3 and {101} of the EEC Treaty that competition shall not be distorted implies the existence on the market of workable competition.

undertaking, so called 'primary' markets, but also to conduct threatening levels of competition in secondary, particularly, downstream markets. It is this concern with existing levels of competition in 'aftermarkets' that as we shall see, has profound implications for IPRs.

The CJEU has proceeded on the theory that the Treaty requires a protection of levels of competition in markets which have already been weakened by the presence of a dominant firm. Conduct aimed at driving existing competitors from markets or denying entry to competitors to markets, such as refusals to supply and license, discriminatory pricing, predatory pricing, and tie-ins in the form of product bundling,[60] has been held to be abusive, limiting certain forms of exploitation of exclusive IPRs in secondary markets.[61] There is no unifying principle for exclusionary abuse in the application of Article 102 but in Article 102(b) there is a clear statement that an abuse under that Article must go beyond limiting production or technological development to show that there will be sufficient harm to consumers. There are two caveats here. The first is that the test of harm to consumers can be indirect; a reduction in 'efficient competitors' can be sufficient.[62] Indeed, some cases suggest that a reduction in 'not yet as efficient competitors' can be viewed as harmful to consumers.[63] Secondly, the proof of harm to consumers does not require proof of actual harm; it may take the form of proof of conduct that creates a risk of harm to consumers by creating a risk of harm of eliminating effective competition. Article 102 is aimed not only at practices which may cause prejudice to consumers directly but also at those which are detrimental to them through their impact on an effective competition structure.[64] This will be discussed further in Chapter 6 on the concept of abuse.

2.6 THE GOAL OF FAIR COMPETITION

The protective functions of Articles 101 and 102 have been reinforced by their second goal; the goal of ensuring that there is a degree of fairness on the market. The concept of undistorted competition has been interpreted to require a set of Marquis of Queensbury rules for competition so that smaller and medium-sized firms in particular are not driven out or excluded from markets by illegitimate means, unrelated to business efficiency or innovation. This applies particularly to market dominance, but it is also relevant to cartels and market sharing agreements.[65]

The inclusion of this goal was first suggested in *United Brands*[66] when the CJEU found the decision of United Brands to stop dealing with a long-term distributor

[60] See *Michelin v Commission* [1983] ECR 3461 at para 70.
[61] See Part II.
[62] Case 62/86 *AKZO*.
[63] See eg Case C-95/04 P *British Airways v Commission* [2007] ECR I–2331.
[64] Ibid. at para 106.
[65] See eg *Ninth Report on Competition Policy* [1979] Luxembourg, pp 9–10.
[66] Case 27/76 *United Brands v Commission* [1978] ECR 207.

abusive because it was an excessive or 'disproportionate' penalty for the actions of the small distributor's minor transgressions. The CJEU held that the refusal to continue to sell to the distributor amounted 'to a serious interference with the independence of small and medium-sized firms in their commercial relations with the undertaking in a dominant position'. The CJEU objected to the use of excessive force because such conduct could have a 'serious adverse effect on competition . . . by allowing only firms dependent upon the dominant undertaking to stay in business'.[67]

The case introduced into EU competition law the general principles of 'proportionality' and 'dependence'. Thus, where a dominant undertaking has dealings with a dependent customer, it must be 'proportionate' in its treatment, ie it must not behave unreasonably or unfairly, even where the dominant undertaking is not actually operating in the secondary market. Secondly, the concern of the CJEU with the need to preserve the independence of small and medium-sized firms in their dealings with dominant undertakings incorporates an assumption that the damage to the individual competitor is invariably accompanied by damage to the economy.[68]

The Commission and Courts' concern with the protection of the independence of small and medium-sized firms is also in evidence in the *AKZO* case, a case of predatory pricing by a Dutch chemical multinational against a small English competitor. The Commission's view was that '[any] unfair commercial practices on the part of the dominant undertaking intended to eliminate, discipline or deter smaller competitors would . . . fall within the scope of the prohibition of [Article 102] if other conditions are fulfilled'.[69]

The Commission was, however, prepared to include within the notion of fairness, a concept of legitimate competition by performance:

> A dominant firm is entitled to compete on the merits ... The maintenance of a system of effective competition does, however, require that a small competitor be protected against conduct by a dominant undertaking designed to exclude it from the market not by virtue of greater efficiency or superior performance, but by abuse of power. If a dominant undertaking uses its market power to obtain a competitive advantage other than competition on the merits, and it has a substantial effect on the structure of competition, it is abusive.[70]

The concern with the protection and preservation of small and medium-sized firms is part of a wider concept of EU competition law which is designed to encourage their development because of their potential to contribute to innovation and employment. In the *XXIInd Report on Competition Policy* (1992), the Commission referred to 'the active policy towards SMEs which the Commission has been pursuing for many

[67] Ibid.

[68] The concept of dependence derives from German law but has been enacted into French law. It reflects a concern with the vulnerability of small firms to exploitation by dominant firms. See J. Kallaugher and J. Venit, 'Essential Facilities: A Comparative Law Approach [1994] *Fordham Corp Law Inst* 315, pp 325–30. See also D. Gerber, 'Law and the Abuse of Economic Power in Europe' 62 *Tulane Law Rev* 57 (1987).

[69] Case 62/86 *AKZO.*

[70] Ibid.

years. . . . that SMEs are an engine for economic growth . . . and that the development of SMEs should be encouraged'.[71]

In the competition context, this policy has translated into special treatment on State Aids and a special exemption from Article 101 under the Commission's Notice on Agreements of Minor Importance, which stipulates that agreements between SMEs generally fall outside the scope of Article 101(1).[72]

2.7 THE GOAL OF INTEGRATION

The third goal of competition policy under the Treaty is that of assisting in the integration of the national markets of the Member States into a common market.

The effect on Article 102 of the integration goal has been relatively undramatic. Article 102 in effect presupposes integration because it allows firms to grow internally through efficient performance to a position of dominance in a market.[73] It is only after an undertaking has achieved dominance that it is regulated closely. However, in the definition of abusive conduct, Article 102 is influenced by the integration principle to the extent that it finds certain forms of geographic, or interstate, price discrimination abusive which might on purely economic criteria be of less concern.[74]

The effect of the integration goal on the interpretation of Article 101 has been more fundamental. The Court of Justice in *Consten and Grundig*[75] interpreted the objectives of Article 101 to include the prohibition of market partitioning agreements in addition to the prohibitions listed in Article 101. Faced with a sole distribution agreement granted by a German supplier to a French distributor, combined with an exclusive trade mark right, the CJEU held that the infringement of Article 101(1) consisted of the attempt by the supplier and distributor to 'isolate the French market for Grundig products and maintain . . . artificially, for products of a very well known brand, separate national markets within the community'. This was prohibited under Article 101(1) as an attempt to distort competition in the common market and could not be exempted under Article 101(3):

> An agreement between producer and distributor which might tend to restore the national divisions in trade between Member states might be such as to frustrate the most fundamental object of the Community. The Treaty, whose preamble and content aim at abolishing the barriers between States, and which in several provisions give evidence of a stern attitude with regard to their reappearance, could not allow undertakings to reconstruct such barriers. [Article 101(1)] is designed to pursue this aim, even in the case of agreements between undertakings placed at different levels of the economic process.[76]

[71] Ibid. at para 78.

[72] See Commission Recommendation 2003/361/EC concerning the definition of micro, small, and medium sized enterprises OJ L124, 20 May 2003, p 36

[73] See eg T. Kauper, 'Article 86, Excessive Prices and Refusals to Deal' [1991] *Antitrust Law Journal* 441, p 443.

[74] See Chapter 10.

[75] Cases 56 and 58/64 *Consten and Grundig*.

[76] Ibid, at p 343.

In *Consten and Grundig*, the CJEU was concerned with three types of barriers to interstate trade associated with the exclusive distribution agreement conferred on the French distributor: the first was the restriction on sales by the exclusive distributor directly into the territories of other distributors in other Member States. The second was the contractual obligations placed on the exclusive distributors to prevent customers from engaging in parallel exports into the territories in other Member States, ie the export bans. The third was the use of the exclusivity of the trade mark to reinforce the boundaries of the exclusive national territories by use of the infringement proceeding. Although there were strong arguments that the protection for Consten from the competition of other distributors in the Grundig distribution network provided a necessary economic incentive to Consten to invest in the distribution activity, the CJEU insisted that the costs of the barriers to integration overrode the pro-competitive benefits of the arrangement. All these elements in the arrangement were held to be *per se* distortive of competition under Article 101(1) and *per se* not capable of qualifying for exemption under Article 101(3).

The applicability of this reasoning to IP licences is all too evident. Where an exclusive licensing agreement is part of a wider network of parallel licences, there is always potential for competition between the licensees who have been allocated national territories for the same product or process. The nature of the IPR does not restrict the free movement of the goods made incorporating that right. Under EU law the right of free circulation attaches to goods as soon as they are placed on the market. Consequently, the licensees can engage in direct sales both actively by advertising or passively by responding to unsolicited orders. Moreover, the customer of licensees can engage in parallel trading, exporting or importing the licensed goods and services between the different national territories of the licensees. Insofar as this interpretation of Article 101 stresses the need to protect interstate trade, it insists on the preservation of intra-brand competition even to the point of deterring investment in licensing and the consequent spread in the manufacturing of the technology in new Member States. The reconciliation of the integration policies of Article 101 with IPRs has to confront this dilemma in the short term: if it concentrates too heavily on protecting the bridges of trade between national markets it discourages the diffusion of manufacture and new technologies.[77]

In the longer term, as the common market becomes a single continental market, the integration objective will play a less important role in the application of Article 101 to licensing agreements. Until then, it has resulted in a highly interventionist approach to regulation and creates a direct confrontation with the system of territorial protection which is necessary to convince licensees to accept the risks of investing in the manufacturing and distribution facilities necessary to exploit the licence.

From the viewpoint of the competition rules as a regulatory system for IPRs, it is useful in legal argument and analysis to recognize the way in which a narrow economic definition of the goals of competition policy has been displaced by the goals of fairness and integration in the wider concept of 'distortion' applied by the Court of Justice.

[77] See eg H. Ullrich, 'Patents and Know how, Free Trade, Interenterprise, Cooperation and Competition within the Internal European Market' [1992] *IIC* 583.

Part II

ARTICLE 102 AND INTELLECTUAL PROPERTY RIGHTS

3

ARTICLE 102 AND INTELLECTUAL PROPERTY RIGHTS

The role of Article 102 TFEU in the system of EU competition law is to regulate undertakings which have been found to occupy dominant positions on particular markets, ie those firms with extensive market power, such as near monopolies. In common with Article 101, its aim is to prohibit the use of market power to damage effective competition in markets by preventing access to markets or driving out existing competition, as well as to fix prices at higher than competitive levels. This means that both Articles 101 and 102 can occasionally apply to the same agreement or practice, but they apply independently on their own terms.[1]

Unlike Article 101, however, the method used by Article 102 is to concentrate on individual undertakings[2] which have acquired a dominant position in a particular market and closely regulate their conduct. As long as a firm is not dominant it is not touched by Article 102. Article 102 does not prohibit the legitimate acquisition of extensive market power by superior efficiency or innovativeness. Dominance itself is not unlawful. Once, however, an undertaking achieves a position of dominance it has a special responsibility 'not to allow its conduct to impair genuine undistorted competition on the common market'.[3]

The framework for the regulation of dominant undertakings under Article 102 is established by its prohibition of abusive conduct. It states:

[1] See eg *Hoffman La Roche* [1979] ECR 461; *Tetra Pak II* [1990] ECR II–309; *Italian Flat Glass* [1992] ECR II–1403. The Commission can choose to take action on one Article alone even when both may apply. See eg *IGR Stereo Television, Eleventh Report on Competition Policy*, point 63, *Fourteenth Report on Competition Policy*, point 76, discussed *infra*.

[2] This wording of Art 102 makes it clear that the concept of dominance can include more than one undertaking, ie joint dominance. See eg Case IV M.190 *Nestle/Perrier* [1992] OJL 356/1, [1993] 4 CMLR M17. For a discussion of the complications raised by this point, see eg M. Schödermeir, 'Collective Dominance Revisited: An Analysis of the EC Commission's New Concept of Oligopoly Control' [1990] ECLR 28.

[3] Case 322/81 *Nederlandsche Banden-Industrie Michelin v Commission* [1983] ECR 3461, [1985] 1 CMLR 282.

Any abuse by one or more undertakings of a dominant position within the common market or in a substantial part of it shall be prohibited as incompatible with the common market insofar as it may affect trade between Member States.[4] Such abuse in particular may consist in:

(a) directly or indirectly imposing unfair purchase or selling prices or other unfair trading conditions;

(b) limiting production, markets or technical development to the prejudice of consumers;

(c) applying dissimilar conditions to equivalent transactions with other trading parties, thereby placing them in a disadvantaged position;

(d) making the conclusion of contracts subject to acceptance by the other parties of supplementary obligations which, by their nature or according to commercial usage, have no connection with the subject of such contracts.

In its definition of abusive conduct, Article 102 havers between two different concepts of abuse. The first is the narrower economic concept of 'exploitative abuse', ie conduct which consists of using market power to extract supra-competitive gains from customers by unfairly high prices (Article 102(a)) and limiting supply to markets (Article 102(b)).

These same paragraphs have also been interpreted to include a second concept of abuse, predatory or 'exclusionary abuse,' ie conduct attempting to evict or exclude competitors from markets. This is hinted at by the abuses set out in Article 102(c), discriminatory treatment, and Article 102(d), tie-ins, which refer to conduct which appears to be directed to customers but has the indirect effect of eliminating and deterring competitors, and Article 102(b), refusals to supply.[5]

The concern with the protection of competitors has been read into Article 102 as part of a wider view of its function in preventing distorted competition as originally stated under Article 3(g) of the EC Treaty. The Court of Justice has proceeded on the theory that the Treaty requires the competition authorities to preserve and maintain existing competitive *structures* in markets which have already been weakened by the presence of a dominant undertaking.[6] At the same time, however, the Court of Justice has acknowledged that since dominant undertakings can achieve a dominant position by virtue of greater efficiencies and innovativeness than competitors, they cannot be required to refrain from competing on the basis of legitimate competitive means even if such conduct has the effect of further weakening residual competition on a dominated market.[7]

[4] See discussion of this concept in Chapter 13.

[5] Case 6/72 *Europemballge & Continental Can v Commission* [1973] ECR 215, [1973] CMLR 199.

[6] As the CJEU put it in Case 6/72 *Continental Can*, at para 24: 'if [Article 3g EC] provides for the institution of a system ensuring that competition in the Common Market is not distorted, then it requires a fortiori that competition must not be eliminated'. See the discussion in Chapter 6. Despite the removal of Art 3(g) EC from the TFEU, it is presumed that the CJEU will maintain the same policy towards competition; see Chapter 2.

[7] Case 85/76 *Hoffman-La Roche v Commission* [1979] ECR 461, [1979] 3 CMLR 211.

Applying these dual principles, the CJEU has expanded the list of abuses to include refusals to deal,[8] refusals to license,[9] predatory pricing,[10] and inappropriate acquisitions of competitors.[11] It has been prepared to protect individual customers who have become dependent upon dominant undertakings from unfair treatment.[12] It has also been prepared to protect competitors in secondary markets where a dominant undertaking attempts to integrate vertically or already has been engaged in operations in two related markets. Thus, a dominant undertaking may now be required to supply or license products to competitors in secondary markets.[13] Moreover, its pricing and product packaging decisions, choice of customers, and exercise of IPRs may be found to be unlawful because of their effect on existing competitors in primary or secondary markets.[14]

To understand how this concept of regulation of market power applies to IPRs requires an appreciation of two steps: first, what types of exploitation of IPRs are likely to be regarded as *prima facie* abusive under the new expanded definition of abuse.[15] Secondly, to what extent does the normal exploitation of IPRs coincide with the concept of legitimate competitive means for a dominant undertaking, or is otherwise justified under Article 102.[16]

Before assessing how the widened concept of abuse applies to IPRs, however, it is necessary to examine the preconditions to the application of Article 102.[17]

In the first place, before an IPR can be regulated by Article 102, its owner must be found to occupy a dominant position in a particular market, which is either the common market as a whole or a substantial part thereof. An exclusive right to exploit an IPR conferred by legislation does not automatically result in a finding of dominance. There must be a further finding that there are so few substitutes for the protected product or technology that the right-holder has the power in a relevant product market to

[8] Cases 6 and 7/73 *Istituto Chemioterapico Italiano SpA & Commercial Solvents Corp. v Commission* 1974 ECR 223, [1974] 1 CMLR 309.

[9] C-241–2/91P *Radio Telefis Eireann v Commission (Magill)* [1995] ECR I–743.

[10] Case 62/86 *AKZO-Chemie v Commission* [1991] ECR I–3359, [1993] 5 CMLR 215.

[11] See eg Case 6/72 *Continental Can* at para 24.

[12] See eg Case 27/76 *United Brands v Commission* [1978] ECR 207.

[13] Case 241–242/91P *Magill.*

[14] See eg C-53/92P *Hilti AG v Commission* [1994] ECR I–667, [1994] 4 CMLR 164.

[15] See eg Case 85/76 *Hoffman-La Roche.*

[16] See Chapters 5-11.

[17] One precondition for the application of Art 102 is that the abuse has an 'effect on trade between the Member States'. See Case 22/78 *Hugin v Commission* [1979] ECR 1869 for a rare case where a complaint under Art 102 has been dismissed on this ground. This precondition has been discussed in connection with Art 101 and the Commission's *de minimis* Notice (Commission Notice on agreements of minor importance which do not appreciably restrict competition under Article 81(1) of the Treaty establishing the European Community [2001] OJ C 368/13 22 December 2001). See Chapter 13. A second precondition is that the dominant position must be held on a substantial part of the common market, if not the whole of it. This is a type of *de minimis* test requiring that the dominant position be held either in a Member State or an important subdivision thereof, such as a region, a city, or even a port. The test is partly physical size but if the pattern and volume of production and consumption of the product is significant that can be enough. See eg *Striker Line v Commission* [1975] ECR 1663.

enable it to prevent effective competition being maintained on that market.[18] To assess dominance under Article 102, therefore, the first step is to determine the relevant product market upon which dominance is measured, and its geographic dimension.

For IP owners, this first step is particularly important. If the market is defined in sufficiently narrow terms, it can limit the field of legitimate exploitation of an IPR. A narrowly defined market can produce the result that possession of an IPR can coincide with or contribute to a position of dominance on a market by reducing the possibilities of substitution. This then places the IP owner into a regulated category under Article 102. Secondly, it can have the effect of making the exercise of exclusive IPRs in one 'market', which may have been perfectly acceptable as a lawful exploitation of a property right, unlawful in the second 'market' under Article 102 because it threatens the existence of competition on that 'market'[19] or because it goes beyond the scope of the IPR.[20] In other words, the narrow definition of markets can have an effect on the treatment of IPRs in the test of dominance as well as abuse.

Under Article 102, the determination of whether or not a firm has a dominant position on that market depends in general on whether the firm can behave independently of other firms in the market in respect of pricing and other decisions. For IP owners, however, it is important to recognize that there are different degrees of dominance with different legal consequences. There is, firstly, a general category of dominance which applies to undertakings in a powerful position in a market in which, however, some effective competition continues to exist. Secondly, there is a special category of dominance in a market, the extreme form of dominance—a *de facto* monopoly. If an IPR coincides with a monopoly, and that monopoly happens to be or become an essential infrastructure or essential facility, upon which other firms in related markets are dependent for their existence, competition law may place stricter limits upon the exercise of IPRs by requiring supply or access to essential inputs.

Since the whole structure of regulation by prohibition of abuse in Article 102 only applies if there is a finding of dominance upon a particular market, let us first examine the concepts of dominance (Chapter 5) and relevant market (Chapter 4) as they apply to IPRs before studying the concept of abuse and IPRs (Chapters 6-11).

[18] Case 27/76 *United Brands* at 215.
[19] See eg Case 241–242/91P *Magill*.
[20] See eg C-53/92P *Hilti*.

4

THE RELEVANT MARKET AND INTELLECTUAL PROPERTY RIGHTS

4.1 Introduction 37
4.2 The Relevant Product Market 38
4.3 The Relevant Geographic Market 53

4.1 INTRODUCTION

According to the logic of the competition rules, a preliminary step in the assessment of the market power of the owner of a product is the definition of the relevant market in which the market power is to be assessed. The relevant market definition therefore establishes a framework in which to assess whether the company in question holds market power. The relevant market definition is therefore not only relevant for an Article 102 perspective, but also an important tool under both Article 101 and merger regulation. Indeed, the approach applied to defining the relevant market has under Article 101 and its Block Exemption Regulations (BER) been more economic and to some degree more sophisticated.

The importance of the relevant market definition was highlighted by the Court of Justice in *United Brands*:[1]

> The opportunities for competition under Article [102] of the Treaty must be considered having regard to the particular features of the product in question and with reference to a clearly defined geographic area in which it is marketed ... for the effect of the economic power of the undertaking concerned to be evaluated.[2]

It is this preliminary step that has undoubtedly made a major contribution to the modern collisions between certain predatory commercial strategies and competition law. The competition authorities display a predilection for defining product markets

[1] Case 27/76 *United Brands v Commission* [1978] ECR 207.

[2] Ibid, at 287.

narrowly and narrow product markets tend to create single product markets. This approach is not aimed solely at IP owners; it is a standard feature of EU competition policy. However, it has had a direct impact upon IP owners. The EU Courts and the Commission have made it clear that the determination of a 'relevant market' requires two separate steps: the identification of a market for a particular product and its geographic dimension.[3] In addition to this, the Commission has in its Technology Transfer Block Exemption Regulation (TTBER) adjoined a technology market and an innovation market. Both are essential to the treatment of IPR, in particularly under Article 101.

4.2 THE RELEVANT PRODUCT MARKET

To identify a product market, one must start with an initial reference to a particular product, ie a good or service or group of related goods or services. There is an important distinction between a product market and a product. A product market is measured with initial reference to a single product but it is frequently wider than a single product. For any good or service there are substitutes and the analysis of competitive relationships between firms with respect to a product would normally require an assessment of the possible substitutes for that product taking into account its function, its suitability for satisfying user needs, and its price.

Hence, the traditional analysis of the relevant market by the Commission and the EU Courts has tended to place great weight upon the exploration of competitive relationships in terms of the possible substitutes for the product on the demand side in particular but also on the supply side. As the CJEU put it in *Hoffmann-La Roche*:

> The concept of the relevant market in fact implies that there can be effective competition between the products which form part of it and this presupposes that there is a sufficient degree of interchangeability between all the products forming part of the same market insofar as a specific use of such products is concerned.[4]

In the Commission Notice on the Definition of the Relevant Market, the relevant product market has been defined as '[comprising] all those products and/or services which are regarded as interchangeable or substitutable by the consumer, by reason of the products' characteristics, their prices and their intended use'.[5]

In other words, if other goods exist which are substitutable from the point of view of users, they must be considered to be within the same product market. Moreover, if suppliers would be prepared to switch their production capacity to a new product, then

[3] The CJEU also looked at a third dimension, temporal markets in Case C-27/76 *United Brands* although this has not been included in the Commission Notice on the definition of the relevant market for the purposes of Community competition law [1997] OJ C372/5, [1998] 4 CMLR 177.

[4] Case 85/76 *Hoffmann-La Roche & Co AG v Commission* [1979] ECR 461, [1979] 3 CMLR 211 at para 28.

[5] Commission Notice on the definition of relevant market (n 3 above), para 7.

they must be included in the measure of the supply side of the market. In theory, therefore the initial choice of product does not automatically define the relevant product market. Much still depends on the extent to which there are substitutes which are interchangeable in function with that product. Interchangeability can be tested by reference to the cross-elasticity of demand for a product. This is the response of demand to a small but significant increase in price such as 5 per cent.[6] To what extent do users of the product switch to other products? If there was a higher than 5 per cent shift of demand to another product, that product would be included in the market. If there was a disproportionately lower switch in demand to other products, then the relevant market would have been established according to the CJEU's guidelines of inelastic need and limited interchangeability.[7]

To measure cross-elasticity in this way would require extensive econometric and statistical analysis but this the Commission is not always willing to resort to. Instead, the Commission has also tended to rely on a consideration of other types of evidence to determine which products are sufficiently similar to be regarded by users as reasonable substitutes for one another. The first step for the Commission is to select a product and analyse its characteristics and intended use to limit the field of investigation of possible substitutes.

The Commission then may look at the following types of evidence to determine whether two products are substitutes: substitution in the recent past; views of customers and competitors; consumer preferences; barriers to switching demand; different categories of customers. Throughout the case law, there are examples of the Commission using the intended end use of the product as the starting point for the definition of markets. In *United Brands*,[8] the Commission chose bananas as a separate market from fruit after receiving evidence of different patterns of use from different consumer groups. In *Hoffmann-La Roche*,[9] there were seven groups of vitamins, each with its own market. Vitamin C could be used for two purposes, 'bio-nutritive' and 'technical'. The Commission classified Vitamin C into two markets based on different use.

The tests of substitutability are largely demand side orientated taking into account consumer and user preferences. The Commission has tended to favour demand side tests partly because the exercise emphasizes product markets from the viewpoint of consumers and customers. It has been less regular in its consideration of supply side substitutability, such as the tendency of suppliers of other products (B, C, and D) to switch their resources to the production of good A in response to a rise in price in good A.[10] It has tended to rely on supply side responses only when their effects are

[6] Ibid, para 17.

[7] See eg Case 6/72 *Europemballage Corp. & Continental Can Co Inc v Commission* [1973] ECR 215 at para 32. See also Commission Notice on the definition of the relevant market.

[8] Case 27/76 *United Brands*.

[9] Case 85/76 *Hoffmann-La Roche*.

[10] See Case 6/72 *Continental Can* at paras 32–3 in which the CJEU criticizes the Commission for not assessing the supply side of the relevant product market.

sufficiently immediate to be equivalent to demand side factors. On the other hand, even if supply substitutability does not always figure in the Commission's determination of the issue of product market, it partly compensates by considering this factor at the later stage of assessing dominance.

At some point the possibility of substitution diminishes to the point where it becomes so limited that the product can be discounted as a source of real competition. The Court of Justice has defined that point where the products in the market 'are only to a limited extent interchangeable with other products'.[11] The precise cut-off point can be a matter of judgement, whether economic, administrative, or judicial.

Although the CJEU has made much of the role of substitutability as the determinant of markets, for IP owners the initial determination of the product or service upon which the market is based may be an even more important step.

4.2.1 Defining the relevant product

If a firm accused of an abuse of a dominant position is providing a simple product, then the initial determination of the 'relevant product' calls for little discretion on the part of the competition authorities. If the product is bananas, the initial product defines itself. The Commission or EU Courts can move directly to the issue of interchangeability, ie testing whether the product forms part of a wider market. For example in *United Brands*, the major issue in the test of relevant product market was whether the market for bananas could be viewed as part of a wider market for fruit in general or was a separate product market from other fruits. The Commission could test this issue by obtaining evidence relating to the characteristics of bananas from the viewpoint of consumers, for example the way they particularly satisfy the needs of the young, the elderly, and the infirm. The EU Courts could support the Commission's decision, holding that bananas were 'only to a limited extent interchangeable with' other fruits and 'only exposed to their competition in a way that is hardly perceptible'. The initial selection of the product upon which the market analysis was to be based, itself, created no legal issue.[12]

When, however, the product is more technically complex, the selection of the initial product involves the exercise of greater discretion by the competition authorities. They can decide whether and to what extent to view the various sub-products or raw materials as components of an integrated product and to what extent to view each sub-product or raw material as a product in its own right.[13] In the case of products such as consumables and spare parts, they can decide whether they are part of the product package

[11] Case 322/81 *Nederlandsche Banden-Industrie Michelin v Commission* [1983] ECR 3461, [1985] 1 CMLR 282 at para 37.

[12] Case 27/76 *United Brands*.

[13] See also Commission Regulation (EC) No 772/2004 of 27 April 2004 on the application of Article 81(3) of the Treaty to categories of technology transfer agreements OJ L 123, 27 April 2004, pp 11–17 *(TTBER)* Art 1(1)(e) and Commission Notice, Guidelines on the application of Article 81 of the EC Treaty to technology transfer agreements [2004] OJ C101/2, paras 19–25.

presented by the firm to users and consumers or separate products creating separate markets. Furthermore, where a firm has integrated two different levels of economic activity within the same company, the Commission can decide whether these operations constitute an integrated operation offering one 'product' or are separate activities offering separate products on separate markets despite the corporate form of the operations.

From a commercial point of view, firms consider decisions such as the selection of product and product packaging to be the essence of their commercial judgement in marketing generally and in the exploitation of IPRs in particular. Moreover, the organization of business operations is a matter of corporate strategy.

From the viewpoint of the competition authorities charged with protecting effective competition in markets, however, the choice of product market for the purpose of enforcing Article 102 is governed by considerations of regulatory policy. Even where a firm may be convinced that its product package or its business operation is an integrated whole, the Commission may choose a narrower definition of product in line with its regulatory priorities and thereby set the stage for a finding of narrow product market.

The significance of the step of selecting the initial product in defining markets for IP owners can be illustrated by looking at *Hilti*.[14] Hilti was and is a firm that specializes in producing nail guns, cartridges, and nails as parts of a powder-activated fastening (PAF) system for the construction industry. Eurofix and Bauco, two independent manufacturers of Hilti-compatible nails, complained to the Commission that Hilti was engaged in the practice of tying the sales of cartridges with requirements to buy nails and that this was having the effect of driving them out of the market. Hilti's response was to maintain that it had no dominant position in the relevant product market because that market was the market for PAF systems consisting of a combination of their nail guns, cartridge strips, and nails into an integrated product. This product competed with other types of fastening systems in the construction sector. The Commission, however, decided that Hilti-compatible cartridge strips and Hilti-compatible nails formed separate products and separate product markets. This finding then provided a springboard for the further finding that Hilti was dominant in the market for Hilti-compatible cartridge strips. Prominent in this finding of dominance was the existence of a patent on the cartridges held by Hilti which allowed it legitimately to exclude competition. In addition, the strong economic position of Hilti in the nail gun market reinforced its dominance in the cartridge strip market.

In *Hilti*, moreover, the definition of market went beyond the issue of dominance and influenced the issue of abuse. Since there were separate markets for cartridge strips and nails, and only the cartridge strip was a patented product, the tie-in with the unpatented nails was caught by Article 102 as a case of attempted leveraging of the patent protection going beyond the scope of the patent. The Commission could characterize the commercial practices of Hilti in tying in sales of their patented product in the cartridge market to sales of non-patented nails as an abuse of its dominant position in the

[14] C-53/92P *Hilti AG v Commission* [1994] ECR I–667, [1994] 4 CMLR 614.

cartridge strip market. Furthermore, since Hilti's patents in the UK were subject to licences of right, the Commission could examine the level of royalties charged by Hilti to determine whether they were set so high as to constitute an indirect refusal to supply under Article 102. Both findings of abuse, as well as the finding of dominance, could only be sustained because of the prior definition of product markets.[15]

The General Court (GC) supported this narrow view of the relevant product market stating that Hilti's argument that nail guns, cartridge strips, and nails 'should be regarded as forming an indivisible whole . . . is in practice tantamount to permitting producers of nail guns to exclude the use of consumables other than their own branded products in their tools'.[16] The GC added that as far as EU competition law is concerned, 'any independent producer is quite free . . . to manufacture consumables intended for use in equipment manufactured by others, unless in so doing it infringes a patent or some other industrial or intellectual property right'.[17]

Once the GC had accepted that the market in nail guns had been designated as the relevant product, the finding of dominance was assured by Hilti's high market share of between 70–80 per cent. The GC also agreed with the Commission that the existence of a patent on cartridge strips strengthened Hilti's position in the market for Hilti-compatible consumables in general.[18]

On appeal, Advocate General Jacobs raised the point that if the PAF system competed with non-PAF systems in a wider market, which included both systems, Hilti would not be dominant. The CJEU, however, was not to be drawn on this substantive issue. The CJEU was reluctant to attack the determination of the relevant market decision which was a conclusion of law by the GC, because it would in effect require the CJEU to reappraise the evidence before the GC.[19] As an appellate court, the CJEU was willing only to investigate whether there was an error of law involved in the GC's decision on the substitutability issue. As Advocate General Jacobs pointed out, however, the CJEU would be bound to consider an argument that the GC omitted to take relevant facts into consideration because this could amount to an error of law and a ground to annul the judgment.[20] Barring such an error, however, the CJEU is reluctant to intervene in the question of measuring substitutability of products in a particular case.

In the event, the discretion allowed to the Commission to define 'products' narrowly as the basis of product markets can predetermine the scope of the jurisdiction of Article 102. If the product selection allows the Commission to find that an undertaking is operating in two markets rather than one, it can lead to a finding of dominance in a

[15] See also Chapter 8 'tying'.

[16] Case T-30/89 *Hilti v Commission*, [1991] ECR II–1439 at para 68.

[17] Ibid, at para 68.

[18] Ibid, at paras 92–3.

[19] As the CJEU put it: 'It should be pointed out, before considering Hilti's pleas, that the Court of Justice has consistently held that . . . Article 51 of the Statute of the Court of Justice of the EEC an appeal may rely only on grounds relating to the infringement of rules of law to the exclusion of any appraisal of the facts.' C-53/92P *Hilti* at para 10.

[20] Ibid, at para 28.

secondary market, even where the firm may be engaged in robust competition in the primary market. Moreover, the definition of the product market can lead to the characterization of the conduct of the firm in exploiting its IPRs as an attempt to extend its dominance in one 'market' into related 'markets'. Since IPRs are regulated by Article 102 largely because of the characterization of markets, it is useful to look closely at the Commission's practice in this sphere as a separate step in the chain of steps leading to a finding of dominance.

A similar approach was taken by the Commission in *Tetra Pak II*, in which it found that there were four separate products and four separate product markets: aseptic carton machinery, aseptic cartons, non-aseptic carton machinery, and non-aseptic cartons. Tetra Pak had argued that the machinery and cartons were an integrated packaging system within its own market. They also argued that separating machinery and cartons could give rise to health risks and to potential damage to reputation.

In this case the Commission was more forthcoming about its motivation. It stated that: 'Article [102] precludes the manufacturer of a complex product from hindering production by a third party of consumable products intended for use in its systems.'[21] Again, this approach of the Commission received support from the GC which stated that: 'In the absence of general and binding standards or rules, any independent producer is quite free, as far as EU competition law is concerned, to manufacture consumables intended for use in equipment manufactured by others, unless in so doing it infringes a competitor's intellectual property right.'[22]

The implication of this statement is that unless a consumable itself is protected by the IPR, it is viewed as a separate product and cannot be bundled with another product which is protected by an IPR. The method used by the Commission to pursue this regulatory policy is to define each product as the base for a separate market.

4.2.2 Narrow product markets and Commission practice

The technique of defining product markets narrowly in *Hilti* (and *Tetra Pak II*) could be traced back to the case of *Hugin*,[23] in which the cash register manufacturer ended a relationship with a distributor repairer, Lipton, and refused to supply him with spare parts once he was no longer part of Hugin's dealer network. In analysing the complaint under Article 102, the CJEU was prepared to find that there was a separate market for spare Hugin parts required by independent undertakings specializing in maintenance and repair of Hugin cash registers from the market for cash registers generally. This then led to a finding that Hugin was dominant in the 'market' for new spare parts for Hugin cash registers despite the robust degree of interbrand competition on the general cash register market.

The method of reasoning of the Commission and CJEU involved as a first step their acceptance of Hugin spare parts as separate products from new cash registers because of

[21] Case T-83/91 *Tetrapak v Commission* [1994] ECR II–755 at para 81.

[22] Ibid, at para 83, affirmed. CJEU Case C-333/94P [1997] 4 CMLR 662 at para 36.

[23] Case 22/78 *Hugin v Commission* [1979] ECR 1869.

the existence of demand from independent undertakings specializing in the maintenance and repair of cash registers, the reconditioning and sale of used machines, and the rental of Hugin machines. In other words, in *Hugin*, the CJEU reasoned that a separate product market could be said to exist if there was a separate demand for the product.

Once the initial product could be defined as narrowly as new Hugin spare parts, they could then be found to be part of a single product 'market' because (1) they were not interchangeable with the spare parts for other cash registers, and (2) they were not interchangeable with old Hugin spare parts, for the purpose required by independent undertakings in the maintenance market.[24]

One significance of this finding for IP right-holders is that if the initial choice of product is defined by reference to demand, there is little room for arguments that product markets should be defined by conditions of supply, such as product packaging. Similarly, it leaves little scope for strategies of exploitation of IPRs which attempt to override consumer or user preferences.

Thus in *Volvo* and *Maxicar*, the issue arose whether it was possible to designate a market for spare parts as separate from the market for new cars. The car firms had argued that the replacement parts could not be viewed as a separate market from new cars because they were part of a package deal offered to the customer. The relevant market was the market for new cars and/or maintenance and repair work.

Again, there was no doubt of the commercial logic to the car manufacturers' arguments. For as a result of keeping their car prices low in relation to costs in order to compete they had increasingly taken their profits in the after-sales maintenance market. In other words, from the point of view of commercial strategy, or considerations on the supply side of the market, the two separate stages of economic activity were viewed as a comprehensive package.

In the framework of competition policy, however, the issue of selection of initial product depends on the viewpoint of consumers and users. Thus Advocate General Mischo in the two spare parts cases distinguished between the individual purchasers of cars who might be affected by the relationship between the price of spare parts and the new vehicle and those who were simply interested in repairs. The demand of the latter 'creates' a separate market:

> The fact remains that the owner of a vehicle who, at a given moment decides to repair the bodywork of his vehicle rather than change model is obliged to purchase (either directly, if he repairs the car himself, or indirectly through a garage in the manufacturer's network or through an independent repairer) a body panel which is identical in shape to the original part. Consequently, for the owners of a vehicle of a particular make the relevant market is the market made up of the body panels sold by the manufacturer of the vehicle and of the components which, being copies, are capable of being substituted for them.[25]

On similar grounds the Advocate General also rejected the arguments that there was a spare parts market in general. In all such cases, the governing factor from the

[24] Ibid, at paras 7–8.

[25] Case 53/87 *CICRA et Maxicar v Renault* [1988] ECR 6039, [1990] 4 CMLR 265 at paras 47–8 and Case 238/87 *Volvo v Veng (UK)* [1988] ECR 6211 at paras 7–8.

viewpoint of competition policy was whether there was a specific consumer demand for the product in question, ie the relevant spare parts, and whether *that* demand could be met by any other substitute products. The car makers' argument that some consumers might view the product mix as a package could not be sustained as the determinant of the relevant market if it could be shown that there were other consumers who had a need for separate spare parts either to repair cars themselves or to have their cars repaired by independent repairers.

One implication of this analysis is that the only effective defence against an initial Commission designation of product in narrow terms is to show that it is too narrow from a demand point of view. For example in *Alsatel v Novasam*,[26] the Commission had made the finding that the relevant product was the service of renting and maintaining telephone equipment. On appeal, the telephone company succeeded in convincing the CJEU that the relevant market was the market for telephone installations in general including telephones sold to the public. The CJEU's view was that since consumers would choose between buying the equipment or renting it with maintenance support, the relevant market had to be defined more widely to take account of the interchangeability.

The problem for an IP right-holder who fails to widen the initial choice of product by the Commission, is that it can face a form of double jeopardy. The narrow definition of product in the first place can reduce the possibilities of substitutes to nil and this in turn can result in a product market so narrow as to amount to a single product market. The CJEU's decision in *Hugin* has been criticized because it failed to consider possible alternative sources of supply in the form of copies made by independent undertakings. Yet Advocate General Reischl found that there were significant barriers to entry for independent undertakings to manufacture Hugin spare parts. These barriers consisted of the existing doubts and threat of considerable penalties to such manufacture rather than the legal barriers of a design right. In the event a finding of a narrow market could be justified by the absence of substitutes.

Secondly, the finding of narrow product market can result in the IPRs so curtailing substitutes that the IP owner is found to be dominant to the point of constituting a *de facto* monopoly.[27] In *Maxicar v Renault* and *Volvo v Veng*,[28] once it was accepted that the relevant market could be defined by reference to the supply of goods or provision of services protected by an IPR, then ownership of the right itself would in practice have the effect of converting a narrowly defined product as the base for a market into a single product market.

We shall see in the next chapter that this in turn can also in practice make the holder dominant.[29] What is important to see at this stage is that whether or not an IPR has the

[26] Case 247/86 *Alsatel v Novasam* [1988] ECR 5987, [1990] 4 CMLR 434 at para 17.

[27] C-241–242/91P *Radio Telefis Eireann v Commission (Magill)* [1995] ECR I–743, [1995] 4 CMLR 718.

[28] Case 237/87 *Volvo v Veng*.

[29] For example, if the relevant market was reduced to the market for body parts which could fulfil the same function as those covered by the registered design right, it would extend to those which were identical in appearance to the latter. However, any part which is identical to the protected design, infringes it, since it is precisely the appearance of the part which is protected by the right. This means that the relevant market would consist solely of the manufacturer's parts and infringing parts, the manufacture and sale of which is prevented by the IPR.

effect of converting a narrowly defined product into a single product market is an important question of fact. A narrow product market does not automatically result in an IPR creating a position of dominance. The effect of an IPR in curtailing substitutes is dependent on whether there are substitute products capable of performing the same function as the relevant product. If, in a rare case, the product which is chosen as the base for the relevant market is dependent on a particular form to fulfil its function and the IPR precludes substitutes for that form, the IPR can effectively extinguish substitutes in that market and produce dominance. For example, in the case of *Volvo*, the product was a body panel protected by design rights. If the component in question had been, say, a distributor or alternator or any part which could have been made using another design, then the IPR would not have had the effect of narrowing the product market. As long as components performing the same function were available and they were 'interoperable' with Volvo cars, the existence of the design right would not have the effect of precluding substitutes from the product market. If, however, the function of the component is inseparable from its appearance, as in body panels, and the IPR gives an exclusive right to products with that appearance, the existence of the IPR can have the effect of narrowing down the product market to a single product market. This in turn sets the scene not only for a finding of dominance on that product market for the right-holder; it could also convert a position of dominance into a monopoly.

In the *Volvo* case, the narrow market definition divided related products offered by the same firm into primary and secondary markets, a manufactured spare part and a maintenance market. Competition law thereby acknowledged that the owner of the IP-protected spare part product was a lawful monopolist in the primary market for manufacturing and selling a spare part, but found that it effectively had special responsibilities towards competitors in a secondary market. In the primary market, the IP owner was entitled to returns on his investment in the IPR as well as protection from copying. In the second or 'after' market, the IP owner had obligations to supply the IP protected product. This case introduced the concept in competition law that exploitation in neighbouring markets, even when protected by an IP, was not immune from the competition law rules. In other words, these rules prevent an IP owner from unlawfully leveraging its dominance in the primary market to obtain added market power in a secondary market.

4.2.3 'Technologies' and secondary product markets

A related feature of narrow product markets definition in recent cases has been the way in which IPRs such as patents and industrial copyright 'products' have been identified as technologies and not as end products for the purpose of 'market' definition. In the EU, as well as in the USA, 'technology markets' have been defined as essentially 'licensing markets', consisting of markets for a licensed technology and its close substitutes.[30] This concept of 'technology markets' has been applied in the assessment

[30] That is, 'the technologies or products that are close enough substitutes to constrain the exercise of the market power with respect to the intellectual property that is licensed'. See *US Antitrust Guidelines for the Licensing of Intellectual Property*, issued by the US Department of Justice and the Federal Trade

of the SIEC (Significant Impediment of Effective Competition) test in the EU and the SLC (Substantial Lessening of Competition) test in the USA to mergers as well as to IP licensing in technology transfers.[31]

In cases of abuse of dominance, this designation of markets allows a licensed technology to be viewed as an upstream product and the licensed product as a downstream product, allowing the characterization of the licensed technology as a primary market and the product market as a secondary market.[32]

This in turn can result in a finding that the IP owner is dominant in a market and even that it is an essential facility. In the *IMS*[33] case, for example, the CJEU thought that even if the '1860 brick structure', a database for storing and updating pharmaceutical sales data in Germany, may not have been established as a separate market, it could nevertheless be viewed as an indispensable input:

> it is sufficient that a potential market or even hypothetical market can be identified. Such is the case where the products or services are indispensable in order to carry on a particular business and where there is an actual demand for them on the part of undertakings which seek to carry on the business for which they are indispensable...Accordingly, it is determinative that two different stages of production may be identified and that they are interconnected, inasmuch as the upstream product is indispensable for the supply of the downstream product.[34]

Similarly in the *Microsoft*[35] case, the GC confirmed this approach by stating: 'The fact that the indispensable product or service is not marketed separately does not exclude from the outset the possibility of identifying a separate market.'[36]Again, this treatment of technology markets can be viewed as logical under the competition rules. It applies the approach directed to tangible upstream infrastructures, such as ports and ferries, to IPRs when they enjoy the real market power of essential facilities. The competition rules only distinguish between IPRs and physical infrastructures in the analysis of the concept of abuse when the test of 'exceptional circumstances' is applied.

4.2.4 Technology markets and primary markets

The demand orientated method of defining product markets by reference to substitutes can also make its contribution to a finding of narrow product markets for IPRs.

Commission 6 April 1995 (<http://www.justice.gov/atr/public/guidelines/0558.htm>) (accessed 17 November 2010), para 3.2.2; see also the *EU Technology Transfer Guidelines*, para 22.

[31] See Marcus Glader, *Innovation Markets and Competition Analysis, EU Competition Law and US Antitrust Law* (Cheltenham: Edward Elgar, 2006).

[32] A. Heinemann, 'The Contestability of IP-Protected Markets' in J. Drexl (ed), *Research Handbook on Intellectual Property and Competition Law* (Edward Elgar, 2008), p 60; see also Case C-418/01 *IMS Health GmbH & Co OHG v NDC Health GmbH & Co KG* [2004] ECR I-5039, [2004] 4 CMLR 1543 at paras 44-5.

[33] Case C-418/01 *IMS Health GmbH & Co OHG v NDC Health GmbH & Co KG* ('IMS') [2004] ECR I-5039.

[34] C-418/01 *IMS* at paras 44-5.

[35] Case T-201/04 *Microsoft Corp v Commission* (*Microsoft*) [2007] ECR II–3601.

[36] In retrospect, in C-241–242/91P *Magill* the programme listings could have been viewed as a separate product instead of a market and, as such, treated as an indispensable input for the programme guides.

For example in the *AstraZeneca* case,[37] involving a finding of the abuse of misusing the patent process in relation to its patent on Losec, a proton pump inhibitor used to treat ulcers, the product market chosen by the Commission was the market for proton pump inhibitors (PPIs). PPIs were a subset of anti-ulcer drugs but the Commission found that PPIs had progressively replaced the previous generation of anti-ulcer drugs—H2 Blockers—even though the PPIs were more expensive. It also found that there was no sign of substitution in the other direction—from PPIs to H2 Blockers. In addition, non-price factors in consumer demand were taken into account. In the event AstraZeneca could be found to have considerable market power by virtue of the position of its product, Losec, in that 'market'. This method of defining the relevant market is used regularly by the Commission even where no IPRs are involved in a product. It is Commission policy to look only at actual substitutes and not potential substitutes at the market definition stage unless they will be available within two years.[38]

Thus, in the *Rambus* case,[39] a case of abuse consisting of misusing market power to obtain higher than FRAND (Fair, Reasonable and Non-Discriminatory) royalties for certain patented technologies in the context of a technology pool and standardization process, the four patented technologies owned by Rambus would initially have been viewed as competing players in technology markets containing substitute technologies and not viewed as indispensable inputs Once the standard was selected and they were chosen as essential patents in the Joint Electron Device Engineering Council's (JEDEC) standards, SDRAM and DDR-SDRAM, they were treated as technology monopolies and indispensable inputs. This treatment of technology markets is logical under the competition rules. It is similar to the treatment of tangible upstream and downstream products such as ports and ferries. It also throws light upon the role of IPRs in contributing to a finding of dominance in relation to a protected product.

This method of defining the relevant market is used regularly by the Commission even where no IPRs are involved in a product. It is Commission policy to look primarily at actual substitutes at the market definition stage because the Commission pursues a policy of measuring the process of competition in the here and now. Potential substitutes can be taken into account to enlarge the relevant market only where they meet a strict test of being real potential substitutes.[40] In the event, current methods of market definition have the consequence for IPRs that with narrow product markets, the IPR can be found to make a significant contribution to a finding of market power.

Finally, although generally under Article 102 TFEU, product markets have tended to be defined as separate components of complex products rather than the assembled product itself, it is theoretically possible in alleged tie-in cases to counteract these

[37] Case COMP/A. 37.507/F3. *AstraZeneca* Commission decision of 15 June 2005, partly upheld on appeal GC Case T-321/07 *AstraZeneca AB (Sodertalje, Sweden) and AstraZeneca plc (London, United Kingdom) v Commission* Judgment 1 July 2010.

[38] Heinemann (n 32 above), p 56.

[39] Case COMP/38.636–*Rambus* Commission decision 9 December 2009.

[40] See Commission Notice on the definition of the relevant market, paras 20 *et seq*. See also the discussion in Heinemann (n 32 above), p 56.

narrow product market definitions if one has a case of genuine technological integration.[41] By and large, EU competition distinguishes between purely commercial strategic bundling and technological bundling. The first will not deter narrow product market definition. The second, if there is genuine evidence of technological advantage in integration, could and should preclude a narrow market definition because the bundling has in effect produced a new single product.[42] However, this presupposes that the IP owner can produce adequate evidence of technological benefit resulting from the product integration. In the *Microsoft* case, the Microsoft Corporation made the claim that its media player was integrated with its Windows operating system and consequently there was no unlawful tie-in but it failed to adduce adequate evidence of technological benefit produced by the bundling.[43]

4.2.5 Dependence, 'essential facility', and market definition

The Commission's practice of narrowly defining markets is not directed specifically at the holders of IPRs. Its designation of spare parts and consumables as separate markets has been part of a wider tendency to regulate essential infrastructures which create dependency relationships in neighbouring markets. Its actions are in part prompted by the desire to exercise regulatory control over emerging markets in particular sectors. Thus as the Commission argued to the GC in *Magill*,[44] it was determined to use Article 102 to supervize effective competition particularly in the computer software and telecommunications industries.

Moreover, the Commission's choice of relevant product market has on occasion been heavily influenced by the type of abuse that is alleged to have occurred. In *Hilti*,[45] the complaint came from the manufacturers of Hilti-compatible nails complaining that Hilti was attempting to exclude them from the market. In *Tetra Pak*[46] the abuse alleged was that of extinguishing competition in the market for aseptic cartons and machinery by the acquisition of the exclusive rights to the technology. In *Magill*[47] the abuse was the control over the publication of advanced TV programme listings. In *Soda Ash*,[48] the Commission was quite open about its approach. It stated that in determining 'the area of business in which conditions of competition and the market power of the allegedly dominant undertaking fall to be assessed . . . account has to be taken of the nature of the

[41] See eg Hedvig Schmidt, *Competition Law, Innovation and Antitrust, An Analysis of Tying and Technological Integration* (Cheltenham, UK and Northampton, MA, USA: Edward Elgar, 2009).

[42] See eg Communications from the Commission—*Guidance on the Commission's Enforcement Priorities in Applying Article 82 EC Treaty to Abusive Exclusionary Conduct by Dominant Undertakings* OJ C45, 24 February 2009, pp 7–20, para 61.

[43] Case T-201/04 *Microsoft* at para 1160.

[44] T-69–70/89, 76/89 *RTE, ITP, BBC v Commission (Magill)* [1991] ECR II–485, [1991] 4 CMLR 586.

[45] Case C-53/92P *Hilti.*

[46] Case T-83/91 *Tetrapak II*

[47] Case C-241–242/91P *Magill.*

[48] *ICI v Solvay* OJ L 152/21 [1991].

abuse being alleged and of the particular manner in which competition is impaired in the case in question'.[49]

The Commission's desire to supervize markets and prohibit abuse is particularly strong where it can be shown that the market in question consists of a natural monopoly which is an essential infrastructure for another related market. In such a case, the Commission sees its role as preventing the extinction of other competitors on that second market whether or not IPRs are involved. The desire to maintain effective competition on markets has led to the technique of narrow market definition as a jurisdictional method. The fact that the establishment of two markets as the basis for the regulation of 'essential facilities' may itself confuse jurisdictional issues with supervision issues does not appear to inhibit the Commission. Nor has it often been found to have exceeded its brief by the EU Courts. In the event, it is useful to chart in greater detail how the Commission and the EU Courts in cases other than *Hugin* have been influenced by the dependence upon essential facilities in their designation of the product market.

In the early case of *Commercial Solvents*,[50] the CJEU approved of the distinction drawn by the Commission between the raw materials market for nitropropane and aminobutanol and the final product market for the drug ethambutol, used in the treatment of tuberculosis. The raw materials were derived from the process of nitration of paraffin which at one stage had been protected by patents. In the ensuing years, Commercial Solvents had been able to protect its near monopoly position because of the capital costs of the manufacturing equipment and the lack of other commercially viable products which could be made from the raw materials. The CJEU accepted that the two markets were separate and that Commercial Solvents and its subsidiary ICI between them had a dominant position on the market for the raw materials.

This case signalled that the corporate form would not interfere with the Commission's designation of markets. Unlike Article 101, it was irrelevant that the undertaking had decided to vertically integrate from the raw material to the pharmaceutical product market. What counted was that there were two separate markets by virtue of the existence of demand on the pharmaceutical product market for the raw material. As it happened, Commercial Solvents also had a dominant position on the raw materials market because of its ownership of the production facilities for the raw materials which were indispensable for the downstream ethambutol market. However, it was a necessary condition of the finding of dominance that there were separate markets for the raw materials and the pharmaceutical product.

In *Télémarketing*,[51] a TV company in a relationship with an independent telemarketing firm attempted to vertically integrate into the lucrative market of TV advertising by

[49] Ibid. at para 42.

[50] Cases 6 and 7/73 *Istituto Chemioterapico Italiano SpA & Commercial Solvents Corp. v Commission*, 1974 ECR 223, [1974] 1 CMLR 309.

[51] Case 311/84 Centre *Belge d'Etudes du Marché-Télémarketing v Compagnie Luxembourgeoise de Télédiffusion SA and Information Publicité Benelux SA* [1985] ECR 3261, [1986] 2 CMLR 558.

ending its contractual relationship and setting up a subsidiary of its own in that field. When the advertising firm, Télémarketing, complained to the Commission, the Commission began its analysis under Article 102 by finding that there were two separate markets: the TV programme sending market and the TV advertising market. This led to a finding that the TV company was dominant in the TV programmes market and that it was abusing its dominance in that market to exclude a competitor from the secondary market.

The characterization of separate markets can be used as a method to identify dominance and regulate its effects in related markets. Thus, in the *IBM* case[52] in 1984, after receiving complaints from independent software companies about IBM's use of its information as a hardware provider to create advantageous marketing conditions for its own software providers, the Commission analysed the business operations of IBM's Systems 370 Central Processing Units and operating systems as falling into three separate markets. The Commission first isolated the market for mainframe computer systems of which IBM's Systems 370 Central Processing Unit was one product as a separate market. It then designated (1) the market for main memory attached to IBM's System 370 CPU; and (2) the market for software usable in IBM System 370, as two separate markets. The main factor in viewing the latter categories as separate markets was that once customers had chosen to buy and use IBM System 370s, they could not readily switch to competitors in the mainframe market. By defining the market narrowly, the Commission placed itself in a position to allege in its statement of objections that IBM was dominant in the markets for the supply of (1) main memory and (2) basic software for IBM System 370s and had abused its dominant position by 'tying' memory and software to the purchase of its mainframe.

More recently, we can see this technique employed in the *Microsoft* case.[53] In June 1993, the Commission received a complaint from Novell that Microsoft's licensing practices were abusive under Article 102 because they foreclosed competitors from the market for PC operating systems software. In their investigation of the abuse, the Commission made the finding that the three layers of software which could be installed upon a PC constituted separate markets: disk operating systems (DOS); graphical user interfaces (GUI); and software applications, such as word processing, etc. Again, this then led to findings of dominance, ie *de facto* industry standard, on the DOS market, and tying and discrimination in its pricing, rebates, and licensing in the GUI and software applications markets.

This technique is not limited to the large-scale operation. It can also be applied to differentiate markets to regulate situations where the owner of a smaller scale infrastructure itself engages in the secondary market. In such a case, the definition of product and relevant product market can be stretched beyond traditional market categories into concepts such as essential inputs or facilities. In the *Decca Navigation*

52 *IBM Personal Computer* EC Comm. December 84/233 (1984).

53 *XXIVth Report on Competition Policy* (1994) Annex II, p 364–5; see also *AT&T/NCR Merger* [1992] 4 CMLR M41; *Digital Kienzle* [1992] 4 CMLR M99.

Systems case,[54] for example, the Commission was prepared to characterize the provision of navigation signals as a 'market' with a downstream 'market' consisting of Decca-compatible receivers.

We can also see it in the 'essential facilities' cases in which for example the underlying railway track infrastructure is viewed as a market separate from the market for operating rail services, an electricity grid is viewed as a market separate from the market for transmitting electricity, a port is viewed as a market separate from a ferry service. In such cases the characterization of markets appears to be prompted as much by the purpose of establishing dominance as by the requirement of establishing whether in fact more objectively the jurisdictional requirements of Article 102 have been met.

In *Magill*,[55] both the GC and the CJEU, by implication if not explicitly, gave their approval of this practice. In that case, the Commission had divided the relevant product markets into three, each based upon a particular product: (1) the market for TV listings and (2) the market for weekly TV guides, both of which were ancillary to (3) the market for TV programmes. The CJEU upheld the finding that there was a market for weekly TV guides which was secondary and dependent upon the 'market' for information used to compile programme listings in which the TV companies had a *de facto* monopoly. Thus, a narrow and somewhat artificial view of product markets led to a finding of dominance in the TV listings market and a special responsibility for the TV guides market.

The finding of a separate market in TV listings information in *Magill* was a continuation of the pattern established in other cases involving IPRs in which the CJEU and the GC have accepted the Commission's practice of using a narrow product definition as the basis of a narrow market definition in order to establish dominance and hence a platform to regulate essential infrastructures in various forms.[56] We shall look more closely at this development in the next chapters after examining the geographic dimension of the product market. To a large extent IPRs seem to be caught in the crossfire of a wider policy problem. The Commission's task-orientated definition of product market is part of its concern to be an effective enforcement authority giving it regulatory control over emerging markets in particular sectors such as information technology and telecommunications. Moreover, the EU Courts appear to be willing to countenance this approach.[57]

From the viewpoint of IPRs, this practice of the Commission and the EU Courts requires careful scrutiny. For insofar as the Commission is able to establish narrow markets, it is able to place limits upon the scope for exploiting such rights. In *Volvo*,[58] the use of spare parts markets did not prevent full scope for exclusive exploitation in the spare parts market. In *Magill*, however, the CJEU accepted the point, hinted at in

[54] EC Comm. December 89/113 [1989].

[55] T-69–70/89, 76/89 *Magill*.

[56] C-22/78 *Hugin*; C-53/92P *Hilti*; C-333/94 *Tetra Pak II*.

[57] Case 481/01 *IMS Helath* at paras 44–5.

[58] Case 237/87 *Volvo v Veng*.

Volvo, that in the case of markets dependent upon another market in which an undertaking is dominant or owns an essential input or facility, the whole range of Article 102 rules relating to abuse are applicable to the exercise of IPRs.

The CJEU's decisions in *Magill* and *Hilti* suggest that the Commission's approach to narrow markets and vertical slicing can be acceptable from a competition point of view. The EU Courts are prepared to back the Commission on its designation of product. There could still be an issue of whether a complex product can be designed to be so integrated that it cannot be unbundled by the Commission's definition of product. At all events, once the Commission takes a decision to define the product narrowly, the only barrier to a finding of dominance will be finding that there are other products which are substitutable.[59]

4.3 THE RELEVANT GEOGRAPHIC MARKET

A similar phenomenon can be seen in the definition of the relevant geographic market. In the general run of competition cases, as the CJEU pointed out in *United Brands*, the geographic market is determined by reference to the area in which the product is marketed where the conditions of competition are sufficiently homogeneous to allow an evaluation of the economic power of the undertaking concerned.[60] As the Court put it in *United Brands*:

> The conditions for the application of [Article 102] to an undertaking in a dominant position presuppose the clear delineation of the substantial part of the common market in which it may be able to engage in abuses which hinder effective competition and this is an area where the objective conditions of competition applying to the product in question must be the same for all traders.[61]

In *United Brands*, a rough and ready consideration of transport costs resulted in the inclusion of six other Member States, while the presence of specific regulations of imports and marketing arrangements in the UK, France, and Italy led to their exclusion from the relevant geographic market for bananas. In later cases, both economic factors, such as transport costs and the location of production facilities, and regulatory factors have figured prominently in the determination of the relevant geographic market.

From the viewpoint of IPRs, it is significant that the economic criteria used regularly in the assessment of relevant markets under the Merger Regulation are not always used as regularly under Article 102. Under the Merger Regulation, a more economic approach is taken to the assessment of the relevant geographic market, with the result that the degree of interpenetration of trade features in the assessment. In such cases, the

[59] *Commission's Enforcement Guidelines on Article 82* (n 42 above) para 51.

[60] Case 76 *United Brands* at paras 10–11; see also Commission Notice on the definition of the relevant market (n 32 above), paras 8, 28–30, and 44–52.

[61] Ibid, at para 44.

geographic market has been drawn widely as consisting of Western Europe[62] or the Union,[63] depending upon the actual trade flows or supply patterns.

Under Article 102, in contrast, the geographic market has often been chosen as the area in which a state monopoly is conferred, as in telecommunications, or an area in which a firm enjoys IP protection, without the follow up of an empirical analysis of interpenetration of trade. In part this is because the choice of the state as the relevant geographic area has been prompted more by regulatory than economic criteria. Thus in *British Telecom* and *Magill* the choice of national markets was dictated by the absolute monopoly conferred by legislation.

In some cases, the geographic area has been narrowed to the area in which the abuse has occurred. This could be seen in *Michelin*[64] in which the Netherlands was taken as the relevant market. This helped to support a finding of dominance which in turn provided the basis of a finding of abuse by Michelin. However, the Commission's criterion for the determination of the geographic market was that the tyre manufacturers had chosen to organize themselves into national markets. Yet this ignored the possibilities of competing suppliers obtaining supplies outside the Netherlands either from passive or active sellers. In all such cases, the determination of the relevant geographic market looks less like an objective economic assessment of homogeneous market conditions and more an administrative device for underpinning findings of dominance and abuse. The definition of the geographic market in *Michelin* was therefore heavily criticized,[65] yet the Commission, despite greater attention to detail, took the same approach in *Michelin II*,[66] and found that the relevant geographic market was France.

Further examples of this tendency can be seen in the application of the test of whether the relevant geographical market is a substantial part of the common market. In some dependence and essential facility cases the choice of geographic market is so narrow that it can consist of a single port.[67] It is not at all clear that the Commission has the firm support of the EU Courts on this issue. Although the Commission cites *Hugin* for support, some cases have cast doubt on the EU Courts' willingness to accept the Commission's assessment of narrow markets which ignore competitive forces. In

[62] See eg *Mannesman/Vallourec/Ilva* [1994] OJ L 102/15.

[63] See eg *Pilkington-Technint/SIV* OJ L 158, 25 June 1994.

[64] Case C-322/81 *Michelin I*; see also Case C-286–8/96P *Commission v Solvay* [2000] ECR I–2391; Case T-65-89 *BPB Industries and British Gypsum Ltd v Commision* [1993] ECR II–389, [1993] 5 CMLR 32.

[65] See Valentine Korah, 'The Michelin Decision of the Commission' [1982] 7 *EL Rev* 130, 131.

[66] *Michelin* [2001] OJ L 143/1, [2002] 5 CMLR 388, at paras 119–71, upheld upon appeal Case T-203/01 *Manufacture française des pneumatiques Michelin v Commission* [2003] ECR II–4071, [2004] 4 CMLR 923.

[67] See eg Case 179/90 *Merci Conventzionale Porto di Genova* [1991] ECR I–5889; C-18/93 *Corsica Ferries Italia SRL v Corpo del Piloti del Porto di Genova* 7 May 1994; and more controversially *Sea Containers v Stena Sealink* [1993] OJ L 15/8 [1995] 4 CMLR 84 in which the Commission held the port of Holyhead to be the relevant geographic market for the central corridor between the UK and Ireland, despite the obvious possibility of setting up a competing ferry route from Liverpool. After having been granted access in the Commission decision, Sealink did precisely that; Simon Bishop and Derek Richard, 'Oscar Bronner–Legitimate Refusal to Supply' in John Grayston (ed), *European Economics and Law: competition, single market and trade* (Bembridge: Palladian Law, in association with Lawfully Simple, 1999).

Italian Flat Glass,[68] for example, the Commission's assessment of Italy was rejected by the CJEU because the Commission had failed to examine the competitive effects of competing products from other countries.[69] Even more significant for IP owners was the case of *Tetra Pak II*[70] in which the GC rejected the Commission's decision that significant price differences in different Member States were relevant to a finding of the relevant geographic market.

In the more recent *British Airways* case, the GC confirmed what it had said in *Tetra Pak II* that the conditions need not be 'perfectly homogeneous' for a territory to be established as the geographic market.[71] In this case, it upheld the Commission's finding of the UK as the relevant geographic market, but not after considering competition from outside the market.

In *Intel*, a case very much concerned with IPR, the Commission was rather more lenient with the scope of the geographic market and defined as 'worldwide' based on the fact that 'the main suppliers compete globally, CPU (Central Processing Unit) architectures are the same around the world, the main customers (OEMs) operate on a worldwide basis, and the cost of shipping CPUs around the world is compared to their cost of manufacture'.[72]

In sum, if the definition of geographic markets underestimates substitutabilities, it can be used more readily as a springboard to a finding of dominance by the Commission.

Other elements, such as the expansion of the Internet and other high-technological products and services, the further integration of the European internal market, and the adoption of the Euro, should all in fact lead to the broadening of the geographic market. These developments have yet to be clearly reflected in case law and therefore the policy of narrow market definitions both in relation to product and geographic markets still stands.

[68] [1990] 4 CMLR 535 at para 77.

[69] Although an Art 101 case, the GC also rejected the Commission's definition of the relevant market in Case T-374/94 *European Night Services v Commission* [1998] ECR II–3141.

[70] T-83/91 *Tetra Pak II*; see also C-333/94 *Tetra Pak II*.

[71] Case T-219/99 *British Airways v Commission* [2004] 4 CMLR 1008 at para 108, and Case T-83/91 *Tetra Pak II*, at para 91.

[72] Case COMP/C-3/37.990–*Intel* Commission decision of 13 May 2009, D(2009) 3726 final (<http://ec.europa.eu/competition/elojade/isef/index.cfm?fuseaction=dsp_result> (last accessed 28 June 2010)), para 836.

5

THE CONCEPT OF DOMINANCE AND INTELLECTUAL PROPERTY RIGHTS

5.1 Introduction 57
5.2 Dominance and Intellectual Property Rights 58
5.3 The Methods of Assessing Dominance 59
5.4 Dominance, Intellectual Property Rights, and Barriers to Entry 63
5.5 A Note on Ordinary and Special Dominance 64

5.1 INTRODUCTION

Once the relevant market has been defined, the next step under Article 102 is to determine whether in fact the accused undertaking is in a dominant position on that market. If dominance was measured according to purely economic criteria, the test would consist of the power to limit output in order to raise prices and to extract profits above the competitive level from that market.

Under Article 102, however, the test of dominance has been traditionally defined by a legal assessment of prevention of effective competition and market independence. As the Court of Justice put it in *United Brands*, a dominant position is:

> a position of economic strength enjoyed by an undertaking which enables it to prevent effective competition being maintained on the relevant market by affording it the power to behave to an appreciable extent independently of its competitors, its customers and ultimately of its consumers.[1]

In *Hoffmann-La Roche*, the CJEU went on to indicate that the definition of dominance does not apply solely to monopolies:

> Such a position does not preclude some competition, ... but enables the undertaking which profits by it, if not to determine, at least to have an appreciable influence on the conditions under

[1] Case 27/76 *United Brands v Commission* [1978] ECR 207 at para 38; similar formulations were used in Case 85/76 *Hoffmann-La Roche v Commission* [1979] ECR 461, [1979] 3 CMLR 211, and Case 322/81 *Nederlandsche Banden-Industrie Michelin v Commission* [1983] ECR 3461, [1985] 1 CMLR 282.

which that competition will develop, and in any case to act largely in disregard of it so long as such conduct does not operate to its detriment.[2]

On the other hand, dominance can extend to monopoly. In *Commercial Solvents*,[3] the dominant undertaking was found to have a world monopoly over the production facilities for raw materials. In *Magill*,[4] the TV companies were found to have *de facto* monopoly over the TV listings which were necessary for the production of TV guides. In all these cases, the more intense degree of dominance had an effect on the standards of conduct required under the test of abuse. For IP owners, therefore, it is necessary to be aware not merely of the threshold definition of dominance but also the special category of monopoly or essential input.

5.2 DOMINANCE AND INTELLECTUAL PROPERTY RIGHTS

The CJEU has long reassured IP owners that the ownership of an IPR does not amount to dominance. In *Deutsche Grammophon*, the CJEU stated that possession of an IPR did not automatically amount to a position of dominance:

> The manufacturer of sound recordings who holds a right related to copyright does not occupy a dominant position within the meaning of [Article 102] merely by exercising his exclusive rights to distribute the protected article. [Article 102] further requires that the manufacturer should have the power to impede the maintenance of effective competition over a considerable part of the relevant market—in particular to the existence of any producers making similar products and to their position on the market.[5]

This indicates that exclusive IPRs are not equated with dominance. It gives recognition to the reality that exclusive rights are essentially negative rights; they do not automatically result in positive right to exploit a protected product. The actual possibilities of commercial exploitation depend upon the extent of demand and competition in the market for the protected product or process.

The CJEU's formulations have never precluded the possibility that the ownership and exercise of IP can coincide with dominance. In *Télémarketing*, for example, the CJEU stated that: 'The fact that the absence of competition or its restriction on the relevant market is brought about or encouraged by provisions laid down by national law in no way precludes the application of [Article 102].'[6] There are situations where the power to exclude the marketing of infringing goods can create a dominant position by impeding

[2] Case 85/76 *Hoffmann-La Roche*.

[3] Cases 6 and 7/73 *Istituto Chemioterapico Italiano SpA & Commercial Solvents Corp. v Commission* [1974] ECR 223, [1974] 1 CMLR 309.

[4] C-241–242/91P *Radio Telefis Eireann v Commission (Magill)* [1995] ECR I–743, [1995] 4 CMLR 718.

[5] Case 78/70 *Deutsche Grammophon Gesellscharft mbH v Metro-SB-Grossmarketete GmbH & Co* [1971] ECR 487, [1971] CMLR 631 at para 16.

[6] Case 311/84 *Centre Belge d'Etudes du Marché-Télémarketing v Compagnie Luxembourgeoise de Télédiffusion SA and Information Publicité Benelux SA* [1985] ECR 3261, [1986] 2 CMLR 558 at para 16.

competition. Similarly, there are situations where the ownership of an IPR can be viewed under Article 102 as producing a *de facto* monopoly. Much depends upon the criteria used to establish when they will coincide with dominance or monopoly.

5.3 THE METHODS OF ASSESSING DOMINANCE

The assessment of dominance by the Commission often begins with the market share of a firm. As the Court of Justice said in *Hoffmann-La Roche*:[7]

> although the importance of the market shares may vary from one market to another the view may legitimately be taken that very large shares are in themselves and save in exceptional circumstances, evidence of a dominant position. An undertaking which has a very large market share and holds it for some time by means of the volume of production and scale of the supply which it stands for … is by virtue of that share in a position of strength which makes it an unavoidable trading partner …[8]

For example, in *Commercial Solvents* there was a finding of a 'world monopoly'.[9] In *Continental Can* market shares of 70–90 per cent[10] or in the *Sugar* case of 85–95 per cent[11] were clear cases of dominance. In the case of undertakings with IPRs, a sufficiently narrow definition of markets can produce a finding of similarly high market shares. In *Tetra Pak II*,[12] for example, Tetra Pak was found to have 92 per cent of the market for non-aseptic milk cartons. In both *Magill* and *IMS,* the dominant companies were found to hold *de facto* monopolies in the markets surrounding their IPR and in *Intel*[13], Intel was found to hold 80 per cent market shares in the x86 CPU market.

Yet a high market share by itself is rarely sufficient to establish dominance. If used alone it offers only a static picture of relative shares at one point in time. The Commission regards the market share of the accused undertaking only as a preliminary indication of the existence of a dominant position. It looks at the market shares of any other products that may exist in the relevant market but it also looks at the dynamics of the market, product differentiation, barriers to expansion and entry, and countervailing buying power.[14] In the case of IPRs the analysis of the extent of actual and potential competition raises the issue of how the IPRs protecting a product affect the possibilities of substitution both in respect of actual substitutes and potential substitutes, ie the extent to which they constitute real barriers to entry and impediments to competition.

[7] Case 85/76 *Hoffmann-La Roche.*

[8] Ibid, at para 41.

[9] Cases 6 and 7/73 *Commercial Solvents.*

[10] Case 6/72 *Europemballage Corp & Continental Can Co Inc v Commission* [1973] ECR 215, [1973] CMLR 199.

[11] [1975] ECR 1663 at pp 1973, 1977–8.

[12] Case C-333/94P *Tetra Pak International SA v Commission (Tetra Pak II)* [1996] ECR I–5951, [1997] 4 CMLR 662.

[13] Case COMP/C-3/37.990–*Intel* Commission decision of 13 May 2009, D(2009) 3726 final (<http://ec.europa.eu/competition/elojade/isef/index.cfm?fuseaction=dsp_result> (last accessed 28 June 2010)) at para 852.

[14] Communications from the Commission—*Guidance on the Commission's Enforcement Priorities in Applying Article 82 EC Treaty to Abusive Exclusionary Conduct by Dominant Undertakings* OJ C45, 24 February 2009, pp 7–20, paras 13–18.

However, the essential factor to be examined closely is the existence of actual competition. The starting point for the Commission is usually the market shares and market power of competitors. In *Michelin I*, for example, the CJEU confirmed that the Commission was entitled to rely upon the fact that Michelin's share of the market for new replacement tyres for heavy vehicles of 57–65 per cent established dominance when the market shares of its main competitors were only 4–8 per cent.[15]

In contrast, in *Rhone Poulenc/SNIA*,[16] the Commission could find that the market share of the proposed joint venture of 53 per cent for nylon fibres would not impede competition on that market where another firm, Dupont—a powerful American multinational, had a market share of 20 per cent and the resources to compete fairly aggressively.

In cases where there are *actual* substitutes for the protected product in the market, there is still a need to investigate their real possibilities of substitution. First mover advantage, brand name, and distribution system may all impede competitors in competing with the dominant undertaking in the primary market. An IPR can be associated with a dominant undertaking enjoying market power deriving from factors in addition to the IP protection against copies.

For example in the *AstraZeneca* case, its product Losec was found to be dominant in certain national markets for proton pump inhibitors (PPI), by virtue both of its high market share and by its position of incumbent on that market because Losec was the first PPI and AstraZeneca had considerable financial resources. Losec's market share was also protected by its patent on omeprazole and its brand name. However, its position as first mover and its financial resources were at least as important as the patent in enabling AstraZeneca to obtain and maintain higher prices than later entrants on the market.[17] The Commission also found that the power of monopsony buyers was considerably reduced in the case of innovative new products. As evidenced by its premium pricing, AstraZeneca's market power was not seriously constrained by existing competition in the market. On these issues, the Commission's decision was supported by the General Court (GC).[18] Moreover, the GC emphasized the contribution to market power offered by the patent protection of Losec when used as a means to put significant pressure on competitors and force their hand in entering patent settlements.[19]

A second, behavioural indicator of dominance along with a high market share, is evidence of control over price. For example, in *AKZO*,[20] the ability of the undertaking to maintain its overall profit margins by regular price increases and increases in volume even in periods of general recession was a factor which led to a finding of dominance. Moreover, in *Hoffmann-La Roche* the CJEU indicated that, 'the fact that an undertaking is compelled

[15] Case 322/8 *Michelin I* at para 52.

[16] OJ C 212/23 [1992].

[17] Case T-321/05 *AstraZeneca* at paras 276–83 and 284–6.

[18] Ibid, at para 261.

[19] Ibid, at para 272.

[20] Case 62/86 *AKZO-Chemie v Commission* [1991] ECR I–3359, [1993] 5 CMLR 215.

by the pressure of its competitors' price reductions to lower its own prices is in general incompatible with that independent conduct which is the hallmark of a dominant position'.[21] This is not to say that price cuts during a time period, even if allied with market share reductions, are necessarily a defence to dominance. In *Hoffmann-La Roche* the CJEU found that the price cuts of vitamins varied with the volume of production and costs as opposed to being imposed by the pressure of competition.[22] In *AstraZeneca*,[23] the way in which the firm was able to maintain premium pricing even when facing a monopsony of buyers was taken by the Commission as evidence of dominance.[24]

Even if there is little actual competition on the market, there still may be real potential competition which can convince an undertaking with a high market share to behave as if it was in a competitive market simply in order to discourage entry by other firms. Along with proof of the existence of real potential competitors outside the market and ready to move in,[25] the Commission will look to evidence of any existing barriers to entry which can reinforce a high market share and prevent access to the relevant market.[26] If the market share of the product of the accused firm is very high, even approaching 100 per cent there will still be a need for an assessment of *potential* substitutes and the extent to which they are barred from entry by the IPRs of the incumbent. An enhanced understanding of the potential contestability of markets has drawn the regulators' attention to the role of IPRs as a barrier to entry to potential competitors.[27]

In some rare cases, the IPR itself can operate as a barrier to entry, creating a *de facto* monopoly. For example in *Volvo v Veng (UK) Ltd*,[28] the design right prevented all substitution because the design of the front wing coincided with its function, to provide a wing with the correct shape to fit in with the design of the car. Similarly in *Hilti*, the designation of the stapling gun and cartridges as separate products on separate markets meant that the legal monopoly of the patent resulted in a finding of real monopoly. Further, in the *Rambus* case, the finding of monopoly power was linked to the selection of the patented technology as an essential patent in the industrial standard. Prior to this step, the market power of the patented products was limited by the existence of substitute technologies. Once the patented products were chosen as essential to the Joint Electron Device Engineering Council's (JEDEC) standards: SDRAM and DDR-SDRAM, the market power of the Rambus patented technology

[21] Case 85/76 *Hoffmann-La Roche* at para 71.

[22] Ibid, at para 72.

[23] Case COMP/A. 37.507/F3 *AstraZeneca* Commission decision 15 June 2005.

[24] Ibid, at para 547, confirmed by the GC Case T-321/05 *AstraZeneca* at paras 255–69.

[25] See eg *Mannesman-Vallorec* OJ L 102/15 [1994].

[26] Case COMP/C-3/37.792 *Microsoft* Commission decision of 24 March 2004, [2005] 4 CMLR 965 at para 429.

[27] See eg A. Heinemann, 'The Contestability of IP-Protected Markets' in J. Drexl (ed), *Research Handbook on Intellectual Property and Competition Law* (Cheltenham UK, Northampton MA: Edward Elgar, 2008), p 54.

[28] Case 238/87 *AB Volvo v Erik Veng (UK) Ltd* [1988] ECR 6211.

became an indispensable input and it enjoyed a lawful monopoly of that input owing to its patent.

However, the barriers to entry encountered by a firm attempting to enter a market often consist of factors other than IPRs. One example is the resources of a firm with a high market share which are or can be used to raise the costs of or otherwise discourage potential competitors from taking the decision to invest in the market. These can include high expenditure on advertising. They can also apply to the extent to which a dominant firm has developed capital intensive operations, raising the minimum level of investment needed to enter. If the capital equipment is highly specialized and would be difficult to sell off in the event of business failure, this tends to raise the ante even higher. A firm's high degree of vertical integration has also been viewed as giving firms a competitive advantage and thereby deterring entry.[29] In *United Brands*, for example, the extent to which the United Brands group extended into banana growing and shipping tended to reinforce its dominance on the upstream banana distribution market. Moreover, a firm's cushion of capital has been viewed as having the effect of deterring competitors.[30]

Another resource viewed by the competition authorities as reinforcing dominance has been the technological superiority of the firm vis-à-vis its rivals. In *Hilti*,[31] the Commission identified a strong research and development function as a factor reinforcing its position of dominance. In *Tetra Pak I*,[32] technological superiority achieved through capital investment was a factor in dominance. In *Michelin I*,[33] the CJEU stressed the lead established over competitors in matters of investment and research and the special extent of the range of its tyres. In the case of certain types of tyre, the Michelin group was the only supplier on the market. In *Hoffmann-La Roche*,[34] for example, there was a finding of technological superiority despite the fact that Roche's patents for the manufacture of vitamins had expired. Roche attempted to argue that the expiry of patent protection was a factor suggesting the absence of dominance. The CJEU, however, accepted the Commission's arguments that the extensive know-how of the company was a factor giving it a lead over its competitors and that exclusive rights preventing third parties from entering the market were not essential to a finding of technological advantage.

If technological supremacy is viewed as helping to establish dominance, it could be argued that EU competition law appears to be levying a penalty for R&D investment and high quality of product.[35] The Court's view, however, has been that a finding of dominance is not itself unlawful; it simply imposes a special responsibility on the dominant undertaking not to engage in prohibited conduct.

[29] Case 27/76 *United Brands*.
[30] Case 6/72 *Continental Can*.
[31] C-53/92P *Hilti AG v Commission* [1994] ECR I–667, [1994] 4 CMLR 614.
[32] Case T-83/91 *Tetrapak Rausing SA v Commission (Tetra Pak II)* [1990] ECR II–309, [1991] 4 CMLR 334.
[33] Case 322/81 *Michelin I*.
[34] Case 85/76 *Hoffmann-La Roche*.
[35] This argument was made by the French Government in Case 322/81 *Michelin I*.

5.4 DOMINANCE, INTELLECTUAL PROPERTY RIGHTS, AND BARRIERS TO ENTRY

A similar issue arises in cases in which it has been held that the exclusivity created by protection of IPRs is an important barrier to entry, reinforcing dominance. In *Hilti*,[36] for example, the firm's cartridge strips were protected by patents in all Member States apart from Greece and Germany and the firm claimed copyright protection in the UK and this was viewed as an important factor reinforcing dominance. In *Tetra Pak I*[37] the acquisition of the exclusive patent licence was viewed as a barrier to entry because it prevented access to the technology by potential competitors.

For right-holders the main risk of dominance occurs if the product market is defined in sufficiently narrow terms as to create a single product market. For then, the existence of an IPR could extinguish competition and thereby confirm the dominant position of the undertaking owning the right incorporated in the product.

In some rare cases, the IPR itself can operate as a barrier to entry, creating a *de facto* monopoly. For example in *Volvo v Veng*,[38] the design right prevented all substitution because the design of the front wing coincided with its function, to provide a wing with the correct shape to fit in with the design of the car.[39] In *Volvo v Veng* and *CICRA & Maxicar v Renault*,[40] the Advocate General alerted the Court that when the relevant market is reduced to a product covered by an IPR, the fact that the IPR precludes substitutes itself ensured a finding of dominance. This suggests that the mere holding of the right could amount to dominance because the enforcement of the manufacturer's right makes it impossible for the consumer to obtain a substitute product. Similarly in *Hilti,* the designation of the stapling gun and cartridges as separate products on separate markets meant that the legal monopoly of the patent resulted in a finding of real monopoly.

However, more frequently, the IPR acts in conjunction with other restrictive forces. For example, in *Rambus*, the finding of monopoly power was linked to the selection of the patented technology as an essential patent in the industrial standard rather than the patent as such. Prior to the selection of the standard, the market power of the patented products was limited by the existence of substitute technologies. Once the patented products were chosen as essential to the Joint Electron Device Engineering Council's (JEDEC) standards, SDRAM and DDR-SDRAM, the market power of the Rambus patented technology became an indispensable input and it enjoyed a lawful monopoly of that input owing to its patent. Further, in *Magill,* the CJEU found that the *de facto* monopoly was created by the TV companies' control over the source of the information

[36] C-53/92P *Hilti*.

[37] Case T-83/91 *Tetra Pak II*.

[38] Case 238/87 *Volvo v Veng (UK)* [1988] ECR 6211.

[39] Ibid. See also Case 22/78 *Hugin v Commission* [1979] ECR 1869, [1979] 3 CMLR 345.

[40] Ibid.

about programme listings as well as the existence of copyright protection.[41] And in *Intel*, the IPR themselves were seen as significant barriers to entry. The Commission found that not only was a new entrant to the market faced with substantial expenditure to develop the necessary know-how to design and produce competitive x86-microprocessors for use in computers, but was also in need of access to, ie licence of the x86 instruction set which was held by Intel.[42]

In *Microsoft*, the GC found that the major source of market power was the applications barrier to entry and 'network effects'. These barriers to entry precluded substitutes far more effectively than the IP protection as such.

The method used by the Commission is to assess the factual market power of the IP owner and not make any assumptions about the market power of the legal monopoly. Consequently, as long as the competition authority concentrates on assessing the existence of market power empirically and recognizes that not all patents are automatically monopolies because of the real possibilities of product substitution, it is difficult to criticize a finding of dominance based on a factual matrix.

5.5 A NOTE ON ORDINARY AND SPECIAL DOMINANCE

Finally, in the case of a finding of a primary market protected by an IPR and a derivative market, whether a downstream 'aftermarket' or a 'neighbouring' market, the competition rules apply an important filtering rule that restricts remedies for compulsory access to IPRs to extreme cases. Unlike other abuses, which often only require a prior finding of ordinary dominance, generally defined as above 40 per cent or 50 per cent.[43] In some cases, such as the discriminatory pricing cases, ordinary dominance can go as low as 39.7 per cent.[44] One criticism of these cases is that there is insufficient market power to justify calling the pricing conduct abusive.[45] However, the same cannot be said about the abuse of refusal to license, because that abuse requires proof of a special degree of dominance, defined as consisting of two elements. The first is that there is a *de facto* monopoly over an input. The second is that that input is indispensable to a second product in a secondary market. This type of dominance is sometimes called 'super-dominance' or 'essential facilities' dominance although this latter label is rarely applied in IP cases.[46]

[41] A similar finding was made in Case C-418/01 *IMS Health v NDC Health* [2004] ECR I-5039.

[42] *Intel* at paras 854–8; see also paras 129–30.

[43] Case 27/76 *United Brands* and C-62/86 *AKZO*.

[44] See eg Case T-219/99 *British Airways v Commission* at para 211 and T-203/01 *Michelin Commission (Michelin II)* [2003] ECR II-4071.

[45] See Brian Sher and John Kallaugher, 'Rebates revisited: anti-competitive effects and exclusionary abuse under Article 82' [2004] ECLR 263–85.

[46] Steven Anderman, 'The New Interface between Intellectual Property and Competition Law' in Steven Anderman and Ariel Ezrachi, *Intellectual Property and Competition Law: New Frontiers* (Oxford: OUP, 2011).

Technically, the *de facto* monopoly may be less important to prove than the indispensability requirement. In some cases it is even enough for the IP owner to be the owner of a near monopoly as long as it has control over an indispensable technology.[47] The reason for this is that quasi-monopolies as well as essential facilities have the capacity to create a basis for leveraging the dominance of the incumbent firm in a primary market into a derivative market and to thereby create a risk of unlawfully eliminating effective competition in a secondary market. This is reinforced by the GC's holding in *Microsoft* that a risk of elimination of effective competition, may be a basis for a finding of the abuse of refusal to supply. In the *Oscar Bronner* case, the Court of Justice chose to give a very strict definition of indispensability. It stated that even if the IPR created a monopoly, the IPR had to be indispensable to access a related market before the IP owner was forced to grant access. Therefore it would only be an abuse under Article 102 if:

> the refusal of the service . . . be likely to eliminate all competition in the . . .[related] market on the part of the person requesting the service and that such refusal be incapable of being objectively justified, but also that the service in itself be indispensable to carrying on that person's business, inasmuch as there is no actual or potential substitute in existence for that [service].[48]

In the *IMS* case the test was changed to 'the elimination of all effective competition in the market'. In *Microsoft*, the GC modified the *IMS* test of indispensability by defining it as not allowing competitors in neighbouring markets to compete viably on the market.[49]

Where a firm owns an indispensable technology, this will create special responsibilities of providing access that go beyond the scope of ordinary dominance. For example it may be required to share interoperability information with downstream competitors or supply IP-protected products with competitors in aftermarkets.[50]

The definition of this special category of dominance had its origins in the case of *Commercial Solvents*.[51] In that case, it will be recalled, Commercial Solvents was a multinational producer of the raw materials, nitropropane and aminobutanol, necessary for the production of the pharmaceutical product ethambutol. When Commercial Solvents decided to extend its operations from the raw materials market into the pharmaceutical market, it simultaneously stopped deliveries of the raw materials to its long-term customer in the pharmaceutical market, Zoya. The Commission found that the raw materials produced by Commercial Solvents by itself and through its subsidiary ICI were indispensable for the continued presence of Zoya on the upstream market for ethambutol. Without supplies from ICI, Zoya would be effectively eliminated from that market. There were no effective substitutes even though Commercial Solvents'

[47] Case T-201/04 *Microsoft Corp v Commission* [2007] ECR II–3601 at para 392.

[48] C-7/97 *Oscar Bronner GmbH & Co KG v Mediaprint Zeitungs-und-Zeitschriftenverlag GmbH & Co KG* [1998] ECR I–7791, [1999] 4 CMLR 112.

[49] T-201/04 *Microsoft* at para 230. See the discussion in I. Forrester and K. Czapracka, 'Compulsory Licensing in European Competition Law: The Power of the Adjective' in Anderman and Ezrachi (ed), *IP and Competition Law: New Frontiers* (Oxford: OUP, 2011).

[50] Case 238/87 *Volvo v Veng* and Case C-241–242/91P *Magill*.

[51] Cases 6 and 7/73 *Commercial Solvents*.

patents had expired. Moreover, Zoya's manufacturing investments had made its production of ethambutol dependent upon supplies of raw materials from Commercial Solvents. The key to the ultimate decision by the Commission that Commercial Solvents had to resume supplies to Zoya was the finding that Commercial Solvents was not only dominant in the raw materials market: it had a monopoly and the existence of the monopoly made its refusal to sell to one of its principal users unlawful under Article 102.

If there had been an alternative supplier in competition with Commercial Solvents, the refusal to supply would not necessarily have constituted an abuse. As the CJEU stated, it would have required the presence of, on the raw material market, another raw material which could be substituted without difficulty for nitropropane or aminobutanol to invalidate a finding of dominance.[52]

Commercial Solvents had argued that another Italian company produced ethambutol from butaname and that there were other methods of producing the raw material nitropropane. The Commission found that these were not realistic alternatives. The company existed but the alternatives were of an experimental nature and had not been tested on an industrial scale. The development of the possibility involved considerable capital and considerable risk. It was not possible at present to have recourse to methods of manufacture on an industrial scale which made use of other raw materials.[53]

In *Hugin*[54] as well, the Commission had found an extreme form of dominance. Hugin was the sole supplier of Hugin spare parts. Lipton would have been driven out of business if supplies from Hugin were not available.

In *Télémarketing*,[55] the decision of the TV company to end the commercial relationship with Télémarketing was found to be abusive in a situation where the TV company enjoyed a *de facto* monopoly over access to telemarketing services. Anyone wishing to remain or enter the latter market was dependent upon access to the essential infrastructure of mention on the TV programme. In these cases, the existence of two markets and the monopoly over the infrastructure in the first market which was essential to the second market created the basis for a tight regulation of the commercial behaviour and freedom of contract in the second market.

The characterization of separate markets as a method of identifying dominance and regulating its spill-over effect in related markets is a technique the Commission has employed to regulate immensely powerful firms who seek to extend their power into contiguous markets. Thus, in the *IBM* case in 1984,[56] as we have seen, the Commission analysed the business operations of IBM's Systems 370 Central Processing Units and operating systems as falling into three separate markets: (1) the market for mainframe computer systems of which IBM's Systems 370 Central Processing Unit was one

[52] Ibid, at para 15.
[53] Ibid, at para 16.
[54] Case 22/78 *Hugin*.
[55] Case 311/84 *Télémarketing*.
[56] *IBM Corp v Commission* [1981] ECR 2639.

product; (2) the market for main memory attached to IBM's System 370 CPU; and (3) the market for software usable in IBM System 370, as two separate markets. The main factor in viewing the latter two categories as separate markets was that once customers had chosen to buy and use IBM System 370s, they could not readily switch to competitors in the mainframe market. This then created a basis to regulate certain commercial activities of IBM, in particular memory and software bundling, and delays in supplying other manufacturers of memory and software with interface information, etc. These practices would have been perfectly lawful had IBM been non-dominant but because it was found to be dominant, they could be characterized as abusive conduct under Article 102. Hence by defining the market narrowly, the Commission placed itself in a position to allege in its statement of objections that IBM was dominant in the markets for the supply of (1) main memory and (2) basic software for IBM System 370s and had abused its dominant position by 'tying' memory and software to the purchase of its mainframe.[57]

This technique was also employed in the 1994 *Microsoft* case.[58] The Commission acted upon a complaint it received from Novell that Microsoft's licensing practices were abusive under Article 102 because they foreclosed competitors from the market for PC operating systems software. In their investigation of the abuse, the Commission made the finding that the three layers of software which could be installed upon a PC constituted separate markets: disk operating systems (DOS); graphical user interfaces (GUI); and software applications, such as word processing, etc. Again, this then led to findings of dominance, ie *de facto* industry standard, on the DOS market, and tying and discrimination in its pricing, rebates, and licensing in the GUI and software applications markets.

This technique is not limited to the large-scale operation. It can also be applied to differentiate markets to regulate situations where the owner of a smaller scale infrastructure itself engages in the secondary market. In such a case, the definition of product and relevant product market can be stretched beyond traditional market categories into concepts such as essential inputs or facilities. In the *Decca Navigator Systems*[59] case, for example, the Commission was prepared to characterize the provision of navigation signals as a 'market' with a downstream 'market' consisting of Decca-compatible receivers. Decca's dominance in the navigation signals market gave it a special responsibility towards the operators in the downstream market for Decca-compatible receivers.

This idea was further developed by the Commission in a series of 'essential facility' cases. Thus in *Sea Containers v Stena Sealink*,[60] a case in which Sea Containers, attempting to introduce a high speed catamaran ferry service in the port of Holyhead for

[57] See also *AT&T/NCR* [1992] 4 CMLR M41.

[58] Undertaking to the Commission 15 July 1994, *XXIVth Report on Competition Policy* (1994), 443–5.

[59] [1990] 4 CMLR 627.

[60] [1995] 1 CMLR 84.

the Holyhead-Ireland route, encountered resistance from Stena Sealink, the owner of the port facilities. Stena refused access to the new entrant because it was afraid of competition with its own traditional ferry service. The Commission found that Stena Sealink occupied a dominant position as port owner because it was the only British port serving the market for the provision of maritime transport services for cars and passengers on the 'central corridor' route between the United Kingdom and Ireland. It also found that there were no realistic substitutes for this facility. The Liverpool port was not substitutable for Holyhead because of the added length of the journey and the possibilities of Sea Containers building a second port for itself were not realistic economically or physically. In this case, the Commission referred for the first time to the special responsibilities of '[a]n undertaking which occupies a dominant position in the provision of an essential facility and itself uses that facility (ie a facility or infrastructure without access to which competitors cannot provide services to their customers) . . .'[61] From the Commission's viewpoint, the definition of dominance now included a subcategory which could be defined in this way. It applied to physical facilities such as ports, railways, airline computer systems, etc.[62] It also appeared to apply to intangible facilities or inputs such as IPRs.

The application of essential facility analysis to IPRs would appear to depend on whether the owner of the product incorporating the IPR had a natural monopoly as opposed to a more traditional dominant position. Much depends upon whether there were alternative methods of achieving the same commercial step.

The complication for IPR owners is that in some situations, the right itself can have the effect of creating a *de facto* monopoly. In such a case, Article 102 can be used as a basis to override the essential nature of the IPR, the right to exclude rivals at least in the second dependent market.[63] At that point competition law will subject IPRs to an essential facility analysis.[64]

In such cases, the argument has been made that the possession of an IPR cannot be viewed as a barrier to entry reinforcing dominance because it is identical to the existence of the IPR. However, as early as 1975, in *GM/Continental*,[65] the CJEU held that a monopoly right granted by the state may give rise to a dominant position, at least when combined with the power to determine prices. In *Télémarketing*,[66] the CJEU reiterated that the fact that the 'absence of competition' was brought about by law did not prevent the application of Article 102 and a finding of dominance.

[61] Ibid, at para 66. Such an undertaking may not refuse other companies access to that facility without objective justification or grant access to competitors on terms less favourable than those which it gives its own services without infringing Art 102.

[62] See John Temple Lang, 'Defining Legitimate Competition: Companies Duties to Supply Competitors, and Access to Essential Facilities' [1994] *Fordham Corp Law Inst* 245.

[63] See Venit and Kallaugher, 'Essential Facilities: A Comparative Approach' [1994] *Fordham Corp Law Inst* 315, at 337.

[64] Ibid, p 337.

[65] Case 26/75 *General Motors Continental NV v Commission* [1975] ECR 1367, [1976] 1 CMLR 95.

[66] Case 311/84 *Télémarketing*.

In *Magill*, the Court of Justice did not appear to allow that concern to prevent the application of an essential facility type of analysis to a situation where as a result of narrow market definition the IPR contributed to 'a factual monopoly'. The Commission had decided that the TV broadcasting companies held a dominant position under Article 102 by virtue of their factual monopoly over their respective weekly listings which placed third parties interested in publishing a weekly TV guide 'in a position of economic dependence'. The Commission further found that by claiming copyright protection for their TV programme listings, the TV organizations strengthened their factual monopoly into a legal monopoly, creating a situation where 'no competition from third parties is permitted to exist on the relevant markets'.[67]

The GC accepted the Commission's definition of the relevant product markets[68] and its finding that the copyright in the TV listings, together with the factual monopoly of the TV companies over their programme schedules, gave the TV companies a dominant position in the TV listings 'market', placing third parties such as Magill in a position of economic dependence. This in turn created a platform for a finding that Magill was an entrant in a market for TV guides, separate from, but related to, the market for TV listings in which the TV broadcasters owned a facility or infrastructure which was essential.

The Court of Justice showed a greater awareness of the sensitivities of IP owners to the issue of dominance. It began by excluding the possibility that the finding of dominance could be based on the 'mere ownership of an intellectual property right'.[69] It then went on to make the point that the dominant position of the television companies was based on the *de facto* monopoly enjoyed by them by force of circumstances over the information used to compile listings for television programmes. As the only source of listings information for firms like Magill, the television companies were placed in a position to prevent effective competition on the market in weekly television magazines.[70]

Though the CJEU agreed with the GC and the Commission's conclusion that the television companies occupied a dominant position, it chose not to make any reference to their finding that the dominant position of the television companies was reinforced by their legal monopoly based on copyright protection for the listings. The CJEU was concerned to underline that the existence of the IPR in this case was only incidental to the finding of dominance. It emphasized the point made in *Michelin I* that the true test of market dominance was possession of economic strength in a market, ie the ability to behave independently of competitors and consumers,[71] a test which presupposes an economic analysis of market strength.

[67] *Magill TV Guide* Commission Decision [1989] OJ L 78/43, [1989] 4 CMLR 757, para 22.

[68] That is (1) the market for TV listings and (2) the market for weekly TV guides, both of which were ancillary to (3) the market for TV programmes. Cases T-69–70/89, 76/89 *RTE, ITP, BBC v Commission* [1991] ECR II-485, [1991] 4 CMLR 586.

[69] C-241–242/91P *Magill* at para 45.

[70] Ibid, at para 47.

[71] Case 322/81 *Michelin I*.

In *Intel*, Intel specifically argued that it was unable to behave independently on the market due to its customer pressure. The Commission rejected this argument for several reasons amongst them the fact that its customers were equally dependent upon Intel and that Intel was able to offer fidelity rebates even when prices were falling showing that Intel was 'able or free to adopt a price policy to forestall competitive pressure'.[72]

Another way of viewing this approach is to acknowledge that it is a special definition of dominance, one which is based on a situation of dependence on an indispensable input or facility. While this special version of dominance and indispensability may have been foreshadowed in discussions in other Article 102 cases of the Court of Justice,[73] and applied more widely, its use in *Magill* made it plain that it was applicable to the exercise of IPRs. In the event, it is an issue which must be taken into account by IP owners in assessing the curbs imposed by EU competition law.[74]

In recent cases involving abuse of dominance allegations, the Commission and the EU Courts have been prepared to view a technology that has no substitutes as an essential facility under Article 102, if it consists of an indispensable input into a downsteam product market.

In the *IMS* case, for example, the CJEU thought that even if the 1860 brick database may not have been established as a separate market, it could be viewed as an indispensable input. It held that, as the owner of an indispensable input, IMS had a special responsibility to offer access to undertakings in the derivative market for marketing services based on the database. Similarly in the *Microsoft* case, the GC confirmed this approach by stating: 'The fact that the indispensable product or service is not marketed separately does not exclude from the outset the possibility of identifying a separate market.'[75]

5.5.1 The legal status of dominance under Article 102 TFEU

If 'mere ownership' of the IPR occurs in conjunction with a *de facto* monopoly on a market and that is sufficient to justify a finding of dominance, then we are not too far from a position where the existence of ownership alone can confer dominance.

However, it is important to remember that an integral feature of dominance as defined by Article 102 as it applies to an IP-protected product, or even super-dominance, is that it does not by itself make an IP owner guilty of unlawful conduct. Article 102 jurisprudence has from its inception accepted that the achievement of dominance by a firm unilaterally using its business acumen, its R&D, and its IPRs to create successful new products is lawful. The French effort to make dominance unlawful *per se* in the original EC Treaty was thwarted by the German insistence that it remain lawful and the concept of unlawful be encapsulated in the definition of abuse. In common

[72] *Intel* at para 910; see also paras 883–5 and 893.
[73] See eg comments by the AG in Case 322/81 *Michelin I* at pp 297–9.
[74] Cf the decision of the CJEU in Case C-333/94 *Tetra Pak II*.
[75] Case T-201/04 *Microsoft* at para 335.

with the US Sherman Act, s 2, Article 102 TFEU embodies an understanding that where a system encourages and protects legitimate competition, it should not 'punish its winners.' This philosophy applies to firms that succeed by imaginative exploitation of IPRs as an incidental consequence of a wider principle that applies equally to firms that base their success on exploiting other types of goods and services. The fact that an IP owner like Microsoft devises a business strategy of interoperability with applications makers and thereby obtains dominance in the operating systems market through its business acumen is perfectly lawful under the competition law rules. Similarly, when IP owners cooperate to select a technology that becomes a standard, the process of cooperation in R&D and standard setting, if legitimate in other respects, can itself be a lawful means of achieving dominance. It is not the acquisition of the power of an industrial standard itself that is unlawful; it is conduct that attempts to use that market power for certain ends that can be unlawful. Moreover, in examining the acquisition of dominance by IP owners, there is an important distinction between unilateral and bilateral (or multilateral) acquisitions of market power. Whereas the unilateral acquisition of market power through internal growth is a form of competition on the merits, it can be unlawful to obtain dominance by an acquisition of the only effective competing technology in the market.[76] The acquisition of dominance solely owing to the size of the treasury of the acquiring company in this way is impermissible because it offers no guarantee of efficiency or innovation and extinguishes competition by substitution.

Furthermore, there is also a distinction to be drawn between different types of bilateral and multilateral acquisitions of market power. If a joint venture has been created to produce a new product that otherwise would not have been created and that creates a monopoly, it can be lawful because the acquisition of the monopoly is due to actual innovative efficiency. The collaboration creates a new market and thereby fosters competition by substitution; it does not repress existing competition.[77] Similarly collaboration between competitors in joint R&D and industrial standard setting that results in a new technological standard for an industry can be lawful, assuming that the actual standard setting process was not a cover for a technology limiting effort or cartel to squeeze higher royalty rates from manufacturing licensees.[78] This reasoning indicates that on this issue the competition rules are in harmony with the IP rules. Both encourage innovative efficiency by stimulating 'competition by substitution'.[79]

[76] See eg *Tetrapak I (BTG Licence)* [1988] OJ L72/27.

[77] Commission Notice, Guidelines on the application of Article 81 of the EC Treaty to technology transfer agreements [2004] OJ C101/2 refer to innovation markets and will only restrict certain licensing agreements where there is a risk that innovation or new products are hindered or delayed in being brought to market because of the agreement—not if the agreement can generate new products, para 25.

[78] See Chapter 9, section 9.5 on collecting societies.

[79] A phrase originally coined by H. Ullrich and mentioned by J. Drexl 'Is there a More Economic Approach to Intellectual Property and Competition Law?' in J. Drexl (ed), *Research Handbook on Intellectual Property and Competition Law* (Cheltenham, UK, Northampton MA, USA: Edward Elgar, 2008).

6

THE CONCEPT OF ABUSE AND INTELLECTUAL PROPERTY RIGHTS

6.1 The Expansion of the Concept of Abuse under Article 102 from Exploitative to Exclusionary Conduct 75
6.2 The Expanded Concept of Abuse and Restrictions on Intellectual Property Rights 85

Once an undertaking owning an IPR achieves a position of dominance it has a special responsibility not to allow its conduct to impair effective competition on the common market.[1] This definition of abuse under Article 102 has been used by the EU Courts and the Commission to place curbs on the exploitation of IPRs. A dominant IPR owner, particularly one in an enhanced dominant position, can be restrained from acquiring other firms with competing technology.[2] It may be required to supply or license the protected products or processes to competitors in secondary markets.[3] Its pricing, discounting, and product bundling decisions may be found to be unlawful because of their effect on existing competitors whether in primary[4] and secondary markets.[5] In principle, the normal exercise of an IPR will not be an abuse. These remedies of competition law are meant to be applied to IPRs only in exceptional circumstances. However, the use of IPRs as an instrument of commercial strategy has in fact resulted in a number of cases where IP owners have been found guilty of abusive conduct.

[1] The original phrase was 'genuine undistorted competition.' Case 322/81 *Nederlandsche Banden-Industrie Michelin v Commission* [1983] ECR 3461, [1985] 1 CMLR 282.

[2] Case T-51/89 *Tetra Pak Rausing SA v Commission (Tetra Pak I)* [1990] ECR II–309, [1991] 4 CMLR 334.

[3] C-241–242/91P *Radio Telefis Eireann v Commission (Magill)* [1995] ECR I–743, [1995] 4 CMLR 718, and Case C-418/01 *IMS Health GmbH & Co OHG v NDC Health GmbH & Co KG* [2004] 4 CMLR 1543.

[4] See eg Case COMP/C-3/37.990–*Intel* Commission decision of 13 May 2009, D (2009) 3726 final (<http://ec.europa.eu/competition/elojade/isef/index.cfm?fuseaction=dsp_result> (last accessed 28 June 2010)).

[5] Case C-333/94 *Tetra Pak International SA v Commission (Tetra Pak II)* [1996] ECR I–5951, [1997] 4 CMLR 662, Case 53/92P *Hilti v Commission* [1994] ECR I–667, [1994] 4 CMLR 614, and Case COMP/C-3/37.792 *Microsoft* [2005] 4 CMLR 965, confirmed in Case T-201/04 *Microsoft Corp v Commission* [2007] ECR II-3601.

Article 102 itself gives only four examples of abuse:

(a) directly or indirectly imposing unfair purchase or selling prices or other unfair trading conditions;

(b) limiting production, markets or technical development to the prejudice of consumers;

(c) applying dissimilar conditions to equivalent transactions with other trading parties, thereby placing them at a disadvantaged position;

(d) making the conclusion of contracts subject to acceptance by the other parties of supplementary obligations which, by their nature or according to commercial usage, have no connection with the subject of such contracts.

On first reading, these abuses suggest a concern to place limits on the capacity of a dominant firm to exploit its customers or consumers by extracting monopoly rents from them by such practices as excessive pricing, limiting markets, tie-ins, etc. For example, the first two abuses, (a) unfair pricing and (b) limiting production, suggest a conscious policy of limiting the damage caused to customers and consumers by excessive pricing. Insofar as that was the case, they were not likely to impinge upon the exercise of IPRs except in a marginal way. Competition law has long recognized that the pricing of IPRs included a reward element that could take it above price levels which would apply in a more normal competitive market.[6] Moreover, the EU Courts have also accepted that the logic of the exclusive right allows its holder to eliminate competition from unauthorized manufacturers and sellers of the protected product.[7]

However, Article 102 has been interpreted to apply more widely than merely prohibiting exploitative abuses; it is also aimed at 'structural' or 'exclusionary' abuses directed against competitors, both in primary and related markets. These abuses include acquisitions,[8] predatory pricing,[9] and refusals to supply[10] and license,[11] none of which are explicitly mentioned in Article 102. The theory is that maintaining existing levels of competition in markets which have already been weakened by the presence of the dominant firm in a market operates indirectly to protect consumers[12] and contributes to innovation. Where an IP owner holding market power uses that power to attempt to eliminate existing competition which may contribute to innovation, it has been difficult to argue that possible long-term innovative efficiencies can provide a justification under Article 102.[13]

To understand how this widened concept of Article 102 has virtually redrawn the borderline between EU competition law and IPRs requires us to trace two steps: (1) the development of a general rule of structural or exclusionary abuse in primary and related markets; and (2) the way this wider interpretation of Article 102 has impinged upon the exploitation of IPRs.

[6] Case 53/87 *CICRA et Maxicar v Renault* [1988] ECR 6039, [1990] 4 CMLR 265, at para 17. See also *Scandlines Sverige v Port of Helsingborg* COMP/36.568 [2006] 4 CMLR 1298.

[7] Ibid, at para 15.

[8] Case T-51/89 *Tetra Pak I.*

[9] See Case 62/86 *AKZO-Chemie v Commission* [1991] ECR I-3359, [1993] 5 CMLR 215.

[10] Case 53/87 *Maxicar.*

[11] See C-241–242/91P *Magill* and Case C-418/01 *IMS Health.*

[12] Case 6/72 *Europemballage & Continental Can v Commission* [1973] ECR 215, [1973] CMLR 199 at para 24.

[13] Ibid, at para 26.

6.1 THE EXPANSION OF THE CONCEPT OF ABUSE UNDER ARTICLE 102 FROM EXPLOITATIVE TO EXCLUSIONARY CONDUCT

Although Article 102 may appear to be primarily concerned with exploitative abuses,[14] the Court of Justice has interpreted it to apply to conduct causing damage to the competitive structure of markets already weakened by the presence of a dominant firm. In other words, it has been interpreted to protect competitors as well as consumers and customers. In *Michelin I*,[15] in one of the clearest statements of this wider approach as a general rule for Article 102,[16] the CJEU reaffirmed that:

> Article [102] covers practices which are likely to affect the structure of a market where, as a direct result of the presence of the undertaking in question, competition is weakened and which through recourse to methods different from those governing normal competition in products or services based on traders' performance, has the effect of hindering the maintenance or development of the level of competition still existing in the market.[17]

This general rule of Article 102 contains three notable constituent elements:

(a) conduct which is likely to weaken the structure of a market by restricting competition, ie driving out existing competitors or denying entry to new firms, will be *prima facie* abusive;

(b) it must be shown that the methods used to achieve this effect are different from those which govern normal competition on the basis of traders' performance; and

(c) the nature of the evidence required to establish that the conduct in question has the effect of hindering the maintenance or development of the level of competition still existing in the market. Currently, despite the desire for a policy change suggested by the Commission, the EU Courts have insisted that it is not necessary to prove actual harm or likely harm.[18] It is sufficient to prove that the conduct gives rise to a risk of eliminating existing levels of 'effective' competition. The law is designed to deter and to act preventively. This interpretation of Article 102 shapes it into what is effectively a *per se* rule. Let us look at each of these in turn.

[14] See R. Joliet, *Monopolization and Abuse of a Dominant Position: A Comparative Study of American and European Approaches to the Control of Economic Power* (The Hague, 1970). See also Temple Lang, 'Monopolisation and the Definition of Abuse of a Dominant Position under Article 86 EEC Treaty' [1970] 16 *CML Rev* 345.

[15] Case 322/81 *Michelin I* at para 70. See also Case 85/76 *Hoffman-La Roche* [1979] ECR 461, [1979] 3 CMLR 211 and Case 62/86 *AKZO v Commission* [1991] ECR I–3359.

[16] See eg J. Venit and J. Kallaugher, 'Essential Facilities: A Comparative Law Approach' [1994] *Fordham Corp Law Inst* 315 at p 328.

[17] Case 322/81 *Michelin I* at para 70.

[18] T-219/99 *British Airways v Commission* [2003] ECR II–5917, [2004] 4 CMLR 1008, upheld C-95/04 *British Airways v Commission* [2007] ECR I–2331, [2007] 4 CMLR 22.

6.1.1 Weakening levels of competition in markets

The foundation of the structural interpretation of Article 102 was the early case of *Continental Can*,[19] in which the alleged abuse consisted solely of an acquisition of a competitor. The CJEU held that even though this was a purely structural change and the language of Article 102 presupposed abusive conduct, where the acquisition of a competitor by a dominant firm would virtually eliminate all competition in the market there was a distortion of the market which made it abusive. The CJEU stated that if the test of abuse was whether there was a distortion of the market, then *a fortiori* the elimination of competition was abusive.[20]

In two subsequent cases, the CJEU developed the point that conduct by an undertaking which damaged or attempted to damage residual levels of competition on a market, which fell short of the complete elimination of competition, could also be caught by Article 102. In *Commercial Solvents*,[21] an undertaking with a monopoly of an indispensable raw material was found to be abusive when it refused to continue to supply a long-standing customer because it wanted to eliminate that firm *as a competitor* in a market into which it had decided to enter. The CJEU affirmed the finding of abuse, stating that:

> an undertaking being in a dominant position as regards the production of raw material and therefore able to control the supply to manufacturers of derivatives, cannot just because it decides to start manufacturing those derivatives (in competition with former customers) act in such a way as to eliminate competition which in the case in question, would amount to eliminating one of the principal manufacturers of ethambutol in the common market.[22]

In that case, the CJEU also indicated that the damage to competition could occur in *a market* other than the one in which the undertaking was dominant, where the dominant undertaking was using its dominant position to get a competitive advantage over a rival in that related market.

In *Hoffmann-La Roche*,[23] the CJEU confirmed that less than complete forms of damage to competitive structures in markets could be abusive because of their exclusionary effect on competitors as well as their restrictive effects on customers. In that case, the use of fidelity rebates, exclusive supply contracts, and tied sales to deny access to the market to competitors were held to be abusive.

Hoffmann-La Roche was the first case to grapple with the obvious question raised by the structural interpretation given to Article 102. If the test of abuse consisted of whether the conduct of the firm damaged the remaining level of competition in the market, and damage short of an elimination of all effective competition could be

19 Case 6/72 *Continental Can.*

20 Ibid, at para 24.

21 Cases 6 and 7 *Istituto Chemioterapio Italiano SpA & Commercial Solvents Corp. v Commission* [1974] ECR 223, [1974] 1 CMLR 309.

22 Ibid, at pp 250–1.

23 Case 85/76 *Hoffman-La Roche.*

regarded as abusive, then how could a dominant firm continue to function? For even organic growth through investment in R&D and increasing efficiencies in production and distribution could result in a further weakening of the competitive structure in that market. In effect, unless some exception for legitimate competition by dominant firms was built into Article 102, its prohibition of abuse would be so wide that it would call into question the lawfulness of the very existence of a dominant position. In *Hoffmann-La Roche*, the CJEU acknowledged this point by requiring that in addition to distorting the competitive structure of the market, the dominant firm's conduct must involve 'recourse to methods different from those which condition normal competition in products and services'. If the dominant firm engaged in 'normal competition', it was entitled to compete to the point of eliminating rivals and discouraging new entrants.[24]

6.1.2 Methods of normal competition: 'competition on the merits' and 'objective justification'

The requirement that the dominant undertaking must have used methods differing from normal competition is technically a precondition for the finding of abuse and therefore part of the burden of proof for the Commission. The concept of normal competition embraces both the concept of competition on the merits and business or objective justification. At one stage it was thought that

> Although there is clearly a relation between business justifications and performance based competition, the better view would probably be that the concepts are distinct. That is the burden is on the dominant firm to prove a business justification, while the burden of proving abuse, including proof that conduct is not performance related, should rest with the Commission (or the plaintiff in a private action).[25]

However, recent case law of the EU Courts suggest that rather than viewing objective justification as a 'defence,' its absence should be viewed as a constituent element of an abuse overlapping with competition on the merits. For example in *Magill*, the three conditions necessary to establish exceptional circumstances for the remedy of a compulsory licence under Article 102(b) included 'the absence of an objective justification'[26] And in *Microsoft*, the General Court (GC) was firmly of the view that while the defendant had the burden of coming forward with the evidence of an objective justification, it was up to the Commission to respond by meeting the burden of proving an absence of justification.[27]

[24] Ibid, at para 91.

[25] Venit and Kallaugher (n 16 above), p 339. The authors add: 'This conclusion is supported by the fact that the objective justification defense appears to be based on a proportionality analysis (i.e. do the interests of the dominant firm justify the impact of its conduct on third parties and is there a less restrictive alternative for protecting those interests?) whereas the criterion of "normal methods of competition based on performance" looks to a categorization of types of conduct without regard for the effect of that conduct in a particular case.'

[26] Case C-241–242/91P *Magill* at para 55.

[27] Case T-201/04 *Microsoft* at para 1144.

The concept of 'normal' or legitimate competition by performance is a creature of competition policy concerns and is not to be confused with normal commercial practice. This point was graphically illustrated in *Continental Can*,[28] where the decision by a dominant firm to take over a competitor was found to be abusive because of its structural effects. In *Commercial Solvents*,[29] the decision to vertically integrate into a related market as a means of assuring a continued return on an expanding capital base was found to be abusive because of its exclusionary effect. In neither case did the fact that the means used were normal commercial practice preclude the finding of abuse. In the later cases of *Hilti*[30] and *Tetra Pak II*,[31] the dominant undertakings argued that their practice of product bundling was normal commercial usage. Again, neither Commission nor Courts were prepared to accept commercial usage as an objective justification for a practice which had the likely effect of excluding existing competitors from and preventing entrants to the market. Further in *Tetra Pak I*, an attempt to purchase the only existing competitor is a normal commercial tendency. However, it was found abusive because it would have meant the elimination of existing competition.

On the other hand, the concept of legitimate competition by performance clearly extends to the use of internal economic efficiencies to grow and compete with other firms by passing on those economic efficiencies in the form of lower prices. For example, in *AKZO*,[32] a case concerning alleged predatory pricing,[33] the CJEU held that charging prices which were lower than average total costs could be presumed to be anti-competitive, and pricing below average variable costs was *per se* anti-competitive.[34] The clear implication of these presumptions, however, was that, as long as a dominant undertaking priced above average total cost, it could pass on its efficiencies in the form of low prices and legitimately compete with and weaken competitors remaining in the market without acting abusively. This is a case where the concept of competition on the merits is integrated into the norm defining the abuse.

Similarly, the development of a competitive edge through innovation is legitimate competition by performance which can be translated into practices which result in the elimination of competitors, either those who attempt to copy the protected product or those who are forced out of the market owing to the superior quality of the innovation in relation to their products. For example, in *Volvo*,[35] the CJEU acknowledged that the dominant manufacturer of spare parts could eliminate competition from other

[28] Case 6/72 *Continental Can*.

[29] Cases 6 and 7/73 *Commercial Solvents*.

[30] Case 53/92P *Hilti*.

[31] Case C-333/94 *Tetra Pak II*.

[32] Case T-51/89 *Tetra Pak I*.

[33] See the discussion in Chapter 11 below.

[34] If prices were lower than average variable costs, they could be presumed to be conduct designed to eliminate competition because of the sacrifice of any contribution to relevant fixed costs. If prices were fixed at levels above average variable costs but below average total costs they could still be found to be anti-competitive where they were part of a deliberate plan to eliminate a competitor. See Chapter 11 (predatory pricing) below.

[35] Case 238/87 *Volvo v Veng*.

manufacturers of spare parts by using its design right.[36] The CJEU only qualified that right in respect of the supplying of spare parts to secondary markets, such as maintenance markets.[37]

The issue of self-defence under Article 102, is probably better characterized as an objective justification. As the Court of Justice said in *United Brands*:

> ... the fact that an undertaking is in a dominant position cannot disentitle it from protecting its own commercial interests if they are attacked, and that such an undertaking must be conceded the right to take such reasonable steps as it deems appropriate to protect its said interests.[38]

The self-defence of 'reasonable steps' incorporates an 'objective' measure of justification. It can apply to discriminatory pricing[39] as well as to predatory pricing.[40] Its scope, however, is limited to 'meeting competition' and not 'beating competition'. As the Commission indicated in *AKZO*,[41] AKZO as a dominant undertaking could offer or supply below a determined minimum price 'only in respect of a particular customer and only if it is necessary to do so in good faith to meet (but not to undercut) a lower price shown to be offered by a supplier ready and able to supply to that customer'.[42] This also implies that it is left to the dominant undertaking to verify the information about the pricing practices of its opposition.[43]

Under Article 102, the concepts of competition on the merits and objective justification apply to a dominant undertaking's relationships with customers. For example, in *Hoffmann-La Roche*,[44] the CJEU made it plain that if the dominant firm offered discounts to customers based on quantities ordered as opposed to 'loyalty rebates', that would be normal competition on the merits and objectively justified. Similarly, in *Hilti*[45] and *Tetra Pak II*,[46] the CJEU was prepared to accept in principle that issues of safety and hygiene and quality control were legitimate grounds for tie-ins[47] as long as these could be shown to be objectively justified. In *Microsoft*, the GC held that if the tie led to 'superior technical product performance' then it could be justifiable for a dominant company to technologically integrate its products.[48]

[36] Ibid, at para 8.

[37] Ibid, at para 9.

[38] Case 27/76 *United Brands v Commission* [1978] ECR 207 at para 189.

[39] See the discussion in Chapter 10.

[40] Case 62/86 *AKZO*.

[41] [1983] 3 CMLR 694.

[42] Ibid, at para 36 of the legal assessment and Art 4 of the Interim Decision. This may create difficulties of verification for the dominant undertaking, but the principle must be respected. See the discussion in Chapter 11.

[43] See U. Springer, 'Meeting competition: Justification of Price Discrimination under EC and US Antitrust Law' [1997] *ECLR* 251, p 254.

[44] Case 85/76 *Hoffman-La Roche*.

[45] Case 53/92P *Hilti*.

[46] Case C-333/94 *Tetra Pak II*.

[47] See the discussion in Chapter 8.

[48] Case T-201/04 *Microsoft* at paras 1159–61.

Furthermore, Article 102 also incorporates a legitimate means test by applying a limiting principle of proportionality. The dominant undertaking may act as efficiently as it wishes in its attempts to gain profits and improve its market position but only by employing methods which are necessary to pursue its legitimate aims, ie methods which limit competition no more than is necessary. In *United Brands*,[49] the CJEU declared that a prohibition imposed by a dominant undertaking upon the resale of green bananas by its customers was abusive because its effects went beyond the object to be attained. In *Hoffmann-La Roche* there was an indirect reference to the proportionality concept when the CJEU held that the exclusive purchasing agreements concluded with customers could only be admissible subject to the conditions of Article 101(3).[50] In *BRT v SABAM and Fonier*[51] the CJEU held that conditions imposed by a copyright-management association in contracts intended to protect members' rights were abusive because they encroached more severely on members' freedom to exercise their copyrights than was necessary to protect its rights. Implicit in this decision was a view that measures requiring members to assign their present and future rights on a global basis could be justified by a test of necessity or indispensability. In GEMA,[52] the CJEU held that the decisive factors in assessing a collecting society's rules in the light of the competition rules were (1) the indispensability test, ie whether they exceed the limits absolutely necessary for effective protection; and (2) the equity test, ie whether they would limit the individual copyright holder's freedom to dispose of his work no more than necessary.

In the case of a refusal to supply, there are special reasons why a justification test is necessary. Kallaugher and Venit suggest the following:

> It could be argued ... that there is a legitimate presumption that a dominant firm will supply any customer that is willing and able to pay the purchase price for its goods and services. Thus in the special case of refusals to supply, a burden could be put on the dominant firms to rebut the presumption by showing that it had a good reason for refusal.[53]

For example in *Commercial Solvents*,[54] the decision to refuse to supply Zoya was not compelled by necessity; ICI had sufficient capacity to supply itself and Zoya. Moreover, in *United Brands*, the CJEU indicated that a proportionality principle was a constituent element of the necessity test. It found that the decision to discontinue deliveries to its distributor for selling competing bananas and taking part in its competitor's advertising campaign was a disproportionately severe sanction, implying that a less severe sanction related to the action of the distributor may have been justified.

[49] Case 27/76 *United Brands*.

[50] Ibid, at para 120.

[51] Case 127/73 *BRT v SABAM and Fonier* at p 316. See also Cases 110/88, 241–242/88 *Ministère Public v Tournier* in which the Court decided that proportionality was the test for ascertaining whether the royalties charged by the French copyright-management agency SACEM were abusive because it insisted that licensees took the whole of its repertoire rather than just the works they were interested in.

[52] [1979] ECR 3173.

[53] Venit and Kallaugher (n 16 above), p 329.

[54] Cases 6 and 7/73 *Commercial Solvents*. See also Case 311/84 *Centre Belge d'Etudes du Marché–Télémarketing v Compagnie Luxembourgeoise de Télédiffision SA and Information Publicité Benelux SA* [1985] ECR 3261, [1986] 2 CMLR 558 in which it was held to be abusive to exclude firms other than its subsidiary from the telemarketing market because there was no objective necessity for such exclusion.

It could also be possible to argue, for example, that there was no space capacity. In *British Plasterboard*,[55] the CJEU was prepared to accept that a sudden shortage of oil supplies justified a refusal to supply a former customer since it would have meant that existing customers could not have been accommodated. Finally, a legitimate basis for justification for refusing to supply is that the creditworthiness of the buyer was questionable.[56]

A further feature of the normative approach to the definition of abuse under Article 102 is its treatment of assertions of innovative efficiencies by the defendant. At one point it was argued unsuccessfully that the exercise of IPRs should enjoy an objective justification amounting to a complete immunity under the competition law rules because of the property right prerogatives of IP owners.[57] More recently, a more plausible innovative efficiency defence has been raised based on the argument that if the competition rules provide compulsory licences of IPRs as a remedy they will reduce the incentives of undertakings to innovate and thereby reduce dynamic efficiency. For example in the recent *Microsoft* case, Microsoft asserted that it would have less incentive to develop a given technology if it would be required to make that technology available to its competitors.

The Commission initially attempted to deal with this assertion by Microsoft as a balancing exercise which balanced the negative impact of an order to license its IPRs on Microsoft's incentives to innovate against the counter-argument that the compulsory licence would produce improved innovative efficiency for the industry as a whole because interoperability would maintain plural sources of innovation.

The GC clearly had other ideas about how the efficiency defence should be treated as an objective justification under Article 102. It made it clear that what was called for was not a balancing exercise of the two theories of innovation but a more legally structured assessment of Microsoft's arguments. It held that Microsoft's assertion could only be raised under the head of objective justification as an integral part of the proof of abuse.[58] It stated that once the constituent elements of the abuse have been established, in this case that there were exceptional circumstances requiring an obligation to provide interface information, the burden shifts to the dominant firm to raise any plea of objective justification and support it with arguments and evidence.[59]

In the event, Microsoft did not meet its burden. Its arguments were vague, general, and theoretical. It merely stated that '[d]isclosure would . . .eliminate future incentives to invest in the creation of more intellectual property', without specifying the technologies or products to which it thus referred.[60]

The GC concluded that the Commission's conclusion was not based on a balancing of the two conflicting views of innovation but rather upon its factual findings: that there

[55] See Case T-65/89 *BPB Industries and British Gypsum v Commission* [1993] ECR II–389.

[56] Case T-27/76 *United Brands*.

[57] It has also been suggested that there should be some irreducible minimum area of non-interference with IPRs by the competition rules based on the specific subject matter or essential function of the IPR. However, the courts and competition authorities seem clear that the grant or 'existence' of an IP right may be based on public law but, once granted, the IPR is exercised by its owner as a private right subject to the limits of the competition rules in the Treaty.

[58] Case T-201/04 *Microsoft* at para 659.

[59] Ibid, at para 688; see also para 709.

[60] Ibid, at para 698.

was no basis to Microsoft's claims that its products would be cloned; that disclosure of interoperability was widespread in the industry—IBM had already committed to this course in the 1980s; and that Directive 91/250 was consistent with this policy.[61]

This indicates first of all that under Article 102, assertions about innovative efficiencies by the defendant are probably best viewed as an objective justification, a constituent element of proving an abuse. However, under EU law, this test of objective justification will be limited to arguments about pro-consumer efficiencies and incentives to innovate only insofar as they are rooted in findings of fact about current conduct or information known at the time the conduct was engaged in. Predictions about the future may be too speculative to find acceptance in analysing the issue of objective justification. The lawfulness of a firm's actions must be assessed at the time when the firm acts.[62]

This does not preclude the possibility that the innovative efficiency of a dominant firm can be found to be an objective justification but such a defence must meet two 'structural' tests. The first is that there is some evidence in the here and now of the existence or reality of these efficiencies. Secondly, there must be evidence in the present conditions of the markets that those efficiencies will be passed on to consumers.[63] In a sense, the values and structure of Article 101(3) are built into the objective justification test.[64] For example, if a firm can show that two products can be integrated to create a third product of greater quality and functionality that will meet consumer needs, and that eliminates existing competition because the new product provides a more desirable alternative to consumers or users, that will offer a business justification or be viewed as competition on the merits.[65] Moreover, patent owners may have strong case of objective justification for refusing to license in cases where they have prepared plans to meet demand themselves but have delayed implementation to allow a sequencing of products.

The actual burden of proof of the abuse, including the absence of an objective justification remains with the Commission.[66] However, the calculus of innovative efficiencies will be restricted by the distinctive European approach prizing the existence of effective competition. Thus, if conduct by an IP owner actually deprives consumers of a new product or creates a risk of elimination of effective competition through exclusionary

[61] Ibid, at para 710.

[62] Case T-271/03 *Deutsche Telekom v Commission* [2008] ECR II 477.

[63] Communications from the Commission–*Guidance on the Commission's Enforcement Priorities in Applying Article 82 EC Treaty to Abusive Exclusionary Conduct by Dominant Undertakings* OJ C45, 24 February 2009, pp 7–20, para 29.

[64] This is a reminder that Art 102 shares with Art 101 and the Merger Regulation (see Art 2(1)(b)) a treatment of innovative efficiencies defences that is subjected to the two conditions of consumer benefit and non-elimination of effective competition. See also Ekaterina Rousseva, 'Modernising by Eradicating how the Commission's New Approach to Article 81 EC Dispenses with the need to apply Article 82 to Vertical Restraints' (2005) 42 *CML Rev* 587.

[65] See Commission, *Enforcement Guidance on Article 82*, para 61.

[66] Council Regulation 1/2003 on the implementation of the rules on competition laid down in Articles 81 and 82 of the Treaty, OJ L 14 January 2003, Art 2.

strategies, the possible innovative efficiencies of the firm are not likely to be treated as a pro-competitive benefit to be 'balanced' against the anti-competitive conduct. By carefully controlling excesses of dynamic efficiency defences, the European approach ensures that the test of abuse gives a priority to real effective competition in the short term and ignores less easily provable assertions about dynamic efficiencies in the long term. This feature, although directly emphasizing the protection of competitors, is viewed as an indirect method of protecting consumers from harm.[67]

6.1.3 Proof of harm

The concept of abuse as it applies to exclusionary abuse as well as exploitative abuse is concerned with avoiding consumer harm. In the case of exclusionary abuse, however, the more immediate harm is to competitors and the ultimate harm is to consumers. Hence, the legal norm defining abuse is primarily concerned to offer protections for the continued participation of competitors still existing in a market weakened by the existence of a dominant firm.[68] There have been two notable features of this definition of abuse.

Firstly, it is well established that if abusive conduct is found to be capable of having exclusionary effects, there is no need to prove actual effects upon or actual harm to competitors; the law is meant to apply preventively before the damage is done, because once done it can be irretrievable. Hence, certain types of conduct can be abusive *per se* if they consist of conduct which has as its purpose the further weakening of a market by means other than competition on the merits.[69] The mere finding that a firm engages in such conduct will be sufficient to prove abuse; such conduct is thought to be inherently capable of having exclusionary effects.[70]

The Commission and EU Courts have indicated that proving the likelihood of harm is sufficient and that this can be inferred from the harm to the process of effective competition.[71]

However, the judicial interpretation of Article 102 goes one step further, maintaining that there may be no need even to prove *likely* effects on all occasions. For example

[67] Case C-95/04P *British Airways* at para 106.

[68] Article 102 TFEU covers practices which are likely to affect the structure of a market where, as a direct result of the presence of the undertaking in question, competition has already been weakened, and which, through recourse to methods different from those governing normal competition in products and services based on trader's performance, have the effect of hindering the maintenance or development of the level of competition still existing on the market; Case 322/81 *Michelin I* at para 70.

[69] See eg Opinion of AG Kokott in *British Airways*: '. . . a line of conduct of a dominant undertaking is abusive as soon as it runs counter to the purpose of protecting competition in the internal market from distortions..', Case C-95/04P Opinion of AG Kokott, 23 February 2006, paras 68–9.

[70] See eg G. Monti, *EC Competition Law* (Cambridge: Cambridge University Press, 2007) p 171.

[71] Case C-95/04 *British Airways*; Case T-203/01 *Michelin v Commission (Michelin II)* [2003] ECR II–4071; Commission's *Enforcement Guidance on Article 82* (n 63 above), paras 19–20; and Commission Notice, Guidelines on the Applicability of Article 81 [now 101] of the EU Treaty to Horizontal Cooperation Agreements OJ [2001] C3/02, p 2.

in *Microsoft,* Microsoft had argued that in IP cases, following the case law, there must be a strict test of effects: it must be shown that the conduct was 'likely to eliminate' all competition or that the conduct of the dominant undertaking had a 'high probability' of elimination of all competition. The GC, however, accepted the Commission's argument that it was enough to prove that the refusal to supply gave rise to 'a *risk* of elimination' (italics added) of competition in the second market in order to establish an abuse under Article 102. The test did not require the Commission to establish that competition had been eliminated or that its elimination was imminent.[72] The GC stated that Microsoft's complaint was purely one of terminology and wholly irrelevant.[73] The GC said the two tests 'reflect the same idea, namely that Article [102] does not apply only when there is no more competition in the market or that elimination is imminent'.[74] This would be counter to the objective of the provision which is to maintain undistorted competition in the market and safeguard the competition that still exists.[75]

The GC went on to state that under Article 102 what matters to establish an infringement, is that the refusal *is liable to or likely to eliminate all effective competition on the market.*[76] The fact that some competitors 'retain a marginal presence in some niches of the market' does not constitute the existence of such competition.[77] By lessening the importance of the difference between the two standards of proof: 'liable to' and 'likely to' eliminate competition, the GC emphasized that the test of Article 102 is not concerned with proof of effects but rather of proof of conduct that *could possibly* produce effects and this is in line with previous CJEU case law on Article 102.[78]

This part of the decision should be read in the light of two further points. In the first place there was actually strong evidence that the *likely* effect of the abuse would have been to eliminate competition because of the prior finding that access to MS Windows operating system was 'necessary to maintain viability in the market for work servers'[79] and that such information was essential to viability on the market.[80] Indeed, insofar as the interface information was indispensable to a continued presence on the workgroup server market, it was in fact not only likely that elimination would occur, but also that once ejected, it would not be possible for competitors to return to the market because of the existence of the 'network effects' barrier to entry.[81]

[72] T-201/04 *Microsoft*, at para 457.

[73] Ibid, at para 561

[74] Ibid, at para 561.

[75] The GC also noted that 'network effects' would make it harder for competitors once ejected to come back into the market. T-201/04 *Microsoft* at para 562.

[76] T-201/04 *Microsoft* at para 563. See also para 1089 regarding the tying abuse, where the GC applies a similar wording in relation to finding anti-competitive effects.

[77] Ibid, at para 563.

[78] See eg Cases 6 and 7/73 *Commercial Solvents* ('risks eliminating competition'); Case 311/83 *Télémarketing* ('possibility of eliminating all competition').

[79] Case T-201/04 *Microsoft* at paras 392–3.

[80] Ibid, at paras 421–2.

[81] The approach to anti-competitive effects applied by the GC to the refusal to license abuse in *Microsoft* was more or less duplicated in the latter part of the case relating to the tying abuse.

The Commission has recently argued that it intends to take a more 'effects-based' approach to the interpretation of Article 102.[82] However, this approach has been called into question by recent judgments of the EU Courts.[83] One implication of the *Microsoft* judgment is that the GC is not particularly impressed by the concept of reforming Article 102 to add a stronger test of effects as a constituent element of the abuse of refusal to license. The judgment reiterates that the test of abuse under Article 102 is conduct to which objectively abusive intent could be attributed and which creates a plausible risk of the harm of elimination of effective competition. Finally, the Commission itself has not entirely consistently pushed for an effects-based test. It has stated that it will not apply where conduct seriously restricts competition.[84]

6.2 THE EXPANDED CONCEPT OF ABUSE AND RESTRICTIONS ON INTELLECTUAL PROPERTY RIGHTS

This wider concept of abuse under Article 102 raises important issues in the context of IPRs. For example, how can it be reconciled with the entitlement to eliminate competition which is an inherent part of the grant of the exclusivity of an IPR? Further, to what extent does the concept of normal exploitation of IPRs constitute competition on the merits or an objective justification?

The answers to these questions appear to be shaped by the EU Courts' and Commission's determination of whether an abuse is being committed on a primary or a secondary market. In principle, the exclusive exploitation of an IPR is acceptable in the market for a specific product which incorporates it. Attempts to extend the method of exclusive exploitation into neighbouring markets or related products could be caught by Article 102, either as a specific abuse such as a tie-in or as a refusal to supply or license in cases where the dominant position precludes alternative sources of supply. In other words, exclusive exploitation could be legitimate competition on the merits in the primary market but could become abusive in a secondary, dependent market in certain exceptional circumstances because of the leveraging of market power from one market to the other.

Where an IP owner enjoys a quasi-monopoly in a product market, and the exploitation of the IPR is used in conjunction with a practice designed to foreclose new competitors or drive out existing competitors in secondary markets, the EU courts are prepared to restrict the exercise of an IPR if it is contrary to the requirements of Article 102. As the lawyers for the TV companies in *Magill* discovered, the fact that the exercise of IPRs was within the scope of national law by itself offered no defence to

[82] Commission's *Enforcement Guidance on Article 82* (n 63 above), paras 5–6.

[83] Case C-95/04, *British Airways*; Case T-203/09 *Michelin II*; Case T-201/04 *Microsoft*.

[84] DG Competition Commission 'DG Competition discussion paper on the application of Article 82 of the Treaty to exclusionary abuses' (Brussels, December 2005) (<http://ec.europa.eu/comm/competition/antitrust/art82/discpaper2005.pdf> (Last accessed 3 October 2010)), para 91.

complaints of anti-competitive abuse.[85] In effect, the Commission, with the support of the EU Courts, is entitled to draw the borderline between IPRs and competition law in its definition of abuse with reference to its definitions of relevant product markets.

However, before further exploring the way the concern of the EU Courts to protect competition levels in secondary markets has impinged on the exploitation of IPRs, let us examine a case where the widened general concept of abuse has impinged on the conduct of a dominant IP owner in its primary market.

6.2.1 Structural abuse and intellectual property rights in the primary market

In the primary market in which an undertaking is dominant, the main effect of Article 102 is to regulate exploitative abuses, such as excessive pricing,[86] predatory pricing,[87] tie-ins,[88] and discriminatory pricing.[89] *Continental Can*, however, raised an issue whether, within a relevant market, the acquisition of an IPR by a dominant undertaking might be abusive. The internal development of innovation was clearly competition by performance, entitling the right-holder to exclude potential competitors from the market. Could an acquisition of relevant technology be viewed differently? In *Tetra Pak I*[90] the CJEU and Commission gave their answer. Tetra Pak had a 91.8 per cent share of the market for the supply of machines for sterilizing and filling aseptic cartons, as well as the cartons themselves. Elopak, a licensee of Liquipak, was attempting to develop a product to compete in the aseptic market making use of Liquipak's exclusive patent licence from BTG. On the threshold of development, Tetra Pak acquired the entire Liquipak group of companies putting to an end the entry of the Elopak/Liquipak product. Elopak complained to the Commission and when the Commission commenced infringement proceedings, Tetra Pak relinquished the exclusive licence, agreeing to keep it on a non-exclusive basis. The Commission continued with the proceedings finding that Tetra Pak had behaved abusively in acquiring the exclusive licence by buying the Liquipak group because it strengthened its monopoly and frustrated the attempts of potential competitors from entering the field.

In *Tetra Pak I*,[91] Advocate General Kirschner was of the view that under Article 102 the normal exploitation of originated rights should be distinguished from acquisition through purchase:

> I do not consider that the principles which the Court of Justice has developed in regard to the original acquisition of industrial property rights, can be transposed directly upon the derived acquisition of an exclusive license. Where a patent or registered design is obtained by its originator, the

[85] Cases 241–242/91P *Magill.*
[86] See Chapter 9.
[87] See Chapter 11.
[88] See Chapter 8.
[89] See Chapter 10.
[90] Case T-51/89 *Tetra Pak I.*
[91] Ibid. at p 364.

undertaking is protecting its own development work from imitation by third parties. An undertaking occupying a dominant position may also protect itself in that way, even when in so doing, as in the *Maxicar* case, it drives out from the market undertakings whose business previously consisted in imitating the products in question .

In contrast, the acquirer of a patent licence procures for himself the development work carried out by others. That is legitimate, but it distinguishes his legal position from that of the original proprietor of the protective right. It is to the latter that the exclusive entitlement belongs and it is intended to allow him to obtain the reward for his creative effort.[92]

These differences persuaded the Advocate General to recommend that 'the special position which the proprietor of an industrial property right enjoys in the context of Article [102]' should not be extended to the licensee:[93]

The fact that an inventor occupying a dominant position on the market may exclude third parties from exploiting his own invention without his conduct constituting an abuse does not signify that undertakings occupying a dominant position may, by acquiring an exclusive license, invariably exclude their potential competitors from using the research findings made by third parties.[94]

The Advocate General also made the case that not only was the acquisition of the exclusive right not protected by the existence of the IPR, it was disproportionate conduct and therefore an infringement under Article 102 because a non-exclusive licence would have allowed Tetra Pak to use the protected product for its own improvements and would not have had adverse effects on competitors and new entrants. The acquisition of the exclusive licence not only extinguished the threat of potential competition from Liquipak, it removed the possibility that any other potential competitors could use the alternative sterilization process to get access to the market.

The GC held that the mere fact that an undertaking in a dominant position acquires an exclusive licence does not *per se* constitute abuse within the meaning of Article 102. For the purpose of applying Article 102, the circumstances surrounding the acquisition and, in particular, its effects on the structure of competition in the relevant market must be taken into account.[95]

It agreed with the Commission that it was not the acquisition as such that was abusive. It was the acquisition given the position of Tetra Pak on the market. The exclusivity of the licence strengthened Tetra Pak's already very considerable dominance. It also had the effect of preventing or considerably delaying the entry of a competitor into a market in which very little, if any, competition is found because access to the 'use of the process protected by the BTG license was alone capable of giving an undertaking the means of competing effectively with Tetra Pak in the field of aseptic packaging

[92] Ibid, at p 364.
[93] Ibid.
[94] Ibid, at p 365.
[95] Ibid.

of milk'.[96] In the light of those circumstances, the acquisition of the exclusive licence was abusive.

In *Intel,* the IPR held by Intel also strengthened Intel's position on the market for x86 Central Processing Units (CPUs) to a degree where it was in fact in control of who could enter into competition with it.[97] Intel had only issued one licence to its competitor AMD, but the conduct it was found to engage in by the Commission, such as offering loyalty discounts and taking measures aimed at preventing or delaying the launch of computers based on competing product, demonstrated that it was intent on excluding AMD from the market.[98] Although the IPR did not play a significant role in relation to the actual abuse, it was central to Intel's dominant position. The Commission found that Intel was an 'unavoidable trading partner' and therefore in a powerful position to control its customers, the OEMs, and more importantly punish them if they did not remain loyal to Intel.[99] It concluded that Intel's behaviour was anti-competitive and 'resulted in a significant reduction of consumer choice and in lower incentives to innovate'.[100]

6.2.2 Specific abuses, second markets, and intellectual property rights

As we have seen, as long as the exclusive exploitation remains in the primary market for a protected product, Article 102 is not unduly restrictive of IPR exploitation. Discrimination (c) and tie-ins (d) can apply to exploitative abuses in the primary market even to IPRs; but the latter would probably limit only tie-ins consisting of a combination of a protected product with unprotected products.

Once, however, the exclusive exploitation of IPRs extends into a second market, particularly a dependent market, or to a second product unprotected by the right, the balance between lawful exploitation and the exclusion of competitors can be struck at less favourable levels for IP owners because of the application of the structural rule of abuse. Under Article 102, the policy of maintaining effective competition in secondary markets can in exceptional circumstances trump the policy of encouraging the process of innovation through reward to inventors.

The specific abuses listed in Article 102 have been adapted to a two-market situation to protect against attempts to foreclose competition in both markets. For example, in Article 102(c) and (d)—applying discriminatory conditions to customers and tying arrangements—we have examples of exclusionary action against rivals. At first sight, these specific prohibitions appear to be concerned with protecting customers rather than competitors. Yet whilst the conduct is directed at a different level of economic

[96] Ibid.
[97] *Intel* at paras 854–8; see also paras 129–30.
[98] See Art 1 of *Intel* Commission decision.
[99] *Intel* at para 1599.
[100] Ibid, at para 1616.

activity, its underlying motivation is to exclude competitors from the primary market. As the CJEU put it in *Continental Can*:

> As may be further seen from letters (c) and (d) of Article 102, the provision is not only aimed at practices which may cause damage to consumers directly, but also at those which are detrimental to them through their impact on the effective competition structure as mentioned in Article 3(f) of the [EC Treaty] ...[101]

Refusal to supply offers an example of abuse which can arise under either main head. If the second market is not being supplied by a good or service wanted by consumers or users, a refusal to supply can be classified under Article 102(b), as in *Commercial Solvents* or *Magill*. On the other hand, if the issue is that the dominant firm has a subsidiary in the secondary market, the refusal to supply may be abusive because of its discriminatory effect. For example in *Commercial Solvents*, the Advocate General made the point that if paragraph (c) of Article 102 makes discrimination between trading parties an abuse, then it 'must, a fortiori, be an abuse for a dominant undertaking to place another trading party at a disadvantage by refusing to supply to him a raw material which the dominant undertaking supplies to others in an equivalent position'.[102]

6.2.3 The concept of related markets under Article 102

For Article 102 to apply to conduct in a second market, ie one other than the dominated market, there must be a link between the two markets. The general rule is that conduct must be such as to threaten the level of residual competition in a market where, as a result of the presence of that dominant undertaking, competition is already weakened. This presupposes that there is a sufficient link between the dominant position and the residual levels of competition in the second market. The way the EU Courts and the Commission have defined the nature of associative links between markets under Article 102 has varied widely, depending on the nature of the abuse.

In one line of cases starting with *Commercial Solvents*,[103] the relationship between markets has been vertical, with the dominant undertaking controlling supply to a downstream market by virtue of dominance or monopoly in the upstream market. In such cases, the EU Courts and the Commission have held that the undertaking which was dominant in the upstream market, could not without objective justification use its market power in that market to reserve to itself an operation in the downstream market. In those cases, since the dominance in the primary market was clearly the source of the power to control the downstream market, a sufficient nexus was established between dominance and the second market.

[101] Case 6/72 *Continental Can* at para 26.

[102] Cases 6 and 7/73 *Commercial Solvents*.

[103] Ibid, see also Case 311/84 *Télémarketing*. See the discussion in Chapter 7.

In a second line of cases, the link between the two markets was vertical but the dominant undertaking acted in the secondary market to reinforce its dominant position in the primary market. For example, in *BPB Industries and British Gypsum*,[104] an undertaking, dominant in the market of manufacturing plasterboard, used a system of loyalty rebates in the secondary market to discriminate against distributors using the plasterboard of foreign manufacturers. The CJEU held that the basis for the association between the two markets was the fact that the dominant undertaking was dealing with customers who were operating simultaneously in the two markets. This placed BPB and British Gypsum in a position to use their market power in the dominated market to cross-subsidize pricing in the second market. The GC held that because this discriminatory treatment was used to strengthen the dominant position in the primary market, it could be viewed as abusive conduct despite the fact that it occurred on a secondary market. Similarly, in *AKZO*,[105] a case of predatory pricing, the giant chemical firm was dominant in the market for organic peroxide used for plastics, but was found to have acted abusively in the flour preservative market to preserve its position in the plastics market. At this point in time, there was an assumption that there had to be a nexus between the market in which there was a dominant position and the market in which the abuse was committed. Commentators thought that there was no authority for the application of Article 102 to actions committed by a dominant undertaking on a secondary market for the purpose of strengthening its position on that secondary market.[106] Yet this was to underestimate the scope of the associative links which the CJEU was prepared to take into account under Article 102. In *Tetra Pak II*,[107] the Courts were prepared to apply Article 102 to an abuse committed by a dominant undertaking on a market upon which the undertaking was not dominant and where the conduct and the effects of that abuse were concentrated on that secondary market.

The CJEU acknowledged 'that the application of [Article 102] presupposes a link between the dominant position and the alleged abusive conduct, which is normally not present where conduct on a market distinct from the dominant market produces effects on that distinct market'.[108] It went on to add, however, that: 'in the case of distinct, but associated, markets, as in the present case, application of [Article 102] to conduct found on that associated, non-dominated market and having effects on that associated market can . . . be justified by special circumstances,'[109] in this case the fact '. . . that the quasi monopoly enjoyed by Tetra Pak on [one] market and its leading position on the [other] market placed it in a position comparable to that of holding a dominant position on the markets in question as a whole.'[110]

[104] Case T-65/89 *BPB Industries and British Gypsum*.
[105] Case 62/86 *AKZO*.
[106] See eg Alison Jones, 'Distinguishing Predatory Prices from Competitive Ones' [1995] *EIPR* 252, 255.
[107] Case 333/94 *Tetra Pak II*.
[108] Ibid, at para 27.
[109] Ibid, at para 31.
[110] Case C-333/94P *Tetra Pak II* at para 31.

The Court of Justice drew attention to the detailed findings of associative links between the two markets:

> The fact that the various materials involved are used for packaging the same basic liquid products shows that Tetra Pak's customers in one sector are also potential customers in the other.... It is also relevant to note that Tetra Pak and its most important competitor, PKL, were present on all four markets. Given its almost complete domination of the aseptic markets, Tetra Pak could also count on a favoured status on the non-aseptic markets. Thanks to its position on the former markets, it could concentrate its efforts on the latter by acting independently of the other economic operators on those markets.[111]

The CJEU added that these circumstances, 'taken together and not separately', justified a finding that Tetra Pak enjoyed freedom of operation vis-à-vis other economic operators which made a finding of dominance on the second market unnecessary.[112]

Consequently, in an assessment of the constraints placed by the definition of abuse on the legitimate exercise of IPRs, it is necessary to take into account the market context as well as the type of abuse. The designation of markets is highly relevant to the existence of abuse as well as the existence of dominance. In the next five chapters, we shall look at seven main heads of specific abuse largely in terms of their relevance as limits on the exercise of IPRs:

1. Refusals to supply (Chapter 7)
2. Tie-ins (Chapter 8)
3. Excessive pricing (Chapter 9)
4. Discriminatory pricing and conditional rebates in a single market (Chapter 10)
5. Predatory pricing and margin squeezing (Chapter 11).

[111] Ibid, at para 29.
[112] Ibid, at para 30.

7

REFUSALS TO SUPPLY AND LICENSE AND INTELLECTUAL PROPERTY RIGHTS

7.1 Refusals to Supply: The Court of Justice and Commission 93
7.2 From Refusal to Supply to Refusal to License: The Commission Decisions 98
7.3 *Magill* and the 'Exceptional Circumstances' Test 102
7.4 Refusals to Continue to License or Supply Interface Information on an 'Aftermarket' 109
7.5 The *Microsoft* Case in Europe and 'Exceptional Circumstances' 111
7.6 Competition and IP Remedies 119
7.7 The Pricing of Compulsory Licensing 120

7.1 REFUSALS TO SUPPLY: THE COURT OF JUSTICE AND COMMISSION

From an early stage, the Court of Justice was prepared to give strong support to the Commission's policy of treating a refusal by a dominant firm to supply existing, dependent customers as an abuse of a dominant position. In *Commercial Solvents*,[1] a manufacturer of a raw material for ethambutol, a pharmaceutical product useful in treating tuberculosis, decided to vertically integrate into the downstream, ethambutol market. In consequence, it stopped supplying its long-standing customer, Zoya, who was dependent upon it for commercial survival as a producer of the drug. The Court of Justice held that the dominant firm's plans to begin producing ethambutol itself did not justify its refusal to continue to supply the raw material to its long-standing customer, even though it would now be a competitor, when the refusal would eliminate the competitor, who was one of the principal manufacturers of ethambutol, from the market.

[1] Cases 6 and 7/73 *Istituto Chemioterapico Italiano SPA & Commercial Solvents Corp. v Commission* [1974] ECR 223, [1974] 1 CMLR 309.

The abuse was an extreme form of discrimination under Article 102(c). The CJEU further confirmed the Commission's order to Commercial Solvents to resume supply as a legitimate exercise of its powers under Regulation 17.[2]

The CJEU was particularly concerned about the dominant undertaking's use of its market power in the dominated market to acquire power for itself in the downstream market. The abuse consisted of refusing to supply an existing customer 'with the object of reserving such raw material for manufacturing its own derivatives'.[3] The CJEU also observed that Commercial Solvents had the capacity to continue meeting the needs of Zoya as well as its own new subsidiary and hence had no objective justification for the refusal. In effect, the special responsibility of a dominant firm under Article 102 could be used in such circumstances to curb its freedom of contract and place limits on its business strategy to vertically integrate.

The reasoning of the Court of Justice in *Commercial Solvents* was later applied in *Télémarketing*.[4] Télémarketing was a phone-in marketing company providing phone lines and telephone operators to deal with responses to television advertisements. After working with Télémarketing for several years, the TV broadcasting company decided to enter the field itself and stopped supplying services to Télémarketing by the device of withholding advertising time from advertisers who did not make use of the telemarketing services of its own associated phone-in marketing company. The CJEU held that such a refusal was abusive where, without objective necessity, a firm in a dominant position on a particular market reserves to itself 'an ancillary activity which might be carried out by another undertaking as part of its activities on a neighbouring but separate market, with the possibility of eliminating all competition from such undertaking'.[5]

These cases made it clear that, where a dominant undertaking's refusal to supply drives an existing customer/competitor out of business on an ancillary market, it would be viewed as acting abusively under Article 102.[6] What was less clear were the responsibilities of a dominant undertaking to a new entrant to such a market. Nor was it clear from these cases whether and to what extent the obligation of a dominant undertaking not to refuse supply of a product could be extended to a refusal to license where the dominant undertaking held a copyright, patent, or other IPR entitling the firm to exclusive exploitation. To what extent did the right of exclusive exploitation of an IPR operate as a defence or justification under the competition rules?

At one point, the Commission was prepared to accept that 'a dominant undertaking should not have to subsidize its competitors', but this was in circumstances where the

[2] Now replaced by Council Regulation 1/2003 on the implementation of the rules on competition laid down in Articles 81 and 82 of the Treaty, OJ L 1, 4 January 2003.

[3] Cases 6 and 7/73 *Commercial Solvents* at pp 250–1.

[4] Case 311/84 *Centre Belge d'Etudes du Marché-Télémarkeeting v Compagnie Luxembourgeoise de Télédiffusion SA and Information Publicité Benelux SA*. [1985] ECR 3261, [1986] 2 CMLR 558.

[5] Ibid.

[6] See eg R. Subiotto, 'The Right to Deal with Whom One Pleases under EEC Competition Law' [1992] *ECLR* 234.

customer of a dominant firm reorganized itself to promote a competing brand.[7] By the time of the *IBM*[8] case, however, it had begun to formulate a view that in special circumstances an IP-owning firm in a dominant position could have a positive obligation both to allow new competition to enter, as well as to ensure that existing competition was not illegitimately lessened in markets in which the firm was dominant.[9] Over the years, the EU Courts have taken an active role in defining the nature of those 'exceptional circumstances' in which an IPR owner can be compelled to license its IPR to existing competitors and new entrants in markets affected by the IPR. These cases take it as a starting point that there is normally no obligation of an IP owner to share its technology but there can be exceptional circumstances in which the failure to do so can amount to an infringement of Article 102(b).

7.1.1 Primary and secondary markets and IPRs

For IP owners, a key feature in the development of the EU Courts' determination of the entitlement of dominant firms to refuse to license under Article 102(b) is the distinction made between primary and secondary markets for the purpose of defining abuses. Firms are allowed to enjoy the essence of their exclusive IPR protection in the product or technology market in which they are dominant, ie in the 'primary market'. However, in 'secondary' markets, or 'aftermarkets', ie those markets for which the dominant product or technology is an indispensable input, the CJEU has limited the freedom of exclusive exploitation.

This guideline to the interpretation of Article 102 was introduced by the CJEU in *Volvo UK v Veng AB*,[10] a case referred to the Court of Justice by a UK court for a preliminary ruling under Article 267 TFEU. When Veng was enjoined from importing the infringing wing panels by a Volvo infringement action in the UK court, he claimed as a defence that Article 102 required Volvo to supply or license him to make panels. He argued that Volvo's refusal to license him to supply spare parts for Volvo motor cars was an abuse of its dominant position. The Court of Justice refused to overturn the injunction Volvo obtained under national law, stating quite emphatically that:

The Court of Justice held first that there were three separate markets: the market for cars, the market for Volvo spare parts and the market for repair and maintenance of Volvo cars. It also held that Volvo was not dominant in the car market but was dominant in the spare parts market for

[7] Thus, in *BBI/Boosey & Hawkes* OJ [1987] L 286/36, [1971] CMLR D35 it stated: 'A course of conduct adopted by a dominant undertaking with a view to excluding a competitor from the market by means other than legitimate competition on the merits may constitute an infringement of [Article 102]. The injury to competition would be aggravated where the stated purpose of the action is indirectly to prevent the entry into the market of a potential competitor to the dominant producer. A dominant undertaking may always take reasonable steps to protect its commercial interests, but such measures must be fair and proportional to the threat.'

[8] *IBM v Commission* [1981] ECR 2639; see also [1984] 3 CMLR 147.

[9] Subiotto (n 6 above).

[10] Case 238/87 *Volvo v Veng (UK)* [1988] ECR 6211.

Volvo front wing panels. Moreover, by virtue of its design right and the nature of the product, this was an unusual degree of dominance, a monopoly with no substitutes of a product that was indispensable to the repair and maintenance market.

The Court of Justice held that in the primary market for which Volvo had a monopoly owing to its design right, the exclusive right to make or sell, which was the very purpose of the IPR protection, would be fully respected.[11] There was no duty to supply or license competitors in that market.

As the CJEU put it:

> the right of a proprietor of a protected design to prevent third parties from manufacturing and selling or importing, without its consent, products incorporating the design constitutes the very subject matter of its exclusive rights. It follows that an obligation imposed upon the proprietor of a protected design to grant to third parties, even in return for a reasonable royalty, a license for the supply of a product incorporating the design would lead to the proprietor being deprived of the substance of its exclusive right.

It went on to add that, 'a refusal to grant such a license cannot itself constitute an abuse of a dominant position'.[12]

In this case, the CJEU was suggesting a particular accommodation to the normal exercise of IPRs. IPRs, such as design rights, would enjoy a complete monopoly in the market for manufacturing and selling new Volvo spare parts; they could also price quite highly without breaking the competition rule against unfair pricing.

However, while in the 'primary' market for the product, there was to be normally no requirement for a dominant firm to license competitors to make or sell its IP-protected product. The Court of Justice in *Volvo* went on to indicate that in the 'secondary' and dependent market for Volvo spare parts, Volvo as the monopoly supplier of spare parts, could not always refuse to supply competitors in the maintenance market. Nor could it price so high as to make supplies of the protected product inaccessible to the secondary market. The concern of Article 102 was to maintain access and prevent abusive use of dominance in one market to foreclose competitors in secondary markets. As the CJEU put it:

> It must however be noted that the exercise of an exclusive right by the proprietor of a registered design in respect of car body panels may be prohibited by Article [102] if it involves, on the part of an undertaking holding a dominant position, certain abusive conduct . . .[13]

The CJEU gave three examples of such abuse:

(a) if the intellectual property right-holder 'arbitrarily' refuses to supply spare parts to independent repairers;

[11] The Court also applied its decision in Case 144/81 *Keurkoop v Nancy Kean Gifts* [1982] ECR 2853 to Art 102. It stated that, 'in the absence of Community harmonization of intellectual property law, the determination of the conditions and procedures under which protection of designs is granted is a matter of national rules', para 18. In other words, competition law would not question the basis for the grant of the IPR.

[12] Case 238/87 *Volvo v Veng (UK)*.

[13] Ibid, at para 9.

(b) if it fixes prices for spare parts at an unfair or excessively high level; or

(c) if it decides no longer to produce spare parts for a particular model though many cars of that model are still in use.[14]

These three examples in *Volvo* of additional circumstances going beyond legitimate exercise of IPRs under Article 102 were not meant to be exhaustive. For they all related to the examples of conduct specifically prohibited under Article 102(a)–(d). Moreover, they contained a hint that a refusal to license an IPR could in certain circumstances be abusive under Article 102. It is true that in all three examples the offence could be remedied by a simple order to supply. In the first two examples the conduct complained of has little reference to the IPR; they are simple refusals to supply the goods under Article 102(b) or the charge of unfair prices under Article 102(a), which could be remedied without affecting the specific subject matter of the IPR. In the third case, however, if the right-holder has refused to supply, and also refuses to license, such behaviour would be abusive under Article 102, and ultimately susceptible to a remedy of compulsory licence. Similarly, dominant undertakings which exploit their IPRs by a process of discriminatory licensing or by demanding unreasonably high royalties would be acting abusively under Article 102 despite exercising rights allowed under national law.[15]

In the *Volvo* case, the abusive conduct of the IP owner in the secondary market was thought to consist of 'leveraging' its dominant market power in the primary market in a secondary market to exclude existing competitors and to deny access to new entrants to that market.[16] The implication of the *Volvo* judgment was that in exceptional cases where a dominant firm refuses to supply with the purpose of preventing competition on a secondary market, competition authorities may under Article 102 TFEU order compulsory supply or license of an IP protected good. The case hinted that this duty to supply would not be limited to those who had previously been supplied. The duty appeared to be owing to all those on an existing dependent market.

This case was to prove to have far-reaching implications for IP owners whose concept of exploitation of IPRs increasingly extended to systems of complementary products in aftermarkets, such as spare parts, consumables, and applications of software programs etc. In subsequent case law it also appeared unnecessary to prove the existence of a primary 'market'. The important issue was whether the protected technology or copyright work was 'indispensable' to a related market.[17]

It is important too to see at this point that the Court of Justice was not suggesting a complete exemption for IP owners from the competition rules in a primary market in

[14] Ibid.

[15] See eg *GEMA I and II* [1971] ECR 791; 1979 [ECR] 3173; Cases 110/88, 241–242/88 *Ministère Public v Tournier* [1989] ECR 2521; Case 395/87 *Lucazeau v SACEM* [1989] ECR 2811; Case 402/85 *Basset* [1987] ECR 1747 discussed in Ch 9.

[16] Cases 6 and 7/73 *Commercial Solvents*; see also Case T-83/91 *Tetra Pak International SA v Commission* [1994] ECR II–755, [1997] 4 CMLR 726.

[17] See discussion in Chapter 5.

which it holds a dominant position. For example, in primary markets, the CJEU has found it to be abusive conduct for a dominant firm to acquire control over potentially competing innovative technology by another firm[18] because this type of conduct would foreclose access to the competing technology to that market. Moreover, the limits of Article 102(a) to excessive or unfair pricing are in principle still applicable in the first market.[19] Thus, while paragraph 8 of *Volvo* stands as a powerful statement by the competition rules that in primary markets the legal monopoly created by IP laws will be respected, paragraph 9 stands out as an equally powerful statement that the way the IP is exercised in secondary, dependent markets, is subject to more comprehensive regulation by the competition rules.

7.2 FROM REFUSAL TO SUPPLY TO REFUSAL TO LICENSE: THE COMMISSION DECISIONS

7.2.1 The 'exceptional circumstances' test

After the *Volvo* case, there was little conceptual difficulty for the Commission to extend obligation not to refuse to supply into an obligation not to refuse to license an IP in a dominant position. Where a firm in a dominant position engaged in exclusionary behaviour in secondary markets, it mattered little that the dominance was associated with an IPR. The fact that IP laws confer exclusive rights of exploitation upon proprietors for a limited period of time in the interests of encouraging innovation and creativity was accepted by the Commission. It also understood that without the exclusive rights to exploit the innovation or creation there would be insufficient financial reward for the innovator because others could copy the innovation and sell it more cheaply.

The Commission's particular concern, however, was to regulate the conduct of a firm which occupied a dominant position amounting to an indispensable infrastructure which gives it control over a downstream market for the supply of compatible products. The fact that such a position was created or reinforced by an IPR could not preclude the application of Article 102. If the dominant firm used its market power as a lever to prevent potential competitors from entering markets, or to attempt to drive out existing firms from markets in which the proprietor firm was itself operating, this was an offence under EU competition law whatever the logic of intellectual property law.

In the *IBM* case in 1984 the Commission had taken the position that IBM had acted abusively under Article 102. By delaying disclosure of interface information on its new IBM 375 mainframe computers while taking orders for them, IBM had, the Commission asserted, created an artificial advantage for its own 'peripheral' products (known today as applications) and denied its competitors an opportunity to adapt their

[18] Case T-51/89 *Tetra Pak Rausing SA v Commission (Tetra Pak II)* [1990] ECR II-309, [1991] 4 CMLR 334.

[19] See Chapter 9.

peripheral products to the new IBM 375 mainframe computer.[20] The Commission accepted IBM's undertakings, particularly in relation to interface information and memory binding.[21]

Further, in *IGR Stereo-Television*,[22] the Commission dealt with a case involving IGR, a firm owned by all the TV manufacturers in Germany, which was also the proprietor of the patents for stereo receivers needed to equip German TV sets for stereo TV reception. IGR granted patent licences to its members, but planned to license non-members at a later date and subject to quantity limits. The patent rights were used to stop Salora, a Finnish company, from supplying stereo TV sets to German mail order firms since a patent licence for the stereo receivers was essential in order for a firm to enter the German stereo TV market. After the Commission began proceedings against IGR, it agreed to license immediately and without a quantity limit. Though the case involved an unlawful agreement under Article 101, the Commission also viewed IGR as a firm in a dominant position, abusing its market power by refusing to supply Salora. The Commission did not consider that the patent rights, which were the foundation for the dominant position, could justify the refusal to supply or the imposition of restrictions on supplies to outsiders. If necessary, the Commission would have been prepared to order compulsory licences under Articles 101 or 102. In the event, after the Commission had begun proceedings against IGR, the latter agreed to license Salora immediately and without limit.

7.2.2 New entrants and Commission decisions

The Commission's views on the extension of the duty not to refuse to supply new entrants as well as existing customers were further developed in two airline cases. In *London European/Sabena*,[23] Sabena, which was dominant in Belgium in the market for computer reservation services (CRS), refused access to its CRS to London European because it was entering the London-Brussels route and undercutting Sabena's fare rates. The refusal effectively prevented London European from operating that route. When London European complained to the Commission, it applied the reasoning of *Commercial Solvents* and treated Sabena's conduct as an abusive refusal for competitive reasons to supply an essential service. It observed that there was little competition on the route in question and that Sabena had sufficient CRS capacity.

In *British Midland/Aer Lingus*,[24] Aer Lingus decided to end its 'interlining agreement' with British Midland, ie its arrangement to issue tickets reciprocally on behalf of the other airline, once British Midland began to compete on the Dublin-London route.

[20] See n 8 *op cit*. The Commission also accused IBM of committing the abuse of tying by refusing to supply the software for use with non-IBM mainframe computers. IBM thus wrongfully created a disadvantage for its competitors selling non-IBM mainframe computers.

[21] See also *Decca Navigation Systems* [1990] 4 CMLR 627.

[22] EC Commission, *XIth Competition Policy Report* (1982), p 63.

[23] [1988] OJ L 317/47, [1989] 4 CMLR 662.

[24] [1992] OJ L 96/34, [1993] 4 CMLR 596.

The Commission decided that the potential loss of revenue that Aer Lingus might suffer from the new entrant's competition did not justify the refusal to interline and the handicap it would impose on the new entrant in the form of higher start up costs.

The Commission said:

Refusing to interline is not normal competition on the merits...the argument that interlining would result in a loss of revenue would not of itself make the refusal legitimate...Both a refusal to grant new interline facilities and the withdrawal of existing interline facilities may, depending on the circumstances, hinder the maintenance of competition.[25]

In both cases, it was not clear that the denial of access to the new entrants threatened their survival as opposed to merely creating a competitive disadvantage. In *Aer Lingus*, the Commission summed up the issue in the following way:

Whether a duty to interline arises depends on the effects on competition of the refusal to interline; it would exist in particular when the refusal or withdrawal of interline facilities by a dominant airline is objectively likely to have a significant impact on the other airline's ability to start a new service or sustain an existing service on account of its effects on the other airline's costs and revenue in respect of the service in question, and when the dominant airline cannot give any objective commercial reason for its refusal (such as concerns about creditworthiness) other than its wish to avoid helping this particular competitor.[26]

In these cases, the Commission applied a test which differed from an essential facility test similar to *Commercial Solvents* and *IBM* in two important respects. First, it imposed an obligation to interline without first investigating whether the interlining service was indispensable and incapable of duplication. Secondly, the Commission did not appear to be concerned with the issue whether Aer Lingus, the airline with the dominant CRS, was also dominant in the airlines market.

It might be more helpful to characterize *Aer Lingus, Boosey & Hawkes*,[27] and *United Brands*[28] as cases of 'dependence' rather than 'essential facilities'. They were all cases of retaliation by dominant firms against customers who either entered into, or joined with competitors to enter into, competition with their 'supplier'. In such a situation Article 102 can apply even if the degree of dominance is such that there are some alternative sources of supply and the legal test is one of objective justification and proportionality for the dominant undertaking's use of the sanction of refusal to supply as a punishment. It would be wrong in principle, however, for the Commission to adopt a test for essential facility which falls short of both indispensability and non-duplicability. To impose the obligations on an essential facility which the Commission has envisaged presupposes a strict test on both counts: that the facility is an indispensable input; and TINA applies, ie there is no alternative source of supply.

[25] Ibid, at paras 25–6.

[26] Ibid, at para 26.

[27] *BBI/Boosey & Hawkes: Interim Measures* [1987] OJ L 286/36, [1988] 4 CMLR 67.

[28] Case 27/76 *United Brands v Commission* [1978] ECR 207, [1978] 1 CMLR 429.

7.2.3 The Commission's 'essential facility' doctrine

In its refusal to deal cases in general, the Commission had begun to formulate a view, based on the reasoning of the Court of Justice in *Commercial Solvents* and *Télémarketing*, that the preservation of effective competition required dominant companies which owned 'essential facilities' to offer access to competitors as well as customers on a non-discriminatory basis. One of the first cases where the doctrine was mentioned explicitly was *Sea Containers v Stena Sealink*.[29] In this case, Sea Containers, wishing to introduce a high-speed catamaran ferry service from Holyhead to Ireland, asked Stena Sealink, the owner of the port facilities, to provide access to its new ferry service. Stena Sealink declined because of the competition that it would create to its ferry service on the same route. The Commission stated that an undertaking which:

> occupies a dominant position in the provision of an essential facility and itself uses that facility (ie a facility or infrastructure without access to which competitors cannot provide services to their customers) and which refuses other companies access to that facility without objective justification or grants access to competitors only on terms less favourable than those which it gives to its own services, infringes [Article 102] if the other conditions for applying that Article are met.[30]

The Commission found that Stena Sealink's rejection of Sea Containers' application was not consistent with the obligations of an undertaking which enjoys a dominant position in relation to an essential facility nor conduct which would have been expected from an independent port authority. The Commission's conclusion was that by denying access to its competitor on non-discriminatory terms, Stena Sealink had abused its dominant position as the harbour authority for Holyhead. The Commission had little doubt that the principle of access to essential facilities applied to new entrants in the relevant market, particularly where, as in this case, it was offering a new service. Abuse could be defined in terms of a dominant firm hindering the development of growth in competition in a market as well as the maintenance of the degree of existing competition in that market. Again, as if to pre-empt a claim of objective justification for refusing access, the Commission indicated that the capacity of the harbour was such that an additional competitor could be accommodated without undue inconvenience.[31]

The Commission justified its development of the essential facilities doctrine by reference to the decisions of the Court of Justice in *Commercial Solvents* and *Télémarketing*. However, in two important respects *Stena Sealink* and its successors differ from those cases. First, the Commission's decision in *Stena Sealink* appears to suggest that where a firm controls an essential facility it is under a stricter duty not to discriminate, stemming from its dual role both as administrator of an infra-structure and an operator on a

[29] [1995] 5 CMLR 84.

[30] Ibid, at para 66.

[31] See also the Commission's decision, *Europort AIS v Denmark* [1993] CMLR 457 (re access to facilities of Port of Rødby); see further *Irish Continental Group v CCI Morlaix* [1995] 5 CMLR 177.

market utilizing that infrastructure. For example, in the *Port of Rødby*[32] decision, the Commission indicated that even if the existing facilities at the port were fully utilized and could not accommodate additional sailings, it would be desirable to introduce competition by providing access to the new entrant. Secondly, there may be additional procedural obligations on firms that control an essential facility. In *Stena Sealink*, for example, the fact that Stena Sealink had failed to negotiate and consult with its customers as an independent operator contributed to the finding of abuse.[33]

At all events, by the time of the *Magill* case, the Commission viewed its mission under Article 102 to require dominant firms owning essential facilities or infrastructure in a market to make such facilities available, on a non-discriminatory basis, to enable competitors to compete in the same or related markets. As John Temple Lang described it:

> In Europe, important sections of industry are being deregulated or at least liberalised by the European Union. These measures would be of little value if the companies concerned, most of which are dominant in their own areas, were free to integrate forward and to discriminate in favour of their own downstream operations. Regulated or state-owned companies often own facilities that are essential for all or most of their downstream competitors. The essential facilities principle is, in part, derived from [Article 106 of the TFEU].[34]

This development in EU competition policy enforcement applied to a wide range of commercial activities: airlines, harbour facilities, railways, telecommunications, and energy. It was not directed solely at IPRs. However, if ownership of an IPR amounted to, or was associated with, an essential facility, and unlicensed competitors could not gain entrance to the market, then in the Commission's view, compulsory licensing of IPRs could be an appropriate remedy.[35]

7.3 *MAGILL* AND THE 'EXCEPTIONAL CIRCUMSTANCES' TEST

In the IP licensing context, the implications of paragraph 9 of *Volvo* were considerably extended in the landmark case of *Magill*.[36] Magill was a compiler of a comprehensive weekly TV guide combining the contents of the three individual weekly TV guides sold separately by the respective TV companies. After losing a copyright infringement action at the national level, Magill successfully complained to the Commission that the

[32] Ibid.

[33] See J. Venit and J. Kallaugher, 'Essential Facilities—A Comparative Law Approach' [1994] *Fordham Corp Law Inst* 315.

[34] John Temple Lang, 'Defining Legitimate Competition: Companies' Duties to Supply Competitors, and Access to Essential Services' [1994] *Fordham Corp Law Inst* 245, p 281.

[35] Ibid.

[36] Joined Cases C-241/91P and C-242/91P *RTE and ITP v Commission (Magill)* [1995] ECR I–743, [1995] 4 CMLR 718.

TV companies' refusal to license the programme listings was abusive conduct under Article 102 and won an order for a compulsory licence of the listings material from the TV companies to produce its comprehensive TV guide. The General Court (GC) affirmed the Commission's order. On further appeal to the Court of Justice, the TV companies were supported in their arguments by the Intellectual Property Organisation (IPO), representing software makers internationally. The appeal resulted in a lengthy opinion by the Advocate General recommending that the Court of Justice should set aside the judgments of the GC and annul the decision of the Commission on the grounds that the IPR should be protected against competitors in secondary markets as well as primary markets. Advocate General Gulman (later promoted to the Court of Justice) began by recalling that 'the aim of copyright is precisely to give the proprietor the possibility of restricting competition and that possibility must also be afforded to a dominant undertaking'.[37] He accepted that Article 102 could apply to regulate and restrict the exercise of an IPR which falls within the specific subject matter but in such a case, there must be 'such special circumstances in connection with a refusal to license that it can no longer be regarded as a refusal to license in itself'.[38]

His view was that the fact that the refusal to license resulted in the frustration of a new product—the comprehensive TV guide—was not a special circumstance where the new product competed with that of the copyright holder because the right to refuse a licence must be regarded as necessary to provide a reward for its creative effort, even if its product was inferior to that of its competitors. He said it would only be abusive to refuse to license if the new product did not compete with a product of the copyright holder. Nor did he think that the fact that the product was on a derivative market was a special circumstance justifying the application of Article 102, since it was normal for copyright holders to exploit derivative markets. The Advocate General asserted that:

> if copyright is used in order to prevent the emergence of a product which is produced by means of the work protected by the copyright and which competes with the products produced by the copyright owner himself it should. Even if that product is newer and better, the interests of consumers should not in such circumstances justify interference in the specific subject matter of the copyright where the product is one that largely meets the same needs of consumers as the protected product, the interests of the copyright owner carry great weight. Even if the market is limited to the prejudice of consumers, the right to refuse licenses in that situation must be regarded as necessary in order to guarantee the copyright owner the reward for his creative effort.[39]

7.3.1 The judgment of the Court of Justice in *Magill*

The Court of Justice was not persuaded by the Advocate General's version of special circumstances and upheld the decision of the GC and the Commission on the finding

[37] Ibid, at para 63.
[38] Ibid, at para 40.
[39] Ibid.

of abuse and the entitlement of the Commission to award a remedy of compulsory licence for a violation of Article 102.

On the issue of abuse, the CJEU began by emphasizing that it was wrong to presuppose that all forms of exercise of copyright which are legitimate under national law can never be reviewed under Article 102.[40] It reiterated that in the absence of Community harmonization, the determination of the conditions and procedures for granting protection of an IPR are a matter for national rules. It also admitted that the exclusive right of reproduction is part of the author's rights, so a refusal to grant a licence, even by a firm in a dominant position, cannot in itself constitute abuse of a dominant position.[41] Nevertheless, it insisted that in exceptional circumstances, the exercise of such an exclusive right by a proprietor may amount to abusive conduct.[42]

The Court of Justice was prepared to uphold the GC's finding that 'exceptional circumstances' made the refusal of the TV companies to license the TV listings to Magill abusive conduct on the basis of three circumstances in particular. The first circumstance was that there was no actual or potential substitute for a weekly guide offering comprehensive listings of the programmes for the week ahead, a product for which there was a strong potential consumer demand. This meant that the television companies' refusal to provide basic listings information, for which they were the only source, by relying on their copyright prevented the emergence of a new product, one moreover which they themselves did not offer. The result gave viewers no choice but to buy weekly guides from the three TV companies and was an abuse under Article 102(b), ie 'limiting production, markets or technical development to the prejudice of the consumer'.[43] Secondly, the CJEU found that there was no objective justification for the refusal of the TV companies to license Magill, either in the activity of television broadcasting or in that of publishing television magazines. The implication here is that in the face of a violation of Article 102(b), the mere possession of the IPR is not an objective justification for exclusionary conduct. There must be evidence of some other objective justifying factor such as poor creditworthiness, safety, etc.

The third circumstance was that the TV companies reserved to themselves the secondary market for weekly television guides by excluding all competition on that market, since they denied access to the basic information which was indispensable to the publication of such a guide. Effectively, they used a *de facto* monopoly position on one market, consisting of an essential input or facility, to maintain a monopoly on a secondary, dependent market. This was an abuse of the type prohibited in *Commercial Solvents*. By approving the holding of the GC on this point, the Court of Justice effectively endorsed the basis of the 'essential facilities' doctrine promoted by the Commission, albeit under certain conditions. One precondition was that the facility in the first market was not merely dominant; it was a *de facto* monopoly. Secondly, it must

[40] Ibid, at para 48.
[41] Ibid, at para 49.
[42] Ibid, at para 50.
[43] Ibid, at para 54.

be an indispensable input to the secondary market. There was no alternative source of supply. Thirdly, the direct result of the refusal to make that essential facility available was to maintain a monopoly for the firm on the second market.

The 'new product' rule suggests that one test of exceptional circumstances is that if an IP owner owns an indispensable raw material for a new product with clear consumer demand and (a) that raw material is a *de facto* monopoly, ie there are no existing or potential substitutes for it; (b) it uses it without objective justification to prevent the emergence of that new product; (c) which it does not offer itself, then the refusal to supply or license the raw material could be an abuse of a dominant position. The interest protected by this abuse is apparently consumer demand.

In such a case, the limiting conditions are (a), (b), and (c) cumulatively. For example if, as has been suggested,[44] a firm owns a unique biotechnology invention which it uses to cure clinical obesity but refrains from offering it as a general slimming drug, can another firm use this first holding of *Magill* as a springboard for compulsory access? It may be argued that the decision to limit the technical field of application is part of the company's commercial strategy of exploitation, but the logic of competition law suggests that the better argument is that one of the three conditions are not met, ie either there are substitutes for the raw material or there are safety reasons for not releasing it for general consumption as a slimming pill.

Similarly, if the second test of *Magill*, the 'essential facility' test, is to offer a separate test of abuse, there must be a showing of (a) a firm who owns an indispensable raw material for a secondary market; (b) a *de facto* monopoly; (c) the effect of the refusal is to enable the IPR holder to reserve for itself that secondary market by excluding all competition on it. Inevitably, there will be difficulties in establishing how these guidelines apply to specific fields such as computer software, telecommunications, and other media industries, in which copyright is conferred on information as opposed to artistic or literary work. How does one identify secondary markets which require licensing to competitors at different stages of product development?[45] How can one distinguish between improvements and completely new products? Again, the answers will depend upon an understanding of the logic of competition law as it applies to the particular field.

For example, in the field of IT law, in cases of products which are industry standards, particularly software operating systems, the principles applied in the *IBM* case in the 1980s and the *Microsoft* case in the 1990s are likely to be applied to rights of access to information about interfaces to other secondary products such as software applications, peripherals, and hardware. Moreover, technological products which grow into industrial standards will have an obligation to license to manufacturers other than those already in the technology pool that formed the basis of the standard. The effect of the *Magill* decision will be to reinforce the interoperability obligations under the EC

[44] See Case 333/94 *Tetra Pak International SA v Commission (Tetra Pak II)* [1996] ECR I–5951, discussed in V. Korah, 'The Paucity of Economic Analysis in the EEC Decisions on Competition—Tetra Pak II' [1994] *Current Legal Problems* 148.

[45] Ibid.

Computer Program Directive,[46] particularly where the essential facility owner is itself operating in the second market.

In addition, where a dominant firm owning an indispensable industry standard decides at some point to vertically integrate into a secondary market, there will be an obligation towards other firms already working in that market on the basis of licences, and there may be an obligation to license new entrants with competing products. The principles of *Commercial Solvents*, as affirmed in *Magill*, will apply to place limits upon the dominant firm's use of its licensing power to foreclose or exclude competitors from such secondary markets.

What remains unclear after the decision, however, is when a product will be viewed as an essential input or facility for another product or market as opposed to being simply part of another product. Take, for example, a firm with a hardware product which has a major share of a market. As part of its product package it provides an application in the form of diagnostic software for maintenance purposes which is then used exclusively by its own maintenance contractors. Are the diagnostic software and the hardware to be viewed as integral parts of the same 'product'? Or, is the diagnostic software to be viewed as a separate product constituting an essential input for the maintenance 'market' for the hardware? If the latter is the case, would the undertaking be required to license it to competing third party maintenance companies even where it offers maintenance contracts along with the sale of its hardware package?

Of course, if it had already allowed third party maintenance firms to enter the market and license its diagnostic software and then suddenly stopped licensing in order to vertically integrate into the maintenance market, that would probably be caught by Article 102 under the reasoning in *Commercial Solvents*. If, however, it has all along viewed its investment in the diagnostic software as part of its programme to exploit the value of its innovative hardware and insists on retaining exclusive rights to use it in the secondary market, will that be viewed as a normal exercise of IPRs?[47]

The obvious difference with the facts of *Magill* is that consumers are in fact being supplied by the IPR holder with the product. The charge cannot be levied under Article 102(b). To win, the third party maintenance companies will have to succeed with two arguments. First, they must show that the diagnostic software is both indispensable to their entry into the maintenance market for that product and that there are no substitutes, ie that the diagnostic software is itself an 'essential' input for the maintenance market requiring the firm to license it even to competitors. Secondly, they will have to show that the hardware company is discriminating between its own company in the

[46] Vinje argued presciently that the provision in the EC Software Directive's (91/250) Recital 27 (now replaced by Directive 2009/24/EC), that Art 102 may still apply 'if a dominant supplier refuses to make information available which is necessary for interoperability', could apply to strengthen the hands of competitors' rights under Art 6 where access to interface information is not complete as a result of reverse engineering or decompilation. See T. Vinje, 'Comment: The Final Word on Magill' [1995] 6 *EIPR* 297, p 302.

[47] It cannot be viewed as a tie-in under Art 102(d). It does not require customers to use it as a condition of buying the hardware; it simply makes it available exclusively with its own maintenance service.

maintenance market and the new entrant, with a view to excluding all competition. In such a case, they would succeed if a court would be prepared to find that the second test of *Magill* can be applied independently of the first. This interpretation of the case should not be altogether excluded.[48] These issues of abuse which arise in the post-product market can arise at different stages of production prior to the final product phase in cases of novel software as well as to other industries such as telecommunications, as the Commission has already acknowledged.[49]

If the guidelines to conduct after *Magill* may be unclear on this point, the case is clear that the principles from which they must be derived require a deep understanding of Article 102. Two lines of guidance are provided by the decision. First, if an IP owner has a dominant position by virtue of the IPR, its exercise of the IPR is limited by the prohibitions in Article 102(a), (c), and (d) as well as (b).[50] Secondly, if the IP owner has a dominant position in the form of an essential facility it will have certain positive duties towards competitors which may be inconsistent with the full exclusive exploitation of the IPR in a downstream market. These principles will not normally impinge on the exercise of the exclusivity of IPRs in primary markets and even secondary markets, but there will be cases of dependence and exclusionary refusals to supply or license which will be found to be abusive under Article 102 and thereby place constraints on the exclusive exploitation of IPRs, particularly in secondary markets.

7.3.2 The post-*Magill* cases

In *Oscar Bronner*,[51] the CJEU had an opportunity to develop the 'exceptional circumstances' test developed in *Magill*. The case did not actually involve IPR, instead it revolved around a newspaper distribution system owned by a larger newspaper, Mediaprint, which a smaller newspaper, Bronner wanted access to. Mediaprint refused access and Bronner complained to the Commission.

The CJEU ruled that a refusal to supply or give access to a facility would only be unlawful if (1) it would eliminate all competition on the downstream market; (2) there was no realistic actual or potential alternative to find; and (3) access to an existing system would therefore be indispensable. Furthermore, the CJEU held that the requirement of indispensability could only be satisfied if there were no technical, legal, and economic obstacles capable of making it impossible, or even unreasonably difficult, for another to replicate the product or service.[52] It continued: 'For such access to be capable of being regarded as indispensable, it would be necessary at the very least to

[48] See eg Case T-504/93 *Tiercé Ladbroke v Commission* [1957] ECR II–923.

[49] See Vinje (n 46 above), p 303.

[50] For example, following the third exception in *Volvo* there may be an obligation under Art 102 to continue to produce spares to allow maintenance of an outdated technical product even if the dominant undertaking would like to shift all consumer demand to a new upgraded product.

[51] Case C-7/97 *Oscar Bronner GmbH & Co KG v Mediaprint Zeitungs-und-Zeitschriftenverlag GmbH & Co KG* [1998] ECR I–7791, [1999] 4 CMLR 112.

[52] Ibid, at para 44.

establish . . . that it is not economically viable to create a second [product or service] with a [production] comparable to that of . . . the existing [product or service]'.[53] Although, *Oscar Bronner* did not deal with IPRs, the case echoes the ruling of *Magill* and actually introduces the 'exceptional circumstances test' to the 'essential facility' doctrine, which originally did not include IPRs.[54] Secondly, the CJEU confirmed *Magill* by building its ruling in *Bronner* upon *Magill*, clarifying its views on 'indispensability' and the requirements needed for such as a claim.

In *IMS Health Inc*,[55] the Commission attempted to answer this question by relying solely on essential facilities reasoning. It ignored the necessity to prove a new product where the applicant for a licence was a new entrant to the market. In *IMS* the Commission ordered a compulsory licence of information contained in a database, consisting of an '1860 brick structure' which provided a format for storing regularly updated information about the sales of pharmaceutical products in Germany region by region. The beneficiaries of the compulsory licences were firms started *inter alia* by former senior management to market regional sales data services which proved to be dependent upon access to the IMS database.

The Commission distinguished between the brick structure database, which it found to be copyright protected, and the related market of regional sales data services. It then found that the IMS 1860 brick structure was an essential facility because it had become a market standard demanded by customers including the wholesalers as well as the pharmaceutical companies and that it was not economical for competitors in the second market of selling regional sales data services to reproduce it. It found that the refusal to license was abusive because once the tests of essential facility and dependent product were met, it was not necessary that the competitors in the 'aftermarket' were offering a product which was new in relation to the product offered by IMS.

IMS appealed to the GC which stayed the order of compulsory licence pending the result of the appeal because there was a serious doubt that the decision would be upheld on appeal, in part because the Commission had proceeded on the supposition that the new product requirement was not an indispensable condition of the exceptional circumstances test. The CJEU's view was that this was a misreading of the existing judicial authority provided by the *Magill* judgment.

When the *IMS* case was referred to the Court of Justice, it confirmed that all three main conditions of *Magill's* 'exceptional circumstances' test had to apply. They were cumulative, ie that in order for a refusal to license new entrants to a market dependent upon an indispensable IP protected input to be abusive, the refusal must meet three conditions:

(a) the undertaking which requests the licence intends to offer, on the market for the supply of data in question, new products or services not offered by the copyright owner and for which there is potential consumer demand;

(b) the refusal is not justified by objective considerations; and

[53] Ibid, at para 46.

[54] Ibid, at para 41.

[55] Case T-148/01R *IMS Health v Commission* [2001] ECR II–3193, [2002] 4 CMLR 58.

(c) the refusal is such as to reserve to the copyright owner the market for the supply of data on sales of pharmaceutical products in the Member State concerned by eliminating all competition on that market.[56]

This interpretation of the 'exceptional circumstances' test based on *Volvo* and *Magill* could be seen as offering in its own right a reconciliation between competition law and IPRs based on their mutual interest in innovation by stressing that the 'exceptional circumstances' for a compulsory licence for new entrants to a market is limited only to cases of new products or 'follow up' innovation and not 'me too' competition. To refuse a licence in such a situation would clearly be a case of limiting technical development under Article 102(b). It also happened to be consistent with the distinction between competition by substitution and competition by copying within IP law.[57]

7.3.3 Are there other categories of exceptional circumstances?

In its *IMS* judgment, the Court of Justice seemed to make it a point to indicate that the *Magill* conditions did not offer the only test of 'exceptional circumstances'. It held 'that "it is sufficient" (rather than "it is necessary") to meet the three Magill criteria in order to show an abusive refusal to license'.[58] That proposition would seem to follow from the purpose of Article 102(b) which in principle prohibits as abusive conduct by dominant firms which limits technical development of markets to the detriment of consumers. Limiting technical development is a wider concept than the particular factual circumstances and conditions of the *Magill* case. Hence, both the language of Article 102(b) and the ECJ judgment in *IMS* offer good grounds for concluding that other types of abuse can also fall within the category of 'exceptional circumstances'.

7.4 REFUSALS TO CONTINUE TO LICENSE OR SUPPLY INTERFACE INFORMATION ON AN 'AFTERMARKET'

A second category of 'exceptional circumstances' in which Article 102 might well apply to IP owners can occur where a dominant firm with an IPR-protected monopoly in the form of an indispensable input refuses to supply or license a competitor in a second dependent market *whom it had been supplying* with a view to obtaining that secondary market for itself.

Article 102(b) as interpreted by the Court of Justice suggests that there is a possible second category of 'exceptional circumstances' that may be relevant to this set of facts.

[56] Case C-418/01 *IMS Health GmbH & Co OHG v NDC Health GmbH & Co KG* [2004] 4 CMLR 1543 at para 52.

[57] J. Drexl, 'Is there a More Economic Appreoach to IP and Competition Law' in J. Drexl (ed), *Research Handbook on Intellectual Property and Competition Law* (Cheltenham: Edward Elgar, 2008), 47.

[58] Cases 241–242/91P *Magill* at para 38.

This second category of cases was introduced by *Commercial Solvents*,[59] a case involving a US dominant supplier of chemical raw materials to an Italian firm making those chemicals into a pharmaceutical product. After a period of supply, the US firm making the 'essential raw material' for the pharmaceutical product decided belatedly to enter the pharmaceutical product market itself and as part of that vertical integration decision stopped supplying its downstream competitor. The CJEU upheld the Commission's finding of abuse on the principle that the refusal of a dominant firm to continue to supply, where there were no alternative sources of supply and where it had sufficient capacity to continue to supply the competitor and its own subsidiary in the aftermarket was conduct unjustifiably intended to eliminate its major competitor in the market.

In the information technology field, this principle has been extended to IP owners of industrial standards who have been compelled by the European competition authorities to supply or license or provide proprietorial information about interface codes on 'reasonable' terms.[60] The starting point for the imposition of this second category of competition law restriction on the conduct of copyright protected industrial standards was the IBM undertaking of 1984.[61] The Commission had initiated proceedings against IBM based upon Article 102 as early as 1980 claiming that IBM was dominant in the markets for the supply of the main memory and basic software for IBM Systems 370 Central Processing Units (CPUs) and had abused its dominant position by tying or bundling memory and software to the purchase of its CPUs and discriminating against other manufacturers of memory and software by delaying the supply of changes in interface codes to them even though they had taken orders for the supply of the CPUs. This created an artificial advantage for itself in the downstream markets by denying competitors an opportunity to adapt their products to the new IBM products. At this stage, the Commission did not explicitly use essential facility reasoning; it relied on the dependence of the peripheral product makers on the IBM Systems 370 CPUs owing to the high costs of 'switching' to other mainframe computers.

In 1984, IBM negotiated with the Commission to accept its unilateral undertaking to provide other manufacturers with technical interface information needed to permit competitive products to be used with IBM's System 370 mainframe computers. IBM agreed to provide interface information to software developers in a timely manner and to announce changes affecting interoperability in advance of general availability. The information could be supplied in source code or special documents setting out interface information specifically. This information was to be freely available to any relevant company doing business in the EU and any fees were to be reasonable and non-discriminatory. IBM was required to support international standards for open system interconnection for products, systems, and networks of different manufacturers.[62]

[59] Cases 6 and 7/73 *Commercial Solvents*; see also Case 311/84 *Télémarketing*. Cf *Otter Tail Power Co v United States* 410 US 366 (1973).

[60] See eg *IBM Personal Computer* EC Comm. December 84/233 (1984); *Microsoft IP* (94) 643 [1994] 5 CMLR 143.

[61] *IBM Personal Computer* EC Comm. December 84/233 (1984).

[62] [1984] 3 CMLR 147.

What was noteworthy about the IBM undertaking in the mid-1980s was that it applied the obligation of interoperability more widely than *Commercial Solvents*. It applied it to all competitors, existing and new entrants. The Commission gave little weight to the right of IBM as the inventor of the mainframe system to prevent competing manufacturers of peripheral applications for the IBM system from enjoying the position of 'free riders' who hadn't contributed to the costs of researching and developing the system. It gave priority to interoperability over reward-incentives to innovation, seeking only to ensure that IBM as the owner of the essential infrastructure received a fair and reasonable return for any licences. Interestingly, this was not inconsistent with the reasoning of paragraph 9 of the *Volvo* case.

7.5 THE *MICROSOFT* CASE IN EUROPE AND 'EXCEPTIONAL CIRCUMSTANCES'

The answer to some of these questions was offered in the *Microsoft* case[63] arising again out of relationships in the information technology sector. In 2000 and 2001, the Commission investigated Microsoft after a complaint by Sun Microsystems, one of Microsoft's most important competitors in the workgroup server market. Sun complained that Microsoft provided inadequate information about interface codes for Sun to equip its Solaris servers to interoperate smoothly with Microsoft's 'integrated' package of Windows 2000, Office Suite, and workgroup server operating system because it refused to disclose how the integration between Windows and Office Suite and its server operating system worked. This refusal had the effect of preventing Sun from offering certain services to Windows-based users of its high quality Solaris workgroup server. The Commission in a decision issued on 24 March 2004 found that Microsoft had abused its near monopoly in the Windows operating system under Article 102 by deliberately restricting interoperability between the Windows operatimg system and non-Microsoft workgroup servers such as those operated by Sun Microsystems. The Commission found that by refusing to disclose interface protocols to other workgroup server makers to allow them *to continue to* interoperate with MS Windows, Microsoft was attempting to lever its dominant position in the Windows PC operating system market to obtain dominance in the workgroup server operating system market and media player markets.[64]

There was a separate abuse relating to the bundling or tying of the Windows Media Player with the Windows PC operating system with Microsoft's media player, which will be dealt with below in Chapter 8.

The remedies imposed by the Commission for the refusal to supply interface information included a fine of €497.2 million for its infringements of Article 102 and an order that Microsoft must divulge all necessary interface information to *allow non-MS*

[63] Case COMP/C-3/37.792 *Microsoft Corp* [2005] 4 CMLR 965, upheld in Case T-201/04 *Microsoft v Commission* [2007] ECR II–3601.

[64] *Microsoft* Commission Decision.

workgroup server OS to achieve full interoperability with Windows PCs and MS workgroup servers within 120 days. This was to enable *rival vendors* to compete on a level playing field in the workgroup server operating system market. Insofar as this information was copyright protected, the Commission indicated that it would require a compulsory copyright licence to be given to competitors in the workgroup server market in order to bring the infringement of Article 102 to an end. Microsoft was to receive remuneration that was reasonable and was based on non-discriminatory terms. The Commission also required Microsoft to update the disclosed information each time it brings to the market new versions of its relevant products. The Commission also indicated that it planned to appoint a monitoring trustee to oversee that Microsoft's interface disclosure is complete and accurate. This remedy of compulsory disclosure of interface information was reminiscent of the remedy agreed in the IBM undertaking of 1984.[65] It was noteworthy too that the remedy of compulsory disclosure was not restricted to any one particular complainant but appeared to be aimed at all participants in the work server market.

Microsoft appealed to the GC against the fine and remedies imposed by the Commission. Before the appeal was heard, and following an adverse report by the monitoring trustee and its own experts, the Commission adopted a further decision in 2006 to penalize Microsoft another 280.5 million for continued non-compliance with its 2004 decision.

The Commission's finding that Microsoft had abused its near monopoly in the Windows operating system by deliberately restricting interoperability between the Windows OS and Sun Microsystems workgroup server operating systems was based on an 'entirety of the circumstances' test which asserted that its decision must be based on the results of a comprehensive investigation and not be bound by an exhaustive checklist of exceptional circumstances.

There was little doubt that Microsoft met the threshold test of a monopoly which was an indispensable input to a secondary product.[66] There was little doubt as well that Sun Microsystems was offering an innovative product for which there was substantial and demonstrable demand. The Sun workgroup server OS was not a 'me too' product of the Microsoft server and may in fact have preceded it in the market. The Commission could therefore legitimately impute to Microsoft the exclusionary motive of using its control over the PCOS market to evict an *innovating* competitor, ie conduct which amounted to an abuse of 'technological' leveraging of its dominance.[67] If a dominant firm with a monopoly of an IP-protected product which is an indispensable input, chose to 'compete on the merits', it would have to continue to license the relevant

[65] See *XIVth Report on Competition Policy* (Commission, 1984), paras 94–5.

[66] Judging from the statement of objections and the recent press release, the Commission revealed its acceptance of the network effects analysis of barriers to entry in high tech markets that had influenced the US Justice Department and Federal Trade Commission in the US *Microsoft* case (*US v Microsoft Corp* 253 F 3d 34 (DC Cir 2001)).

[67] See *Microsoft* Commission Decision.

interface information to its innovating competitors and compete directly in that secondary market on the basis of quality and price, etc. For a dominant firm with a *de facto* monopoly which is an indispensable input to other products to be allowed to use its power in any other way would have a 'chilling effect' on innovation by competitors in the dependent aftermarket and limit technical development in that market, conduct which is characterized as an abuse by Article 102(b). Without access to interface information, competitors in the workgroup server market would be gradually deprived of their opportunity to develop servers with new or added functionality that Microsoft does not offer to the consumer.[68] This tended to place the facts of the Microsoft case squarely within the 'exceptional circumstances' test of Article 102(b) because the conduct of the dominant firm unjustifiably limited the technical development of the market.

In addition, it is important to see that embedded in the *Microsoft* facts was the further circumstance, not present in *Magill*, which could significantly change the calculus in, and thereby expand, the 'exceptional circumstances' test. Following the authority of the reasoning of *Commercial Solvents*, and subsequent CJEU decisions,[69] if a dominant firm has been engaged in a course of dealing with a contractor in an aftermarket and suddenly chooses directly to compete with it by vertically integrating its operations and introducing its own product on that market, it has an obligation to continue to 'supply,' ie license or inform its existing customers (now competitors) in the downstream market, unless it can offer a justification for that refusal. To fail to do so would mean that the dominant firm was not 'competing on the merits' in an already weakened market. By initially opting for an open system as a strategy to grow and achieve dominance, the owner of an IP-protected industrial standard has created expectations and under EU competition law would have difficulties refusing to continue to supply downstream contractors under Article 102(b) and possibly 102(c) for discriminating between its own subsidiary and competitors, particularly where there are no capacity restraints. In such a case, a dominant firm can be found to be acting abusively by refusing to continue to supply information or to license a firm with which it has been dealing where its motive is self-evidently one of using its dominance to *evicting* that competitor from the market.

In other words, the 'exceptional circumstances' in which a compulsory copyright licence can be awarded by a competition authority would include refusals to supply interface code information or license *existing* innovative downstream operators with predatory intent. In such cases, the Commission would be relying on the authority of Article 102(b) but with a theory that in the IT sector, Article 102(b) can be infringed when a company such as Microsoft with an industrial standard, limits technical development by refusing to *continue* to share interface information and thereby prevents competitors on related markets from developing their interoperable systems. If Microsoft had opted for a closed system in the way say of Apple Mac initially, the circumstances might have

[68] See M. Dolmans and N. Levy, *EC Commission v Microsoft: Win, Lose or Tie?* (Brussels: Cleary, Gottlieb, Steen & Hamilton, 2004).

[69] See eg Case 311/84 *Télémarketing*.

been different because the company would have achieved its dominance on the basis of originally integrated products and it would normally have been entitled to continue to compete on that basis. To hold otherwise would be to make dominance itself unlawful. However, having built up its dominant position on the basis of interoperating with downstream applications makers, it seems arguable that Microsoft cannot freely resort to a policy of 'closing up' interoperability by withholding interface information once it establishes its Windows OS as an industrial standard. That type of commercial strategy would be viewed as predatory under Article 102 rather than 'competition on the merits' and even if the interface information were copyright protected, the Commission would be entitled to order a resumption of the supply of such information. The compulsory licence of the copyright protected information was essentially to ensure the resumption of that supply.

Upon appeal by Microsoft, the GC gave its judgment[70] modifying and extending the test of exceptional circumstances established by the CJEU in its *Magill*[71] and *IMS Health* judgments[72].

The starting point in analysing the judgment of the GC is to understand that the GC determined that its review of the Commission's findings of fact was to be a limited one. Early on the GC made it clear that in so far as the Commission's findings of fact were based on complex economic and technical assessments, it would undertake only a limited review, as opposed to its normal general review of the Commission's decisions. By restricting itself to a limited review, the GC accepted that it could not substitute its own assessment of matters of fact for that of the Commission. It was limited to checking the accuracy of the facts, whether the evidence contained all the relevant data, and whether the data were capable of substantiating the conclusions drawn, ie it would not overturn the Commission's findings unless it could find manifestly incorrect findings of fact or errors of assessment of law. This respected the Commission's margin of appreciation in economic and technical matters. In addition its new approach to the 'exceptional circumstances' in which competition law will find that a refusal to license an IPR will be an infringement of Article 102, the GC gave important guidance on three other related issues: (1) the significance of the findings of 'indispensability' of the interface protocols to interoperability in the 'second market'; (2) the significance of the finding that there was a 'risk' of elimination of competition in the second market; and (3) by emphatically limiting the standard of proof of risk of elimination of effective competition, the judgment suggests a lesser role for economic argument in the legal rules defining the concept of *effects* of abuse under Article 102 and may affect the current discussion of reform of Article 102.

The modification of the 'exceptional circumstances' test in *Microsoft* In *Magill*[73] and *IMS Health*,[74] the Court of Justice maintained that where an IP was involved, it was

[70] Case T-201/04 *Microsoft*.
[71] Cases C-241–242/91P *Magill*.
[72] C-418/01 *IMS Health*.
[73] Cases-241–242/91P *Magill*.
[74] Case 418/01 *IMS Helath*.

necessary to show that there must be 'exceptional circumstances' present before Article 102 could be used to override the free exercise of an IPR. The 'exceptional circumstances' test as expounded in these two cases consisted of three cumulative conditions. (This of course was in addition to the requirement that the nature of dominance in the first market was a monopoly which was an indispensable input into the second market). The first condition was that the undertaking asking for a compulsory licence must offer a new product for which there was potential or demonstrable consumer demand. Secondly, the Commission needed to show that the refusal to license would lead to an elimination of all competition on the secondary market. Thirdly, it had to be shown that the dominant undertaking had no objective justification for refusing to license.

Microsoft argued that in this case too there should be a strict test based on the 'new product' rule as set out in the *IMS Health* case.[75] This argument was not entirely convincing since the Court of Justice in *IMS Health* said that the facts of *Magill* were 'sufficient' to meet the exceptional circumstances test, implying that other categories of exceptional circumstances could exist.[76]

Microsoft also attempted to establish that competitors would not be providing a new product but replicating MS Windows server operating systems, 'mimicking their functionality' and that therefore consumers would not be harmed by its refusal to share interface information. Had Microsoft succeeded in proving this assertion, the case might have been otherwise decided but the Commission argued somewhat more successfully that Microsoft's competitors could use the interface disclosures to develop the advanced features of their own products[77] and liven up the competitive landscape.[78] It argued therefore that the refusal to continue to supply interface information stopped 'follow on' innovation. The facts as found supported this point since the Solaris workgroup server offered more functions, eg reliability/availability of the network and security than the Microsoft workgroup servers.[79]

In its argument on appeal, the Commission reiterated its position but in the process of responding to the GC's questioning, it seemed to achieve a clearer focus.

(1) The Commission refined the new product argument by arguing that the definition of 'new product' is one that doesn't duplicate existing products but adds substantial elements arising from competitors' own research efforts.

(2) It took a far more effective line on the crucial issue of adapting the exceptional circumstances categories to the facts of the case partly in response to the questioning of the GC.[80] It reiterated the point that *IMS Health* did not establish an exhaustive list

[75] At one point, Microsoft also argued that none of the criteria of the Case C-7/97 *Bronner* case were satisfied but this was on the basis that *Bronner* should apply if there were no intellectual property rights at stake. See Case T-201/04 *Microsoft* at para 301.

[76] *IMS Health* at para 107.

[77] Ibid, para 695.

[78] See ibid, para 725.

[79] See eg at para 652.

[80] Ibid, para 317.

of exceptional circumstances. But this time it seemed to be more strategic by making the point that the framework for analysing the test of refusal to supply was provided by Article 102(b) which declares it *an abuse to limit technical development* to the prejudice of consumers. It argued that the refusal to provide the indispensable interface information amounted to a blockage of interoperability in the specific sector of information technology and a blow to 'follow on' innovation in the secondary market. It also explained that this factor differentiated the facts of the case from the *IMS Health* and *Magill* type cases.[81] This was more focused than its earlier insistence that the framework could be established simply by looking at the entirety or totality of the circumstances.

(3) Finally, it also drew attention to the fact that Microsoft was disrupting an existing pattern of a history of supply of interface information to the sector and the discontinuation of supply had occurred after Microsoft had made use of interoperability in the sector to build up its market for Windows operating systems.[82] This point also reminds us that on this point too the facts of Microsoft can be significantly distinguished from a refusal to supply a new entrant to the sector (as was the case in the facts of *Magill* and *IMS*).[83]

The GC accepted almost all of the Commission's arguments and indeed developed them in certain respects.

The GC emphasized that the test of new product must be considered under Article 102 which makes it *an abuse to limit . . . technical developments* to the prejudice of consumers.[84] It pointed out that the new product rule in *Magill* was meant to protect consumers from the harm of preventing the appearance of a totally new product, *one not offered by the dominant firm and one for which there was a potential consumer demand.*[85]

It also stressed that in *IMS Health*, the CJEU had emphasized the damage to consumer interests that can arise where the refusal to grant a licence *prevents the development of a secondary market* to the detriment of consumers.[86]

It then concluded that the *Magill* and *IMS Health* new product rule *cannot be the only parameter which determines whether a refusal to license an IPR is capable of causing prejudice to consumers within the meaning of [Article 102(b)].*[87] That provision refers to limiting not only production or markets, but also a limitation of *technical development.*[88]

[81] Ibid, para 305.
[82] Ibid, para 307.
[83] See S. Anderman, 'Does the Microsoft Case Offer a New Paradigm for the "Exceptional Circumstances" Test and Compulsory Licenses under EC Competition Law?' (2004) 1(2) *Competition Law Review* 13–14.
[84] Case T-201/04 *Microsoft* at para 644.
[85] Ibid, at para 643.
[86] Ibid, at para 646.
[87] Ibid, at para 647.
[88] Ibid, at para 647.

The GC went on to find that the Commission had evidence for its finding that the refusal to supply would prevent the competitors from 'developing the advanced features of their own products available in the web of interoperability relationships that underpin the Windows domain architecture' and evidence for its finding that 'the refusal caused prejudice to consumers'.[89]

Hence the GC concluded that the Commission's findings were not manifestly incorrect.[90]

7.5.1 What are the implications of this judgment for future cases of attempts to obtain compulsory licences?

In the first place we must recognize that this judgment is one that is explicitly rooted in its findings of facts: interoperability issues in the information technology sector; obstruction to innovative competitors by an owner of a *de facto* industrial standard after a history of a continued relationship of sharing code information.

Nevertheless, it is clear that after the GC's judgment, the 'exceptional circumstances' test has wider parameters than the 'new product' rule in *Magill.* We had an intimation of this possibility in *IMS Health* but now we have a confirmation. The only issue is how wide are the parameters?

The parameters are probably not as wide as suggested by a literal reading of para 664 which states that:

> Article [102] covers not only those practices which may prejudice consumers directly but also those that which indirectly prejudice them by impairing an effective competitive structure?

It is wise to remind ourselves first of all that the test of exceptional circumstances set out in CJEU judgments presupposes that the IP-protected product in the first market must be both a monopoly and an indispensable input into the second market. Secondly, a constituent element of the abuse must be that there is strong evidence that the practice of the IP owner *will give rise to the risk of 'eliminating effective competition' in the market.* This probably places limits on the definition of impairment of 'an effective competitive structure'.

The crucial test of 'exceptional circumstances' after the *Microsoft* judgment is to discern how the new product test has been redefined. In this case there were two factors that seemed to be influential in the GC's judgment: First this was a case concerning the need to maintain interoperability in the information technology sector to ensure the *continuation of demonstrable* plural sources of innovation, sources which were also demonstrably satisfying consumer needs that were not satisfied by Microsoft. Sun had demonstrated that it was a real source of innovation and promised to continue to be so. This case did not concern a new entrant seeking access. Sun and other work server makers had enjoyed a long period of interoperability with Windows based on its

[89] Ibid, at paras 651–6.

[90] Ibid, at para 665.

willing supply of interface information, albeit to a predecessor of Sun. Microsoft's decision to discontinue this practice after receiving the letter from Sun, whatever its obvious irritation at the scope of the request, could objectively be viewed as an abuse comparable to the definition of abuse in a line of cases since *Commercial Solvents*. Moreover, the refusal in such circumstances could legitimately be construed as exceptional circumstances satisfying a modified new product test *owing to its limitation of technical development in the sector to the prejudice of consumers*.[91]

After *Microsoft*, the category of exceptional circumstances when applied to *new entrants* will continue to require that the new entrant offers a new product, however that is defined by the case law. As we know, the definition of new product continues to be opaque. All we know is that the new entrant may not offer a replica or clone of the product already offered by the owner of an IP-protected industrial standard. What is less clear is the extent to which and the way in which the new product must be different from the old. In the *Microsoft* case, a close look at the facts of workgroup servers indicated a recognizable difference in the functionalities of the Solaris servers from those of Microsoft.

But of course the *Microsoft* case was not a case of a new entrant similar to *Magill* and *IMS Health*. It was a case of a dominant firm disrupting an existing relationship of interoperability on grounds which could be found to be anti-competitive. Following *Microsoft*, we can assume that where an incumbent has already been dealing with undertakings operating in a dependent secondary market and the competitor in the secondary market (1) already has advanced features in its own products and (2) requires access to the interface information in order to viably continue to develop such advanced features, Article 102(b) will apply. Innovators will get such protection because a refusal in such circumstances will limit the 'technical development' of the market.

Yet will it stop there? In the *Microsoft* case, the Commission did not seem to consider the distinction between the new entrant and established relationship dichotomy particularly significant.[92] It merely drew attention to the fact that this was the case in *Microsoft*. The GC thought it more significant but only as an added factor. Yet the GC judgment in the *Microsoft* case drew attention to the fact that the language and purpose of Article 102(b) now guides us in defining the outer limits of the competition rules. And, in respect of monopoly undertakings with an indispensable product which have historically provided access to competitors in secondary markets, the test of exceptional circumstances may be even wider and possibly moving closer to cases of essential facilities which are not IP protected. *Commercial Solvents* continues to provide possible authority for the interpretation of Article 102(b) and that provision refers to limiting 'markets', as well as 'technical development', to the prejudice of consumers. Where a monopolist with an indispensable input disrupts a relationship of previous supply for reasons that could be viewed as anti-competitive, it may be sufficiently egregious behaviour to bypass the established exceptional circumstances test for IP owners.[93]

[91] Ibid, at para 665.

[92] Ibid, at para 307.

[93] See Anderman and Kallaugher, *Technology Transfer and the New EU Competition Rules* (Oxford: OUP, 2006), Ch 10.

The finding of an absence of objective justification In *Magill*, the objective justification argument was that the existence of the IP justified a refusal to licence. However, in *Microsoft* the justification argument was taken a step further. Microsoft asserted that it would have less incentive to develop a given technology if it was required to make that technology available to its competitors. The Commission treated this argument as an invitation to engage in a balancing exercise.

However the GC ruled that it could only be raised under the head of objective justification.[94] It held that once the constituent elements of the abuse have been established, the burden shifts to the dominant firm to raise any plea of objective justification and support it with arguments and evidence.[95] In this case Microsoft did not meet its burden. Its arguments were vague, general, and theoretical. It merely stated that '[d]isclosure would . . .eliminate future incentives to invest in the creation of more intellectual property,' without specifying the technologies or products to which it thus referred.[96]

The GC made it clear that what was called for was not a balancing exercise of the two theories of innovation but a more legalistic assessment of Microsoft's arguments. The GC concluded that the Commission's conclusion was not based on a balancing of the two conflicting views of innovation but its findings: that there was no basis to Microsoft claims that its products would be cloned; that disclosure of interoperability was widespread in the industry—IBM had already committed to this course in the 1980s; and that Directive 91/250[97] was consistent with this policy. [98]

So the GC did not engage with the Commission's attempt to balance the possible negative impact of an order to supply on Microsoft's incentives to innovate and the positive impact on the whole industry including Microsoft.[99] It contented itself with the conclusion that Microsoft had not made out an adequate case for objective justification. This suggests that the GC will in future deal with arguments about pro-consumer efficiencies and incentives to innovate as an attempted objective justification. They will be dealt with not as a simple balancing test, along the lines of a US-style rule of reason analysis, but more as a legal claim that can be overridden if the practice also deprives consumers of a new product or creates a risk of elimination of effective competition.

7.6 COMPETITION AND IP REMEDIES

The relationship of EU competition law as a 'second tier' of regulation of the exercise of IPRs is reinforced by this judgment. There will continue to be an internal balance between exclusivity and access within the law of each IPR and the possibility of an

94 Case T-201/04 *Micrsoft* at para 659.

95 Ibid, at para 688.

96 Ibid, at para 698.

97 Now replaced by Directive 2009/24/EC.

98 Case T-201/04 *Microsoft* at para 710.

99 See discussion in C. Ritter, 'Refusal to Deal and Essential Facilities: Does Intellectual Property Require Special Deference compared to Tangible Property?' (2005) *World Competition* (3) 281, 298.

external limit created by the competition law rules. A feature of this is the treatment of the decompilation issue under Article 6 of the Computer Programs Directive.[100,101] Even where the rules of IP law may provide an alternative method of resolving the dispute, if the conduct of the IP owner transgresses the prohibition of Article 102, competition law will provide a remedy to ensure access. This raises the interesting issue whether IP laws should reform themselves to minimize intervention by competition law or whether they should leave it to competition law to intervene whenever its rules are contravened by the exercise of an IPR.

One point that makes its appearance at the margins of the *Microsoft* case is the argument suggested by Microsoft that Sun's right to reverse engineer through decompilation under Article 6 of the Computer Programs Directive made the Article 102(b) complaint unnecessary.[102] Yet, in principle, Article 102(b) TFEU and Article 6 of the Computer Programs Directive are separate and independent laws even if they apply to certain types of overlapping conduct. The Computer Programs Directive does not only promote interoperability in the form of a limited decompilation right in Article 6 and a reminder of the idea/expression dichotomy in Article 1; Recital 17 of the Directive also states that:

> Whereas the provisions of this Directive are without prejudice to the application of the competition rules under [Article 101 and 102] if a dominant supplier refuses to make information available which is necessary for interoperability as defined in this directive.

In the *Microsoft* case, Sun seems to have given evidence to make it plain that the decompilation option was not adequate to meet the need for full interoperability in the circumstances, if for no other reason than the reverse engineering process was so complex that it handicapped them in their efforts to provide software compatible with a new Windows version in sufficient time for the new version of Windows OS. The Commission's view, which is a legitimate interpretation of Article 102, is that Article 102 offers a source of authority which may exist alongside but applies independently of Article 6 of the Computer Programs Directive.

It is worth noting, however, that if IP law were to take a form offering a more extensive guarantee of interoperability of interface information for software, then the effect would be that Article 102 would be called upon even more rarely to adjudicate cases of non-supply of interface information.

7.7 THE PRICING OF COMPULSORY LICENSING

While the category of 'exceptional circumstances' has been opened up to meet the purposes of Article 102(b), little new light has been thrown on the nature of the

[100] Directive 2009/24/EC of the European Parliament and of the Council of 23 April 2009 on the legal protection of computer programs, OJ L 111/16, which replaced Council Directive 91/250/EEC of 14 May 1991 on the legal protection of computer programs, OJ L 122, 17 May 1991, p 42.

[101] Case T-201/04 *Microsoft* at para 228.

[102] Note the *Microsoft* case refers to the old Computer Programs Directive 91/250/EEC.

'reasonable and non discriminatory' terms which are meant to govern compulsory access. Indeed, the GC's reversal of the Commission's appointment of an independent monitoring trustee to oversee the issue of fair pricing of compulsory access raises new questions.

Similarly in *Magill* the CJEU approved the Commission's decision to order a licence on terms which were 'reasonable' and 'non-discriminatory', but it gave little indication how these concepts were to be defined. This standard appears to be used by the Commission more generally in its regulation of access in the telecommunications sphere.[103]

Broadly, it is necessary to distinguish between the issue of excessive pricing under Article 102(a) and the formula of reasonable and non-discriminatory pricing in the case of compulsory access or licence under Article 102(b). In the case of Article 102(a), it is necessary to avoid pricing which is so extremely high, and can be shown to be so, that it is outside the range of permissible pricing even in a free market context. At its most extreme, it could be set so high as to amount in practice to a refusal to supply or trade. The important point is that Article 102(a) is not meant to put the EU Courts or Commission in the position of being an industrial regulator. It presupposes a wide range of 'fair' prices and is meant to step in only in the extreme case when a price is set which no fair dominant undertaking would set. That room for high pricing includes considerable space for a dominant undertaking with an IPR to obtain an extensive reward for innovation.

In contrast, to set fee levels under the formula of reasonable and non-discriminatory pricing of compulsory access in a two market situation, where those markets are vertically integrated, requires the EU Courts and Commission to attempt to approximate a regulator's task. In the *Magill* case itself the issue was eventually referred to a Copyright Tribunal set up under the Copyright, Designs and Patents Act 1988 to determine fees in cases of disputes between the parties. In other cases, there will be a need for regulatory principles to be applied to determine the issue of 'reasonable' royalties.

The starting-point in most cases is that the essential facility owner, whether or not an IPR is involved, is often engaged in some capacity in the downstream market. The first element in a reasonableness test of pricing in the second market must be to separate the proprietor of the essential infrastructure from the downstream operation in any calculation of its costs so as to ensure that there are no hidden cross-subsidies or discrimination. Insofar as there are two or more organizations under common ownership or control, there are bound to be shared costs and some method must be devised to ensure that these common costs are properly allocated to the relevant operation.[104] This will require a method of regulating the internal 'transfer pricing' of the two organizations. It might help if two separate sets of books are kept, but there may be a need for a

[103] See eg the Commission's Guidelines on the Application of EEC Competition Rules in the Telecommunications Sector, 91/C 233/02 [1991] OJ C233/2.

[104] Economists might prefer to use concepts such as incremental and stand-alone costs.

system of imputing costs to ensure that even separate books accurately reflect the division of costs between the two operations.

At the same time, it must be recognized that compulsory access allows in effect a sharing of an asset, whether the asset is material such as a gas line, port, railway track, or telephone line, or an IPR embedded in a product or process, such as a digital transmitter or software. In either case, therefore, some compensation must be given for the costs to the owner of creating and maintaining the shared asset.

In the IP licensing context, it is worth recalling the words of Advocate General Mischo in *Maxicar*, that 'the proprietor of protective rights may lawfully call for a return on the amounts he has invested in order to perfect the protected design'.[105]

This suggests that a reasonable fee would be set at a higher level than the access costs and the incremental costs of adding the compulsory licensee. The fee must include provision for an additional element to compensate for the costs of originating and maintaining the infrastructure. In the context of compulsory licensing, a licensing fee set too low could have the effect of allowing compulsory access to create an institutionalized form of 'free riding'. This would act as an even greater deterrent to investment in innovation than the fact of a compulsory licence itself.

On the other hand, the terms of a compulsory licence are not meant to compensate an IP owner for the full appropriation value of the right in the second market. An important reason for regulating the exercise of the essential infrastructure in a downstream market is to ensure that price levels approximate those of a market with workable competition rather than monopoly. If one allowed monopoly prices in both markets, this would defeat the object of the exercise. Moreover, in the licensing context, there may be a case for taking into account the reward to the manufacturer of an upstream product in the calculation of a reasonable return in a downstream market. For example, in *Maxicar*, Advocate General Mischo made the point that, when fixing the price of bodywork components sold as spare parts, due account should be taken of the fact that the manufacturers have already recovered part of the expenditure on perfecting the protected design.[106] It would be wrong in principle to adopt a standard based on compensation for loss of profits based on sales of licensed products[107] since this would approximate monopoly conditions for the IP owner in the downstream market.

What basis can be used to calculate a reasonable royalty in such cases? In principle the approach must be cost based with an element added on to compensate for a proportionate return on investment. A short cut could be available where the proprietor of the essential infrastructure has already set a royalty in the downstream market. This would represent its view of the part of the investment costs which should be returned along with the payment for the extra costs of the licensing process. Although this figure

[105] Case 53/81 *CICRA et Maxicar v Renault* [1988] ECR 6039, [1990] 4 CMLR 265 at para 17.

[106] Ibid, at paras 17 and 63.

[107] This is the usual measure of damages for patent infringement which presupposes a return based on enforcement of the IPR 'monopoly' return. See eg *Catnic Components Ltd and another v Hill & Smith Ltd* [1983] FSR 512 (Ch Patents Ct).

would have to be adjusted to take into account the state of competition on the licensee market, it represents a potential benchmark.

There is still the major problem of assessing the appropriate return either to compare with the existing royalty or where there is no existing royalty set. The EU Courts or Commission has to construct a basis for approximating a reasonable royalty in a workably competitive market. In the telecoms sector, an issue has arisen over whether the loss of market caused by the undertakings who have received compulsory access should be added to the 'reasonable return' to an essential infrastructure holder. In *Telecom Corporation of New Zealand v Clear Communication Ltd*,[108] the Privy Council appeared to have been persuaded that the application of the 'Baumol-Willig rule' or 'efficient component pricing rule' could allow the inclusion of opportunity costs (ie lost profit) as the basis of calculating a fair return to the monopoly provider of telecoms infrastructure when interconnecting other network operators.

The basis of the Baumol-Willig rule is the claim that the efficient component pricing rule is a necessary condition for efficiency and competitive neutrality in the provision of access to essential facilities. Only the efficient component pricing rule gives neither the owner nor its rivals a competitive advantage aside from any derived from superior efficiency. It is a test of discrimination that a reasonable price can be calculated in a perfectly contestable market to include opportunity costs, the sacrifice of profit entailed in supplying access to the essential facility to another firm instead of carrying out the operation itself.

In the *New Zealand Telecoms* case, the issue raised was the application of the Baumol-Willig rule of parity pricing under s 36 of the New Zealand Commerce Act which *inter alia* prohibits the use of a dominant position to prevent or deter any person from engaging in competitive conduct on that or any other market.

The High Court held that the application of the Baumol-Willig rule as the basis of New Zealand Telecoms pricing was not a breach of s 36 because, despite the risks of monopoly rents initially, it was a method which was likely to improve efficient competition rather than prevent or deter it.

The New Zealand Court of Appeal was more concerned about the risks of following the Baumol-Willig rule under s 36. Gault J was deeply sceptical about the inclusion of opportunity costs in the price demanded by a firm controlling an essential service in a perfectly contestable market. If that meant that the price charged could include monopoly rents for the firm in the dependent market, he doubted the validity of the model. He could 'not accept that the objects of the Commerce Act are served by a method of pricing that secures the profits of a firm in a dominant position'. Cooke J agreed with Gault but added that if the principle in Baumol-Willig was to set a price which made the supplier indifferent as to whether the other components of the final product are provided by itself or others, then the principle was anti-competitive because it would 'amount to

[108] [1995] 1 NZLR 385.

allowing a new entry into a market on condition only that the competitor indemnify the monopolist against any loss of custom'.

The Privy Council, in a judgment delivered by Lord Browne-Wilkinson, held that the terms for interconnection set by Telecom did not contravene Article 36 of the New Zealand Commerce Act. With the pricing based on the Baumol-Willig rule, Telecom could not be shown to have used its dominant position, as was required of the New Zealand Act, for the purpose of preventing or deterring competition from the competing service operator.

Underlying the Privy Council's decision, however, was its acceptance of the finding that s 36 did not have as its purpose the elimination of monopoly profits obtained by the dominant market position as such. This was the target of the price control provisions of Part IV of the Act and not s 36. In effect, as long as the pricing was comparable between the different service operators, including Telecom's subsidiary, the Privy Council accepted that it was not contrary to s 36; it accepted Baumol's evidence that the efficient component pricing rule was not designed to decide if there were monopoly rents in the original pricing of the dominant market position, but only if the pricing was unfair as between existing service operators.

Insofar as the efficient component pricing rule is aimed at non-discriminatory competition and does not preclude monopoly rents, it appears to be only partly relevant for the purposes of assessing the level of reasonable terms for compulsory access under Article 102(b) and analogous regulatory legislation. As we have seen, the purpose of the reasonableness test is to attempt to create charges in a related market which are both non-discriminatory and set at a reasonable level when that market is dependent upon an essential facility. This requires a method of assessing prices which is cost based but includes a return for the investment in the asset which is compulsorily 'shared'.

A more relevant model from the telecoms field is offered by the Guidelines issued by OFTEL in the UK on The Regulation of Conditional Access for Digital Television Services.[109] These Guidelines offer a discussion of the pricing issues raised by the obligation to offer technical conditional access services on a fair, reasonable, and non-discriminatory basis. The Guidelines distinguish between a fair and reasonable element and a non-discriminatory element. The latter is primarily concerned with the comparison of prices offered to different organizations for the same or similar services. Fair and reasonable prices are primarily concerned with the relationship between prices and the costs involved in providing the services. The starting-point for the Guidelines is that the costs of each service should be calculated separately on an incremental basis. Consequently, any specific cost associated with technical conditional access services which is identifiable, measurable, and attributable to the activities of specific

[109] Oftel, *Guidelines to the Regulation of Conditional Access for Digital Television Services*. (<http://www.ofcom.org.uk/static/archive/oftel/ind_info/broadcasting/conacc.htm#INTRODUCTION> (last accessed 27 June 2010)). These are contained in a statement issued by the Director-General in March 1997.

broadcasters must form the base for the price of or charges for the provision of services to those broadcasters.

In addition, where there are common costs not directly attributable to any individual set of activities, it suggests several methods of allocation, all subject to the requirement that the provider of common services must choose a method which is independent of any interests as a broadcaster (downstream operator).

It is in its treatment of fixed costs that the Guidelines suggest a useful method of calculating reasonable prices. It proposes that account should be taken of the position *ex ante* when the investment was made in the shared service. The Guidelines state:

> A related issue is the impact the uncertainty of demand for conditional access services has on the actual costs of provision of units of conditional access service. Many of the costs of setting up the infrastructure . . . might be fixed irrespective of the use that is subsequently made of those services. . . . Variations in the level of demand are likely to have a significant impact on the unit costs. OFTEL considers that it would be appropriate to take into account the risk that predictions of demand may turn out to be wrong (in either direction).[110]

Its treatment of the costs of capital takes a similar *ex ante* approach. In assessing the fairness or otherwise of the pricing of services, OFTEL will need to take into account the cost of capital 'and' the possibility that any investment may fail to make a return at all. It also uses a methodology for evaluating the appropriate cost of capital.[111]

The Guidelines also make allowance for the timing of the recovery of costs including front loading and variability. OFTEL uses a calculation of 'net present value' which takes into account the prices charged over the project period.[112] Finally, there is a check on input costs to ensure that these are not excessive. The method used is to give particular attention to the allocation of common costs between related companies and the licensee as well as the transfer prices of inputs from associated companies.[113] In cases of monopoly suppliers, for example because it is the only supplier with an IPR, then an external evaluation is made.[114]

[110] Ibid, A72.

[111] The appropriate cost of capital would be calculated with reference to eg the risk-free rate of return; the level of systemic risk incurred by investors in the conditional access business; the returns available from comparable investments; the debt-equity ratio. See para A79.

[112] Ibid, A73–75.

[113] Ibid, A76.

[114] Ibid, A77.

8

TYING[1]

8.1 Introduction	127
8.2 The EU Courts' Approach to Tying in Case Law	130
8.3 Tying and Intellectual Property Rights	142

8.1 INTRODUCTION

Tying is the selling or leasing of a product on the condition that the buyer or lessee also purchase or lease another product from the seller. Importantly, it is a common business strategy applied in many industries and by many companies to reduce costs, create production efficiencies, and spread the risk when entering into a new market. Yet, the conduct of tying is specifically mentioned in Article 102 under the subheading of 102(d), '*as making the conclusion of contracts subject to acceptance by the other parties of supplementary obligations which, by their nature or according to commercial usage, have no connection with the subject of such contracts.*'[2] In other words, once a company is found dominant, tying in principle becomes an abuse under the EU competition rules. Although, the definition applied in Article 102(d) only covers contractual tying, a broad range of tying practices have been caught under this heading in case law.[3]

[1] This chapter is based on 'Tying Arrangements under Article 82 EC' in H. Schmidt, *Competition Law, Innovation and Antitrust, An Analysis of Tying and Technological Integration* (Cheltenham, UK, Northampton, MA, USA: Edward Elgar, 2009).

[2] The conclusion of such a contractual obligation is also viewed as a restriction of competition under Art 101(1)(e) and is applicable to the terms of patent licences.

[3] T-201/04 *Microsoft Corp v Commission* [2007] ECR II–3601 at paras 860–1 and Case COMP/C-3/37.792–*Microsoft* Commission decision of 24 March 2004, [2005] 4 CMLR 965 at paras 794 and 801. The Enforcement Guidelines on Art 82 distinguish between contractual tying and technological integration, but merely note that the foreclosure effects are greater for technological integration; *Guidance on the Commission's Enforcement Priorities in Applying Article 82 EC Treaty to Abusive Exclusionary Conduct by Dominant Undertakings* (Brussels, 3 December 2008), para 53, OJ C45, 24/02/2009, p. 7–20. Compare with DG Competition, Commission: 'DG Competition discussion paper on the application of Article 82 of the Treaty to exclusionary abuses' (Brussels, December 2005), (<http://ec.europa.eu/comm/competition/antitrust/art82/discpaper2005.pdf> (last accessed 3 October 2010)), p 55. The paper is a Staff

It includes tying applied as a contractual tying,[4] mixed bundling,[5] and technological integration.[6] In contractual tying the buyer is forced to take the additional tied product in order to purchase the tying product. Cases such as *Hilti* and *Tetra Pak II* demonstrate that this form of tying has been treated by the Commission and the Courts as practically illegal *per se*. *Hilti* and *Tetra Pak II* set the standards for the specific requirements for finding tying abusive. Since these two cases revolved around contractual tying, the standards applied fit less well with other forms of tying such as technological integration.

Mixed bundling appears to be the odd one out; mixed bundling is when the company offers the tying and tied product in a bundle and separately. Therefore in principle there is no coercion of the customer. In fact, the Commission's remedy in *Microsoft I* was to require Microsoft to offer its products in a mixed bundle.[7] However, there may be a financial incentive upon the customer to purchase the bundle rather than the products individually and this can result in exclusionary effects, as was the case in *Digital Undertaking*.[8] In *Digital Undertaking*,[9] the Commission found Digital dominant in the service market for both hardware and software of its own products despite the primary market for computer systems being extremely competitive. Digital applied a pricing policy whereby it offered its software services together with its hardware services in a package which was considerably cheaper than the stand-alone prices of the software services thereby making its software services more attractive to the consumers with the hardware services.

There have been two more mixed bundling cases, both involving Coca-Cola. In the 1989 case, Coca-Cola had allegedly abused its dominant position by offering discounts on cola and non-cola packages to retailers.[10] The case was settled by Coca-Cola agreeing not to offer discounts based on conditions of retailers having to purchase non-cola products. In the 2005 case Coca-Cola again agreed to not condition its sale of its

Discussion paper published by the DG Competition and not actually an official Commission Notice. For simplicity however, it will be referred to as the Commission *Discussion Paper*.

[4] Case IV/30.787 *Eurofix-Bauco/Hilti*, OJ (1988) L 65/19, confirmed in T-30/89 *Hilti v Commission* [1991] ECR II–1439, [1992] 4 CMLR 16 and on appeal C-53/92P *Hilti AG v Commission* [1994] ECR I–667, [1994] 4 CMLR 614 and *Tetra Pak II* Commission decision, 92/163, OJ L 72, 18 March 1992, [1992] 4 CMLR 55, confirmed in T-83/91, *Tetra Pak International SA v Commission (Tetra Pak II)* [1994] ECR II–755, [1997] 4 CMLR 726 and on appeal C-333/94 *Tetra Pak International SA v Commission (Tetra Pak II)* [1996] ECR I–5951, [1997] 4 CMLR 662.

[5] *Digital Undertaking* Commission Press Release IP/97/868 and *XXVIIth Report on Competition Policy 1997*.

[6] Case COMP/C-3/37.792–*Microsoft* Commission decision [2005] 4 CMLR 965, confirmed in T-201/04 *Microsoft Corp v Commission* [2007] ECR II–3601 (*Microsoft I*).

[7] *Microsoft I* Commission decision at para 1011.

[8] *Digital Undertaking, XXVIIth Report on Competition Policy 1997* and Commission Press Release IP/97/868, 'The European Commission accepts an undertaking from Digital concerning its supply and pricing practices in the field of computer maintenance services' (Brussels, 10 October 1997); see also Robert O'Donoghue and A. Jorge Padilla, *The Law and Economics of Article 82 EC* (Oxford and Portland, Oregon: Hart Publishing, 2006) p 500.

[9] *Digital Undertaking, XXVIIth Report on Competition Policy 1997* and Commission Press Release IP/97/868, 'The European Commission accepts an undertaking from Digital concerning its supply and pricing practices in the field of computer maintenance services' (Brussels, 10 October 1997).

[10] Commission's *XIXth Report on Competition Policy* 1989, para 50.

stronger brands with its less-selling brands or require the retailers to reserve shelf space for Coca-Cola's entire range of products.[11]

The cases demonstrate that the Commission will intervene where exceptional price discounts are given when two products or services are purchased together, but only where the discount given by the dominant company makes it financially unattractive for the customer to go elsewhere and where the discount is not proportionate to costs.[12]

Technological integration is where the tying and tied product has been combined into one product, so it is in principle physically impossible for the consumer to separate the components.[13] So far three cases have involved technological integration: *IBM Undertaking*,[14] *Microsoft I*,[15] and *Microsoft II*.[16]

In *IBM Undertaking*, which was a settlement between the Commission and IBM, the issue of technological integration was raised for the first time. The Commission used Article 102(d) as part of the regulatory framework to make IBM agree to discontinue its practice of integrating its memory devices with the CPU and 'bundling' its main memory function with the sale of its System 370 Central Processing Units by including the price of its main memory function in the price of its CPU and refusing to supply the CPU separately.[17]

In *Microsoft I*, the Commission sought to cease Microsoft's tying of its Windows Media Player (WMP) to its Windows operating system. The case has been seen as controversial for various reasons. Firstly, the case confirmed that the inflexible list of conditions applied to contractual tying also applies to technological integration despite the Commission acknowledging that the two forms of tying are different, and economists arguing that the latter is not always harmful, but can induce pro-competitive effects.[18] Secondly, the case mirrored the US *Microsoft* case[19] although in this case the alleged tying was between Microsoft's operating system and its web browser, Internet Explorer.

Although technological integration like contractual tying imposes a risk of foreclosure in the tied product market, the purpose of technological integration may not be

[11] *Coca-Cola Undertaking* [2005] OJ L 253/21 and Commission decision COMP/A.39.116/B2–*Coca-Cola*, paras 34–7(<http://ec.europa.eu/competition/antitrust/cases/decisions/39116/commitments_fr.pdf> (last accessed 3 October 2010)).

[12] See also P. Andrews, 'Aftermarket Power in the Computer Service Market: The Digital Undertaking' *ECLR* 1998, 19(3), 176–81.

[13] Kai-Uwe Kühn, Robert Stillman, and Christina Caffarra, 'Economic Theories of Bundling and their Policy Implications in Abuse Cases: An Assessment in Light of the Microsoft Case' Vol 1, no 1, *European Competition Journal* March 2005, 85–121, p 88.

[14] *IBM Undertaking*, 1984 OJ L 118/24.

[15] Case COMP/C-3/37.792–*Microsoft* Commission decision of 24 March 2004 (*Microsoft I*) [2005] 4 CMLR 965 confirmed in T-201/04 *Microsoft*.

[16] *Microsoft* (COMP/C-3/39.530) [2009] OJ C242/20 (the decision on tying).

[17] There was also an issue of implicit tying of software by IBM's practice of refusing to disclose interface information. See Refusal to Supply, Chapter 7.

[18] *Microsoft I* Commission decision at para 841, see also the Commission's *Enforcement Guidance on Article 82* (n 3 above), paras 47 and 52.

[19] *US v Microsoft Corp* 253 F 3d 34 (DC Cir. 2001) (*US Microsoft III*).

purely anti-competitive. In fact, it is a method of innovation and product development commonly applied by businesses. A too strict treatment of such forms of tying can therefore undermine companies' incentive to innovate, which will in the long run affect competition and consumer welfare negatively. Also from the IP owners' view, a strict approach to technological integration will adversely affect their ability to develop IP protected products through technological integration, where only parts of the product are covered by an IPR or are covered by different IPR.

The different types of tying affect the markets and competition differently and thus cause different levels of pro- and anti-competitive effects. It is therefore interesting that the Commission and the EU Courts have chosen to only apply one approach to all the different types of tying.

In comparison, economists make an effort to distinguish between the different forms of tying under the assumption that they all create different effects upon the market, some being anti-competitive and others offering clear pro-competitive benefits.[20] The competition authorities mainly fear that where a company holds a dominant position tying will be applied as a leveraging device to foreclose a related market, the tied product market, or to protect the tying product market, resulting in limiting the consumer choice and excluding competition. Other anti-competitive incentives include entry deterrence, price discrimination, and mitigating competition and gaining a competitive advantage by creating network externalities or through technological integration.[21] However, other motivators for tying have been highlighted by economists, such as economies of scale in production and distribution, price discrimination, product improvement, quality assurance, and avoidance of double marginalization, all of which can be pro-competitive.[22] A company may apply tying for one particular reason, for instance as a form of quality assurance, but by doing so also gain a competitive advantage, price discriminate, or even foreclose the tied product market in the process. The purpose of the tying can therefore be completely innocent, but the outcome nevertheless harmful. Likewise the opposite could also occur, the tying intended to restrict competition, yet the effects are nonetheless harmless.

8.2 THE EU COURTS' APPROACH TO TYING IN CASE LAW

In EU competition law a comparatively small number of cases has made it to the Commission and the EU Courts, when compared with other forms of abuse; however,

[20] See Robert H. Bork, *The Antitrust Paradox: A Policy at War with Itself* (New York: The Free Press, 1993), p 372–5; Ward S. Bowman, 'Tying Arrangements and the Leverage Problem' (1957) 67 *The Yale Law Journal*, 19; David S. Evans and Michael Salinger, 'Why Do Firms Bundle and Tie? Evidence from Competitive Markets and Implications for Tying Law' Winter 2005, 22 *Yale Journal on Regulation* 37.

[21] Barry Nalebuff, 'Bundling, Tying, and Portfolio Effects' *DTI Economics Paper No 1, Part 1–Conceptual Issues*, February 2003, p 18.

[22] O'Donoghue, R. and Padilla, A. J. (n 8 above), pp 480–3.

interestingly, the majority of the tying cases have involved some form of IPR. This therefore merits a closer inspection of the relationship between IPR and tying and raises questions of the IPR influence upon tying cases; in particular, has the presence of IPR had a crucial role in the outcome of the cases or has its presence has been merely incidental?

Tying is also subject to the competition rules under Article 101.[23] This means not only that tying is seen as a form of conduct, which can cause severe harm, but also that Articles 101 and 102 may apply to the same tying conduct or agreement, but on their own terms. The modernization of Article 101 has in recent years created a gap and inconsistencies in the treatment of tying under Article 101 and 102 respectively. This is because the approach under Article 101 (especially to tying as a vertical restraint) is more economic and focused upon consumer welfare, compared with the more form-based and rigid approach applied under Article 102.[24]

For instance, tying is not a hard core restriction in either the Vertical Block Exemption Regulation[25] or the Technology Transfer Block Exemption Regulation (the TTBER),[26] demonstrating that the Commission, when it comes to licensing agreements, views it as less harmful especially without the presence of market power.

Under Article 102 however, the Commission and the EU Courts view tying as almost illegal *per se*, almost because, uniquely to tying, certain conditions must be present before abuse can be established. First, there must be two separate products, second, the company must be dominant in the tying product market, third, the customer must be coerced into purchasing the two products together, fourth, the tying must be likely to foreclose competition, and finally, there must be no objective justification for the tying practice.[27]

8.2.1 Two separate products

Without the establishment of two separate products there cannot be a tying arrangement.[28] In *Microsoft I*, the General Court (GC) described the two separate products assessment as a two-part test: an assessment of the product's nature, physical

[23] See *Vaassen/Moris* [1979] OJ L 19/32, [1979] 1 CMLR 511.

[24] Commission Notice, Guidelines on the Application of Article 81(3) of the EC Treaty, OJ C101, 27 April 2004, pp 97–118 and IP/00/520 'Commission finalises new competition ruled for distribution' (Brussels, 24 May 2000) and Ekaterina Rousseva, 'Modernising by Eradicating how the Commission's New Approach to Article 81 EC Dispenses with the need to apply Article 82 to Vertical Restraints' (2005) 42(3) CML Rev 587, p 589.

[25] Commission Regulation 330/2010 of 20 April 2010 on the application of Article 101(3) of the Treaty on the Functioning of the European Union to categories of vertical agreements and concerted practices. OJ L 102, 23 April 2010, pp 1–7 and Commission Notice, Guidelines on Vertical Restraints, OJ C130, 19 May 2010, p 1 paras 214–22.

[26] Commission Regulation (EC) No 772/2004 of 27 April 2004 on the application of Article 81(3) of the Treaty to categories of technology transfer agreements OJ L 123, 27 April 2004, pp 11–17, Art 4.

[27] T-201/04 *EC Microsoft* at paras 839–71 and *Enforcement Guidelines on Article 82*, para 50.

[28] *US Microsoft III* at 85.

appearance, and commercial usage and second, a requirement of consumer demand for the tied product.[29]

However, case law demonstrates that the focus has primarily been on the consumer demand and, in particular, evidence of independent manufacturers of the tied component has played a decisive role.[30] The lack of focus upon the first part of the assessment is due to its closeness to the definition of the relevant product market, an assessment undertaken in all Article 102 cases. The relevant product market definition provides a framework for the establishment of dominance, but case law shows that when two product markets are established under the relevant product market assessment, the finding of two separate products is more or less given. The outcome of a tying case can therefore often already be determined at this stage.

The second part of the separate product assessment, consumer demand test is applied to identify whether the tied product is distinct from that of the tying product. The test simply asks whether the consumers, given a choice, would purchase the tying and tied product separately. This can manifest itself in whether there are independent manufacturers of the tied product, whether non-dominant undertakings in the markets tend not to tie, especially where the markets are competitive, if so there is also considered to be a separate consumer demand for the tied product. This test was applied in *Hilti*, *Tetra Pak II*, and *Microsoft*. However, another indicator of a product's stand-alone status is the company's own commercial conduct. For instance, in *Microsoft I*, the Commission found that Microsoft offered upgrades of WMP separately from Windows and sold WMP to other operating systems such as Apple on its own, indicating that Microsoft itself did not perceive WMP and Windows as fully integrated.[31]

Hilti[32] was the first major tying case. In the case, the Commission had responded to a complaint by Eurofix-Bauco that Hilti was tying the sale of its cartridge strips to sale of its nails. The Commission, applying its policy of a narrow market definition, found that there were three separate markets: the market for nail guns, cartridge strips, and nails. Three facts influenced the Commission's decision. First, Hilti held a patent on the cartridge strips allowing Hilti legally to exclude competition, and thereby gain market power.[33] Second, Hilti's market power was further enhanced by its products being technologically advanced, its R&D, and a well-organized distribution system in the nail gun market.[34] Third, there were independent nail manufacturers in the market for nails. This was further confirmed by the fact that the nail guns and consumables (nails and cartridge strips) were not purchased together.[35]

[29] Case T-201/04 *Microsoft* at paras 925 and 927.

[30] Case C-333/94 *Tetra Pak II* at para 36; Case T-30/89 *Hilti* at para 67; Case T-201/04 *EU Microsoft I* at para 927; Commission's *Enforcement Guidance on Article 82* (n 3 above), at para 51.

[31] *Microsoft I* Commission decision at paras 805 and 813.

[32] Case C-53/92P *Hilti v Commission* [1994] ECRI–667.

[33] *Hilti* Commission decision at paras 55 and 66.

[34] Ibid, at para 67.

[35] Ibid, at para 57.

The Commission found that Hilti was reinforcing the tie-in by a practice of charging excessively high royalties to deter independent nail manufacturers from obtaining licences of right in the cartridge strips. The Commission concluded that these and other practices were abusive because they prevented or limited the entry of independent producers into those markets.

Hilti appealed to the GC on the grounds that the cartridge strip, nails, and gun were an integrated product, a powder-actuated fastening system, and that they were not separate product markets. The GC rejected Hilti's arguments and upheld the Commission's view that there were three separate markets and that Hilti was dominant on the cartridge market. It accepted the existence of independent nail manufacturers as evidence of a separate market and went on to state that, 'in the absence of general and binding standards and rules, any independent producer is quite free, as far as Community competition law is concerned, to manufacture consumables intended for use in equipment manufactured by others, unless in doing so it infringes a patent or some other industrial or intellectual property right'.[36] Effectively Article 102(d) was to be used to prevent Hilti from extending the scope of its exclusive exploitation rights beyond the patented product to unpatented products.

The definition of relevant product markets appears to reinforce that decision because it separated the patented and the unpatented goods into separate markets. It also provided the foundation for the finding of dominance.

A similar approach was taken in *Tetra Pak II*. Here the Commission identified four product markets: the market for aseptic cartons, aseptic machines, non-aseptic cartons, and non-aseptic machines.[37] In comparison, Tetra Pak had argued that these were all part of an integrated packaging system for packaging liquid food. The main reason for finding four separate markets was the patents that Tetra Pak held on the technology of the machines, cartons, and processes.[38] Again, the presence of independent producers played an important role in separating the markets. The GC reiterated what it had said in *Hilti*, that independent manufactures are 'quite free' to produce and offer consumables intended for use in third party products, as long as these do not infringe IPR.[39] The upshot of the GC's statement is that where products contain both IP protected and unprotected components, there is likelihood that these will be seen as separate products and not one under Article 102(d). This strict definition of a product essentially permits the competition authorities to regulate IPR and ensure that they are not applied to extend the scope of the IPR itself.

In *Microsoft I*, the Commission identified two product markets: the market for the operating system and the market for media players. It based its market definitions on

[36] Case T-30/89 *Hilti v Commission* [1991] ECR II–1439, [1992] 4 CMLR 16 at para 68.

[37] Case T-83/91 *Tetra Pak II* at para 34.

[38] Ibid, at para 10.

[39] Case T-83/91 *Tetra Pak II* at para 34, and see also paras 83–4.

the fact that there were manufacturers of stand-alone media players,[40] barriers to entry into the media player market, such as network effects and IPR.[41] The Commission's market definition was never questioned by the GC, which merely accepted the Commission's findings.[42] Yet, the Commission's market definition played a significant role in identifying whether there were two separate products rather than an integrated product as Microsoft argued.[43] It relied again on the fact that some media players are offered separately and that there was therefore a distinct consumer demand for media players, which could be distinguished from that of the operating system.[44] Nonetheless, the Commission ignored Microsoft's argument that there was not a separate demand for an operating system without a media player.[45]

The Commission has in its *Enforcement Guidelines of Article 82* confirmed the use of the consumer demand test.[46] However, the guidelines do not require that the tying and tied products are in separate markets, they merely need to be distinct.[47]

Two products are distinct if, in the absence of tying or bundling, a substantial number of customers would purchase or would have purchased the tying product without also buying the tied product from the same supplier, thereby allowing stand-alone production for both the tying and the tied product.[48]

This statement indicates that where it is still economically viable to produce the tied product separately, the consumer demand requirement is fulfilled. Such interpretation is in line with the approach taken in the US in *Jefferson Parish*[49] and *Eastman Kodak*[50], where the Supreme Court also demanded that consumer demand was assessed in relation to economic viability. However, this does not take into account technological integrated products and the benefits these can generate.

In contrast, the GC in *Microsoft I* held that only 'in the absence of independent demand for the allegedly tied product, there can be no question of separate products and no abusive tying'.[51] In other words, the GC's standard of proof for technological integration requires all demand for the tied product to have ceased. This is an unrealistically high threshold because even if consumer demand dictates a need for an integrated product, the demand for the products separately can continue for a significant period after the integrated product has become available and until the market has fully adapted. This is, for instance, the case with PCs. When these originally came upon the

[40] *Microsoft I* Commission decision at para 405.

[41] Ibid, at paras 418–20.

[42] Case T-201/04 *EC Microsoft* at paras 23–9.

[43] *Microsoft I* Commission decision at para 800.

[44] Ibid, at para 804; see also para 405.

[45] Ibid, at paras 404–5.

[46] The Commission's *Enforcement Guidance on Article 82* (n 3 above), para 51, see also Commission *Discussion Paper* (n 3 above), para 185.

[47] Ibid, para 51.

[48] Ibid.

[49] *Jefferson Parish Hospital District No 2 v Hyde* 466 US 2 (1984) at 21.

[50] *Eastman Kodak Co v Image Technical Services, Inc. et al.* 504 US 451 (1992) at 462.

[51] T-201/04 *Microsoft* at para 918.

market, the consumer had to purchase hardware, software, desktop, screen, keyboard, and mouse separately. Now some thirty years later, these are offered in a simple package, although they can be purchased separately as well.

The problem with the test is two-fold. First, products can continue to be divided into smaller components or parts and the question is when is it reasonable to stop the separation. As Bork notes:

> Every person who sells anything imposes a tying arrangement. This is true because every product or service could be broken down into smaller components capable of being sold separately, and every seller either refuses at some point to break the product down any further or, what comes to the same thing, charges a proportionally higher price for the smaller unit.[52]

Second, the test does not sufficiently take into account product development and innovation and this is of particular concern to IP owners. The US Court of Appeals labelled the test 'backward-looking' and therefore a 'poor proxy' for 'overall efficiency in the presence of new and innovative integration'.[53] As part of healthy competition companies are expected to develop and improve their products and one natural way could be through tying or technological integration. In its *Enforcement Guidelines of Article 82*, the Commission has indirectly acknowledged the product development issue, by stating that it will be willing to consider whether the combination of two products 'into a new, single product' may benefit the consumer.[54]

8.2.2 Dominance

It is clear that without market power, tying as a unilateral conduct is unlikely to cause significant harm to competition. Case law dictates that dominance must be found at least in the tying product market.[55] In *Hilti,* the Commission clarified the importance of dominance in relation to the abuse:

> The ability to carry out its illegal policies stems from its power on the markets for Hilti-compatible cartridge strips and nail guns (where its market position is strongest and the barriers to entry are highest) and aims at reinforcing its dominance on the Hilti-compatible nail market (where it is potentially more vulnerable to new competition).[56]

It is interesting to note that so far in all the cases, the dominant company held market shares well above 60 per cent. In *Tetra Pak II*, Tetra Pak had 90 per cent market share in both the aseptic machines and cartons markets.[57] Likewise Microsoft was found to hold 90 per cent of the operating systems market for personal computers in both

[52] Bork (n 20 above), p 378–9.

[53] *US Microsoft III* at 89.

[54] The Commission's *Enforcement Guidance on Article 82* (n 3 above), para 62.

[55] Case C-333/94 *Tetra Pak II* at paras 25 and 30–1, and Case T-201/04 *Microsoft* at para 842; see also Case T-30/89 *Hilti* at paras 87, 89–92, and 94. Hilti was found to be dominant in both the tying and tied product markets.

[56] *Hilti* Commission decision at para 74.

[57] *Tetra Pak II* Commission decision at para 104.

Microsoft I and *II*.[58] In *Hilti*, Hilti was found to hold 70 per cent of the cartridge strips market and 55 per cent of the market for nail guns.[59] However, *Hilti* was special, because it also held 70–80 per cent market share in the nail market, the tied product market.

There is therefore good reason to suggest that for tying to be harmful the company must hold significant market power, which indicates that the normal lower threshold for dominance, around 40 per cent, may only suffice in situations where additional factors make the tying company more powerful than its competitors.

In case law, the finding of dominance has also been influenced by the presence of IPR. This was clearly illustrated in both *Hilti* and *Tetra Pak II*.[60] The use of an IPR to establish dominance is not unique to tying cases as Chapter 5 has shown, nor is it unique to EU case law. In the US, patents in particular, have frequently played the leading role in finding market power. In *International Salt*[61] and *Loew's*,[62] the question was not about the company's market power but the scope of the IPR. In *International Salt*, the 'uniqueness' of the patent was assumed to confer significant market power for the tying arrangement to be harmful.[63] It was not until 2006, in *Illinois Tool*[64] that the Supreme Court firmly moved away from this notion, by stating that a presumption of market power based on the presence of an IPR does not suffice as evidence for market power, instead evidence thereof must be shown.[65]

In EU case law, IPRs have affected the establishment of dominance in two ways. First, indirectly, through the relevant market definition, which is often curtailed along the scope of the IPR. Second, directly, through the assumption that an IPR will inevitable confer some level of market power.

8.2.3 Coercion

Coercion or forcing the sale of two products together is the very heart of tying and thus the abuse. Coercion may be contractual as it was in *Hilti* and *Tetra Pak*; financial, where the customer is awarded so great a discount that it leaves no commercial meaningful choice not to accept the second, tied product;[66] or by removing certain benefits, such as not honouring guarantees, where customers have used third party products.[67] Finally, through technological integration, coercion may occur due to the fact that the products are physically integrated and therefore the consumer is left with no choice but

[58] *Microsoft I* Commission decision at para 432 and *Microsoft II* Commission decision at para 24.
[59] *Hilti* Commission decision at para 70 and T-30/89 *Hilti* at para 85.
[60] Cases T-30/89 *Hilti* at para 93 and T-83/91 *Tetra Pak II* at para 23.
[61] *International Salt Co v United States*, 332 U.S. 392, (1947).
[62] *United States v Loew's Inc* 371 US 38, 83 S. Ct. 97, 9 L.Ed.2d 11 (1962) 46.
[63] *International Salt* at 395.
[64] *Illinois Tool Work Inc v Independent Ink Inc* 547 US 1 (2006).
[65] Ibid. at 16.
[66] *Digital, XXVIIth Report on Competition Policy—1997*, and Commission Press Release IP/97/868.
[67] *Hilti* Commission decision at para 75.

to purchase the combined product, as was the case in *Microsoft I*. The test applied by the Commission and the Courts has been whether the customer is permitted a choice between purchasing the bundle of products or separately.[68]

In *Microsoft I*, the Commission stated that the consumers did not have a choice as to whether to obtain the operating system without the media player.[69] It found this despite the fact that the WMP was given away for free with the Windows operating system: 'it is immaterial that consumers are not forced to "purchase" or "use" WMP. As long as the consumers "automatically" obtain WMP—even for free—alternative suppliers are at a competitive disadvantage'.[70] The GC confirmed this viewpoint noting that it is irrelevant for fulfilling the conditions of Article 102(d) that the WMP was obtained for free, that there was no obligation upon the consumers to make use of the WMP, and that the consumers could obtain other media players for free to work with Windows.[71] Instead it highlighted its concerns of giving the WMP away for free because it found that it would deter Original Equipment Manufacturers (OEMs) from pre-installing a second media player on the PCs as well as encouraging the consumers to use only the WMP rather than a later downloaded media player, notwithstanding that the latter may be of better quality.[72]

8.2.4 Likelihood of foreclosure

In tying case law, the EU Courts and the Commission seemed to have applied the general low threshold of the conduct being capable of having or likely to have an anti-competitive effect without necessarily excluding all competition from the market.[73] In *Napier Brown/British Sugar*,[74] it was sufficient evidence that British Sugar had reserved to itself the sugar delivery market by tying its sale of sugar to the delivery for the Commission to conclude that the behaviour was abusive although no real evidence of anti-competitive effects was ever provided.[75] A similar approach was applied in *Hilti*,[76] and in *Télémarketing* where the CJEU held that Télémarketing had reserved to itself an ancillary market with the 'possibility of eliminating all competition' in that market.[77]

In *Microsoft I*, the Commission engaged in an exceptionally thorough analysis of the anti-competitive effects of Microsoft's tying, outlining factual evidence of the risk

[68] Ibid, decision at para 75 and Case T-83/91 *Tetra Pak II*, at para 137.
[69] Ibid, at para 834.
[70] Ibid, at para 833.
[71] T-201/04 *EC Microsoft* at paras 968–70.
[72] Ibid, at para 971.
[73] Case T-219/99 *British Airways v Commission* [2003] ECR II–5917, [2004] 4 CMLR 1008 at para 293, confirmed in C-95/04 *British Airways v Commission* [2007] ECR I–2331, [2007] 4 CMLR 22.
[74] *Napier Brown/British Sugar* Commission decision 88/519/EEC, 1988 OJ L 284.
[75] Ibid, at para 46.
[76] *Hilti* Commission decision at para 75.
[77] Case 311/84 *Centre Belge d'Etudes du Marché-Télémarketing v Compagnie Luxembourgeoise de Télédiffusion SA and Information Publicité Benelux SA* [1985] ECR 3261, [1986] 2 CMLR 558 at para 27.

of foreclosure and concluding that Microsoft's tying had the potential to risk foreclosure of the media player market in the future.[78] The Commission argued that an extensive analysis was necessary because it was unclear whether the tie was anti-competitive because downloading still permitted consumers to obtain a third party media player.[79]

The GC on the other hand did not find the downloading option significant enough to eliminate the risk of foreclosure.[80] Its main concern was the pressure Microsoft put on OEMs to ship Windows with WMP, thus barring them from offering third party media players to their customers, and therefore providing Microsoft with a competitive advantage not pertinent to the quality of the product and likely to affect related markets.[81]

Although the GC agreed with the conclusion of the Commission's extensive anti-competitive effects assessment, it indicated that a less extensive analysis would have brought forth the same result.[82] It thereby confirmed the low threshold applied first in *Napier Brown/British Sugar* and held that where there is a 'reasonable likelihood' that the tying arrangement 'will lead to the lessening of competition so that the maintenance of an effective competition structure would not be ensured in the foreseeable future' the anti-competitive effects requirement is fulfilled.[83] The wording is similar to the one the GC applied in *British Airways,*[84] a price discrimination case under Article 102.

The consequence of the GC's low standard of proof for tying is that once two separate products have been identified, abuse can relatively easily be established. The Commission notes in its *Enforcement Guidelines of Article 82* that where the tie-in is a lasting one, ie technological integration, the risk of anti-competitive foreclosure is considered to be even greater.[85] However, it is unclear whether this will result in an even lower standard of proof for anti-competitive effects, albeit such an interpretation is not unlikely.

The low standard of proof has to be seen in relation to the high standard of proof, which the Courts and the Commission have persisted on for the objective justifications.

8.2.5 Objective justifications

Unlike Article 101, Article 102 does not contain a general exemption clause. However, Article 102(d) does indicate that the nature of the products or their commercial usage can make it acceptable to sell the products tied together. It is unclear though how the wording of Article 102(d) should be interpreted. One way could be to see the absence

[78] *Microsoft I* Commission decision at paras 841–954.
[79] Ibid, at para 841.
[80] T-201/04 *Microsoft* at paras 1045–50.
[81] Ibid, at paras 1058–69 and 1076.
[82] Ibid, at para 1058–9.
[83] Ibid, at para 1089.
[84] Case T-219/99 *British Airways* at para 293.
[85] The Commission's *Enforcement Guidance on Article 82* (n 3 above), para 53.

of 'commercial usage' as a prerequisite for seeing tying as abusive.[86] An alternative reading would be to see 'commercial usage' and the 'nature of the product' as a form of objective justification or exemption.[87]

Though the GC made it quite clear in *Tetra Pak II* that '[even] a usage which is acceptable in a normal situation, on a competitive market, cannot be accepted in the case of a market where competition is already restricted'.[88] The statement leaves the objective justification requirement in a strange limbo and no clear guidance as to what qualifies as an objective justification.[89]

Although the EU Courts and the Commission have allowed the defending companies to bring forth a so-called objective justification for the alleged abusive behaviour, which will then be weighted against the anti-competitive effects of the conduct, so far all companies facing a tying as an abuse claim have failed the high standard of proof of objective justifications set by the Commission and the EU Courts. The shortage of cases makes it is difficult to assess whether the rejection of the objective justifications is because of insufficient evidence and poor defence by the dominant companies or the applied threshold is significantly high for these types of case.[90] Three types of objective justifications have been attempted: health and safety, product quality, and reduction in costs.

In *Tetra Pak II*,[91] the Commission found that Tetra Pak's practice of tying the sale of machines for the sterilization and filling of aseptic liquid food cartons to the purchase of the cartons, the maintenance of the machines, and the purchase of spare parts was abusive in a situation where it was part of a deliberate strategy of excluding existing competitors in the carton manufacturing market, maintenance, and spare parts markets. The company gave undertakings to the Commission that it would no longer tie spare parts and maintenance services to the sale of the machines. However, it chose to contest the Commission's findings that the tie-in between the machines and the cartons was abusive. Its appeals to the GC and later to the CJEU were based on the ground that there was a natural link between the two products and that their integration was in accordance with commercial usage and Article 102(d) presupposed no link between the additional services and the subject matter of the contracts.[92]

The GC rejected the argument that commercial usage supported the conclusion that the machinery for packaging a product was indivisible from its cartons in a situation where 'for a considerable time there have been independent manufacturers who specialize in the manufacture of non-aseptic cartons designed for use in machines

[86] See Ahlborn, Evans, and Padilla (n 86 above), pp 315–16.
[87] C-333/94 *Tetra Pak II* at paras 34–5.
[88] T-83/91 *Tetra Pak II* at para 137.
[89] See Ahlborn, Evans, and Padilla, p 315–16.
[90] Ibid, p 314.
[91] Case C-333/94 *Tetra Pak II*.
[92] Ibid, at para 34.

manufactured by other concerns, and who do not manufacture machinery themselves'.[93] Its judgment did not rule out the legitimacy of the defence as such but only its application to the facts of *Tetra Pak*. Importantly, in rejecting Tetra Pak's defence the GC relied on the presence of independent manufacturers, the evidence also applied for identifying consumer demand, and establishing that the two products were distinct.

The GC also rejected the second ground for the company's appeal, that there was an objective justification for their linkage based on concern with the hygiene standards of other producers. It noted that it was not for Tetra Pak to impose measures on its own initiative on the basis of technical considerations, product liability, protection of public health, or its own reputation.[94] It continued holding that the tying clauses in Tetra Pak's contracts clearly were beyond their 'ostensible purpose' and were excessive for the protection of public health.[95] The GC concluded that Tetra Pak was not alone in being able to manufacture cartons for its machines. On appeal, the CJEU endorsed the judgment of the GC on these issues. However, it insisted on a residual regulatory role for Article 102(d) and tied sales even where there was evidence of a natural link between the two products or where tied sales were in accordance with commercial usage: 'such sales may still constitute abuse within the meaning of [Article 102] unless they are objectively justified.'[96]

In *Hilti*, the dominant firm's argument that safety considerations objectively necessitated the bundling was given short shrift by the GC. It stated that considerations of product safety which were enforced by other laws and public bodies could not override EU rules on competition. It was 'clearly not the task of an undertaking in a dominant position to take steps on its own initiative to eliminate products which, rightly or wrongly, it regards as dangerous or at least inferior in quality to its own products'.[97] This statement has now been incorporated into the *Enforcement Guidelines of Article 82*.[98]

In *Microsoft I*, Microsoft attempted to rely on three defences. First, an efficiency defence in relation to transaction costs, claiming that having the WMP as a default option on the operating system reduced time and confusion for consumers.[99] The Commission rejected this argument, holding that the pre-installed media player did not need to be the WMP.[100]

Second, Microsoft argued that shipping the two products together reduced transaction costs by saving on maintaining a separate distribution system for the second product and that this reduction in costs was passed on to the consumer.[101] Although the

[93] T-83/91 *Tetra Pak II* at para 82.
[94] Ibid, at para 138.
[95] Ibid, at para 139–40; see also *Hilti* Commission decision at para 90 and AG Cosmas' Opinion in C-344/98 *Masterfoods Ltd v HB Ice Cream Ltd* [2000] ECR I–11369, [2001] 4 CMLR 449, para A101.
[96] C-333/94 *Tetra Pak II* at para 37.
[97] T-30/89 *Hilti* at para 118–19.
[98] The Commission's *Enforcement Guidance of Article 82* (n 3 above), para 28.
[99] *Microsoft I* Commission decision at paras 956.
[100] Ibid, at paras 956–7.
[101] Ibid, at para 958.

Commission accepted the defence as valid, it found that the efficiencies gained from the reduction in cost were insufficient or in fact insignificant to outweigh the anti-competitive effects.[102]

Third, Microsoft argued that Windows and WMP were technologically integrated. This argument was dismissed by the Commission, because Microsoft had not demonstrated that the integration was indispensable to achieve the works of application developers.[103] The GC, on the other hand, seems to have applied a slightly lower standard of proof. It commenced by holding that Microsoft's reason for the integration of ensuring a stable and well-defined Windows platform for the benefit of both software developers and Internet site creators was not an acceptable defence as this was the main cause of foreclosure.[104] It also rejected Microsoft's argument that the removal of the WMP would result in the degrading and fragmentation of the operating system.[105]

The GC did not see the actual integration as a major problem, but the fact that Windows was not available on its own. It relied upon two things; first an email sent from a Microsoft executive to Bill Gates, which suggested that the threat posed by RealPlayer should be met through the integration of the WMP with Windows, to ensure WMP remained more competitive than RealPlayer.[106] Second, the fact that Microsoft had not sufficiently demonstrated that the integration of WMP into Windows led to 'superior technical product performance',[107] all, Microsoft had noted was that Windows operated faster with WMP integrated, but it never provided clear evidence for this.[108]

Although, the GC concluded that there were no objective justifications for Microsoft's integration of its WMP with its Windows operating system, it has with this statement provided guidelines, albeit not very elaborate, as to what can constitute a valid justification for technological integration of products by dominant companies. It is clear that the company must demonstrate that the technological integration provides some superior form of technology than what the consumers could have achieved themselves by adding the tying and tied product together.

The standard of proof put forward by the GC corresponds to the one applied by the Court of Appeals in *US Microsoft II*,[109] which held that for a technological integration to be justified the defendant would have to demonstrate that the integration took place on the design stage of the product and added 'some technological value', which was more than the mere bolting of the two products.[110]

[102] Ibid, at para 958.
[103] Ibid, at para 963.
[104] T-201/04 *EC Microsoft* at paras 1146 and 1151.
[105] Ibid, at paras 1147.
[106] Ibid, at paras 911 and 937.
[107] Ibid, at para 1159 and Commission decision at paras 962 and 967.
[108] T-201/04 *EC Microsoft* at para 1160.
[109] *United States v Microsoft Corp* 147 F 3d 935 (DC Cir. 1998) (*US Microsoft II*).
[110] Ibid, at paras 949 and 950.

8.3 TYING AND INTELLECTUAL PROPERTY RIGHTS

As mentioned in the beginning of this chapter, the tying case law mainly consists of cases involving some form of IPR. Their presence appears to have an effect on the cases in two specific manners, namely in respect of the relevant market definition and in the establishment of dominance. Conversely IPR seem to have had little influence on the actual finding of abuse and thereby the assessment of anti-competitive effects.

Both *Hilti* and *Tetra Pak II* demonstrate the Commission and the EU Courts' general approach to IPR in relation to Article 102 offences. In both cases the relevant product markets were very much defined along the scope of the IPR, and although the CJEU has held that an IPR on its own cannot lead to the assumption of dominance, the presence of IPR played a significant role in finding dominance in the two cases.[111]

In *Microsoft I*, the IPR played a less prominent role in respect of tying. The feared foreclosure on the tied product market was mainly due to Microsoft's near-monopoly in the operating systems market and the network effects in this market than the IPR Microsoft held on the tying product. It could be questioned whether this was due to the actual IPR, a copyright, in comparison to the patents that Hilti and Tetra Pak held, given that patents are often seen as stronger rights than copyrights because patents can exclude third parties from producing the same product whereas copyright can only cease the copying of a product, not the production of a similar one.

In principle, Article 102(d) could still apply to attempts to bundle patented and unpatented goods in the same product market unless such a tie-in was objectively necessary or had 'a connection with the subject of such contracts'.[112] However, in *Tetra Pak II,* Tetra Pak attempted to use the IPR it held on the aseptic machines and cartons to justify the tie-ins.[113] The GC repeated its mantra that 'any independent producer is quite free, as far as Community competition law is concerned, to manufacture consumables intended for use in equipment managed by others, unless in so doing it infringes a competitor's intellectual property right',[114] thereby reiterating its view that an IPR protection of a particular product is a necessary condition for an entitlement to exclusive rights of manufacture and sale. If sales of a protected product—the machines—were tied to sales of an unprotected product—the cartons—there would be an abuse because of the extension of the IPR protection to an unprotected product, which would lead to exclusionary and exploitative effects unless there could be an objective justification.

In other words, an IPR can dictate whether a company can engage in tying and technological integration or not.

[111] Case T-30/89 *Hilti* at para 93 and T-83/91 *Tetra Pak II* at para 23.

[112] See C-333/94 *Tetra Pak II* at paras 36–7.

[113] T-83/91 *Tetra Pak II* at para 131.

[114] Ibid, at para 83.

9

EXCESSIVE PRICING AND INTELLECTUAL PROPERTY RIGHTS

9.1 Introduction 143
9.2 Article 102(a) Generally 145
9.3 Article 102(a) and Intellectual Property Rights 150
9.4 Dual Markets, Intellectual Property Rights, and Unfair Pricing 154
9.5 Collecting Societies and Excessive Pricing 155
9.6 Conclusion 159

9.1 INTRODUCTION

Excessive pricing is considered an exploitative abuse, because it directly harms consumers[1] and is therefore in principle open to scrutiny by the Commission and the EU Courts. In fact, it is one of the most obvious forms of abuse that a dominant undertaking can engage in to explore its market power. Yet, competition authorities have been reluctant to intervene[2] largely because, unlike sectoral regulators, they recognize that they have limited skills to determine what is an 'excessive' price and need to leave a margin of appreciation to undertakings to fix prices in competitive markets.[3] Economists have argued that under normal competitive market conditions excessive pricing could be corrected by the market itself through the entrants of new competitors,[4]

[1] However, EU competition law will also condemn excessive pricing where it has exclusionary effects upon competitors and thus indirectly harms consumers. See eg Case 238/87 *Volvo v Veng (UK) Ltd* [1988] ECR 6211 at para 9.

[2] Note in US antitrust law, excessive pricing is not caught under s 2 of the Sherman Act; Michael Gal, 'Monopoly Pricing as an Antitrust Offense in the US and EC: Two Systems of Belief about Monopoly' (2004) 49 *Antitrust Bulletin* 343; although 'monopolizing trade' is caught (*Berkey Photo, Inc v Eastman Kodak Co.* 603 F 2d 263, 274 n. 12 (2d Cir. 1979) and *Verizon Communications Inc v Law Offices of Curtis Trinko* 540 US 398 (2004).

[3] *Scandlines Sverige v Port of Helsingborg* COMP/36.568, [2006] 4 CMLR 1298.

[4] See Ariel Ezrachi and David Gilo, 'Are Excessive Prices Really Self-Correcting?' (2009) 5 *J. Competition L. & Econ.* 249–67 who argue that the markets are not always self-correcting.

that intervention by competition authorities may restrict this 'invisible hand' effect of market forces if they are too interventionist,[5] and that 'price regulation' may restrict the monopolist in carrying out expensive R&D.[6] However, the EU competition authorities are not convinced that market forces are self-correcting and that excessive prices inevitably draw in new entrants.[7] Their motives for not applying Article 102(a) robustly are more a reflection of their recognition of the inherent limits of competition policy to regulate pricing.

In relation to IPRs, the idea that a company will fix its price where it is 'cost-reflective' ie in the sense of reflecting its marginal cost, is completely inappropriate because this ignores the need to allow the IP owner to recoup the money invested into developing the product as an incentive to innovation. Especially in high tech markets where IPRs are essential elements of the industry and competition is moved from competition *in* the market to *for* the market, pricing at marginal cost is not a realistic yardstick. These markets are often characterized by high sunk costs (the investment in the development of the innovation) and low marginal costs (once developed, the actual production of the innovation is cheap).[8] The issue is to find a way to define excessive or unfair pricing that gives sufficient weight to a 'fair' price for an IPR.

Under Article 102(a), a dominant firm is prohibited from 'directly or indirectly imposing unfair purchase or selling prices or other unfair trading conditions'. From an early stage, the CJEU has held that in principle, a particularly high price, unjustified by any objective criteria, may be an abuse of a dominant position.[9] The CJEU at one stage described the abuse as attempting to reap trading benefits which are higher than an undertaking would have reaped if there had been normal and sufficiently effective competition in the market.[10]

At first glance, this appears to call into question the entitlement of an IP owner to a just reward for originating the IPR because of the effect on competition of the exclusive right. As economists have often pointed out, the ability to charge higher than competitive prices for a protected product, and to restrict competition, is 'the very essence of patents'.[11] The regulation of the pricing of IPRs therefore places Article 102(a) right at the heart of the patent-antitrust interface.

[5] Ezrachi and Gilo, p 251.

[6] Robert O'Donoghue and A. Jorge Padilla, *The Law and Economics of Article 82 EC* (Oxford and Portland, Oregon: Hart Publishing, 2006), p 626 and Ezrachi and Gilo (n 4 above), p 250.

[7] Ezrachi and Gilo (n 4 above).

[8] R.C. Lind, and P. Muysert, 'Innovation and Competition Policy, Challenges for the New Millenium' *ECLR* 2003 24(2) 87–92, p 89; see also David S. Evans and A. Jorge Padilla, 'Excessive Prices: Using Economics to Define Administrable Legal Rules' (2005)1 *J. Competition L. & Econ*. 97, p 99.

[9] See Case 40/70 *Sirena Srl v Eda Srl* [1971] ECR 69, [1971] CMLR 260.

[10] Case 27/76 *United Brands v Commission* [1978] ECR 207, [1978] 1 CMLR 429 at para 249.

[11] See eg F. Machlup, 'An Economic Review of the Patent System, Study of the Committee on Patents, Trademarks and Copyright', Senate Judiciary Committee, US 85th Congress, Study no 15 (Washington DC, 1958), p12.

The CJEU has accepted that there is considerable room for a high return on IPRs based on the amounts which IP owners have invested in order to perfect the protected right.[12] It has never said, however, that under Article 102 IP owners in a dominant position can recoup the full value to which they would be entitled if the commercial exploitation of the IPR were regulated solely under national law. How in practice can the requirement of a fair price and a lawful return under Article 102(a) be reconciled with the concept of just reward under IPRs? To answer this requires three steps. First, we must look at how Article 102(a) has been interpreted generally. Second, we shall examine how that interpretation applies to IPRs. In the course of this second step we shall move to the third step by asessing how Article 102(a) applies differently depending on whether the pricing of the IPR occurs in a single market or in two related markets.

9.2 ARTICLE 102(a) GENERALLY

General Motors[13] was the first case to deal with excessive pricing, although the CJEU had previously in an IPR case indicated that Article 102 could be applied to such circumstances.[14] In *General Motors*, the CJEU gave an initial definition of abusive pricing under Article 102(a) by stating that when a charge for inspecting vehicles imported by parallel importers from other Member States was 'excessive in relation to the economic value of the service provided', it could constitute an abuse.[15] The case was however, quashed by the CJEU for insufficient evidence.

British Leyland,[16] decided a year later, offered a good example of how Article 102(a) can result in a finding of excessive charges. In that case, British Leyland had sole authority under British law to issue certificates of conformity for traders of left-hand drive Metros wanting access to the British market. After a period of charging a single fee of £25 for both right- and left-hand drive vehicles, it raised its fee for left-hand vehicles to £150. The CJEU found that British Leyland had abused its dominant position in respect of the supply of certificates of conformity by refusing to approve certificates and by charging excessive fees.

British Leyland illustrates two important points about Article 102(a): first, the charge of excessive prices may be proved by evidence of the dominant undertaking's own previous pricing conduct, particularly when the discrepancy is so great. Secondly, excessive pricing under Article 102(a) could be abusive because of its exclusionary effects, where it is linked to a policy of discouraging competitors by refusing to approve.[17]

[12] Case 24/67 *Parke Davis & Co v Probel, Reese, Beintema-Interpharm and Centrafarm* [1968] ECR 55, [1968] CMLR 47.

[13] Case 26/75 *General Motors Continental v Commission* [1976] ECR 1367.

[14] Case 78/70 *Deutsche Grammophon GmbH v Metro-SB-Grossmärkte GmbH* [1971] ECR 487, [1971] CMLR 631 at para 19.

[15] Case 26/75 *General Motors* at para 16.

[16] Case 226/84 *British Leyland v Commission* [1986] ECR 3263, [1987] 1 CMLR 185.

[17] Ibid, at paras 27–30.

In *United Brands v Commission*,[18] the CJEU restated the definition of Article 102(a) in *General Motors*, amending it only slightly to, 'charging a price which is excessive because it had no reasonable relation to the economic value of the product supplied'.[19] It also emphasized the importance of making this assessment on the basis of an analysis of production costs. The method to be used to make an objective determination of whether the sales price exceeded the economic value of a product was to compare sales prices with production costs to determine the profit margin. If that difference appeared excessive, the next step was to decide 'whether a price has been imposed which is unfair itself. . .'[20]. Alternatively, a test of unfairness could consist of a comparison of product prices with the selling prices of 'competing products'.[21] It could also include a comparison of its own costs in a different market, although this meant that careful consideration had to be given to the cost structures and other conditions in the local markets which could influence profit margins.[22]

While in *United Brands*, the CJEU overturned the Commission's finding of excessive prices based on the comparative prices test, it did not reject the comparative price method as such.[23] It merely insisted that if a comparison of prices was to be used, it should be based on adequate evidence that the lower prices actually covered costs.[24] To the extent that the CJEU accepted the need for price comparisons as supplementary tests to an analysis of the price/cost on its own, it acknowledged the problems the Commission faced in implementing Article 102(a) by looking solely at the cost structure and price levels of any one firm. The CJEU recognized that there were difficulties entailed in:

> working out production costs which may sometimes include a discretionary apportionment of interest costs and general expenditure and which may vary significantly according to the size of the undertaking, its object, the complex nature of its set up, its territorial area of operations, whether it manufactures one of several products, the number of its subsidiaries and their relationship with each other.[25]

[18] Case 27/76 *United Brands v Commission* [1978] ECR 207, [1978] CMLR 1 429.

[19] Ibid, at para 250.

[20] Ibid, at para 252.

[21] Ibid, at para 252.

[22] Siragusa points out that these factors are also relevant to the analysis of discriminatory pricing under Art 102(a). See M. Siragusa, 'The application of Article 86 to the Pricing Policies of Dominant Companies: Discriminatory and Unfair Prices' (1979) 16 *CML Rev* 179, 188.

[23] In Case 27/76 *United Brands*, the Commission had found that United Brands had charged excessive prices based on a comparison of the price in Ireland with that in other countries. This was the 'comparative cost' method borrowed from German jurisprudence. The Commission had found that the price in Belgium was 80% higher than in Ireland and ordered United Brands to reduce its prices wherever they were higher than the Irish baseline. The CJEU rejected the Commission's finding of excessive prices because of the failure of the Commission to refute United Brands' contention that the Irish price was making a loss and therefore constituted a false base.

[24] Case 27/76 *United Brands*, at paras 255–6, see also Machlup (n 11 above).

[25] Ibid, at para 255.

Yet it may have underestimated the complications inherent in a cost-based assessment of 'economic value'.[26]

In the *SACEM* cases,[27] an Article 263 reference from the French Court ten years later, the complications of such an assessment were made clearer. The CJEU found that the royalties charged by the French copyright-management society were abusive under Article 102. On this occasion, the CJEU introduced a more sophisticated version of the test of excessive pricing by indicating that where there was a cost-based justification for a particular price, there must be some indication that the costs were not themselves inflated by the inefficiencies of the dominant firm. Again, this test makes a valid conceptual point but it also creates doubts about its practical application. One doubt concerns the capability of the Commission or the EU Courts to evaluate evidence that the dominant firm was acting inefficiently and pricing inequitably.

The contrast with US practice under the Sherman Act is instructive here. Under US antitrust law, it is recognized that the regulation of pricing is so demanding an exercise that first, excessive pricing is not covered by s 2 of the Sherman Act and second, if it requires regulation this is dealt with by the establishment of a specific regulatory commission.[28] In interpreting Article 102(a) to involve hands-on regulation of excessive pricing[29] the CJEU may have underestimated the handicap of not having dedicated regulatory institutions to carry out the type of sophisticated analysis of prices and costs which is needed in most cases to substantiate a charge of excessive prices.

It is implicit in the evaluation of efficiency in an assessment of excessive pricing that the Commission and EU Courts must define the legitimate rewards to firms whose growth has come about through greater efficiency and reduced production costs. If the gap between costs and prices is used as the yardstick, there is the possibility that the

[26] Siragusa has pointed out, 'the cost of production is not necessarily a sure indication of the economic value of the product' (n 22, above, p 187). On the other hand, economic value could be the CJEU's shorthand for a price which reflects the market clearing price on a workably competitive market, in which case it could, according to economic microtheory, be closely cost related.

[27] Case 395/87 *Ministère Public v Tournier* [1989] ECR 2521 and Case 110/88 *Lucazeau v* SACEM, [1989] ECR 2811, [1991] 4 CMLR 248.

[28] See Gal, n 2 above. As Fox has described it, 'American law rests on the principle that price should be controlled by the free market unless Congress has in effect determined that the market cannot work and has established a regulatory commission.' E. Fox, 'Monopolization and Dominance in the United States and the European Community: Efficiency, Opportunity, and Fairness' (1986) 61 *Notre Dame L Rev* 981, p 993. Note that the Commission has on occasions applied legislation as a means of regulating high prices in specific sectors where *ex ante* regulation was needed, for instance to regulate high tariffs for international mobile roaming services (Regulation 717/2007, OJ [2007] L 171/32) instead of applying Art 102. Article 17 of Regulation 1/2003 grants the Commission powers to review and investigate a specific sector of the economy or type of agreement where there appears to be a restriction on competition. The Commission's latest sectoral enquiry was into the pharmaceutical industry, which concluded on 8 July 2009 (<http://ec.europa.eu/competition/sectors/pharmaceuticals/inquiry/communication_en.pdf> (last accessed 4 October 2010)).

[29] EU law rejects the concept of US antitrust policy which holds that if a firm attains monopoly on its competitive merits and prices at monopoly levels, the high price itself will invite new entry and market forces would gradually wear away the monopoly power. See T. Kauper, 'Article 86, Excessive Prices and Refusals to Deal' [1991] 59 *Antitrust Law Journal* 441.

more efficient firms could be penalized by the regulatory standard. One problem here is that the test appears to make little allowance for the way the dominant position was acquired.[30] If a firm achieves dominance through efficiencies and maintains that dominance through continued internally generated efficiencies, it could nevertheless be penalized for its pricing decisions as excessive and exploitative. One would expect the defence of legitimate competition by performance to apply to such a position should it ever arise in practice.[31]

Analogous problems arise where the dominance of the undertaking has arisen as a result of innovation protected by IPRs. To what extent in principle does the concept of competition by performance apply to the just reward for IPR exploitation?

A further issue is of course that this form of yardstick competition assessment can only work in practice where there is an appropriate comparable situation, ie a company facing similar cost structure and restrictions on the market.[32] Yardstick competition is therefore further problematical in relation to IP owners.

Although not an IP case, *Deutsche Post*[33] demonstrates a situation where the Commission could not make such comparable analysis because of Deutsche Post's near-monopoly on the German postal market and it was therefore forced to apply an alternative benchmark.[34] In the case, Deutsche Post was accused by the British Post Office of excessive pricing in relation to a levy on incoming mail from the UK that had (wrongfully) been classified as unauthorized remail. As the Commission could not compare Deutsche Post's cost with an equivalent competitor, it compared instead the cross-border charges on mail with those Deutsche Post charged for domestic mail and found that former to be excessive.[35] In comparison, in *Micro Leader*[36] the same copyright protected products, French-language editions of Microsoft software packages,

[30] Ibid, p 449.

[31] See the discussion in Chapter 6.

[32] R. Whish, *Competition Law* (6th edn, Oxford: OUP, 2008), p 714. In the UK case, *Napp Pharmaceutical Holdings Ltd*, the Office of Fair Trading (OFT) successfully applied the yardstick competition approach. Napp was found to have abused its dominant position under Chapter II of the UK Competition Act 1998 by charging excessive prices for its sustained release morphine (MST) to its Community customers (ie patients not in hospitals). The OFT found that Napp had 90% of the MST market having held a patent on MST from 1980–92, there were high barriers to entry, and MST was an essential pain relief. The prices Napp charged to Community customers were typically ten times higher than the prices charged to hospitals. The OFT applied a 'preponderance-of-the-evidence' approach, which consists of using several comparables and using Napp's prices during its patent protection as price benchmark. The OFT thus compared Napp's MST prices against those of its competitors, over time and in different markets, and found that the margin between Napp's costs and its prices was excessive. (OFT Decision, 30 March 2001, [2001] UKCLR 597. Upon appeal, the Competition Appeal Tribunal endorsed the methods applied by the OFT and upheld its findings although it found mitigating factors in favour of Napp and therefore reduced the fine (Case No 1000/1/1/01 *Napp Pharmaceutical Holdings Ltd v Director General of Fair Trading* [2002] CAT 1, CompAR 13.

[33] *Deutsche Post AG–Interception of cross-border mail* Commission decision OJ [2001] L 331/40, [2002] 4 CMLR 598.

[34] Ibid, at para 159.

[35] Ibid, at paras 160–7.

[36] Case T-198/98 *Micro Leader Business v Commission* [1999] ECR II–3989, [2000] 4 CMLR 886.

were offered at different prices in two geographically separate markets, Canada and the European Union. However, the Commission dismissed Micro Leader's complaint because of insufficient evidence. The General Court (GC), on the other hand stated that the Commission had made a manifest error of assessment as it was clear that the evidence provided '[constituted], at the very least, an indication that, for equivalent transactions, Microsoft [the copyright owner] applied lower prices on the Canadian market than on the Community market and that the Community prices were excessive'.[37] A full-blown assessment of the alleged abuse would have required the Commission to engage in price and costs comparison analysis of the two markets. The GC clarified that the Commission had made too swiftly a presumption of legality based on the copyright protection.[38]

The complexity of cost analysis and the determination of what is a fair price on a given market has led to a less interventionist approach by the Commission to such cases. The Commission explained its policies on the issue in its 1994 Competition Report:

> The existence of a dominant position is not itself against the rules of competition. Consumers can suffer from a dominant company exploiting this position, the most likely way being through prices higher than would be found if the market were subject to effective competition. However, the Commission in its decision-making practice does not normally control or condemn the high level of prices as such. Rather it examines the behaviour of the dominant company designed to preserve its dominance, usually directed against competitors or new entrants who would normally bring about effective competition and the price level associated with it.[39]

This statement was more or less repeated by the Director General of the Commission's Directorate General for Competition, Philip Lowe, in a speech in 2003.[40] Importantly, the recent *Enforcement Guidelines on Article 82* only encompasses exclusionary practices and there is therefore no mention of excessive prices within them, which reinforces the notion that this is an area the Commission is not notably interested in from an enforcement perspective.[41]

Another aspect is of course the difficulties involved in demonstrating that the price is indeed excessive. The Commission has in two recent cases, *IPS*[42] and *Scandlines Sverige*,[43] attempted full cost-price analysis. In both cases the claimant failed owing to insufficient evidence. The *IPS* case demonstrates that even in an industry involved in

[37] Ibid, at para 54.

[38] Ibid, at paras 55–7.

[39] *XXIVth Report on Competition Policy* (Commission, 1994), p 207.

[40] Philip Lowe, 'How Different is EU Antitrust? A Route Map for Advisors, An Overview of EU Competition Law and Policy on Commercial Practices' *Conference d'automne de l'American Bar Association*, (Brussels, 16 October 2003) (<http://ec.europa.eu/competition/speeches/text/sp2003_038_en.pdf> (last accessed 4 October 2010)).

[41] See however, n 28 above regarding the Commission's regulatory intervention approach.

[42] Case T-5/97 *Industrie des Poudres Spherique (IPS) v Commission* [2000] ECR II–3755, [2001] 4 CMLR 1020—the Commission decision was not published).

[43] *Scandlines Sverige v Port of Helsingborg* COMP/36.568, [2006] 4 CMLR 1298.

the production of a relatively simple product (calcium) a full cost-price analysis requires a very detailed level of analysis and fact-finding.[44]

In *Scandlines Sverige*, two ferry operators complained that the port owners were charging excessive fees for the services provided on the Helsingborg/Helsingør ferry route between Sweden and Denmark. In rejecting the claims of excessive pricing, the Commission repeated the *United Brands* mantra that 'whether the difference between the costs actually incurred and the price actually charged is excessive, and, if the answer to this question is in the affirmative, whether a price has been imposed which is either unfair in itself or when compared to competing products'.[45] It thereby confirmed this as the legal standard for excessive pricing although it indicated that recognition could be given to 'the intangible value' represented by the advantageous location of the ferry port, which 'must be taken into account as part of the assessment of the economic value of the services provided by Helsingborgs Hamn AB (HHAB), and which is not reflected in the costs actually incurred by HHAB'.[46] However, the decision also emphasized the relatively high legal standard required to prove that prices are excessive still stands.

9.3 ARTICLE 102(a) AND INTELLECTUAL PROPERTY RIGHTS

The difficulties of measuring unfair pricing in general under Article 102(a) are intensified when an assessment must be made of a fair return to innovators exploiting their IPRs under Article 102(a). As Lind and Muysert note in relation to high technology industries where IPRs flourish:

> The very high ex ante risks of failure mean that the returns to 'winners' in high technology markets should be very high. . . [T]he risks of ex post appropriation of rewards that were not ex ante excessive are very high and that competition authorities should in general avoid using profitability measures in high technology industries.[47]

Applying the *United Brands* yardstick competition test to IPR to restrict IP owners from extracting maximum returns for their inventions through their monopoly position would seriously weaken the value of the IPR.

However, in *Parke Davis*, the CJEU held that 'a higher sale price for a patented product as compared with that of an unpatented product does not necessarily constitute an abuse'.[48] This indicated that in principle, the concept of a higher than competitive return being a fair return where IP is concerned is partly based on an acceptance of the

[44] T-5/97 *IPS*, paras 157–67. See also David Howarth, 'Pricing Abuse' in Giuliano Amato and Claus-Dieter Ehlermann (eds), *EC Competition Law, A Critical Assessment* (Oxford and Portland, Oregon: Hart Publishing, 2007), p 270.

[45] Case 27/76 *United Brands* at para 252 and *Scandlines Sverige* at para 145.

[46] *Scandlines Sverige* at para 235.

[47] Lind and Muysert (n 8 above), p 91.

[48] Case 24/67 *Parke Davis* [1968] ECR 55 at p 72.

costs of innovation, including the need to reward the individual firm for its investment in research and development.[49]

As the CJEU noted in *Maxicar*,[50] the higher price for components sold by the manufacturer as compared to those sold by the independent producers 'does not necessarily constitute an abuse, since the proprietor of protective rights in respect of an ornamental design may lawfully call for a return on the amounts which he has invested in order to perfect the protected design'.[51]

This case also gave some indication that the principle of a return on amounts invested does not necessarily embody a narrow cost-plus approach. In *Maxicar*, Advocate General Mischo stated that 'the inventor is entitled to recover not only his production costs in the strict sense and a reasonable profit margin but also his research and development expenditure'.[52] The approach taken by the Commission in *Scandlines Sverige*, where it permitted 'intangible value represented by the advantageous location of the ferry port' to be taken into the cost and economic value calculations, provides a similar indication that some flexibility is permitted when assessing costs and 'economic value'.[53]

Moreover, as Korah has pointed out, 'the concept of costs can be reconciled with providing incentives to investment provided that factors for the risk of failure and delay in obtaining a return are included in the costs that can be recovered before prices are considered unreasonable'.[54]

Furthermore, the principle of return on amounts invested allows some flexibility in assessing a fair return for different types of IPRs. For example, R&D costs are particularly applicable to IPRs such as design rights and patents and perhaps informational copyright.[55] In the case of other rights such as trade marks, the costs can include the expense involved in promotion, advertising, and systems of quality control.[56] There is room to develop a separate type of calculation under Article 102(a) depending upon the particular character of the IPR.

Nevertheless, the concept of fair pricing as based on a fair return on costs under Article 102(a) does not give full recognition to the reward function of the grant of the IPR. Even though the CJEU has recognized that charging a higher than competitive price is legitimate competition by performance, this does not go so far as to allow right-holders to appropriate the full value of their IPR as that value is conceived under national law. In *DSD*,[57] DSD was found to have abused its dominant position by

[49] Ibid, at p 90.

[50] Case 53/87 *CICCRA v Renault (Maxicar)* [1988] ECR 6039, [1990] 4 CMLR 265.

[51] Ibid, at para 17.

[52] Ibid.

[53] *Scandlines Sverige*.

[54] V. Korah, 'No Duty to License Independent Repairers to Make Spare Parts: The Renault, Volvo and Bayer Henneke Cases' (1988) *EIPR* 381, p 383.

[55] See eg I. Govaere, *The Use and Abuse of Intellectual Property Rights in EC Law* (London: Sweet & Maxwell, 1996), Ch 2.

[56] See G. Tritton, *Intellectual Property in Europe* (London: Sweet & Maxwell, 1995).

[57] *Duales System Deutschland AG (DSD)* [2001] OJ L 166/1, [2001] 5 CMLR 609, upheld T-151/01 *Der Grüne Punkt–Duales System Deutschland GmbH v Commission* [2007] ECR II-1607.

charging excessive prices for the use of its trade mark, Der Grüne Punkt. DSD operated the only German-wide waste disposal system for taking back used sales packaging on behalf of other companies as part of an environmental scheme adopted by the German Government. DSD forced its contracting manufacturers and distributors to label all packaging for return with the Der Grüne Punkt logo regardless of whether DSD would be the one responsible for removing the used packaging. It then charged its customers based on the packaging carrying the logo. The Commission found that the fee charged was disproportionate to the service provided and the GC concurred.[58] In doing so the Commission looked at the actual service provided, but did not take into consideration the intangible value of the trademark. The Commission's concern was related to making a distinction between the fee charged for using the trade mark and using the DSD recovery system. In agreeing with the Commission the GC recognized the economic value a trade mark could have and therefore concluded that the Commission's decision should be interpreted as permitting DSD to charge an adequate fee for the use of its trade mark even when the DSD system was not used.[59]

The case is another demonstration of the Commission and EU Courts limiting the use of IPRs where they are applied strategically to extend the scope of the IP protection to gaining market power or extra profits.

The argument for a high return on products or processes protected by IPRs is that the return is not simply a reward to the individual inventor; it is also designed to act as an incentive for other inventors or originators to invest in innovation. Machlup has described this as the monopoly-profit-incentive theory of patent protection, emphasizing its incentive for innovation.[60] It also includes an element to compensate for the failures of other efforts at commercial exploitation.[61]

From an IP point of view, this incentive function of 'just reward' results in a figure which is established by what consumers and customers are willing to pay for the added value the IPR confers on a product compared with another product which does not incorporate that right, in other words what the market will bear. As Friden has pointed out:

> It represents not the possibility to charge reasonable prices and obtain reasonable profits but rather the possibility, for the holder of an exclusive right, to charge whatever the market will pay, one of the main justifications being the need to give the innovator an incentive to bear the risk of innovation which he might refuse to do if only promised a reasonable profit.[62]

Moreover, economists have made the point that the methodological difficulties of measuring what is a reasonable or unreasonable reward are so great that it is best left to a regulation of the duration of the period of the grant of the exclusive right.

[58] *DSD* Commission decision at para 111 and T-151/01 *DSD*, at paras 119 and 121.

[59] T-151/01 *DSD* at paras 191–6.

[60] Machlup (n 11 above).

[61] See eg V. Korah, *EC Competition Law and Practice* (5th edn, London: Sweet & Maxwell, 1994) p 99.

[62] G. Friden, 'Recent developments in EEC Intellectual Property Law: The Distinction Between Existence and Exercise Revisited' [1989] 26 *CML Rev* 193, 211.

Machlup has suggested that:

Since it is the very essence of patents to restrict competition and permit output to be kept below, and price above, competitive levels, it is difficult to conceive economic criteria by which one could judge whether output is less than reasonably 'practicable' and price is 'unreasonably high'.[63]

Moreover, as Evans and Padilla note:

While it is true that patent law grants firms a certain period of time in which to recoup up-front costs, that time period is no magic number. There is no reason to believe that the exact number of years under a patent is the time necessary to fully recoup the investment costs and provide sufficient incentives to innovation. And there is no reason to suggest that prices should suddenly revert to marginal cost once the legally sanctioned monopoly is over.[64]

The CJEU has not been willing to stretch the logic of Article 102(a) to entitle the right-holder to charge what the market can bear during the period of the patent or design right. The reason for this is that Article 102(a) requires a differentiation between dominant and non-dominant undertakings, including undertakings whose position coincides with, or is reinforced by, ownership of an IPR. In the case of non-dominant firms they can charge what the market will bear. However, those in a dominant position are entitled only to fair return, not an excessive one.[65] EU competition law appears to take the position that the 'just reward' for the exclusive right is not the standard to be applied to the right-holder with the market power of dominance. Although competition law accepts that an exclusive right is not automatically a dominant position, it can require a modification of the exploitative possibilities of a right-holder when in a dominant position.

It can be argued that where the right owner is merely seeking to appropriate the full value of its IP, ie by charging prices as high as the market can afford, this is no more than the economic corollary of the 'existence' of the right, ie the grant under national laws of the exclusive rights of exploitation, and should not *per se* amount to an abuse of a dominant position. Nevertheless, that misinterprets the role of Article 102(a) as a safeguard against exploitative pricing.

Korah reminds us of this because, while she criticizes the cost-plus approach, drawing attention to its failure to allow sufficient room for the IPR concept that the person financing innovation should be able to obtain the prices that the market will bear, she also acknowledges 'it is difficult to criticise the CJEU for condemning excessive prices given the wording of Article 102(a)'.[66]

The implication of the above analysis is that Article 102(a) could potentially impose a limit on the pricing of IPRs. In practice, however, this is not likely to affect IP owners unless their conduct is both egregious and can easily be demonstrated to be excessive

[63] See Machlup (n 11 above), p 12.

[64] Evans and Padilla (n 8 above), p 109.

[65] See eg *Sirena v Eda*: 'A higher price for a trademarked product does not per se constitute sufficient proof of abuse but it may nevertheless become so, in view of its size, if it does not seem objectively justified.' [1971] ECR 3169 at para 17.

[66] V. Korah (n 61 above), p 98. This sentence was deleted in the subsequent editions.

in the light of their own previous conduct.[67] In *Qualcomm*,[68] the Commission initiated proceedings against the patent owner of the third generation (3G) mobile telephony technology owing to claims that its licensing terms and royalties were excessively high and in breach of its FRAND commitments (Fair, Reasonable, and Non-Discriminatory). The Commission was, in particular, concerned that the high prices would stall the development of the 3G standard and would leave the consumers to pay higher prices for handsets. However, after two years' investigations, the Commission closed the proceedings owing to all complainants withdrawing and not having reached a conclusion as to whether there was an abuse.[69]

There is considerable room for IP owners to price at high levels to obtain a return on their IP investment. As the Advocate General expressed it in *Maxicar*, 'the proprietor of protective rights. . .may lawfully call for a return on the amounts which he has invested in order to perfect the protected design'.[70] Furthermore, prices charged by a right-holder which are considerably higher than those charged by competing independents are not necessarily abusive because of this right of return.

9.4 DUAL MARKETS, INTELLECTUAL PROPERTY RIGHTS, AND UNFAIR PRICING

Yet it is important to recognize that this analysis of Article 102(a) is limited to the situation where the effects of the high pricing are purely exploitative. If the effects of the high pricing are exclusionary of competitors, then there may be a conflict between a just reward for the IPR and the need to prevent a weakening of competition on a secondary market. In *Maxicar*, the CJEU referred to the fixing of prices at an unfair level as an alternative abuse to refusing to supply spare parts to an independent repairer.[71] Insofar as a high price has the effect of excluding demand in a secondary market, it could be abusive on that ground.

Moreover, in analysing the fairness of prices in a secondary market like spare parts, the reward can be reduced because of the consideration that part has been recouped on the sale of the original manufactured product. In *Maxicar*, the Advocate General stated in the case of 'bodywork components sold as spare parts the problem displays an unusual aspect in so far as part of that expenditure has probably already been recovered from the sale of new cars. It is therefore necessary, when fixing the prices of spare parts, to take due account of that factor'.[72]

67 See eg *British Leyland*, *op cit*, n 16 above.
68 Commission MEMO/07/389, 1 October 2007.
69 Commission MEMO/09/516, 24 November 2009.
70 Case 53/87 *Maxicar* at para 17.
71 Ibid, at para 16.
72 Ibid, at para 63.

In practice, the issue of high pricing in the two market context is likely to be governed by the rules applicable to the obligations to set a reasonable price when an IP owner has been ordered to license (see Chapter 7). Insofar as commentators consider the regulation of the pricing of IPRs to be 'unworkable',[73] they quite legitimately describe the methodological difficulties facing Courts and indeed the Commission dealing with a complaint under Article 102(a). Nevertheless, that does not mean that right-holders can price freely as if Article 102(a) does not exist. That sub-article must be taken into account in pricing decisions along with the limits on discriminatory pricing imposed by Article 102(c) and predatory pricing (see the following chapters).

9.5 COLLECTING SOCIETIES AND EXCESSIVE PRICING

Collecting societies manage and enforce copyright on behalf of their members covering different categories of works eg music, writings, films, arts, and photography. This includes issuing licences and collecting royalties, both on an individual basis between one member and one user, but also collectively, for instance through blanket licences which permit the users the right of performance of the society's catalogue for a set period. Broadcasters, cable TV companies, or discos, etc will thus have access to thousands of works through one annual licence. The idea behind collecting societies is that by acting collectively copyright holders receive just rewards for their work at reasonable costs and licensees gain access to a vast amount of copyrighted material through a 'one-stop shop'.

The Commission's concern at collecting societies' effects on competition was addressed in a Communication in 2004.[74]

It highlighted that the Commission is keen to establish common grounds or to be more precise, hard law on the regulation of collective management 'to achieve a genuine Internal Market for both the off-line and on-line exploitation of intellectual property'.[75]

From a competition law perspective, collecting societies can negatively affect the markets in two ways. First, as associations they enable authors/publishers/performers

[73] See eg Govaere (n 55 above), p 260.

[74] Communication from the Commission to the Council, European Parliament and ESC on the Management of Copyright and Related Rights in the Internal Market COM (2004 216 final (<http://eur-lex.europa.eu/LexUriServ/LexUriServ.do?uri=COM:2004:0261:FIN:EN:PDF> (last accessed 4 October 2010).

The Commission is currently holding several 'Online Commerce Roundtable' discussions, the latest on 19 October 2009, revolving around music, which resulted in a joint statement (<http://ec.europa.eu/competition/sectors/media/joint_statement_1.pdf> (last accessed 4 October 2010)), in which the participants committed to: (1) pursuing new EU licensing platforms comprising the repertoires of several collecting societies; (2) an agreement that collective rights managers should adhere to certain objective, transparent, and non-discriminatory criteria to allow other entities to deliver multi-territorial licences; and (3) set up a working group to create a common framework for the identification and exchange of rights ownership information. Commission Press Release IP/09/1548, 20 October 2009.

[75] Ibid, Section 3.6.

to operate jointly and offer joint licensing agreements wherein common conditions are set, such as price. Second, they are often national in scope and often *de facto* monopolies in their country, which not only affects Article 102,[76] but also EU competition law's second goal, that of maintaining the functioning of the internal market.[77]

In *SABAM II*, the CJEU held that when determining whether a particular conduct was abusive in relation to collecting societies, 'account had to be taken of all relevant interests, for the purpose of ensuring a balance between the requirement of maximum freedom for authors, composers and publishers to dispose of their works and that of the effective management of their rights by an undertaking. . .'.[78] The CJEU here indicated that abusive behaviour by collecting societies, owing to their special characteristics, could in principle be justified, subject to the principles of proportionality and indispensability.[79]

Both the *SACEM*-cases[80] revolved around the terms upon which discotheques obtained licences to SACEM's, (a French copyright collecting society), catalogue of music. The discotheques complained about excessively high royalty rates. The CJEU took a different approach from that in *United Brands,* as it did not compare like for like, but based its price comparison on other undertakings' prices in other Member States.[81] It concluded that when a dominant company 'imposes scales of fees for its services which are *appreciably higher* than those charged in other Member States and where a comparison of the fee levels has been made on a consistent basis, that difference must be regarded as indicative of an abuse. . .'[82] (Emphasis added).

The CJEU noted that the burden of proof shifted to the dominant undertaking to justify price differences.[83] It held that a price difference could be justified by 'objective dissimilarities'.[84] SACEM argued that high prices charged by discotheques, the peculiar features of the French copyright laws, combined with high staff costs due to special French collection methods, meant that its costs were higher in comparison to collecting societies in other Member States.[85] In response, the CJEU held that 'it is precisely the lack of competition on the market in question that accounts for the heavy burden of administration and hence the high level of royalties'.[86] The CJEU left it

[76] Case 127/73 *BRT v SABAM* [1974] ECR 51, [1974] 2 CMLR 23.

[77] Rafael Allendesalazar, and Roberto Vallina, 'Collecting Societies: The Usual Suspects' in Claus-Dieter Ehlermann, and Isabela Atanasiu (eds) *European Competition Law Annual 2005: The Interaction between Competition Law and Intellectual Property Law* (Oxford and Portland, Oregon: Hart Publishing, 2007), p 371.

[78] Case 127/73 *BRT v SABAM and Others* [1974] ECR 313 at para 8.

[79] Allendesalazar and Vallina (n 77 above), p 373.

[80] Case 395/87 *Ministère Public v Tournier* [1989] ECR 2521 and Case 110/88 *Lucazeau v* SACEM [1989] ECR 2811, [1991] 4 CMLR 248.

[81] Howarth (n 44 above), p 267.

[82] C-395/87 *Ministère Public v Tournier* [1989] ECR 2521, [1991] 4 CMLR 248 at para 38.

[83] Ibid, at para 38.

[84] Ibid.

[85] Ibid, at paras 39–42.

[86] Ibid, at para 42.

however, for the national court to make the final judgment of whether the royalty rates were excessive.

The CJEU also alluded to the notion that the assessment of excessiveness was not just a question about the royalty rates being comparable with that charged by other collecting societies, but a question of proportionality as well, when it stated:

> [the] fact that a flat-rate royalty is charged can only be criticized by reference to the prohibition contained in [Article 102] if other methods might be capable of attaining the same legitimate aim, namely the protection of the interests of authors, composers and publishers of music, without thereby increasing the costs of managing contracts and monitoring the use of protected musical works.[87]

The cases demonstrate a harsh treatment of collecting societies because the comparable applied in the price comparison-test was not an accurate equivalent, whereas true 'yardstick competition' can only be performed where a 'suitable comparable can be found'.[88] The CJEU's approach emphasizes the concerns with collecting societies namely that with their *de facto* monopoly in individual Member States they cannot only manipulate competition within the national markets, they can also hinder the effectiveness of the internal market.

Moreover, the *SACEM* cases raise four uncertainties. First, there is no legal certainty as to whom the Commission or the EU Courts choose to compare with. Second, the standard of 'appreciably higher' is an equally uncertain term. Allendesalazar and Vallina point to the CJEU's own comment in the *SACEM* cases that the royalty rates were 'many times higher'[89] and compare this with *United Brands* where a price difference of 7 per cent could not automatically be regarded as excessive or unfair.[90] Yet it still leaves a comparatively big gap between what is 'appreciable higher' and what is not. Third, the introduction of a proportionality test by the CJEU raises questions as to whether that test can be applied alone or only in conjunction with the 'economic value–yardstick competition test' and whether its application is reserved to collecting societies or available for other companies.

Fourth, it is unclear what evidence will suffice for reaching the 'objective dissimilarities' standard of proof. The CJEU was not persuaded by SACEM's argument of high administrative costs, stating that that was a result of lack of competition.[91] However, as Howarth points out, one common factor amongst all collecting societies in the Member States was their monopoly status and thus lack of competition could not be the real reason for SACEM's high administrative costs.[92]

[87] Ibid, at para 45.
[88] Whish (n 32 above), p 714.
[89] Case C-395/87 *Ministère Public v Tournier* at para 37.
[90] Allendesalazar and Vallina (n 77 above), p 379 and Case 27/76 *United Brands* at para 266.
[91] Case C-395/87 *Ministère Public v Tournier* at para 42.
[92] Howarth (n 44 above), p 268.

In *CISAC*,[93] which is an Article 101 case, the Commission addressed the lack of competition by ordering twenty-four European collecting societies to remove certain territorial restrictions from their agreements and membership contracts. In particular, the Commission found that the reciprocal representation agreements resulted in parallel territorial delineation, dividing the European market into national segments and causing media companies to apply for individual national licences instead of one broad European one.[94] Another concern was the membership clause in the collecting societies' contracts with authors, which prevented authors from moving between collecting societies and in particular to collecting societies outside the author's Member State.[95] By removing this clause, the authors are free to chose a collecting society and can now do so based on a rational decision in relation to costs, services, benefits derived from membership, and 'the ability to collect the highest proportion of rights due to the authors', ensuring that competition is generated between the collecting societies.[96]

In *Kanal 5*,[97] two television broadcasters claimed that the national collecting society, STIM, was abusing its *de facto* monopoly by charging them royalties based on a remuneration model, where the royalties partly corresponded to the television channels' revenues.[98] The CJEU held that as a collecting society, STIM was protecting the authors' rights by ensuring appropriate remuneration for the use of that right, and this would have to be taken into consideration in assessing whether the royalties charged were excessive.[99] The CJEU referred to *Tournier*[100] of the *SACEM* cases and stated that as long as,

> the amount of the royalties [which] corresponds partly to the revenue of those channels. . . is proportionate overall to the quantity of musical works protected by copyright actually broadcast or likely to be broadcast unless another method enables the use of those works and the audience to be identified more precisely without however resulting in a disproportionate increase in the costs incurred for the management of contracts and the supervision of the use of those works.[101]

STIM's remuneration model is not in itself abusive under Article 102, but a normal exploitation of copyright.[102]

Although the CJEU initially has indicated a willingness to treat collecting societies in a more lenient manner by taking into consideration the purposes behind them, it has

[93] Case COM/C2/38.698–*CISAC*, Commission decision, on appeal to the GC T-442/08 *International Confederation of Societies of Authors and Composers (CISAC) v Commission.*

[94] Case COM/C2/38.698–*CISAC*, Commission decision at para 204.

[95] Ibid, at para 124.

[96] Ibid, at 134.

[97] Case C-52/07 *Kanal 5 Ltd, TV 4 AB v Föreningen Svenska Tonsättares Internationella Musikbyrå (STIM) upa* [2008] ECR I–9275.

[98] Ibid, at para 16.

[99] Ibid, at paras 29–32.

[100] Case C-395/87 *Tournier* at para 45.

[101] Case C-52/07 *Kanal 5* at para 41.

[102] Ibid, at para 34.

adopted an unusually harsh treatment of them, by the fact that it has adopted a different price comparative test than the one applied for other companies. It has also introduced a proportionality test, which although has not been interpreted in detail, will force collecting societies to explain or defend their royalty charges not only in relation to price, but also in terms of rates.

9.6 CONCLUSION

For both the primary market and the secondary market there remain difficulties in assessing what is 'excessive pricing' and a 'fair return' of the investment made. Although both have proved difficult for the Commission and the EU Courts to measure, and the CJEU has accepted the right of an IP owner to recoup some of his losses, it does not mean that when it comes to IPR-protected products one can completely ignore Article 102(a). There will always be a possibility that extremely high pricing in a primary or secondary market can result in a complaint under Article 102(a). However, the case law suggests that there will be wide margins allowed for entrepreneurial pricing before the limits of 'unfair' pricing are reached.

10

EXCLUSIONARY PRICING POLICIES: DISCRIMINATORY PRICING, REBATES, AND DISCOUNTS

10.1 Discriminatory Pricing 161
10.2 Conditional Rebates in a Single Market 174

10.1 DISCRIMINATORY PRICING

10.1.1 Introduction

Discriminatory pricing is prohibited by Article 102(c) which defines it as 'applying dissimilar conditions to equivalent transactions with other trading parties thereby placing them at a competitive disadvantage'.

Discrimination caught under Article 102(c) can be either treating 'similar situations differently or different situations the same'.[1] Case law indicates that discrimination as an abuse is closely linked with or overlaps other varieties of pricing practices; for instance, price differentiation which has the effect of excluding competitors from markets, such as predatory pricing and loyalty rebates,[2] as well as pricing practices which cause injury directly to customers and consumers.[3] Many of the cases discussed here are therefore also relevant for the sections on rebates and loyalty discounts and predatory pricing. The prohibition under Article 102(c) can also apply to differential pricing in separate product markets and in separate geographic markets. Despite the relationship to other forms of exclusionary abuses, discriminatory pricing has been left out of the Commission's *Enforcement Guidelines on Article 82*. In relation to rebates, the Commission states that individualized rebates are illegal because they are likely

[1] Case 13/63 *Italy v Commission* [1963] ECR 165 at 177–8.

[2] This is sometimes referred to as primary line injury.

[3] This is referred to as secondary line injury.

to be loyalty-inducing and therefore presumably exclusionary, yet although the Commission does not mention it, they are also discriminatory and would be caught under Article 102(c).[4]

From an economic perspective price discrimination has not been seen as *a priori* good or bad for consumer welfare.[5] In particular, in high -technology industries with high fixed cost and low marginal costs, customers can benefit from price discrimination. Economists therefore argue that a strict *per se* illegality approach to price discrimination is not favourable, and that clear evidence of anti-competitive effects is needed before the behaviour can be seen as abusive.[6] 'Price discrimination, if successful, increases firms' profits. What effect this has on consumer welfare, however, can only be decided in individual cases, since it is generally ambiguous.'[7] However, these arguments have not been accepted by the EU Courts who continue to apply the prohibition in Article 102(c) as a *per se* abuse. In *British Airways*[8] the Court of Justice confirmed the General Court's judgment that the loyalty discount scheme of the airline constituted an abuse because of its potential to exclude competitors and irrespective of a finding of direct consumer harm. As the CJEU put it Article 102 'is aimed not only at practices which may cause prejudice to consumers directly but also those which are detrimental to them through their impact on an effective competition structure...'[9]

If Article 102(c) is viewed as a basis for regulation, two main issues arise: (1) what is meant by 'equivalent transactions'? and (2) what types of justifications can be offered for differential pricing?

10.1.2 The concept of equivalent transactions

In principle, price differences are only discriminatory under Article 102(c) if they can be shown to apply to 'equivalent transactions'. This implies that the products themselves must either be identical[10] or substitutable.[11] It also suggests that the commercial

[4] Communications from the Commission—*Guidance on the Commission's Enforcement Priorities in Applying Article 82 EC Treaty to Abusive Exclusionary Conduct by Dominant Undertakings* OJ C45, 24 February 2009, pp 7–20 (hereinafter *Commission's Enforcement Guidelines on Article 82),* para 45; see cases such as Case 85/76 *Hoffmann-La Roche v Commission* [1979] ECR 461, [1979] 3 CMLR 211; Case T-288/97 *Irish Sugar plc v Commission* [1999] ECR II–2969, [1999] 5 CMLR 1300; and Case T-219/99 *British Airways v Commission* [2003] ECR II–5917, [2004] 4 CMLR 1008; see also Temple-Lang, 'Article 82 EC—The Problems and the Solutions' Institutions and Markets Series Fondazione Eni Enrico Mattei Nota di Lavro 65.2009, pp 8–9.

[5] Robert O'Donoghue and A. Jorge Padilla, *The Law and Economics of Article 82 EC* (Oxford and Portland, Oregon: Hart Publishing, 2006), p 555.

[6] Ibid.

[7] Ibid, p 561.

[8] See eg C-95/04P *British Airways v Commission* [2007] ECR I–2331 at para 106.

[9] Ibid. See the discussion in H. Schweitzer, 'The Role of Consumer Welfare in EU Competition Law' in Josef Drexl, Reto M. Hilty, Laurence Boy, Christine Godt, Bernard Remiche (eds), *Technology and Competition - Technologie et concurrence. Contributions in Honour of Hanns Ullrich—Mélanges en l'honneur de Hanns Ullrich* (Brussels: Larcier, 2009).

[10] See eg the bananas in Case 26/76 *United Brands v Commission* [1978] ECR 207.

[11] See eg *HOV SVZ/MCN* [1994] OJ L 104/34.

context in which the goods or services are sold will be of significance in finding them 'equivalent'.[12] The concept of 'transaction', however, is wider than the good or service on its own; it includes other conditions of sale such as terms of payment and delivery.[13] For example, in *United Brands*, the CJEU found that the price differences were discriminatory in a situation where the bananas were sold to the different distributor ripeners under the same conditions of sale, terms of payment, and costs of unloading.[14] Had any of those factors varied from distributor to distributor, that would have raised questions about the equivalence of transactions.[15]

This may also mean that goods covered by trade marks and similar, but unbranded goods are not equivalent transactions, because the consumers differentiate in terms of value between branded and unbranded goods. Where such differentiation by the consumers is substantial, the goods cannot be seen as equivalent for the purpose of Article 102(c).[16] The same could be said for the licensing of IPRs, where the value of the first licence issued by a dominant company will significantly decrease if a second licence is issued within the same territory.[17] Here the assessment of 'equivalence' would be based on the terms of the contracts.

The concept of equivalence also raises questions about different prices when the product is sold in different product markets or in different geographic markets.[18]

10.1.2.1 *Non-equivalent transactions: different quantities*

From an early stage the Court of Justice was prepared to acknowledge that discounts were not abusive if they differed according to different quantities ordered. There was no need to show elaborate proof of being cost-related by being related to lorry load, etc as long as such discounts were open to all customers on the same basis, ie the same percentage discount for the same quantities of the product ordered. In *Hoffmann-La Roche*, for example, the CJEU indicated that quantity discounts exclusively linked to the volume of purchases fixed objectively and open to all customers were lawful.[19] In *Hilti*,[20] the Commission made the point that it was the fact that Hilti's customers bought in equivalent quantities that made the different treatment abusive. In *Tetra Pak II*,

[12] See eg Case COMP/38/096–*Clearstream* Commission decision [2005] 5 CMLR 1302, confirmed in T-301/04 *Clearstream v Commission* 9 September 2009.

[13] Ibid, at para 235.

[14] [1978] ECR 207 at para 225.

[15] See U. Springer, '*Borden* and *United Brands* Revisited' [1997] *ECLR* 42, 44.

[16] O'Donoghue and Padilla (n 5 above), p 565.

[17] Ibid, p 566.

[18] See eg Case T-198/98 *Micro Leader Business v Commission* [1999] ECR II–3989, [2000] 4 CMLR 886.

[19] In one case where the Commission found that a dominant firm had adopted a pricing policy which was discriminatory, it made an order that any further discounts offered by the firm had to reflect actual cost savings. The decision was later annulled on procedural grounds. See T-30/91 *Soda Ash-Solvay et Cie v Commission* [1995] ECR II–1775, [1996] 5 CMLR 57.

[20] Case C-53/92P *Hilti AG v Commission* [1994] ECR I–667, [1994] 4 CMLR 614.

the GC indicated that quantity discounts might be the sole objective justification for differential pricing.[21]

There is of course an element of discrimination in quantity rebates, ie they discriminate against small firms with small orders.

In *Portuguese Airport*,[22] which involved a discount granted on landing charges, the discount was based on the frequency of landing and additional discounts that were attached to domestic routes. This meant that the national airlines were able to achieve much higher discounts than airlines from other Member States despite the fact that all airlines needed the same landing and take-off services.[23] The CJEU clarified that even if the discount granted is not exclusionary, it must be actually non-discriminatory, otherwise it will be abusive under Article 102(c). Moreover, the CJEU also reflected upon the legality of discounts in relation to efficiencies, economies of scale, and cost savings:

> where as a result of the thresholds of the various discount bands, and the levels of discount offered, discounts (or additional discounts) are enjoyed by only some trading parties, giving them an economic advantage which is not justified by the volume of business they bring or by any economies of scale they allow the supplier to make compared with their competitors, a system of quantity discounts leads to the application of dissimilar conditions to equivalent transactions.[24]

In *British Airways*, the Commission found BA's rebates schemes discriminatory under Article 102(c), because two travel agents selling the same amount of tickets would under BA's scheme achieve different commission due to the fact that the bonus would relate to the sales that the agencies achieved the year before rather than the actual sales of the current year. Conversely, travel agents selling a different amount of tickets could through the scheme end up achieving the same bonus. BA was thereby applying dissimilar conditions to equivalent transactions with different customers so placing one customer at a competitive disadvantage.[25] The Commission concluded that not only would these schemes place travel agents at a competitive disadvantage relative to each other and thus restrict their ability to compete effectively with each other, but BA's bonus schemes would also distort competition in the markets for air transport services between BA and other airlines.[26]

10.1.2.2 *The effects of the discriminatory practice*

Article 102(c) prohibits discriminatory pricing only if it has the effect of placing trading parties at a competitive disadvantage. It would have been possible to give this

[21] Case T-83/91 *Tetra Pak International SA v Commission* [1994] ECR II–755, [1997] 4 CMLR 726.

[22] Case C-163/99 *Portugal v EC Commission* [2001] ECR I–2613, [2002] 4 CMLR 1319. Article 102(c) has been applied to condemn similar discount schemes at other airports within Europe by the Commission: *Alpha Flight Services/Aéroports de Paris* OJ [1998] L 230/10, [2001] 4 CMLR 611; *Brussels National Airport (Zaventem)* [1995] OJ L 216/8, [1996] 4 CMLR 232; *Ilmailuaitos/Luftfartsverket (Finnish Airports)* [1999] OJ L 69/24, [1999] 5 CMLR 90; *Spanish Airports* [2000] OJ L 208/36; see also Commission Press Release IP/01/673, 10 May 2001, in which the Commission announced that it had concluded its investigations into discriminatory landing fees.

[23] Ibid, at para 11.

[24] Ibid, at para 52.

[25] *Virgin/British Airways* [2000] OJ L 30/1, [2000] 4 CMLR 999, at para 109.

[26] Ibid, at para 111.

element of Article 102(c) an economic interpretation. However, it has been given a more formalistic interpretation. In fact, 'placing trading parties at a competitive disadvantage' covers both customers of the dominant company being placed at a competitive disadvantage in relation to the dominant company itself (primary line injury) and in relation to other customers (secondary line injury).[27]

The exploration of competitive effect in *Hoffmann-La Roche*, for example, was limited to a supposition that the difference in rates of rebate caused damage to those customers who received less favourable rates. In *United Brands*, the differences in prices as such had no competitive effect on competition between the distributor ripeners. They were only potential competitors because the ripening clauses prevented arbitrage between them. It was enough to state that the differential pricing had an effect on the potential freedom of action of customers rather than the actual effect on competitors. In *Corsica Ferries*[28], the CJEU did not even refer to 'competitive disadvantage' when it explained the purpose of Article 102(c). It merely held that a Member State, which approves tariffs by a company holding a legal monopoly that distinguishes between 'maritime transport undertakings, depending on whether they operate transport services between Member States or between ports situated on national territory',[29] 'induces [the monopolist] to abuse its dominant position inter alia by applying dissimilar conditions to equivalent transactions with its trading partners, within the meaning of Article [102(c)] of the Treaty'.[30]

The CJEU has applied a similar approach in its airport cases[31] and also in the *Deutsche Post* case.[32] Whish suggests that the CJEU may have adopted this rather liberal interpretation of Article 102(c) to deal with cases where the discrimination is applied along national borders thereby harming undertakings in other Member States (rather than placing them directly at a competitive disadvantage).[33] Oliver contends another reading; namely that 'once discriminatory treatment by a dominant undertaking is shown, trading partners can be presumed to have suffered competitive harm'.[34] This interpretation is coherent with a wider range of cases under Article 102(c).[35]

British Airways reinforces this interpretation. In the case, the CJEU was offered another opportunity to comment on the concept of 'competitive disadvantage', because BA claimed that the GC had misapplied paragraph (c) of Article 102 by not requiring

[27] Faull and Nikpay (eds), *The EC Law of Competition* (Oxford: OUP, 2007), para 4.324.

[28] Case C-18/93 *Corsica Ferries Italia Srl v Corporazione dei Piloti del Porto di Genoa* [1994] ECR I–1783.

[29] Ibid, at para 38.

[30] Ibid, at para 43.

[31] Case C-163/99 *Commission v Portugal* and Case C-82/01P *Aéroports de Paris v Commission* [2002] ECR I–9297, [2003] 4 CMLR 609.

[32] *Deutsche Post AG–Interception of cross-border mail* Commission decision OJ [2001] L 331/40, [2002] 4 CMLR 598.

[33] R. Whish, *Competition Law* (6th edn, Oxford: OUP, 2008), p 752.

[34] Peter Oliver, 'The Concept of "Abuse" of a Dominant Position Under Article 82 EC: Recent Developments in Relation to Pricing' [2005] 1 *European Competition Journal* 315–39, p 334.

[35] See also Faull and Nikpay (n 27 above), who make a distinction between cases dealing with discrimination of an exclusionary character and cases of an exploitative nature arguing that that in cases dealing with the former the CJEU has 'neglected' this latter part of Art 102(c), para 4.325.

concrete evidence of competitive disadvantage.[36] The CJEU held that Article 102(c) contains two conditions: first, the behaviour is discriminatory and second, 'it tends to distort that competitive relationship, in other words to hinder the competitive position of some of the business partners of that undertaking in relation to the others'.[37] The CJEU confirmed that the GC had been correct when it had not required concrete evidence for competitive disadvantage; the fact that the behaviour was likely or 'tends' to create competitive disadvantage was sufficient.[38]

Although from an economic perspective, this low standard of proof appears inadequate, it makes sense from a legal perspective because it permits the competition authorities to intervene if necessary *ex ante* and thereby limit the harm caused by the abusive behaviour.

10.1.3 Separate markets and price discrimination

In cases of intermarket discrimination, as opposed to intramarket discrimination, Article 102(c) has been more realistically applied. In principle, where a similar product is put to different uses in separate product markets, a dominant undertaking can differentiate its price for the same product in the two markets. The fact of different use could operate as an objective factor distinguishing one transaction from another, allowing an undertaking in a dominant position to take into account in its pricing practices the different market conditions on different product markets, assuming the markets are separate. At least to this extent, Article 102(c) allows a commercial pricing strategy which extracts from each separate market what that market will bear. In *Tetra Pak II*,[39] the GC appeared to endorse this proposition when it suggested that for the purpose of determining a case of price discrimination, each relevant market had to be assessed separately. This suggests that there is no general policy of equalizing prices across markets under Article 102(c).[40]

In cases, however, where the price differentiation occurs on two markets which are 'linked',[41] either because one is 'downstream'[42] or 'neighbouring',[43] the price differences may be abusive because they are part of a two market commercial strategy by a dominant undertaking which has an exclusionary aim or effect in one of those markets. For example, in the case *BPB and British Gypsum v Commission*,[44] where there was an associative link between the two markets, with customers operating on both markets,

[36] Case C-95/04P *British Airways* at para 142.

[37] Ibid, at para 144.

[38] Ibid, at paras 145 and 146-8.

[39] T-83/91 *Tetra Pak II* at para 162 upheld in C-333/94 *Tetra Pak International SA v Commission (Tetra Pak II)* [1996] ECR I–5951, [1997] 4 CMLR 662.

[40] See Springer (n 15 above), p 45.

[41] See eg Case C-310/93P *BPB Industries plc and British Gypsum Ltd v Commission* [1995] ECR–865, [1997] 4 CMLR 238; see also Case T-83/91 *Tetra Pak II*.

[42] See eg C-53/92P.

[43] Case T-83/91 *Tetra Pak II*.

[44] Case C-310/93P *BPB Industries*.

profits made in one market and used to subsidize pricing on the second market, particularly with the purpose of preserving dominance upon the separate market, could be viewed as abusive even if the conduct was concentrated on the market other than the one in which the undertaking was dominant.

10.1.3.1 *Intellectual property rights and separate markets*

In cases where the dominant firm enjoys the protection of an IPR, the IP owner can, by defining the field of technical application of a protected product, create separate markets in which the product can be offered on different terms. For example, the commercial licensing strategy of an IP owner can include licensing the same patent for different fields of use and charging different rates of royalty. This is recognized as non-discriminatory under Article 101 TFEU in the Technology Transfer Block Exemption[45] and it would be non-abusive under Article 102(c) as long as the different treatment applied to non-equivalent transactions.

However, the rules of Article 102(c) in relation to separate markets continue to apply. The issue is essentially one of establishing non-equivalence rather than a justification for the use of the IPR. Consequently, as long as the markets are separate, Article 102(c) will not interfere with a differentiated exploitation policy in each market. If, however, there are associative links established between different product markets, the prohibition in Article 102(c) can apply to intermarket price differentials.

For example, in the case of *Tetra Pak II*,[46] the GC held that the practice of Tetra Pak of offering widely varying discounts to customers for their aseptic and non-aseptic milk carton machines, ie from 20–40 per cent and in some cases from 50–60 per cent higher discounts in the non-aseptic market in which Tetra Pak was not dominant, was itself discriminatory pricing under Article 102(c). Tetra Pak had argued that if one looked at the pricing of the overall package of machines with cartons, a 50 per cent difference in the discount for machines would produce a considerably narrower discount, ie about 4 per cent, for the package of products as a whole, presumably because of correspondingly higher prices for cartons. However, the GC agreed with the Commission that it was correct to look solely at the pricing of the machines, as such, since users must be perfectly free to use cartons from other manufacturers on Tetra Pak machines.

The GC added that, 'discounts on cartons should be granted solely according to the quantity of each order, and orders for different types of carton should not be aggregated for that purpose'.[47] The GC was decidedly unsympathetic to the argument that Tetra Pak could treat its packaging system as integrated and indivisible as a justification for its abusive differential pricing. Similarly, all arguments about technical considerations, product liability, protection of public health and public reputation were not accepted as objective justifications for differential pricing. They could not outweigh

45 See Part III.

46 Case T-83/91 *Tetra Pak II*.

47 Ibid, at para 215.

the point that the products were separate and it was not up to the dominant undertaking to 'take steps on its own initiative to eliminate products which rightly or wrongly it regards as dangerous or inferior in quality to its own products'.[48] . The GC added that reliability and hygiene 'could be ensured by disclosing to users of Tetra Pak machines all the technical specifications concerning the cartons to be used on those systems, without the applicant's intellectual property rights being thereby prejudiced'.[49]

It is clear that the IPR holder must take into account the legal ground rules for defining separate product markets in assessing whether or not a pricing practice is abusive. This is particularly true when the IPR holder has been designated as an 'essential facility'. In such cases, the test laid down by Article 102(c) can be expected to be even more stringent particularly on the issue of justification.

Another possible objective basis for different rates of royalty or licence fees is differing frequency of use. For example, in *Coditel v Cine Vog*,[50] the copyright holder was able to limit the number of acts of exploitation of the right which was offered to third parties and charged amounts which varied with the frequency of use. In these respects, the treatment of IPRs under Article 102(c) gives recognition to the discretion given to IPR holders under national legislation. When an IP owner divides up an IPR, each component is viewed as a different product entitling the owner to apply dissimilar conditions. This entitlement to slice IPRs is subject to restraints when an attempt is made to package services and charge for the package rather than the individual product. For example, in its Guidelines on the Application of EEC Competition Rules in the Telecommunications Sector, the Commission has ruled that a telecommunications operator may not charge an additional price for the supply of a leased line based on the use made by the lessee of that line, but can base such charges only upon differences in costs directly entailed to the telecommunications operator.[51] Although the Commission acknowledges that the value of the use of the leased circuit may be different depending upon the profitability of the service supplied on the circuit, a dominant undertaking cannot, consistent with Article 102(c), use this difference as a basis for a difference in price. Waelbroeck suggests that if the supplier owns an IPR covering the use of the product, the situation will be different because the IP owner will be entitled to charge a fee based on the acts of utilization.[52] However, there may be a distinction to be drawn between fields of use and usage under Article 102(c). The former are separate markets coinciding with the use of the IPR and reinforcing it. An essential facility owner may not be able to justify charges based on usage simply because an IPR is involved if the effect in a particular market is discriminatory. There would have to be a closer link between the IPR leased and a performance right.

[48] Ibid, at para 138.

[49] Ibid, at para 139.

[50] Case 262/81 *Coditel v Ciné Vog Films (Coditel II)* [1982] ECR 3381, [1983] 1 CMLR 49.

[51] Guidelines on the application of EEC competition rules in the telecommunication sector OJ C233/2 6 September 1991 at paras 95–7.

[52] See Michael Waelbroeck 'Price Discrimination and Rebate Policies under EU Competition Law' [1995] *Fordham Corp Law Inst* 142, p 157.

From an economic perspective, there appears to be a limited if not zero incentive for IP owners who are not vertically integrated to price discriminate between licensees, because upstream licensors will benefit from higher royalty income if there is greater competition in the downstream market.[53] On the other hand, vertically integrated licensors in markets where these control essential inputs are more likely to commit secondary line injury price discrimination as was the case in *HOV-SVZ/MCN*.[54]

The discretion given to an IP owner to divide and price separately under Article 102(c) does not extend to attempts to bundle and tie separate products. In certain circumstances, the offer of different conditions for similar components can be an offence under Article 102(c). For example, in *Hilti*,[55] the dominant firm's use of selective pricing policies included two types of discrimination. It gave particularly favourable discounts to targeted customers of competitors who were prepared to switch to Hilti. This was abusive conduct towards competitors. Secondly, it reduced discounts to Hilti customers who bought Hilti cartridge strips without Hilti nails, thus effectively charging higher prices to those customers who bought nails from competitors. This conduct was held to be discriminatory to customers. Since the source of the latter abuse was Hilti's commercial strategy of attempting to 'bundle' its cartridge strips sales with its nail sales, it suggested that Article 102(c) set limits to the commercial pricing strategies of dominant firms which were based on product packages.

10.1.4 Geographic price discrimination

A further constraint on pricing decisions by IP owners is the way the case law applies Article 102(c) to the commercial practice of pricing differently in different geographic markets. Where a dominant firm, whether in possession of an IPR or not, attempts to maximize returns by charging different prices in different geographic markets, that can be prohibited as an exercise in market partitioning. The Commission, with the support of the EU Courts, has read into Article 102(c) the objective of preventing private companies in their pricing decisions reintroducing 'the barriers which the single market has abolished'.[56]

In *United Brands*,[57] the Commission and the CJEU were confronted by a pattern in which identical bananas packed in identical boxes were sold free on rail at either Rotterdam or Bremerhaven at widely differing prices depending upon which one of six countries was their country of destination. Although the CJEU announced at the outset that 'the responsibility for establishing a single banana market did not lie with the applicant', it added that United Brands might only charge 'what the market can bear

[53] Damien Geradin, 'Pricing Abuses by Essential Patent Holders in a Standard-Setting Context: A View from Europe' [2008] (<http://ssrn.com/abstract=1174922> (last accessed 1 June 2010)), p 9.

[54] Case COMP. 94/210 *HOV SVZ/MCN* Commission decision [1994] OJ L 104/34, upheld in Case T-229/94 *Deutsche Bahn AG v Commission*, [1997] ECR II–1689, confirmed in Case C-436/97P.

[55] [1994] ECR I–667.

[56] See *XXIst Report on Competition Policy* [1991], point 43.

[57] Case 27/76 *United Brands*.

provided that it complies with the rules for the regulation and coordination of the market laid down by the Treaty'.[58] In the end, the CJEU concluded that a rigid partitioning of the market was created at price levels which were artificially different, placing certain distributor ripeners at a comparative disadvantage, thus 'distorting' competition.[59] What was slightly curious about this judgment was its failure to acknowledge that the main cause of partitioning was not the different prices but the 'green banana' clause which prevented distributors from parallel importing from low to high price countries. In principle, different prices in different Member States as such should not be abusive since interstate trade can help to level the differences. On the other hand, obstacles to parallel trading would create market partitioning. It would have been possible for the CJEU to strike down the green banana clause and leave pricing to find its own level. However, the CJEU decided effectively to treat the clause and the differential pricing as two independent infringements.[60]

The CJEU accepted that differences in costs such as transport, tax, customs duties, wages, conditions of marketing, and density of competition could result in differences in retail prices. But it held that United Brands should only take such factors into account to 'a limited extent' since it sold the same product in the same place to distributors who alone bore the risks of the consumers' market. In fact, United Brands priced on its view of the expected market price in each market about four days before the ship was unloaded, taking into account the effect on demand of weather, strikes, currency fluctuations, etc. The CJEU claimed that this direct pricing by the producer to the consumer left out the stage of the market consisting of the exchange between producer and distributor and thereby adversely affected the mechanisms of the market.[61] According to the CJEU, 'the interplay of supply and demand should, owing to its nature', only be taken into account at the stage where the supplier sells to the consumer.[62] The distortion to competition consisted of the producer operating a centralized system of pricing which effectively took away from the local distributors their opportunity to maximize monopoly profits in the local market.

In principle the judgment of the CJEU in *United Brands* implied that there could be a defence of 'meeting competition' at least at local levels. This defence would apply to dominant undertakings to enable them to defend themselves against lower pricing by competitors. The CJEU had no objection to the pricing by each of the distributors being different, as indeed it would have no objection to the pricing of different licensees or subsidiaries of an IP owner being different, as long as the different prices reflected differences in the risks attached to different market conditions. The abuse in *United Brands* consisted of the extension of market power by United Brands, the dominant producer, into the distribution market in the way that it did it.

[58] Ibid, at p 227.

[59] Ibid, at p 298.

[60] See eg M. Siragusa, 'The Application of Article 86 to the Pricing Policies of Dominant Companies: Discriminatory and Unfair Prices' (1979) 16 *CML Rev* 179.

[61] Case 27/76 *United Brands* at 230.

[62] Ibid, at p 229.

In the more recent case of *Irish Sugar*,[63] Irish Sugar was found to have abused its dominant position on the Irish market for industrial and retail sugar where it held 90 per cent market share. It was also the sole producer of sugar beet in Ireland. Three of its pricing strategies were found to be discriminatory, one of which was geographical price discrimination: Irish Sugar had offered special rebates to retailers in border areas of Ireland to deter the imports of cheaper sugar from Northern Ireland out of the Irish market whether this was from competing suppliers or re-imports of its own sugar.[64] The GC found that Irish Sugar had funded the rebates with the profits gained from its sale in the rest of Ireland.[65] 'By conducting itself in that way, the applicant abused its dominant position in the retail sugar market in Ireland, by preventing the development of free competition on that market and distorting its structures, in relation to both purchasers and consumers'.[66] In other words, Irish Sugar foreclosed the Irish sugar market from competition from other Member States, distorting thereby not only competition, but also the maintenance of the internal market.

The decisions in *United Brands*[67] and *Irish Sugar* should not be read to suggest that dominant IP owners cannot price differently in different geographic markets within the EU and be lawful under Article 102(c). Much depends on the basis for the price differences. For example in *Tetra Pak II*,[68] the Commission found that Tetra Pak had been charging different prices to customers in different Member States for non-aseptic milk cartons and milk packaging machines. It was prepared to accept that price differences could be justified where they resulted solely from the specific local market conditions as long as they did not involve discriminatory discounts. However, the Commission found that the price differences were not based on objectively justifiable economic differences but instead were evidence of a market partitioning policy which could be artificially maintained by Tetra Pak.[69] It therefore ordered Tetra Pak to refrain from discriminatory pricing and discounting. The Commission ordered Tetra Pak to ensure that any differences between the prices charged for its products in the various Member States must result solely from the specific local market conditions. It also required that any customer within the Community should be supplied by any Tetra Pak subsidiary it chose and at the price it practised.

The issue of price discrimination has also arisen in a number of collecting society cases. Insofar as the national society prices at different levels simply because the licensee comes from a different Member State, it will be unlawful. For example, in GEMA,[70] the Commission found that the rules of the German Performing Rights Society

[63] *Irish Sugar* Commission decision [1997] OJ L 258/1, [1997] 5 CMLR 666, confirmed in Case T-228/97 *Irish Sugar plc v Commission* [1999] ECR II–2969, [1999] 5 CMLR 1300, and upheld by dismissal Case C-497/99P *Irish Sugar plc v Commission* [2001] ECR I–5333, [2001] 5 CMLR 1082.

[64] T-228/97 *Irish Sugar* at para 173.

[65] Ibid, at para 188.

[66] Ibid, at para 188.

[67] Case 26/76 *United Brands* at paras 208 and 233.

[68] Case T-83/91 *Tetra Pak II*.

[69] Ibid, at para 1154.

[70] [1971] CMLR D 35.

violated Article 102 *inter alia* by requiring higher royalties on records imported or reimported from other Member States, discriminating against the nationals of other Member States.[71] The Commission required GEMA to apply the same licence fee for domestic and imported records even though the latter required more expensive controls. Nationality as such could not justify price differences where all other aspects of the transaction are equivalent. What, however, is the position where there are differences in the national IP legislation which result in differences in treatment based on nationality?

In *Basset v SACEM*,[72] for example, the French collecting society levied a fee from Basset which consisted of a performance royalty for playing music in discotheques and a supplementary fee which applied regardless of whether or not such a fee was levied by the collecting society in the Member State from which the import had come. The CJEU held that since the French licensing fee, including the supplementary fee, did not vary depending upon the origin of the product, it could be viewed as the normal exploitation of the copyright and did not in principle constitute an abuse of Article 102(c).[73] The fact that the price differences were due to the different legislation of the Member States[74] meant that the situation was not comparable to *United Brands* because that case was concerned with the dominant undertaking's exploitation of different market conditions.

The CJEU's willingness to accept differences in national legislation as a justified basis for differences in pricing rests in part on its acceptance of the fact that in the case of IP legislation, it would not be realistic to force private bodies to take pricing decisions which compensate for differences in national conditions for IPR protection. In the event, differences in national legislation can justify differences in prices even where the effect is to treat some customers more favourably than others on the basis of their nationality.[75]

The CJEU's insistence in *United Brands* that the degree of involvement of the dominant firm in the local consumer market was the key to the availability of the 'meeting competition' defence of justification for differences in prices is not altogether defensible in purely economic terms.[76] However, the basis for the CJEU's concern was more a concept of appropriateness of conduct by a dominant undertaking. If a dominant IP owner licensed a product to licensees in different national territories or invested in subsidiaries in different national territories, that would not preclude the respective licensees or subsidiaries meeting the competitive conditions of competition locally.

[71] See also Case 7/82 *GVL v Commission* [1983] ECR 483 where a German collecting society refused to make management agreements with artists who were not German residents.

[72] Case 402/85 *Basset v SACEM* [1987] ECR 1747, [1987] 3 CMLR 173.

[73] Nor was it contrary to then Arts 30 or 36 of the EEC Treaty (now 34 and 36 TFEU).

[74] L. Zanon, 'Price Discrimination under Article 86 of the EEC Treaty. A Comment on the UBC Case' (1982) 31 *ICQL* 36; W. Bishop, 'Price Discrimination under Article 86: Political Economy in the European Court' [1981] *MLR* 282.

[75] See Springer (n 15 above), p 51.

[76] See eg Siragusa (n 15 above), p 253.

The gravamen of the abuse in *United Brands* was that the producer asserted the defence that it was responding to local competition in its pricing when it did not 'bear the risks of the consumers market'.[77] The CJEU thought that Article 102 required that the 'interplay of supply and demand should only be applied to each stage where it is really manifest'.[78]

It is not altogether the case, therefore, that Article 102(c) requires standard pricing throughout the common market. If it did so, it would of course artificially require higher prices in certain countries than would otherwise be the case if the producer could price at levels adjusted to local conditions. However, the Commission's rules allow for price differentiation as long as it reflects local conditions and as long as the operator in the local market bears the risk and reaps the benefit of those local conditions. Nevertheless, the Commission and the EU Courts' approach to geographic price discrimination under Article 102(c) could be improved if they took greater account of whether or not a differential pricing practice is accompanied by measures to prevent parallel imports.[79]

10.1.5 Article 102(c) as a regulatory framework for an essential facility

Where a dominant undertaking is an essential facility for a downstream market, Article 102(c) applies to prevent discrimination on any of the terms which it offers to operators in that market where such discrimination would restrict competition. The discrimination could take the form of imposing different conditions upon different operators, whether of price or other conditions of access, without any difference in cost, technical factors, or differences in intensity of use or operation in different sub-markets.[80] The application of dissimilar conditions to equivalent transactions is unlawful discrimination because it could discourage entry or expansion of the competitor on the downstream market.

Article 102(c) also applies where an essential facility owner offers the same price and other conditions to competitors or customers for different types of 'transactions'. For example if a dominant firm in an upstream market cross-subsidizes its downstream subsidiary by funding its operations by capital remunerated substantially below the market rate or provides activities, premises, equipment, experts, and/or services with a remuneration substantially below the market rate, this will be regarded as a cross-subsidization of costs which would make identical tariffs discriminatory.[81] A dominant undertaking operating an essential facility will need to use accounting

[77] Case 26/76 *United Brands* at para 228.

[78] Ibid. See Springer (n 15 above), p 253.

[79] See Case T-228/97 *Irish Sugar* at paras 185–90 and eg Waelbroeck (n 52 above), p 154.

[80] See eg Notice on the Application of the Competition Rules To Access Agreements in the Telecommunications Sector [1998] OJ C265/02.

[81] See eg an analysis of cross-subsidization as discrimination in the Commission's Guidelines on the application of the Competition Rules in the Telecommunications Sector (n 51 above), paras 102–4.

methods which make its allocations of cost transparent to avoid suspicion of hidden cross-subsidization.[82]

10.2 CONDITIONAL REBATES IN A SINGLE MARKET

10.2.1 Introduction

The Commission and the EU Courts have long viewed certain discounting strategies of dominant firms as abusive because they were motivated by exclusionary aims towards competitors. Thus in *Hoffmann-La Roche*,[83] a case in which a dominant pharmaceutical manufacturer offered discounts for its vitamins in the form of 'fidelity rebates', ie an extra discount applied to the quantities ordered conditional upon the customer obtaining from the one manufacturer all or most of its requirements, the CJEU held that the discount was abusive under Article 102 as an indirect method of binding a customer to an exclusive relationship. The CJEU was concerned with the business strategy of Hoffmann-La Roche in using discounting as a method of supplementing the more formal exclusive agreements it had reached with some of its customers. It even viewed the dominant firm's use of an 'English clause' not so much as a method of competition but as a method of finding out about rivals' pricing policies and underpricing them. The 'English clause' encouraged customers to inform Hoffmann-La Roche of any competitors offering lower prices. It provided that if Hoffmann-La Roche would not match the competitor's price, the customer would be free to obtain supplies from the competitor without forfeiting its loyalty rebate. The CJEU held the clause to be *per se* abusive. The machinery of the English clause was not viewed as an aid to meeting competition but as a device to allow the dominant supplier 'to decide whether by adjusting its prices, it will permit competition'.[84]

Hoffmann-La Roche and cases that followed demonstrate that the Commission and the EU Courts have taken a formalistic approach to rebates and discounts and it is presumed that these discounts are granted only by exclusionary motives.[85] The CJEU has repeatedly said that quantity discounts linked exclusively to volume of the purchases are in general permissible.[86] This corresponds to economic thinking that has identified that the offering of rebates and discounts can have pro-competitive incentives, such as efficient recovery of fixed costs, providing better incentives to retailers,

[82] Ibid, paras 105–6.

[83] Case 85/76 *Hoffmann-La Roche*.

[84] Ibid, at para 107.

[85] Case T-203/01 *Manufacture française des pneumatiques Michelin v Commission (Michelin II)* [2003] ECR II–4071, [2004] 4 CMLR 923 at para 56; see also paras 65 and 100.

[86] Case 322/81 *NV Nederlandsche Banden-Industrie Michelin v Commission Michelin I* [1983] ECR 3461, [1985] 1 CMLR 282 at para 71; Case C-163/99 *Portugal v Commission* at para 50; Case T-203/01 *Michelin II* at para 85; and Case C-95/04 *British Airways* at paras 246–7, although see further below as to how the EU Courts have curtailed this statement.

reduction of double marginalization, and resolving 'hold-up' problems.[87] That said the Commission and the EU Courts appear to have made an arbitrary distinction between the different forms of rebates and discounts, viewing some as quantity discounts and therefore in principle legal and some as loyalty-inducing.[88] These have been presumed to have exclusionary effects and to be harmful to consumers. In other words, loyalty-inducing discounts have been treated as *per se* illegal without consideration to potential pro-competitive effects. In the few cases where the competition authorities have looked at objective justification, these have been restricted to cost savings: 'a rebate can only correspond to the economies of scale achieved by a firm as a result of the additional purchases which consumers are induced to make'.[89]

The concern of the EU Courts and Commission with exclusionary motives of dominant firms has been a regular feature in discount cases. In *British Plasterboard*,[90] the Commission found loyalty rebates based on exclusive requirements agreements abusive because they went beyond normal methods of competition. In *Soda Ash*,[91] the Commission held that the technique of 'top slice' discounts was abusive. Further, in *Irish Sugar*,[92] the GC noted that the EU Courts have consistently held loyalty-inducing rebates to be illegal under Article 102, and held that the Court:

> must therefore appraise all the circumstances, and in particular the criteria and detailed rules for granting rebates, and determine whether there is a tendency, through an advantage not justified by any economic service, to remove or restrict the buyer's choice as to his sources of supply, to block competitors' access to the market, to apply dissimilar conditions to equivalent transactions with other trading parties, or to reinforce the dominant position by distorting competition.[93]

It concluded by upholding the Commission's finding of loyalty-inducing rebates infringing Article 102.

In all these cases, the use of discounts which varied from rates which applied to quantities of individual products ordered were seized upon as evidence of abusive exclusionary activity directed against competitors (primary line injury).

The price differences in such cases had the added element of abuse that they placed customers at a disadvantage in relation to other customers (secondary line injury). For example, in *Hoffmann-La Roche*[94] an added discount in the form of a rebate was paid

[87] O'Donoghue and Padilla (n 5 above), pp 376–8; see also Vito Auricchio, 'Discount Policies in US and EU Antitrust Enforcement Models: Protecting Competition, Competitors or Consumer Welfare?' [2007] 3 *European Competition Journal* 373–409, pp 375–6.

[88] Note though, as will be discussed below, the distinction between the two has become more blurred over the years.

[89] COMP/E-2/36.041/*PO—Michelin* Commission decision (*Michelin II*) [2002] OJ L 143/1, para 216; see also Whish (n 33 above), pp 719–20.

[90] [1995] ECRI–865, [1997] 4 CMLR 238.

[91] [1991] OJ L 152/21 at 33; L 152/40 at 50.

[92] Case T-228/97 *Irish Sugar v Commission*.

[93] Ibid, at para 197.

[94] Case 85/76 *Hoffmann-La Roche*.

to customers for all vitamins ordered across the whole range of vitamin products rather than on the basis of the order for each vitamin. The CJEU held that the use of aggregated rebates was a bundling exercise which unlawfully restricted competition between Roche and its competitors because it deprived Roche's customers of their freedom to choose their source of supply.

In *Michelin I*,[95] the CJEU found the more subtle conduct of rebates based on sales targets abusive because of their exclusionary purpose. Michelin granted discounts to its tyre dealers based on their annual turnover of Michelin tyres in the previous year. The CJEU held that 'it is necessary to consider all the circumstances particularly the criteria and rules for the grant of the discount and to investigate whether, in providing an advantage not based on any economic service justifying it, the discount tends to remove or restrict the buyers freedom to remove or to choose its sources of supply'.[96] In this case, the actual criteria to qualify for the discount were unknown to the dealers and also changed regularly causing uncertainty for the dealers and prohibiting them from setting sales targets.[97] The lack of transparency for the customers of when they had reached their target clearly added to the finding of abuse.[98]

Moreover, the target rebates were set for Michelin's customers individually and were often higher than the previous year. The CJEU noted that when discounts are granted according to quantities sold during a relatively long reference period it will increase the pressure upon the customer to achieve that purchase figure which triggers the discount to obtain the discount or avoid a loss.[99] The issue of what is a reasonable reference period has been discussed in subsequent case law.[100] In *Michelin II*, [101] for instance, the GC stated that the CJEU had never said that a non-abusive reference period could not be longer than three months, despite the Commission arguing the opposite.[102]

In all these cases, the seller was offering identical goods for different prices to customers without any objective justification. The CJEU's view was that the only conceivable commercial return to the dominant undertaking in exchange for the loyalty or fidelity discounts was the unlawful one of driving competitors out of the market.

Michelin II demonstrated the complexity between non-abusive quantity discounts and abusive loyalty discounts. Michelin was granting different forms of discounts to its customers in the French new replacement tyres market for trucks and buses and the French retreaded tyres market for trucks and buses. In particular, three types of

[95] Case 322/81 *Michelin I*.

[96] Ibid, at para 73.

[97] Ibid, at para 83.

[98] Ibid.

[99] Ibid, at para 81.

[100] See eg *Coca-Cola/San Pellegrino* Commission's *XIXth Report on Competition Policy (1989)*, point 50, which accepted a three months' reference period as non-abusive.

[101] *Michelin* Commission decision (*Michelin II*) confirmed in T-203/01 *Michelin II*.

[102] Case T-203/01 *Michelin II* at para 88 and *Michelin* Commission decision (*Michelin II*) at para 216.

discounts caught the Commission's attention: standardized target quantity rebates, service bonuses, and the Michelin Friends' Club, an agreement between Michelin and dealers regarding closer business cooperation and services assistance. The GC commenced by noting that

> quantity rebate systems linked solely to the volume of purchases made from an undertaking occupying a dominant position are generally considered not to have the foreclosure effect prohibited by [Article 102]. . . Quantity rebates are therefore deemed to reflect gains in efficiency and economies of scale made by the undertaking in a dominant position. It follows that a rebate system in which the rate of the discount increases according to the volume purchased will not infringe [Article 102] unless the criteria and rules granting the rebate reveal that the system is not based on an economically justified countervailing advantage, but tends. . . to prevent customers from obtaining supplies from competitors.[103]

However, it continued:

> a quantity rebate system in which there is a significant variation in the discount rates between the lower and higher steps, which has a reference period of one year and in which the discount is fixed on the basis of total turnover achieved during the reference period, has the characteristics of a loyalty-inducing discount system.[104]

In other words, the GC curtailed the definition of *per se* legal quantity rebates in comparison to the distinction originally made in *Hoffmann-La Roche,* to now distinguishing between lawful economically justifiable quantity rebates and the unlawful loyalty-inducing rebates. The GC's distinction shifts the focus from the form of the rebate to the effects or rather efficiencies of the rebates, ie where the dominant company is unable to demonstrate clearly that the discounts are of a clear economical nature, the discounts are seen as loyalty enhancing. In the case, Michelin's rebates were seen as abusive because Michelin failed to provide adequate justification for their economic efficiencies.[105]

In response to Michelin's argument that its conduct did not have the effect of limiting the degree of competition in the market nor reinforcing its position on the market,[106] the GC referred to the *Hoffmann-La Roche* mantra that the conduct would be abusive if it had 'the effect of hindering the maintenance of the degree of competition still existing in the market or the growth of that competition'.[107] It continued by stating that this effect need not be *actual*, instead it held it would be 'sufficient to show that the abusive conduct. . . *tends to restrict competition*, or in other words, that the conduct is capable of having that effect'.[108] (Emphasis added). The GC concluded that for the purpose of Article 102, the object of restricting competition was equivalent to the

[103] Case T-203/01 *Michelin II* at paras 58–9.
[104] Ibid, at para 95.
[105] Ibid, at paras 107–9.
[106] Ibid, at para 236.
[107] Ibid, at para 238, referring to Case 85/76 *Hoffmann-La Roche*, para 91.
[108] Ibid, at para 239.

effect of limiting competition, because if the aim of the conduct was to restrict competition it would 'also be liable to have such an effect'.[109]

The statement clearly supports the formative approach the EU Courts have applied over the years to Article 102 cases, although this approach has been highly criticized by scholars.[110]

British Airways[111] is another recent case in which loyalty-inducing rebates were scrutinized. The case dealt with target incentive rebates, but from the buyer's side. Virgin in a complaint to the Commission argued that British Airways (BA) was abusing its dominant position by paying bonus commissions to travel agents based on the degree of increase of the sales of BA tickets by the travel agents in relation to a reference period.

The Commission found that BA had applied three bonus schemes: 'marketing agreements', 'global agreements', and, a 'performance reward scheme'; all having one important feature in common:

> ... In each case meeting the targets for sales growth leads to an increase in the commission paid on all tickets sold by the agent, not just on the tickets sold after the target is reached. In the [marketing agreement] schemes the cash bonus per ticket paid to the travel agent increases for all tickets sold. In the [performance reward scheme] the percentage commission paid increases for all ticket sales by the travel agent. This means that when a travel agent is close to one of the thresholds for an increase in commission rate selling relatively few extra BA tickets can have a large effect on his commission income. Conversely a competitor of BA who wishes to give a travel agent an incentive to divert some sales from BA to the competing airline will have to pay a much higher rate of commission than BA on all of the tickets sold by it to overcome this effect.[112]

The increase of the commission payable on *all* ticket sold meant that in comparison to previous rebate cases; the loyalty-inducing effect of the commission was further enhanced.

The Commission established that BA was a dominant buyer in the United Kingdom market for air travel agency services. The services being the promotion of the air transport services, helping travellers choose the appropriate services, issuing tickets,

[109] Ibid, at para 239; this reaffirms the GC's statement in T-228/97 *Irish Sugar* at para 170.

[110] Joanna Goyder and Albertina Albors-Llorens, *Goyder's EC Competition Law* (5th edn, Oxford: OUP, 2009), p 331; M. Motta, 'Michelin II—The treatment of rebates', 27 November 2006, available at <http://www.barcelonagse.eu/tmp/pdf/motta_MichelinII.pdf> (last accessed 29 June 2010); F. Maier-Rigaud, 'Article 82 Rebates: Four Common Fallacies' (2006) 2 *European Competition Journal* 85; D. Spector, 'Loyalty Rebates: An Assessment of Competition Concerns and a Proposed Structured Rule of Reason' (2005) 1(2) *Competition Policy International* 89; D. Waelbroeck, 'Michelin II: A Per Se Rule against Rebates by Dominant Companies?' (2005) 1 *J. Competition L. & Econ.* 149; J. Kallaugher and B. Sher, 'Rebates Revisited: Anti-Competitive Effects and Exclusionary Abuse under Article 82' [2004] *ECLR* 263; J. Temple Lang and R. O'Donoghue, 'Defining Legitimate Competition: How to Clarify Pricing Abuses under Article 82' (2002) 26 *Fordham Int'l LJ* 83; Lars Kjolbye, 'Rebates under Article 82 EC: Navigating Uncertain Waters' *ECLR* 2010, 31(2), 66–80.

[111] T-219/99 *British Airways v Commission* [2003] ECR II-5917, [2004] 4 CMLR 1008 upheld in C-95/04 *British Airways v Commission* [2007] ECR I-2331, [2007] 4 CMLR 22.

[112] *Virgin/British Airways* Commission decision, OJ L 30/1, [2000] 4 CMLR 999 at para 29.

collecting money from travellers, and remitting it to the airline. In return the airlines paid the travel agencies' commissions based on the sales of tickets. BA held from 1992 46.3 per cent market share to 39.7 per cent market share in 1998. In other words, although BA was dominant its market share was in fact decreasing, despite its use of the target schemes.

However, the Commission stated that the schemes were loyalty inducing similarly to the ones found abusive in *Hoffmann-La Roche* and *Michelin I*.[113] It noted that the schemes were more 'related to loyalty' than efficiencies, even though BA had provided evidence for some efficiencies gained through the scheme when dealing with larger travel agents.[114] Instead it argued that BA was using the scheme to create loyalty by rewarding travel agents that met or exceeded their sales of BA tickets in comparison to previous years' sales.[115]

BA appealed the case to the GC who upheld the Commission decision in its entirety.[116] The GC's ruling mirrored closely that of *Michelin II*, again requiring a demonstration of BA's commission being 'based on an economically justified consideration'.[117] The GC did so with reference to *Michelin II* and *Portuguese Airport*.[118] It is unclear whether the GC intended to develop its line of attack further from that of *Michelin II*, or merely attempted to reiterate it in relation to the facts of *British Airways*.[119] In any case, BA did not meet the required standard.

In relation to anti-competitive effects, the GC repeated *Michelin II* almost word for word:

> for the purposes of establishing an infringement of [Article 102], it is not necessary to demonstrate that the abuse in question had a concrete effect on the markets concerned. It is sufficient in that respect to demonstrate that the abusive conduct of the undertaking in a dominant position tends to restrict competition or, in other words, that the conduct in question is capable of having or likely to have such an effect. [120]

However, as Whish notes, the Commission did not provide any persuasive evidence for the finding that BA's commission affected the ability of other airlines to compete and in particular that Virgin was being excluded from the market.[121] The GC's judgment was upheld upon appeal to the CJEU.[122]

[113] *Virgin/British Airways* at para 96.
[114] Ibid, at para 102.
[115] Ibid.
[116] T-219/99 *British Airways*.
[117] Ibid, at para 271.
[118] Case C-163/99 *Portugal v Commission*.
[119] See Alison Jones and Brenda Sufrin, *EC Competition Law, Text, Cases and Materials* (3rd edn, Oxford: OUP, 2008), p 504.
[120] T-219/99 *British Airways* at para 293.
[121] Whish (n 33 above), p 724.
[122] C-95/04 *British Airways*.

The CJEU distinguished between quantity discounts, loyalty schemes, and target rebates as applied in *British Airways* and *Michelin I*, holding that the latter were abusive if:

those discounts or bonuses can produce an exclusionary effect, that is to say whether they are capable, first, of making market entry very difficult or impossible for competitors of the undertaking in a dominant position and, secondly, of making it more difficult or impossible for its co-contractors to choose between various sources of supply or commercial partners.[123]

The CJEU thereby seems to state that there are three types of discounts: legal quantity discounts (it is unclear whether the curb the GC made in *Michelin I* of quantity rebates having to be lawful economically justifiable is the one applicable, or a *per se* legal group of quantity discounts still exists; paragraph 67 of the judgment indicates that the GC's restriction is now the chosen definition for legal quantity discounts); loyalty-inducing rebates as in *Hoffmann-La Roche* (which are considered virtually illegal *per se*);[124] and rebates or discounts which are neither of the above (in *British Airways* and *Michelin I* they were target rebates, but the CJEU's definition is broad enough to cover other forms of reward schemes). For these latter two groups, the CJEU noted that it must be assessed whether there is an objective economic justification.[125] It is clear from the judgment that that assessment is closely related to that of whether the discounts have any exclusionary effects. The CJEU explained that the relationship is that of a balancing test between the pro- and anti-competitive effects of the practice:

It has to be determined whether the exclusionary effect arising from such a system, which is disadvantageous for competition, may be counterbalanced, or outweighed, by advantages in terms of efficiency which also benefit the consumer. If the exclusionary effect of that system bears no relation to advantages for the market and consumers, or if it goes beyond what is necessary in order to attain those advantages, that system must be regarded as an abuse.[126]

The CJEU thus confirmed the low standard of proof that the GC had set in the case, ie that there is no need to prove actual harm, instead it is sufficient to demonstrate that the conduct tends to restrict competition or is capable of having or likely to have such an effect.[127]

In the case, the CJEU confirmed the GC's finding both in relation to exclusionary effects and lack of objective economic justification because it found that BA was requesting a reassessment of the facts and not appealing on a question of law.[128]

The cases on rebates and discounts suggest that the conditions of Article 102 have been applied highly legalistically. The emphasis has been placed on differences in

[123] Ibid, at para 68.
[124] Oliver (n 34 above), p 331.
[125] Case C-95/04 *British Airways* at paras 69 and 84.
[126] Ibid, at para 86.
[127] Case T-219/99 *British Airways* at para 293.
[128] Case C-95/04 *British Airways* at paras 78, 80, and 86–90.

price, other terms of the contract, and the method of performance of the contract as such rather than the economic effects of the discounts.[129] It has been claimed, with some justice, that the rules are applied rather rigidly and are not easy to reconcile with the commercial realities of companies' pricing policies.[130]

The Commission's *Enforcement Guidelines on Article 82* attempts to compensate for this by introducing the as efficient as competitor test to so-called conditional rebates. The Commission has already applied this approach in two cases, *Prokent-Tomra*[131] and *Intel.*[132] The latter is discussed below.

10.2.2 Conditional rebates and intellectual property rights

IPR has not played a significant role in relation to rebates cases. However, the Commission, with backing from the EU Courts, has made it clear in several types of pricing cases that regardless of the presence of IPR it will assess and find abusive pricing practices which have the effect of excluding competitors. Thus in *Duales Systems Deutschland AG*[133] discussed in Chapter 9 on 'Excessive Pricing', the Commission prohibited the use of a trade mark as part of a fee system, which allowed DSD to charge excessive prices and exclude competitors from the market for the collection and recycling of sales packaging in Germany through exclusive dealing.

In *Hilti*,[134] which was a tying case involving IPR, the Commission also found that the tying effect was exacerbated through rebates or rather the reduction of them.

In *Digital Undertaking*,[135] the Commission found that the bundling of software services in a package with hardware services was abusive because it left little choice (especially financially) for the consumer but to accept the bundled package. The Commission argued that the bundle was a deliberate policy from Digital to exclude its competitors from the hardware services market. Digital was also found to have offered loyalty-inducing rebates to customers if they did not obtain supplies from other service providers during their contracts with Digital.

In *Intel*,[136] Intel was found to have deployed a series of conditional rebates to its customers and other measures aimed at preventing or delaying the launch of

[129] See eg Zanon (n 74 above) and Bishop (n 74 above).

[130] See eg Waelbroeck (n 52 above), p 148.

[131] Case COMP/E-1/38.113–*Prokent-Tomra* Commission decision, OJ C219, 28 August 2008, pp 11–15.

[132] Case COMP/C-3/37.990–*Intel* Commission decision of 13 May 2009, D (2009) 3726 final (<http://ec.europa.eu/competition/elojade/isef/index.cfm?fuseaction=dsp_result> (last accessed 28 June 2010)).

[133] *Duales System Deutschland AG (DSD)* [2001] OJ L 166/1, [2001] 5 CMLR 609, upheld T-151/01 *Der Grüne Punkt–Duales System Deutschland GmbH v Commission* [2007] ECR II–1607.

[134] *Eurofix-Bauco v Hilti* Commission decision OJ (1988) L 65/19.

[135] *Digital Undertaking XXVIIth Report on Competition Policy 1997* and Commission Press Release IP/97/868, 'The European Commission accepts an undertaking from Digital concerning its supply and pricing practices in the field of computer maintenance services' (Brussels, 10 October 1997).

[136] Case COMP/C-3/37.990–*Intel* Commission decision of 13 May 2009, D (2009) 3726 final (<http://ec.europa.eu/competition/elojade/isef/index.cfm?fuseaction=dsp_result> (last accessed 28 June 2010)).

computers based on competing products (so-called 'naked restrictions'—these will not be discussed here). Intel was found to hold a dominant position on the market for x86 Central Processing Units (CPUs) amongst other things because of its IPR. Intel and AMD were the main manufacturers of CPUs produced for use in different segments of the computer industry; the major segments being desktop, laptop, and server computers. The market was further divided into x86 and non-x86 architecture.[137] The x86 architecture produced by Intel was originally chosen by IBM in the 1980s, when IBM was the *de facto* standard for PCs. This was also the time when it chose Microsoft Windows as its operating system.[138] The Intel x86 architecture and Microsoft Windows are therefore compatible with each other, whereas other non x86 CPUs are not compatible with Windows. In effect, IBM via its own *de facto* industry standard for PCs created the *de facto* industry standards that Intel holds in PC hardware and Microsoft holds in software respectively. Furthermore, Intel holds 'substantial intellectual property rights protection' on the x86 CPU architecture and the x86 CPU design, known as the x86 instruction set, making it near impossible for a new entrant to the market to compete directly with Intel. '[Critical] technology and intellectual property necessary to design, manufacture, and sell a CPU that executes the x86 instruction set is owned and vigorously enforced by Intel. It will therefore be very costly, time consuming and difficult to develop a product which is compatible with the x86 instruction set and may ultimately be impossible.'[139]

The Commission found that the sunk costs in the form of substantial investment in research and development and production facilities that companies would be required to undertake if they were to enter the market created significant barriers to entry and expansion of the market, not to mention the need to negotiate licensing fees and terms with Intel for the x86 CPU instruction set. This together with the strong product differentiation Intel had placed on its x86 CPU making it a 'must-stock' product equally added to the Commission's conclusion that Intel was dominant in the x86 CPU market.[140] Additionally the Commission noted that more or less all other companies who had previously produced x86 CPUs had now exited the market. In fact, only Intel and AMD remained.[141]

Intel contested the Commission's finding of dominance, arguing that it was in fact dependent on the Original Equipment Manufacturers (OEMs) and that they possessed significant market power that meant that Intel was unable to behave independently of its customers.[142] Moreover, Intel argued that prices had fallen in the market over the recent years indicating healthy competition in the market.[143] The Commission rejected both arguments holding that Intel was an unavoidable trading partner for the OEMs,

[137] *Intel* at para 120.
[138] Ibid, at para 121.
[139] Ibid, footnote 137.
[140] Ibid, at para 881; see also paras 912, and 854–66.
[141] Ibid, at para 882.
[142] Ibid, at paras 883–4.
[143] Ibid, at para 884.

supplying 70 to 80 per cent of the market for a considerable period of time and falling prices were not inconsistent with market power. The Commission outlined three points for this: First, the microprocessor industry 'is characterised by rapid technological progress. . . over time, this translates into either increased performance of the CPU at equivalent cost or equal performance at lower cost'.[144] Second, assessing the true value of the products in relation to price is particularly difficult in high tech industries because new products are frequently developed, which are of better quality but lower costs.[145] Finally, the fact that Intel was able to impose loyalty-inducing rebates on the OEMs despite falling prices demonstrated that Intel was 'able or free to adopt a price policy to forestall competitive pressure'.[146]

In relation to abuse, the Commission commenced by noting that its *Enforcement Guidance on Article 82* did not apply to the Intel proceeding as the latter was started before the paper was published; yet, the Commission still asserted that its decision was in line with its policies outlined in the guidance paper.[147] Moreover, its approach to the alleged abuse was first to apply the traditional form-based approach and then move on to add reasoning of likely effects. Despite holding that no evidence of anti-competitive effect was needed to find the conduct abusive, the Commission nevertheless engaged in such a discussion raising the question as to why? One commentator states lack of confidence and to avoid criticism from applying a form-based approach.[148] However, considering that the Commission itself is interested in moving to a more effect-based approach, applying both a form-based and effect-based approach to the case makes sense if it is to tempt the EU Courts to move in that direction as well. It is therefore perfectly sensible to apply both methods.

The Commission assessed Intel's pricing policies with five of its customers finding that it had applied various forms of rebates to these companies in return for exclusive purchase of the Intel x86 CPU or the majority (80–95 per cent) of their CPU needs from Intel.[149] It also found that these conditional rebates made it difficult for the OEMs to source AMD's CPUs. In the case of Dell, the conditional rebates granted to it by Intel were based on Dell purchasing all its CPU needs from Intel. Intel made it clear to Dell that it would lose a significant amount of its discounts, if it did not remain Intel exclusive. However, Intel did not provide Dell with objective criteria from which to assess how much of the discount it would lose if it partially switched to AMD x86 CPUs. Referring to *Michelin I* the Commission found this lack of transparency adding to the effect of enforcing the exclusivity of the conditional rebates.[150] Moreover, when

[144] Ibid, at para 908.

[145] Ibid, at para 909.

[146] Ibid, at para 910.

[147] Ibid, at para 916.

[148] Damien Geradin, 'The Decision of the Commission of 13 May 2009 in the *Intel* case: Where is the Foreclosure and Consumer Harm', pp 9 and 10, available at: <http://papers.ssrn.com/sol3/papers.cfm?abstract_id=1490114> (last accessed 30 June 2010).

[149] *Intel*, at para 926.

[150] Ibid, at paras 927–50, and, in particular, para 942.

Dell did obtain x86 CPUs from AMD its rebates from Intel decreased with immediate effect.[151] Intel subsequently contacted Lenovo another OEM to offer it additional rebates owing to Dell having lost theirs.[152] Again Lenovo was forced to obtain all its x86 CPUs from Intel to gain the discounts.[153] Lenovo had originally been forced to cancel its AMD notebook projects to obtain the discounts from Intel. HP and NEC's rebates from Intel were conditional upon them purchasing between 80 and 95 per cent of their CPU needs from Intel. The Commission found that not only were these conditional rebates loyalty-inducing and abusive under Article 102, they also had the effect of restricting HP's and NEC's freedom to choose their sources of x86 CPU supply and preventing other competitors from supplying HP and NEC with x86 CPUs.[154] Finally, the Commission found that the payments Intel had made to Media Saturn Holding (MSH) were conditional upon MSH selling only PCs based on Intel x86 CPUs and that had an effect equivalent to fidelity rebates as well as restricting MSH's freedom to choose its suppliers.[155]

Having established the abusive nature of the rebates granted by Intel, the Commission went on to look at the anti-competitive effects of them, although it had noted in the beginning that case law dictated that there was no need for the Commission to demonstrate actual effects, despite Intel arguing the opposite.[156] Instead the Commission referred to *Microsoft* and *British Airways*, noting that it would suffice to demonstrate that the behaviour tended to restrict competition or 'is capable of having or likely to have such an effect'.[157] It went on to observe with reference to *Michelin II* and *Compagnie maritime belge* that a violation of Article 102 could also occur from the anti-competitive object of the conduct under investigation.[158]

In the Commission's assessment of anti-competitive effects, it applied the efficient competitor test, as outlined in its *Enforcement Guidelines on Article 82*. The Commission commenced by establishing that it regarded Intel as 'an unavoidable trading partner' and its product a 'must-stock' for OEMs. This meant that Intel could leverage its market power from the non-contestable share of demand for its x86 CPU into the contestable share of demand, ie the share for which customers would look for substitutes.[159] The fact that Intel's x86 CPU was highly popular amongst final

[151] Ibid, at para 946.

[152] Ibid, at para 948.

[153] Ibid, at paras 982–9.

[154] Ibid, at paras 972 and 981.

[155] Ibid, at paras 990–1000.

[156] Ibid, at para 925; see also paras 922–3.

[157] *Intel* at para 923 and Case T-219/99 *British Airways* at para 293.

[158] *Intel* at para 923 and Case T-203/01 *Michelin II* at para 241; Joined Cases T-24/93, T-25/93, T-26/93, and T-28/93 *Compagnie Maritime Belge Transport SA v Commission* [1996] ECR II-1201, [1997] 4 CMLR 273 at para 149, confirmed by Joined Cases C-395/96P and C-396/96P *Compagnie Maritime Belge Transports SA v Commission* [2000] ECR I-1365, [2000] 4 CMLR 1076 at paras 118–120. See also Case C-202/07P *France Télécom v Commission* [2009] ECR I-2369 at paras 107–113.

[159] *Intel* at para 1005.

customers reinforced its 'must-stock' nature, made it less realistic for customers to switch to alternative suppliers, and thereby expanded the non-contestable share of demand for it.[160] Moreover, the Commission found that the relevant time horizon within which it was realistic to switch or a share was contestable was also relatively low, lasting no more than a year.[161] It based this finding on the fact that there were significant difficulties associated with entering into long-term commitments in the market, one being that new products are constantly replacing older versions within a short time frame of three to four months, referred to as 'refresh cycles'.[162] A final parameter on which to base the efficient competitor test is the assessment of the relevant measures of viable costs; ie to be viable in the long run, a company must recover at least the total cost of producing its output. The Commission noted that in a market such as the x86 CPU where there are very high fixed costs, the average prices must be significantly above marginal cost for a company to remain viable.[163]

For this parameter the Commission chose to rely on average avoidable costs (AAC) as its benchmark. Unsurprisingly, Intel disagreed with the Commission as to which costs should come under this heading.

The Commission has been criticized for its chosen parameters for the efficient competitor test in particular in relation to the contestable share, because of the difficulties involved for the dominant company to assess this without access to often confidential information from the competitors and customers.[164] One commentator even suggests that this parameter should be seen as a 'thought experiment that is used to frame the analysis of likely effects based on a variety of factors'.[165]

One buyer's contestable share may not be the same as another's, meaning that a dominant company will have to look at each individual customer. This however, is equally difficult to calculate (requiring increased costs for the company to accountants, economists, and so on to estimate the production capacity) and would force cautious dominant companies not to engage in price competition, even perhaps raise their prices and not grant often essential rebates to their customers.[166] The *Intel* case clearly demonstrates the complexities the parameters raise and indicates that the Commission's effect-based approach may not be as effective after all.

When assessing the rebates granted by Intel to each of its five customers, the Commission found in each case that the rebates were capable of having or likely to have anti-competitive foreclosure effects, since even an efficient competitor would have been prevented from supplying these five customers' x86 CPU requirements.[167]

[160] Ibid, at paras 1009–12.
[161] Ibid, at paras 1013–14.
[162] Ibid, at para 1018.
[163] Ibid, at para 1036.
[164] Temple-Lang (n 4 above) and Lars Kjølbye 'Rebates under Article 82 EC: Navigating Uncertain Waters' *ECLR* 2010, 31(2), 66–80.
[165] Lars Kjolbye (n 164 above), p 80.
[166] John Temple-Lang (n 164 above), p 16.
[167] *Intel* at paras 1281, 1406, 1456, 1507, and 1573.

The Commission went on to assess the importance of the OEMs on the x86 CPU market; in effect the buyer power and control they possessed over Intel. It found that Dell and HP in particular, owing to their large market shares, their strong presence in the more profitable part of the market, and their ability to 'legitimise a new x86 CPU in the market' by providing an important springboard for an x86 supplier wanting to penetrate the market, were 'strategically more important OEMs'.[168] Therefore targeting those two OEMs particularly had an added effect on the market and further enhanced the anti-competitive effects of the rebates granted by Intel. Through the conditional rebates Intel induced loyalty from the OEMs, which artificially prevented consumer choice, foreclosed the access to the market for competitors (actual or potential), and lowered the incentive to innovate.[169]

Two arguments were put forward by Intel as objective justifications for the rebate schemes. Firstly, Intel argued that it merely responded to price competition from its rivals and through the rebates met competition.[170] Secondly, Intel applied the rebates to achieve four important efficiencies; (1) lower prices; (2) scale of economies; (3) other cost savings and production efficiencies; and (4) risk sharing and marketing efficiencies.[171] It further claimed that the conditions placed on the rebates were indispensable to achieve those efficiencies and their impact would have been minimal upon the market because AMD was expanding.[172] All were rejected by the Commission.[173]

As regards, the meet competition defence, the Commission stated:

> Intel's argument is also flawed because Intel did not simply lower its overall prices in order to respond to a competitive threat, but it created an individualised pricing system in which certain customers received special rebates that were conditioned upon exclusivity or quasi exclusivity. Thus, the abuse in this case is not determined by the size of the rebate but by the conditions attached to the payment of the rebate, namely the exclusivity and quasi-exclusivity conditions. Such conditions are unnecessary for responding to price competition and therefore their principal aim cannot be considered to be addressing price competition. Consequently, Intel's specific individualised conditional exclusivity rebates cannot be justified by a meet competition defence.[174]

Although from the reading of the Commission decision the conclusion seems obvious—Intel's behaviour was abusive—it should be viewed in conjunction with the European Ombudsman's decision that the Commission was in fact guilty of maladministration by not having taken proper notes during a meeting with Dell.[175]

[168] Ibid, at paras 1577–96.
[169] Ibid, at paras 1597, 1598, 1603, and 1616.
[170] Ibid, at para 1625.
[171] Ibid, at para 1632.
[172] Ibid, at para 1632.
[173] Ibid, at para 1639.
[174] Ibid, at para 1630.
[175] Decision of the European Ombudsman closing his inquiry into complaint 1935/2008/FOR against the European Commission (<http://www.ombudsman.europa.eu/cases/decision.faces/en/4164/html.bookmark> (last accessed 30 June 2006)).

Moreover, the Commission relied heavily on email correspondence as evidence, as Geradin points out:

> absent the ability to cross-examine the authors of these emails, distinguishing anticompetitive from competitive intent is very difficult, and subject to interpretation mistakes. After all, the very purpose of competition, and the job description of sales executives, is to take away business from competitors. It is thus hardly surprising that all sorts of 'juicy language' can be found in emails and internal presentations.[176]

These issues combined raise doubt as to whether Intel's rebate schemes were as harmful as made out to be by the Commission. However, based on the form-based approach the very presence of the schemes suffices for a finding of abuse under Article 102, and the Commission's conclusion was therefore correct albeit its decision a tad colourful.

10.2.3 Conclusion on conditional rebates

The case law on discounts and rebate schemes has not in relation to the actual abusive behaviour shown any special treatment of IPRs nor the opposite. In fact, IPRs seem not to play a significant role in the finding of abuse; where the IPR has played a role has been in the establishment of the relevant market and dominance. This corresponds to other forms of abusive behaviour under Article 102, such as tying and predatory pricing.

[176] Geradin (n 148 above), p 13.

11

EXCLUSIONARY PRICING: PREDATORY PRICING AND MARGIN SQUEEZE

11.1 Predatory Pricing 189
11.2 Margin Squeeze 194

11.1 PREDATORY PRICING

Article 102 has been applied by the Commission with the approval of the EU Courts to cases of predatory pricing. The abuse consists of pricing below cost with an intention to eliminate competitors. Insofar as Article 102 is used to regulate predatory pricing because of its exclusionary effects, courts must be careful not to prevent firms from competing on the basis of performance. If firms have achieved a dominant position by virtue of efficiency and innovation, they must be allowed to pass on the benefits to consumers even if that damages competitors.

In *AKZO v Commission*,[1] the CJEU indicated that there were two basic methods of analysis to determine whether or not an undertaking has practised predatory pricing. The first is that pricing below average variable costs is *per se* abusive in the sense that no proof of intent is necessary. For in such a case, there is no conceivable economic purpose other than the elimination of a competitor, since each item produced and sold entails a loss for the undertaking.[2] The second method is that pricing products below average total costs but above average variable costs is only to be considered abusive if an intention to eliminate can be shown.[3] In *AKZO*, the Commission found that AKZO had offered products to ECS's customers at unreasonably low prices with a view to

[1] *ECS/AKZO* Commission decision [1985] OJ L 374/1, [1986] 3 CMLR 273; on appeal Case 62/86 *AKZO Chemie BV v Commission* [1991] ECR I–3359, [1993] 5 CMLR 215.

[2] Case 62/86 *AKZO* at para 71.

[3] Ibid, at para 72.

damaging ECS's chances of survival. The dominant company had sought out the customers of ECS offering to supply at prices below cost and below the prices it charged its own customers. AKZO's low pricing was below average total costs but above average variable costs but its clearly expressed intent, combined with its targeting of ECS customers, was sufficient to prove predatory pricing under Article 102.

In *Tetra Pak II*,[4] the Commission found that the pricing by Tetra Pak of non-aseptic cartons in Italy was considerably below average variable costs from 1976 to 1981 though it showed no proof of intention to eliminate competitors. This finding was supported by the General Court's (GC's) own examination of the facts.[5] In 1982, the Commission found that prices for the cartons were between average variable costs and average total costs and the GC stressed the need to find evidence of intent to eliminate a competitor.[6]

Tetra Pak argued that there was inadequate proof of predatory pricing because the Commission had not shown that Tetra Pak had a realistic prospect of recouping its losses once it had eliminated the competitor in question. Underlying this argument was the model of predation occurring in two stages: the dominant undertaking first prices below cost attempting to drive out a competitor and then, in a subsequent stage, attempts to recoup its losses by charging at supra-competitive prices. Tetra Pak, relying on the theories of US economists and the decision of the US Supreme Court in *Brook Group*,[7] maintained that where there was no prospect of recoupment that could be evidence of non-predatory intent. The GC held that, 'it is not necessary to demonstrate specifically that the undertaking in question had a reasonable prospect of recouping losses'.[8] On appeal, the CJEU agreed, stating:

> it would not be appropriate in the circumstances of the case to require in addition proof that Tetra Pak had a realistic prospect of recouping its losses. It must be possible to penalise predatory pricing whenever there is a risk that competitors will be eliminated. [The General Court] found . . . that there was such a risk in this case. The aim pursued, which is to maintain undistorted competition, rules out waiting until such a strategy leads to the elimination of competitors.[9]

The GC also reaffirmed that the precepts of the *AKZO* test provided the correct basis to assess whether a pricing practice was predatory or came within the scope of competition on the basis of quality.[10] The GC added that the period during which

[4] *Tetra Pak II*, Commission decision 92/163, OJ L 72, 18 March 1992, [1992] 4 CMLR 55, confirmed in T-83/91, *Tetra Pak International SA v Commission (Tetra Pak II)* [1994] ECR II–755, [1997] 4 CMLR 726 and on appeal C-333/94 *Tetra Pak International SA v Commission (Tetra Pak II)* [1996] ECR I–5951, [1997] 4 CMLR 662.

[5] T-83/91 *Tetra Pak II* at para 150.

[6] Ibid. The same reasoning was applied by the GC to sales of aseptic machines in the UK from 1981 to 1984 (paras 189–91).

[7] *Brook Group Ltd v Brown and Williamson Tobacco Group* 405 US 209 (1993).

[8] T-83/91 *Tetra Pak II* at para 150.

[9] C-333/94 *Tetra Pak II* at para 44.

[10] T-83/91 *Tetra Pak II* at paras 147–9.

prices are applied as part of a plan to damage a competitor is a factor to be taken into account.[11]

Tetra Pak II dealt with leveraged recoupment, whereas in *Deutsche Post/UPS*,[12] the predation was in relation to cross-subsidization. Deutsche Post was supplying parcel services at below-cost prices from 1990–1995, having funded the loss with profits gained from the letter services market where it held exclusive rights under German law.[13] The Commission saw the reserved letter services as a 'permanent source of funding' for Deutsche Post.[14] Only if Deutsche Post did not have to continue to subsidize the parcel services would it make financial sense for Deutsche Post to make the subsidization. Therefore, Deutsche Post was attempting with the subsidy to prevent competitors from gaining sufficient hold of the market so that eventually it could earn profits on the parcel services.[15] The case is of interest from an IPR perspective because it demonstrates that if an IPR was applied in a similar manner, ie where the profits of the sale of the IP-protected product or service or the licensing of an IPR is used to subsidize below-cost sales of other unprotected products or services, it could be seen as abusive under Article 102.[16]

In *France Telecom*,[17] the core issue was again the application of the AKZO test to predatory pricing. The CJEU reaffirmed its application and in particular the absence of a need to demonstrate recoupment. It also confirmed the Commission's finding of predatory pricing in the French market for ADSL high-speed internet access for residential customers.[18]

Wanadoo, France Telecom's subsidiary, had from March 2001 to October 2002 charged prices below average variable costs for its residential broadband services. The Commission had found that this was part of a pre-emptive plan 'designed to maximise revenue and margins on ADSL subscriptions, stabilise that same revenue by increasing subscriber loyalty, and maximise revenue on neighbouring markets. . .'.[19]

[11] Ibid, at para 149.

[12] Case COMP/35.141, *Deutsche Post AG* Commission decision of 20 March 2001 [2001] OJ L 125/27.

[13] Ibid, at para 5.

[14] Ibid, at para 6.

[15] David Howarth, 'Pricing Abuses Unfair and Predatory Pricing Under Article 82 EC: From Cost-price Comparisons to the Search for Strategic Standards' in Giuliano Amato and Claus-Dieter Ehlermann (eds), *EC Competition Law, A Critical Assessment* (Oxford and Portland, Oregon: Hart Publishing, 2007) p 289.

[16] Communications from the Commission—*Guidance on the Commission's Enforcement Priorities in Applying Article 82 EC Treaty to Abusive Exclusionary Conduct by Dominant Undertakings* OJ C45 24 February 2009, pp 7–20 (hereinafter *Commission's Enforcement Guidelines on Article 82*), para 62 and footnote 2.

[17] Case COMP/38.233–*Wanadoo Interactive* Commission decision of 16 July 2003, unpublished. (<http://ec.europa.eu/competition/antitrust/cases/decisions/38233/en.pdf> (last accessed 5 October 2010)) confirmed in Case T-340/03 *France Telecom SA (formerly Wanadoo Interactive SA) v Commission* [2007] ECR II–107 and upheld in C-202/07P *France Telecom SA v Commission*, 2 April 2009.

[18] T-340/03 *France Telecom* at paras 73–91.

[19] *Wanadoo Interactive* Commission decision at para 292.

France Telecom itself held almost 100 per cent of the market for wholesale ADSL services for internet services providers in France. In January 2001 Wanadoo held 46 per cent of the market for ADSL high-speed internet access for residential customers; this had risen to 72 per cent by September 2002, and over the same period the market itself had increased five-fold in size.[20] Alternative internet access, such as low-speed connections, were considered but rejected because of the differences in use, features, performances, and lack of substitutability between them.[21] In its challenge of the Commission decision to the GC, France Telecom argued that the market was an emerging and dynamic market with few customers and potential as well as actual competitors should be looked at.[22] The GC held that the fact that it was a fast-growing dynamic market did not stop the competition rules from applying; moreover, Wanadoo's 'link-up' with France Telecom gave it technical advantages over both actual and potential competitors and the Commission had therefore been right in finding Wanadoo dominant.[23] From an IPRs perspective, the assessment of dominance in *France Telecom* indicates that new markets, where innovation is in its infancy, will not be seen as a justification for abuse to flourish unchallenged.

In respect of abuse, France Telecom argued that the wrong test of predation had been applied; it claimed that it was permitted to align its prices with its competitors, its below-cost pricing was not part of a plan, and the Commission had not proved that France Telecom could recoup its loses.[24] The GC stated that as a dominant company France Telecom did not have an absolute right to align its prices with its competitors if this meant selling at below cost.[25] The case should be contrasted with *Digital Undertaking*[26], where the Commission in its settlement agreement with Digital recognized that dominant companies should be able to 'meet' competitors in respect of price.[27]

The GC also rejected France Telecom's argument that there was no plan to preempt competition, noting that the Commission had provided sufficient evidence for this.[28] Importantly, the GC rejected France Telecom's claim that there is a need for the Commission to demonstrate recoupment. The GC's ruling was upheld by the CJEU, which confirmed that proof of recoupment was not a precondition for finding predatory pricing.[29] 'In particular, the [CJEU] has taken the opportunity to dispense with such proof in circumstances where the eliminatory intent of the undertaking at issue could be presumed in view of that undertaking's application of prices lower than

[20] Commission Press Release IP/03/1025, 16 July 2003.

[21] T-340/03 *France Telecom* at paras 73–91.

[22] Ibid, at paras 105–11.

[23] Ibid, at paras 115–18 and 121.

[24] Ibid, at para 170.

[25] Ibid, at para 182.

[26] Commission Press Release IP/97/868.

[27] See Alison Jones and Brenda Sufrin, *EC Competition Law, Text, Cases, and Materials* (Oxford: OUP, 2008), p 465 for a discussion on this.

[28] T-340/03 *France Telecom* at paras 195–218.

[29] C-202/07 *France Telecom* at para 110.

average variable costs.'[30] The CJEU continued to state that the impossibility for the dominant company to recoup the losses does not justify the predatory behaviour, because it will still permit the company to reinforce its market power.[31]

The judgment in *France Telecom* should be compared with the Commission's *Enforcement Guidelines on Article 82*, in which the Commission has attempted to apply a more economic approach,[32] although it has been somewhat restricted in doing so because of the clarity of the case law on the matter.[33] Yet, in the *Enforcement Guidelines on Article 82* the Commission applies average avoidable costs (AAC) as a benchmark for predation instead of average variable costs (AVC), which seems to be the EU Courts' preferred standard. The Commission makes the assumption that AAC better reflects the possible sacrifice the company is making.[34] It also employs Long-Run Average Incremental Costs (LRAIC) instead of Average Total Costs (ATC).[35] On the face of it, this change is unlikely to affect the outcome of a cost analysis in relation to predation. It is the expansion of the AKZO test which is of greater risk to dominant undertakings. In addition to the two situations confirmed by the EU Courts as predatory pricing, pricing below AVC (which in the guidance paper is below AAC) and pricing below ATC (now below LRAIC) when part of a plan to exclude a competitor, the Commission seems to have included a third situation, namely where the dominant undertaking is 'deliberately incurring losses or foregoing profits in the short term' to foreclose a competitor.[36] If this conduct '[leads] in the short term to net revenues lower than could have been expected from a reasonable alternative conduct, that is to say, whether the dominant undertaking incurred a loss that it could have avoided' it is illegal.[37] In other words, the Commission will see pricing above LRAIC, but where the undertaking is still making a profit sacrifice as abusive.[38] However, the EU Courts' persistent use of the AKZO test, most recently in *France Telecom*, does not support above-cost predatory pricing.[39] Second, according to Gravengaard and Kjaersgaard, the only competitors a dominant company is likely to exclude through profit sacrifice above costs are *less* efficient competitors,[40] rather than 'as efficient' competitors, which the

[30] Ibid, at para 110.

[31] Ibid, at para 112.

[32] See Chapter 1.

[33] See Joanna Goyder and Albertina Albors-Llorens, *Goyder's EC Competition Law* (5th edn, Oxford: OUP, 2009), pp 323–4.

[34] *Commission's Enforcement Guidelines on Article 82* (n 16 above), para 64 and footnote 3.

[35] Ibid, para 26.

[36] Ibid, para 63.

[37] Ibid, para 65.

[38] See Martin A. Gravengaard and Niels Kjaersgaard, 'The EU Commission Guidance on Exclusionary Abuse of Dominance – and Its Consequences in Practice' [2010] 31(7) *ECLR* 285–305, p 303 and John Temple-Lang, 'Article 82 EC – The Problems and The Solution' *Institutions and Markets Series*, Fondazione Eni Enrico Mattei, Nota di Lavro 65.2009, (<http://papers.ssrn.com/sol3/papers.cfm?abstract_id=1467747> (last accessed 26 May 2010)), p 17.

[39] Cases C-395/96P and C-396/96P *Compagnie Maritime Belge Transports SA v Commission* [2000] ECR I–1365, [2000] 4 CMLR 1076 is the only exception, but the case is unique owing to its specific facts. See also Gravengaard and Kjaersgaard (n 38 above), p 303.

[40] Gravengaard and Kjaersgaard (n 38 above), p 303.

Commission claims to have targeted the enforcement guidelines towards protecting.[41] The ambiguity of this third situation if it were, against the odds, to be upheld by the EU Courts would cause severe legal uncertainty, in particular considering the lack of clear guidance and consideration of defences provided by the *Enforcement Guidelines on Article 82*.[42] Notably, defences such as start-up of big investments, reaching economies of scale in network industries, promotional expenditure, excess capacity in recessions, and meeting competition (at least above AAC) should be permitted for predatory pricing.[43] Only defences of economies of scale and 'efficiencies related to expanding the market' are listed in the *Enforcement Guidelines on Article 82*.[44] Unfortunately, the GC avoided a discussion of the meeting of competitors in *France Telecom* when it held that a dominant company does not have an absolute right to align prices.[45] The jury is therefore still out as to whether a defence of meeting of competitors is possible and if so when?

In general, the case law and the Commission's *Enforcement Guidelines on Article 82* suggest that ownership of an IPR confers no special position under Article 102 should a product incorporating an IPR be sold at below cost. Such conduct is governed in the usual way by the case law of the EU Courts interpreting Article 102.

11.2 MARGIN SQUEEZE

11.2.1 Introduction

Margin squeeze[46] has long been seen by the Commission as a separate abuse under Article 102 TFEU. However, it has only recently (since 2000) come within the Commission searchlight in cases involving companies in the telecommunications, gas, electricity, and water industries. This has mainly been in relation to the liberalization of those industries, and where companies in downstream markets are heavily relying on former state monopolies' infrastructures or essential raw materials.[47] Moreover, prior to *Deutsche Telekom*,[48] margin squeeze cases revolved around simple raw materials in mature markets. *Deutsche Telekom* is the first opportunity that the Court of Justice has had to examine margin squeeze abuse and confirm its stand-alone presence

[41] *Commission's Enforcement Guidelines on Article 82* (n 16 above), para 23; however, see para 24, where the Commission notes that 'in certain circumstances a less efficient competitor may also exert constraint which should be taken into account . . .'.

[42] Ibid, para 74 and Temple-Lang (n 38 above), p 18.

[43] Temple-Lang (n 38 above), p 18.

[44] *Commission's Enforcement Guidelines on Article 82* (n 16 above), para 74.

[45] T-340/03 *France Telecom*, para 187.

[46] Also sometimes referred to as 'price squeeze'.

[47] Robert O'Donoghue and A. Jorge Padilla, *The Law and Economics of Article 82 EC* (Oxford and Portland, Oregon: Hart Publishing, 2006), p 304.

[48] *Deutsche Telekom* Commission decision of 21 May 2003, [2003] OJ L 263/9, [2004] 4 CMLR 790, upheld upon appeal T-271/03 *Deutsche Telekom AG v Commission* [2008] ECR II–477, confirmed in Case C-280/08P *Deutsche Telecom v Commission* 14 October 2010.

as an abuse.[49] The case also marks a new generation of margin squeeze abuse in new products and emerging markets. It highlights not only the problems these types of markets cause in terms of defining the markets and dominance, but also raises an important policy concern of when to intervene: while the market is volatile and developing, thereby risking impeding the market expansion; or waiting until the market has matured and settled, risking that intervention becomes ineffective?[50]

Margin squeezing as an abuse arises where a vertically integrated dominant company uses its market power in the upstream market to leverage market power into the downstream market. This is achieved by pricing its upstream product to its rival at higher prices than what it charges its own downstream subsidiary, to squeeze the profit margins of the rivals and thereby decrease their profits and their ability to compete effectively in the downstream market. Eventually the rivals are forced to leave the downstream market.

The GC defined margin squeezing in *Industrie des Poudres Sphériques*:[51]

> Price squeezing may be said to take place when an undertaking which is in a dominant position on the market for an unprocessed product and itself uses part of its production for the manufacture of a more processed product, while at the same time selling off surplus unprocessed product on the market, sets the price at which it sells the unprocessed product at such a level that those who purchase it do not have a sufficient profit margin on the processing to remain competitive on the market for the processed product.[52]

In other words, margin squeezing can occur in two ways: either by the dominant company offering its own products in the downstream market at low prices or charging high prices for its upstream products.[53] Margin squeezing is a form of leveraging abuse and is thought to be applied by dominant companies to gain market power in the downstream market, although other anti-competitive strategies are restoring monopoly power in the upstream market or defensive leveraging. The latter is particularly potent for companies in high-tech markets with rapid growth and product development.[54]

Margin squeezing is therefore closely linked with refusal to supply and the issue of a duty to deal under Article 102, because of its ability to leverage market power from one market to another.[55] Margin squeezing is also closely linked to predatory pricing, because both can exclude 'as efficient as' competitors on the downstream market, but in contrast to predatory pricing, a margin squeeze abuse does not require that the dominant company has priced below cost. Finally, margin squeezing also shares similarities with excessive pricing.[56]

[49] Case C-280/08P *Deutsche Telekom AG v Commission, opinion of Advocate General* Ján Mazák delivered on 22 April 2010, at para 44.

[50] O'Donoghue and Padilla (n 47 above), p 332.

[51] T-5/97 *Industrie des Poudres Sphériques v Commission*, [2000] ECR II–3755, [2001] 4 CMLR 1020.

[52] Ibid, at para 178.

[53] Alison Jones, 'Margin Squeezes in Telecommunications Markets' in Steven Anderman and Ariel Ezrachi, *Intellectual Property and Competition Law: New Frontiers* (Oxford: OUP, 2011); O'Donoghue and Padilla (n 47 above), p 304.

[54] O'Donoghue and Padilla (n 47 above), p 308.

[55] Ibid, p 325.

[56] See *Deutsche Telekom* Commission decision at para 199, but note the legal tests applied to assess the two forms of abuse are remarkably different: for excessive pricing, the company's own costs are

In *Napier Brown/British Sugar*,[57] the Commission found that British Sugar had 'engaged in a price cutting campaign leaving an insufficient margin for a packager and seller of retail sugar, as efficient as British Sugar itself in its packaging and selling operations, to survive in the long term.'[58] British Sugar was dominant in both the market for sugar beet and retail sugar and had engaged in other forms of anti-competitive practices, such as tying, refusal to supply, and offering fidelity rebates.[59]

In *Industrie des Poudres Sphériques*, the GC rejected the claim of margin squeezing because of insufficient evidence, illustrating that for margin squeezing to be effective and thereby abusive, it must be able to eliminate an equally efficient competitor from the market. Industrie des Poudres Sphériques had argued that Péchiney Électrométallurgie (PEM) had abused its dominant position in the low-oxygen primary calcium metal market, the raw material for broken calcium metal, by selling the low-oxygen primary calcium metal at excessively high prices and offering the derived product thereof, the broken calcium metal, at very low prices.[60] The GC held that predatory pricing cannot be based on a competitor's cost performance. In other words, the actual 'squeeze' on the company's price margin may stem from the fact that the company is not as efficient as the dominant company rather than the dominant company behaving in an abusive manner.[61] The GC went on to note that, equally, a dominant company cannot be forced to sell at prices below its own manufacturing costs.[62]

In *Deutsche Telekom*,[63] Deutsche Telekom was accused of charging unfair prices to wholesale customers for access to its local network. Deutsche Telekom was found to have a dominant position in the 'local loop' market; that is the physical circuit connecting the end-user's premises to the local switching point.[64] Deutsche Telekom provided both retail services in the 'local loop' market and also wholesale availability in terms of access to the local loop for other operators to offer the same retail service to end-users. The complainant argued that the prices Deutsche Telekom was charging for wholesale availability to the local loop exceeded the prices it charged for retail services of that local loop, leaving its price margins so low that competitors could not compete

compared to similar products in the same or related markets, whereas for margin squeezing, the 'excessiveness' of the price is measured in relation to the relevant price and profit margin on the downstream market. One is focused upon costs, the other upon profits. O'Donoghue and Padilla (n 47 above), p 322.

[57] *Napier Brown/British Sugar* [1988] OJ L 284/41.

[58] Ibid, at para 65.

[59] Ibid, at paras 64 and 75–6.

[60] Ibid, at paras 177–9.

[61] Faull and Nikpay (eds), *The EC Law of Competition* (Oxford: OUP, 2007), para 4.291.

[62] *Napier Brown/British Sugar* at para 179.

[63] *Deutsche Telekom* Commission decision upheld upon appeal in T-271/03 *Deutsche Telekom* and C-280/08P *Deutsche Telecom*. The case should be compared with the US cases *Verizon Communications Inc v Law Offices of Curtis v Trinko LLP*, 540 US 398 (2004) and *Pacific Bell v linkLine Communications Inc*, 555 US (2009), in particular the latter shares factual similarities with *Deutsche Telekom Deutsche Telekom*, yet the US Supreme Court took a very different approach and found no antitrust violation.

[64] *Deutsche Telekom* Commission decision at para 96.

with Deutsche Telekom efficiently.[65] The case was further complicated by the fact that the wholesale prices were in fact set by the German regulatory authorities, but Deutsche Telekom still had control over the retail services pricing.[66] The Commission applied a margin squeeze test, stating that

> there is an abusive margin squeeze if the difference between the retail prices charged by a dominant undertaking and the wholesale prices it charges its competitors for comparable services is negative, or insufficient to cover the product-specific costs to the dominant operator of providing its own retail services on the downstream market . . . especially where other providers are excluded from competition on the downstream market even if they are at least as efficient as the established operator.[67]

Deutsche Telekom however, argued that there could not be any abuse as it had not engaged in below-cost selling or predation.[68] The GC upheld the Commission decision upon appeal and at the same time confirmed the Commission test to margin squeeze abuses.[69] It held that the abusive nature of Deutsche Telekom's conduct derived from 'the unfairness of the spread between its prices for wholesale access and its retail prices' and the Commission was not required to demonstrate that the retail prices were abusive as such.[70] The GC also rejected the defendant's claim that the margin squeeze had no effect on the market. Instead the GC held that owing to Deutsche Telekom's monopoly its wholesale services were

> indispensable to enabling a competitor to enter into competition with the applicant on the downstream market in retail access services, a margin squeeze between the applicant's wholesale and retail charges will in principle hinder the growth of competition in the downstream markets. If the applicant's retail prices are lower than its wholesale charges, or if the spread between the applicant's wholesale and retail charges is insufficient to enable an equally efficient operator to cover its product-specific costs of supplying retail access services, a potential competitor who is just as efficient as the applicant would not be able to enter the retail access services market without suffering losses.[71]

11.2.2 Margin squeeze and intellectual property rights

Although there have so far not been any margin squeeze abuses in relation to IPRs, the concerns raised in the telecommunications industry cases are to some extent transferable to IPRs. In particular, IPR cases involving refusal to license, because in these cases, similarly to the cases in telecommunications industry, the questions of whether, when and if on what conditions access to the essential facility or IPR should be granted

[65] Ibid, at paras 1–4 and 102.
[66] Ibid, at para 104.
[67] Ibid, at paras 1078.
[68] Ibid, at para 104.
[69] T-271/03 *Deutsche Telekom AG v Commission* [2008] ECR II–477 at paras 183–93.
[70] Ibid, at para 167.
[71] Ibid, at para 237.

are of great importance to provide competition in a downstream market to flourish.[72] The main difficulty is to ensure that competition in the downstream market is not encouraged with detriment to innovation and product development in the upstream market.[73]

In the *Enforcement Guidelines on Article 82,* the Commission sees margin squeezing as a form of refusal to supply and notes that where an equally efficient competitor is not able to trade profitably on the downstream market because the price charged by the dominant company on the upstream market is comparatively too high, this will be seen as a refusal. The refusal will become an enforcement priority when (a) it relates to a product or service indispensable for the effective competition in the downstream market; (b) the refusal is likely to lead to the elimination of effective competition on the downstream market; and (c) the refusal is likely to lead to consumer harm.[74] A prime example of the application of these three conditions in relation to IPR is the *EU Microsoft* case discussed in Chapter 7.[75] The Commission continues to observe that consideration should be given to the effects a supply obligation may have on the input owner's incentive to invest and innovate upstream and realize an adequate return on its investments.[76] However, in markets where regulation already places an obligation upon the dominant company to supply, the Commission will presume that the 'necessary balancing of incentives has already been made by the public authority' when imposing such supply obligation.[77] An example is in markets where the company's dominance has been sheltered because of 'special or exclusive rights or has been financed by state resources'.[78] The Commission is clearly referring here to the *Deutsche Telekom* cases; however, the situation is undoubtedly applicable to IPR and other essential facilities, and certainly regulatory industries are not exempted from the competition rules.

72 Jones (n 53 above).

73 Ibid. This is also recognized by the Commission: *Commission's Enforcement Guidelines on Article 82* (n 16 above), para 75.

74 *Commission's Enforcement Guidelines on Article 82* (n 16 above), para 82.

75 Case T-201/04 *Microsoft Corp v Commission* [2007] ECR II–3601.

76 *Commission's Enforcement Guidelines on Article 82* (n 16 above), paras 82 and 89.

77 Ibid, para 82.

78 Ibid, para 82.

Part III

ARTICLE 101 AND INTELLECTUAL PROPERTY LICENSING IN A MODERNIZED SETTING

12

INTRODUCTION: INTELLECTUAL PROPERTY RIGHTS LICENSING AND COMPETITION POLICY GENERALLY

12.1	Introduction	201
12.2	The Modernization of EU Law Applicable to IP Licensing Agreements	203
12.3	The New Analytical Tools Provided by the New *More* Economic Approach	207

12.1 INTRODUCTION

To IP owners, an entitlement to exploit IPR such as patents not only includes the right to make use of and sell the protected technology; it also includes the right to license it to another to make use of or sell it. Many inventors who have invested in R&D find themselves unable to exploit the full commercial potential of their investment. Either they cannot enter and manufacture in all territories in the EU or they cannot manufacture all possible technical applications of the invention. As we have seen in Part II, some firms choose a business strategy of being purely research-led organizations leaving manufacturing to other organizations taking part in standard setting projects.

In such situations, a licence may be the only acceptable way in which a reward to invention can be obtained while still keeping a measure of control over the exploitation of the invention. The restrictions in the field of technical application or geographical territory in the licence appear to be merely subdivisions of the original right conferred by legislation; they seem to have no adverse effects on third parties who would otherwise be subject to the exclusive rights of the original right owner. Certainly, to the parties to IP licensing agreements, the case for the licensor's entitlement to pass on the exclusivity enjoyed under the statutory grant seems unanswerable.

To a large extent, however, IP owners have tended to underestimate the importance of the difference between individual exploitation and contractual exploitation within the logic of competition law, particularly where the exclusivity of the licensor is shared with the licensee. From a competition law perspective, bilateral and multilateral agreements entail a risk that the parties may be using the agreement as a means to obtain dominance or to share markets or fix prices in a way that individual undertakings acting autonomously would not be able to do. Indeed, in certain circumstances a licensing agreement *by itself* may be regarded as a merger within the meaning of the Merger Regulation[1] and be subject to an assessment for substantial impediment to effective competition.

Modern competition law recognizes that the process of technology transfer, essentially the process of technological IP licensing, is on balance a highly pro-competitive activity and compatible with Article 101 because it helps to increase the reward for innovative effort and the incentives for others to invest in R&D. It spreads the level of technology by creating incentives for the introduction of production of the product in new territories. Because a licensing agreement invariably requires some degree of manufacture as well as sale, it results in a technological lift to the licensee that would not occur if the licensor merely manufactured elsewhere and exported the finished product into the EU for distribution. Technology licensing agreements also introduce new products to existing markets adding to competition and in some cases actually creating new markets. Hence, many licensing agreements are now not caught at all by Article 101.

Competition policy also recognizes that many specific restrictions in licences are necessary to induce licensees to enter into a licensing agreement.[2] In the course of drafting the IP licensing agreement, the parties must inevitably place certain contractual restrictions upon each other to achieve the object of the agreement. Many licensees will be reluctant to undertake the risks of manufacture and sale of a new product without the protection of an exclusive licence that limits competition from the licensor and other licensees within the licensed territory. Most licensors will not give an exclusive licence without the quid pro quo of a minimum royalties clause. In addition they will not license their IP without an array of clauses designed to protect the integrity and value of their IP once it is licensed to the licensee. They will, for example, insist on certain obligations of confidentiality in respect of know how, limits on sublicensing, quality controls on materials used, and limits on the use of the licensed IP once the licensing agreement has expired. They may also insist on obligations by the licensee to grant back licences for improvements and not to exploit technologies that compete with the licensor as well as an obligation not to challenge the validity of the licensed IPR. Many of these may be viewed as commercially indispensable both to induce licensors to license their technology in the first place. Hence many individual provisions in licensing agreements will fall outside the scope of Article 101.

[1] Council Regulation (EC) No 139/2004 of 20 January 2004 on the control of concentrations between undertakings (the Merger Regulation), OJ L 24, 29 January 2004, pp 1–22.

[2] Commission Notice, Guidelines on the application of Article 81 of the EC Treaty [now Article 101 TFEU] to technology transfer agreements [2004] OJ C101/2 (hereafter TTA Guidelines), paras 9 and 17.

On occasion, however, contractual restraints can be used as a device to create restrictions on the process of competition. Some royalty arrangements can help to underpin a price fixing scheme. In some technology transfer agreements the exclusive territorial protection needed by licensees or output restrictions can, on occasion, be used by clever draftsmen as a cover for market sharing agreements. In a European perspective, they can also reinforce the isolation of national markets from the single market by excessive territorial protection. Moreover, some IP licensing agreements have the potential to create conditions of dominant market power or collusion in the licensed market which foreclose competitors from entering that market. These practices harm consumers and can be used to exclude competitors from markets, either for the products made using the licensed technology or for the IP-protected technology itself.

Competition policies have long sought sifting mechanisms that could accurately distinguish between pro-competitive IP licences and those employed in anti-competitive commercial practices. For a long period the method used within the EU was to define anti-competitive harm in terms of contractual restraints on the economic freedom to compete and/or those that disturbed rivalry on existing markets. Once potentially harmful IP licensing agreements were identified with this broad brush approach, the parties were required to consult formalistic block exemption regulations to obtain exemption to assure the enforceability of the agreement under the competition law rules. In recent years, the need to use more economic analysis in appraising licensing agreements and measuring their competitive effects has become widely accepted. Following the lead established by the USA in 1996, the EU eventually adopted a *more* economic approach as part of its modernization reform of Article 101 generally.

12.2 THE MODERNIZATION OF EU LAW APPLICABLE TO IP LICENSING AGREEMENTS

The wider 'modernization' reform of Article 101, generally, has introduced four new features to the regulatory framework for IP licensing agreements.

First, the new framework of analysis contained in the Technology Transfer Block Exemption Regulation (TTBER)[3] and its Guidelines (the TTA Guidelines)[4], in common with the other block exemption regulations (BERs) and their Guidelines,[5] which have been part of the modernization reform, introduce a more economic goal to EU competition policy. While not abandoning its earlier goals of protecting freedom of action and vertical integration, the new framework modifies these goals by adding the

[3] TTA Guidelines (n 2 above), paras 9 and 17.

[4] Commission Regulation (EC) No 772/2004 of 27 April 2004 on the application of Article 81(3) of the Treaty [now Article 101(3) TFEU] to categories of technology transfer agreements OJ L 123, 27 April 2004, pp 11–17 (hereafter the TTBER).

[5] TTA Guidelines (n 2 above).

more economic goal of testing agreements according to the criterion of effect on consumer welfare.

Second, following the realignment of goals, the instruments of EU competition policy have been re-oriented to use economic analysis to concentrate upon the potential anti-competitive harms of unilateral and coordinated effects. As a result, lawyers must now be aware of the distinction between vertical and horizontal agreements and the extent of market power created by licensing agreements. One effect of this reform is that competition policy has become less interventionist with many more licensing agreements not caught by the competition rules.

Third, the nature of the block exemption system and along with it TTBER, has changed. The new BERs only offer a safe harbour and not the legal certainty of the old style BERs. Previous BERs in the IP licensing field offered an exemption to the parties without a market share limit and subject only to a formal power of withdrawal by the Commission or a national competition authority. The current TTBER is given a reduced role within the legal framework. Today if the agreement falls outside the scope of the safe harbour offered by the TTBER, it may nevertheless qualify for exemption under Article 101(3) using the TTA Guidelines and the general Article 101(3) Guidelines.[6] The new TTBER is no longer as useful as a source of legal protection standing on its own.

Fourth, the enforcement of Article 101 has been changed procedurally. There is no longer a requirement of prior notification of agreements to the Commission to obtain provisional validity. The legal status of agreements is to be assessed at any time the issue of enforceability arises on the basis of the compatibility of the agreement and its provisions with the prohibition in Article 101. Moreover, the enforcement process as a whole has been decentralized. The national authorities and courts now have jurisdiction to apply the balancing test of the four conditions of Article 101(3) as well as 101(1).[7]

These reforms have been intended to usher in a greater reliance upon self-assessment by the parties to commercial agreements under Article 101, either by finding that an agreement fits within a block exemption regulation or by legal advisers assessing the validity of the contents of the agreement in the light of Article 101(1) and 101(3) and the Guidelines accompanying the new BERs, EU Courts' cases, and Commission decisions and Notices. They were also instituted to free up the Commission to concentrate upon important competition issues such as cartels, mergers, and abuses of dominant positions, rather than becoming too involved in examining agreements with only marginal significance for competition concerns.

[6] See eg Commission Regulation 330/2010 of 20 April 2010 on the application of Article 101(3) of the Treaty on the Functioning of the European Union to categories of vertical agreements and concerted practices OJ L 102, 23 April 2010, pp 1–7 and Commission Notice, Guidelines on Vertical Restraints OJ C130, 19 May 2010, p 1.

[7] Commission Notice, Guidelines on the application of Article 81(3) of the Treaty, OJ C101, 27 April 2004, pp 97–118.

The use of a *more* economic approach offers competition law a much improved sifting mechanism to distinguish between the pro-and anti-competitive IP licensing agreements. The greater acceptance that IP licensing agreements are generally pro-competitive and compatible with Article 101[8] allows the authorities to concentrate far more on the pathology of IP licensing, leaving the greater portion of pro-competitive licensing to freedom of contract. They do this by more clearly identifying the potential anti-competitive harms of licensing agreements, by introducing a more nuanced approach to the market power of the parties to licensing agreements, and by drawing a clearer distinction between IP licensing agreements between competitors and those between non-competitors. This allows the introduction of two different regulatory regimes. There is a more extensive assessment of IP licensing agreements between competitors because of their greater anti-competitive risks and there is a far more lenient regime applied to agreements between non- competitors because of their higher propensity to create economic benefits and lower propensity to cause harmful effects. However, the benefits of a less interventionist regime for agreements between non-competitors are accompanied by a major change in the nature of the competition assessment of IP licensing agreements in four important respects.

The Commission has chosen to fit the assessment of IP licensing into the modernized framework of Article 101 and keep the special treatment of IP licensing agreements to a minimum. As the TTA Guidelines proclaim, the new TTBER's assessment of IP licensing takes 'due account of the dynamic aspects of technology licensing' making 'in particular... no presumption that intellectual property rights and licensing agreements as such give rise to competition concerns'.[9] This appears to echo the assertion of the 1995 US IP Licensing Guidelines[10] that the characteristics of IPRs that make them distinct 'can be taken into account in the standard antitrust analysis ... and do not require the application of fundamentally different principles'.[11]

Thus, the new TTBER and the TTA Guidelines have been drafted to harmonize the treatment of IP licensing agreements with that of other agreements under the modernized application of Article 101. The TTBER provides a 'safe harbour' exemption for licensing agreements and the TTA Guidelines both explain the approach embodied in the TTBER and give guidance on the application of Article 101(3) to licensing agreements that fall outside the scope of the TTBER.

Yet by harmonizing the treatment of IP licensing with the other BERs, the *more* economic approach removes much of the special treatment of IP licensing enjoyed under the 1996 TTBER[12] which provided a dedicated self-contained exemption

[8] Council Regulation 1/2003 on the implementation of the rules on competition laid down in Articles 81 and 82 of the Treaty, OJ L 1, 4 January 2003, Recital 4 and Arts 5 and 6.

[9] See TTA Guidelines (n 2 above), paras 9 and 17.

[10] Ibid, para 9.

[11] *Antitrust Guidelines for the Licensing of Intellectual Property*, issued by the US Department of Justice and the Federal Trade Commission, 5 April 1995 (<http://www.usdoj.gov/atr/public/guidelines/0558.htm> (last accessed 10 June 2006)).

[12] Ibid, Section 2.1.

providing legal certainty for the length of the agreement. With modernization, the competitive assessment of licensing agreements under the 2004 TTBER and the TTA Guidelines takes some account of the special features of IP licensing but it is an integral part of the wider reform of Article 101 and there is a common analytical framework for all the new BERs. The Commission's General Guidelines to Article 101(3) apply across the board to IP licensing agreements as well as other commercial agreements.[13]

One adverse impact of this reform is the dramatic reduction in legal certainty in the assessment of IP licensing agreements. In the past, BERs in the IP licensing field offered an exemption to the parties without a market share limit and subject only to a formal power of withdrawal by the Commission or a national competition authority. The current TTBER, instead of providing a source of certain legal protection standing on its own, now offers only a conditional 'safe harbour' which is no longer applicable once the parties' market share exceeds the market share limits.[14]

A second effect of the new legal regime is the premium it now places upon self-assessment by the parties and their legal advisers. If a licensing agreement falls outside the scope of the safe harbour offered by the TTBER, it is neither presumed lawful or unlawful and may still qualify for exemption under Article 101(3).[15] However, at that stage the assessment of its legal status must be done by the parties themselves bearing the burden of proving that the agreement is exemptible using the TTA Guidelines, the general Article 101(3) Guidelines, and the prohibition in Article 101. There is no longer a requirement of prior notification of agreements to the Commission to obtain provisional validity or the option of applying to the Commission for individual exemption.

Finally, the nature of the method of self-assessment has changed in fundamental respects. It has entailed the abandonment of more than two decades of a purely legal formalism which allowed lawyers to analyse licensing agreements clause by clause and compare each clause with the black lists, white lists and grey lists of the block exemption regulations available from 1984 to 1996. The new methods of self-assessment require lawyers to make an accurate *legal* assessment of the enforceability of IP licensing agreements by using analytical tools which are now heavily influenced by economic principles. It requires lawyers today to appreciate how economic thinking now permeates the legal rules.

At the same time, the *more* economic approach is not a pure economic approach. The modernized interpretation of Article 101 does not entirely jettison its foundations in the earlier case law. There is an important place for many of the earlier judgments of the Court of Justice. There are earlier judgments of the EU Courts that reinforce the new methodology adopted by the Commission. But equally importantly, the new model adopted in the TTBER and TTA Guidelines is subject to modification by the

[13] Commission Regulation 240/96 on technology transfer Agreements [1996] OJ L 31/2.

[14] Guidelines on the application of Article 81(3) [now 101(3) TFEU] (n 7 above), paras 3–6.

[15] TTBER (n 4 above), Arts 3 and 8; see also Recitals 10–12 and TTA Guidelines (n 2 above), paras 65–73.

new judgments of the General Court and Court of Justice.[16] For example, some of the recent case law has stressed a continued role for older doctrines associated with a less economic approach to Article 101.[17] Nevertheless, much of the assessment of the limits on IP licensing established by the competition rules now consists of the application of economic analysis within the framework of the legal rules.

12.3 THE NEW ANALYTICAL TOOLS PROVIDED BY THE NEW *MORE* ECONOMIC APPROACH

The new *more* economic approach therefore requires lawyers to develop an appreciation of four new economic concepts that influence the legal rules in order to make an assessment of IP licensing agreements:

(1) a new approach to defining markets for IP licensing agreements;

(2) a new appreciation of the differences between agreements between competitors and those between non-competitors as well as the different anti-competitive risks attached to each. This has resulted in virtually two separate competition law regimes, one for each type of agreement;

(3) a new approach that incorporates the market power of the parties to the agreement more centrally into the competition assessment; and

(4) a new approach to defining the anti-competitive harms from IP licensing agreements.

Together these analytical tools help the competition authorities and the parties more accurately to assess the potential risks of harmful effects of licensing agreements. They will also apply both to the assessment of exemption and to the assessment of whether or not an agreement or provision is caught in the first place by Article 101.

12.3.1 A new method of defining the relevant market for IP licensing agreements

The definition of markets for the purpose of assessing IP licensing shares most of the characteristics of the general approach to defining markets under EU law. The Commission reiterates that its approach to defining the relevant market is laid down in its general market definition guidelines.[18] This assessment requires an economic awareness of methods of testing for substitutes. But it also requires an understanding about how the competition authorities will exercise their discretion in choosing the relevant product with which to begin the search for substitutes. If there are no

[16] TTBER (n 4 above), Recital 12, see also TTA Guidelines (n 2 above), paras 17–18 and 37.

[17] See eg Case T-328/03 *O2 (Germany) GmbH & Co v Commission*, 2 May 2006.

[18] See Case C-209-07 *Competition Authority v Beef Industry Development Society Ltd et al* [2008] ECR I-8637; Case C-501/06P *GlaxoSmithKline v Commission* [2009] ECR I-9291.

substitutes then the IPR is in a market of its own. If there are substitutes, the relevant market can be used as a basis of measuring market shares and other components of market power. Furthermore by defining relevant markets, it is possible to get clearer definitions of the difference between licensing agreements between competitors and those between non-competitors.

The TTA Guidelines give considerable assistance in seeing how the Commission will exercise its discretion in defining relevant markets in relation IP licensing agreements.

The starting point is the distinction drawn in the TTA Guidelines between product markets and technology markets.[19] There is a further type of market called an innovation market[20] but this is more relevant for merger cases than licensing agreements.

The 'product market' refers to the market for the licensed product involved in the dispute. As used in Article 3 of the TTBER it refers to the relevant goods and service markets in both their geographic and product context.[21] The method used to define the 'product market' is to include all products that are regarded by buyers as substitutes for the contract products incorporating the licensed technology.[22] It is meant to be viewed as the downstream market in relation to the 'technology' market.

The 'technology' market refers to the licensed technology itself and its substitutes, ie other technologies regarded by licensees as substitutable for the licensed technology by virtue of their intended use and their royalties The method is similar to the product market definition. It starts with the technology marketed by the licensor and identifying other technologies to which licensees could switch if royalties rise. It is viewed as an upstream or input market.

It is often necessary to examine both markets when assessing the object and effects of an IP licensing agreement.[23] Both markets are important for determining the market power of the parties and both markets are relevant to the determination of whether or not an agreement is between non-competitors or competitors.

12.3.2 The distinction between IP licensing agreements between competitors and those between non-competitors

The second economic tool that has dramatically altered the new legal framework is the distinction drawn between IP agreements between competitors and those between non-competitors. This distinction is more refined than the old division between vertical and horizontal agreements. A relationship between licensor and licensee is 'vertical', if the parties to a licensing agreement operate in different markets. The typical example would be an agreement between an inventor and a manufacturer or between

[19] Commission Notice on the definition of relevant market for the purposes of Community competition law OJ C 372, 9 December 1997, pp 5–13, [1998] 4 CMLR 177 p 5. See the discussion in Chapter 4 of this book.

[20] See TTA Guidelines (n 2 above), paras 19–25.

[21] Ibid, para 25.

[22] Ibid, para 20.

[23] Ibid, para 21.

specialist component manufacturers and assembly manufacturers; these are viewed as a significantly smaller risk to competition than 'horizontal' licensing agreements, ie those between competitors on the same market or likely potential competitors.

However, the vertical/horizontal distinction is too crude from an economic perspective particularly in high tech sectors. The distinction between agreements between competitors and non-competitors offers a more accurate sifting mechanism and results in a widening of the category of relatively harmless agreements.[24]

All earlier BERs regulating IP licensing took the view that most IP licensing agreements should be treated as potentially 'horizontal' agreements between competitors possibly because of a concern that the licensee often evolves into a potential competitor to the licensee as the result of obtaining experience with manufacturing the new technology. Yet the overwhelming evidence is that at the time a licensing agreement is signed, most are actually agreements between non-competitors. The economic realism of the new TTBER has resulted in a re-evaluation of prohibited restraints in the case of licensing agreements between non-competitors and the creation of a deservedly more benign regulatory regime. This reform is far-reaching because it applies not only within the confines of the safe haven but also up to a point of where the parties' market shares may be as high as 40–50 per cent as long as they fall below dominance.

Moreover, the TTBER gives an expansive definition of 'agreements between non-competitors'. It applies not only to the paradigm vertical case of an agreement between an inventor and a manufacturer but also to an agreement between two manufacturers as long as they are not competitors in respect of the licensed product. In 'product markets' competitors are defined as 'actual' competitors, ie competing undertakings who in the absence of the technology transfer agreement would have been active on the relevant product and geographic markets on which the contract products are sold without infringing each other's IPRs.[25] In 'product markets', in addition to actual competitors, there is a need to look at 'potential' competitors who realistically are in a position to undertake the necessary investments and accept the switching costs of entering the same market had the price of the product been raised. In 'technology markets', only 'actual' competitors are considered.

A further feature of the TTBER that is helpful to IP licensing is that it defines the parties as 'competitors' or 'non-competitors' at the time the contract is made and will not allow the natural competition that may develop as the result of the licensing agreement as the manufacturing expertise of the licensee matures to affect the designation of the contract. If the parties are non-competitors at the time the agreement is made, they will not be redesignated for the purposes of the exemption during the duration of the agreement unless the agreement itself is materially amended. The distinction between agreements between competitors and agreements between non-competitors

[24] Ibid, para 20.

[25] See TTBER (n 4 above), Art 1(j)(i) and (ii) and TTA Guidelines (n 2 above), para 27.

has led to two sets of rules both in respect of the market share limits in the TTBER[26] and the types of hard core restrictions prohibited in licensing agreements.[27]

The distinction between agreements between competitors and those between non-competitors is a vital indicator but it is only an indicator. Agreements between competitors using IP licences are not always anti-competitive; indeed, R&D joint ventures, new technology production joint ventures, and technology pools and standard setting organizations are often highly pro-competitive. However, agreements between competitors are a more fertile seedbed for anti-competitive practices. There are greater temptations and opportunities for collusion between competitors in the form of price-fixing or market sharing cartels for goods designed to extract higher returns from customers and to prevent entry by other competitors. IP licences, both genuine and sham, can be used to reinforce such collaborative arrangements. Consequently, the restraints in horizontal agreements such as cross-licences and patent pools are often prime candidates for close examination by competition authorities.

In the case of agreements between non-competitors too, examples can be found of anti-competitive collusion: for instance, where both licensor and licensee have a manufacturing capacity, or where such relationships help to reinforce collusion between competitors. However, the risks are significantly lower than in the case of agreements between competitors, and this is so for four main reasons.

First, the motive for licensing is often the need to complement the existing capabilities of each firm. The licensor needs the manufacturing capabilities of the licensee. The licensee needs the R&D results of the licensor. It has often been pointed out by economists that it is only through cooperative relationships such as licensing that the efficiencies of scale and scope can be achieved to allow innovation to occur. There are often good indications when a relationship is essentially between non-competitors. For example, the manufacturing capacity of the licensor at the start of the relationship could make it plain that the possibility that it could be active on the market is unlikely. A second and separate indication would be whether or not the licensee is committed to using the licensor's trade mark for the duration of the contract. The absence of a trade mark obligation does not imply collusion but the use of the licensor's trade mark creates a strong presumption that the relationship is between non-competitors and at least in the latter case is likely to remain so for the period of the contract.

Secondly, agreements between non-competitors, in contrast to agreements between competitors, introduce a new competitor into a market and help to diffuse the licensed product or process throughout the economy.

Thirdly, restraints in agreements between non-competitors can promote efficiencies by allowing the licensor to induce the licensee to invest in the new product or process, achieve efficiencies in production and distribution, and compete more effectively in the new market.

[26] TTBER (n 4 above), Art 1(j)(ii); TTA Guidelines (n 2 above), paras 24 and 31.

[27] Ibid, Art 3.

Finally, as with all relationships between non-competitors, as long as there is robust competition in the product market between brands, such 'inter-brand' competition can operate to regulate the effects on price of the absence of competition within each manufacturing and distribution chain, ie 'intra-brand' competition. If there is strong competition in the final product market, market forces operate to limit the amount that any one brand can extract from consumers. The main economic effects of intra-brand collusion in such a case would be limited to influencing the distribution of the overall profit of the brand within the distribution chain itself and possibly improving the quality of inter-brand competition. For these reasons, most competition law systems operate with different presumptions about agreements between competitors and those between non-competitors.

Given these well established premises of regulation of IP licensing by competition policies, the EU now introduces two different legal regimes within the same TTBER and its Guidelines: one for agreements between competitors and one for agreements between non-competitors. This offers an essential analytical tool to distinguish anti-competitive licensing practices from the pro-competitive licensing practices by concentrating on the high-risk categories of agreements between competitors.

12.3.3 The new approach to the measurement of the market power of the parties to IP licensing agreements

A further feature of the new EU competition policy is the more nuanced approach to market power in the legal rules. Thus, depending upon the extent of market power enjoyed by the parties to IP licensing agreements, there will be different rules of assessment to be applied. The most obvious example is the market share limits to the safe harbour of the BER: 20 per cent for agreements between competitors and 30 per cent for agreements between non-competitors. This applies to agreements as a whole. The less obvious examples are the way the assessment of individual clauses in the IP licensing agreement will be affected by the degree of market power enjoyed by the parties.

An IP licensing agreement is likely to have anti-competitive effects in only a narrow range of market conditions: ie where the parties to the agreement will have considerable market power after the agreement is made; where there is a high degree of concentration in the licensor's market; where a high proportion of licensees in that market are subject to similar restraints; and where access to the market is restricted by entry barriers. Again, these factors are indicators. Even high levels of market concentration are not necessarily conclusive evidence of anti-competitive effect. Much depends upon the overall evaluation. The new approach is to examine the parties to licensing agreements to determine the extent of their market power. If the market power of the parties is significant even though short of being dominant there may be risks attached to extending exclusivity. If the market power is sufficiently low then the risks are smaller. The TTBER and TTA Guidelines identify the main categories of anti-competitive provisions as hard core restrictions but they also introduce a methodology for assessing all provisions that takes into account the fact that agreements are between competitors and the market power of the parties to the agreement in assessing possible unilateral or coordinated effects.[28] These restrictions in licensing agreements are not always anti-competitive but they are the main categories of provisions in licensing agreements which require the most careful monitoring. Again, these tools are needed for assessment both for the purposes of exemption under Article 101(3) but also for the purposes of deciding whether or not Article 101(1) applies in the first place.

12.3.4 The new categorization of the potentially harmful effects of IP licensing agreements

The modernized legal framework in TTBER and the TTA Guidelines classify the potential anti-competitive effects of licensing agreements into two categories: 'unilateral' or 'coordinated' effects. This categorization brings the assessment of licensing agreements into line with assessment of other commercial agreements and mergers.[29]

'Coordinated effects' include the harms produced by collusion between competitors either in a market for the licensed products, 'the product market', or in a market for the IP-protected technologies, 'the technology market.' The collusion often takes the form of price fixing or market sharing which results in the harm of reducing *inter-brand* competition. In the IP licensing context, the harm is the reduction to *inter-technology* competition, that is to say competition between licensors of IP-protected products in a relevant product market or competition between different technologies in a relevant technology market. Coordinated effects can also harm *intra-technology* competition, ie competition between licensees. For example a ban on all selling of a licensed product by one licensee into the territories of other licensees might reduce intra-technology in a national market. Of course there are partial limits on the possibilities of IP licensing agreements being used to curb intra-technology competition because of the doctrine of exhaustion. The licensor can bind the licensee but not the purchaser of the licensed product from the licensee. According to the doctrine of exhaustion, once the licensed product is placed on the market anywhere in the EU, it can be freely bought and sold anywhere else in the EU. Nevertheless, an IP licensing agreement has the capacity to reduce *intra-technology* competition between licensees of the same licensor.

'Unilateral effects' include the possibility of foreclosure of competitors from a technology market or a market for the licensed product either by raising rivals' costs or restricting their access to essential inputs or otherwise raising barriers to entry. The harm caused by unilateral effects almost always is the reduction in *inter-technology* competition.

To understand the nature of this new approach to assessing IP licensing agreements under Article 101, it is first necessary to look more closely at the conditions for clearance under Article 101(1) and exemption under Article 101(3) in general terms (Chapter 13) and then examine its detailed application to IP licensing agreements (Chapters 14–17).

[28] Ibid, Art 4.

[29] Resale price maintenance, tying arrangements, non-competition clauses, or exclusive dealing and grant backs.

13

THE STRUCTURE OF ARTICLE 101 TFEU AND IP LICENSING AGREEMENTS

13.1 Introduction 213
13.2 The Process of Exemption under Article 101(3) TFEU 215
13.3 Article 101(2) TFEU and Unenforceability 217
13.4 The Clearance of IP Licensing Agreements under Article 101(1) TFEU 218

13.1 INTRODUCTION

Article 101 contains a two-part structure, each part contributing to the determination whether any form of collaboration between two or more undertakings is pro- or anti-competitive. Article 101(1) provides the jurisdictional test to determine whether an agreement or concerted practice comes within the scope of the Article as a whole. It states:

1. The following shall be prohibited as incompatible with the internal market: all agreements between undertakings, decisions by associations of undertakings and concerted practices which may affect trade between Member States and which have as their object or effect the prevention, restriction or distortion of competition within the internal market, and in particular those which:

(a) directly or indirectly fix purchase or selling prices or any other trading conditions;

(b) limit or control production, markets, technical development, or investment;

(c) share markets or sources of supply;

(d) apply dissimilar conditions to equivalent transactions with other trading parties, thereby placing them at a competitive disadvantage;

(e) make the conclusion of contracts subject to acceptance by the other parties of supplementary obligations which, by their nature or according to commercial usage, have no connection with the subject of such contracts.

2. Any agreements or decisions prohibited pursuant to this Article shall be automatically void.

3. The provisions of paragraph 1 may, however, be declared inapplicable in the case of:
   — any agreement or category of agreements between undertakings,
   — any decision or category of decisions by associations of undertakings,
   — any concerted practice or category of concerted practices,

which contributes to improving the production or distribution of goods or to promoting technical or economic progress, while allowing consumers a fair share of the resulting benefit, and which does not:

(a) impose on the undertakings concerned restrictions which are not indispensable to the attainment of these objectives;

(b) afford such undertakings the possibility of eliminating competition in respect of a substantial part of the products in question.

In principle Article 101 can apply to a wide range of acts of collaboration between two or more undertakings.

In the IPR context, for example, Article 101(1) has been held to apply widely to individual licensing agreements; to Research & Development joint ventures[1] and standard setting organizations, to concerted practices involving licensing agreements;[2] to assignments of IPRs to third parties;[3] to trade mark delimitation agreements,[4] to cross-licensing agreements arising out of patent settlements[5] and patent or technology pools.[6] Moreover, in principle Article 101(1) applies to 'vertical agreements', ie agreements between non-competitors as well as to 'horizontal agreements,' ie agreements between competitors.[7] It is worth noting that the Court of Justice has repeatedly stated that an IP licensing agreement, as such, is not a 'restriction on competition',[8] but may fall within the scope of Article 101(1) whenever it is 'the subject, the means or the consequence of',[9] or 'serves to give effect to',[10] a commercial practice which has as its object or exercise the prevention, restriction, or distortion of competition in the common market.

13.1.1 The conditions of Article 101(1) TFEU

Under 101(1), an agreement is only prohibited if it meets all three of the provision's main conditions.

[1] See eg Commission's Notice on applicability of Article 101 to horizontal cooperation agreements 2001 OJ C3/2.

[2] See eg Case 395/87 *Lucazeau v SACEM* [1989] ECR 2811.

[3] See eg Case 40/70 *Sirena v Eda* [1971] ECR 3169.

[4] See eg Case C-9/93 *IHT Internationale Heiztechnik GmbH v Ideal-Standard GmbH* [1994] ECR I–2789.

[5] See Commission Notice, Guidelines on the application of Article 81 of the EC Treaty [now Article 101 TFEU] to technology transfer agreements [2004] OJ C101/2 (hereafter TTA Guidelines), para 204.

[6] Ibid, para 210.

[7] Cases 56 and 58/64 *Establissements Consten SA & Grundig-Verkaufts-GmbH v Commission* [1966] ECR 299, [1966] CMLR 418.

[8] See eg Case 262/81*Coditel v Ciné Vog Films (Coditel II)* [1982] ECR 3381, [1983] 1 CMLR 49 at para 14; see also Case 24/67 *Parke Davis v Probel* [1968] ECR 55, [1968] CMLR 47.

[9] See eg Case 78/70 *Deutsche Grammophon Gesellscharft mbH v Metro-SB-Grossmarketete GmbH & Co* [1971] ECR 487, [1971] CMLR 631, para 6.

[10] See eg *Coditel II, op cit* at para 14.

The first condition in Article 101(1) is that there must be evidence of *agreement or other form of collaboration between two or more 'undertakings'*. Insofar as the conduct of an IP owner consists of unilateral enforcement of such a right under national law, it will not be caught by Article 101 although it might be regulated by Article 102.

The second condition of Article 101(1) is that it applies only to agreements, decisions, and concerted practices which have an 'appreciable' quantitative *effect on interstate trade*. This condition is essentially a jurisdictional test for the application of the system of EU competition law in two important respects. It first establishes a territorial point: whether an agreement made inside or outside the EU is caught by EU competition law by virtue of its effects. Secondly, it defines the jurisdictional borderline between EU competition law and the domestic competition law of the Member States.

The third condition and the central regulatory condition in Article 101(1) is the requirement that the agreement has the *object or effect of preventing, restricting, or distorting competition*. If an IP licensing agreement is made between independent undertakings and has an appreciable effect on interstate trade, it is still necessary to show that it has as its *object* or *effect* the prevention, restriction, or distortion of competition before it is contrary to Article 101(1). This test is jurisdictional too in the sense that it constitutes a precondition to the application of Article 101(1). However, it is more complex because it involves a preliminary substantive assessment of the pro- or anti-competitive nature of the agreement and this assessment has changed quite dramatically in recent years. As we shall see, this test has been interpreted to incorporate (1) a concept of freedom of action which is designed to protect the economic autonomy of existing competition in markets, (2) an assessment of the object and effects of the agreement in its specific legal and economic context to ensure that its restrictive effects are significant or 'appreciable.' It also includes (3) an assessment of the effects of an agreement on the integration of the internal market and with modernization it introduces (4) an assessment of whether an agreement reduces consumer welfare in the market owing to unilateral or coordinated effects. We shall discuss these four factors in some depth in Section 13.4.

13.2 THE PROCESS OF EXEMPTION UNDER ARTICLE 101(3) TFEU

If an agreement or provision is caught by Article 101(1), it can nevertheless be saved from non-enforceability by being exempted under Article 101(3) as long as it meets four conditions.

(1) It must contribute 'to improving production and distribution of goods and promoting technical progress' as a necessary condition of exemption.

Article 101(3) formally recognizes the pro-competitive value of innovative agreements by this stipulation. Such agreements can provide economic benefits in the form of static as well as dynamic efficiencies.[11] Other appreciable benefits may also be able to meet this condition [12]

However, before these efficiency benefits can be accepted as a justification for a restrictive agreement under Article 101(1), three other conditions must be met.

(2) The first of these conditions is that the agreement must allow consumers a fair share of the resulting benefit.

This condition appears to require proof of economic benefits to consumers in the form of lower prices, delays in raising prices, increased production of goods or services, products of better quality, and new products which are demanded by consumers. This test also requires a fair balance to be struck between the profits gained and the benefits passed on to consumers. This condition could extend to a requirement that the benefits must compensate for the disadvantages they cause to competition.[13] Further, this condition includes the requirement that the benefits must be passed on to consumers in the same market in which the anti-competitive effects occur.[14] The fair share to consumers condition is therefore the clearest expression that the EU embraces a test of consumer welfare and not total welfare in assessing the net effect of agreements.

(3) The second condition is that the agreement must not contain restrictions on competition which are not 'indispensable to the attainment' of the above objective.

The indispensability requirement on its face indicates a proportionality test. However, the Guidelines on Article 101(3) suggest that 'the decisive factor is whether economic benefits are produced as a result of the agreement that would not be fully realized in the absence of the agreement.'[15]

(4) The final condition is that the agreement must not afford the parties to it 'the possibility of eliminating competition in respect of a substantial part of the products in question.'

This condition expresses the concern of the Treaty as interpreted by the Court of Justice that the agreement does not lead to a position where existing effective competition in a market is reduced to a point where competition is no longer effective.[16] This condition is not part of the economic balance of benefits and harms. Instead it emphasizes the overriding concern of EU competition policy to ensure that existing

[11] See Commission Notice, Guidelines on the Applicability of Article 101 of the EU Treaty to Horizontal Cooperation Agreements OJ [2001] C3/02, para 32.

[12] See eg C-501/06P *GlaxoSmithKline v Commission* [2009] ECR I–9291.

[13] Commission Notice, Guidelines on the application of Article 81(3) of the Treaty [now 101(3) TFEU], OJ C 101, 27 April 2004, pp 97–118, paras 85–6.

[14] Ibid, para 43.

[15] Ibid, para 74. See discussion in S. Anderman and J. Kallaugher, *Technology Transfer and the New EU Competition Rules* (Oxford: OUP, 2006), p 59.

[16] See Case 26/76 *Metro-SB Grossmärkte GmbH v Commission (no 1)*, [1977] ECR 1875, [1978] 2 CMLR 1.

effective competition is not undermined by bilateral or multilateral conduct as well as by unilateral conduct.

Under Article 101(3) as part of the process of exemption, the Treaty requires consideration of the innovative benefits of an agreement or provision but it requires any risks that might not benefit consumers or be unnecessarily wide, or foreclose existing competitors in a particular market, or the denial of access to new entrants to be taken into account as well. In any one case, the parties to an agreement have the burden of proving that it meets these four conditions.

The Commission has historically assisted the parties in this task by providing group or block exemption regulations which apply the four conditions to specific types of commercial agreements. Since modernization, the Commission has adopted Guidelines, based on the application of the four conditions, which offer the methodology to assess agreements that fall outside the safe harbour of a BER. In addition to Guidelines for specific types of agreements,[17] the Commission has also provided general rules for interpreting Article 101(3).[18]

The current block exemption for licensing agreements, the TTBER,[19] offers a template for exemption based upon an analysis of IP licensing agreements and its provisions. Moreover, the accompanying Guidelines, the TTA Guidelines,[20] offer a new methodology to the parties, the national courts, and national competition authorities to analyse agreements that fall outside the safe harbour of the TTBER. If an agreement complies with the criteria for exemption in the Guidelines and the case law, it is enforceable as far as the competition rules are concerned because the prohibition in Article 101(1) is no longer applicable.

13.3 ARTICLE 101(2) TFEU AND UNENFORCEABILITY

If the prohibition in Article 101(1) applies to an agreement and it cannot be exempted under Article 101(3), the agreement as a whole will be automatically void and unenforceable under Article 101(2) in national courts as well as the EU Courts. In the event, the parties to the agreement may in principle be subject to a fine, and either party to the agreement can treat it as no longer binding upon it.[21] Article 101(2) can thus operate as a competition defence to any action in a Member State court to enforce an agreement.

[17] See eg Commission Regulation 330/2010 of 20 April 2010 on the application of Article 101(3) of the Treaty on the Functioning of the European Union to categories of vertical agreements and concerted practices. OJ L 102, 23 April 2010, pp 1–7 and Commission Notice, Guidelines on Vertical Restraints, OJ C130, 19 May 2010, p 1.

[18] Art 101(3) Guidelines (n 13 above).

[19] Commission Regulation (EC) No 772/2004 of 27 April 2004 on the application of Article 81(3) of the Treaty to categories of technology transfer agreements, OJ L 123, 27 April 2004, pp 11–17.

[20] TTA Guidelines (n 5 above).

[21] See eg Case C-453/99 *Courage Ltd v Crehan* [2001] ECR I-6297, [2001] 5 CMLR 28. (Automatic voidness under Art 101(2) does not preclude a damages action by an injured party to the contract. Moreover, severance may be allowed under national law.)

If the prohibition applies to a particular clause in the licensing agreement, that may have the legal effect of either voiding the whole agreement or merely preventing the enforceability of the clause while maintaining the legal enforceability of the remainder of the licensing agreement. If the provision is a 'hard core restriction' as defined by the TTBER, the agreement as a whole will be void and unenforceable. If the provision is defined as an excluded restriction, it alone will be severable and void and unenforceable as such leaving the rest of the agreement intact.

Hence, it is necessary for parties to an IP licensing agreement to engage in a careful process of self-assessment in order to be in a position to face any challenges to the lawfulness or enforceability of an agreement under the competition rules. In the IP licensing context, the types of challenges presented often take the form of licensees attempting to be free of the royalty obligation after they reach the point of independence in manufacturing the licensed technology efficiently and independently. That is a factor that serves wonderfully to concentrate the mind of the licensor when drafting the agreement.

In the event, the most useful way to analyse Article 101 as a regulatory framework for IP licensing agreements today is to look separately at the two methods of assessment: (1) the process of exemption under Article 101(3) and (2) the process of clearance under Article 101(1).

As we have seen, the new style TTBER has changed the rules of the game. It offers more flexible, less interventionist conditions for exemption but the nature of the exemption has changed from an automatic exemption to a conditional exemption with market share limits, a conditional 'safe harbour'. Where the parties' market share exceeds the established limits, the agreement no longer enjoys the exemption provided by the BER and they must engage in a process of self-assessment using the more economic methodology of the Guidelines published by the Commission to ascertain the compatibility of their agreement with Article 101(1) and (3).

Because the exemption offered by the TTBER is now *conditional* in its effect, the method of applying the conditions of exemption *outside the scope* of the TTBER through individual assessment will now be as important to understand as the application of the TTBER itself. We will look more closely at the process of exemption under the new style TTBER and TTA Guidelines in Chapter 15. However, under the new framework for IP licensing, the issue of clearance under Article 101(1) also requires more detailed consideration.

13.4 THE CLEARANCE OF IP LICENSING AGREEMENTS UNDER ARTICLE 101(1) TFEU

The method of attempting to 'clear' an agreement under Article 101(1), ie designing it so that its contents do not come within the scope of Article 101(1), is now an easier option for the parties to licensing agreements after modernization. With the *more* economic approach the Commission has construed Article 101(1) more narrowly. Hence, the assessment of IP licensing agreements to determine their possibilities to be 'cleared' under Article 101(1) has taken on a new importance. Nevertheless, 'clearance' continues to require that the licensing agreement does not meet at least one of the Article's three conditions for application.

13.4.1 Agreements between independent undertakings

The first condition required for the prohibition in Article 101(1) to bite is that there must be evidence of an agreement or other form of collaboration between two or more 'undertakings'. Insofar as the conduct of an IP owner consists of unilateral enforcement of such a right under national law, it will not be caught by Article 101(1),[22] though it might be regulated by Article 102.

The concept of an undertaking in Article 101(1), though not defined in the Treaty, has been held to apply widely to individuals, partnerships, joint ventures,[23] and companies. The Court of Justice has defined it as 'any entity' engaged in a commercial activity.[24] Public authorities are caught if they are engaged in a commercial or economic activity but are excepted if they are acting as a public authority.[25]

However, an undertaking has also been defined as being an independent entity. If it is part of a wider 'economic unit', consisting of a group of companies, the group rather than the individual company may be the 'undertaking'. The Court of Justice has stated that the concept of undertaking is not identical with the question of legal personality for the purposes of company law. The corporate veil can be lifted[26] to show the underlying economic and commercial reality. If a licensing agreement is made between two companies within the same corporate group it may be viewed as excluded from Article 101(1) because, despite the corporate form, the two parties can be viewed as part of the same 'economic unit', and the agreement is not one between separate undertakings. As the CJEU stated in *Centrafarm v Sterling Drug*,[27] an agreement or concerted practice between a parent and a subsidiary does not fall within the scope of Article 101 where the agreement between two companies is in fact an internal allocation of functions between members of the same economic unit. If, however, the reality is that a subsidiary has a measure of independence in determining its commercial policy, then the subsidiary will be viewed as a separate undertaking for the purposes of Article 101(l).[28]

[22] Case 78/70 *Deutsche Grammophon Gesellschaft*, at para 5.

[23] Joint ventures can also be 'agreements' depending on their structure.

[24] See eg *Polypropylene* [1988] 4 CMLR 34 at para 99.

[25] Case 30/87 *Corinne Bodson v Pompes Funebres de Region Liberees SA* [1985] ECR 2479, [1989] 4 CMLR 984.

[26] It is also lifted to establish the jurisdiction of EU law over the foreign parent of a subsidiary within the EU (see eg Cases 6 and 7/73 *Istituto Chemioterapico Italiano SpA & Commercial Solvents Corp. v Commission* [1974] ECR 223, [1974] 1 CMLR 309) or when holding a parent company attributable for the guilty conduct of the subsidiary (see eg *Johnson and Johnson* [1981] 2 CMLR 287).

[27] Case 15/74 *Centrafarm BV and Adnaan De Pejper v Sterling Drug Inc and Winthrop BV* [1974] ECR 1147 at 1183; see also *Kodak* [1970] CMLR D31 (Comm).

[28] See eg Case 85/74 *Commission v Solvay and La Porte* [1985] 1 CMLR 481. The issue of autonomy is raised again in the context of the relationship between parents and joint ventures.

The effect of this jurisdictional condition is to offer to companies the option of avoiding the regulatory effects of Article 101 by acquiring the licensor, or vertically integrating, rather than obtaining a licensing agreement.[29] In the case of *Viho Europe*,[30] the General Court (GC) was faced by a complaint from a distributor that Parker Pen had an arrangement with its wholly-owned subsidiaries which required them to refer all orders from customers from other EU countries to the subsidiary established in the customer's country. The GC noted that the arrangement contributed to preserving and partitioning the various national markets, but held that when such a policy is 'followed by an economic unit . . . within which the subsidiaries do not enjoy any freedom to determine their conduct in the market', it 'does not fall within the scope of [Article 101(1)]'.[31] The Commission was told by the GC that it cannot fill a gap that may exist in the scheme of regulation by stretching Article 101 to apply to circumstances for which it is not intended.

If the network involves independent dealers, Article 101(1) can apply. For example, when Parker Pen had put a similar contractual clause in its distribution agreement with its independent distributor in Germany, Herlitz, prohibiting all sales to resellers from other EU countries, its practices were subject to a fine of 700,000 ECU.

The EU Courts have on occasion blurred the distinction between unilateral and bilateral action by implying agreement between two independent undertakings in cases where one undertaking issued a unilateral prohibition on exports to which the other undertaking acquiesced. For example in *AEG Telefunken*, the refusal of a manufacturer to admit a known discount reseller to a selective distribution system was deemed to be by agreement with the other resellers contractually involved in the chain because of their 'tacit' acceptance of its exclusionary policy.[32] In such cases, however, there must be evidence of tacit acceptance by an independent undertaking in order to allow a finding of implied agreement to fall within Article 101(1).

In *Adalat-Bayer*,[33] the Commission attempted to take the process a step further by charging the Bayer company with an infringement of Article 101(1) in a situation where it had established a company policy of monitoring its own subsidiaries to restrict the quantities supplied to independent wholesalers based on national market orders. The Commission concluded that there was a 'quasi-contractual arrangement' between the subsidiaries and the wholesalers because the latter were clearly influenced

[29] After *Consten Grundig*, for example, Grundig simply acquired Consten and integrated it within the Grundig organization.

[30] Case T-102/92 *Viho Europe BV v Commission* [1995] ECR II–117, [1997] 4 CMLR 469, upheld by the CJEU in Case C-73/95P *Viho Europe BV v Commission* [1996] ECR I–5457, [1997] 4 CMLR 419.

[31] Ibid, at paras 52–4.

[32] Case 107/82 R *AEG Telefunken v Commission* [1983] ECR I–3151 at para 38; see also Cases 25 and 26/84 *Ford Werke AG & Ford of Europe v Commission* [1985] ECR 2725; Cases 32, 36–82/78 *BMW Belgium v* Commission [1979] ECR 2435 (unilateral instructions by manufacturers to distributors in0 the form of a circular); *Sandoz* [1990] ECR 145 (supply of printed invoice stating 'exports prohibited').

[33] [1996] 5 CMLR 416; see H. Lidgard, 'Unilateral Refusal to Supply: An Agreement in Disguise' [1997] *ECLR* 352.

by Bayer's conduct to adapt their own practices to fall into line with Bayer's objectives. The Commission's decision was upheld by both the GC and CJEU.[34]

13.4.2 Is the agreement capable of appreciably affecting 'trade between the Member States?'

13.4.2.1 *Introduction*

The second jurisdictional condition of Article 101(1) is that it applies only to agreements, decisions, and concerted practices which have an 'appreciable' quantitative effect on interstate trade. This condition is essentially a jurisdictional test for the application of the system of EU competition law in two important respects. It first establishes a territorial point: whether an agreement made inside or outside the EU is caught by EU competition law by virtue of its effects.[35] Secondly, it defines the jurisdictional borderline where EU competition law applies alongside the domestic competition law of the Member States.[36] Even if an agreement is anti-competitive by object, it will not be unlawful under Article 101(1) if it does not have an appreciable effect on interstate trade.

This test of effect on interstate trade has been given an extremely wide interpretation by EU Courts and Commission, applying as long as the agreement 'may have an influence direct or indirect, actual or potential on the pattern of trade between Member States'.[37]

The influence can be future as well as present, and possible as well as probable.[38] For example in *Vacuum Interrupters*,[39] the Commission held that a joint venture agreement between two British manufacturers was caught by Article 101(1) because it was reasonable to assume that had they proceeded independently they would have each marketed the product in other Member States. Similarly, in *Pronuptia*,[40] the Court of Justice held that where clauses in a distribution franchise partitioned markets between licensor and licensee, it *per se* affected interstate trade even if both were in the same Member State, insofar as they prevented licensees from setting up in other Member States.

[34] Case T-41/96 *Bayer AG v Commission* [2000] ECR II–3383 and Joined Cases C-2/01P and C-3/01 *Bundesverband der Arzneimittel-Importeure v Commission* [2004] ECR I–23, [2004] 4 CMLR 653. See also the discussion in S. Kon and F. Schaeffer, 'Parallel Imports of Pharmaceutical Products: A New Realism or Back to Basics' [1977] *ECLR* 123.

[35] An agreement relating to trade outside the EU, whether made inside or outside the EU, can be caught by Art 101(1) if its side-effects are to restrict or distort competition. See eg Joined Cases 40 to 48, 50, 54 to 56, 111, 113, and 114/73 *Zuiker Unie v Commission* [1975] ECR 1663, [1976] 1 CMLR 295; see also Joined Cases 89, 104, 114, 116, 117, 125–29/85 *Ahlström Oy v Commission (Woodpulp II)* [1988] ECR 5193, [1988] 4 CMLR 901.

[36] The jurisdiction is concurrent in the sense that if Art 101(1) does not apply for any reason, domestic law can still apply. Moreover, even where Art 101(1) does apply, it only supervenes where a formal Commission decision has been taken or where the application of the law by Member States will not threaten the full and uniform application of Community law. See *Walt Wilhelm v BundesKartelamnt* [1969] ECR 1.

[37] Case 56/65 *STM v Maschinenbau Ulm* [1966] ECR 235 at 249; [1966] CMLR 357 at 375.

[38] See eg Case 107/82 *AEG Telefunken* at para 60.

[39] [1977] 1 CMLR D 67.

[40] Case 161/84 *Pronuptia de Paris v Schillgalis* [1986] ECR 353.

There has, however, long been an important quantitative dimension to the test of effect on interstate trade. Even a licence between undertakings in two different Member States would only be found to satisfy the condition of affecting interstate trade if its effect were 'appreciable' in terms of volume of trade.[41] The Court of Justice made it clear that for an agreement to fall within Article 101(1), it must have a more than *de minimis* effect upon interstate trade.[42]

13.4.2.2 *The Commission's Notice on effect upon interstate trade*[43]

The Commission has defined the concept of 'capable of appreciably affecting trade between Member States' in its 2004 Guidelines on the effect of trade concept contained in Article 81 and 82 of the Treaty (now 101 and 102 TFEU)[44] (Trade Guidelines) by setting out two rebuttable presumptions:

For agreements between non-competitors, para 52 of the Trade Guidelines states that the Commission holds the view that such agreements are not capable of affecting interstate trade when they meet two cumulative conditions:

(1) An aggregate market share in any market within the Community of 5 per cent or less; *and*

(2) An annual aggregate turnover within the Community of no more than €40 million.

An aggregate market share in any market within the Community According to Paragraph 52 (a) of the Trade Guidelines the only relevant market share is that of the licensor. However, even if the licensor had a market share of 5 per cent or more, (which is by no means certain) it would still be necessary to meet the test of turnover in para 52(b).

An annual aggregate turnover within the Community The purpose of para 52(b) is to identify the relevant turnover. It makes it clear that in the case of licensing agreements the relevant turnover shall be the aggregate Community turnover of both licensee and licensor.

In the case of licensing agreements, the Trade Guidelines make a particular stipulation that the turnover of the licensor in his capacity of licensor is limited to the royalties received from licensee(s). The Trade Guidelines recognize that since royalties are calculated as a percentage of the product or a fixed amount per product sold by the licensee, a royalty income of €40 million could reflect a much higher turnover on the market for products incorporating the licensed technology which is generally the market on which the effects of an agreement are analysed. The Trade Guidelines therefore provide that in respect of licence agreements the relevant turnover is taken to be that of

[41] See Case 56/65 *STM*.

[42] Case 5/69 *Volk v Vervaecke* [1969] ECR 295, [1969] CMLR 277. The Court had also referred to this test in the earlier test of Case 56/65 *STM*.

[43] Commission Notice on Guidelines on the effect on trade concept contained in Articles [101] and [102] [2004]OJ C101/81 (Trade Guidelines).

[44] Ibid.

the licensees on the market where they sell the products incorporating the licensed technology.

13.4.2.3 *The Notice on Agreements of Minor Importance*

There is a related *de minimis* test for agreements under Article 101(1) which 'clears' commercial agreements if they have an insignificant effect on competition as well as on the movement of interstate trade. Where the market shares of the parties to an agreement are extremely low, its effect on competition is viewed as *de minimis*. In *Volk v Vervaecke*,[45] the Court of Justice held that an exclusive distribution agreement between a German firm and a Belgian firm was not caught by Article 101(1) because the total market share of Volk in Germany was 0.2 per cent and altogether only 200 machines were sold. The CJEU stressed that even if the Commission found that the purpose of an agreement was to restrain competition because it was an exclusive dealing imposing absolute territorial protection, if its overall effect on the market was insignificant because of the weak market position of the parties, then Article 101(1) would not apply.

This decision was followed by a series of *de minimis* notices, ie Commission Notices on Agreements of Minor Importance. The legal status of the current Notice before national and EU Courts is as 'only a factor which the courts may take into account in a pending case', but the Commission has agreed not to open proceedings under Regulation 1/2003 and if an agreement covered by the Notice were in fact to be caught by Article 101(1), there would be no fine.

In the current version of the *de minimis* Notice,[46] the Commission has applied market share thresholds below which it considers that agreements will not have an appreciable effect on competition.

In para 9 of the Notice, the Commission states that agreements between undertakings engaged in the production or distribution of goods or in the provision of services do not fall under the prohibition in Article 101(1) if (a) the aggregate market share held by the parties to the agreement does not exceed 10 per cent, on any of the relevant markets where the agreement is made between undertakings who are actual or potential competitors ('horizontal agreements') or (b) if the market share held by *each* of the parties to the agreement does not exceed 15 per cent on any of the relevant markets affected by the agreement where the agreement is made between undertakings which are not actual or potential competitors ('vertical agreements'). In the case of a mixed horizontal/vertical agreement or where it is difficult to classify the agreement as horizontal or vertical, the 10 per cent threshold is applicable.[47] The threshold is reduced to 5 per cent where there are parallel networks of agreements having foreclosure effects.

[45] Case 5/69 *Volk v Vervaecke*. The CJEU had also referred to this test in the earlier test of Case C-56/65 *STM* (at 375–6) in which it had stated that an appreciable restriction was one which restricted sales to and from other Member States in the agreement or 'limited the opportunities allowed for other commercial competitors in the same products by way of parallel re-exportation and importation'.

[46] Notice on Agreements of Minor Importance (*de minimis*) [2001] OJ C368/13.

[47] The Commission adds that agreements can exceed these thresholds by no more than 10% for two years in succession and still remain outside the scope of Art 101(1).

The thresholds provided in the Notice do not preclude agreements with higher market shares falling outside Article 101(1) if they meet the test of non-appreciability elaborated in the judgments of the CJEU which is discussed in the next section.[48] However, the Notice curiously maintains that even below the thresholds (a) *horizontal* agreements which have as their object to fix prices or limit production or sales; or to share markets or sources of supply and (b) vertical agreements which have as their object to fix resale prices or to confer territorial protection on the participating undertaking or third undertaking, may not enjoy the benefits of the *de minimis* exception. However, this is at odds with the judgments of the Court of Justice in *Delimitis*[49] and *Miller*[50] and should be viewed in the light of the authority of those judgments.[51]

13.4.3 The *object* or *effect* of preventing, restricting, or distorting competition

13.4.3.1 *Introduction*

If a licence agreement is made between independent undertakings, and has an effect on interstate trade, it will only be contrary to Article 101(1) if it can be further shown that it has as its *object* or *effect* the prevention, restriction, or distortion of competition. As mentioned, this test involves a preliminary assessment of the pro- or anti-competitive nature of the licensing agreement. Under Article 101(1), the test is an alternative one; an agreement can be unlawful either by virtue of its *object* or its *effects*. The test of its object is a test of the content of the agreement. It requires an analysis of its clauses of the agreement to determine its *specific purpose* and whether *by virtue of its clauses* its effect on competition is likely to be sufficiently deleterious.[52] In deciding whether an agreement is prohibited by Article 101(1), there is therefore no need to take account of its actual *effects* once it appears that its *object* is to prevent, restrict, or distort competition within the common market.[53]

If no *object* to restrain competition can be inferred from the agreement or its provisions, then it is necessary to examine the *effects* of the agreement to see whether they are restrictive or distortive of competition. This requires an assessment of the likely consequences of the agreement and for it to be caught by the prohibition in Article 101(1) it is necessary to find that those factors are present which show that competition has *in fact* been prevented or restricted or distorted.

[48] See eg T-374/94 *European Night Services (ENS) v Commission* ECR II–3141.

[49] Case C-324/89 *Delimitis v Henninger AG* [1991] ECR I–935.

[50] Case 19/77 *Miller v Commission* [1978] ECR 131, [1978] 2 CMLR 334.

[51] See discussion in J. Faull and A. Nikpay (eds), *The EC Law of Competition* (Oxford: OUP, 2007), paras 3.337 *et seq.*

[52] See also Joined Cases 29/83 and 30/83 *Compagnie royale asturienne des mines and Rheinzink* v *Commission* [1984] ECR 1679 at para 26, and Case C-551/03 P *General Motors v Commission* [2006] ECR I–3173 at para 66.

[53] Joined Cases 56/64 and 58/64 *Consten and Grundig v Commission* [1966] ECR 299 at 342 and Case C-105/04 P *Nederlandse Federatieve Vereniging voor de Groothandel op Elektrotechnisch Gebied v Commission* [2006] ECR I–8725 at para 125.

In both cases, effect on competition is to be measured by comparing the results of the agreement with the likely state of affairs which would exist in the absence of that restriction.[54]

It is important to identify four strands in the development of the ideas about the nature of Article 101(1). The first strand is the early EU approach to competition law which stressed the idea of 'freedom of action' and freedom to compete in the new European markets. This was influenced by the German/Ordoliberal goal of limiting private economic power by prohibiting agreements[55] that limited the economic autonomy of firms on the market. The second strand was the 'appreciability' doctrine consisting of the judgments of the Court of Justice insisting that agreements must be examined in their legal and economic context and be found to have 'appreciable' effects before being prohibited by Article 101(1). The EU Courts showed some concern that agreements with insignificant effects on competition should not be caught in the drift net of Article 101(1)

The third strand was the 'integration' concern, the concern of the competition authorities to promote the integration of the market by preventing agreements from reinforcing existing barriers to trade between Member States. This had the effect of reinforcing the extent to which the prohibition in Article 101(1) could apply to agreements between non-competitors particularly in the European-wide IP licensing sector.

The fourth strand is the modernized view of Article 101(1), introduced in 2003/2004, which maintains that the goal of competition is consumer welfare and the purpose of Article 101 is the *more* economic one of protecting competition on the market as a means of enhancing consumer welfare and of ensuring an efficient allocation of resources. This has meant that the key issue in applying Article 101(1) is to ensure that it will not lead to unilateral or coordinated effects producing increases in prices, limitations of output, or reduced quality, all of which result in reduced consumer welfare.

All four strands have received judicial support. The most recent reform of the Commission has had both support[56] and modification[57] from the judiciary in the past and since the modernization regulations and notices were put into force. This makes it necessary to consider each of the four strands more carefully.

13.4.3.2 *Freedom of action and restraints of competition*

Before modernization, the test of objects and effects under Article 101(1) was based on the earlier Germanic/Ordoliberal goal of limiting private economic power by prohibiting agreements that limited the economic autonomy of firms on the market.[58] The goal was to protect 'freedom of action' in markets as a political aim, providing the basis of

[54] Case 56/65 *STM* at para 80.

[55] See Faull and Nikpay (n 51 above), p 218.

[56] See eg T-328/03 *O2 (Germany) GmbH v Commission* [2006] ECR II–1231, [2006] 5 CMLR 5; Case C-501/06P *GlaxoSmithKline v Commission* [2009] ECR I–9291.

[57] See eg C-209/07 *Competition Authority v Beef Industry Development Society Ltd* [2008] ECR I–8637.

[58] See Faull and Nikpay (n 51 above), p 218.

a fair social order. This doctrine defined the goal of competition law *inter alia* as preserving existing rivalry in markets and emphasized the need to preserve existing structures in markets. The concept of 'freedom of action' as part of the test of *object* in Article 101(1) was described in *Consten and Grundig* when the CJEU stated: 'Competition may be distorted within the meaning of Article 101(1) not only by agreements which limit it as between the parties, but also by agreements which prevent or restrict the competition which might take place between one of them and third parties.'[59] The Commission also endorsed the doctrine: 'The exclusive nature of a contractual relationship between a producer and a distributor is viewed as restricting competition since it limits the parties' freedom of action in the territory covered.'[60] However, the Commission added an economic dimension to the Ordoliberal goal by claiming that the process of rivalry on markets produced the best economic results. [61] Hence for the Commission, the protection of rivalry and the freedom of action of the parties to the agreement and others on the market was the goal of Article 101.

Whilst the doctrine of 'freedom of action' originated in German law and was derived from the regulation of relationships between competitors,[62] it was applied in EU competition law to vertical agreements like distributorships.[63] If a distribution agreement was exclusive, it was caught by Article 101(1) and required exemption because it contained a restriction on the supplier selling to anyone in the contract territory apart from the distributor and barred other distributors in that territory from buying from the supplier.[64] The application of the 'freedom of action' doctrine to exclusive vertical distribution agreements by the Commission was given strong support by the Court of Justice when an agreement between non-competitors had the effect of partitioning national markets and reinforcing the tendency of Member States' markets to resist integration.[65]

The application of the freedom of action doctrine had the result that a contractual restraint on the freedom of action of the parties on the market could be equated to a 'restriction of competition' by *object* under Article 101(1) without any reference to the

[59] Joined Cases 56/64 and 58/64 *Consten and Grundig* v *Commission* [1966] ECR 299.

[60] See *XXIIIrd Report on Competition Policy* (1993) Com (94) 161 final, p 212.

[61] See discussion in Faull and Nikpay (n 51 above), p 218.

[62] In the case of horizontal agreements, it can perhaps be defended as a reasonable basis for a rebuttable presumption of anti-competitiveness. Where firms are competitors any restriction on their action is probably a restriction on the process and possibly the structure of competition. As the Court of Justice has acknowledged in *Zuiker Unie*: 'The criteria of coordination and cooperation laid down by the caselaw of the Court . . . must be understood in the light of the concept inherent in the competition provisions of the EEC Treaty according to which each economic operator must develop independently the policy which he intends to adopt on the common market including the choice of the person or undertaking to which he makes, offers or sells.' Joined Cases 40–48, 50, 54–56, 111, 113, and 114/73 *Zuiker Unie* at 1942. See also S. Anderman and J. Kallaugher, *Technology Transfer and the New EU Competition Rules*, (Oxford: OUP, 2006) pp 46–7.

[63] See eg *Bendix/Ancien Ets. Mertons & Strae* 1 June 1964 5 OJ EC 1496 (1964).

[64] The ideal agreement from a 'freedom of action' perspective is a non-exclusive distributorship which leaves the supplier free to appoint other distributors in the same territory and to distribute its own products in the same territory.

[65] See Joined Cases 56/64 and 58/64 *Consten and Grundig* v *Commission* [1966] ECR 299.

actual process of competition on the market or the effects of the agreement on that process. The test was legalistic and focused on the form of the restraints in the contract. Close regard must be paid to the wording of its provisions and to the objectives which it is intended to attain. Subjective intent was less important than the test of what the provisions viewed objectively purported to do, in particular whether the agreement could be classified into one of the types of agreements covered by Article 101(1)(a) to (e). Infringement by *object* was a test of whether an agreement 'could be regarded by its very nature as being injurious to the proper functioning of normal competition'.[66] In principle, Article 101(1) was to provide a wide net, sweeping in potential threats to existing market structures and rivalries as well as market partitioning, leaving to Article 101(3) the task of assessing the effects and merits of the agreement using the criteria of its four conditions. This wide definition of Article 101(1) was long controversial and criticized because of its schizophrenic approach to the treatment of commercial agreements,[67] as well as its excessive formalism.[68]

13.4.3.3 *'Appreciability'*

The concept of preserving economic autonomy by preventing the restriction of economic rivalry was not a sufficient condition to find a restriction of competition under Article 101(1). The Court of Justice has long maintained that the concept of restriction of competition under Article 101, whether under the *object* test or the *effects* test,[69] must not be applied mechanically, but must be accompanied by a second stage test of 'appreciability', particularly in the case of the *object* and *effects* of agreements between non-competitors.[70] The CJEU was concerned that agreement with insignificant restrictive objects or effects should not be caught by the drift net of Article 101(1). The Commission was required to ask whether the specific clauses in the agreement,

[66] Case C-209/07 *Beef Industry*, paras 17, 21–3.

[67] The Commission, it was said, first condemned in principle an inordinate number of vertical agreements under Art 101(1) as restrictions on competition, creating a 'drift net' approach to jurisdiction, and requiring inordinate numbers of notifications in order to achieve legal validity. It then exempted considerable numbers of agreements because they readily met the four-fold balancing test of not on balance restricting competition under Art 101(3). See C. Bright, 'Deregulation of EC Competition Policy: Rethinking Article 85(1)[now 101(1)]' and I. Forrester, 'Competition Structures for the 21st Century' in [1994] *Fordham Corp Law Inst*, pp 505 and 405 respectively.

[68] Its mode of analysis takes no account of the actual economic effects of an agreement or provision, let alone basic economic arguments that strong inter-brand competition in the final product market can operate to curb the effects of anti-competitive restrictions within a vertical chain of manufacturing and distribution. The analysis consists of an examination of the terms of agreements to determine whether they limit, or are intended to limit, the freedom of action of the parties to the agreement or third parties in the market.

[69] Case 56/65 *STM*.

[70] Even at the time of the *Consten and Grundig* decision, the Court of Justice had the conviction that the freedom of action concept should not apply as comprehensively to vertical agreements as it should to horizontal agreements. Having insisted in *Consten and Grundig* that Art 101 applied to vertical agreements as well as horizontal agreements, and accepted that a version of the freedom of action test was applicable, the Court was equally insistent that the test of restriction should be subject to a qualitative as well as a quantitative appreciability test.

though restrictive in form, are, or would be, 'appreciable' in their market and legal context.[71]

The appreciability test was directed by the Court of Justice from the outset at the Commission's automatic assumption that territorial exclusivity in a vertical distribution contract was a 'restriction of competition' under Article 101(1). Thus, in the case of *STM v Maschinenenbau Ulm*,[72] the CJEU stated that 'an agreement whereby a producer entrusts the sale of his products in a given area to a sole distributor cannot automatically fall under the prohibition in Art 101(1)'.[73] The CJEU added that in order to decide whether a clause granting an exclusive right of sale is to be prohibited by reason of its object or its effect, it was 'appropriate to take into account in particular the nature and quantity, limited or otherwise, of the products covered by the agreement', and the position of each of the parties on the market for the products concerned.[74] The other factors were 'the isolated nature of the agreement, or alternatively its position in a series of agreements', and 'the severity of the clauses protecting the exclusive dealership. . .'.[75]

There were two distinct strands in the 'appreciability' doctrine which allowed agreements to clear Article 101(1) in spite of restricting rivalry. The first consisted of those cases developing the 'appreciability' doctrine as an issue of appreciable quantitative *effect*.

13.4.3.4 *Appreciability and restrictions by effect*

The Court of Justice made it clear in *STM* that where an agreement does not have the object of restricting competition:

> the consequences of the agreement should then be considered and for it to be caught by the prohibition, it is then necessary to find that those factors are present which show that competition has in fact been. . . restricted. . .to an appreciable extent. The competition in question must be understood within the actual context in which it would occur in the absence of the agreement in dispute.[76]

In a series of cases since *STM*, the EU Courts have held that where vertical restraints in an agreement do not have a foreclosure effect or where there are real concrete possibilities for competitors to enter and grow in a market or where the agreement does not

[71] The Court in *STM* went on to indicate that the appreciability test also had a qualitative dimension. It extended to '. . . the severity of the clauses intended to protect the exclusive dealership or alternatively the opportunities allowed for other commercial competitors in the same products by way of parallel re-exportation and importation'. This indicated that the appreciability test was also concerned with an analysis of clauses in part to determine the extent of their market partitioning effect. There was a suggestion that the absence of such an effect might help to create a basis for clearance under Art 101(1) thus foreshadowing the category of 'open' exclusive licence that was recognized in the later *Maize Seed* case.

[72] Case 56/65 *STM*.

[73] Ibid, at p 248.

[74] Ibid, at p 250.

[75] Ibid, at p 250.

[76] See ibid, at pp 249–50. See also Case 23/67 *SA Brasserie de Haecht v Consorts Wilkin Janssen Case* [1967] ECR 407; T-328/03 *O2 (Germany)*.

make a significant contribution to a sealing-off effect, particularly in a network of agreements, the agreement or restraint will not be caught by Article 101(1).[77]

The GC summed up this line of authority in *European Night Services*:

> Before any examination of the parties' arguments as to whether the Commission's analysis as regards restrictions of competition was correct, it must be borne in mind that in assessing an agreement under Article 85(1) [now 101(1)] of the Treaty, account should be taken of the actual conditions in which it functions, in particular the economic context in which the undertakings operate, the products or services covered by the agreement and the actual structure of the market concerned . . .[78]

These cases make the point that an agreement with parties having higher than *de minimis* market shares may not be caught by Article 101(1). This effects doctrine was long advocated by the Court of Justice and the General Court and suggests that in its modernization reform the Commission is not working against the grain of the legal framework established by the EU Courts.

13.4.3.5 *Appreciability and restrictions by object*

The second strand in the case law was a more qualitative approach to appreciability based upon several different views about specific provisions as restrictions of competition. In *STM,* the Court of Justice stated that the assessment of the *object* of an agreement under Article 101(1), particularly in the case of agreements between non-competitors, required an assessment by an analysis of its clauses of the *specific purpose* of the agreement in the *economic context* in which it is to be applied to determine whether by virtue of its clauses its effect on competition is likely to be sufficiently deleterious.[79]

After *STM* there were a series of cases from *Nungesser*[80] to *Pronuptia*[81] finding reasons to provide an exception to the wide interpretation of 'restriction of competition' as it was based on the 'freedom of action' doctrine. These cases included the 'market opening' and 'ancillary restraints' judgments and have sometimes been referred to as the 'rule of reason in Article 101(1)' cases.[82] These cases as they apply to IP licensing agreements will be discussed in detail in Chapter 14.

[77] Case C-324/89 *Delimitis v Henninger*, paras 21 and 27.

[78] Cases T-374, 375, 384, and 388/94 *European Night Services v Commission* [1998] ECR II–3141, [1998] 5 CMLR 718. The CJEU supported this statement by referring to judgments in Case C-324/89 *Delimitis v Henninger*; C-250/92 *Gottrup-Klim* [1994] ECR I–5641 at para 31; Case C-399/93 *Oude Luttikhuis and Others v Verenigde Coöperatieve Melkindustrie* [1995] ECR I–4515 at para 10; and Case T-77/94 *VGB and Others v Commission* [1997] ECR II–759 at para 140.

[79] See also Joined Cases 29/83 and 30/83 *Compagnie royale asturienne des mines and Rheinzink* v *Commission* [1984] ECR 1679 at para 26, and Case C-551/03 P *General Motors v Commission* [2006] ECR I–3173 at para 66.

[80] Case 258/78 *Nungesser v Commission* [1982] ECR 2015, [1983 1 CMLR 278.

[81] Case 161/84 *Pronuptia de Paris GmbH v Pronuptia de Paris Irmgard Schillgallis* [1986] ECR 353, [1986] 1 CMLR 414.

[82] See eg R. Whish and B. Sufrin, 'Article 85 The Rule of Reason' [1987] *Ox Yrbk in Eur Law*; I. Forrester and C. Norall, 'The Laicisation of Community Law Self Help and the Rule of Reason' [1984] 21 *CML Rev* 11.

13.4.3.6 *Market integration*

The third strand was the strong concern of the EU Courts to promote the integration of the market by preventing agreements from reinforcing existing barriers to trade between Member States. This reinforced the extent to which the prohibition in 101(1) could apply to agreements between non-competitors.[83] It also drew attention to the cumulative effects of large numbers of agreements of the same type as sealing-off national markets.[84] These cases focused on interstate rivalry and reinforced the traditional freedom to compete concept.[85]

13.4.3.7 *The new modernized approach to restriction of competition*

After modernization, the competition authority has proposed to apply a different test as a third step: does the contractual restraint have a harmful effect upon *consumer welfare*, ie does it result in identifiable unilateral or coordinated effects which can reduce consumer welfare by raising prices, limiting output, and or limiting quality of products. As suggested in the new TTBER and TTA Guidelines, the interpretation of the test of *object* and *effect* of restricting competition under Article 101(1) should ask whether the contractual restraint has identifiable unilateral or coordinated effect which can harm the process of competition and reduce consumer welfare by resulting in higher prices, lower output or lower quality or variety of products. If a contractual restraint in an agreement *between non-competitors* cannot be shown to have the potential to harm consumer welfare *in that sense,* it will not be viewed as a restriction of competition. For example, using a *more* economic approach, where the parties are *not* competitors in a market, the agreement itself cannot have the economic *effect* of restricting *inter-technology* competition. Much like a 'vertical merger,' a licensing agreement between non-competitors will not have a structural effect in either a technology or licensed product market.

In such cases, Article 101(1) will only apply where the licensing agreement contains a particular *provision* that has the *object* or *effect* of constituting a restriction on *intra-technology* competition, ie competition between licensees of the same technology. Yet, using a more economic approach, the new test of *object* as applied to individual contractual provisions has also been considerably narrowed down owing to the greater economic realism of the legal framework. The Commission has created a reduced list of contractual restrictions which are *per se* restrictions by *object* defining them as 'hard core restrictions'[86] 'that are presumed in light of the objectives pursued by the competition rules to have such a high potential of negative effects on competition that it is unnecessary for the purposes of Article 101 to demonstrate that there are any actual *effects* on the market', [emphasis added]. The inclusion of any of these hard core provisions in the IP licensing contract makes the whole agreement unenforceable under

[83] *Distillers Company Limited* [1978] OJ 50/16.

[84] See eg Case 23/67 *SA Brasserie de Haecht v Consorts Wilkin Janssen Case* [1967] ECR 407; Case C-234/89 *Delimitis v Henninger* AG [1991] ECR I–935.

[85] See discussion in Faull and Nikpay (n 51 above), pp 232–3.

[86] See TTBER (n 19 above), Art 4.

Article 101(2). It has also introduced a list of contractual restrictions, called excluded restrictions, that are themselves non-enforceable without affecting the enforceability of the remainder of the agreement.[87] Hence, in the event of an agreement between *non-competitors* it may be enough to ensure that the licensing agreement contains no 'hard core' or 'excluded' restrictions to clear the agreement under Article 101(1) without moving on to the next stage analysis of exemptibility under the TTBER and TTA Guidelines.

The new *more* economic test under Article 101(1) is markedly less generous for agreements between *competitors* because such agreements have a *prima facie* effect on the structure of the market and therefore a potential effect on *inter-technology* competition. The TTA Guidelines suggest that such agreements are best assessed under the four criteria of the exemption.

Moreover, the *more* economic approach of the Commission remains subject to the judgments of the Courts. It has been endorsed in some recent judgments of the GC and CJEU.[88] But the EU Courts have also set limits to its application. Thus, where the 'nature' of the object of the agreement is to partition national markets, that can offend Article 101(1) without any showing of harm to consumers and such agreements must seek enforceability, if at all, under the test of Article 101(3).[89] As well, in respect of agreements between *competitors*, the test of the restrictive object of the agreement may be satisfied with reference to the protection of rivalry or economic autonomy of the parties because of its inevitable effect on the existing market structure.[90] Hence, for agreements *between competitors* generally, and IP licensing agreements in particular, the formula remains that the potential negative effects of structural change are presumed and the agreement must be exempted, if at all, under the test of Article 101(3).[91]

[87] Ibid, Art 5.

[88] Case T-328/03 *O2 (Germany)* in which the GC chided the Court of Justice for not applying its new approach more diligently.

[89] See Case 506/06 *GlaxoSmithKline*.

[90] See C-209/07 *Beef Industry*, paras 17, 21–3.

[91] Ibid.

14

THE JUDICIAL CONCEPT OF RESTRICTION OF COMPETITION AND IPR LICENSING

14.1 Introduction 233
14.2 Judicial Authority before Modernization 234
14.3 The Scope of the Patent Doctrine and Restriction on Competition 235
14.4 The *Consten and Grundig* Judgment 236
14.5 The Commission's Change of Policy 238
14.6 The Court of Justice's Application of the Appreciability Test to Intellectual Property Rights 242

14.1 INTRODUCTION

Under the new modernized regime for Article 101(1) there is a greater prospect that the agreement and its provisions can be shown not to constitute 'preventions, restrictions or distortions of competition'. The *more* economic approach to the assessment of IP licensing under Article 101 has given new meaning to the concept of an agreement having the *object* or *effect* of 'restricting competition' and has narrowed the scope of 'restriction of competition' in Article 101(1), particularly in the case of agreements between *non-competitors*. The *more* economic approach, however, has not entirely ousted the judicial approach to Article 101(1). The earlier doctrines of freedom of action, scope of the patent, market opening, and ancillary restraints sit side by side with the Commission's new rules offering both support and, on occasion, limitation of its reach. Their continued relevance is two-fold. The Commission must work within the framework established by the judgments of the EU Courts interpreting the Treaty. And the parties in a dispute will want to cite to judgments of the EU Courts to reinforce a case based upon the Commission's TTBER and TTA Guidelines when appearing before a court or arbitration tribunal.

14.2 JUDICIAL AUTHORITY BEFORE MODERNIZATION

As we have seen, before 2004, the interpretation of 'restriction of competition' in Article 101(1) was based on a finding whether the agreement or a contractual restraint within it restricted the freedom of action or economic autonomy of individuals. The goal of competition policy was strongly influenced by the ordoliberal/Germanic conception of preserving existing rivalry on markets. It was enough to show that an agreement limited one party's ability to sell competing products or an agreement provided territorial exclusivity and thereby could foreclose third parties from the market to find the provision restrictive of competition. Its overall effect was to interpret these essential contractual restraints in IP licensing agreements as automatically equivalent to the Treaty concept of 'restrictions of competition' without reference to their effects. This conception also lay behind the two-part structure of Article 101 as a whole. Article 101(1) would cast a wide net leaving the assessment of agreements to the structured balancing test of Article 101(3). This wide net was reinforced by the cases deciding that freedom of action should be extended into freedom of interstate trade within the competition rules.[1] The approach also meant that Article 101(1) was strongly influenced by a legalistic approach to assessing provisions.

However, there were three doctrines that were relevant to the application of the test of restriction of competition to IP licensing. The first was the early 'scope of the patent' doctrine which provided a period of non-regulation until the 1970s but still has some role in the legal analysis today.[2] The other two are the 'new technology/market opening' doctrine originating in the *Nungesser*[3] case and the 'ancillary restraints' doctrine from *Remia*[4] to *Pronuptia*[5]. These two lines of cases arose from the CJEU's efforts to ameliorate the wide interpretation of 'restriction of competition' in Article 101(1) by subjecting it to a test of qualitative 'appreciability'. These lines of authority all played a role in the past and have a capacity to influence decisions under Article 101(1) today along with the more economic analysis available in the TTA Guidelines.

[1] Joined Cases 56/64 and 58/64 *Consten and Grundig v Commission* [1966] ECR 299; Case C-234/89 *Delimitis v Henninger AG* [1991] ECR I-935. See also Case 23/67 *SA Brasserie de Haecht v Consorts Wilkin Janssen Case* [1967] ECR 407.

[2] This concept is related to the patent misuse doctrine in US law and the inherency theory in German law. See I Rahnasto, *Intellectual Property Rights, External Effects and Antitrust Law* (Oxford: OUP, 2003), pp 42–9; see also J. Drexl, 'Is there a more Economic Approach to IP and Competition Law?' in J. Drexl (ed), *Research Handbook on Intellectual Property and Competition Law* (Cheltenham, UK, Northampton, MA, USA: Edward Elgar, 2008).

[3] Case 258/78 *Nungesser v Commission* [1982] ECR 2015, [1983] 1 CMLR 278.

[4] Case 42/84 *Remia BV and Verenigde Bedrijven Nutricia v Commission* [1985] ECR 2545, [1987] 1 CMLR 1.

[5] Case 161/84 *Pronuptia de Paris GmbH v Pronuptia de Paris Irmgard Schillgallis* [1986] ECR 353, [1986] 1 CMLR 414.

14.3 THE SCOPE OF THE PATENT DOCTRINE AND RESTRICTION ON COMPETITION

IP licensing historically enjoyed a special position under the test of restriction of competition in Article 101(1). In the period prior to *Consten and Grundig*, many restrictions in patent licensing agreements were found to be acceptable under Article 101(1), provided that they did not go beyond the scope of the patent rights of the licensor, as patentee.

The concept of scope of the patent was derived from US antitrust law[6] and the German law against restraints on competition,[7] both of which maintained that certain practices which extended the original grant of exclusivity, such as tie-ins of non-patented products with patented products; price and territorial restrictions on the sale of a patented product, post expiration royalties; licensee veto of other licensees; territorial restrictions on a sale of unpatented products made with a patented process as misuse of the patent, were illegal *per se*.[8]

The Commission's concept of scope of the patent accepted that certain clauses in IP licences which simply divided and shared the licensor's rights as patentee were not restrictions of competition. At this stage, the Commission was prepared to draw a distinction between provisions in the licensing agreement which flowed from the inherent subject matter of the licensed right and formed part of the right itself and which should be compatible with Article 101(1) and those clauses which were an attempt to extend the economic power of the licensor beyond its inherent scope.[9] This first category formed a notable exception to the Commission's freedom of action concept of restriction on competition which applied more widely to exclusive distribution and other agreements. Implicit in the Commission's reasoning was that because the licence was a subdivision of a right granted by legislation, it deprived no third party of its freedom of action.[10]

The influence of the doctrine of scope of the patent reached its high point in the Commission's Notice on Patent Licensing Agreements of 1962 (the so called 'Christmas Message'). This Notice provided that a patent licence containing only limitations as to technical applications or fields of use, quantity of products to be manufactured, or restrictions on time, or persons to carry out the licensing role would not

[6] Under US law, the patent misuse doctrine evolved from patent law and was later taken up by antitrust law to find clauses which extended the scope of the original exclusivity beyond the patentee itself to be patent abuse. See eg *Mercoid Corp v Mid Continent Investment Co* 320 US 661 (1943).

[7] Section 20(1) of the Act against Restraints of Competition provides that patent licensing agreements are void to the extent that they impose restraints on the licensee which exceed the scope of the patent grant. Certain restrictions are deemed not to exceed the patent right.

[8] EU Case 193/83 *Windsurfing International v Commission* [1986] ECR 61 remains on the books as an example of the way an extension of a licensing agreement, beyond the scope of a patent by tying a patented product with a non-patented product, could make the agreement unenforceable.

[9] See eg *First Report of Competition Policy (1972)*, pp 65–74; *Fourth Report on Competition Policy (1974)*, point 20.

[10] In Joined Cases 40–48, 50, 54–56, 111, 113, and 114/73 *Zucker Unie v Commission* [1975] ECR 1663, [1976] 1 CMLR 295, an analogous argument was attempted that since the government regulation had already restricted competition, the contractual cooperation was not itself restrictive of competition.

be caught by Article 101(1). What was particularly significant about the Notice was its acceptance that licensors involved in a single licensing relationship could give an 'exclusive' licence to a licensee for a particular territory, ie a licence which restricted the licensor not only from appointing any other licensee in that territory but also from making, using, or selling itself in that territory, and not be caught by Article 101(1).

The Commission's reasons for clearing patent licensing agreements in this way were also pragmatic.[11] It thought at the time that patent licences were 'not likely to affect trade between Member States as things stand in the Community at present'.[12] Moreover, it was preoccupied with the issues of formulating a block exemption for distribution agreements and would not have welcomed a flood of notifications of patent licensing agreements.[13]

In the event, the scope of the patent doctrine as incorporated in the Notice helped to shelter patent licensing from the effects of the Commission's 'freedom of action' doctrine throughout the 1960s.

It provided a basis to reconcile IP licensing with Article 101 which allowed considerable weight to be given to the legislative policy underpinning an IPR.[14] Unlike distribution agreements, patent licensing agreements could remain free of the notification/exemption decision under Article 101 because such agreements were not caught by Article 101(1) in the first place. There was little pressure for a block exemption at this stage.

By the early 1970s, the attitude of the Commission to licensing of IPRs had dramatically changed. This was in part due to the greater awareness of the potential of IPR licences to seal off markets and limit interstate competition created by the *Consten and Grundig* judgment.[15] It was also due, however, to the Commission's overzealous interpretation of its role as protector of the flows of direct and parallel trade between the Member States. Instead of drawing a distinction between exclusive territorial manufacturing licences and territorial sales restrictions, it chose to apply *per se* prohibitions to both. It is worth considering each point in greater detail.

14.4 THE *CONSTEN AND GRUNDIG* JUDGMENT

If one were to read Article 101(1) literally, it would appear to be confined to the type of anti-competitive agreements specified in Article 101(1) (a)–(e)—fixing prices, limiting production, limiting markets, price discrimination, etc. In *Grundig*, however, the CJEU widened the scope of the prohibition in Article 101(1) by defining it to apply to market partitioning agreements. Thus it stated that the infringement of Article 101

[11] See eg W. Alexander, 'Patent Licensing Agreements in the EC' [1986] *IIC* 1.

[12] See D. Goyder, *EC Competition Law* (2nd edn, Oxford: OUP, 1993), p 290.

[13] See Alexander (n 11 above).

[14] Although directed essentially at patent licensing, it could also have been developed to fit other types of intellectual property licensing such as trade marks, copyright, and design rights.

[15] Cases 56 and 58/64 *Establissements Consten SA & Grundig-Verkaufts-GmbH v Commission* [1966] ECR 299, [1996] CMLR 418.

consisted of the attempt by the licensor and licensee to isolate 'the French market for Grundig products and maintain . . . artificially, for products of a very well-known brand, separate national markets within the community'.[16] This was prohibited under Article 101 as an attempt 'to distort competition in the common market'.

An agreement between producer and distributor which might tend to restore the national divisions in trade between Member States might be such as to frustrate the most fundamental object of the Union. The Treaty whose preamble and content aim at abolishing the barriers between states, and which in several provisions gives evidence of a stern attitude with regard to their reappearance, could not allow undertakings to reconstruct such barriers. Article 101(1) is designed to pursue this aim, even in the case of agreements between undertakings placed at different levels of the economic process.

In the course of the judgment in *Grundig*, too, the case was made that the distribution agreement was not a restriction of competition because it added a new competitor to the French market to compete with other brands. Consten and Grundig argued that the Commission should have based its approach on a rule of reason and considered the economic effects of the disputed contracts on competition between the different brands. More specifically, it should have taken into consideration the fact that a vertical sole dealer relationship, by introducing a new competitor into the French market, increases interbrand competition in that market. The CJEU accepted that 'competition between producers is generally more noticeable than that between distributors of the same make'.[17] However, it was particularly concerned to exclude this as a mitigating factor in a situation where an agreement inhibited interstate trade. As the CJEU put it:

> The principle of freedom of competition concerns the various stages and manifestations of competition. Although competition between producers is generally more noticeable than that between distributors of the same make, it does not . . . follow that an agreement tending to restrict the latter kind of competition should escape the prohibition in Article 101(1) merely because it might increase the former.[18]

This decision to group vertical agreements together with horizontal agreements as equal subjects of competition law regulation was a new departure in the practice of competition law systems.

The legacy of *Consten and Grundig* was a framework establishing two important parameters for the regulation of IPR licensing both stemming from the constitutional role of Article 101 to promote the integration of the separate markets of the EU into a single market. The first parameter it established was that an agreement which contained measures to partition markets was restrictive of competition under Article 101(1), thus creating curbs on the scope for the normal exercise of the option of IP licensing. The second was the creation of a *per se* restriction which was not only prohibited by Article 101(1) but was also non-exemptible under Article 101(3), again because of the market integration imperative.

[16] Ibid.
[17] Ibid.
[18] Ibid.

14.5 THE COMMISSION'S CHANGE OF POLICY

In the period after *Consten and Grundig*, and with the exclusive distribution block exemption approved, the Commission decided that it could turn its attentions to the need to monitor restrictions in networks of licensing agreements which affected interstate trade. The large number of licensing agreements which had been notified to it had made it plain that networks of multiple parallel licensing agreements created exclusive territories which coincided with the territory of Member States. Yet the exclusive territorial rights to manufacture did not in themselves contribute to the sealing off effects; it was the accompanying territorial sales restrictions.

Where an exclusive licensing agreement restricted to one territory is part of a wider licensing network, there is always the potential for competition between the licensees who have been allocated exclusive territories. The territorial nature of the manufacturing and sales right does not restrict the free movement of goods which incorporate the right. Under EU law, the right of free circulation attaches to the goods as soon as they are placed on the market and possibly as soon as they are manufactured.[19] Consequently, the licensees can engage in direct sales to other licensees' territories, whether actively, by advertising, or passively by responding to unsolicited orders. Moreover, the customers of a licensee can engage in parallel trading, exporting and importing the licensed goods and services between the different territories of the licensees as well as that of the licensor. In such a situation, the territorial sales restrictions imposed on the licensees might reduce interstate trade but not exclusive territorial restrictions on manufacture by themselves. The only effect of an exclusive licence is to limit the number of licensees with a right to manufacture and sell in the protected area. By itself, an exclusive licence to manufacture and sell has no effect on direct or parallel sales from other Member States.[20]

The Commission's *First Report on Competition Policy* summed up the change in position by stating its renewed concern with the freedom of action or economic autonomy of the parties. It stated that where the owner of a patent conferred an exclusive right to another undertaking in an assigned area, 'he loses the freedom to enter into agreements with other applicants. The exclusive character of such a licence may amount to a restriction of competition and thus fall within the category of prohibited agreements in so far as it has an appreciable effect on market conditions.'[21]

The Commission was prepared to apply a quantitative appreciability test to such agreements, but not a qualitative appreciability test. It preferred such licensing agreements to be tested under Article 101(3). This change in Commission practice resulted in cases that called into question the assumptions of the scope of the patent doctrine in

[19] See eg B. Van der Asch, 'Intellectual Property Rights under EC Law' [1983] *Fordham Corp Law Inst* 539.

[20] Cf R. Joliet, 'Trademark Licensing under the EEC Law of Competition' [1984] *IIC* 31.

[21] Annex to the Fifth General Report on the Activities of the Communities, April 1972, at pt 78.

the Notice and meant that there was a greater need for patent licensing agreements to be notified to the Commission for exemption.[22]

The parties to licensing agreements now found themselves in a similar position to the parties to exclusive distribution agreements but without the benefit of the exclusive dealing block exemption. Industry was faced with the need to notify patent licensing agreements to the Commission in order to obtain certainty as to their legal validity, and responded by engaging in intensive lobbying of national governments. There were also efforts made to introduce provisions in the drafting of the Community Patent Convention in 1975 to offset the Commission's policy.[23] Article 43(1) of the draft Convention provided that a Community patent may be licensed in whole or in part for the whole or parts of the territories in which it is effective and that a licence may be exclusive or non-exclusive. Article 43(2) then added that the rights conferred by the Community patent may be invoked against a licensee who contravenes any restriction in his licence which is covered by Article 43(1). These were meant to be a signal that such restrictions were not contrary to the treaty.[24]

The Commission responded to this concern by preparing a new patent licensing block exemption to deal with the expected large numbers of notifications. It also introduced a Notice on Sub-Contracting Agreements to help certain types of subcontracting agreements involving licences to be cleared by a group notice.[25] It was not prepared to bow to the lobbying pressure in respect of territorial exclusivity under Article 101(1).

In its *Fourth Report on Competition Policy* in 1975, the Commission attempted to reconcile its decisions with the earlier pronouncements of the Court of Justice concerning IPRs:

> On a legal plane, the Commission faces the problems exposed by the Court of Justice in its distinction between the existence of nationally protected industrial property rights, which is not to be affected by community law, and the exercise of these rights, which can be subject to the Treaty rules.
>
> The assessment of patent licensing agreements under the Treaty calls upon a consideration of interests and issues which go beyond the field of competition policy . . .

It has been suggested that the policy of the Commission was that it would 'in future . . . regard all export restrictions as needing an exemption under Article [101(3)] and thus as not belonging to the "essence" of the patent'. The Commission's policy, however, went further; it seemed to treat the sharing of exclusivity geographically as outside the scope of the patent under Article 101(1) without applying an appreciability test.

During this period too the Commission adjusted the concept of the 'essence' or 'scope of the patent' in respect of non-territorial restrictions in order to meet

[22] See eg *Burroughs-Geha-Werke* OJ L 13/53 (1972); *Burroughs-Delplanque* OJ EC L 13/50 (1972); see also *Davidson Rubber* OJ EC L 143/31 (1972).

[23] See Alexander (n 11 above).

[24] Ibid.

[25] Notice on Contractors and Subcontractors [1979] 1 CMLR 264.

competition concerns. In *AOIP v Beyrard*,[26] for example, the Commission found that certain non-territorial provisions were prohibited by Article 101(1), for example the no-challenge clause, non-competition clause, the obligation to pay royalties during the lifetime of the most recent original or improvement patent, whether or not the original patent was being exploited by the licensee. These were all viewed as going beyond the scope of the patent and not only caught by Article 101(1) but also inherently non-exemptible under Article 101(3).

In its *Fourth Report on Competition Policy*, however, the Commission indicated that subdivisions of the grant of the IPR could be compatible with Article 101(1) *subject to the absence of competition effects* (our emphasis). For example, restrictions on the duration of the licence were allowed within the frame of the duration of the original grant. Restrictions on field of use were allowed but only as long as they were not disguised market sharing arrangements. Quantitative output restrictions were caught by Article 101(1).[27]

This restrictive policy towards both territorial and non-territorial restraints in licensing agreements was reflected in the draft block exemption for patent licensing officially published in 1979. It allowed territorial exclusivity to all licensees but restricted all territorial sales restraints and export bans to SMEs only, defining these as undertakings with a turnover of less than 100 million ECU. It incorporated a 'black list' of fourteen clauses, the presence of any of which would preclude the application of the block exemption. It also offered a 'white list' of nine restraints which would not prevent exemption which were more based on the test of clearance under Article 101(1), stating only that they may or may not be caught under Article 101(1).

A factor that appears to have reinforced the Commission's attitude towards non-territorial restrictions in patent licensing agreements was the knowledge that the Antitrust Division of the US Justice Department, under the influence of the 'patent misuse' doctrine developed by the US Supreme Court,[28] had developed a set of administrative guidelines to antitrust enforcement[29] in the form of 'Nine No-Nos' for patent licensing.[30]

[26] OJ EC L 6/8 (1976).

[27] Annex to Seventh General Report on the Activities of the Communities, 1975 pts 19 and 20.

[28] Under the impetus of Mr Justice Douglas. See eg *Morton Salt Co v G. S. Suppiger Co*, 314 US 488 (1941); *United States v United States Gypsum Co* 333 US 364 (1947).

[29] Wilson, Dept. of Justice Luncheon Speech, 'Law on Licensing Practice—Myth or Reality Straight Talk from Alice in Wonderland'.

[30] The following restrictions were viewed as *per se* unlawful:

(1) tie-ins; (2) grant backs; (3) resale restraints; (4) tie-outs; (5) licensee vetoes; (6) mandatory package licences; (7) royalties not reasonably related to the licensees' sales of the patented product; (8) restrictions on the sale of an unpatented product manufactured with a patented process; (9) price restrictions on sales of a licensed product. Oppenheim, Weston, and McCarthy, *Federal Antitrust Laws Tenth Commentary* (4th edn, 1981), 885–7.

At this stage, the Justice Department appeared to be unconcerned about the effects of strict antitrust rules upon the process of innovation.[31]

The influence of the 'Nine No-Nos' reached into the European Commission in the preparation of the draft block exemption. As Hartmut Johannes, the administrator within DGIV (the Competition Directorate) with responsibility for IPRs, put it in 1978, 'In the art of antitrust, the Americans are the teachers and the Europeans are the pupils.' He indicated that US thinking was not accepted uncritically; in particular, its *per se* rules and the horizontal/vertical distinction were not transferable. However, he also acknowledged that when the Commission prepared its draft patent licensing block exemption, 'It knew the no nos but of course not the American critics of these no nos; the critics dated from 1981.'[32]

For IP owners in the EU, the main worries created by the Commission's policy surrounded its refusal to accept the logic of the need for protection of new licensees against competition from other licensees as well as the licensor during the period the licensee was tooling up and familiarizing itself with the new technology. These were not allayed by the draft block exemption with its relatively low turnover limits.

Industry was uneasy because, until an appropriate block exemption could be prepared, it was faced with a pervasive notification requirement for IP licences. The Commission's policy at this stage appeared to be doubly unfriendly towards innovation. It insisted upon an automatic prohibition of exclusive territorial licences under Article 101(1), in spite of the costs and delays of notification. Yet in its draft block exemption it appeared to be unwilling to translate Article 101(3) to allow protection for territorial sales restrictions to any but the smallest firms.

Competition policy at that stage was so focused on monitoring exclusivity in licensing agreements that it risked deterring investment in innovation and technology transfer. It appeared to ignore the need under the Treaty to strike a balance between the protection of interstate trade and the promotion of the diffusion of the manufacture of new technologies throughout the common market.

[31] In 1967, the Assistant Attorney General announced: 'I do not believe that the impact of antitrust on patent licensing restrictions has any effect on innovative activity whatsoever . . . to me it seems probably so even if antitrust law were to go so far as to prohibit not only price fixing but also field of use restrictions, quantity restrictions, territorial restrictions, and any other restriction on the complete freedom of the licensee.' In Turner, 'Antitrust and Innovation' (1967) 12 *Antitrust Bulletin* 277, 281.

[32] This was a reference to the groundswell in antitrust thinking which had been introduced by a combination of the writings of Chicago School adherents such as Bork and Posner and the experience of the administrators within the Justice Department. See E. Fox, 'The New American Competition Policy—from Antitrust to Pro-Efficiency' [1981] 2 *ECLR* 439; see also eg R. Bork, *An Antitrust Paradox: A Policy at War with Itself* (2nd edn, New York: Basic Books, 1978, reissued 1993); R. Posner, *Antitrust Law. An Economic Perspective* (University of Chicago Press, 1976). By 1987 the Department's views had begun to change quite radically. It signalled the change by suggesting that there was a need to differentiate between horizontal and vertical restraints and to move away from a formalistic approach to an economic approach consisting of an evaluation of licensing restraints. See Abbot Lipsky, 'Current Antitrust Division Views on Patent Licensing Practices' Antitrust Section of the ABA, 15 November 1981, (1981) *Trade Regulation Reporter* (CCH) 55, 985.

14.6 THE COURT OF JUSTICE'S APPLICATION OF THE APPRECIABILITY TEST TO INTELLECTUAL PROPERTY RIGHTS

14.6.1 Exclusive territoriality

In the early 1980s, it fell to the Court of Justice to lead the way in easing the competition law framework for IP licensing. The CJEU had previously indicated that the test for territorial exclusivity in vertical contracts should include a qualitative appreciability test in *STM*.[33] In the much awaited decision of *Nungesser v Commission*,[34] the Court of Justice introduced a concept of qualitative appreciabilty that stipulated if the exclusive territorial obligation in the licensing agreement was an indispensable inducement to the licensee to invest in the new technology this could make the agreement compatible with Article 101(1). The case concerned an assignment of breeders' rights to a maize seed variety by INRA, a French research institution, to Eisele who registered the right in Germany. Under the agreement, Eisele was given an exclusive right to manufacture and sell INRA's maize seed variety in Germany. In addition, INRA agreed to refrain, and to prevent others, from importing its maize seed variety in Germany. Eisele had relied upon its IPR to prevent a parallel importer from importing into Germany from another French source and had obtained a court-approved settlement. Receiving a complaint, the Commission decided, following its policy of the 1970s, that all provisions of the agreement were caught by Article 101(1) and could not be exempted under Article 101(3). This meant that the Commission was prepared to treat exclusive territorial licences to manufacture and sell as equally anti-competitive as territorial sales restrictions under Article 101(1). Both required exemption under Article 101(3).

The CJEU objected to the Commission's insistence that an exclusivity clause in a vertical agreement such as an IPR licence was by its nature caught by Article 101(1) as a restriction on competition,[35] because this gave insufficient weight to the fact that the new seed technology could only move to new Member States if the exclusive territorial restriction was part of the contract and was the only means to promote competition.

It thought that there was a need to distinguish between exclusive licences to manufacture and sell in a particular territory on the one hand, and territorial sales restrictions —which consisted of a contractual obligation on other licensees not to sell directly into a protected territory—on the other. The first case, which it called an 'open exclusive licence' was one where 'the exclusivity of the license relates solely to the contractual relationship between the owner of the right and the licensee, whereby the owner merely undertakes not to grant other licenses in respect of the same territory and

[33] Case 56/65 *STM v Maschinenbau Ulm* [1966] ECR 235 at 249, [1966] CMLR 357.

[34] Case 258/78 *Nungesser*.

[35] Ibid, para 2(c).

not to compete himself with the licensee on that territory'.[36] In the second case, which it called a 'closed exclusive licence', the exclusive licence is joined with territorial sales restrictions and IPRs to create an absolute territorial protection under which the parties to the contract propose, as regards the products and the territory in question, to eliminate all competition from third parties, such as parallel importers or licensees for other territories.[37]

The CJEU held that an open exclusive licence, ie an exclusive licence to manufacture and sell in a particular territory, was 'not in itself incompatible with Article 101(1)',[38] reasoning as follows: in case of a licence of breeders' rights over hybrid seeds newly developed in one Member State, an undertaking established in another Member State which was not certain that it would not encounter competition from other licensees for the territory granted to it, or from the owner of the right himself, might be deterred from accepting the risk of cultivating and marketing that product. Such a result would be damaging to the dissemination of a new technology and would prejudice competition in the Union between the new product and similar existing products.

One problem with this exception for open exclusive licences as defined by the CJEU was that it only allowed for a limited form of protection from the other manufacturers within the licence network.[39]

The CJEU indicated that any attempt to place limits on other licensees, as well as on the more obvious category of parallel importers, not to sell into the territory would take the licence outside the scope of an open licence.[40]

14.6.2 The new technology/market opening test

Although the CJEU defined 'open exclusive licences' as a category which is not automatically caught by Article 101(1), it did not hold that all 'open' licences were cleared. Instead, it held that the exception was to be limited to cases where the technology was (1) new to the licensee's market, (2) where the technology had been developed after years of research and experimentation; (3) where, without the exclusivity, the licensee might not have been willing to take on the risks of developing and marketing that new product; and (4) where the exclusive protection offered in the agreement applied only to manufacturing and selling the products produced by that manufacture in the territory.[41] It did not extend to limits on selling rights outside the territory or any

[36] Ibid.

[37] Ibid, at para 53.

[38] Case 258/78 *Nungesser* at para 53.

[39] Thus, the licensee could have protection under the contract against either the licensor or other licensees locating manufacturing operations in the territory. The Court reasoned that this limited form of security to the licensee was necessary to induce risky investment and it offered no contractual protection against technical products sold in other territories and imported into the territory.

[40] Case 258/78 *Nungesser*; see M. Siragusa, 'Technology Transfers under EEC Law, A Private View' [1983] *Fordham Corp Law Inst* 95.

[41] Ibid, at paras 55–8.

attempts to place limits on other licensees to sell into the territory. In taking this decision, the CJEU was not concerned to draw a line between IPRs and competition policy as such, but rather between the need for adequate incentives for the integration of manufacturing processes and the need to protect interstate trade. No mention was made of the existence/exercise distinction or the specific subject matter issue. The case turned on the specific nature of the technology and the extent of protection against risks that was necessary to achieve its dissemination.[42]

In *Coditel II*,[43] the CJEU went a step further and held that an agreement conferring an exclusive right to exhibit a film for a specified period in the territory of the Member States with absolute territorial protection is not necessarily caught by Article 101(1).

In the *Coditel* cases, a Belgian company, Cine Vog Films, had obtained exclusive exhibition rights to a French film, *Le Boucher*, for a five-year period. It discovered that Coditel, a group of Belgian cable companies, had obtained the film from a transmission broadcast by the German licensee with exclusive rights in Germany. In *Coditel I*,[44] Cine Vog was able to obtain an injunction to prohibit Coditel from transmitting the film on Belgian television without offending Article 56 TFEU (free movement of services). Coditel had argued that such exclusive rights limited to Member States would result in a partitioning of the common market as regards the undertaking of economic action in the film industry. The CJEU, however, took note of the specific characteristics of the product, ie that it was a literary or artistic work available to the public which may be infinitely repeated and presented problems of copyright different from other works such as books which are circulated in a material form. It also took note of the contract which stipulated that the right to show the film on Belgian television could not be exercised until a fixed number of months after the first showing of the film in cinemas in Belgium. The CJEU considered that this highlighted the fact that the right of a copyright owner and his assigns to require fees for any showing is part of the essential function of copyright in this type of literary and artistic work. The CJEU reasoned that the effect of these factors was that:

> while copyright entails the right to demand fees for any showing or performance, the rules in the Treaty cannot in principle constitute an obstacle to the geographical limits which the parties to a contract of assignment have agreed upon in order to protect the author and his assigns in this regard. The mere fact that these geographical limits may coincide with national frontiers does not point to a different solution in situations where television is organized in the Member States largely on the basis of legal broadcasting monopolies.[45]

The CJEU held that the assignee could rely on his performing right to prohibit an unauthorized showing by cable television without offending Article 56 TFEU.

[42] See eg Jan Peeters, 'The Rule of Reason Revisited: Prohibition on Restraints of Competition in the Sherman Act and the EEC Treaty' (1989) 37 *The American Journal of Comparative Law* 521, 526.

[43] Case 262/81 *Coditel v Ciné Vog Films (Coditel (II))* [1982] ECR 3381, [1983] 1 CMLR 49.

[44] Case 62/79 *Coditel v Ciné Vog Films (Coditel I))* [1980] ECR 881, [1981] 2 CMLR 362.

[45] Ibid, at para 16.

In *Coditel II*, the cable company group Coditel appealed from the decision of a Belgian court awarding damages to Cine Vog for the unauthorized transmission. The theory of Coditel on this occasion was that Article 101 could be applied to the agreement and that its prohibition applied to the exclusive licence or assignment of the copyright as an improper exercise as the means of a restrictive agreement. The CJEU accepted that in principle the exercise of an IPR in the form of an agreement may be incompatible with Article 101 but it held that:

> The mere fact that the owner of a copyright in a firm has granted to a sole licensee the exclusive right to exhibit that film in the territory of a Member State and consequently to prohibit, during a specified period, its showing by others is not sufficient to justify the finding that a contract must be regarded as the purpose, the means or the result of an agreement, decision or concerted practice prohibited by the Treaty.[46]

The CJEU was willing to allow the licensor to bestow absolute territorial protection upon the licensee because the industry was engaged in an integrative activity and investment in licensing the product protected by the IPR could only be secured if the full territorial protection was allowed. The CJEU reiterated the distinction it drew in *Coditel I*, ie between licences of works which are performing rights which can be infinitely repeated without anything physical being put on the market and other types of literary and artistic works such as books or records which cannot be circulated in the market apart from their material form. In the Article 101(1) context, this was not so much an attentiveness to the nature of the IPR; rather, the CJEU was willing to justify the absolute territorial protection on the basis that it was necessary to prevent the purpose of the licensing agreement from being entirely frustrated.[47]

The CJEU's concern for the protection of the IPR and a need to ensure a just return on the investment made in developing the industrial property should also be seen as prompted more by the need to ensure that the film industry continued to penetrate national markets than to an insistence upon allowing inventors to appropriate their just return. The CJEU indicated that its indispensability test for territorial protection was related to the special 'characteristics of the [film] industry and its markets in the Community, especially those relating to dubbing and subtitling for the benefit of different language groups, to the possibilities of television broadcasts, and to the system of financing [film] production in Europe'.[48] In other words, where the financing of the integration of film production through the medium of television throughout Europe would be jeopardized by inadequate IPR protection, and the only adequate protection was absolute territorial protection, the CJEU was prepared to allow such protection to ensure that the process of interstate film distribution would actually take place.

46 Case 262/81 *Coditel II*.

47 See R. Joliet, 'Territorial and Exclusive Trade mark Licensing under the EEC Law of Competition' [1984] *IIC* 21.

48 Case 262/81 *Coditel II*.

The Advocate General had suggested that a just return for IPRs in the film industry related to the specific object of the IPR and was therefore not caught by Article 101(1) but this was not referred to in the CJEU's judgment. Instead, the CJEU referred only to a fair return upon the investment made. It was the task of the national court to determine whether the exclusive agreement created barriers which were artificial or unjustifiable in terms of the needs of the industry, of undue duration, or based on fees which exceeded a fair return on investment.[49] Moreover, the CJEU was careful to set limits to the width of the exception it was creating for Community-wide film. It would be curtailed where the object or effect was to prevent or restrict the distribution of films or where competition within the film market was distorted.[50] Nevertheless, the CJEU had created the basis for a further exception in the definition of restraint of competition under Article 101(1).

In *Erauw Jacquery*,[51] the CJEU showed once again that the width of the exception in Article 101(1) would vary with the type of product protected by an IPR and the industry in which it is used. In this case, the CJEU was prepared to find an export ban indispensable but the circumstances were unusual. The licence was for basic seed (ie seeds used to produce the seeds used by growers for the production of cereals) from the licensor to the propagator and the licensor insisted on an export ban for the purpose of quality control. The export ban and customer restrictions on licensees were held to be compatible with Article 101(1) because they were objectively justified by the need to ensure the proper handling of seeds by the growers who enjoyed a licence only for propagation. The CJEU stated that 'a person who has made considerable efforts to develop varieties of basic seed which may be the subject matter of plant breeders rights must be allowed to protect himself against any improper handling of those varieties of seed'.[52] The protection against improper handling of seed could only be assured by a restriction of propagation to selected licensees. To that extent the clause prohibiting the licensee from selling and exporting basic seeds did not come within the prohibition laid down by Article 101(1) of the Treaty.[53].

The Advocate General compared the risk of the technology in the seed finding its way into the hands of rivals as comparable with the risk faced by a franchisor that its franchised know-how might benefit competitors. The CJEU was also strongly influenced by the substantial financial commitment made in investing in the development of the seed.[54] Although the CJEU referred to *Nungesser*, this reference was to the financial commitment of the licensor in developing the product and the urgency of the need for protection for the licensor's investment rather than to the need for an adequate incentive of territorial protection for the economic risks undertaken by the licensee.

[49] Ibid, at para 19.

[50] Ibid, at para 20.

[51] Case 27/87 *Erauw–Jacquéry Sprl v La Hesbignonne Société Coopérative* [1988] ECR 1919, [1988] 4 CMLR 576.

[52] Ibid.

[53] Ibid, at para 10.

[54] Ibid. It has been argued that the Court did not base its findings on the existence/exercise distinction but rather the value of the IPR. J. Derbyshire, 'Computer Programs and Competition Policy: A Block Exemption for Software Licensing' [1994] 9 *EIPR*, 370.

It would be a mistake to conclude from the indispensability analysis of these exceptions that a general doctrine of ancillary restraints is more widely available to clear *territorial* IPR restraints, given the CJEU's concerns with market partitioning under Article 101(1). Instead, the test appears to be two-fold: is the degree of territorial protection essential to ensure that the licensing agreement will result in a market opening for the product? Are its effects on intra-brand interstate outweighed by the benefits of the extension of manufacture of goods or provision of service? In the case of *Erauw Jacquery*, for example, the CJEU placed great weight on the need for protection for quality control purposes. The costs of the ban on exports were outweighed by the penetration benefits of the basic licence. In *Pronuptia*,[55] the CJEU made it clear in the context of franchise agreements where brands were well-known, that territorial exclusivity incentives for franchising were not to be regarded as genuine ancillary restraints for the purposes of Article 101(1) unless the franchise brand *was relatively unknown*. However, for established franchise operations, territorial exclusivity as such could be caught by Article 101(1).

Nevertheless, the sequence of cases since *Nungesser* has made the point that the test of 'qualitative' appreciability applies to territorial exclusivity in IPR licensing agreements. The Commission has acknowledged the existence of these as exceptions to its general rule, but applied them sparingly. The new technology exception in *Nungesser* has been strictly construed so that the test of 'newness' can be difficult to meet. For example, in *Velcro/Aplix*, the Commission refused to clear an exclusivity clause because the technology was not new.[56] In *Rich Products/Jus Rol*, the fact that other firms in the UK and in other Member States had developed processes for freezing yeast, even though they were not easily accessible, meant that the technology was not 'new' under Article 101(1).[57] In *Delta Chemie* the fact that the licensee had previously acted as the distributor meant that the technology was not new. Moreover, the Commission stated that the exception in *Erauw Jacquery* was to be limited to licences for the propagation of basic seed.[58]

14.6.3 Non-territorial restraints and restrictions on competition

In the field of non-territorial restraints, there has been more of a consensus between Commission and EU Courts over the concepts applicable to clear the provisions of licensing agreements.[59] The EU Courts' endorsement of the concept of 'ancillary

[55] Case 161/84 *Pronuptia*.

[56] [1989] 4 CMLR 157.

[57] [1988] 4 CMLR 527.

[58] [1939] 4 CMLR 535.

[59] The concept of the 'scope of the IPR' has been accepted in relation to non-territorial restrictions as a partial exercise of the IPR granted by legislation and therefore one which deprives no third party of its freedom of action. However, this concept has proved to be a two-edged sword in the sense that a contractual provision which goes beyond the scope of the IPR could not only be caught by Article 101(1); it would also be non-exemptible under Article 101(3). See Case 193/83 *Windsurfing International Inc v Commission* [1986] ECR 611.

The earlier importance of scope of the patent in defining restriction on competition has waned owing largely to the growth of the overlapping doctrine of ancillary restraints developed by the Court of Justice.

restraints' has led to an important second basis for finding clauses in licensing contracts to be not appreciably restrictive of competition.[60] During the 1970s, the Commission actually began to acknowledge that in the case of certain agreements which were pro-competitive, some of their contractual restraints which were objectively indispensable to the nature and purpose of the agreement could be regarded as not being restrictive of competition. The concept originated in transfer of business cases but its logic was soon applied to IP licences. In *Reuter/BASF*,[61] the Commission was confronted with a non-competition clause contained in a sale of a business agreement, which was indispensable if the agreement were to be made. Without it, the buyer would be prey to competition from the seller and would be deterred from entering the agreement in the first place. Since the sale itself was not an anti-competitive agreement, the Commission was prepared to accept the presence of a necessary contractual restraint as a restriction or distortion of competition, as long as it was of reasonable duration. The Commission also held that a prohibition of the transferor divulging secret know-how was not caught by Article 101(1).

The test of indispensability, while giving recognition to commercial logic, was essentially formalistic in method. If a contractual restraint was indispensable to the overall purpose of an agreement which was acceptable in competition terms, the provision could be viewed as an exception from the category of contractual restraints which are *ipso facto* 'restrictions on competition'.

In *Remia and Nutricia*,[62] the Court of Justice applied similar reasoning to a case where the non-competition clause placed on the seller in the first transaction was then extended to the buyer in the second transaction. Again, the issue under Article 101(1) was not whether the agreement had a pro-competitive effect but whether the restriction was necessary to make the transfer of assets fully effective.

In the case of *Pronuptia*,[63] the CJEU had the occasion to apply ancillary restraints reasoning under Article 101(1) to the licensing of know-how together with a trade mark in a distribution franchising agreement. The franchisee, wishing no longer to be bound by the royalty obligation, claimed that the franchise agreement was prohibited by Article 101(1) and was therefore unenforceable under Article 101(2). The CJEU held first of all that the compatibility of such agreements with Article 101(1) could only be assessed by reference to the provisions in the agreement in their economic context. The franchise system allows a franchisor to profit from its success by extending a business through the exploitation of its know-how without further capital investment. The franchisee obtains access to the methods and name of an established business in return for an upfront payment and a royalty. The effect of the agreement is to allow the franchisor to penetrate new markets with the financial help of independent resellers.

[60] See discussion in E. Gonzalez Dias, 'Some Reflections on the Notion of Ancillary Restraints' [1995] *Fordham Corp Law Inst* 325.

[61] [1976] 2 CMLR D44.

[62] Case 42/84 *Remia and Nutricia*.

[63] Case 161/84 *Pronuptia*.

The CJEU identified two conditions which were indispensable to the proper functioning of the system. The first was 'the franchisor must be able to communicate his know-how to the franchisees and provide them with the necessary assistance in order to enable them to apply his methods without running the risk that his know-how and assistance might benefit his competitors even indirectly'.This made the following clauses essential:

1. The franchisee's obligation not to open a shop of the same or a similar nature in an area where he may compete with a member of the network, during the period of validity of the contract and for a reasonable period after its expiry (ie one year).

2. The franchisee's obligation not to transfer his shop to another party without the prior approval of the franchisor.

The second condition the CJEU identified as essential was 'the franchisor must be able to take the measures necessary for maintaining the identity and the reputation of the network bearing his business name or symbol'. It followed that provisions which establish the means of control necessary for that purpose were also not restrictions on competition for the purpose of Article 101(1). The CJEU accepted that there were six provisions justified as ancillary restraints under this criterion. As mentioned, the CJEU was unwilling to extend the logic of the concept of ancillary restraints to territorial exclusivity incentives for franchising where brands were well-known. It stated that territorial restrictions in the franchising agreement were not genuine ancillary restraints nor indispensable. This view reinforced the point that territorial restrictions in franchise agreements, and by implication other types of vertical IP licensing agreements, normally required exemption.

These judgments both reinforce and overlap with the economic reasoning in the TTA Guidelines that clears agreements between non-competitors. They will be useful to support arguments based on the methodology of the TTA Guidelines because of their greater legal authority before a court or arbitration tribunal. Moreover, other judgments calling into question some of the tenets of the modernized approach will undoubtedly be used by whichever side finds it helpful to produce a result.

The Court of Justice's recent judgments suggest that the economic assessment of the Guidelines will not always be the final word in decisions under Article 101(1). In *Competition Authority v Beef Industry Development Society Ltd,* the Court of Justice made it clear that the two-step test did not apply to agreements between *competitors*.[64] For such agreements, the test remained the old test: whether the rivalry between the parties was reduced. Moreover, there is still some strength in the older Court judgments on market opening and ancillary restraints to assess the possibilities of clearing clauses under Article 101(1).[65]

[64] Case C-209/07 *Competition Authority v Beef Industry Development Society Ltd et al* [2008] ECR I–8637.

[65] See discussion in J. Faull and A. Nikpay, *The EC Law of Competition* (Oxford: OUP, 2007), Ch 3.

15

THE TECHNOLOGY TRANSFER BLOCK EXEMPTION REGULATION AND TECHNOLOGY TRANSFER AGREEMENT GUIDELINES

15.1 Introduction: The Evolution of EU Competition Policy towards IP Licensing Agreements 251
15.2 The Current Phase 255
15.3 The Main Features of the New Technology Transfer Regulation and Guidelines 257
15.4 The New Methods of Assessing Individual Restraints in Licensing Agreements outside the Safe Harbour of the TTBER 266

15.1 INTRODUCTION: THE EVOLUTION OF EU COMPETITION POLICY TOWARDS IP LICENSING AGREEMENTS

The current TTBER and TTA Guidelines represents the third main phase in the evolution of EU competition policy towards IP licensing. In the first phase in the 1960s and 1970s there was a strong concern by EU regulators to limit the scope for IP licensing. This was partly because of the influence of the doctrines of the US Supreme Court about patent monopoly and the 'Nine No-Nos' of the US Department of Justice and Fair Trade Commission in respect of patent licensing and partly because of internal EU worries about market partitioning heightened by the *Grundig*[1] case. During this period inadequate thought was given to the pro-competitive features of IPRs and IP licensing

[1] Cases 56 and 58/64 *Establissements Consten SA & Grundig-Verkaufts-GmbH v Commission* [1966] ECR 299, [1966] CMLR 418.

or the damaging economic effects of a restrictive competition policy upon investment in IPRs.

By the mid-1980s, there was a sea change in the regulation of IP licensing. US regulators, courts, and legislators led the way by changing the rules to reflect a more economically realistic assessment of the market power of patent holders. The regime of 'the Nine No-Nos' was dismantled under the IP friendlier policy of the DOJ/FTC. This change coincided with a new approach in the EU Courts—the acceptance of vertical exclusive IP licences as pro-competitive in the *Nungesser* case in the CJEU.[2]

During this second phase of the regulatory framework for IP licensing, the Commission adopted the regulatory device of form-based and legalistic block exemption regulations (BERs). The first IP licensing block exemption regulations were adopted, the Patent Licensing BER (2467/84) in 1984 and the Know-how BER (556/89) in 1989 by the European Commission and Council. During this period, too, EU concerns about market partitioning were partially eased by the growth of the doctrine of exhaustion and the build-up of established pathways of interstate trade.

The two IP licensing BERs of the 1980s were replaced in 1996 by a single Technology Transfer Block Exemption Regulation 240/96 (Regulation 240/96), applying both to pure or mixed patent licensing and know-how agreements. The scope of the new unified block exemption was slightly widened by its definition of certain other IPRs like utility models, semi-conductor topographies, and plant breeder certificates as 'patents' for the purpose of the Regulation. However, Regulation 240/96 continued the practice of allowing the licensing of certain other IPRs, such as trade marks and copyright protection, to be exempted as part of the package, only if they were not the main purpose of the agreement, ie if such IPRs were 'ancillary' to the main purpose of the agreement which had to be that of licensing patents and/or know-how.[3]

Shortly before, in 1995, the US Fair Trade Commission and the Antitrust Division of the Justice Department had produced their Antitrust Guidelines to the Licensing of Intellectual Property, offering a more economic regulatory model.[4] The legal framework for technology transfer created by Regulation 240/96, however, continued to be form-based and legalistic in the sense that certain clauses were either exemptible or non-exemptible depending almost entirely on their form. To qualify for exemption the parties were required to draft an agreement that was consistent with the Commission's three-fold categorization of numerous restraints in licensing agreements: its 'white'

[2] Case 258/78 *Nungesser v Commission* [1982] ECR 2015.

[3] Commission Regulation (EC) 240/96 on the application of Article 81(3) of the Treaty of certain categories of technology transfer agreements, OJ L 031, 9 December 1996, pp 2–13, Recital 6: see also Arts 1(1) and 5(1)(4).

[4] US Department of Justice and the Federal Trade Commission, *Antitrust Guidelines for the Licensing of Intellectual Property* (5 April 1995) (<http://www.usdoj.gov/atr/public/guidelines/0558.htm> (last accessed 10 June 2010)). See comparison of the two regulatory regimes in S. Anderman, *EC Competition Law and Intellectual Property Rights: The Regulation of Innovation* (Oxford: OUP, 1998); see also V. Korah, *Technology Transfer and the EC Competition Rules* (Oxford: OUP, 1996).

list of twenty-six clauses, the clearly exemptible clauses under the block exemption;[5] its 'black list' of seven clauses which consisted of clearly non-exemptible clauses. If a clause was blacklisted, the *agreement* as a whole was non-exemptible and unenforceable. There was no severance policy for blacklisted clauses. Instead, there was a third category of 'grey' clauses (all those that were not whitelisted or blacklisted). These clauses could be approved or non-opposed under a 'quick look' procedure subject to a deadline of four months for the Commission.

The Commission's three-fold characterization encompassed a wide variety of typical clauses in licensing agreements: territorial restraints, customer allocation, field of use, output restrictions, price restrictions, non-compete obligations; tying, grant-backs, and no-challenge clauses. It somewhat controversially subjected the contractual restrictions on territorial restriction to micro-regulation owing more to its concern to promote market integration than for conventional competition reasons.

The Commission claimed in the Regulation 240/96 that it recognized that the EU's ability to draw abreast of its competitors in the rest of the world depended upon the capacity of European industry to devise new technologies and to spread them throughout the Member States of the Community. It acknowledged that its licensing policy as incorporated in Regulation 240/96 'was designed to play a pivotal role in the development of innovation within the EU economy and in contributing to the competitiveness of businesses operating in the Community'.[6] It also asserted in Recital 3 that it 'wished to encourage the dissemination of technical knowledge in the Community and to promote the manufacture of technically more sophisticated products'.

Yet, although on the whole Regulation 240/96 allowed industry to transfer the more conventional technology sufficiently freely and with legal certainty, within the EU, its regulatory structure did not display a light touch. Its draftsmen never tackled the task of differentiating between genuinely vertical and horizontal agreements. Their concern with the political/economic problems of maintaining intrabrand competition and integration of the Member States into a single market led them to give less than optimum incentives to technology licensing agreements from a purely economic competition point of view. In particular, their strict rules for territorial exclusivity, even where the economic costs and benefits, or 'efficiencies,' suggested little competition risk, meant that the needed incentives for second and subsequent waves of licensees were reduced. The Commission itself has openly acknowledged that its territorial restrictions have been imposed 'because of the added market integration objective which [EU] competition policy has'.[7]

On the other hand, Regulation 240/96 facilitated licensing by not setting market share limits to the safe harbour of the block exemption and leaving high market share

[5] In fact they consisted of a mix of cleared clauses, ie those not caught by Art 101(1) and exemptible clauses, ie those caught by Art 101(1) but automatically exempted under Art 101(3).

[6] TTBER 1996, para 9.

[7] See Commission Evaluation Report on the Transfer of Technology Block Exemption Regulation No 240/96, 'Technology Transfer Agreements under Article 81' COMM(2001) 786 final, 20 December 2001, para 55; see also Guidelines on Vertical Restraints (OJ C291 of 13 October 2000), point 7.

agreements to be regulated by Article 102 or by a 'withdrawal procedure' whereby the benefits of the block exemption for an agreement could be formally withdrawn in carefully defined cases by the Commission or the competition authority of a Member State. This approach was adopted in the final draft of Regulation 240/96 after a strong campaign by industry was waged throughout Europe against a Commission proposal to introduce market share limits to the Regulation 240/96.

By 2001, the Commission had decided that there was a clear need to change its policy towards technology transfer agreements even before Regulation 240/96 was due to expire in April 2006. This was caused partly by the change in the Commission approach to the regulation of vertical agreements, more generally under Article 101. It had begun to move away from a legalistic and form-based approach to a more economic and effects-based approach to the regulation of other types of agreements, taking into greater account the economic analysis of possible costs and benefits, or 'efficiencies', of certain restrictions, and recognizing the different economic effects of vertical and horizontal agreements respectively. This could be seen in the main characteristics of the Commission's reforms of vertical distribution agreements, such as exclusive and selective distribution and franchising (the Vertical Agreements Block Exemption (EC 2790/1999)) and horizontal agreements, such as research and development (EC 2659/2000) and specialization agreements (EC 2658/2000). The new Vertical Agreements Block Exemption introduced a more flexible regulatory approach by widening its scope to include a variety of categories of agreement. It also abandoned white and grey lists of clauses, retaining only an outright prohibition upon a limited number of 'hard core' restrictions. This easing of the regulatory straitjacket allowed the parties greater freedom to draft their agreements but the benefits of the safe haven offered by the block exemption were restricted by the market shares limit of 30 per cent built into the block exemption as part of a more economic approach to regulation. The new regulatory framework placed a premium upon self-certification by the parties in cases where their market shares exceeded the limits. To offer assistance in this endeavour, the Regulation was supplemented by guidelines.

At a more technical level, the reform by the Commission resulting in the replacement of Regulation 17 by the new Regulation 1/2003 gave the courts and competition authorities of the Member States the power to apply Article 101(3) directly. This not only ended the need for precautionary notification of agreements; the Commission decided that it also meant that the opposition procedure or 'quick look' facility for grey clauses would have to be abandoned and clauses would 'either be covered by the block exemption or treated as hardcore'.[8]

A second important factor was the publication of the Commission's *Evaluation Report on the Technology Transfer Regulation*[9] which evoked a response from Member States and the licensing community that strongly favoured reform. The Report stressed that the 1996 Regulation had a number of shortcomings.

[8] Commission Evaluation Report on the Transfer of Technology Block Exemption Regulation No 240/96, 'Technology Transfer Agreements under Article 81', p 6.

[9] Ibid.

First, because of its legal formalism and narrow definitions of scope, Regulation 240/96 was described as creating a 'legal straitjacket' in the sense that companies often had to redraft their commercial agreements to fit within its confines. Secondly, Regulation 240/96 was too narrow in scope, covering only a limited number of exclusive licensing arrangements, mainly to pure and mixed patent and know-how licences. Other criticisms related to the lack of economic realism of the regulatory framework. Regulation 240/96 was too restrictive in the sense that the black list covered items that were not always anti-competitive and which could have efficiency enhancing effects. On occasion, restrictions with different legal form but with similar economic effects on markets were given different treatment.[10] Finally, some exempted clauses had the potential for economic harm.

These criticisms were taken on board by the Commission in its decision to reform the regulatory framework for technology transfer. In choosing the form of a new technology transfer regulation, the Commission used the Vertical Agreements Block Exemption regulation as a role model and gave priority to a harmonizing TTBER with its other block exemption regulations as part of its preparation for competition policy in the post-modernist world of twenty-five Member States.

15.2 THE CURRENT PHASE

With the modernization of EU competition law we have entered the third phase—a period of regulation consisting of the new TTBER (772/2004) and TTA Guidelines with a more flexible and economic approach, a partial harmonization with the Vertical Agreements BER, and a new paradigm for assessing the enforceability of licensing agreements. The modernization of competition policy within the Commission, necessary to adapt it to the realities of an enlarged Europe of twenty-five Member States, consists of a number of procedural reforms set out in Regulation 1/2003, including those discussed in the following paragraphs.

The new TTBER and TTA Guidelines have been drafted to harmonize the treatment of certain IP licensing agreements ('technology transfers'[11]) with that of other agreements under the modernized application of Article 101. The TTBER thus provides only a 'safe harbour' type of exemption for licensing agreements and the TTA Guidelines explain the approach embodied in the TTBER and perhaps more importantly give guidance on the application of Article 101(3) to licensing agreements that fall outside the scope of the TTBER.

The new safe harbour is created by TTBER for 'technology transfers' which can be assumed with sufficient certainty to satisfy the conditions of Article 101(3). Thus licensing agreements between non-competitors are assumed to be highly unlikely

[10] For example, territorial and customer restrictions were treated differently.

[11] As defined by Art 1 in the Commission Regulation (EC) No 772/2004 of 27 April 2004 on the application of Article 81(3) of the Treaty of categories of technology transfer agreements, OJ L 123 of 27 April 2004, pp 11–17 (hereafter the TTBER).

to cause substantial competitive harm if the market share of the parties in either the market for the licensed product or the market for the technology protected by the IPR is 30 per cent or less. Licensing agreements between competitors are assumed to be highly unlikely to cause substantial competitive harm if the market share of the parties in either the market for the licensed product or the market for the technology protected by the IPR is 20 per cent or less. Moreover, the TTBER refuses access to the safe harbour to agreements that include hard core restrictions, ie those restrictions that are by their nature severely anti-competitive.

If an IP licensing agreement cannot fit within the confines of the safe harbour, the parties must attempt an individual assessment with the help of the TTA Guidelines. Outside the safe harbour, IP licensing agreements are not presumed to be unlawful but the burden will lie upon the parties to prove that their agreements are compatible with Article 101(3) using the methodology which the TTA Guidelines provide to apply Article 101(3) to an IP licensing agreement as a whole and to a number of typical provisions within IP licensing agreements. The TTA Guidelines embody the more economic approach and therefore offer a sliding scale for agreements and provisions that vary with the extent of market power of the parties. Thus, outside the safe harbour, if the parties to licensing agreements avoid hard core restrictions and if the market shares and market conditions suggest that the market power of the parties to the agreement will not produce a foreclosure of the market for the licensed product or the market for the technology protected by the IPR, there is now a good case for exemption outside the safe harbour. Under the new regime, the closer the market shares and market power of the parties come to definitions of dominance the less readily exemptible will be the licensing agreement or provision.

The Commission makes it clear in its reform of TTBER and the TTA Guidelines that the great majority of IP licensing agreements are pro-competitive and compatible with Article 101. Moreover, the recitals of the TTBER and the TTA Guidelines indicate that the Commission has made a considerable effort to understand the nature of IPRs and IPR licensing. Thus, they acknowledge that the creation of IPRs often entails substantial investment and that it is often a risky endeavour. They state plainly that 'in order not to reduce dynamic competition and to maintain the incentive to innovate, the innovator must not be unduly restricted in the exploitation of the IPRs that turn out to be valuable'.[12] In particular, they must be able to 'seek compensation for successful projects that is sufficient to maintain investment incentives, taking failed projects into account'.[13] The Commission also acknowledges that technology licensing may require the licensee to make considerable sunk investments in the licensed technology and production assets necessary to exploit it and that Article 101 'cannot be applied without considering such *ex ante* investments made by the parties and the risks thereto'.[14]

[12] Commission Notice, Guidelines on the application of Article 81 of the EC Treaty [now Article 101 TFEU] to technology transfer agreements [2004] OJ C101/2 (hereafter TTA Guidelines), para 8.

[13] Ibid.

[14] Ibid.

Nevertheless, by choosing to fit the assessment of IP licensing into the modernized framework of Article 101 the Commission has kept the special treatment of IP licensing agreements to a minimum. As the TTA Guidelines proclaim, the new TTBER's assessment of IP licensing takes 'due account of the dynamic aspects of technology licensing' making 'in particular . . . no presumption that intellectual property rights and licensing agreements as such give rise to competition concerns'.[15] This appears to echo the assertion of the US Guidelines that the characteristics of IPRs that make them distinct 'can be taken into account in the standard antitrust analysis . . . and do not require the application of fundamentally different principles'.[16] At the same time, however, in order to take due account of the dynamic aspects of IP licensing, it has been necessary for the Commission to make some special adjustments in the competition rules as they apply to IP licensing agreements. One example is the Commission's acceptance of the idea that the test of whether the parties are competitors or non-competitors at the time of the agreement is meant to determine the status of agreement throughout the duration of the agreement, even though the status of an agreement under the modernized rules is meant to be determined at the time of any dispute. A second, is the recognition that licensees will need special protection against passive sales from other licensees of the same licensor for a period of two years after they first put the licensed product on the market in their licensed territory.

15.3 THE MAIN FEATURES OF THE NEW TECHNOLOGY TRANSFER REGULATION AND GUIDELINES

The new regulatory framework can perhaps best be described in two parts. First, there are the seven main heads of TTBER: (1) the new wider scope for IP licensing; (2) the duration of IP licensing agreements; (3) the new distinction between 'horizontal' and 'vertical' licensing agreements; (4) the new market shares limits; (5) the prohibited restrictions; (6) the excluded restrictions; and (7) withdrawal and disapplication. Secondly, there is the new way of assessing licensing agreements and restrictions outside the safe harbour of the TTBER. Let us look at each in turn.

15.3.1 The scope of the TTBER

The TTBER extends to a wide range of IPR licensing agreements and assignments. Pure and mixed patent[17] and know-how agreements have been expanded to include software copyright licensing agreements and design rights licensing agreements. All these IPRs are viewed as the 'core' technology to be licensed.[18]

[15] Ibid, para 9.

[16] The US *Antitrust Guidelines for the Licensing of Intellectual Property* (n 4 above), Section 2.1.

[17] 'Patents' are widely defined to include utility models, designs, topographies of semiconductor products, and plant breeder's certificates: TTBER Art 1(1)(h).

[18] TTBER Art 1(1)(b).

The TTBER also allows a wider variety of IPRs to be included in the licensing[19] package along with the core 'technology' as long as they are 'ancillary' provisions.[20] To meet the test of ancillarity, they must (1) not constitute the primary object of the agreement and (2) be directly related to the manufacture or provision of the contract products. This formula is clearer than its predecessor. The test is whether the other IPR is included essentially to enable the licensee to better exploit the core licensed technology. If it appears that the one licensing the 'ancillary' IPR, say a trademark, is the real purpose of the agreement, it will not be exempted under TTBER.

The TTBER offers both a wider, and more clearly defined scope for IP licensing than its predecessor. Moreover, although the TTBER itself does not extend to copyright licensing other than software licensing, the TTA Guidelines state that the principles set out in the TTBER and TTA Guidelines will apply to traditional forms of copyright by analogy.[21] The TTA Guidelines are less positive about pure trade mark licensing; they state that the TTBER is not intended to extend to pure trade mark licensing, even by analogy.[22]

The application of the block exemption is also conditional upon the fact that the licensing agreement must be concluded for the purpose of *producing* contract products, ie products incorporating or produced with the licensed technology. [23] Licences contained in agreements which are primarily for *reselling* or *distribution* purposes are excluded and parties to such agreements will have to look to the vertical distribution agreements exemption regulation for exemption. In respect of sublicensing, agreements by licensees to *sublicense* the licensed technology are covered but pure *sublicensing* agreements are not exempted by TTBER although the principles of the TTBER will apply by analogy to such agreements.[24] Finally, since the TTBER only deals 'with agreements where the licensor permits the licensee to exploit the contract products', it 'should not deal with licensing agreements for the purpose of *sub-contracting research and development*'. Recital 5 indicates that the exemption could apply to exploitation by the licensee in the form of manufacturing and selling 'possibly after further research and development by the licensee'. [25]

15.3.2 The allowed duration of licensing agreements under the TTBER

The exemption conferred by the TTBER has a potentially longer duration than its predecessor; it can last 'as long as the intellectual property right in the licensed technology has not expired, lapsed or been declared invalid or, in the case of know how for as long as the know how remains secret'.[26] If the know-how becomes publicly known

[19] TTA Guidelines, para 53.
[20] TTBER, Art 1(1)(b).
[21] TTA Guidelines, para 51
[22] Ibid, para 53.
[23] TTBER, Art 2. TTA Guidelines, para 41.
[24] TTA Guidelines, para 42.
[25] Ibid, para 44.
[26] TTBER, Art 2.

as a result of action by the licensee, the exemption will continue to apply for the duration of the agreement. The block exemption will apply separately to each licensed property right covered by the agreement but will continue in effect until the date of expiry, invalidity, or the coming into the public domain of the last intellectual property right which constitutes core 'technology' as defined by Article 1 of TTBER. This means that if the patent protection should expire, the know-how component can ensure that the agreement lasts until the end of the original term, even if that term is greater than ten years.[27] The TTBER itself expires in 2014 so contracts cannot be expected to remain block exempted after that date. On the other hand, licensing agreements which are self-certified as exempted can last longer than ten years, if the know-how remains secret or the patent remains valid.

15.3.3 The distinction between licensing agreements between 'competitors' and those between 'non-competitors'

The economic realism of the new TTBER has resulted in a division of licensing agreements into two categories—agreements between *non-competitors* and agreements between *competitors.* The TTBER now recognizes that anti-competitive concerns are considerably greater in the case of agreements between *competitors,* has re-evaluated its prohibited restraints in the case of licensing agreements between *non-competitors*, and created a deservedly more benign regulatory regime. This reform is far-reaching because it applies not only within the confines of the safe haven but also up to a point where the parties' market shares may be as high as 40–50 per cent, as long as they fall below dominance.

Moreover, under the TTBER the definition of agreements between *non-competitors* is much wider than the definition of 'vertical' agreements. It applies not only to the paradigm vertical case of an agreement between an inventor and a manufacturer but also to an agreement between two manufacturers as long as they are not competitors in respect of the licensed product. In 'product markets' competitors are defined as 'actual' competitors, ie competing undertakings who in the absence of the technology transfer agreement would have been active on the relevant product and geographic markets on which the contract products are sold without infringing each other's IPRs.[28] The one complication is that in product markets, 'competitors' also includes a narrow category of 'potential' competitors who realistically are in a position to undertake the necessary investments and accept the switching costs of entering the same market had the price of the product been raised.[29] In 'technology markets', the definition of competitor is limited to 'actual' competitors.[30]

A further feature of the TTBER that is important for IP licensing is that it defines the parties as 'competitors' or 'non-competitors' at the time the contract is made and will

[27] The limit imposed by TTBER 1996 on know-how.

[28] TTBER, Art 1(j)(ii); TTA Guidelines 24 and 31.

[29] Ibid.

[30] TTBER, Art 1(j)(i).

not allow the natural competition that may develop as the result of the licensing agreement, as the manufacturing expertise of the licensee matures, to affect the designation of the contract. Thus, if the parties are non-competitors at the time the agreement is made, they will not be redesignated for the purposes of the exemption during the duration of the agreement unless the agreement is materially amended.[31] The distinction between agreements between competitors and those between non-competitors is particularly noticeable in two regulatory contexts: the market share limits to the TTBER[32] and the types of hard core restrictions in licensing agreements.[33]

15.3.4 The distinction between *competitors* and *non-competitors* under the TTBER and the TTA Guidelines

The modernization reform has resulted in an important change to the treatment of licensing agreements by drawing a careful and more enlightened distinction between agreements between competitors and those between non-competitors. Historically the BERs rather crudely distinguished between 'vertical' and 'horizontal' agreements. Vertical agreements were defined as agreements between undertakings each of which operates at a different level of the production or distribution chain. Horizontal agreements were defined as agreements between undertakings operating at the same level of the production and distribution chain. While relatively easy for lawyers to apply, this distinction meant the vertical agreements were defined narrowly and horizontal agreements too widely and as a consequence, competition concerns were incorrectly aimed at many agreements between non-competitors.

As part of the Commission's new economic approach, the Guidelines on Vertical Agreements stress that the test should be whether the relationship between the parties operating *for the purposes of the agreement* is at a different level of the production and distribution chain. This means that there could be a 'vertical agreement' between firms on the same level, ie two manufacturers, as long as they are manufacturing products which are not in competition with each other. The Guidelines to Vertical Agreements state that an undertaking could be active at more than one stage of the production and distribution chain.[34]

The TTBER and the Commission's TTA Guidelines have also adopted a more economically enlightened view of the distinction between the two types of agreement, adhering to the spirit if not the letter of the Vertical Agreements Guidelines. The test in the TTBER is whether the parties would have been actual or potential competitors *in the absence of the agreement*. If without the agreement, the parties would not have been competitors, they will be deemed to be non-competitors.[35] This requires a careful

[31] TTBER, Art 4 (3); TTA Guidelines, para 31; see also paras 32–3.
[32] TTBER, Art 3.
[33] Ibid, 4.
[34] Guidelines on Vertical Restraints (n 7 above), para 25(c).
[35] TTBER, Art 1(j)(ii).

understanding of the two parties as well as the commercial nature of the markets in which they operate.

The TTBER draws a distinction between 'product markets' and 'technology markets' [36] and defines competing undertakings differently in each market. Under the TTBER, the licensor and licensee can either be *actual* or *potential* competitors in the product market but only *actual* competitors in the technology market.

The licensor and licensee will be viewed as *actual* competitors when in the absence of the agreement they are both active on the same *relevant product market and the same geographic market(s)* or the same *technology market* [37]without infringing each others' IPRs.[38] Consequently, the existence of blocking patents will be important in the analysis.[39]

The licensor and licensee will be viewed as *potential competitors* on the relevant product market and geographic market(s) if in the absence of the agreement and without infringing the IPRs of the other party, it is likely that they would have undertaken the necessary additional investment to enter the relevant market in response to a small but permanent increase in product prices within a short period such as a year or two.[40]

[36] Outside the safe harbour of the TTBER, potential competition can be taken into account to some extent in technology markets; TTA Guidelines, para 66.

[37] A 'technology market' is defined under TTA Guidelines, para 22 as consisting of the technologies which are rivals to the technology of the licensor. If any technologies would be substitutable for licensees faced with a SSNIP, then those technologies are in the same market. TTA Guideline 23 suggests that an alternative approach is to calculate the shares of the technology by reference to the market share of its licensed product on the relevant product market. See TTBER Art 3(3).

[38] TTA Guidelines, para 28.

[39] If the parties own technologies that are in a one-way or two-way *blocking patent position* the parties are considered to be non-competitors on the technology market. A one-way blocking position exists when a technology cannot be exploited without infringing another technology. This is, for instance, the case where one patent covers an improvement of a technology covered by another patent. In that case the exploitation of the improvement patent presupposes that the holder obtains a licence to the basic patent. A two-way blocking position exists where neither technology can be exploited without infringing upon the other technology and where the holders thus need to obtain a licence or a waiver from each other. In assessing whether a blocking position exists, the Commission will rely on objective factors as opposed to the subjective views of the parties. Particularly convincing evidence of the existence of a blocking position is required where the parties may have a common interest in claiming the existence of a blocking position in order to be qualified as non-competitors, for instance where the claimed two-way blocking position concerns technologies that are technological substitutes. Relevant evidence includes court decisions including injunctions and opinions of independent experts. In the latter case the Commission will, in particular, closely examine how the expert has been selected. However, other convincing evidence, including expert evidence from the parties that they have or had good and valid reasons to believe that a blocking position exists or existed, can also be relevant to substantiate the existence of a blocking position: TTA Guidelines, para 32.

[40] TTA Guidelines, para 29. However, in individual cases longer periods can be taken into account. The period of time needed for undertakings already on the market to adjust their capacities can be used as a yardstick to determine this period. The parties are, for instance, likely to be considered potential competitors on the product market where the licensee produces on the basis of its own technology in one geographic market and starts producing in another geographic market on the basis of a licensed competing technology. In such circumstances, it is likely that the licensee would have been able to enter the second geographic market on the basis of its own technology, unless such entry is precluded by objective factors, including the existence of blocking patents.

Finally, the TTA Guidelines make special provision for 'breakthrough' products such as drastic inventions which make the competitor's technology obsolete.

A good example is offered by Example 5 in the US Licensing Guidelines,[41]

AgCO, a manufacturer of farm equipment, develops a new, patented emission control technology for its tractor engines and licenses it to FarmCo, another farm equipment manufacturer. AgCo's emission control technology is far superior to the technology currently owned and used by FarmCo, so much so that FarmCo's technology does not significantly restrain the prices that AgCo could charge for its technology. AgCo's emission control patent has a broad scope. It is likely that any improved emission's control technology that FarmCo could develop in the foreseeable future would infringe AgCo's patents.

Note that they are not *actual* competitors in emission control technology despite both being manufacturers of emission control technology.

Note also that they are not likely *potential* competitors in emission control technology because of the blocking patent.

A second feature of the TTBER is that if the parties are non-competitors *at the time the agreement is concluded*, they will continue to enjoy the more liberal regime of hard core restrictions for the duration of the agreement unless the agreement itself is materially altered.[42] This will be true even if the licensees and licensors become actual competitors at a later date because 'the licensee starts licensing out his technology or the licensor becomes an actual or potential supplier of products on the relevant market'.[43] This was a concession made by the Commission who had originally intended a reassessment at any time that commercial conditions called for one. Outside the TTBER the position is more complex and we shall come back to it in context.[44]

15.3.5 The market share limits

The TTBER may have been helpful to IP licensing in many respects, but it has created complications for IP licensing by introducing a system of market share limits to its scope to harmonize it with the regulatory methods used in the Vertical Agreements BER. By introducing a new legal regime whereby its 'safe harbour' is limited by market share limits, the TTBER radically alters the nature of the block exemption and the overall legal framework for IP licensing. Under the guise of giving greater recognition

[41] The US *Antitrust Guidelines for the Licensing of Intellectual Property* (n 4 above).

[42] TTBER, Art 4(3). In some cases it may also be possible to conclude retrospectively that even though the licensor and the licensee produced competing products at the time the agreement was made, they are nevertheless non-competitors on the relevant product market and the relevant technology market because the licensed technology represents such *a drastic innovation* that the technology of the licensee is rendered obsolete or uncompetitive. This classification can be made at any stage when it becomes clear that the licensee's technology has become obsolete or uncompetitive on the market. TTA Guidelines, para 33.

[43] TTA Guidelines, para 68.

[44] Ibid, para 31.

of the economic realities of IP licensing, it creates legal uncertainty for the parties in volatile new technology markets. For licensing agreements between non-competitors, the block exemption will not apply where the licensed product exceeds 30 per cent of the relevant market because such agreements normally impose a lower risk to competition. For the parties to agreements between competitors or 'horizontal' licensing agreements, the exemption will not apply where the licensed product exceeds a 20 per cent market share. In defining the market for the licensed *product,* both actual and potential competition is relevant. In *technology* markets only actual competition will be considered.

If the product which is the subject of a technology transfer agreement exceeds the market share ceiling at any time during the course of the contract, it will lose the benefit of the block exemption, after a transitional period of two years. The TTBER makes no other concession to the volatility of relationships during the term of the licensing agreement as it did in respect of status of the parties as competitors or non-competitors.[45] If an agreement loses its exemption under the TTBER, it will not be automatically prohibited by Article 101(1); nor will any notification be required to the Commission. Indeed, the agreement may still be exempted by self-assessment, ie an analysis of Article 101(3) as it applies to the agreement using the TTA Guidelines and the case law of the EU Courts and Commission. However, to lawyers accustomed to the old style block exemption regulation, the legal security offered by self-assessment seems more precarious than the legal security of the safe harbour of the block exemption.

15.3.6 The hard core restrictions

The TTBER places considerable emphasis upon a narrow black list of prohibited 'hard core' restrictions whose presence in a licensing agreement make it unexemptible under the TTBER but also almost always unenforceable under Article 101 generally. The hard core restrictions have been drafted on the supposition that they are 'almost always anti-competitive'.[46] They have been defined differently depending upon whether the licensing agreement that contains them is between competing undertakings or between non-competing undertakings.

15.3.6.1 *Restrictions on agreements between competitors*

Where the licensee competes with the licensor at the time the agreement is concluded, the TTBER contains four main hard core restrictions. The first three are basic anti-cartel competition rules: bans on price fixing,[47] reciprocal output limitations,[48] and

[45] TTBER, Art 3.1; TTA Guidelines, para 31.
[46] TTA Guidelines, para 74.
[47] TTBER, Art 4(1)(a), TTA Guidelines, paras 79–80, 156.
[48] TTBER, Art 4(1)(b), TTA Guidelines, paras 82–3, 175.

market allocation clauses.[49] The fourth is a prohibition on licensors restricting the licensee's ability to carry out R&D and exploit its own technology.[50]

The TTBER also provides that where the agreement between competitors takes the form of a *non-reciprocal* licensing agreement, the licensor is allowed under an exception to Article 4(1)(c) to offer an exclusive licence, that is a licence to produce and sell the contract products without the licensor himself producing goods in that territory or selling the contract goods from that territory. In such a case, the licensee will merely be doing what the licensor was entitled to do and hence that restriction, on its own, cannot be viewed as anti-competitive. Indeed, it may even be argued that Article 101(1) does not apply to a simple exclusive licence between licensor and licensee as long as the agreement involves no third parties such as other licensees.[51]

A second analogous exception consists of field of use provisions. A field of use restriction limits the exploitation of the licensed technology by the licensee to one or more particular fields of use leaving untouched the licensor's ability to exploit the licensed technology in another field. A good example is offered by a maize seed variety which is licensed for animal food only with the licensor retaining exclusive rights to exploit the seed variety for human foodstuffs. Field of use restrictions may be 'exclusive' or 'sole' and are treated for competition purposes as analogous to exclusive or sole territorial licences. Again, as long as the field of use obligation is limited to the licensing agreement, it is little more than a subdivision of the licensor's own powers and may not even be caught by Article 101(1).

5.3.6.2 *Restrictions on agreements between non-competitors*

For agreements between non-competitors,[52] the hard core restrictions are more varied in their concerns. They include price fixing and they extend to territorial restrictions and to restrictions of active and passive sales to end-users by a licensee who is part of a selective distribution system.

The territorial restriction prohibition is contained in Article 4(2)(b) which states that an agreement may not be exempted if it has as its object,

> (i) the restriction of the territory into which, or of the customers to whom, the licensee may sell the contract products . . .

It then provides a limited list of exceptions consisting of permitted territorial restrictions, including obligations on licensees not to sell *actively* into the exclusive territory of another licensee, not to sell at all into the exclusive territory of the licensor, requiring the licensee to manufacture or provide contract products only for its own use, etc.

[49] Article 4(1)(c), TTA Guidelines, para 84.

[50] The one exception is where the restriction is indispensable to prevent the disclosure of the licensed technology: TTBER, Art 4(1)(d).

[51] Cf Art 4(2) of Regulation 17/62, OJ No 013, 21 February 1962.

[52] TTBER, Art 4(2).

The Commission has acknowledged the indispensability of protection against *passive* sales for licensees.

. . . it is unlikely that licensees would not enter into the licence without protection for a certain period of time against passive (and active) sales into the exclusive territory of a licensee by other licensees.[53]

This statement recognizes the strategic importance of passive sales protection as an incentive in the technology transfer agreement and the TTBER provides that licensors can provide every licensee with protection for two years from the sale of the licensed product in its territory against passive sales by other licensees manufacturing the same licensed product in other territories. The theory is that the two years should be sufficient for each licensee to familiarize itself with the production process to achieve the efficiencies to allow it to catch up and compete on equal terms with other licensees. [54]

15.3.7 The excluded restrictions

The Commission has also created a shortlist of *prima facie* excluded restrictive conditions in Article 5 which, unlike hard core restrictions, are only void in themselves; they will not affect the remainder of the agreement. The Commission has in effect introduced a severability rule for such clauses. Whilst they cannot be exempted as part of the block exemption process, they can be exempted individually if they meet the four conditions of Article 101(3). There are four main excluded restrictions: (a) any direct or indirect obligation by the licensee to assign or to grant an exclusive licence in respect of its own several improvements to the licensed technology; (b) any direct or indirect obligation by the licensee to assign or to grant an exclusive licence in respect of its own several improvements to the licensed technology; (c) any direct or indirect obligation on the licensee not to challenge the validity of the IPRs held by the licensor; and (d) in a licensing agreement between non-competitors, any direct or indirect obligation limiting the licensee's ability to exploit its own technology or limiting the ability of any of the parties to the agreement to carry out research and development unless indispensable to prevent the disclosure of the licensed know-how to third parties.

15.3.8 Withdrawal and disapplication of the TTBER

Article 6 of the TTBER allows the Commission and the competition authorities of the Member States to withdraw its benefits for any individual agreement that does not fulfil the conditions of Article 101(3). This Article is aimed at the problems of parallel networks and their cumulative effects where access of third parties' technology to the market is excluded or access of potential licensees to the market is restricted. In such cases the Commission would have to make a negative decision under Regulation 1/2003.

[53] TTA Guidelines, para 101.

[54] See discussion in TTA Guidelines, paras107–16.

The TTA Guidelines suggest that in the case of exclusive licences between non-competitors, the Commission will only exceptionally intervene.[55] Yet Article 6(1)(b) seems not to recognize that a case where a dominant licensee obtains an exclusive licence would not be within the safe harbour in the first place.

Article 7 of the TTBER provides the Commission with the possibility of excluding by regulation any parallel networks of similar agreements. This possibility is fairly remote because the withdrawal step offers the more effective remedy of rendering the agreement void and unenforceable.

15.4 THE NEW METHODS OF ASSESSING INDIVIDUAL RESTRAINTS IN LICENSING AGREEMENTS OUTSIDE THE SAFE HARBOUR OF THE TTBER

The new TTA Guidelines offer a general methodology for the individual assessment of licensing agreements and individual restrictions under Article 101(1) and outside the safe haven of the TTBER. There is no assumption of illegality of such agreements as long as they do not contain any hard core restrictions of competition. Agreements are to be assessed in their economic and legal context and will only be viewed as restrictive of competition if they will adversely affect actual or potential competitors to such an extent that they will produce higher prices, lower output, lower innovation, or lower quality of goods or services. The TTA Guidelines distinguish between inter-technology competition and intra-technology competition and suggest that the impact of the agreement on both types of competition will need to be assessed.[56] The expectation of the TTA Guidelines is that appreciable anti-competitive effects are only likely to occur where one or both of the parties has a significant degree of market power and the agreement contributes to a strengthening of that market power. The Commission suggests that the following factors *inter alia* are particularly relevant in this assessment:

(a) the nature of the agreement;
(b) the market position of the parties;
(c) the market position of competitors;
(d) the market position of buyers of the licensed products;
(e) entry barriers; and
(f) maturity of the market.[57]

This economic and legal analysis in the TTA Guidelines also places great weight on the differences in the risks of anti-competitive harm between agreements between *non-competitors* and agreements between *competitors*. The TTA Guidelines'

[55] See TTA Guidelines, paras 164 and 165.
[56] Ibid, paras 11 and 12.
[57] Ibid, para 132.

general methodology creates a rather different framework of regulation for each type of agreement.

15.4.1 Licensing agreements between non-competitors

15.4.1.1 *Inter-technology competition*

In the case of agreements between non-competitors, there is normally no inter-technological competition, either actual or potential, at the start of the agreement. Hence the fact of the agreement itself will not restrict competition unless the market power of the licensee threatens consumer harm through foreclosure of competition.[58] Consequently, the test will concentrate on whether any provision within the licensing agreement is a *restriction of competition* by effect.

Moreover, where a licensing agreement is made between non-competitors, whether actual or potential, many restrictions on the conduct of licensor and licensee *inter se* in the licensing agreement will not constitute a restriction of competition under the new framework.[59]

For example, many non-territorial clauses between licensors and licensees will be regarded as *ancillary restraints* and therefore 'almost always *not* restrictive of competition within the meaning of Article 101(1)'.[60]

Some examples of such restrictions are those which are indispensable to achieving the main purpose of the licensing agreement. These include:

(a) confidentiality obligations;

(b) obligations on licensees not to sublicense;

(c) obligations not to use the licensed technology after the expiry of the agreement, provided that the licensed technology remains valid and in force;

(d) obligations to assist the licensor in enforcing the licensed intellectual property rights;

(e) obligations to pay minimum royalties or to produce a minimum quantity of products incorporating the licensed technology; and

(f) obligations to use the licensor's trade mark or indicate the name of the licensor on the product.[61]

[58] TTA Guidelines, para 155. Cf Art 81(3); TTA Guidelines, para 29. It is useful to revive the distinction between non-restrictive and exemptible clauses in licensing agreements. The white lists in previous regulations tended to combine contractual restraints not caught by Art 101(1) with those that were so caught but nevertheless exempted in a single white list of clauses. For parties engaged in individual-certification today, it is wise to make such distinctions clearer.

[59] Ibid.

[60] Para 155. Cf Art 81(3); TTA Guidelines, para 29. It is useful to revive the distinction between non-restrictive and exemptible clauses in licensing agreements. The white lists in previous regulations tended to combine contractual restraints not caught by Art 101(1) with those that were so caught but nevertheless exempted in a single white list of clauses. For parties engaged in individual-certification today it is wise to make such distinctions clearer.

[61] Case 258/78 *Nungesser*.

Moreover, certain territorial restrictions *as between licensor and licensee* can be viewed as not *restrictive of competition* under Article 101(1).

Where a licensor offers a sole and exclusive licence to the licensee, if the parties were not competitors before the contract was made, a pure obligation on the licensor not to appoint another licensee in the territory or not to itself exploit the licensed product in the territory might be *restrictions* but they would not be *restrictions on competition* for the purpose of Article 101(1).[62] The authority for this is the *Nungesser*[63] case.

A similar analysis can be performed for contractual restraints such as field of use restrictions. What is important to note here is that the new methodology recognizes that the IP owner can subdivide its powers of exploitation by contractual restriction and not be caught by Article 101(1) under the analysis of restriction on competition rather than the scope of the patent or limited licence doctrines which stem from IP law. Consequently, in the case of agreements between non-competitors, the new methodology gives a wide scope for contractual restrictions between licensor and licensee not to be caught by Article 101(1) in the first place.

15.4.1.2 *Intra-technology competition*

The second process of competition that is relevant for Article 101(1) is the process of intra-technology competition, normally the competition that can exist *between different licensees* producing the same product.[64]

Under EU law, since the *Consten* and *Grundig*[65] case, there have been specific competition concerns with restrictions on intra-technology competition such as provisions placing obligations on licensees not to sell directly into the territories of other licensees. From the Commission's point of view since such obligations are viewed as restricting the potential competition that could have existed between the licensees in different territories in the absence of such obligations, they are regarded as a restriction of competition for the purposes of Article 101(1). A more universal example of restrictions on intra-technology competition would be a price restraint placed on all licensees by a licensor. In so far as a licensing agreement between non-competitors contains a restriction on intra-technology competition, it will be necessary to resort to the analysis under Article 101(3) to decide whether such restrictions of competition in the licensing agreement are acceptable under Article 101 as a whole.

For example, an obligation placed by the licensor upon the licensee not to sell directly into the territory of another licensee will be caught by Article 101(1) because it restricts intra-technological competition but will be exemptible under the TTBER in respect of *active* sales for the duration of the contract and in respect of *passive* sales for

[62] The TTA Guidelines are more cautious: 'territorial restraints in an agreement between non-competitors may fall outside [Article 101(1)] for a certain duration if the restraints are objectively necessary for a licensee to penetrate a new market.' Para 12(b).

[63] Case 258/78 *Nungesser KG v Commission* [1982] ECR 2015.

[64] Cases 56 and 58/64 *Consten and Grundig*.

[65] See TTBER, Art 4(2).

two years from the time of each licensee's first sale in its territory. This shows a particularly improved understanding of the need to encourage investment in IP licensing because every licensee gets protection against rival licensees and the licensor itself for a minimum of two years from the time it first markets the product in its territory. The thinking is that the licensee gets an initial period to tool up to match the efficiencies of production of its rivals. In previous BERs there was no such guarantee because the period of five years of allowed protection against passive sales in any one territory was dependent on the time left after the product was put on the market by any licensees. Hence 'second' and 'third wave' licensees could end up with less than two years' protection which might discourage investment at that stage and hence inhibit further diffusion of the technology throughout the single market.

Even if the market shares of the licensee exceeds 30 per cent and the two years of the TTBER do not automatically apply, the factual analysis of the licensee's need for such protection could lead to a two-year period of protection, or, in the case of particularly complex and expensive technologies, possibly an even longer period of protection for licensees. In other words, even outside the TTBER, Article 101(3) offers a relatively benign treatment of licensing agreements between non-competitors. First it asks whether there will be any pro-competitive benefits arising from the provision; whether the benefits were objectively necessary [or indispensable] to achieve those benefits; and whether or not competition in the market would be eliminated—note eliminated not merely reduced.

One feature of the new framework which needs careful attention is the assessment of competition between licensor and licensee outside the safe harbour of the TTBER. In principle, once outside the TTBER, a reassessment must be made *at that stage* whether the agreement is one between competitors or non-competitors. The TTBER offers a special *ex ante* treatment of the status of the contractual relationship within the safe harbour for the purpose of applying the hard core restrictions in Article 4(3). This provision was a concession made by the Commission during the course of the final draft and it constitutes special recognition of the dynamic aspects of technology licensing.[66] To what extent does this *ex ante* analysis continue outside the scope of the safe harbour of the TTBER?

In the General Framework for the Application of Article 101, the TTA Guidelines specifically mention a case where the parties become competitors subsequent to the conclusion of the agreement because the licensee develops and starts exploiting a competing technology.[67] They state that it must be taken into account that the parties were non-competitors at the time the agreement was made and that the Commission will therefore mainly focus on the impact of the agreement on the licensee's ability to exploit its own (competing) technology and the hard core restrictions will continue to

[66] The Commission has pointed out that Art 4(3) will apply even if the licensees and licensors become actual competitors at a later date because 'the licensee starts licensing out his technology or the licensor becomes an actual or potential supplier of products on the relevant market'.

[67] See TTA Guidelines, para 31.

apply to the parties as if they are non-competitors unless the agreement itself is materially amended after the parties have become competitors. If the reassessment is made in this way it should take sufficient account of the inherent dynamic of the licensing relationship, ie the fact that almost every IP licence creates potential technological competition after the licensee has mastered the technology but while the contract remains in existence.

Since the technology is inevitably transferred at the early stages of the contract, licensors view as an indispensable inducement to give an *exclusive* licence of its technology the assurance of a return for the period of the contract. That is why the licensor inserts a minimum royalties clause. Moreover, that is also why it inserts a non-compete clause *in respect of the technology transferred.* The non-compete clause in respect of *inter-technological* competition between the parties at the start of the contract cannot limit the licensee's independent development of its own R&D.

The competition rules place limits on the possibilities for licensees opportunistically to opt out of a contractual commitment during the period of the contract. The new legal framework attempts to avoid causing investors either to think twice about investing in new technology within the EU because a chill on investment in IP licensing into the EU will limit the diffusion of technology transfer. The TTA Guidelines offer a reassurance that the designation of the parties as *competitors* or not will take adequate account of the *ex ante* relationship. Even though in principle the reassessment is *ex post,* at the time the agreement loses its position in the safe harbour of the TTBER, it seems that it will be accepted that the contractual non-compete clause continues to operate as a contractual block on potential *intra-technology* competition *during* the course of the agreement.[68]

15.4.2 Licensing agreements between competitors

The treatment of licensing agreements *between competitors* is on the face of it much harsher than agreements between non-competitors largely because of the greater competition concerns with such agreements. At the Article 101(1) level, there are more restrictions by object and the territorial restrictions in the agreement are more susceptible to the charge of being restrictions of inter-technology competition. The longer list of hard core restrictions is accompanied by lower market share thresholds of 20 per cent. Access to the safe harbour of the TTBER is less open to licensing agreements between competitors.

Yet, it is wrong to conclude that the competition authorities are entirely hostile to licensing agreements between competitors. The Commission has clearly felt that it had inadequate knowledge and experience of the permutations of pro-competitive licensing agreements between competitors to regulate them in the TTBER with the light

[68] Further evidence of non-competitor status during the course of the contract will be offered by the licensee's use of the licensor's trade mark.

touch approach they used to regulate licensing agreements between non-competitors. Moreover, the Commission is only too aware that this type of agreement is the source of the most serious risks of anti-competitive licensing agreements even if that were true only in a minority of cases. As a consequence, the Commission has left the application of the full range of Article 101(3) to such agreements to individual assessment using the methodology of the TTA Guidelines.

Moreover, there are important concessions to this tighter approach to licensing agreements between competitors. One such is the creation of the special category of *non-reciprocal* licensing agreements between competitors.[69] Both within and outside the TTBER they are treated as honorary agreements between non-competitors. [70]

The application of Article 101(3) to licensing agreements between competitors is further ameliorated outside the TTBER and above the 20 per cent market share by a 'second safe harbour' where there are at least four other poles of independently controlled technologies and no hard core restrictions in the licensing agreement.[71]

However, under the new methodology, licensing agreements between competitors are generally more easily caught by Article 101(1) because restrictions, even ancillary restrictions, are usually *restrictions of competition* under Article 101(1) and the permitted scope for provisions is carefully regulated by Article 4(1) of the TTBER.

As part of the process of individual assessment of an IP agreement, it is necessary to look at its individual provisions. These will be analysed in two categories: Chapter 16 Territorial Provisions and Chapter 17 Non-territorial provisions.

[69] See definitions in TTBER, Art 1(1)(c) and (d). Are the parties cross-licensing competing technologies or technologies which can be used to produce competing products? See also the special position of one way or two way blocking patents (TTA Guidelines, para 32) and 'drastic innovations' (TTA Guidelines, para 33).

[70] A similar, more lenient treatment is given to reciprocal agreements between competitors where a restriction on output is imposed on one of the licensees only. See eg TTBER Art 4 (1)(b).

[71] TTA Guidelines, para 131.

16

THE REGULATION OF TERRITORIAL RESTRAINTS IN INTELLECTUAL PROPERTY RIGHT LICENSING AGREEMENTS UNDER ARTICLE 101 TFEU[1]

16.1 Introduction	273
16.2 Exemptible Exclusive Territoriality	274
16.3 Field of Use Restrictions	278

16.1 INTRODUCTION

The degree of territorial exclusivity which the licensor can offer the licensee lies at the heart of the commercial exchange in a technology licensing agreement. The licensee is prepared to take on the risks of investing capital in manufacturing premises and plant and a distribution system rather than the costs of an elaborate in-house R&D programme. However, unless there is some protection from competition from the licensor and other licensees in its home territory it will have little incentive to take on such risks. The licensee's need for time to tool up, to acquaint itself with the technology, and to establish itself as a manufacturer with a distribution system before being subjected to competition from the licensor or other prior licensees is often so great that without such contractual protection many licensees would be deterred from making the investment.

If there were no competition policy constraints, the licensing agreement would be used to confer several levels of protection. The first level of protection would be

[1] See further discussion in S. Anderman and J. Kallaugher, *Technology Transfers and the New EU Competition Rules* (Oxford: OUP, 2006), Ch 8.

protection against the licensor itself. This would include an obligation not to grant a licence to manufacture to another licensee in the licensed territory and not to sell directly into the licensed territory. The second level of protection also includes protection against the direct sales from other licensees. These direct sales restrictions could, however restrictive in form the provision in the contract, be limited to 'active' sales in the sense that the other licensees would be prohibited in their licensing agreement from advertising and establishing selling facilities in the territory or could extend to 'passive' sales restrictions which would prohibit a licensee from responding to orders received from within the territory of another licensee.

Licensees would of course prefer to have as much territorial protection as possible but there are limits to what can be secured simply by using the IP licensing contract. It would be unlawful too for a licensor to require licensees to bind their buyers not to export. Moreover, the doctrine of exhaustion keeps open the paths of parallel trading between buyers and sellers in two different licensed territories. Hence the most that can be done lawfully in the licensing agreement is to place limits on the capacity of licensees [or licensor] to sell directly into other licensees' or the licensor's territory.

To the extent that the licensor can offer these protections to the licensee, it will be able to offer an inducement to investment by the licensee which will go a long way towards minimizing the financial risks of manufacturing and introducing new products into a market. However, despite the obvious economic benefits inducing technology transfer, and the indispensability of territorial protection, EU competition law has proved to be cautious in following the logic of incentives preferring to give priority to its concerns to keep open the flow of inter-state, intra-technology trade between exclusive territories. The EU Courts and Commission have acknowledged the importance of territorial exclusivity as an incentive to technology transfer and indeed the general pro-competitive nature of licensing agreements. However, in their decisions on territorial restraints in licensing agreements, they have been reluctant to encourage 'bottom up' integration by the spread of IP-protected technology manufacture throughout the common market, preferring to rely on 'top down' negative integration by using competition law to limit restrictions on sales between licensees.

16.2 EXEMPTIBLE EXCLUSIVE TERRITORIALITY

For historical reasons, as we have seen, the Commission prior to 2004 never fully recognized the indispensability of exclusive territorial restrictions under Article 101(1) and the logic of applying the ancillary restraints doctrine to territorial exclusivity in licensing agreement. The new TTA Guidelines state:

> Where the licensee is facing substantial sunk investments, agreements granting an exclusive licence are likely to fulfil the conditions of Article [101(3)] except where there are no real alternatives to the licensor's technology on the market or where most of the available technologies have been licensed to the same licensee.

Within the safe harbour and presumably under Article 101(3) more generally, in the case of IP licensing agreements between non-competitors, the scope for territorial exclusivity in the block exemption is quite wide. The TTBER and TTA Guidelines distinguish between two types of territorial protection: restrictions on production within a given territory (exclusive or sole licences) and restrictions on the sale of products incorporating the licensed technology into a given territory and to a given customer group (sales restrictions).[2]

16.2.1 Exclusive and sole licences

Under the block exemption, the first form of territorial protection that a licensor can offer a licensee is protection from competition from *manufacture* of the licensed goods within the licensed territory by either the licensor or other licensees.

The TTA Guidelines offer three rules for exclusive and sole licensing. First, an exclusive licence [or sole licence] between non-competitors—if caught by Article 101(1)—is likely to fulfil the conditions of Article 101(3) *up to the level of dominance*. There are probably two reasons for this. First as the guidelines themselves point out,

> The right to grant an exclusive licence is generally necessary in order to induce the licensee to invest in the licensed technology . . . particularly where the licensee must make large investments in further developing the licensed technology. To intervene against the exclusivity once the licensee has made a commercial success of the licensed technology would deprive the licensee of the fruits of his success and would be detrimental to competition, the dissemination of technology and innovation.[3]

In addition, all the licensor is doing is sharing its exclusive rights under a patent or another IPR. The alternative to the exclusive licence realistically would be no new product on the market. The exemption would appear applicable both within and outside the safe haven as long as the technology licensed did not achieve a dominant position in the relevant market.

For similar reasons, an exclusive licence offered by a licensor in a non-reciprocal agreement between competitors (in essence a vertical agreement) is block exempted up to the market share threshold of 20 per cent and above the market share threshold the likely anti-competitive effects of such exclusive licensing must be analysed.

The third category consisting of reciprocal exclusive licensing between competitors is generally viewed as a hard core restriction falling under Article 4(1)(c). Reciprocal sole licensing between competitors is block exempted up to the market share threshold of 20 per cent. Above the threshold, in cases where the parties have a significant degree of market power the TTA Guidelines state that 'such agreements may facilitate

[2] Commission Regulation (EC) No 772/2004 of 27 April 2004 on the application of Article 81(3) of the Treaty to categories of technology transfer agreements OJ L 123, 27 April 2004, pp 11–17, Art 4.

[3] Commission Notice, Guidelines on the application of Article 81 of the EC Treaty [now Article 101 TFEU] to technology transfer agreements [2004] OJ C101/2, (hereafter TTA Guidelines), para 165.

collusion by ensuring that the parties are the only sources of output in the market based on the licensed technologies'.[4]

The second type of territorial protection offered by the licensor as an inducement to agree to a licence are *sales restrictions*, ie obligations not to sell in a particular licensed territory. The TTBER again distinguishes between licensing agreements between competitors and licensing agreements between non-competitors.

In the case of agreements between *non*-competitors sales restrictions between the licensor and a licensee are block exempted up to the market share threshold of 30 per cent. Even above the market share threshold restrictions on all sales by licensees to territories or customer groups reserved for the licensor may fall outside Article 101(1) where the licensor or licensee would not have licensed without such a condition. 'A technology owner cannot normally be expected to create direct competition with himself inside his own technology. . .'[5] Again, this would appear to be the case for restrictions on the sales above the market share limits up to the level of dominance.

The TTA Guidelines add that:

> Above the market share threshold restrictions on active sales between licensees' territories and customer groups limit intra-technology competition and are likely to be caught by Article [101(1)] when the individual licensee has a significant degree of market power. Such restrictions, however, may fulfil the conditions of Article [101(3)] where they are necessary to prevent free riding and to induce the licensee to make the investment necessary for efficient exploitation of the licensed technology inside his territory and to promote sales of the licensed product[6]

In other words, even above the market share limits and below dominance, restrictions on *active* sales are exempted for the period of the validity of the licensing agreement.

In contrast, restrictions on *passive* sales by licensees are permissible for two years from the date on which the licensee benefiting from the restrictions first put the product incorporating the licensed technology on the market inside its exclusive territory.[7] Passive sales restrictions exceeding this two-year period will be viewed as hard core restrictions falling within Article 4(2)(b).

In the case of *non*-reciprocal agreements between *competitors*, restrictions on active and passive sales by the licensee or the licensor into the exclusive territory or to the exclusive customer group of the other are also block exempted.[8] Even above the market share threshold of 20 per cent where such restrictions are indispensable for the dissemination of valuable technologies, they may be exempted under Article 101(3). The TTA Guidelines take a very conservative view of the possibilities of exempting such vertical restrictions. If the *licensor* has a relatively weak market position in the territory where it itself exploits the technology, and if restrictions on active sales are indispensable to

[4] Ibid, para 163.
[5] Ibid, para 172.
[6] Ibid, para 174.
[7] Ibid, para 174.
[8] Ibid, para 170.

induce the licensor to grant the licence, protection against the risk of facing active competition from licensees in its main area of activity may be exemptible.

Similarly, passive sales restrictions could be viewed as indispensable within the meaning of Article 101(3) for the period of time required for the protected *licensee* to penetrate a new market and establish a market presence in the allocated territory or vis-à-vis the allocated customer group. This protection against active sales only partially allows the licensee to overcome the asymmetry, which it faces from other licensees already established on the market.

In a *reciprocal* agreement between *competitors*, restrictions on active and passive sales to customers and territories allocated to a licensee are hard core restrictions. Such restrictions are thought by the competition authorities to have a high potential for market sharing since they prevent both parties from selling actively and passively into territories and to customer groups which they actually served or could realistically have served in the absence of the agreement. But this is further evidence of a broad brush approach adopted by the Commission to horizontal licensing agreements.

Output limitations imposed on the licensee in agreements *between non-competitors* are often pro-competitive because they promote technology transfer.

> As a supplier of technology the licensor should normally be free to determine the output produced with the licensed technology by the licensee. If the licensor were not free to determine the output of the licensee, a number of licence agreements might not come into existence in the first place, which would have a negative impact on the dissemination of new technology. This is particularly likely to be the case where the licensor is also a producer, since in that case the output of the licensees may find their way back into the licensor's main area of operation and thus have a direct impact on these activities.[9]

The Commission has indicated that output restrictions in licence agreements between non-competitors are block exempted up to the market share threshold of 30 per cent, provided that the licensor is not obliged to limit the output of *other licensees* or the total output of *all licensees*. If so, it is considered that the agreement is implementing a concerted practice limiting output at the level of the licensees.

The main anti-competitive risk flowing from output restrictions on licensees in agreements between non-competitors, according to the Commission, is reduced intra-technology competition *between licensees*. The significance of such anti-competitive effects depends on the market position of the licensor and the licensees and the extent to which the licensee, owing to the output limitation, is prevented from satisfying demand for the products incorporating the licensed technology.

In some cases, output limitations may also be used to facilitate the partitioning of markets and to extend territorial protection beyond what is allowed under the TTBER and the present guidelines, for example where quantities are adjusted over time to cover only local demand or where sales restrictions on licensees require them not to sell into a territory or customer group reserved for the licensor.[10]

[9] Ibid, para 178.
[10] Ibid, paras 175–7.

Reciprocal output restrictions in licence agreements *between competitors* constitute a hard core restriction covered by Article 4(1)(b) of the TTBER but output restrictions imposed on the licensee in a non-reciprocal agreement or on one of the licensees in a reciprocal agreement are block exempted up to the market share threshold of 20 per cent.

16.3 FIELD OF USE RESTRICTIONS

Field of use restrictions are limits either on the type of product or the technical field in which the licensee may make, use, or sell a product. Examples offered by the TTA Guidelines are a chipset technology for more than four Central Processing Units (CPUs) or for four or less CPUs and an engine technology for either four or six cylinder engines.[11] A field of use restriction may be viewed as simply a partial allocation of the IP protection conferred upon the right-holder and hence the competition effects are little different from unilateral action. Moreover, the TTA Guidelines make it clear that if the licensor could reserve certain fields of use for its own exploitation, it would either not license or charge a higher royalty. Even when combined with territorial exclusivity, field of use restrictions can be pro-competitive in effect by encouraging the licensor to licence its technology for applications that fall outside its main field of exploitation. The TTA Guidelines point out that in 'agreements between non-competitors the licensor is normally also entitled to grant sole and exclusive licences to different licensees limited to one or more fields of use. Such restrictions limit intra-technology competition between licensees in the same way as exclusive licensing and are analysed in the same way.' The Guidelines require that a distinction be made between *field of use* restrictions in which the licence is limited to one or more technical fields of application or one or more product markets and *customer restrictions* which are hard core restrictions under Articles 4(1)(c) and 4(2)(b) of the TTBER. Field of use agreements between actual or potential competitors are block exempted up to the market share threshold of 20 per cent. Those between non-competitors are block exempted up to 30 per cent.

[11] See TTA Guidelines, para 179.

17

THE REGULATION OF NON-TERRITORIAL RESTRAINTS IN LICENSING AGREEMENTS[1]

17.1 Introduction 279

17.2 Non-Territorial Restraints which are Non-Restrictive of Competition 280

17.1 INTRODUCTION

Under the new legal framework it is also necessary to analyse non-territorial restraints differently depending on whether or not they occur in vertical or horizontal licensing agreements. It is helpful to categorize non-territorial restraints into two main types: non-restrictive and exemptible. The first type consists of certain non-territorial restraints that are normally non-restrictive of competition. The main criterion used by the EU Courts and Commission for finding a contractual restraint to be non-restrictive under Article 101(1) is the 'ancillary restraints' test, that is, those provisions that are absolutely indispensable to IP licensing agreements because, without them, the value of the IPRs could be lost.

The second type of provision commonly found in licensing agreements is one which although caught by Article 101(1) is nevertheless exemptible under Article 101(3). This requires a different calculus, a use of the TTA Guidelines and the relevant case law to make an assessment of the applicability of the four conditions of Article 101(3) to the particular clause. Insofar as a specific non-territorial restraint is block exempted, it offers a promising case for exemption in agreements which are made in respect of licensed products with above market share limits. It is also important to be able to

[1] See further discussion in S. Anderman and J. Kallaugher, *Technology Transfers and the New EU Competition Rules* (Oxford: OUP, 2006), Ch 8.

distinguish when such a provision crosses the line between exemptible and non-exemptible because it overlaps with a hard core restriction.

17.2 NON-TERRITORIAL RESTRAINTS WHICH ARE NON-RESTRICTIVE OF COMPETITION

17.2.1 The 'ancillary' restrictions

With the removal of a white list of exemptible restrictions which was offered in previous regulations, it is useful to revive the distinction between non-restrictive and exemptible clauses in licensing agreements. The white lists in previous regulations tended to combine contractual restraints not caught by Article 101(1) with those that were so caught but nevertheless exempted in a single white list of clauses. For parties engaged in self-certification it is wise to make such distinctions clearer. The TTA Guidelines offer assistance in this endeavour by setting out a list of examples of obligations in licence agreements that are almost always *not* restrictive of competition within the meaning of Article 101(1).[2] These include:

(a) confidentiality obligations;

(b) obligations on licensees not to sublicense;

(c) obligations not to use the licensed technology after the expiry of the agreement, provided that the licensed technology remains valid and in force;

(d) obligations to assist the licensor in enforcing the licensed intellectual property rights;

(e) obligations to pay minimum royalties or to produce a minimum quantity of products incorporating the licensed technology; and

(f) obligations to use the licensor's trade mark or indicate the name of the licensor on the product.[3]

These clauses offer examples of what the EU Courts and Commission have labelled 'ancillary restrictions', ie those restrictions that are indispensable to effectuating the main purpose of the licensing agreement. Each one has been viewed in the context of its role as an indispensable restraint to allow the licensing agreement to be made in the first place.

There are three related types of provisions recognized as 'indispensable' to IP licences which are not restrictions on competition under Article 101(1), at least in their pure form, either because of the scope of the patent doctrine or the ancillary restraints concept.

[2] Commission Notice, Guidelines on the application of Article 81 of the EC Treaty [now Article 101 TFEU] to technology transfer agreements [2004] OJ C101/2 (hereafter TTA Guidelines), para 155.

[3] Ibid, para 155.

17.2.2 The obligation not to divulge secret know-how

It has long been acknowledged by the Commission that a licensor is entitled to place on the licensee an obligation not to divulge know-how communicated by the licensor during the contract. Moreover, the licensor is entitled to hold the licensee to that obligation for a period after the expiry of the contract until the know-how enters the public domain because in both instances non-disclosure is an indispensable condition of know-how licensing. As the Commission stated in *Delta Chemie*,[4] the commercial value of the know-how rests very largely in its confidential character and each disclosure brings prejudice to the holder of that know-how. Since there is no time limit on the know-how protection through contract, it is legitimate to impose an obligation as long as the know-how does not enter the public domain. In *Boussois/Interpane*,[5] the Commission cleared a clause which placed a five-year limit on the secrecy obligation on the licensee. The parties had agreed that that represented the average life of the know-how and accepted that the obligation remained only as long as the know-how was not obtained by third parties from other sources. The Commission noted in clearing the clause that the ban did not extend beyond the useful life of the technology. The then TTBER (Article (2)(1)) whitelisted an obligation on the licensee not to divulge the know-how communicated by the licensor and added that the licensee may be held to this obligation after the agreement had expired. This provision is essential for the licensor; the only issue is whether it offers sufficient protection for sharing secret know-how with the licensee. Often the licensee is required to ensure that its employees are bound by the confidentiality ban as well. Often, as well, the licensor attempts to combine a secrecy obligation with other provisions such as a ban on sublicensing without prior consent, a post-term use ban, and a non-competition clause. As we shall see, EU competition law does not allow the licensor the luxury of all these forms of protection; only some are viewed as objectively indispensable.

17.2.3 The ban on sublicensing and assignment

The obligation not to sublicense the know-how which is communicated under the licence or the patent which is licensed or to assign either of these is not caught by Article 101(1) even if it extends beyond the term of the licence, as long as the know-how has not entered the public domain and the patents are still in force. In *Burroughs Delplanque*,[6] this protection was regarded as within the scope of the patent. In *Jus Rol*,[7] the ban on sublicensing to any undertaking other than a wholly owned subsidiary of either licensor or licensee was cleared because it protects the licensor's right to use the know-how as it sees fit as long as the know-how has not entered the public domain.

[4] *Delta Chemie* Commission Decision [1988] OJ L 309/34, [1989] 4 CMLR 535.
[5] [1988] 4 CMLR 124.
[6] See *Burroughs Delplanque* [1972] CMLR D 67 at para 48.
[7] *Rich Products/Jus Rol* (1988) 4 CMLR 527.

Competition policy would not countenance a ban once the patent expires or the know-how loses its secrecy because the contract would unfairly restrain the licensee whilst its competitors would be free to use the IPR. The main complication involving the ban on sublicensing occurs in the context of grant backs of improvements and post-term use bans which will be discussed below.

17.2.4 Post-term use bans

The third indispensable clause in IP licensing is the post-term use ban. The Commission has long accepted that an obligation placed upon the licensee to cease using the licensed technology after the termination of the agreement is not a restriction on competition. As the Commission puts it in Recital 20 of the 1996 Technology Transfer Regulation:

> The obligation on the licensee to cease using the licensed technology after the termination of the agreement . . . [does] not generally restrict competition. The post-term use ban may be regarded as a normal feature of licensing, as otherwise the licensor would be forced to transfer the know-how or patents in perpetuity.

The presence of this obligation in the agreement distinguishes the licence from the assignment.

In *Jus Rol*[8] the Commission cleared a post-term use ban which applied for ten years following termination noting that it was inherent in this type of agreement. If the owner were to lose its exclusive right to use know-how at the expiry of the licensing agreement it would be less willing to grant a licence and this would be harmful to the transfer of technology. A post-term use ban becomes anti-competitive only if it persists after the know-how becomes freely available to others through no fault of the licensee. In *Delta Chemie*[9] the Commission reiterated that an obligation upon the licensee to cease using the licensed IPR at the end of an agreement is an 'essential condition' insofar as it has not entered the public domain. The limit in time may remove the licensee from the market for the licensed product at the end of the agreement but it is a necessary condition for the transfer of technical knowledge and should not be prohibited by Article 101(1). The 1996 TTBER whitelisted 'an obligation on the licensee not to exploit the licensed know-how or patents after termination of the agreement in so far and as long as the know-how is still secret or the patents are in force'.[10] Presumably, such a clause would be compatible with Article 101(1) today.

17.2.5 Non-compete obligations

Other obligations are less obviously non-restrictive of competition under Article 101(1) and require exemption. In such cases, the competitor/non-competitor distinction

[8] Ibid.

[9] *Delta Chemie* Commission Decision [1988] OJ L 309/34, [1989] 4 CMLR 535.

[10] Commission Regulation (EC) 240/96 on the application of Article 81(3) of the Treaty to certain categories of technology transfer agreements, OJ L 031, 9 December 1996, pp 2–13, Art 2(1)(3).

becomes crucial. For example, a non-competition clause, ie an obligation on the licensee not to use third party technologies which compete with the licensed technology, may have certain pro-competitive functions. It can reassure the licensor to an exclusive licence that the licensed property will be commercially exploited and offer protection should the exclusive licensee be attracted to competing technology.

The TTBER therefore exempts non-compete obligations both in the case of agreements between competitors and in the case of agreements between non-competitors up to the market share thresholds of 20 per cent and 30 per cent respectively. However, they must not directly or *indirectly* limit the licensee's ability to exploit *its own technology* or *limits the ability of any of the parties to the agreement to carry out research and development*, unless such a restriction is indispensable to prevent the disclosure of the licensed know-how to third parties.[11]

Moreover, since the main competitive risk of non-compete obligations is the foreclosure of third party technologies by either individual agreements or cumulative agreements, if the single licensor does not have significant market power or the cumulative effects do not tie up as much as 50 per cent of the market, then these adverse affects are not likely to arise. Above the threshold, there will be a need to look at barriers to entry and apply the analytical framework in the Guidelines on Vertical Restraints.[12]

17.2.6 Grant backs and improvements

A second area of micro-regulation attempting to establish a balance in the TTBER occurs when the licensor requires grant backs of improvements. The licensing of patents and/or know-how, either separately or together, almost inevitably leads to improvements being discovered by licensees. Some improvements can themselves be patentable. Most consist of know-how which can be protected through contract. Some improvements are 'severable'; that is they are products or processes which are capable of being exploited independently of the original IPR. They are defined in the TTA Guidelines as improvements which can be worked without use of the original licensed product.[13] Other improvements are 'non-severable'; they are capable of being used only in conjunction with the protected producer or process in the original licence.

Typically, licensors are reluctant to license without a right of disclosure and use of the licensee's improvements. Disclosure is needed in order to monitor the licensee's development and use of the improvements. The right of use allows the licensor to improve the original product or process for its own use and for the use of other licensees. A number of licensors would prefer such rights to be exclusive or even assigned back,

[11] See Commission Regulation (EC) No 772/2004 of 27 April 2004 on the application of Article 81(3) of the Treaty to categories of technology transfer agreements, OJ L 123, 27 April 2004, pp 11–17, Arts 4(d) and 5(2).

[12] Commission Regulation 330/2010 of 20 April 2010 on the application of Article 101(3) of the Treaty on the Functioning of the European Union to categories of vertical agreements and concerted practices, OJ L 102, 23 April 2010, pp 1–7

[13] TTA Guidelines, para 109.

reasoning that the improvements are derived from the original invention. They would view a contractual commitment to granting back improvements as part of the quid pro quo for granting the licence in the first place. Some recognize that there is more of an incentive to the licensee to develop and communicate improvements if the licensee can share in the fruits of its severable improvements by licensing them to third parties but the concern about creating extra competitors often leads to a reluctance to cede too much freedom to licensees.

From the viewpoint of EU competition policy, the issue of the stimulus to innovation provided by improvements is too important to be left to freedom of contract. Excessive unilateral control over improvements by strong licensors and/or licensees in the form of restraints in licensing contracts must be curtailed in the interest of promoting the development and diffusion of technology. The restraints in licensing agreements must not be drawn so widely that they stifle the incentives of licensees to improve the technology and disclose the results of their improvements more widely. Yet the rules should not be so unfriendly to licensors that they create a chilling effect on licensing.

The balance struck in the new TTBER depends upon whether or not the improvement by the licensee is severable or non-severable, that is whether or not the licensee can work the technology without using the licensed product or process. In the case of severable improvements, the licensor is barred from including a provision requiring the licensee to *assign* any or all of its severable improvements to the licensor. The TTBER also provides that the licensor can only require the licensee to license back *on a non-exclusive basis* any severable improvements made by the licensee to the licensed product or process or any new applications.[14] On the other hand the licensor can require exclusive licenses of non-severable improvements. Moreover, the TTBER places no reciprocal obligation upon licensors to license their improvements to the licensee or indeed to cross-license the improvements of other licensees back to the licensee. The Commission offers an explanation in the TTA Guidelines to the effect that it helps innovation to give freedom to the licensor to require non-reciprocal, non-exclusive grant backs.[15] Yet it places licensees in a difficult position because on the one hand it allows passive sales from other licensees after two years, thus opening up intra-licensee competition, yet it places the licensor in a position to favour some licensees and disfavour others. Is this freedom of contract a step too far?

17.2.7 Quality controls and licensing

A third area of regulation is that of quality controls and licensing. The concern of the licensor to ensure that the licensee preserves quality standards lies at the heart of the licensing decision, particularly where the licensor's trade mark is associated with the licensed product. In general the insistence on minimum *quality* specifications by

[14] TTBER, Art 5(1)(a).
[15] TTA Guidelines, para 111.

itself, as long as they are agreed upon in advance and based on objectively verifiable criteria, has not been viewed as restrictive of competition under Article 101(1). Moreover, the licensor can reserve a right to monitor quality standards by carrying out related checks. These provisions are recognized by the EU Courts and Commission as indispensable to an appropriate exploitation of the invention.

In the previous TTBER the Commission whitelisted an obligation on the licensee to observe minimum quality specifications, including *technical specifications,* for the licensed product or:

> to procure goods and services from the licensor or from an undertaking designated by the licensor, insofar as these quality specifications, products or services are necessary for:
>
> (a) a technically proper exploitation of the licensed technology; or
>
> (b) ensuring that the product of the licensee conforms to the minimum quality specifications that are applicable to the licensor and other licensees.

In other words, it dealt with tie-ins justified by quality specifications as a special exemptible category, applying the restrictions in respect of technical exploitation and conformity with standards for licensor and even allowing a tie-in where necessary for such purposes.

On the other hand, quality specifications can also mask a tie-in. In the context of technology licensing, tying occurs when the licensor makes the licensing of one technology (the tying product) conditional upon the licensee taking a licence for another technology or purchasing a product from the licensor or someone designated by him (the tied product). The TTA Guidelines recognize that tying can actually be pro-competitive in two types of situations: where the tied product is necessary for a technically satisfactory exploitation of the licensed technology; or where it is necessary to ensure that production under the licence conforms to quality standards desired by the licensor.

> In such cases tying is normally either not restrictive of competition or is exempted by Article 101(3). Where the licensees use the licensor's trademark or brand name or where it is otherwise obvious to consumers that there is a link between the product incorporating the licensed technology and the licensor, the licensor has a legitimate interest in ensuring that the quality of the products are such that it does not undermine the value of his technology or his reputation as an economic operator.[16]

The TTA Guidelines also point out that tying is likely to be:

> pro-competitive where the tied product allows the licensee to exploit the licensed technology significantly more efficiently than other available alternatives. For instance, where the licensor licenses a particular process technology the parties can also agree that the licensee buys a catalyst from the licensor, which is developed for use with the licensed technology and which allows the technology to be exploited more efficiently than in the case of other catalysts.[17]

[16] Ibid, para 194.
[17] Ibid, para 195.

In such cases, where the restriction is caught by Article 101(1), the conditions of Article 101(3) are likely to be fulfilled *above* the market share thresholds as well as below them.[18]

In cases where the licensor does not occupy a dominant position and the relationship is predominantly vertical there is no need to prohibit tie-ins. The case law of the Commission reinforces that view particularly in respect of know-how. In *Jus Rol*,[19] for example, an obligation placed upon the licensee to buy a pre-mix from the licensor was regarded as essential to ensure the proper proportions in the preparation of the mix as well as the correct results in the final product. The tie-in was justified as necessary to ensure consistency of quality in the licensed product.[20] In *Delta Chemie*[21] and *Moosehead/Whitbread*[22] the Commission acknowledged that the tie-ins were justified by the need to ensure consistency of manufacture and marketing in situations where the trade mark figured prominently in the agreement.

Under the current TTBER, tying is block exempted in the case of agreements between competitors up to the market share threshold of 20 per cent and in the case of agreements between non-competitors up to the market share threshold of 30 per cent. The market share thresholds apply to any relevant technology or product market affected by the licence agreement, including the market for the tied product. Above the market share threshold it is necessary to balance the anti-competitive and pro-competitive effects of tying. The main restrictive effect of tying is foreclosure of competing suppliers of the tied product.[23] In the absence of market power in the tying product, the licensor cannot use his technology for the anti-competitive purpose of foreclosing suppliers of the tied product. Furthermore, as in the case of non-compete obligations, the tie must cover a certain proportion if the market for the tied product for appreciable foreclosure effects is to occur. So there has been a major loosening of the regulatory framework in respect of tying.

17.2.8 Royalties

From a competition point of view, it is now accepted by the Commission and the EU Courts that, for the most part, Article 101(1) should have little application to the bargain struck over royalty payments as long as they have been freely negotiated between the parties.

The TTA Guidelines state in respect of royalties that the:

> parties to a licence agreement are normally free to determine the royalty payable by the licensee and its mode of payment without being caught by Article 101(1). This principle applies both to

[18] Ibid, para 195.
[19] *Rich Products/Jus Rol* (1988) 4 CMLR 527.
[20] Ibid.
[21] *Delta Chemie* Commission Decision [1988] OJ L 309/34, [1989] 4 CMLR 535.
[22] [1991] 4 CMLR 391.
[23] TTA Guidelines, para 193.

agreements between competitors and agreements between non-competitors. Royalty obligations may for instance take the form of lump sum payments, a percentage of the selling price or a fixed amount for each product incorporating the licensed technology. In cases where the licensed technology relates to an input, which is incorporated into a final product it is as a general rule not restrictive of competition that royalties are calculated on the basis of the price of the final product, provided that it incorporates the licensed technology. In the case of software licensing royalties based on the number of users and royalties calculated on a per machine basis is as a general rule compatible with Article 101(1).[24]

However the parties are not left entirely free of regulation of royalty arrangements in licensing agreements under Article 101. There are competition concerns with bargains which in some way go beyond the pure exchange of royalty for the licensed product in terms of (a) duration and (b) the base for calculating royalties; in both cases, the concern is that the licensor might exceed its entitlement under the scope of the IPR grant.

17.2.8.1 Duration

The freedom to spread royalty payments for the use of the technology over a period extending beyond the duration of the licensed IPRs as well as after the licensed know-how has entered the public domain is now accepted within the safe harbour of the block exemption and more broadly under Article 101(3) even outside the TTBER.

The TTA Guidelines point out that,

> Notwithstanding the fact that the block exemption only applies as long as the technology is valid and in force, the parties can normally without falling foul of Article [101(1)] agree to extend royalty obligations beyond the duration of the licensed intellectual property rights. Once these rights expire, third parties can legally exploit the technology in question and compete with the parties to the agreement. Such actual and potential competition will normally suffice to ensure that the obligation in question does not have appreciable anti-competitive effects.[25]

If an agreement provides that there is a right for either party to terminate the agreement, then there is greater assurance that the period for calculating the royalties is part of the original bargain struck in respect of the original IP package.

Even assuming a right to terminate, however, there is still a residual concern for royalties on expired patents which could reduce the parties' freedom of contract in respect of the method of paying royalties. In the case of licensed patents, under the new TTBER, the agreement may contain an obligation on the licensee to continue paying the royalties over a period going beyond the duration of the licensed patents essentially as a device to facilitate payment of the original bargain that is struck between licensor and licensee.[26]

[24] Ibid, para 156.
[25] Ibid, para 159.
[26] In contrast, in the case of know-how, the parties are given the freedom to determine the nature of the obligation to continue paying royalties until the end of the agreement even if the know-how becomes publicly known (TTBER Art 2(1)(7)(a)).

17.2.8.2 The base for calculating royalties

Connected with the regulation of the duration of royalty payments are the restrictions imposed by Article 101(1) on the basis for calculating royalties. Royalties can take the form of a lump sum payment, a price per unit sold, or a percentage of the sales price.[27] For agreements between competitors, where a royalty rate is set which takes the form of a restriction on a party's ability to determine prices or as a sham for price fixing, it will be viewed as a hard core restriction under Article 4(1)(a).[28] Moreover, for such agreements the use of the royalty rate to extend to products produced solely with the licensee's own technology are hard core restrictions.[29]

This may be a reference to the *Windsurfing*[30] case. In *Windsurfing,* the agreement provided a method of calculating royalties for the patented rig based on the net selling price of the entire sailboard (rig and board). The Commission held that this method contravened Article 101(1) because it regarded the net royalty clause as an attempt to prevent the separate sale of rigs to unlicensed third parties. The CJEU was more understanding of the practicalities in the case and held that once the method of calculation was adjusted to meet some of the Commission's objections, so that the royalty rate for the separate sale of rigs was not lower than the rate under the old agreement, the royalty rate for the rigs based on the product as a whole did not violate Article 101(1). In respect of rigs, its object or effect was not restrictive of competition. Further, the CJEU indicated that the calculation of royalties for the patented part of a product based on the price of the product as a whole could be justified because it was impracticable to establish its value, either because the number of items manufactured or consumed was difficult to establish or because there was no separate demand for the patented product. On the other hand, the CJEU held that insofar as the calculation of royalties based on a 'bundling' of patented with unpatented products restricted the sale of the unprotected product, the board, it was not only caught by Article 101(1); it was not exemptible under Article 101(3).

Otherwise for competitors, other royalty arrangements are block exempted up to 20 per cent even if they are restrictions.[31] Outside the safe haven of the block exemption, cross-licensing and disproportionate running royalties could be restrictive under Article 101(1) where they have an effect upon prices and may not be exemptible under Article 101(3).[32]

For agreements between non-competitors, the parties may legitimately base royalties on both the products produced with the licensed technologies and products produced with technologies licensed from third parties because of their 'metering' value. However, outside the safe harbour of the block exemption, there may be foreclosure

[27] TTA Guidelines, para 156.

[28] See TTBER Art 4(1)(a).

[29] See TTBER Arts 4(1)(a) and (d). Cf Case 193/83 *Windsurfing International v Commission* [1986] ECR 611; see also *Boussois/Interpane* [1987] OJ L 50/30.

[30] Case 193/83 *Windsurfing International.*

[31] TTA Guidelines, para 158.

[32] Ibid.

effects and if these are appreciable, the royalty arrangement will be caught by Article 101(1) and not likely to fulfil the conditions of Article 101(3).[33]

17.2.9 No-challenge clauses

No-challenge clauses are obligations undertaken by the licensee not to challenge the validity of the licensor's IPRs during the contract term after becoming more closely acquainted with the protected product or process as a result of the licence. The desire of a licensor to insert a no-challenge clause in an IP licence is often so strong that, without such contractual protection, many might be reluctant to license their IP at all. The risk of a licensee using its intimate knowledge of the patent process acquired as a result of a patent licence to devalue the investment in the R&D for opportunistic reasons could deter a decision to license at all or at the very least restrict it to partners over which there were extra-contractual controls.

For many years, however, this factor was viewed as completely overshadowed by the issue of public policy, that the rules of competition law should not indirectly encourage the weakening of the integrity of the patenting process.[34] Thus in a number of cases, the Commission found that the presence of a no-challenge clause was a restriction of competition because it prevented the licensee from removing 'an obstacle to his freedom of action'.[35] In *Davidson Rubber*,[36] the Commission insisted upon the licensor removing the no-challenge clause as the price of granting the exemption. Did it feel that the fact that the licensee was in the best position to detect a weakness in the validity of the IPR was a reason not to allow the licensor to restrain him? On the other hand, the right to challenge can be opportunistically misused by licensees seeking to avoid their contractual obligation to pay royalties or to have greater opportunity to use rival technology. In *Bayer and Henneker v Sullhofer*,[37] the Court of Justice held on an Article 267 TFEU reference that before a no-challenge clause could be found to be contrary to Article 101(1), it must be looked at in its legal and economic context and that is a task for the national court.[38]

In the current version of the TTBER, no-challenge clauses are not blacklisted but they are excluded restrictions under Article 5. On the other hand, the licensor may reserve a right in the licence to the effect that if the licensee challenges the validity of the licensor's IPRs held in the common market, the licensor is entitled to terminate the technology transfer agreement.[39]

33 TTA Guidelines, para 160,
34 See eg *Vaessen/Moris* [1979] OJ 119/32 at paras 34–5.
35 Ibid.
36 [1972] OJ L 143/31.
37 Case 65/86 *Bayer AG and Maschinenfabrik Hennecke GmbH v Heinz Sülthöfer*.
38 Ibid, at para 21.
39 TTA Guidelines, para 1040.

Moreover, the TTA Guidelines have acknowledged that no-challenge clauses may be an indispensable restraint in a patent or other IP dispute settlement agreement as long as the IP is not obviously invalid.[40]

In *Bayer & Henneker v Sullhofer*, the Court of Justice suggested that no-challenge clauses were not necessarily unlawful under Article 101(1) and potentially capable of exemption under Article 101(3). It analysed no-challenge clauses as restrictions of contractual autonomy rather than as inhibitions on the process of protecting the integrity of the patent process and asked whether the restriction had an appreciable effect on that autonomy. It held that in the circumstances of the case, where the patent licence was royalty free, the non-challenge clause did not create a problem under Article 101(1) because the licensee would not have to bear the competitive disadvantage of having to pay royalties for the use of the patent which may be invalid. This judgment suggested a move to a less formalistic approach to no-challenge clauses than *Windsurfing*[41] and left room for argument about other circumstances in which such clauses could be cleared under Article 101(1).

[40] Ibid, para 209. For the TTA Guidelines' discussion of patent settlement agreements more generally, see paras 204–10.

[41] See eg Case 193/83 *Windsurfing International* at para 80.

18

TECHNOLOGY POOLS, INDUSTRIAL STANDARDS, AND TTBER

18.1	Introduction	291
18.2	Stage 1: The Product Formulation Stage	293
18.3	Stage 2: The Creation of the Standard and the Selection of Essential Patents	294
18.4	Stage 3: Licensing Out	296
18.5	The FRAND Commitments	297
18.6	The Legal Framework for Technology Pools and Standardization Agreements	298
18.7	Technology Pools, TTBER, and Guidelines	300
18.8	The Competition Concerns and the Creation of the Pool	300
18.9	The Assessment of Individual Restraints	302
18.10	The Institutional Framework Governing the Pool	303
18.11	Conclusions	304

18.1 INTRODUCTION

Producing industrial standard products through patent and technology pools has on occasion dramatically awakened competition concerns on both sides of the Atlantic in recent years. The most obvious examples in the EU are the recent but now closed cases of *Rambus*[1] and *Qualcomm*[2] and the interchange between the European Commission and European Telecommunications Standard Institute (ETSI) in relation to IPCom's role in the Universal Mobile Telecommunications System (UMTS) pool after it accepted Bosch's commitment to a fair, reasonable, and non-discriminatory (FRAND)

[1] The Commission adopted a 'commitments' decision in respect of Rambus Inc which *inter alia* put a cap on royalties it could charge the JEDEC SSO for certain patents for 'Dynamic Random Access Memory Chips' (DRAMS). 'Antitrust: Commission accepts commitments from Rambus lowering memory chip royalty rates' IP/09/1987 (Brussels, 9 December 2009).

[2] 'Commission closes formal proceedings against Qualcomm' MEMO/09/516.

licence of essential patents.[3] These cases all raised specific questions about the role of obligations within patent or technology pools. However, away from the more dramatic incidents of individual firms engaging in conduct that has occasioned investigations by the Commission to determine possible infringements of Article 102, technology pools have developed as an autonomous process of collaboration amongst competitors producing considerable innovative benefits in terms of ICT technologies and interoperable products which are industrial standards. Yet the process of technology pools and standard setting raises new questions for competition authorities about their intrinsic risks of anti-competitive harm under Article 101 as well as Article 102. How should the obvious innovative and pro-competitive benefits of such collaborations be assessed in relation to their anti-competitive risks? On the one hand the collaboration between competitors produces new technology and industrial standards such as DVDs, 2G, 3G, and 4G mobile telephony in a situation that would otherwise be characterized as a 'patent thicket'. On the other hand, the opportunities are created to 'fix' technologies and prices and to foreclose competitors in the course of the process. Above all, this development raises interesting questions about the role of competition policy in regulating processes which are technologically complex and dependent upon entrepreneurial cooperation. Does competition policy have the means to ensure that the process remains open and results in the best technological solution? Or is competition policy so limited in its scope that it can only stand on the sidelines and pick off obvious examples of price fixing or foreclosure activity, leaving the selection process almost entirely to the participants? Commentators advocate both a relatively non-interventionist approach[4] and a relatively interventionist approach[5] to the role of competition law.

There are undoubted competition concerns raised by the prospect of competitors cooperating to produce industrial standards. Some of these concerns have been reflected in the R&D Joint Venture Block Exemption,[6] the Horizontal Guidelines,[7] and the Technology Transfer Block Exemption and Guidelines.[8] However, in a situation where a particular industry attempts to create a new technological product relying on

[3] See 'Antitrust: Commission welcomes IPCom's public FRAND declaration' MEMO/09/549, 10 December 2009.

[4] See eg S. Anderman and J. Kallaugher, *Technology Transfer and the New EU Competition Rules* (Oxford: OUP, 2006), Ch 9; D. Teece and E. Sherry, 'Standard Setting and Antitrust' (2003) 87 *Minn Law Rev* 1911; see also M. Carrier, 'Why Antitrust Should Defer to the Intellectual Property Rules of Standard Setting Organisations: A Commentary on Teece and Sherry' (2005) 89 *Minn Law Rev* 2017; P. Plomben, 'The New Technology Transfer Guidelines as Applied to Patent Pools and Patent Pool Licenses' in C. Ehlermann and I. Atanasiu (eds), *European Competition Annual 2005, The Interaction between Competition Law and Intellectual Property Law*, (Oxford and Portland, Oregon: Hart Publishing, 2007) 295.

[5] See P. Chappiatte, 'FRAND Commitments—The Case for Antitrust Intervention' (2009) 2 *European Competition Journal* 319; see to H. Ullrich, 'Patent Pools-Policies and Problems' in J. Drexl (ed), *Research Handbook on Intellectual Property and Competition Law* (Cheltenham, UK, Northampton, MA, USA: Edward Elgar, 2008), p 139.

[6] Reg 2659/2000 on the application of Article [101(3)] of the Treaty to categories of research and development OJ [2000] L 304/7.

[7] Commission Notice, Guidelines to the Applicability of Article [101] of the EU Treaty to Horizontal Cooperation Agreements OJ [2001] C3/02 (Horizontal Guidelines).

[8] See Chapters 12–17.

hundreds or even thousands of patents which protect relevant and potentially essential technologies, it may be pro-competitive for competitors to cooperate in R&D after a preliminary planning stage, and in a technology pool with a Standard Setting Organization (SSO) after the various contributory technologies have been identified as relevant to choosing a new technology. It has been estimated that the GSM standard for 2G mobile telephony involved more than 4,000 'essential' patents and the UMTS 3G standard involved more than 8,500 'essential' patents. In those and even smaller groups there are overlapping patents and a plethora of micro patents that would impede the achievement of a technical innovation unless some kind of novel form of cooperation can be instituted. The pro-competitive benefits of a technology pool are that a new product can be created that might not otherwise be realized. It constitutes a defeat for the 'tragedy of the anti-commons' in certain sectors by producing a one-stop shop in the form of new technology or technological product. A technology pool offers the potential benefit of attaining and improving product interoperability since many pools are aimed specifically at created interoperable standards. An economist would argue that this process also lowers transaction costs and thereby contributes to consumer welfare. The EU regulators have recognized these contributions in a series of 'safe harbours' in the three regulations mentioned above while at the same time stipulating guidelines as to the types of collaborative activity that they consider to be potentially anti-competitive.[9]

However, to understand the law and guidelines relating to collaboration in technology pools and standard setting it is necessary first to obtain a better picture of the process itself and its somewhat complex structure. We can best approach this by looking at the separate but interrelated stages that are integral features of the process.

18.2 STAGE 1: THE PRODUCT FORMULATION STAGE

The first stage of a patent or technology pool is often a form of preliminary meeting in which actual or potential competitors meet to identify what type of product is being aimed at and what types of research activity may be necessary to produce the technology to create the product. The organizations that engage in research at this stage are often drawn from three disparate groups. The first group are the research departments of manufacturing firms planning to manufacture a new product using the results of the pooled technology. Two examples of this category are Nokia and Sony Ericsson. The second group are university scientists engaged in contracted-out research. The third group are 'research-led' firms, ie firms that concentrate essentially on research and often do not plan to manufacture a new product based upon the technology resulting from the pool. Two examples of this category are Qualcomm and, increasingly, Phillips. As a result of the preliminary stage, we have a potential type of R&D agreement and

[9] These safe harbours and Guidelines have been analysed in detail in Anderman and Kallaugher (n 4 above), Ch 9.

the decision to engage in collaborative research or contract-out research, or even engage in independent research based on a pre-established set of parameters, is regulated—if at all—for competition purposes in the EU by the R&D BER and Horizontal Guidelines.[10]

This research stage often results in a series of patents covering the technologies discovered in the research. Other patent holders, not originally in the pool, may be enticed to enter either as research led-patentees or as manufacturer-patentees. Yet other patentees may gamble that it is in their interests to remain outside the pool and reap the benefits of higher royalties if their patents should prove essential to the selected technology. These decisions are made once the project moves to the standard setting stage. Ordinarily, those firms that are members of a technology pool have accepted an obligation to disclose their ownership of all patents relevant to the proposed technology, to license at a FRAND rate any patents chosen for the standard, and, in some cases, to search for relevant patents.

18.3 STAGE 2: THE CREATION OF THE STANDARD AND THE SELECTION OF ESSENTIAL PATENTS

The next stage consists of the creation of the standard by an SSO based on the evaluation of the results of the research and the selection of the essential patents in the pool. The SSO will sometimes consist of an entity based on an association of patentees within the pool. Increasingly, specialist organizations such as MPEG LA, are contracted specifically for the purpose of forming and running an SSO. In either form the SSO will normally concentrate on identifying an optimal technological solution to create the product and the patents that are 'essential' to the creation of a new product because they have no known substitute. The ETSI IPR policy offers a definition of an 'essential' as meaning:

> that it is not possible on technical (but not commercial) grounds, taking into account normal technical practice and the state of the art generally available at the time of standardization, to make, sell lease, otherwise dispose of, repair, use or operate equipment or methods which comply with a standard without infringing that IPR. For the avoidance of doubt in exceptional cases where a standard can only be implemented by technical solutions, all of which are infringements of IPRs, all such IPRs shall be considered essential.[11]

At this stage, the SSO will also identify those patents which are needed to license the technology but which are non-essential because of the existence of substitutes. What is difficult to determine from the outside is the extent to which the selection of the

[10] In the US, comparable regulation is provided by the National Cooperative Research (and Production) Act NCRPA 15 USCA S.4302

[11] For a case concerning the test of essentiality, see *Nokia Corporation v Interdigital Technology Corporation* [2007] EWHC 3077.

product is determined purely by technological factors or is influenced by the more powerful firms that are amongst the patentees (or industrial copyright holders) contributing to the technology pool.

Before the selection of essential patents, the SSO will have normally secured an obligation from all those participating in the pool that they will license their patents chosen as essential to the pool on FRAND terms or will disclose at an early stage that certain of their patents are unavailable on FRAND terms so as to allow the SSO and contributors to the technology pool to invent around the unavailable patent. The FRAND obligation is a conditional *contract* binding members of the patent pool to license their patents on FRAND terms if those patents are chosen as essential for the pool technology. This is a necessary step for a technology pool to provide a one-stop shop product at a reasonable price and avoid royalty stacking. However, the interesting feature of this process is that the nature of the FRAND obligation itself is not clearly established. (See Section 18.5 below.)

In some cases, the patentees may be asked to undertake an obligation to search for relevant patents but this obligation is increasingly being assigned to the SSO. What is palpably unacceptable conduct, either as a matter of contract or under an Article 102 analysis, is to give the appearance of being a member of the pool and then once the SSO selects the chosen technology to 'ambush' the other pool members by proclaiming that the essential patents held were never disclosed to the pool and were therefore never subject to a FRAND obligation. Equally important from a legal point of view is where a patentee inadvertently omits to disclose a patent which is later chosen as essential and refuses to accept a FRAND obligation.[12] Of course, it is incumbent on the SSO to have a procedure to ensure that a contractual obligations to disclose all relevant patents, not only those held but also those applied for, are obtained prior to the selection process.[13] However, ETSI, while urging members to disclose IPRs, is also concerned not to allow issues about IPR licensing to complicate, delay, or derail the technical processes.[14]

Not surprisingly, in this rough and ready atmosphere where the main players are technologists, there isn't always convincing evidence of the disclosure commitments undertaken by the patentee. In the *Rambus* case in the US, the Court of Appeals for the DC Circuit CA annulled the FTC's ruling that Rambus had deceived the JEDEC SSO and breached s 2 of the Sherman Act by failing to disclose its ownership of essential patents *in part* because the precise extent of the patent disclosure rules of the JEDEC SSO were not sufficiently established by the evidence.[15] The CCA did not rule out a claim under s 5 of the Fair Trade Act

[12] See eg *In re Dell Computer Corp* (1996) 121 FTC 616.

[13] See eg R. Brooks and D. Geradin, 'Taking Contracts Seriously: The Meaning of the Voluntary Commitment to Licence Essential Patents on "Fair and Reasonable" Terms' in S. Anderman and A. Ezrachi, *IP and Competition Law: New Frontiers* (Oxford: OUP, 2011).

[14] See 'ETSI Guide on Intellectual Property Rights' para 4.1. Discussed in L. Zhang, 'IPR Policies among Telecommunication Standard Setting Organizations'.

[15] *Rambus Inc* v *FTC* 522 F 3d 456 CADC 2008.

After *Rambus* ETSI made it a point to recommend to its technology pool coordinators to tighten their rules of disclosure and to bind contributing patent holders more closely to contractual commitments to license their patented technology to the pool on FRAND terms.[16] However, there are still questions raised about the extent to which the new ETSI rules adequately set standards of disclosure and provide checks to determine whether declared IPRs are actually essential.[17]

18.4 STAGE 3: LICENSING OUT

Once the technology has been chosen and the essential and relevant patents selected, the next stage is for the SSO or other entity to license out the pooled technology to manufacturers to produce and distribute a product based on the technology. The IPRs in the technology package are usually offered as a 'one-stop' licence but it is possible to offer different IPRs in different mixes of technology packages for different types of licensees. Licenses of the IPRs in the technology package will be subject to payment of a royalty to the SSO based on a commercial rate and influenced by the demands of the patentees for their royalties. This royalty will tend to be offered to non-member manufacturers on the same terms as pool member manufacturers. The latter may be single firms with two hats but are treated as operating separately for the purposes of the technology pool licensing process. It is not clear whether this parity of treatment of non-members by the SSO is a matter of commercial practice but clearly once the licensed product of the SSO achieves dominant market power in a market, a failure to offer access on non-discriminatory terms would be an infringement of Article 102 TFEU.

Patentees will receive royalties for their individual patents which they contribute to the pool on the basis of their FRAND commitments. As manufacturers, they will pay royalties for licensing the pooled technology.

Finally, the SSO will normally place the manufacturer/licensees under an obligation to grant back a licence of their improvements in the form of a non-exclusive licence and that can be secured contractually on FRAND or non-royalty terms. All members of the pool with essential or relevant licences will normally receive grant backs in the form of a non-exclusive licence of the improvements discovered by the manufacturer licensees. Disclosure rules of the SSO will govern the issue of disclosure of later improvements from patentees to SSOs or from patentees to patentees.

Moreover, all members of the pool will normally receive a cross-licence of the technology for research purposes from the SSO.

[16] See 'ETSI Guide on Intellectual Property Rights'. Discussed in L. Zhang, 'IPR Policies among Telecommunication Standard Setting Organizations'.

[17] Ibid.

18.5 THE FRAND COMMITMENTS

One relatively novel element in these relationships within the process of standardization technology pools is the measurement of the various FRAND commitments. The patent holders joining a patent pool do so normally on the basis of an agreement to license essential patents on FRAND terms to the SSO. This is a recommended course of action by ETSI and a desired one by the Commission in the TTA Guidelines. The FRAND obligation normally extends to the return commitment of the SSO/licensor to license back to individual patent holders. If the SSO becomes a true industrial standard it will have FRAND obligations to manufacturer/licensees particularly if some of the essential patent holders have begun to manufacture. Finally, the FRAND obligation will extend to the manufacturer/licensees to grant back licences for their improvements and to the SSO or licensing entity to grant back improvements to the patent holders who have contributed essential patents to the pool.

In all cases the FRAND commitment is contractual which allows for the commitment to vary with the nature of the contractual arrangement. Even assuming that all essential patents chosen from contributors in a technology pool are bound by FRAND commitments, the nature of what is reasonable can vary with the nature of the parties. For example, a research-led company with no stake in the technology as a manufacturer may argue that it is reasonable to have a higher royalty than a firm that participates both as a contributor of essential patents and as a manufacturer. Alternatively, a firm that has contributed a greater number of patents to the technology pool may argue that size or quantity matters. Another patentee contributing to the pool may argue that it is reasonable for the qualitatively most important contribution to receive a bigger share. All three arguments may be made within the framework of a FRAND commitment and each SSO must work out a dispute settling mechanism as part of its contractual arrangements.

As mentioned, the precise nature of the FRAND obligation itself is not clearly established On the one hand there is literature suggesting that the FRAND commitment is similar to a standard form contract incorporating a number of implied terms. Brooks and Geradin have compiled a list of some of the 'implied terms' in the FRAND obligation suggested by a number of authors:

- must charge no more than the incremental value of his invention over the next best technical alternative;
- must not negotiate for a royalty-free cross-licence as part of the consideration for a licence;
- must set his royalty rate based on a mathematical proportion of all patents essential to the practice of a standard;
- must set his royalty rate in such a way as to prevent cumulative royalties on the standardized product from exceeding a low percentage of the total sale price of that product;

- must not raise requested royalty rates after the standard has been adopted, or after the relevant market has grown to maturity;
- is not entitled to seek injunctive relief against a standard implementer should they fail to agree on licence terms.

Their view, in contrast is that in fact, 'fair and reasonable' are on their face flexible terms, the specific content of which is substantially left to the negotiation between the parties. Far from reading implied terms into a FRAND obligation as if it were some type of standard form contract, or imposing fair and reasonable terms, they argue that the interpretation of the FRAND commitment should take into account all the specific circumstances between the parties and the prevailing market conditions and ask whether the terms proposed by the parties 'fall outside the range of reasonableness contemplated by the FRAND commitment'.

In any case, today, participation in technology pools by inventing firms is often based on uncertainty about their actual share of the royalties received and distributed by the SSO or licensing entity as well as uncertainty about the period of time that will elapse before the royalties will be paid out. Nevertheless, that does not seem to deter participation.

Finally, the role of lawyers in the process is variable. The process thus far seems to be driven by the technologists who are instrumental in choosing the technologies to be researched, the optimal product from a technological perspective, and the selection of the 'essential' patented technologies. Lawyers thus far seem to be more active at the stage when things go wrong. It is possible that some lawyers are becoming more successful in being heard in the earlier planning stages of the process.

18.6 THE LEGAL FRAMEWORK FOR TECHNOLOGY POOLS AND STANDARDIZATION AGREEMENTS

18.6.1 Introduction

The competition law framework for this novel form of collaboration between competitors under Article 101 is somewhat fragmented, There are potentially three block exemption regulations that can apply. The first stage of the process, the joint research and development stage, is discussed in the Horizontal Guidelines[18] and is regulated by the R&D Block Exemption Regulation.[19] The general principles established by these instruments is that pure R&D agreements that do not entail joint commercialization of the results are not normally caught by Article 102 because they are not likely to cause anti-competitive harm and the same is true of R&D contracted out to third parties.

[18] Horizontal Guidelines (n 7 above).

[19] Regulation 2659/2000 on the application of Article 101(3) of the Treaty to categories of research and development [2000] OJ L 304/7.

The main risks from the R&D process arise in cases of agreements between competitors which extend into the joint commercialization of the results of the research. The R&D provides a safe harbour for such R&D agreements subject to a market threshold of 25 per cent. Where the joint commercialization is limited to licensing, the Guidelines suggest that the agreement may still be compatible with Article 101.

The Horizontal Guidelines and R&D BER deal with three different licensing scenarios:

(1) licensing to participants in the R&D exercise;

(2) licensing where R&D involves improvements or refinements in existing products or technology; and

(3) licensing where R&D cooperation leads to creation of an entirely new product or technology.[20]

The competition concern in the first scenario is with access to results of the R&D cooperation. If all parties have full access, regardless of ownership of IPRs, the agreement is likely to be compatible with Article 101. If there is a failure to allow full access or any one company has exclusive access rights, it will be necessary to obtain exemption. The Horizontal Guidelines indicate that exclusive access rights could meet the requirements of Article 101(3) in particular where they 'are economically indispensable in view of the market, risks, and scale of investment, required to exploit the results of the research and development'.[21]

Where R&D arrangements involve improvements of existing products or technologies, the Guidelines suggest that joint exploitation is unlikely to raise competition where it takes the form only of licensing.[22]

Finally, where R&D efforts involve the development of an entirely new product, the Guidelines identify a risk of 'foreclosure from key technology' for third parties but again those risks are lessened when the parties are willing to license their technology to third parties.[23]

The second stage, standard setting, is mainly dealt with in the 1999 Horizontal Guidelines. The Guidelines indicate that standard setting bodies which are 'recognized' and which adopt non-discriminatory, open, and transparent policies are not normally viewed as restrictive of competition under Article 101(1).[24] In principle, any standard setting exercise that meets these conditions and is either 'part of a wider agreement to ensure compatibility of products' or does not impose an obligation on participants to comply with the standard should not be caught by Article 101(1).[25]

[20] See wider discussion in Anderman and Kallaugher (n 4 above), Ch 9.

[21] Horizontal Guidelines (n7 above), para 67.

[22] Ibid, para 64.

[23] Ibid.

[24] Ibid, para 163.

[25] Ibid.

18.7 TECHNOLOGY POOLS, TTBER, AND GUIDELINES

The main source of legal guidance on the competition policy applicable to technology pool arrangements is the TTA Guidelines. The TTBER does not apply to agreements establishing technology pools and setting out the terms and conditions of their operation. Such arrangements do not fit easily into the stereotypical bilateral technology transfer agreement covered by the block exemption. Moreover, pooling arrangements give rise to issues regarding the selection of the included technologies and the operation of the pool which simply do not arise in the context of other types of licensing. However, at the stage where the SSO licenses out to manufacturers, the individual licences granted by the pool to the manufacturer/licensees, are treated as technology transfers and are potentially covered by the TTBER if they meet its conditions.

The TTA Guidelines define technology pools as taking two forms. The first is an arrangement whereby two or more parties agree to pool their respective technologies and license them jointly as a package The second is an arrangement whereby two or more parties license their technologies to a separate entity, entrusting it with the licensing of the assembled package of technologies.[26] In both cases, the pool may allow licensees to operate on the market on the basis of a single licence.

The Guidelines declare that there is no inherent link between technology pools and standards but that in some cases a technology pool may support a *de facto* or *de jure* industry standard. They also acknowledge that different technology pools may support competing standards.

The Guidelines recognize that technology pools can have considerable pro-competitive benefits: reducing transaction costs[27] and providing one-stop licensing of the pooled technology; and setting a limit on cumulative royalties and avoiding royalty stacking.[28] They also recognize that technology pools may be restrictive of competition and give a view about their competition concerns.

18.8 THE COMPETITION CONCERNS AND THE CREATION OF THE POOL

The main anti-competitive concerns arising out of technology pools, as suggested by the Guidelines, are first of all that the creation of a technology pool necessarily involves joint selling of the pooled technologies Nevertheless, as long as a pool is composed

[26] Commission Notice Guidelines on the application of Article 81 of the EC Treaty [now Article 101 TFEU] to technology transfer agreements [2004] OJ C101/2 (hereafter TTA Guidelines), para 210; see also R. Merges, 'Institutions for Intellectual Property Transactions: The Case of Patent Pools' in R. Dreyfus, D. Zimmerman, and H. Furst (eds), *Expanding the Boundaries of Intellectual Property* (Oxford: OUP, 2001).

[27] But see a criticism of this argument in Ullrich (n 5 above).

[28] TTA Guidelines, para 214.

entirely of technologies that are 'essential' [29] the creation of the pool will itself be viewed as compatible with Article 101(1) because of its pro-competitive object and innovative benefits and this will be true regardless of the market position of the parties.[30]

However, where the joint selling operation involves a technology pool consisting of *substantially* 'substitute' or 'non-essential' technologies this could amount to a price fixing cartel. Moreover, even if the pool includes only *some* substitute or non-essential technologies, it could amount to a collective bundling activity. Finally, if the standard should become a *de facto* industry standard it creates a real risk of reducing innovation by foreclosing technological alternatives by creating high barriers to entry. Therefore where a technology pool is composed *to a significant extent* of substitute or non-essential technologies, this will be viewed by the Commission as a 'violation of Article 101(1)' and it is unlikely that the conditions of Article 101(3) will be fulfilled.[31]

In such a case however, the Commission will have to look closely at the actual effect on royalties as part of its assessment. There may be no significant effect on royalty rates if substitutes are included in the technology package because the essential patent owners will be prompted to resist too big a share going to non-essential patent owners.

There are, moreover, competition concerns about substitute technologies outside the pool. The rule of thumb proposed by the TTA Guidelines is that the issue of foreclosure only arises where the pool has a *significant* position in the market. In such case the pool will be caught by Article 101(1) and require exemption and if the market power of the pool is below *dominance* in a particular market, exemption is likely.

The Commission recognizes that the assessment of technologies is an ongoing process and that substitute and complementary technologies can be developed after the creation of the pool. It recommends that once a technology becomes non-essential it should be excluded from the pool. It also suggests that there are other ways to ensure that third parties are not foreclosed. The Commission indicates that it is prepared to consider the following factors in its assessment:

(a) whether there any pro-competitive reasons for the non-essential technologies in the pool;

(b) whether the licensors remain free to license their respective technologies independently:

(c) whether the pool offers the technology only as a single package or whether it offers separate packages for distinct applications; and

[29] A technology is 'essential' if there are no substitutes for that technology inside or outside the pool and the technology is a necessary part of the package of technology chosen for the purpose of producing the product or process which was the object of the technology pool. A substitute technology is one that is not an essential technology for a particular technology pool product.

[30] TTA Guidelines, para 220.

[31] Ibid, para 219.

(d) whether the pooled technologies are available only as a single package or whether licensees have the possibility of obtaining a licence for only part of the package with a corresponding reduction of royalties.[32]

18.9 THE ASSESSMENT OF INDIVIDUAL RESTRAINTS

Even where a pool is composed entirely of technologies that are 'essential' and the creation of the pool itself is viewed as compatible with Article 101(1) the particular conditions on which licences are agreed may be caught by Article 101(1).[33] Certainly, these licensing provisions will be subject to the hard core provisions in Article 4.

The TTA Guidelines recognize that there are licensing issues that are particular to licensing agreements between technology pools and the third party manufacturers that license the technology package. The TTA Guidelines state that the assessment of individual restraints will be guided by three main principles: that the stronger the market position of the pool, the greater the risk of anti-competitive effects; that the pools holding a strong position on the market should be open and non-discriminatory; and that pools should not *unduly* foreclose third party technologies or limit the creation of alternative pools.[34] The choice of the word *unduly* implies some flexibility on this issue.

Where a technology pool and any industrial standard that it might support is compatible with Article 101, the parties to the technology pool are normally free to negotiate and fix royalties for the technology package as a whole as well as the individual shares of the royalties either before or after the standard is set. The TTA Guidelines recommend that royalties should be agreed before the standard is chosen and that the selection of technologies to be included in the pool is carried out by an independent expert but remind itself that 'licensees must be remain free to determine the price of products produced under the licence'.[35] The TTA Guidelines somewhat more firmly 'require' that where a pool has a dominant position on the market, royalties and other licensing terms should be fair and non-discriminatory and that licences should be non-exclusive. Its reasons are fear of foreclosure and other anti-competitive effects on downstream markets. Yet it also accepts that royalty rates can be set differently for different product markets as long as there is no discrimination *within* the same product market. The main fear of discriminatory treatment is between licensees who are also members of the pool and those that are not. The TTA Guidelines state that the Commission will 'take into account whether licensors are also subject to

[32] Ibid, para 222.
[33] Ibid, para 220.
[34] Ibid, para 224.
[35] Ibid, para 225.

royalty obligations'.[36] That is a particularly useful point since the presence of licensors amongst the licensees, combined with a non-discrimination limit on royalties, makes it more difficult for a pool to use the joint selling platform to fix high royalty rates for licensee manufacturers. If pools are composed solely of research-led licensors without manufacturing capacity, there may be a readier basis for a price fixing complaint.

The TTA Guidelines also display a strong concern about non-compete obligations in cases where a technology pool supports a *de facto* industrial standard. The TTA Guidelines argue that licensors and licensees must be free to develop competing products and standards and must also be free to grant and obtain licences outside the pool in order to limit risks of foreclosure of third parties and avoid limiting innovation in the form of competing technological solutions. However, all the TTA Guidelines say is that the presence of a non-compete obligation in licences in a technology pool supporting a *de facto* standard 'creates particular risk of preventing the development of new and improved technologies and standards'.[37]

The TTA Guidelines also adopt an odd tone by merely recommending that grant back obligations should be non-exclusive and be limited to developments that are essential or important to the use of the pooled technology. They reason that, 'This allows the pool to benefit from improvements in the pooled technology and does not foreclose others from benefiting from them'. However, there is no guarantee that members of the pool will license out.

Finally, where a patent pool shelters an invalid patent and there is a right to terminate a licence in the event of a challenge by a licensee, the TTA Guidelines again recommend that the right to terminate should only apply to the licensor who is the addressee of the challenge and must not extend to the technologies owned by other licensors in the pool.[38]

18.10 THE INSTITUTIONAL FRAMEWORK GOVERNING THE POOL

The TTA Guidelines point out that the way a technology pool is created, organized, and operated can reduce the risk of it having the object or effect of restricting competition and offer assurances that the arrangement is pro-competitive. Yet it takes a rather inhibited approach to prescribing the desired elements under Article 101(3). In particular it merely points to the advantages of a creation process that is open to all interested parties as opposed to a limited group of technology owners. Similarly, it simply suggests that if the members of the relevant bodies of the pool include persons representing different interests, presumably licensors who also manufacture as licensees, this will be more likely to produce royalties and licensing terms that reflect the actual

[36] Ibid, para 226.
[37] Ibid, para 227.
[38] Ibid, para 229.

value of the licensed technology as opposed to a pool controlled solely by licensor representatives.[39]

A further factor is the extent that independent experts are involved in the creation and operation of the pool and in particular in the selection of the standard, which patents are 'essential ' to the standard, and whether or not they are valid patents. The Commission states that it will look closely at the way experts are selected and the exact functions they are to perform, and their degree of independence from the undertakings in the pool.[40]

The Commission will look at the arrangements for sharing sensitive information among the parties since in an oligopolistic market, exchanges of information about pricing and output levels could facilitate collusion. An independent expert could play an important role by ensuring that output and sales data that may be needed for calculating royalties is not disclosed to member undertakings on affected markets.[41] Finally, the dispute mechanism is important. However, the TTA Guidelines do no more than merely indicate that if such a mechanism is entrusted to bodies or persons that are independent of the pool the more likely it is that the dispute resolution will be neutral[42]

18.11 CONCLUSIONS[43]

The striking feature of the regulatory framework for technology pools provided by the TTA Guidelines is the evidence that the regulatory framework is still at an early stage of development. It is incomplete, it is tentative in tone, and it is fragmented even within the TTA Guidelines let alone in terms of its relationship to the other BERs and Horizontal Guidelines. There is at this stage no overarching approach to all the stages of the technology pool and standardization process. As Ullrich has pointed out, the reference to the TTBER being applicable to licences between the SSO and the manufacturer/licensee suggests a view that the relationship is a 'vertical' one but there is no acknowledgement that the reality often is that many manufacturer licensees are also patentee/members of the technology pool that created the licensed package. He also makes the point that the Commission's competition tests for technology pools in the TTA Guidelines are derived from the US IP Guidelines of 1995 and the DoJ and FTC Antitrust Enforcement[44] with the result that the four conditions of Article 101(3) are not treated systematically. For example, the TTA Guidelines do not explore the requirement of indispensability as it will apply to technology pools. Moreover, something on

[39] Ibid, para 231.

[40] Ibid, paras 232 and 233.

[41] Ibid, para 234.

[42] Ibid, para 235.

[43] For a deeper and more detailed discussion see Ullrich (n 5 above); see also Anderman and Kallaugher (n 4 above), Ch 9.

[44] See *Antitrust Enforcement and Intellectual Property Rights. Promoting Innovation and Competition*, issued by the US Department of Justice and the Federal Trade Commission, 4 November 2007.

the test of elimination of competition in a substantial part of the internal market was warranted. Finally, the Commission seems very tentative in its approach to the big firms. It stipulates that market standard technology pools should license on FRAND terms,[45] ie fair reasonable and non-discriminatory grounds but does not emphasize the importance of an open process of selecting technology for the standard and open access to the pool.[46] Instead of merely expressing its preferences, the Commission could have defined these obligations as a condition of exemption for the more powerful standards.

It is definitely early days in terms of creating an adequate regulatory framework for all stages of the technology pool and standardization process. There are definite limits to the extent to which competition law can intervene. For example, it is not possible, using the tools of competition, to ensure that the autonomous process of choosing the technology for the standard is second guessed by a regulatory authority. Competition authorities do not have the ability to choose technologies. However, the conditions of Article 101(3) can be used by competition authorities in a more proactive manner to ensure that the procedures are open, that the SSO has a measure of independence from the patentee members of the technology pool, and that the mechanism for resolving disputes is independent. Since these factors are a good insurance of consumer benefit, the Commission is in a position to take a firmer line at the next stage of regulatory reform.

[45] TTA Guidelines, para 230.
[46] Ibid, paras 224 and 226.

19

REMEDIES

19.1 Introduction 307
19.2 Remedies Applied to Article 102 Cases 309
19.3 Article 101 Remedies 312
19.4 Commitment Decisions 315
19.5 Fines and Penalties 315
19.6 Conclusion 317

19.1 INTRODUCTION

Regulation 1/2003[1], also referred to as the Modernisation Regulation, dramatically changed the enforcement of Articles 101 and 102. Introduced in 2004, it lay down the powers of the Commission for the enforcement of the competition rules,[2] seeking to ensure effective and uniform enforcement, while at the same simplifying administration and decentralizing the enforcement to national competition authorities and national courts.[3] It abolished the 'centralized' notification system of agreements for individual exemption under Article 101(3) and removed the Commission's exclusive power to grant exemption under Article 101(3), making Article 101(3) directly applicable on the same basis as Article 101(1) and (2), and 102.

Decentralization was implemented to allow the Commission to focus its resources upon the investigation of serious infringements, such as cartels and Article 102 abuses, rather than devoting time to the approval of agreements of minor importance.

The purposes of the remedies and fines are not only to punish the companies for infringement of the competition rules, but also to deter other companies from engaging in the same behaviour and ultimately to restore effective competition on the market where the violation of the competition rules took place. These purposes have been

[1] Council Regulation 1/2003 on the implementation of the rules on competition laid down in Articles 81 and 82 of the Treaty OJ L 1, 4 January 2003.

[2] It replaced the old Council Regulation 17/62 on 1 May 2004.

[3] Regulation 1/2003, Recitals 1–3.

articulated in cases involving remedies ordering undertakings to cease infringing behaviour and to pay large fines. Occasionally the ordinary remedies of competition policy have resulted in compulsory licences of IPRs.[4]

The remedies at the Commission's disposal include the power to take final decisions ordering a termination of infringements,[5] making commitment decisions,[6] taking procedural decisions during the investigation process, adopting interim measures[7] to prevent irremediable harm occurring before the Commission can draw a final conclusion, and finally to impose penalties in the form of fines and periodic penalty payments for any breaches of either Article 101 or 102.[8]

In terms of remedies the Commission may impose both 'behavioural' and 'structural' remedies as long as these are proportionate to the infringement committed and necessary to bring it to an end.[9] Behavioural remedies are those that require an infringer to cease its infringing behaviour, such as price fixing or awarding fidelity or discriminatory discounts to customers. They also include so-called *positive* remedies such as obliging the infringing company to supply or license a customer. *Commercial Solvents*[10] offers an example of where the Commission could have applied a structural remedy instead of a behavioural remedy. In this case the infringement was, however, brought to an end by forcing Commercial Solvents to supply its former customer, even though it had a subsidiary in the downstream market, which competed with the customer. In a similar situation where a vertically integrated company like Commercial Solvents continued the abuse by discriminating in various ways against the downstream competitors a structural remedy of breaking up the company would be possible according to this new provision. Structural remedies are only to be applied 'where there is no equally effective behavioural remedy or where equally effective behavioural remedy would be more burdensome for the undertaking concerned than the structural remedy'.[11] However, the application of a structural remedy should only take place if 'changes to the structure of an undertaking as it existed before the infringement was committed would only be proportionate where there is a substantial risk of a lasting or repeated infringement that derives from the very structure of the undertaking.'[12] In other words,

[4] See eg *Magill TV Guide/ITP, BBC, and RTE, Re* Commission decision 89/205 (1989) OJ L 78/43, [1989] 4 CMLR 757, upheld in C-241-242/91P *Radio Telefis Eireann v Commission* (*Magill*) [1995] ECR I–743, [1995] 4 CMLR 718 and Case COMP/C-3/37.792–*Microsoft* Commission decision [2005] 4 CMLR 965, upheld in T-201/04 *Microsoft Corp v Commission* [2007] ECR II–3601.

[5] Regulation, Art 7(1).

[6] This is a 'new power' under Regulation 1/2003, Art 9.

[7] Ibid, Art 8.

[8] Note there is a separate regulation for mergers, which also deals with fines and penalties for mergers not compatible with the common market. Council Regulation (EC) No 139/2004 of 20 January 2004 on the control of concentrations between undertakings, OJ L 24, 29 January 2004, pp 1–22.

[9] Regulation 1/2003, Art 7(1).

[10] Case C-6-7/73 *Istitutio Chemioterapica Italiano SpA and Commercial Solvents Corp v Commission* [1974] ECR 223, [1974] 1 CMLR 309.

[11] Regulation 1/2003, Art 7(1).

[12] Ibid, Recital 12.

the use of the structural remedy has been heavily restricted, and the Commission will be prepared to apply such remedies only in relation to the regulation of industries, where it finds that effective competition is hindered by structural factors.[13]

The width of the remedies available to the competition authorities under the Modernisation Regulation stems from the broad interpretation taken in case law by the CJEU, which had allowed *positive* steps to bring infringements to an end.[14] The previous Enforcement Regulation, Regulation 17, had merely stated that upon a finding of an infringement, the Commission could require the involved undertaking/s to bring the infringement to an end.[15]

19.2 REMEDIES APPLIED TO ARTICLE 102 CASES

In *Commercial Solvents,*[16] the CJEU ruled that Article 3 of Regulation 17 'must be applied in relation to the infringement which has been established and may include an order to do certain acts or provide certain advantages which have been wrongfully withheld as well as prohibiting the continuation of certain actions, practices, or situations which are contrary to the Treaty.'[17] In this particular case Commercial Solvents had refused to supply a raw material to another undertaking. Commercial Solvents was ordered by the Commission to resume supplying *a former customer.* Similarly in *Magill*[18] three broadcasting companies were ordered to license their TV listing to each other and third parties after having refused to supply these to a company that wished to make a comprehensive television guide. The actual remedy chosen by the Commission was a compulsory licence on terms which were 'reasonable and non-discriminatory.' It chose this remedy only because an order to supply the information in the listings would not have allowed their use and therefore would not have ended the infringement. The only way the Commission could be sure that Magill could publish the new product

[13] Communications from the Commission COM(2006) 851, 10 January 2007 regarding Commission Energy Section Inquiry. Cases 6 and 7/73 *Commercial Solvents* offers an example where the Commission could have applied a structural remedy instead of a behavioural remedy. In this case the infringement was however brought to an end by forcing Commercial Solvents to supply its former customer, even though it had a daughter company in the downstream market, which competed with the customer. In a similar situation where a vertical integrated company like Commercial Solvents continued the abuse by discriminating in various ways against the downstream competitors a structural remedy of breaking up the company would be possible according to this new provision.

[14] See eg Cases 6 and 7/73 *Commercial Solvents* at para 45.

[15] Council Regulation 17/1962, First regulation implementing Article 101 and 102 of the Treaty, OJ Sp. Ed. 1962, No 204/62, p 87 as amended by Regulation (EC) No 1216/1999 of 10 June 1999 OJ 1999, L 148/5, Art 3, Note this Regulation is no longer in force.

[16] Cases 6 and 7/73 *Commercial Solvents.*

[17] Ibid, at para 45.

[18] *Magill TV Guide/ITP, BBC, and RTE, Re* (Commission decision 89/205) (1989) OJ L 78/43, [1989] 4 CMLR 757 and C-241-242/91P *Radio Telefis Eireann v Commission* [1995] ECR I–743, [1995] 4 CMLR 718.

in the secondary market and the parties to end the infringement was to require a licence to publish along with the supply of the listings. The CJEU upheld the Commission decision.

Furthermore, the Commission has not restricted itself to finding certain conduct unlawful. It has also prohibited similar conduct in the future. This form of remedy was confirmed by the CJEU in *Tetra Pak II.*[19] In that case, Tetra Pak had *inter alia* tied the purchase of cartons together to its lease of machines for packaging milk. The Commission ordered Tetra Pak to bring the infringement to an end by deleting certain abusive clauses in its leasing agreements and to inform any customer purchasing or leasing a machine of the specifications which packaging cartons had to meet in order to be used on its machines.[20] The Commission added that 'Tetra Pak shall refrain from repeating or maintaining any act or conduct described in Article 1 and from adopting any measure having equivalent effect'[21] thereby ensuring that future equivalent action by Tetra Pak would be deemed illegal. The CJEU upheld the Commission's decision.

The remedies laid down in *Tetra Pak II* show that the Commission with the blessing of the CJEU has the power to restrict future conduct even where the illegal conduct has ended.[22]

Although many Article 102 cases relating to refusal to supply or license have involved ordering the parties to supply or license either existing or new customers and in effect forcing the dominant company to enter into contractual relations or share facilities, the EU Courts have conditioned such obligations upon strict requirements.

In *IMS,* the Commission adopted an interim measure against IMS requiring it to license its 1860 brick structure to its competitors as a matter of urgency to prevent irreparable damage to IMS' competitor, NDC, and to the public interest in competition. The Commission had found that the 1860 brick structure, for which IMS claimed a copyright, was indispensable for competitors to compete in the market for German regional pharmaceutical sales data services and without it NDC and Azyx would have to leave the market. When IMS appealed to the General Court (GC), the GC suspended the Commission's remedy of a compulsory licence because the Commission had not correctly applied the 'exceptional circumstances' as in *Magill.*[23] The Commission therefore withdrew its interim measure.[24]

[19] C-333/94P *Tetra Pak International SA v Commission* [1996] ECR I–5951, [1997] 4 CMLR 662. See also *Steel Beams,* Commission decision 94/215, OJ L 116, 1994, at p 1, [1994] 5 CMLR 353.

[20] Article 3 of Commission Decision *Tetra Pak II* 92/163, OJ L 72, 18 March 92, [1992] 4 CMLR 551.

[21] Ibid, Art 3(2).

[22] Although note the CJEU has been less lenient of remedies affecting the future in Art 101 situations, see eg Cases T-7/93 and 9/93 *Langnese-Iglo & Schöller Lebensmittel v Commission* [1995] ECR II–1533, [1995] 5 CMLR 602, upheld by the CJEU in Case C-279/95P *Langnese-Iglo v Commission* [1998] ECR I–5609, [1998] 5 CMLR 933.

[23] Case T-184/01R *IMS Health v Commission* [2001] ECR II–3193, [2002] 4 CMLR 58 (president of GC Order) upheld on appeal Case C-481/01 P (R) *IMS Health v Commission* [2002] ECR I–3401, [2002] 5 CMLR 44 (President of the CJEU Order).

[24] Commission decision of 13 August 2003 relating to a proceeding under Article 82 of the EC Treaty (Case COMP D3/38.044—NDC Health/IMS Health: Interim measures), 2003/741/EC.

In the information technology field the attitude to remedies has been more strongly influenced by the imperative of interoperability. In the *IBM* settlement in 1984, the Commission insisted on undertakings by IBM to provide full interface information to all applications makers comparable to that provided to its own subsidiary operating in a downstream market. The purpose of that settlement was to ensure that the dominant firm, particularly where it operated in a downstream market, adhered to the principle of fair and non-discriminatory treatment of competitors in that market. In the later *Microsoft* cases the issues of shaping a competition law remedy to ensure interoperability became more controversial.

In the *Microsoft* case in the USA after the District Court judge's remedy of compulsory division of Microsoft into two companies was overturned by the Circuit Court, the Department of Justice together with half of the litigating states negotiated a consent decree with Microsoft which stipulated that Microsoft had to cease a number of monopolistic practices. The decree also placed three positive obligations upon Microsoft to assist dependent competitors to achieve full interoperability with Microsoft products. First, Microsoft was required to supply Independent Software Vendors (ISVs), Internet Access Providers, and Original Equipment Manufacturers, among others, the Application Protocol Interfaces (APIs) and related documentation used by Microsoft middleware to inter-operate with a Windows Operating System product in a timely manner. Secondly, there was an obligation to license to third parties, on reasonable and non-discriminatory terms, any communications protocol implemented in a Windows Operating System product when it is installed on a client computer and used to inter-operate 'natively', ie without the installation of additional software code, with a MS Operating System product. Finally, Microsoft agreed to give a compulsory licence to ISVs etc of any IPRs owned or licensable by Microsoft that was required to exercise any of the options or alternatives expressly provided to them under the final judgment on reasonable and non-discriminatory terms.[25]

The difficulty was that these obligations were subject to a wide proviso on security to the effect that Microsoft would not be required to disclose or license to third parties portions of APIs documentation or layers of communications protocols *inter alia* 'if their disclosure would compromise the security of a particular installation'.[26]

In the European *Microsoft* case, Microsoft was also ordered to make certain interoperability information available to companies wishing to develop and distribute workgroup server operating systems and to allow those companies to use that information subject to the application of reasonable and non-discriminatory conditions.

In relation to the tying offence, Microsoft was ordered to offer an unbundled version of Windows, ie Windows without Windows Media Player (WMP), thereby terminating the abuse.[27] However, Microsoft was not required to stop selling the bundled Windows/WMP version; the only condition placed upon Microsoft by the Commission

[25] See Second Revised Final Proposal of 6 November 2001. III D–F.
[26] Ibid, III J.
[27] *Microsoft* Commission decision at para 1011.

in this respect was that Microsoft was not permitted to make the unbundled version of Windows perform less well than the bundled version.[28]

Interestingly, the Commission omitted any comments in respect of the price of the unbundled Windows. From the Commission's perspective, it would be important to ensure that the unbundled version is not sold at an extortionate price and that the price of the unbundled version as a bare minimum should reflect costs of production or be 'reasonable' and 'non-discriminatory'. Though such a requirement is in theory the correct approach and also the one used by the Commission and EU Courts in other cases such as compulsory licensing cases,[29] in practice however, the cost of adding WMP to Windows is minimal. Hence, in principle, if the price should reflect costs, the price difference between the unbundled version of Windows and Windows with WMP will also be minute. What the remedy proposes is, as mentioned above, a 'mixed bundle', which again in theory should eliminate the anti-competitive effects and harm to consumers that the tying conduct caused. Where the unbundled and the bundled versions are offered at almost the same price owing to costs structure, such as would be the case with Microsoft, the effect of the remedy is limited.[30]

In *Microsoft,* the Commission also required that a monitoring trustee should assess whether Microsoft had fulfilled its remedy obligations.[31] The GC upheld the Commission's finding of abuse and its remedy of providing an unbundled version of Windows.[32] However it annulled the request for a monitoring trustee,[33] stating that the Commission had gone beyond its powers (although this was in relation to Regulation 17) and it did not have unlimited discretion to adopt remedies to infringements, but these had to be proportionate to the infringement committed.[34]

19.3 ARTICLE 101 REMEDIES

Cases under this Article either deal with contracts or cartels between companies, which infringe by their nature and hence should be brought to an end. An example is the *Welded Steel Mesh* case, which was a cartel case, where the Commission decided:

> The undertakings . . . which are still involved in the welded steel mesh sector in the Community shall forthwith bring the said infringement to an end (if they have not already done so) and shall

[28] Ibid, at para 1012; see also paras 1013–14.

[29] See for instance *Magill*; the standard has also been applied by the Commission in respect of the telecommunication sector regulation, see Commission's Guidelines on the Application of the EC Competition Rules in the Telecommunications Sector, 91/C233/02 [1991] OJ C233/2.

[30] T-201/04 *EC Microsoft* at para 943, Jean-Francois Bellis, 'The Microsoft Judgment' Conference, 25 September 2007, BIICL, 17 Russell Square, London and Per Hellström, 'The Microsoft Judgment' Conference, 25 September 2007, BIICL, 17 Russell Square, London.

[31] *EC Microsoft* Commission decision at para 1017.

[32] T-201/04 *EC Microsoft* at para 1229.

[33] Ibid, at para 1279.

[34] Ibid, at para 1276.

henceforth refrain in relation to their welded steel mesh operations from any agreement or concerted practice which may have the same object or effect.[35]

However, there are limits to the extent of the remedies which can be enforced upon a company. In the *Langnese-Iglo* case[36], the CJEU held that the Commission could not order a company not to enter into future 'exclusive purchasing agreements', because these types of agreements can in certain circumstances be pro-competitive and hence could be exempted under Article 101(3).

There are differences in the remedies applied under Articles and 101 and 102 owing to their different purposes. Article 101 prohibits agreements and hence the Commission can instruct them to be terminated or determine that they are unenforceable; a refusal to supply a customer is not in itself unlawful under Article 101 and thus a company cannot be ordered to supply under this article.[37] In *Automec II*[38] BMW had informed Automec that it was not going to renew their contract to supply vehicles and spare parts. Automec complained to the Commission and requested the Commission to take a decision ordering BMW Italia and BMW AG to bring the alleged infringement to an end and continue the contract. Automec complained about the potential dealers losing their commission and added that since it was being boycotted by BMW it had become impossible for it to purchase vehicles from Italian and foreign BMW distributors, even though vehicles were available. Consequently, it had recently been unable to meet several orders which it had received.[39] The GC held that:

As the freedom to contract must remain the rule, the Commission cannot in principle be acknowledged to possess, in the framework of its powers of injunction to put an end to infringements of [Article 101(1)TFEU], a power to order a party to enter into contractual relationship where as a general rule the Commission has suitable means at its disposal for compelling an enterprise to end an infringement.[40]

In other words, when there are other ways of ceasing an infringement, these should be applied rather than forcing the company into a contractual relationship. In contrast, Article 102 remedies can consist of an order to enter into a new contract or resume a disrupted contractual relationship with freedom of contract subordinated to the need to maintain effective competition in the relevant market.[41]

In *Automec,* the Commission was strict as to how far its powers extended; however, in *Atlantic Container Line*[42] it went a step too far in putting an end to the infringement.

[35] *Welded Steel Mesh* [1989] OJ L260/1, [1990] 4 CMLR 13.

[36] Cases T-7 and 9/93, *Langnese-Iglo & Schöller Lebensmittel v Commission* [1995] ECR II–1533, [1995] 5 CMLR 602, upheld by the ECJ in Case C-279/95P *Langnese-Iglo & Schöller Lebensmittel v Commission* [1998] ECR I–5609, [1998] 5 CMLR 933.

[37] *Competition Law* (6th edn, Oxford: OUP, 2008), p 254.

[38] Case T-24/90 [1992] ECR II–2223, [1992] 5 CMLR 431.

[39] Ibid, at para 8.

[40] Ibid, at para 51.

[41] See eg Cases 6 and 7/73 *Commercial Solvents.*

[42] Case T-395/94 *Atlantic Container Line AB v Commission* [2002] ECR II–875, [2002] 4 CMLR 1008.

The case dealt with a horizontal agreement, which fixed prices in maritime transport. Fifteen shipping liner companies were parties to a trans-Atlantic agreement. It covered several aspects of maritime transport, laying down, among other things, the prices of the tariffs applicable to maritime transport and intermodal[43] transport.[44] The Commission annulled the agreement and ordered the conduct to cease. It also required that the companies party to the agreement should inform their customers that the rates were now open for renegotiation. It argued that the renegotiation,

> . . . is intended to prevent the applicants from continuing to enjoy the benefits of long-term contracts entered into on the basis of a price-fixing agreement regarded as unlawful. Although these contracts are not themselves void, customers must be entitled to renegotiate them under normal conditions of competition.[45]

The GC held, however, that this clause was not obviously necessary to bring the infringement to an end and pointed out that the clause did not fit in with previous Commission decisions.[46] Finally the GC felt that the Commission had failed to establish the need for the contested clause and hence it should be annulled.[47]

In relation to the licensing of IPRs the Commission has taken a similar approach to other types of agreements. In *Sega and Nintendo*[48] the Commission ordered the parties to delete certain clauses in their licensing agreement for computer software with publishers of video games because it found that by using these clauses Sega and Nintendo could control the market for video games.[49] A similar remedy was imposed upon Microsoft in the 1999 *Microsoft* case.[50] Microsoft had included in its licensing agreements a minimum quantity obligation for the distribution of its Internet Explorer browser and a ban on advertisement of its competitors' browsers. The Commission ordered Microsoft to remove these clauses from the agreement to avoid foreclosing the market for competitors.[51] Although in general, minimum quantity requirements are allowed for in licensing agreements since they are not considered harmful to competition,[52] the Commission was concerned that in this particular situation the clauses would harm competitors.

[43] 'A door-to-door transport, includes, in addition to maritime transport, the inland carriage of maritime containers between the coast and inland locations. The price of an intermodal transport service is made up of two elements, one relating to the maritime service, the other to the inland service. Thus, [the trans-Atlantic agreement] established, in addition to a maritime tariff, a tariff for the inland transport services operated in the territory of the Community in the context of an intermodal transport operation.' Para 27.

[44] Case T-395/94 *Atlantic Container Line AB v Commission* [2002] ECR II–875, [2002] 4 CMLR 1008 at para 27.

[45] Ibid, at para 405.

[46] Ibid, at para 415.

[47] Ibid, at paras 415–16.

[48] *Commission's XXVIIth Report on Competition Policy (1997)*, point 80 and p 148–9.

[49] Whish (n 37 above), p 743.

[50] *Commission's XXIXth Report on Competition Policy (1999)*, points 55–6 and p 162.

[51] Whish (n 37 above), p 743–4.

[52] In the old Block Exemption Regulation on Technology Transfer Agreements (240/96) [1996] OJ L 31/2, Art 2 consisted of a so-called 'white list' which included clauses which are normally found in licensing agreements and normally do not restrict competition. The minimum quantity requirement was on this list. However, in the new TTBER there is no 'white list', anything that is not specifically black-listed in the provisions is now permitted. Minimum quantity requirements are not included.

19.4 COMMITMENT DECISIONS

Where the Commission has identified competition concerns and intends to act upon these, the companies in question can offer commitments to meet the concerns ascertained. This so-called Commitment Decision provides the Commission with a new power in which it can cease infringing behaviour and compel the companies into legally binding commitments in relation to their future behaviour without the Commission actually needing to establish an infringement.[53] These have proven a rather effective tool for the Commission and permit the Commission to attempt broader remedies than those available to it under Article 7 of Regulation 1/2003. They appear to be the new form of 'informal settlements'. The latter was successfully applied to terminate some major cases, such as *IBM Undertaking,*[54] *Microsoft,*[55] and *Digital.*[56] The Commission has adopted two Commitment Decisions under Article 101 in relation to collecting societies and the licensing of online music.[57]

Under Article 102, the Commission opened proceedings against Microsoft in January 2008 regarding the tying of Microsoft Windows with its Internet Explorer. In December 2009 Microsoft entered into a Commitment Decision in which it guaranteed to make available for five years in the European Economic Area a 'Choice Screen' enabling users of Windows XP, Windows Vista, and Windows 7 to choose in an informed and unbiased manner which web browser(s) they want to install in addition to, or instead of, Microsoft's web browser.[58] OEMs and users will also be able to 'turn Internet Explorer on and off' as need be and importantly OEMs will be free to pre-install third party web browsers on any PCs they ship. The Commitment Decision has been made reviewable by either party after two years or later, if 'either (i) the market circumstances have fundamentally changed or (ii) the Choice Screen has manifestly failed to provide consumers with an effective choice among browsers in a reasonable way'.[59]

Although the companies initially avoid a potentially expensive court case and a fine, the Commission reserves the right to re-open the case in certain circumstances.[60]

19.5 FINES AND PENALTIES

The remedies under Article 102 have been accompanied by heavy fines, and these have increased with the adoption of the Modernisation Regulation. The Commission may charge fines of up to 10 per cent of the annual worldwide turnover in the preceding

[53] Regulation 1/2003, Art 9, see also Recital 13.

[54] [1984] 3 CMLR 147.

[55] Commission Press Release IP/94/653, [1994] 5 CMLR 143.

[56] Commission Press Release IP/97/868.

[57] *BUMA and SAMBA* [2005] OJ C200/5 and *Cannes Extension Agreement* IP/06/1311.

[58] Commission decision of 16 December 2009 relating to a proceeding under Article 102 of the Treaty on the Functioning of the European Union and Article 54 of the EEA Agreement (Case COMP/C-3/39.530—*Microsoft* (tying)).

[59] Ibid, in Annex, para 21.

[60] Regulation 1/2003, Art 9(2).

business year of the undertakings involved in the infringement.[61] The Commission has issued a set of guidelines on the setting of fines,[62] which proposes a two-step approach. First, the Commission sets a basic fine, which relates to the value of the sales of goods or services to which the infringement concerns.[63] Second, the basic amount is adjusted to take into account the gravity of the infringement or mitigating circumstance as the case may be. In the case of the former, previous findings of infringements of Article 101, 102, or national competition laws, refusal to cooperate, and being the instigator of the infringement all count towards increasing the size of the fine.[64] Where the infringing company has shown cooperation by terminating the infringing behaviour early or aided the Commission with its investigation (this is separate to the reduction in fine companies can achieve through the leniency notice[65]), having had a limited role in the infringement, or infringed negligently as opposed to intentionally,[66] the Commission will adjust the fine to reflect this.[67] The Commission has over the years increased the size of the fines to reflect the purpose of the fines; namely as a deterrence and a pecuniary sanction to make Treaty prohibitions more effective.[68] The Commission has been supported in this strategy by the EU Courts.[69] The gradual increase of fines can be seen when comparing a case like *Tetra Pak II* in which Tetra Pak was fined 75 million ECU, approximately 2.5 per cent of its overall turnover in 1992 with the recent *Intel* case, in which Intel was fined €1.06 billion for having offered conditional rebates to customers and made payments to OEMs to ensure they did not make use of AMD's, Intel's competitor, product over a period of five years. Intel was also ordered to cease the infringing behaviour.[70]

The Commission may also impose fines of up to 5 per cent of the average daily turnover for every day the undertaking has not complied with the Commission's requirements.[71] For instance in relation to the *Microsoft* case, the Commission found that Microsoft had not fulfilled its obligations to supply the requested interoperability information in accordance with the Decision. The Commission imposed a fine of €280.5 million, €1.5 million for each day Microsoft had not complied.[72]

[61] Regulation 1/2003, Article 23(2).

[62] Guidelines on the method of setting fines imposed pursuant to Article 23(2)(a) of Regulation No 1/2003,OJ C210, 1 September 2006, pp 2–5.

[63] Ibid, para 13.

[64] Ibid, para 28.

[65] Ibid, para 29.

[66] See eg Case 27/76 *United Brands v Commission* [1978] ECR 207, [1978] 1 CMLR 429 at paras 298–301 for a discussion of this.

[67] *Fine Guidelines* (n 62 above), para 29.

[68] *XIIIth Report on Competition Policy*, Commission 1983, para 62.

[69] Cases 101–103/80 *Musique Diffusion Française SA v Commission (Pioneer)* [1983] ECR 1825, [1983] 3 CMLR 221.

[70] Summary of Commission decision of 13 May 2009 relating to a proceeding under Article 82 of the EC Treaty and Article 54 of the EEA Agreement (Case COMP/C-3/37.990—*Intel*) (2009/C 227/07).

[71] Regulation 1/2003, Art 24(1)(a).

[72] Commission decision of 12 July 2006, OJ C138, 5 June 2008 at pp 10–14.

An additional fine of €899 million was subsequently added, for charging unreasonable prices for access to the interface information.[73]

19.6 CONCLUSION

Although the main purpose of the Commission's remedies is to stop the offending behaviour and to restore effective competition, it is clear from cases such as *Microsoft* that the latter does not always occur. Although the remedies for infractions of the competition law are fairly robust, and include dramatic levels of fines they are nevertheless limited in dealing with actual forces of competitive markets. As M. Monti has noted, in respect of high technology industries, competition law remedies are problematic because they are likely to arrive too late because the market may have corrected itself.[74] Equally, the existing fines and structural and behavioural remedies are sometimes helpless to stop strategies that result in increased or sustained market shares even after the fines have been paid and the offending conduct has ceased.

[73] Commission decision of 27 February 2008 OJ C166, 18 July 2009 at pp 20–3.

[74] G. Monti, 'Article 82 EC and New Economy Markets' in C. Graham and F. Smith (eds), *Competition Regulation and the New Economy* (Oxford: Hart Publishing, 2004), p 23.

20

CONCLUSIONS

20.1 Introduction	319
20.2 Article 102 TFEU and IPRs	320
20.3 Article 101 TFEU and IPRs	324
20.4 Conclusion	326

20.1 INTRODUCTION

EU competition law, in its newly modernized form, continues to regulate the exercise of IPRs over an increasingly wide front. This pattern of competition law enforcement is, first of all, a reminder that the new competition rules are a development of an existing 'second tier' of regulation of the exercise of IPRs, an 'external' system of regulation that applies to anti-competitive conduct not prevented by the 'internal' system of regulation offered by IP legislation.[1] All IPRs have a system of protection that balances the exclusivity granted to 'pioneer' inventors and creators with the limits and exceptions in favour of 'follow on' innovators. However, the limits of permitted exercise of IPRs are drawn not only by the laws of IP but also by reference to the rules of competition law.

We have seen that when the competition rules apply to the exercise of IPRs, they apply as a separate system according to their own logic. They treat the exercise of an IPR, once granted, as any other private tangible right, subject to the public law limits of the competition rules. We have also seen that on closer inspection, the logic of competition law reveals a predisposition to accommodations to the exercise of IPRs which include some limited special concessions, but as importantly, the design of the general norms of competition law seem almost customized to leave room for the 'normal' exercise of IPRs and to focus on the extreme cases where their exercise happens to coincide with extreme commercial conduct.

[1] See I. Rahnasto, *Intellectual Property Rights, External Effects and Antitrust Law* (Oxford: OUP, 2002).

The reasons for this are not far to seek. In the first place, there is a natural overlap in the aims of the two fields of law.[2] The exclusive rights created by IP laws provide an incentive to inventors to create substitute products within markets and new products which establish new markets. Similarly, IP licensing is a vehicle to enlarge exploitation of protected technologies and thereby create a wider diffusion of the new technology which either creates new markets or brings substitutes to existing markets. Finally, the internal rules of IP legislation prevent copying but in fact encourage 'competition by substitution' between follow on innovators and pioneer innovators.[3]

A second crucial factor is that the competition rules do not apply to the exercise of IPRs as such. They apply when the IPR is used as an 'instrument of abuse'[4] or as a means of restricting competition.[5]

The modernization of the competition rules has undoubtedly created a better basis for their 'accommodation' to the exercise of IPRs. The more careful assessment of market power of IPRs and the new and more realistic economic approach introduced into the block exemption regulations and guidelines under Article 101, has reduced much of the substantive burden of regulation on IP licensing agreements between non-competitors as well as R&D joint ventures and standardization agreements. These focus regulation more carefully upon agreements in which the IP owning parties have or achieve real market power, and upon agreements between competitors, thus significantly lessening the effect of the competition rules upon licensing agreements between non-competitors.

20.2 ARTICLE 102 TFEU AND IPRS[6]

The noticeable rise in the strategic use of IPRs in new commercial practices, however, has presented a challenge to the competition authorities in terms of enforcing Article 102. Although the logic of the current rules of competition law embodies a far more

[2] 'Indeed, both bodies of law share the same basic objective of promoting consumer welfare and an efficient allocation of resources. Innovation constitutes an essential and dynamic component of an open and competitive market economy. Intellectual property rights promote dynamic competition by encouraging undertakings to invest in developing new or improved products and processes. So does competition by putting pressure on undertakings to innovate. Therefore, both intellectual property rights and competition are necessary to promote innovation and ensure a competitive exploitation thereof.' See eg Commission Guidelines on the applicability of Article 101 TFEU of the EC Treaty to horizontal cooperation agreements [2001] OJ C3/2 para 7.

[3] A phrase originally coined by H. Ullrich and mentioned by J. Drexl in 'Is there a More Economic Approach to Intellectual Property and Competition Law?' in J. Drexl (ed), *Research Handbook on Intellectual Property and Competition Law* (Cheltenham, UK, Northampton, MA, USA: Edward Elgar, 2008).

[4] See eg Case 85/76 *Hoffmann-La Roche v Commission* [1978] ECR 1139 at para 16.

[5] Case 262/81 *Coditel v Ciné Vog Films (Coditel II)* [1982] ECR 3381, [1983] 1 CMLR 49 at para 14.

[6] This part of the chapter draws upon S. Anderman, 'The IP and Competition Interface: New Developments' in S. Anderman and A. Ezrachi (eds), *IP and Competition Law: New Frontiers* (Oxford: OUP, 2011).

nuanced understanding of the pro-competitive nature of IPRs, the way in which this plays out in its treatment of IPRs under Article 102 varies dramatically depending upon the constituent element of the competition prohibition being assessed. Thus, in the first stages of analysis of potentially anti-competitive conduct, the definition of relevant market and the assessment of dominance, there are few if any special concessions to IPRs. As we have seen, these stages consist of a factual analysis, assisted by economic reasoning, which is similar to the analysis of the market power of any other form of property. IPRs are assessed in terms of the extent to which they create real restrictions of competition in the form of barriers to entry or impediments to entry. At this stage IPRs are examined largely in terms of their factual contribution to market power and their innovative features are viewed almost entirely in this light, ie some innovative efficiencies can actually contribute to market power in the form of barriers to entry or restrictive effects. Consequently, even though there is no longer an assumption that a patent is automatically associated with market power, the methodology of the Commission does not rule out the possibility that an IPR can be found to be associated with an asset that enjoys dominance in a market.

In contrast, in the definitions of abuse, there are more concessions to the innovative and pro-competitive features of IPRs within the logic of the norms of the competition rules. There is, for example, the 'exceptional circumstances' rule that applies to refusals to license an IPR. Moreover the application of the general norm of Article 102(a) to the pricing of IPRs leaves room for IP asset pricing that takes into account investment risks as well as costs in the case of IPRs.

At the same time, however, there are other features of the current EU normative definition of abuse that have proved to be less receptive to sweeping arguments that the pro-competitive features and innovative efficiencies of IPRs should allow them more leeway under the competition rules.

Owing to the influence of the EU Courts, the concept of abuse under Article 102 continues to rely on *per se* rules of abuse to implement its regulatory norms. The logic of the EU competition rules is to protect effective competition in the here and now. The first consequence of this is that Article 102 has a low level test of effects as a constituent element of its concept of abuse of dominance. The EU Courts are reluctant to take into account speculative arguments about future events. The second and related consequence is that the EU Courts have tended to confine arguments based on the pro-competitive features of prohibited acts to the category of objective justifications rather than allow benefits to offset current harms in a more balanced way.[7] This approach reduces the scope for arguments based on dynamic efficiency to operate as a defence in cases of alleged abuse in a way that might be possible in a 'rule of reason' style balancing exercise similar to that used in the USA. Thirdly, such an approach appears to make few concessions to the existence of the alternative remedies offered by the IP laws. Let us look more closely at each of these points.

[7] Case T-201/04 *Microsoft Corp v Commission* [2007] ECR II–3601.

20.2.1 *Per se* rules and a weak effects test

The Commission has recently argued that it intends to take a more effects-based approach to the interpretation of Article 102. It has indicated that proving the likelihood of harm is sufficient and that this can be inferred from the harm to the process of effective competition.[8] However, the Commission itself has not been entirely consistent in its advocacy of an effects-based test. It has stated that it will not take this approach in cases where conduct seriously restricts competition[9] because of the need to prioritize existing effective competition as the best guarantee of productive and innovative efficiencies in the long run.[10] Moreover, as we have seen, this approach has been called into question by the recent judgment of the General Court (GC) in *Microsoft*. Furthermore, in *British Airways*,[11] the Court of Justice made it clear that it preferred a *per se* approach to Article 102. To economists as well as lawyers, one implication of these judgments is that the EU Courts are not particularly impressed by the concept of reforming Article 102 to add a stronger test of effects as a constituent element of *this* abuse. The *British Airways* judgment reiterates that the Court of Justice considers that test of abuse under Article 102 TFEU is a *per se* test, ie conduct to which objectively abusive intent could be attributed and which creates a plausible risk of the harm of elimination of effective competition.[12]

20.2.2 Objective justification

A second feature of the normative approach to the definition of abuse under Article 102 is its treatment of the innovative efficiency defence. In the recent *Microsoft* case for example, Microsoft asserted that it would have less incentive to develop a given technology if it would be required to make that technology available to its competitors.

The Commission, in line with its thoughts about a more economic approach to abuse, attempted to tackle this assertion by Microsoft by dealing with it as a balancing exercise which balanced the negative impact of an order to license its IPRs on Microsoft's incentives to innovate against the counter-argument that the compulsory license would produce improved innovative efficiency for the industry as a whole because interoperability would maintain plural sources of innovation.

The GC clearly had other ideas about how the efficiency defence should be conducted under Article 102. The GC made it clear that what was called for was not a balancing

[8] DG Competition, Communication from the Commission, Guidance on the Commission's Enforcement Priorities in Applying Article 82 EC Treaty [now Article 102 TFEU] to Abusive Exclusionary Conduct by Dominant Undertakings [2009] OJ C45/7 paras 19–20 (hereinafter *Commission's Enforcement Guidelines on Article 82*); Guidelines on horizontal cooperation agreements [2001] OJ C3/2, para 19.

[9] *Commission's Enforcement Guidance on Article 82*, para 22.

[10] DG Competition, Commission 'DG Competition discussion paper on the application of Article 82 of the Treaty to exclusionary abuses' (Brussels, December 2005) (<http://ec.europa.eu/comm/competition/antitrust/art82/discpaper2005.pdf>), para 91.

[11] Case C-95/04P *British Airways v Commission* [2007] ECR I-2331.

[12] See also opinion of AG Kokott in Case C-95/04P *British Airways v Commission* [2007] ECR I-2331 at paras 68–9.

exercise of the two theories of innovation but a more legally structured assessment of Microsoft's arguments, holding that Microsoft's assertion could only be raised under the head of objective justification as an integral part of the proof of abuse.[13]

This suggests that the test of objective justification will be limited to arguments about pro-consumer efficiencies and incentives to innovate only insofar as they are rooted in findings of fact about current conduct or information known at the time the conduct was engaged in. Predictions about the future may be too speculative to find acceptance in analysing the issue of objective justification. The lawfulness of a firm's actions must be assessed at the time when the firm acts.[14]

Most importantly, the innovative efficiency 'defence' will be curbed if the practice also deprives consumers of a new product or creates a risk of elimination of effective competition in technology or product markets. There is no sign of judicial acceptance in the EU of an approach that gives equal standing to pro-competitive and anti-competitive arguments in a balancing test and moves in the direction of the rule of reason analysis that is a feature of US antitrust law.

If the Commission can prove that there is a risk of elimination of competition, that cannot be neutralized by greater efficiency. Nor can greater efficiency be a defence where it is merely an improvement in total welfare; there must be a fair 'pass on' of benefit to consumers. In a sense, the values and structure of Article 101(3) are built into the objective justification test. By carefully controlling excesses of dynamic efficiency defences, the European approach ensures that the test of abuse gives a priority to real effective competition in the short term and ignores less easily provable assertions about dynamic efficiencies in the long term. This feature makes its own distinctive contribution to cases involving findings of abuse. Article 102 continues to share with Article 101 and the Merger Regulation a treatment of innovative efficiencies defences that is subjected to the two conditions of consumer benefit and non-elimination of effective competition.

As we have seen, this technique of dealing with assertions of objective justification by the GC will not preclude defences based on genuine objective justification. One could imagine successful defences based on technological innovation in the case of alleged tie-ins. Moreover, patent owners may have strong case of objective justifications for refusing to license in cases where they have prepared plans to meet demand themselves but have delayed implementation to allow a sequencing of products.

However, the calculus will be restricted by the distinctive European approach to claims of innovative efficiency which prizes the existence of effective competition.

20.2.3 The existence of alternative IP remedies

The interface between IP and competition law has been characterized by the overlap in both systems' aims to promote innovation and consumer welfare. Hence there is a

[13] T-201/04 *Microsoft* para 659.

[14] See eg Case T-271/03 *Deutsche Telekom v Commission* [2008] ECR II–477.

number of accommodations to IPRs embodied in the logic of the competition rules. Nevertheless, the boundary between permitted and prohibited forms of exercise of IPRs under the competition rules is determined by the constituent elements of the prohibited conduct rather than the scope of the IPR. While some have argued that competition law applies mainly to cases where the IPR has been exercised outside its lawful scope the fact is that there are times when the IPR can be exercised in a perfectly lawful manner under the IP laws and nevertheless be held to infringe the competition rules.

Moreover, the process of enforcing the competition rules in those cases where the exercise of IPRs is unlawful both under the IP laws and the competition law rules shows little sign of accommodation. This feature has been apparent in a number of cases. For example in *AstraZeneca* generic competitors had a possibility of complaining under the EPC law. The practice seems to be that if the conduct of the IP owner has reached the stage of offending the competition rule, it will attract a competition law remedy. There is no evidence thus far of a policy to defer the competition law case to allow the parties to exhaust their IP remedies. In most cases so far, the existence of an alternative remedy has not prevented the immediate application of the competition rules. At the point of litigation the logic of the competition rules is straightforward. If there has been an infraction, there must not only be a fine as a penalty but the undertaking committing the abuse must discontinue the abuse. At that stage there is no room to consider a possible remedy offered under IP legislation since that possibility has not precluded the abuse. For example in *Microsoft* the argument that the competitor had a right to reverse engineer the interface codes under Article 6 of the Computer Program Directive had no effect on the finding of abuse.

20.3 ARTICLE 101 TFEU AND IPRS

For a long period the method used within the EU was to define anti-competitive harm in terms of contractual restraints on the economic freedom to compete and/or those that disturbed rivalry on existing markets. Once potentially harmful IP licensing agreements were identified with this broad brush approach, the parties were required to consult formalistic block exemption regulations to obtain exemption to assure the enforceability of the agreement under the competition law rules. In recent years, the need to use more economic analysis in appraising licensing agreements and measuring their competitive effects has become widely accepted. The EU has belatedly followed the lead established by the USA in 1995 by adopting a *more* economic approach as part of its modernization reform of Article 101 generally.

20.3.1 The modernization of EU Law applicable to IP licensing agreements

With the adoption of much of the economic reasoning of the 1995 US IP Guidelines in the 2004 EU regulatory framework for IP licensing agreements, there has been a substantial convergence between the systems. However, it is a mistake to view this as complete convergence.

First, the new framework of analysis contained in the TTBER and TTA Guidelines, in common with the other BERs and Guidelines which have been part of the modernization reform, introduce the *more* economic goal of avoiding reductions in consumer welfare but as we have seen in Part III, this has been accompanied by the EU Courts' reminders that the traditional goals of protecting freedom of action and vertical integration cannot be entirely abandoned.[15]

At the same time, the greater use of economic analysis in enforcing Article 101 concentrates the prohibition more carefully upon the potential anti-competitive harms of unilateral and coordinated effects. The most important change is the distinction drawn between agreements between competitors and those between non-competitors. This single change does much to correct the over-regulation that characterized past EU regulatory frameworks.

The use of a *more* economic approach offers competition law a much improved sifting mechanism to distinguish between the pro-and anti-competitive IP licensing agreements. The greater acceptance that IP licensing agreements are generally pro-competitive and compatible with Article 101[16] allows the authorities to concentrate far more on the pathology of IP licensing, leaving the greater portion of pro-competitive licensing to freedom of contract. They do this by more clearly identifying the potential anti-competitive harms of licensing agreements, by introducing a more nuanced approach to the market power of the parties to licensing agreements, and by drawing a clearer distinction between IP licensing agreements between competitors and those between non-competitors. This allows the introduction of two different regulatory regimes. There is a more extensive assessment of IP licensing agreements between competitors because of their greater anti-competitive risks and there is a far more lenient regime applied to agreements between non- competitors because of their higher propensity to create economic benefits and lower propensity to cause harmful effects. However, the benefits of a less interventionist regime for agreements between non-competitors are accompanied by a major change in the nature of the competition assessment of IP licensing agreements in four important respects.

The Commission has chosen to fit the assessment of IP licensing into the modernized framework of Article 101 and keep the special treatment of IP licensing agreements to a minimum. As the TTA Guidelines proclaim, the new TTBER's assessment of IP licensing takes 'due account of the dynamic aspects of technology licensing' making 'in particular . . . no presumption that intellectual property rights and licensing agreements as such give rise to competition concerns.'[17] This appears to echo the

[15] See eg judgment of the CJEU C-209/07 *Competition Authority v Beef Industry Development Society Ltd* [2008] ECR I-8367.

[16] Commission Notice, Guidelines on the application of Article 81 of the EC Treaty [now Article 101 TFEU] to technology transfer agreements [2004] OJ C101/2 (hereafter TTA Guidelines), paras 9 and 17.

[17] Ibid, para 9.

assertion of the 1995 US Guidelines that the characteristics of IPRs that make them distinct 'can be taken into account in the standard antitrust analysis . . . and do not require the application of fundamentally different principles'.[18]

By harmonizing the treatment of IP licensing with the other BERs, the *more* economic approach removes much of the special treatment of IP licensing enjoyed under the 1996 TTBER which provided a dedicated self-contained exemption providing legal certainty for the length of the agreement. The new uncertainty is compounded by the fact that enforcement of Article 101(3) has been decentralized to Member State courts and competition authorities. Moreover, along with the dramatic reduction in legal certainty in the assessment of IP licensing agreements, is the changed nature of the methods of self-assessment. After more than two decades of a purely legal formalism, the new methods of self-assessment require lawyers to make an assessment of the enforceability of IP licensing agreements using analytical tools heavily influenced by economic principles. It requires lawyers today to appreciate how economic thinking now permeates the legal rules.

Yet, as we have seen, the *more* economic approach is not a pure economic approach. The modernized interpretation of Article 101 does not entirely jettison its foundations in the earlier case law. There is an important place for many of the earlier judgments of the Court of Justice. There are post modernization judgments of the EU Courts that reinforce the new methodology adopted by the Commission.[19] But equally importantly, the new model adopted in the TTBER and TTA Guidelines continues to be subject to modification by the new judgments of the GC and Court of Justice. For example, some of the recent case law has stressed a continued role for traditional doctrines associated with a less economic approach to Article 101.[20] Nevertheless, much of the assessment of the limits on IP licensing established by the competitions rules now consists of the application of economic analysis within the framework of the legal rules

20.4 CONCLUSION

Both instruments of the competition law rules–Article 102 and Article 101–have retained a balance between economic reasoning and political/economic norms that represents a singular EU position. While the EU competition rules share many features with the US model they can be differentiated from the US model particularly in respect of their limits on the conduct of dominant firms. As far as Article 101 is concerned, the EU Courts have proved to be receptive to a *more* economic approach. However, in the

[18] *Antitrust Guidelines for the Licensing of Intellectual Property*, issued by the US Department of Justice and the Federal Trade Commission, 5 April 1995 (<http://www.usdoj.gov/atr/public/guidelines/0558.htm> (last accessed 10 June 2010)), Section 2.1.

[19] See eg Case T-32803 *O2 (Germany) GmBH7 Co v Commission* [2006] ECR II–1231, [2006] 5 CMLR; Case C-501/06 *GlaxoSmithKline v Commission* [2009] ECR I–9291.

[20] See eg C-209/07 *Beef Industry*.

case of Article 102 they have stoutly resisted the replacement of the political/legal philosophy expressed in their interpretations of the Treaty provisions in relation to abuse. The German/Ordoliberal concern with abuse of power has become an EU concern with abuse of power that continues to guide the judgments of the EU Courts in relation to Article 102 cases in the ways set out in this book.

These differences reflect deep-seated differences in political/economic approaches to regulating the conduct of firms on markets. It is not too facile to say that the EU competition rules are still suspicious of the damage to markets that can be inflicted by firms with overwhelming market power while the US system has greater faith in the capacity of market forces to curb the worst excesses of market power by bringing in new entrants to challenge that power. This belief may have been modified by the recent experience of the operation of lightly regulated market forces in the banking industry but does not appear to be fundamentally shaken.

These differences provide two different models of competition policy for countries that are in the process of developing their own hybrid approach to regulating the conduct of firms in markets. They also suggest that at this stage we are some way before an international competition authority can be formed which could operate on the basis of harmonized competition rules.

The use of a *more* economic approach to the enforcement of Articles 101 and 102 is ostensibly designed to help avoid Type 1 errors, (ie errors where non-infringing firms are found to have infringed a competition prohibition). The EU courts would appear at this stage to be affirming that the values of the Treaty suggest that the avoidance of Type 2 errors (ie where infringing firms are found not to have infringed a competition prohibition) is of greater concern than the reduction of Type 1 errors. Insofar as this continues to be the case, Article 102 will apply as a relatively robust limit to abuses of corporate power and ensure that compliance with the competition rules will be taken more seriously.

Appendix 1

Excerpts from the Treaty on the Functioning of the European Union

PREAMBLE

... RECOGNISING that the removal of existing obstacles calls for concerted action in order to guarantee steady expansion, balanced trade and fair competition,...

PART ONE
PRINCIPLES

Article 3

1. The Union shall have exclusive competence in the following areas:

   (a) customs union;

   (b) the establishing of the competition rules necessary for the functioning of the internal market;

   (c) monetary policy for the Member States whose currency is the euro;

   (d) the conservation of marine biological resources under the common fisheries policy;

   (e) common commercial policy.

2. The Union shall also have exclusive competence for the conclusion of an international agreement when its conclusion is provided for in a legislative act of the Union or is necessary to enable the Union to exercise its internal competence, or in so far as its conclusion may affect common rules or alter their scope.

CHAPTER 3 PROHIBITION OF QUANTITY RESTRICTIONS BETWEEN MEMBER STATES

Article 34

(ex Article 28 TEC)

Quantitative restrictions on imports and all measures having equivalent effect shall be prohibited between Member States.

Article 36
(ex Article 30 TEC)
The provisions of Articles 34 and 35 shall not preclude prohibitions or restrictions on imports, exports or goods in transit justified on grounds of public morality, public policy or public security; the protection of health and life of humans, animals or plants; the protection of national treasures possessing artistic, historic or archaeological value; or the protection of industrial and commercial property. Such prohibitions or restrictions shall not, however, constitute a means of arbitrary discrimination or a disguised restriction on trade between Member States.

TITLE VII
COMMON RULES ON COMPETITION, TAXATION AND APPROXIMATION OF LAWS

CHAPTER 1 RULES ON COMPETITION

SECTION 1
RULES APPLYING TO UNDERTAKINGS

Article 101
(ex Article 81 TEC)
1. The following shall be prohibited as incompatible with the internal market: all agreements between undertakings, decisions by associations of undertakings and concerted practices which may affect trade between Member States and which have as their object or effect the prevention, restriction or distortion of competition within the internal market, and in particular those which:
   (a) directly or indirectly fix purchase or selling prices or any other trading conditions;
   (b) limit or control production, markets, technical development, or investment;
   (c) share markets or sources of supply;
   (d) apply dissimilar conditions to equivalent transactions with other trading parties, thereby placing them at a competitive disadvantage;
   (e) make the conclusion of contracts subject to acceptance by the other parties of supplementary obligations which, by their nature or according to commercial usage, have no connection with the subject of such contracts.
2. Any agreements or decisions prohibited pursuant to this Article shall be automatically void.
3. The provisions of paragraph 1 may, however, be declared inapplicable in the case of:
   - any agreement or category of agreements between undertakings,
   - any decision or category of decisions by associations of undertakings,
   - any concerted practice or category of concerted practices, which contributes to improving the production or distribution of goods or to promoting technical or economic progress, while allowing consumers a fair share of the resulting benefit, and which does not:
   (a) impose on the undertakings concerned restrictions which are not indispensable to the attainment of these objectives;

(b) afford such undertakings the possibility of eliminating competition in respect of a substantial part of the products in question.

Article 102
(ex Article 82 TEC)
Any abuse by one or more undertakings of a dominant position within the internal market or in a substantial part of it shall be prohibited as incompatible with the internal market in so far as it may affect trade between Member States.
Such abuse may, in particular, consist in:

(a) directly or indirectly imposing unfair purchase or selling prices or other unfair trading conditions;

(b) limiting production, markets or technical development to the prejudice of consumers;

(c) applying dissimilar conditions to equivalent transactions with other trading parties, thereby placing them at a competitive disadvantage;

(d) making the conclusion of contracts subject to acceptance by the other parties of supplementary obligations which, by their nature or according to commercial usage, have no connection with the subject of such contracts.

PART SEVEN
GENERAL AND FINAL PROVISIONS

Article 345
(ex Article 295 TEC)
The Treaties shall in no way prejudice the rules in Member States governing the system of property ownership.

PROTOCOL
ON THE INTERNAL MARKET AND COMPETITION

THE HIGH CONTRACTING PARTIES,
CONSIDERING that the internal market as set out in Article 2 of the Treaty on European Union includes a system ensuring that competition is not distorted,
HAVE AGREED that:
to this end, the Union shall, if necessary, take action under the provisions of the Treaties . . .

Appendix 2

Commission Regulation (EC) No 772/2004 of 27 April 2004 on the application of Article 81(3) of the Treaty [now Article 101(3) TFEU] to categories of technology transfer agreements (Text with EEA relevance)

THE COMMISSION OF THE EUROPEAN COMMUNITIES,

Having regard to the Treaty establishing the European Community,

Having regard to Council Regulation No 19/65/EEC of 2 March 1965 on application of Article 85(3) of the Treaty to certain categories of agreements and concerted practices[1], and in particular Article 1 thereof,

Having published a draft of this Regulation[2],

After consulting the Advisory Committee on Restrictive Practices and Dominant Positions,

Whereas:

(1) Regulation No 19/65/EEC empowers the Commission to apply Article 81(3) of the Treaty by Regulation to certain categories of technology transfer agreements and corresponding concerted practices to which only two undertakings are party which fall within Article 81(1).

(2) Pursuant to Regulation No 19/65/EEC, the Commission has, in particular, adopted Regulation (EC) No 240/96 of 31 January 1996 on the application of Article 85(3) of the Treaty to certain categories of technology transfer agreements[3].

(3) On 20 December 2001 the Commission published an evaluation report on the transfer of technology block exemption Regulation (EC) No 240/96[4]. This generated a public debate on the application of Regulation (EC) No 240/96 and on the application in general of Article 81(1) and (3) of the Treaty to technology transfer agreements. The response to the evaluation report from Member States and third parties has been generally in favour of reform of Community competition policy on technology transfer agreements. It is therefore appropriate to repeal Regulation (EC) No 240/96.

(4) This Regulation should meet the two requirements of ensuring effective competition and providing adequate legal security for undertakings. The pursuit of these objectives should take account of the need to simplify the regulatory framework and its application. It is appropriate to

[1] OJ 36, 6.3.1965, p. 533/65. Regulation as last amended by Regulation (EC) No 1/2003 (OJ L 1, 4.1.2003, p. 1).

[2] OJ C 235, 1.10.2003, p. 10.

[3] OJ L 31, 9.2.1996, p. 2. Regulation as amended by the 2003 Act of Accession.

[4] COM(2001) 786 final.

move away from the approach of listing exempted clauses and to place greater emphasis on defining the categories of agreements which are exempted up to a certain level of market power and on specifying the restrictions or clauses which are not to be contained in such agreements. This is consistent with an economics-based approach which assesses the impact of agreements on the relevant market. It is also consistent with such an approach to make a distinction between agreements between competitors and agreements between non-competitors.

(5) Technology transfer agreements concern the licensing of technology. Such agreements will usually improve economic efficiency and be pro-competitive as they can reduce duplication of research and development, strengthen the incentive for the initial research and development, spur incremental innovation, facilitate diffusion and generate product market competition.

(6) The likelihood that such efficiency-enhancing and pro-competitive effects will outweigh any anti-competitive effects due to restrictions contained in technology transfer agreements depends on the degree of market power of the undertakings concerned and, therefore, on the extent to which those undertakings face competition from undertakings owning substitute technologies or undertakings producing substitute products.

(7) This Regulation should only deal with agreements where the licensor permits the licensee to exploit the licensed technology, possibly after further research and development by the licensee, for the production of goods or services. It should not deal with licensing agreements for the purpose of subcontracting research and development. It should also not deal with licensing agreements to set up technology pools, that is to say, agreements for the pooling of technologies with the purpose of licensing the created package of intellectual property rights to third parties.

(8) For the application of Article 81(3) by regulation, it is not necessary to define those technology transfer agreements that are capable of falling within Article 81(1). In the individual assessment of agreements pursuant to Article 81(1), account has to be taken of several factors, and in particular the structure and the dynamics of the relevant technology and product markets.

(9) The benefit of the block exemption established by this Regulation should be limited to those agreements which can be assumed with sufficient certainty to satisfy the conditions of Article 81(3). In order to attain the benefits and objectives of technology transfer, the benefit of this Regulation should also apply to provisions contained in technology transfer agreements that do not constitute the primary object of such agreements, but are directly related to the application of the licensed technology.

(10) For technology transfer agreements between competitors it can be presumed that, where the combined share of the relevant markets accounted for by the parties does not exceed 20% and the agreements do not contain certain severely anti-competitive restraints, they generally lead to an improvement in production or distribution and allow consumers a fair share of the resulting benefits.

(11) For technology transfer agreements between non-competitors it can be presumed that, where the individual share of the relevant markets accounted for by each of the parties does not exceed 30% and the agreements do not contain certain severely anti-competitive restraints, they generally lead to an improvement in production or distribution and allow consumers a fair share of the resulting benefits.

(12) There can be no presumption that above these market-share thresholds technology transfer agreements do fall within the scope of Article 81(1). For instance, an exclusive licensing

agreement between non-competing undertakings does often not fall within the scope of Article 81(1). There can also be no presumption that, above these market-share thresholds, technology transfer agreements falling within the scope of Article 81(1) will not satisfy the conditions for exemption. However, it can also not be presumed that they will usually give rise to objective advantages of such a character and size as to compensate for the disadvantages which they create for competition.

(13) This Regulation should not exempt technology transfer agreements containing restrictions which are not indispensable to the improvement of production or distribution. In particular, technology transfer agreements containing certain severely anti-competitive restraints such as the fixing of prices charged to third parties should be excluded from the benefit of the block exemption established by this Regulation irrespective of the market shares of the undertakings concerned. In the case of such hardcore restrictions the whole agreement should be excluded from the benefit of the block exemption.

(14) In order to protect incentives to innovate and the appropriate application of intellectual property rights, certain restrictions should be excluded from the block exemption. In particular exclusive grant back obligations for severable improvements should be excluded. Where such a restriction is included in a licence agreement only the restriction in question should be excluded from the benefit of the block exemption.

(15) The market-share thresholds, the non-exemption of technology transfer agreements containing severely anti-competitive restraints and the excluded restrictions provided for in this Regulation will normally ensure that the agreements to which the block exemption applies do not enable the participating undertakings to eliminate competition in respect of a substantial part of the products in question.

(16) In particular cases in which the agreements falling under this Regulation nevertheless have effects incompatible with Article 81(3), the Commission should be able to withdraw the benefit of the block exemption. This may occur in particular where the incentives to innovate are reduced or where access to markets is hindered.

(17) Council Regulation (EC) No 1/2003 of 16 December 2002 on the implementation of the rules on competition laid down in Articles 81 and 82 of the Treaty[5] empowers the competent authorities of Member States to withdraw the benefit of the block exemption in respect of technology transfer agreements having effects incompatible with Article 81(3), where such effects are felt in their respective territory, or in a part thereof, and where such territory has the characteristics of a distinct geographic market. Member States must ensure that the exercise of this power of withdrawal does not prejudice the uniform application throughout the common market of the Community competition rules or the full effect of the measures adopted in implementation of those rules.

(18) In order to strengthen supervision of parallel networks of technology transfer agreements which have similar restrictive effects and which cover more than 50% of a given market, the Commission should be able to declare this Regulation inapplicable to technology transfer agreements containing specific restraints relating to the market concerned, thereby restoring the full application of Article 81 to such agreements.

[5] OJ L 1, 4.1.2003, p. 1. Regulation as amended by Regulation (EC) No 411/2004 (OJ L 68, 6.3.2004, p. 1).

(19) This Regulation should cover only technology transfer agreements between a licensor and a licensee. It should cover such agreements even if conditions are stipulated for more than one level of trade, by, for instance, requiring the licensee to set up a particular distribution system and specifying the obligations the licensee must or may impose on resellers of the products produced under the licence. However, such conditions and obligations should comply with the competition rules applicable to supply and distribution agreements. Supply and distribution agreements concluded between a licensee and its buyers should not be exempted by this Regulation.

(20) This Regulation is without prejudice to the application of Article 82 of the Treaty,

HAS ADOPTED THIS REGULATION:

Article 1 Definitions

(1) For the purposes of this Regulation, the following definitions shall apply:

(a) 'agreement' means an agreement, a decision of an association of undertakings or a concerted practice;

(b) 'technology transfer agreement' means a patent licensing agreement, a know-how licensing agreement, a software copyright licensing agreement or a mixed patent, know-how or software copyright licensing agreement, including any such agreement containing provisions which relate to the sale and purchase of products or which relate to the licensing of other intellectual property rights or the assignment of intellectual property rights, provided that those provisions do not constitute the primary object of the agreement and are directly related to the production of the contract products; assignments of patents, know-how, software copyright or a combination thereof where part of the risk associated with the exploitation of the technology remains with the assignor, in particular where the sum payable in consideration of the assignment is dependent on the turnover obtained by the assignee in respect of products produced with the assigned technology, the quantity of such products produced or the number of operations carried out employing the technology, shall also be deemed to be technology transfer agreements;

(c) 'reciprocal agreement' means a technology transfer agreement where two undertakings grant each other, in the same or separate contracts, a patent licence, a know-how licence, a software copyright licence or a mixed patent, know-how or software copyright licence and where these licences concern competing technologies or can be used for the production of competing products;

(d) 'non-reciprocal agreement' means a technology transfer agreement where one undertaking grants another undertaking a patent licence, a know-how licence, a software copyright licence or a mixed patent, know-how or software copyright licence, or where two undertakings grant each other such a licence but where these licences do not concern competing technologies and cannot be used for the production of competing products;

(e) 'product' means a good or a service, including both intermediary goods and services and final goods and services;

(f) 'contract products' means products produced with the licensed technology;

(g) 'intellectual property rights' includes industrial property rights, know-how, copyright and neighbouring rights;

(h) 'patents' means patents, patent applications, utility models, applications for registration of utility models, designs, topographies of semiconductor products, supplementary protection certificates for medicinal products or other products for which such supplementary protection certificates may be obtained and plant breeder's certificates;

(i) 'know-how' means a package of non-patented practical information, resulting from experience and testing, which is:

(i) secret, that is to say, not generally known or easily accessible,

(ii) substantial, that is to say, significant and useful for the production of the contract products, and

(iii) identified, that is to say, described in a sufficiently comprehensive manner so as to make it possible to verify that it fulfils the criteria of secrecy and substantiality;

(j) 'competing undertakings' means undertakings which compete on the relevant technology market and/or the relevant product market, that is to say:

(i) competing undertakings on the relevant technology market, being undertakings which license out competing technologies without infringing each others' intellectual property rights (actual competitors on the technology market); the relevant technology market includes technologies which are regarded by the licensees as interchangeable with or substitutable for the licensed technology, by reason of the technologies' characteristics, their royalties and their intended use,

(ii) competing undertakings on the relevant product market, being undertakings which, in the absence of the technology transfer agreement, are both active on the relevant product and geographic market(s) on which the contract products are sold without infringing each others' intellectual property rights (actual competitors on the product market) or would, on realistic grounds, undertake the necessary additional investments or other necessary switching costs so that they could timely enter, without infringing each others' intellectual property rights, the(se) relevant product and geographic market(s) in response to a small and permanent increase in relative prices (potential competitors on the product market); the relevant product market comprises products which are regarded by the buyers as interchangeable with or substitutable for the contract products, by reason of the products' characteristics, their prices and their intended use;

(k) 'selective distribution system' means a distribution system where the licensor undertakes to license the production of the contract products only to licensees selected on the basis of specified criteria and where these licensees undertake not to sell the contract products to unauthorised distributors;

(l) 'exclusive territory' means a territory in which only one undertaking is allowed to produce the contract products with the licensed technology, without prejudice to the possibility of allowing within that territory another licensee to produce the contract products only for a particular customer where this second licence was granted in order to create an alternative source of supply for that customer;

(m) 'exclusive customer group' means a group of customers to which only one undertaking is allowed actively to sell the contract products produced with the licensed technology;

(n) 'severable improvement' means an improvement that can be exploited without infringing the licensed technology.

(2) The terms 'undertaking', 'licensor' and 'licensee' shall include their respective connected undertakings.

'Connected undertakings' means:

(a) undertakings in which a party to the agreement, directly or indirectly:

(i) has the power to exercise more than half the voting rights, or

(ii) has the power to appoint more than half the members of the supervisory board, board of management or bodies legally representing the undertaking, or

(iii) has the right to manage the undertaking's affairs;

(b) undertakings which directly or indirectly have, over a party to the agreement, the rights or powers listed in (a);

(c) undertakings in which an undertaking referred to in (b) has, directly or indirectly, the rights or powers listed in (a);

(d) undertakings in which a party to the agreement together with one or more of the undertakings referred to in (a), (b) or (c), or in which two or more of the latter undertakings, jointly have the rights or powers listed in (a);

(e) undertakings in which the rights or the powers listed in (a) are jointly held by:

(i) parties to the agreement or their respective connected undertakings referred to in (a) to (d), or

(ii) one or more of the parties to the agreement or one or more of their connected undertakings referred to in (a) to (d) and one or more third parties.

Article 2 Exemption

Pursuant to Article 81(3) of the Treaty and subject to the provisions of this Regulation, it is hereby declared that Article 81(1) of the Treaty shall not apply to technology transfer agreements entered into between two undertakings permitting the production of contract products.

This exemption shall apply to the extent that such agreements contain restrictions of competition falling within the scope of Article 81(1). The exemption shall apply for as long as the intellectual property right in the licensed technology has not expired, lapsed or been declared invalid or, in the case of know-how, for as long as the know-how remains secret, except in the event where the know-how becomes publicly known as a result of action by the licensee, in which case the exemption shall apply for the duration of the agreement.

Article 3 Market-share thresholds

1. Where the undertakings party to the agreement are competing undertakings, the exemption provided for in Article 2 shall apply on condition that the combined market share of the parties does not exceed 20% on the affected relevant technology and product market.

2. Where the undertakings party to the agreement are not competing undertakings, the exemption provided for in Article 2 shall apply on condition that the market share of each of the parties does not exceed 30% on the affected relevant technology and product market.

3. For the purposes of paragraphs 1 and 2, the market share of a party on the relevant technology market(s) is defined in terms of the presence of the licensed technology on the relevant product market(s). A licensor's market share on the relevant technology market shall be the combined market share on the relevant product market of the contract products produced by the licensor and its licensees.

Article 4 Hardcore restrictions

1. Where the undertakings party to the agreement are competing undertakings, the exemption provided for in Article 2 shall not apply to agreements which, directly or indirectly, in isolation or in combination with other factors under the control of the parties, have as their object:

(a) the restriction of a party's ability to determine its prices when selling products to third parties;

(b) the limitation of output, except limitations on the output of contract products imposed on the licensee in a non-reciprocal agreement or imposed on only one of the licensees in a reciprocal agreement;

(c) the allocation of markets or customers except:

(i) the obligation on the licensee(s) to produce with the licensed technology only within one or more technical fields of use or one or more product markets,

(ii) the obligation on the licensor and/or the licensee, in a non-reciprocal agreement, not to produce with the licensed technology within one or more technical fields of use or one or more product markets or one or more exclusive territories reserved for the other party,

(iii) the obligation on the licensor not to license the technology to another licensee in a particular territory,

(iv) the restriction, in a non-reciprocal agreement, of active and/or passive sales by the licensee and/or the licensor into the exclusive territory or to the exclusive customer group reserved for the other party,

(v) the restriction, in a non-reciprocal agreement, of active sales by the licensee into the exclusive territory or to the exclusive customer group allocated by the licensor to another licensee provided the latter was not a competing undertaking of the licensor at the time of the conclusion of its own licence,

(vi) the obligation on the licensee to produce the contract products only for its own use provided that the licensee is not restricted in selling the contract products actively and passively as spare parts for its own products,

(vii) the obligation on the licensee, in a non-reciprocal agreement, to produce the contract products only for a particular customer, where the licence was granted in order to create an alternative source of supply for that customer;

(d) the restriction of the licensee's ability to exploit its own technology or the restriction of the ability of any of the parties to the agreement to carry out research and development, unless such latter restriction is indispensable to prevent the disclosure of the licensed know-how to third parties.

2. Where the undertakings party to the agreement are not competing undertakings, the exemption provided for in Article 2 shall not apply to agreements which, directly or indirectly, in isolation or in combination with other factors under the control of the parties, have as their object:

(a) the restriction of a party's ability to determine its prices when selling products to third parties, without prejudice to the possibility of imposing a maximum sale price or recommending a sale price, provided that it does not amount to a fixed or minimum sale price as a result of pressure from, or incentives offered by, any of the parties;

(b) the restriction of the territory into which, or of the customers to whom, the licensee may passively sell the contract products, except:
   (i) the restriction of passive sales into an exclusive territory or to an exclusive customer group reserved for the licensor,
   (ii) the restriction of passive sales into an exclusive territory or to an exclusive customer group allocated by the licensor to another licensee during the first two years that this other licensee is selling the contract products in that territory or to that customer group,
   (iii) the obligation to produce the contract products only for its own use provided that the licensee is not restricted in selling the contract products actively and passively as spare parts for its own products,
   (iv) the obligation to produce the contract products only for a particular customer, where the licence was granted in order to create an alternative source of supply for that customer,
   (v) the restriction of sales to end-users by a licensee operating at the wholesale level of trade,
   (vi) the restriction of sales to unauthorised distributors by the members of a selective distribution system;

(c) the restriction of active or passive sales to end-users by a licensee which is a member of a selective distribution system and which operates at the retail level, without prejudice to the possibility of prohibiting a member of the system from operating out of an unauthorised place of establishment.

3. Where the undertakings party to the agreement are not competing undertakings at the time of the conclusion of the agreement but become competing undertakings afterwards, paragraph 2 and not paragraph 1 shall apply for the full life of the agreement unless the agreement is subsequently amended in any material respect.

Article 5 Excluded restrictions

1. The exemption provided for in Article 2 shall not apply to any of the following obligations contained in technology transfer agreements:

(a) any direct or indirect obligation on the licensee to grant an exclusive licence to the licensor or to a third party designated by the licensor in respect of its own severable improvements to or its own new applications of the licensed technology;

(b) any direct or indirect obligation on the licensee to assign, in whole or in part, to the licensor or to a third party designated by the licensor, rights to its own severable improvements to or its own new applications of the licensed technology;

(c) any direct or indirect obligation on the licensee not to challenge the validity of intellectual property rights which the licensor holds in the common market, without prejudice to the possibility of providing for termination of the technology transfer agreement in the event that the licensee challenges the validity of one or more of the licensed intellectual property rights.

2. Where the undertakings party to the agreement are not competing undertakings, the exemption provided for in Article 2 shall not apply to any direct or indirect obligation limiting the licensee's ability to exploit its own technology or limiting the ability of any of the parties to the

agreement to carry out research and development, unless such latter restriction is indispensable to prevent the disclosure of the licensed know-how to third parties.

Article 6 Withdrawal in individual cases

1. The Commission may withdraw the benefit of this Regulation, pursuant to Article 29(1) of Regulation (EC) No 1/2003, where it finds in any particular case that a technology transfer agreement to which the exemption provided for in Article 2 applies nevertheless has effects which are incompatible with Article 81(3) of the Treaty, and in particular where:

(a) access of third parties' technologies to the market is restricted, for instance by the cumulative effect of parallel networks of similar restrictive agreements prohibiting licensees from using third parties' technologies;

(b) access of potential licensees to the market is restricted, for instance by the cumulative effect of parallel networks of similar restrictive agreements prohibiting licensors from licensing to other licensees;

(c) without any objectively valid reason, the parties do not exploit the licensed technology.

2. Where, in any particular case, a technology transfer agreement to which the exemption provided for in Article 2 applies has effects which are incompatible with Article 81(3) of the Treaty in the territory of a Member State, or in a part thereof, which has all the characteristics of a distinct geographic market, the competition authority of that Member State may withdraw the benefit of this Regulation, pursuant to Article 29(2) of Regulation (EC) No 1/2003, in respect of that territory, under the same circumstances as those set out in paragraph 1 of this Article.

Article 7 Non-application of this Regulation

1. Pursuant to Article 1a of Regulation No 19/65/EEC, the Commission may by regulation declare that, where parallel networks of similar technology transfer agreements cover more than 50% of a relevant market, this Regulation is not to apply to technology transfer agreements containing specific restraints relating to that market.

2. A regulation pursuant to paragraph 1 shall not become applicable earlier than six months following its adoption.

Article 8 Application of the market-share thresholds

1. For the purposes of applying the market-share thresholds provided for in Article 3 the rules set out in this paragraph shall apply.

The market share shall be calculated on the basis of market sales value data. If market sales value data are not available, estimates based on other reliable market information, including market sales volumes, may be used to establish the market share of the undertaking concerned.

The market share shall be calculated on the basis of data relating to the preceding calendar year.

The market share held by the undertakings referred to in point (e) of the second subparagraph of Article 1(2) shall be apportioned equally to each undertaking having the rights or the powers listed in point (a) of the second subparagraph of Article 1(2).

2. If the market share referred to in Article 3(1) or (2) is initially not more than 20% respectively 30% but subsequently rises above those levels, the exemption provided for in Article 2 shall continue to apply for a period of two consecutive calendar years following the year in which the 20% threshold or 30% threshold was first exceeded.

Article 9 Repeal
Regulation (EC) No 240/96 is repealed.
References to the repealed Regulation shall be construed as references to this Regulation.

Article 10 Transitional period
The prohibition laid down in Article 81(1) of the Treaty shall not apply during the period from 1 May 2004 to 31 March 2006 in respect of agreements already in force on 30 April 2004 which do not satisfy the conditions for exemption provided for in this Regulation but which, on 30 April 2004, satisfied the conditions for exemption provided for in Regulation (EC) No 240/96.

Article 11 Period of validity
This Regulation shall enter into force on 1 May 2004.
It shall expire on 30 April 2014.
This Regulation shall be binding in its entirety and directly applicable in all Member States.

Done at Brussels, 27 April 2004.
For the Commission
Mario Monti
Member of the Commission

Bibliography

Books

Amato, G. and Ehlermann, C.-D. (eds), *EC Competition Law, A Critical Assessment* (Oxford and Portland Oregon: Hart Publishing, 2007).

Anderman, S., (ed), *The Interface between Intellectual Property and Competition Law* (Cambridge: Cambridge University Press, 2007).

—— and Ezrachi, A., *Intellectual Property and Competition Law: New Frontiers* (Oxford: OUP, 2011).

—— and Kallaugher, J., *Technology Transfer and the New EU Competition Rules* (Oxford: OUP, 2006).

Bently, L. and Sherman, B., *Intellectual Property* (Oxford: OUP, 2008).

Bishop, S. and Richard, D., 'Oscar Bronner–Legitimate Refusal to Supply' in J. Grayston (ed), *European Economics and Law: competition, single market and trade* (Bembridge: Palladian Law in association with Lawfully Simple, 1999).

Bork, R., *The Antitrust Paradox* (2nd edn, New York: Basic Books, 1978).

Cawthra, B.I., *Patent Licensing in Europe* (2nd edn, London: Butterworths, 1986).

Cornish, W. and Llewellyn, D., *Intellectual Property: Patents, Copyright, Trade Marks and Allied Rights* (7th edn, London: Sweet & Maxwell, 2010).

Deakin, S. and Michie, J. *Contracts, Cooperation and Competition* (Oxford: OUP, 1997).

Demaret, P., *Patent Territorial Restrictions and EEC Law: A Legal and Economic Analysis* (Weinheim, Germany: Verlag Chemie, 1978).

Downing, R., *EC Information Technology Law* (Chichester: J. Wiley, 1995).

Drexl, J. (ed), *Research Handbook on Intellectual Property and Competition Law* (Cheltenham, UK, Northampton MA, USA: Edward Elgar, 2008).

Dreyfus, R., Zimmerman, D., and Furst, H., (eds), *Expanding the Boundaries of Intellectual Property* (Oxford: OUP, 2001).

Ehlermann, C.-D. and Atanasiu, I. (editors) 'European Competition Law Annual 2005: The Interaction between Competition Law and Intellectual Property Law' (Oxford and Portland, Oregon: Hart Publishing, 2007).

Frazer, T., *Monopoly, Competition and the Law: The Regulation of Business Activity in Britain, Europe and America* (Brighton: Wheatsheaf Books, 1988).

Faull, J. and Nikpay, A. (eds), *The EC Law of Competition* (Oxford: OUP, 2007).

Glader, M., 'Innovation Markets and Competition Analysis, EU Competition Law and US Antitrust Law' (Cheltenham: Edward Elgar, 2006).

Govaere, I., *The Use and Abuse of Intellectual Property Rights in EC Law* (London: Sweet & Maxwell, 1996).

Goyder, D., *EC Competition Law* (2nd edn, Oxford: OUP, 1993).

Goyder, J. and Albors-Llorens, A., *Goyder's EC Competition Law* (5th edn, Oxford: OUP, 2009).

Guy, D. and Leigh, G., *The EEC and Intellectual Property* (London: Sweet & Maxwell, 1981).

Graham C. and Smith F. (eds), *Competition Regulation and the New Economy*, (Oxford: Hart Publishing, 2004).

Hovenkamp, H., *Federal Antitrust Policy: The Law of Competition and its Practice* (St Paul, Minn, USA: West Publishing Co, 1994).

Howarth, D., 'Pricing Abuses Unfair and Predatory Pricing Under Article 82 EC: From Cost-price Comparisons to the Search for Strategic Standards' in G. Amato and C.-D.Ehlermann (eds), *EC Competition Law, A Critical Assessment* (Oxford and Portland: Oregon Hart Publishing, 2007).

Jaffe, A., Lerner, J., and Stern, S. (eds), *Innovation and the Economy* (National Bureau of Economics, Cambridge, MA: MIT Press 2001).

Joliet, R., *Monopolization and Abuse of a Dominant Position: A Comparative Study of American and European Approaches to the Control of Economic Power* (The Hague: Martinus Nijhoff, 1970).

Jones, A. and Sufrin, B., *EC Competition Law, Text, Cases and Materials* (3rd edn, Oxford: OUP, 2008).

Kerse, C.S., *EEC Antitrust Procedure* (3rd edn, London: Sweet & Maxwell, 1994).

Korah, V., *Patent Licensing and EEC Competition Rules: Regulation 2349/84* (Oxford: ESC, 1985).

—— *Know-how Licensing Agreements and the EEC Competition Rules: Regulation 556.89* (Oxford: ESC, 1989).

—— *An Introductory Guide to EEC Competition Law and Practice* (5th edn, London: Sweet & Maxwell,1994 and 6th edn, Oxford: Hart Publishing, 1997).

—— *Technology Transfer Agreements and the EC Competition Rules* (Oxford: OUP, 1996).

Leveque, F. and Shelanski, H., *Antitrust, Patents and Copyright EU and US Perspectives* (Cheltenham, UK, Northampton MA, USA: Edward Elgar, 2000).

Lowe, J. and Crawford, N., *Innovation and Technology Transfer for the Growing Firm* (Oxford: Pergamon Press, 1984).

MacQueen, H., Waelde, C., and Laurie, G., *Contemporary Intellectual Property: Law and Policy* (Oxford: OUP, 2008).

Maresceau, M. (ed), *The European Community's Commercial Policy after 1992: the Legal Dimension* (The Hague: Martinus Nijhoff Publishers, 1992).

Monti, G., *EC Competition Law* (Cambridge: Cambridge University Press, 2007).

O'Donoghue, R. and Padilla, A. J., *The Law and Economics of Article 82 EC* (Oxford and Portland, Oregon: Hart Publishing, 2006).

Oppenheim, W. and McCarthy, J., *Federal Antitrust Laws Tenth Commentary* (4th edn, St Paul's, US: West Publishing Company, 1981).

Posner, R., *Antitrust Law: An Economic Perspective* (Chicago USA: University of Chicago Press, 1976).

Rahnasto, I., *Intellectual Property Rights, External Effects and Antitrust Law* (Oxford: OUP, 2002).

Scherer, F., *Innovation and Growth–Schumpeterian Perspectives* (Cambridge USA; MIT Press, 1984).

—— *Industrial Market Structure and Economic Performance* (2nd edn, Chicago: Rand McNally College Publishing Company, 1980).

Schmidt, H., 'Competition Law, Innovation and Antitrust, An Analysis of Tying and Technological Integration' (Cheltenham, UK and Northampton, MA, USA: Edward Elgar, 2009).

Schmookler, J., *Invention and Economic Growth* (Cambridge, Mass.: Harvard University Press,1996).

Schumpeter, J., *Capitalism, Socialism and Democracy* (London: George Allen & Unwin, 1976).

Sullivan, L.A., *Antitrust Law* (St Paul, Minn, USA: West, 1977).

Taylor, C. and Silberstone, Z., *The Economic Impact of the Patent System* (Cambridge, Cambridge University Press, 1973).
Tritton, G., *Intellectual Property in Europe* (London: Sweet & Maxwell, 1995).
Whish, R., *Competition Law* (6th edn, Oxford: OUP, 2008).

Articles

Ahlborn, C., Evans, D. S., and Padilla, A. J., 'The Antitrust Economics of Tying: A Farewell to *Per Se* Illegality' *Antitrust Bulletin*, Spring-Summer 2004, 287–341.
Alexander, W., 'Patent Licensing Agreements in the EC' [1986] *IIC* 1.
Anderman, S., 'Copyright, Compulsory Licensing and EC Competition Law' [1995] *Yearbook of Media and Entertainment Law* 215.
—— 'The Aftermath of Magill' [1996] *Yearbook of Media and Entertainment Law* 530.
—— 'Commercial Co-operation, International Competitiveness and EC Competition Policy' in S. Deakin and J. Michie, *Contract, Cooperation and Competitiveness* (Oxford: OUP, 1997).
—— 'Does the Microsoft Case Offer a New Paradigm for the "Exceptional Circumstances" Test and Compulsory Licenses under EC Competition Law?' (2004) 1(2) *Competition Law Review*.
Andrews, P., 'Aftermarket Power in the Computer Service Market: The Digital Undertaking' (1998) *ECLR*, 19(3), 176–81.
Auricchio, V., 'Discount Policies in US and EU Antitrust Enforcement Models: Protecting Competition, Competitors or Consumer Welfare?' [2007] 3 *European Competition Journal* 373–409.
Baden Fuller, C., 'Article 86 EEC: Economic Analysis of the Existence of a Dominant Position' (1979) 4 *EL Rev* 423.
—— 'Economic Issues Relating to Property Rights in Trademarks: Export Bans, differential Pricing, Restrictions on Resale and Repackaging' (1981) 6 *EL Rev* 162.
Beier, F.-K., 'The Significance of the Patent System for Technical, Economic and Social Progress' [1980] *IIC* 563.
—— 'Industrial Property and the Free Movement of Goods in the Internal Market' [1990] *IIC* 131.
—— 'The Future of Intellectual Property in Europe: Thoughts on the Development of Patent, Utility Model and Industrial Design Law' [1991] *IIC* 157.
Bishop, B., 'Price Discrimination under Article 86: Political Economy of the European Court' [1981] *MLR* 282.
—— 'The Modernization of DGIV Analysis' [1997] *ECLR* 481.
Bowman, W. S., 'Tying Arrangements and the Leverage Problem' (1957) *The Yale Law Journal*, Vol 67:19.
Bright, C., 'Deregulation of EC Competition Policy: Rethinking Art. 85(1)' [1995] *Fordham Corp Law Inst* 505.
Carrier, M., 'Why Antitrust Should Defer to the Intellectual Property Rules of Standard Setting Organisations: A Commentary on Teece and Sherry.' (2005) 89 *Minn Law Rev* 2017.
Chappiatte, P., 'FRAND Commitments–The Case for Antitrust Intervention,' (2009) 2 *European Competition Journal* 319.
Contractor, F. J., 'Technology Licensing Practices in U.S. Companies: Corporate and Public Policy Implications' [1983] *Col Jnl Of World Business* 80.

Demaret, P., 'Industrial Property Rights, Compulsory Licences and the Free Movement of Goods under Community Law' [1987] *IIC* 161.

Derbyshire, J., 'Computer Programs and Competition Policy' [1994] *EIPR* 379.

De Souza, N., 'The Commission's Draft Group Exemption on Technology Transfer' [1994] *ECLR* 338.

Evans, D. S. and Padilla, A. J., 'Excessive Prices: Using Economics to Define Administrable Legal Rules' (2005) 1 *J. Competition L. & Econ.* 97.

—— and Salinger, M.,: 'Why Do Firms Bundle and Tie? Evidence from Competitive Markets and Implications for Tying Law' Winter 2005, 22 *Yale Journal on Regulation* 37.

Ewing Jr., K., 'Antitrust Enforcement and the Patent System, Similarities in the European and American Approach' [1980] *IIC*, 279.

Ezrachi, A. and Gilo, D., 'Are Excessive Prices Really Self-Correcting?' (2009) 5 *J. Competition L. & Econ.* 249–67.

Farr, S., 'Abuse of a Dominant Position—The Hilti case' [1992] *ECLR* 174.

Flynn, J., 'Intellectual Property and Anti-trust: ECC Attitudes' [1992] *EIPR* 49.

Forrester, I., 'Software Licensing in the Light of the Current EC Competition Law Considerations' [1992] *ECLR* 5.

—— 'Competition Structures for the 21st Century' [1994] *Fordham Corp Law Inst* 445.

Forrester, I. and Norall, C., 'The Laicisation of Community law, Self help and the Rule of Reason' [1984] 21 *CML Rev.*

Fox, E., 'The Modernization of Antitrust: A New Equilibrium', 66 *Cornell L Rev* 1140 (1981).

—— 'Monopolization and Dominance in the United States and the European Community: Efficiency, Opportunity, and Fairness', 61 *Notre Dame L Rev* (1986).

Frazer, T., 'Vorsprung durch Technik: The Commission's Policy on Know-How Agreements' [1989] *Yearbook of European Law* 1.

Friden, G., 'Recent Developments in EEC Intellectual Property Law: the Distinction between Existence and Exercise Revisited' (1989) 26 *CML Rev* 193.

Gal, M., 'Monopoly Pricing as an Antitrust Offense in the US and EC: Two Systems of Belief about Monopoly' (2004) 49 *Antitrust Bulletin* 343.

Geradin, D., 'Pricing Abuses by Essential Patent Holders in a Standard-Setting Context: A View from Europe' [2008] (<http://ssrn.com/abstract=1174922> (last accessed 1 June 2010)),

Gerber, D., 'Law and the Abuse of Economic Power in Europe' (1987) 62 *Tulane L Rev* 57.

Glasl, D., 'Essential Facilities Doctrine in EC Anti-trust Law: A Contribution to the Current Debate' [1994] *ECLR* 306.

Gonzalez Dias, F., 'Some Reflections on the Notion of ancillary Restraints under EC Competition Law' [1995] *Fordham Corp Law Inst* 325.

Gotts, I. K. and Bent, S. A., 'Heightened Scrutiny of Intellectual Property Transfers by US Antitrust Officials is the Trend' *European Intellectual Property Review* 1994 (6 1994): 245–7.

Gravengaard, M. A. and Kjaersgaard, N., 'The EU Commission Guidance on Exclusionary Abuse of Dominance–and Its Consequences in Practice' [2010] 31(7) *ECLR* 285–305.

Guttuso, S., 'Know How Agreements' [1986] *Fordham Corp Law Inst* 483.

—— 'Technology Transfer Agreements under EC Law' [1994] *Fordham Corp Law Inst* 227.

Hawk, B., 'The American (Antitrust) Revolution: Lessons for the EEC?' [1988] *ECLR* 53.

Hendricks, J., 'The Information Technology Revolution: The Next Phase' [1995] *Fordham Corp Law Inst* 549.

Hoyng, W. and Biesheuvel, M., 'The Know-how Group Exemption' [1989] *CML Rev* 219.

James, H., 'Tetra Pak: Exemption and Abuse of Dominant Position' [1990] *ECLR* 267.

Jebsen, P. and Stevens, R., 'Assumptions, Goals and Dominant Undertaking: The Regulation of Competition under Article 86 of the EU' [1996] *Antitrust Law Jnl* 4.

Jenny, F., 'Competition and Efficiency' [1993] *Fordham Corp Inst* 185.

Joliet, R., 'Patented Articles and the Free Movement of Goods within the EEC' [1975] *Current Legal Problems* 15.

—— 'Territorial and Exclusive Trademark Licensing under the EEC Law of Competition' [1984] *IIC* 21.

Jones, A., 'Distinguishing Predatory Prices from Competitive Ones' [1995] *EIPR* 252.

Kallaugher, J. and Venit, J., 'Essential Facilities: A Comparative Law Approach [1994] *Fordham Corp Law Inst* 315.

Kaplow, L., 'The Patent-Antitrust Intersection: A Reappraisal' [1983–N4] *Harv Law Rev* 1813.

Kauper, T., 'Article 86 Excessive Prices and Refusals to Deal' [1991] Vol 59 *Antitrust Law Jnl* 441.

Kerse, C., 'Block Exemptions under Article 85 (3): the Technology Transfer Regulation—Procedural Issues' [1996] *ECLR* 331.

Kjolbye, L., 'Rebates under Article 82 EC: Navigating Uncertain Waters' ECLR 2010, 31(2), 66–80.

Kon, S. and Shaffer, F., 'Parallel Imports of Pharmaceutical Products: A New Realism or Back to Basics?' [1997] *ECLR* 331.

Korah, V., 'The Michelin Decision of the Commission [1982] 7 *EL Rev* 130.

—— 'EEC Competition Policy—Legal Form or Economic Efficiency' [1986] *Current Legal Problems* 85.

—— 'No duty to License Independent Repairers to Make Spare Parts: the Renault, Volvo and Bayer & Hennecke Cases' [1988] *EIPR* 381.

—— 'The Preliminary Draft of a New EC, Group Exemption for Technology Licensing' [1994] *EIPR* 263.

Kühn, K.-U., Stillman, R., and Caffarra, C., 'Economic Theories of Bundling and their Policy Implications in Abuse Cases: An Assessment in Light of the Microsoft Case' (2005) 1(1), *European Competition Journal* March, 85–121.

Landes, W.M. and Posner,R.A., 'Market Power in Antitrust Cases', 94 *Harv Law Rev* 937.

Lasok, P., 'Assessing the Economic Consequences of Restrictive Agreements: A Comment on the Delimitis Case [1991] *ECLR* 194.

Lidgard, H., 'Unilateral Refusal to Supply: An Agreement in Disguise' [1997] *ECLR* 352.

Lind, R.C. and Muysert, P., 'Innovation and Competition Policy, Challenges for the New Millenium' 2003 *ECLR* 24(2) 87–92.

Lipsky, A., 'Current Antitrust Division Views on Patent Licensing Practices' Antitrust Section of the ABA, 15 November 1981, 1981 *Trade Regulation Reporter* (CCH) 55, 985

MacFarlane, N., Wardle, C. and . Wilkinson, J., 'The Tension between Intellectual Property Rights and Certain Provisions of EC Law [1994] *EIPR* 525.

Machlup, F., 'An Economic Review of the Patent System, Study of the Committee on Patents, Trademarks and Copyright', Senate Judiciary Committee, US 85th Congress, Study no 15, Washington DC, 1958.

Maier-Rigaud, F., 'Article 82 Rebates: Four Common Fallacies' (2006) 2 *European Competition Journal* 85.

Marenco, G. and Banks, K., 'Intellectual Property and the Community Rules on Free Movement of Goods: Discrimination Unearthed' (1990) 15(3) *EL Rev* 224–56.

Moritz, H. W., 'EC Competition Aspects and Software Licensing Agreements'—A German Perspective', Part One [1994] *IIC* 357; Part Two [1994] *IIC* 515.

Motta, M., 'Michelin II—The treatment of rebates', 27 November 2006, available at <http://www.barcelonagse.eu/tmp/pdf/motta_MichelinII.pdf> (last accessed 29 June 2010).

Oliver, P., 'The Concept of "Abuse" of a Dominant Position Under Article 82 EC: Recent Developments in Relation to Pricing' [2005] 1 *European Competition Journal* 315–39.

Oppenheim, Weston and McCarthy, *Federal Antitrust Laws Tenth Commentary* (4th edn, 1981).

Ordover, J., 'A Patent System for Both Diffusion and Exclusion', *Jnl Of Economic Perspectives* [1991] Vol 5, no 1, 430.

Peeters, J., 'The Rule of Reason Revisited: Prohibitions on Restraints on Competition in the Sherman Act and the EEC Treaty', Vol 37 *American Jnl. of Comparative Law* 521 (1989).

Price, D., 'The Secret of the Know-How Block Exemption' [1989] *ECLR* 213.

—— 'Abuse of a Dominant Position—The Tale of Nails, Milk Cartons, and TV Guides' [1990] *ECLR* 80.

Ramsay, T., 'The EU Commission's Use of the Competition Rules in the Field of Telecommunications: A Delicate Balancing Act' [1995] *Fordham. Corp Law Inst* 561.

Reindl, A., 'The Magic of Magill: TV Program Guides as a Limit of Copyright Law?' [1993] *IIC* 60.

—— 'Intellectual Property and Intra-Community Trade' [1996] *Fordham Corp Law Inst* 453.

Ridyard, D., 'Essential Facilities and the Obligation to Supply Competitors' [1996] *ECLR* 438.

Ritter, C., 'Refusal to Deal and Essential Facilities: Does Intellectual Property Require Special Deference compared to Tangible Property?' (2005) *World Competition* (3) 281.

Rousseva, E., 'Modernising by Eradicating how the Commission's New Approach to Article 81 EC Dispenses with the need to apply Article 82 to Vertical Restraints' (2005) 42 *CML Rev* 587.

Schödermeir, M., 'Collective Dominance Revisited: An Analysis of the EC Commission's new Concept of Oligopoly Control' [1990] *ECLR* 28.

Schröder, H., 'The Application of Article 85 of the EEC Treaty to Distribution Agreements—Principles and Recent Developments [1984] *Fordham Corp Law Inst* 375.

Sher, B. and Kallaugher, J. 'Rebates revisited: anti-competitive effects and exclusionary abuse under Article 82' [2004] *ECLR* 263–85.

Singleton, S., 'Intellectual Property Disputes: Settlement Agreements and Ancillary Licences under EC and UK Competition Law' [1993] *EIPR* 48.

Siragusa, M., 'The Application of Article 86 to the Pricing Policies fo Dominant Companies: Discriminatary and Unfair Prices' [1979] 16 *CML Rev* 179.

—— 'EEC Technology Transfers—A Private View' [1982] *Fordham Corp Law Inst* 116.

—— 'Notification of Agreements in the EEC: To Notify or not to Notify?' [1987] *Fordham Corp Law Inst* 243.

Skinner, T., 'The Oral Hearing of the Magill Case' [1994] *ECLR* 103.

Slot, P., 'The Application of Articles 3(f), 5 and 85 to 94 EEC' (1987) 12 *EL Rev* 179.

Spector, D., 'Loyalty Rebates: An Assessment of Competition Concerns and a Proposed Structured Rule of Reason' (2005) 1(2) *Competition Policy International* 89.

Springer, U., 'Borden and United Brands Revisited' [1997] *ECLR* 42.

—— 'Meeting Competition: Justification of Price Discrimination under EC and US Antitrust Law' [1997] *ECLR* 251.

Smith, J., 'Televison Guides: The European Court doesn't know there's so much in it' [1992] *ECLR* 135.

Smith, P., 'The Wolf in Wolf's Clothing: The Problem With Predatory Pricing' (1989) 14 *EL Rev.* 209.

Subiotto, R., 'The Right to Deal with Whom one Pleases under EEC Competition Law: A Small Contribution to a Necessary Debate' [1992] *ECLR* 234.

—— 'Moosehead/Whitbread: Industrial and No Challenge Clauses Relating to Licensed Trade Marks under EEC Competition Law' [1990] *ECLR* 226.

Teece, D and Sherry, E., 'Standard Setting and Antitrust,' (2003) 87 *Minn Law Rev* 1911.

Temple Lang, J., 'Monopolisation and the Definition of Abuse of a Dominant Position under Article 86 EEC Treaty' [1970] 16 *CML Rev* 345.

—— 'Defining Legitimate Competition: Companies Duties to Supply Competitors and Access to Essential Services' [1994] *Fordham Corp Law Inst* 216.

—— 'European Community Antitrust Law—Innovation Markets and High Technology Industries' [1996] *Fordham Corp Law Inst* 519.

—— 'Article 82 EC–The Problems and The Solution' Institutions and Markets Series, Fondazione Eni Enrico Mattei, Nota di Lavro 65.2009, (<http://papers.ssrn.com/sol3/papers.cfm?abstract_id=1467747> (last accessed 26 May 2010)).

—— and R. O'Donoghue, 'Defining Legitimate Competition: How to Clarify Pricing Abuses under Article 82' (2002) 26 *Fordham Int'l LJ* 83.

Turner, D. F., 'Antitrust and Innovation' (1967) 12 *Antitrust Bulletin* 277.

Ullrich, H., 'Patents and Know How: Free Trade Interenterprise cooperation and Competition within the Internal European Market' [1992] *IIC* 583.

Ungerer, H., 'EU Competition Law in the Telecommunications, Media and Information Technology Area' [1995] *Fordham Corp Law Inst* 465.

Vadja, C., 'The Application of Community Competition Law to the Distribution of Computer Products and Parts' [1992] *ECLR* 110.

Van der Asch, B., 'Intellectual Property Rights under EC Law' [1983] *Fordham Corp Law Inst* 539.

Van der Wal, G., 'Article 86 EC: The Limits of Compulsory Licensing' [1994] *ECLR* 230.

Van Kerchkhove, M., 'The Advocate General delivers his opinion on Magill' [1994] *ECLR* 276.

Venit, J., 'EEC Patent Licensing Revisited: The Commission's Patent Licence Regulation' [1985] *Antitrust Bulletin* 457.

—— 'The Commission's Opposition Procedure' (1985) 22 *CML Rev* 167.

—— 'In the Wake of Windsurfing: Patent Licensing in the Common Market' [1987] *IIC* 1, also in [1986] *Fordham Corp Law Inst* 521.

—— and J. Kallaugher, 'Essential Facilities: A Comparative Approach' [1994] *Fordham Corp Law Inst* 315.

Vinje, T., '*Magill*: Its Impact on the Information Technology Industry' [1992] *EIPR* 397.

—— 'The Final Word on *Magill*' [1995] *ECLR* 297.

Vogelenzang, P., 'Abuse of a Dominant Position in Article 86: The problem of Causality and Some Applications' (1976) 13 *CML Rev* 61.

Waelbroeck, D., 'Michelin II: A Per Se Rule against Rebates by Dominant Companies?' (2005) 1 *Journal of Competition Law and Economics* 149.

Waelbroeck, M., 'The Effect of the Rome Treaty on the Exercise of National Industrial Property Rights' (1976) 21 *Antitrust Bulletin* 99.

—— 'Antitrust Analysis under Article 85 (1) and Article 85 (3)' [1987] *Fordham Corp Law Inst* Ch. 28.

—— 'Price Discrimination and Rebate Policies under EU Competition Law' [1995] *Fordham Corp Law Inst* 142.

Whaite, R., 'Licensing in Europe' [1990] *EIPR* 88.

—— 'The Draft Technology Transfer Block Exemption' [1994] *EIPR* 259.

Whish, R. and Sufrin, B., 'The Rule of Reason under Article 85' [1987] *Oxford Year Book of European Law* 1.

White, E., 'Research and Development Joint Ventures under EEC Competition Law' [1985] *IIC* 663.

Winn, D., 'The Commission Know-how Regulation 556/89: Innovation and Territorial Exclusivity, Improvements and the Quid Prop Quo' [1990] *ECLR* 135.

Zanon, L., 'Price Discrimination under Article 86 of the EEC Treaty: A Comment on the UBC Case' (1982) 31 *ICLQ* 36.

—— 'Price Discrimination and Hoffman La Roche' [1981] 15 *Jnl World Trade Law* 305.

Other Sources and Websites

Bellis, J.-F., 'The 'Microsoft Judgment' Conference (BIICL, 17 Russell Square, London, 25 September 2007).

Dolmans, M and Levy, N., *EC Commission v Microsoft: Win, Lose or the Tie?* (Brussels: Cleary, Gottlieb, Steen & Hamilton).

Gilbert, R. J., 'Competition and Innovation' (27 January 2007) Competition Policy Center, Institute of Business and Economic Research, UC Berkeley <http://repositories.cdlib.org/iber/cpc/CPC07-069> (last accessed 13 October 2010).

Hellström, P., 'The 'Microsoft Judgment Conference (BIICL, 17 Russell Square, London, 25 September 2007).

Lowe, P., 'How Different is EU Antitrust? A Route Map for Advisors, An Overview of EU Competition Law and Policy on Commercial Practices' (Conference d'automne de l'American Bar Association, Brussels, 16 October 2003) (<http://ec.europa.eu/competition/speeches/text/sp2003_038_en.pdf> (last accessed 20 May 2010)).

Nalebuff, B., 'Bundling, Tying, and Portfolio Effects' *DTI Economics Paper No 1, Part 1–Conceptual Issues* (February 2003).

OECD, *Competition Policy and Intellectual Property Rights* (Paris, 1989).

Singleton, S., *Legal Times* (2 May 1995).

US Department of Justice and Federal Trade Commission, *Antitrust Enforcement and Intellectual Property Rights: Promoting Innovation and Competition* (2007). <http://www.usdoj.gov/atr/public/hearings/ip/222655.pdf> (last accessed 13 October 2010).

Wilson, Dept. of Justice Luncheon Speech, 'Law on Licensing Practice—Myth or Reality Straight Talk from Alice in Wonderland'.

Index

abuse(s) 27–8, 40–53, 73–91
burden of proof 81–2
definitions/applicability 33–6, 34*n*, 70–1, 118, 321
exclusionary 74, 75–85
expansion of concept 75–91
preventive legislation 33–6
'risk of harm' criterion 75–6, 83–4, 177–8, 180, 322
specific examples 74, 88–9
structural 74, 86–8
see also dominance, abuse of
aftermarkets 109–11
air travel
discriminatory pricing 164
refusal to interline 99–100
ticket commissions 178–80
Allendesalazar, Rafael 157
allocative efficiency 14
ancillary restraints 233, 234, 247–8, 279, 280
antitrust law 147, 147*n*, 240–1, 241*nn*, 252, 257, 304–5
appreciability 225, 227–9
and restrictions by effect 228–9
and restrictions by object 229
test for 227–8, 234, 238–9, 242–9
assignment, bans on 281–2
average avoidable costs 185, 193
average variable costs 193

bananas, trade in 169–70
(definition of) product market 40
Baumol-Willig rule 123–4
block exemptions 6, 10, 37, 131, 203–4, 205–7, 209–10, 279–80, 286, 292–3, 298–9
freed from market share restrictions 253–4
preclusion from application 240
vertical 131
see also **technology transfer**
blocking position 261*n*
Bork, Robert H. 135, 241*n*
Brooks, Roger G. 297–8
Browne-Wilkinon, Lord 124

Canada, pricing of goods 148–9
car industry 43–5, 95–6
Chicago School 241*n*
China 14
Coca-Cola 128–9
coercion 136–7
collaboration, determination of pro-/anti-competitive nature 213–15
collecting societies 155–9, 171–2
courts' treatment of 157–9
negative impact on markets 155–6
commitment decisions 315
comparative prices test 146–7
competition
actual, existence of 60
and remedies 119–20, 307–17
elimination 65–7, 78, 93–4, 216, 269, 323
enforcement of rules 307–17
impediments/reductions 47
inter-technology 267–8
'intra-brand' 211
intra-technology 230, 268–70, 277
'meeting,' as defence 170–3
normal methods, departure from 77–83
'on the merits' 77
proportionality requirement 80, 87
weakening of levels 76–7
see also **restriction of competition**
competition law
dynamic view 14–15
innovation theory 13–16
relationship with dominance 70–1
relationship with IP rights 11–16, 201–12
see also **EU competition law**
compulsory division (of companies, as remedy) 311
compulsory licensing 3, 77, 81–2, 117–19, 120–5, 309–10
computer products 10, 13, 51–3, 55, 88, 98–9
different-language versions 148–9
interoperability 105–6, 111–19, 311–12
loyalty rebates 182–7
original equipment manufacturers (OEMs) 182–3
separate markets 66–7, 133–5
technological integration 129–30
conditions of sale 162–3
confidentiality, obligations of 267, 281
consumers
demand, relevance of 132, 134
differentiation between branded and non-branded goods 163
prejudicing of interests 115–19
welfare, as criterion 216, 225, 230–1
Cooke J 123–4
coordinated effects 212

copyright
compulsory licensing 3
national laws 104
scope of protection 13
in TV schedules 102–7
copyright management societies 80
'corporate veil,' lifting of 219
corporations
commercial strategies 7–9
cost-price analysis 149–50
cost(s)
allocation 124–5
geographic differences 170
pricing below 189
R&D 151
recovery 125
reduction, as defence 140–1
see also **average avoidable costs**
Court of First Instance *see* **General Court**
Court of Justice of the European Union (CJEU) 3, 18–30
and refusal to supply 93–5
application of appreciability test 242–9
approach to rebates 174–5
see also Table of Cases
cross-elasticity 39
cross-licensing 210
customer pressure, corporate arguments based on 70

data storage methods 47
***de minimis* test** 223–4, 229
decentralization, implemetation of policy 307
decompilation 119–20
dependence principle 28
discounts *see* **rebates**
discriminatory pricing 79, 161–74
and downstream markets 173–4
and separate markets
competitive disadvantaging 164–6
cross-border 165–6
defined 161–2
differences in national approach 172–3
different quantities 163–4
equivalent transactions 162–6
geographic 169–73
illegality *per se* 162
'meeting competition' defence 170–3
distribution agreements, exclusive 239
dominance 45–6
abuse of 40–53
and exclusivity 63–4
and IP rights 58–9
and technological superiority 62
and tying 135–6
determination 36
legal status 70–1, 113–14
methods of assessment 59–62
ordinary *vs.* special 64–71
original equipment manufacturers (OEMs), limitation by 182–3
regulation of firms occupying 33–6
responsibilities attendant on 73–4, 94–5
test 57–8
threshold 136
'downstream' markets/operators 113–14, 121–2, 166–7, 173–4, 195–6
'drift net' approach 227*n*
dual markets 154–5

effective competition 25–7
use of market power to damage 33–6
efficiency
as intended aim of rebates 186
defence based on 140–1, 321, 323
forms of 14
see also **allocative efficiency; productive efficiency**
efficient competitor test 184–5
efficient component pricing rule *see* **Baumol-Willig rule**
equivalent transactions 162–6
'essential facility' doctrine 67–70, 101–2, 104–7, 108, 121–2
product qualifying for 106–7
regulatory framework 173–4
ETSI (European Telecommunications Standards Institute) 294
EU competition law
applicability test 215
balancing with IP rights 17–20, 201–12, 319–20, 323–4
decrease in interventionism 204
early approach 225–7, 234
enforcement 307–17
evolution 10–11, 251–5
infringement by IP rights holders 6, 73–4
integration 29–30
legal framework 5–6
modernization 203–7, 225, 230–1, 233, 255–7, 319, 324–6
more economic approach 205–12, 324–7
objectives 25
scope 3–5
'second tier' regulation 119–20, 319
European Commission 3, 4, 40–1
and indispensability requirement 65–6
and refusal to supply 93–5, 101–2, 115–16
approach to licensing 222–4, 230–1, 231–41, 247–9, 252–5, 256–7, 266–7, 314
policy change 238–41
approach to pricing 193–4
approach to rebates 174–5, 185–7
approach to technology pools 301–2

assessment of dominance 59–62, 68
'average avoidable costs' criterion 185, 193
competition policy 9–11, 15–16, 28–9
contractual restrictions 230–1
criticisms 185–7, 227*n*, 254–5
definition of 'effect on trade' 222–4
'drift net' approach 227*n*
'essential facility' doctrine 101–2
extent of powers 313–14
product market definition 49–53, 54–5
prohibitive competence 19–20
remedies available to 308–9
treatment of tying 133–4
see also Table of Cases
European Court of Justice (ECJ) *see* **Court of Justice of the European Union**
European Union
single market 203
see also **EU competition law; European Commission**
Evans, David S. 153
'exceptional circumstances' test 98–9, 102–9, 111–19
additional categories 109
bypassing 118
conditions 108–9
developments in case law 107–9, 120–5
modification 114–17
scope 113–14
second category 109–11
excessive pricing 96–7, 143–59
and proportionality principle 152, 157, 159
authorities' reluctance to intervene 143
burden of proof 156–7
case law 145–50
collecting societies and 155–9
comparative prices test 146–7
correction by market forces 143–4
cost-price analysis 149–50
cross-border postage 148–9
defined 145–6
evaluation of efficiency 147–8
exploitative 154–5
problems of determination 143, 146–7, 159
similarities with margin squeezing 195
exclusionary pricing 189–98
exclusivity 63–4, 74, 86–8
exemption, processess of 215–17
see also **block exemptions**
exercise of IP rights
monitoring through competition policy 11–16
normal 21–2
permitted/prohibited 19–20, 21–5
regulation 319–20
test for permissibility 23–4
exhaustion, doctrine of 212
export bans *see* **territoriality, exclusive**
fair return *see* **legitimate reward**
fairness, as legislative goal 27–9
Faull, Jonathan 165*n*
ferry services 101
field of use restrictions 278
film, exhibition rights 244–5
fines 315–17
foreclosure, likelihood of 137–8
Fox, Eleanor 147*n*
France
competition policy 70–1
computer products 191–3
pricing legislation 172
FRAND (Fair, Reasonable and Non-Discriminatory) criterion/ commitments 297–8, 305
ambushes 4, 8, 291–2
exceeding of 48, 154
pricing 120–1, 124–5
freedom of action, principle of 225–7, 227*n*, 229, 233, 234, 236, 238
Friden, Georges 152

Gates, Bill 141
Gault J 123–4
General Court (GC) 42–3
Gerardin, Damien 297–8
Germany
competition policy/theory 70–1, 225–7, 234, 327
postal services 148–9, 191
telecommunicatons 196–7
gift (of tied product) 137
grant backs 283–4
Gravengaard, Martin A. 193–4
Gulman, Advocate General 103

harm, proof of 83–5
Howarth, David 157–8

indispensability 64–7, 105–6, 107–8, 114, 216, 246–7, 248–9
see also **'essential facility' doctrine**
industrial standards 291–305
competition concerns 292–3
creation 294–5
de facto 303
information
inadequate, provision of 111–19
refusal to supply 109–11, 115–16
innovation
benefits of technology pools 300–1
incentives to 284
undermining 115, 130
theory of 13–16
integration
of the market, EU concern for 225, 230
of products 29–30, 79 *see also* **technological integration**

intellectual property (IP)
see also **IP legislation**; **IP rights**
interim measures 310
Internet 55
access providers 191–3
interoperability 105–6, 111–19, 311–12
deliberate restriction 112–13
interstate trade, impact of agreements on 215, 221–4, 238
defined 222–4
quantitative dimension 222
IP legislation
internal balance 12–13
national variations 172–3
relationship with competition law 4–6, 9–11, 17–20, 319–20
scope 4
IP rights
abuses 35–6
and conditional rebates 181–7
and margin squeezing 197–8
and separate markets 167–9
and unfair pricing 150–9
commercial strategies 7–9, 73–4
creation of *de facto* monopoly 45–6, 58–9, 61–4, 68–9
'grant' *vs.*'existence' 20–1
limits 4–5, 9
market power 6
minimum protection levels 24–5
relationship with tying 130–1, 136, 142
restrictions 85–91
reward function 151–2
strategic use 320–1
types 10
unilateral enforcement 219
see also **EU competition law**; **exercise of IP rights**
Ireland 171
IT (information technology) law 105–6, 111–19
remedies 311–12

Jacobs, Advocate General 42–3
JEDEC (Joint Electron Device Engineering Council) 48, 61–2
Johannes, Hartmut 241

Kallaugher, John J. 77*n,* 80
Kirschner, Advocate General 86–7
Kjaersgaard, Niels 193–4
know-how, obligation not to divulge 281
Korah, Valentine 151, 153

Lang, John Temple 102
legitimate reward
and quality controls 284–6
as function of IP rights 151–2, 245–6
benefits of licensing 202
(problems of) assessment 147–8, 152–3, 159
leveraging 41–2, 190–1
downstream markets 195–6
technological 112–13
licensing 201–12
anti-competitive collusion 210, 212, 275
'closed exclusive' 242–3
collective 9
differences in fees 168–9
distinguished from personal exploitation 201–2
exclusive and sole, regulation 275–6
lack of special treatment 205, 324–5
loss of legal certainty 206
market share limits 262–3
modernization of EU law 203–7, 252
more economic approach 205–12
(need for) restrictions 202–3
new analytical tools 207–12
of technology 46–7
'open exclusive' 242–4
out 296
pro-competitive nature 202, 251–2, 256–7
purpose 201, 210
refusal 24, 98–102, 310
regulatory parameters 237
relevant market definition 207–8
remedies 314
right to 201
self-assessment, role of 204, 206, 218
territorial protection 203, 238
see also **compulsory licensing**; **licensing agreements**
licensing agreements 30
anti-competitive effects 210, 211–12, 215, 224–31, 233–49, 270–1, 277–8
assignment bans 281–2
automatically void 217–18
between competitors 208–10, 259–62, 263–4, 270–1, 275–6
between 'independent undertakings' 219–21
between non-competitors 208–11, 259–62, 264–5, 267–70, 277
between potential competitors 261–2
between subsequent competitors 269–70
'black list' (of clauses) 252–3
clearance 218–31
conditions for prohibition 214–15
confidentiality obligation 267
de minimis test 223–4, 229
dual categorization/legal regimes 211, 259–62
duration 258–9, 261*n,* 282
effects, test based on 224–5, 227, 228–9, 230–1, 322
excluded 265
exemption process 215–17
field of use restrictions 278

grant backs/improvments
internal restraints 227
new methods of assessment 266–71, 324–6
no-challenge clauses 289–90
non-compete obligations 282–3
non-reciprocal 264
non-territorial provisions 239–40, 247–9, 279–90
object, test based on 224, 227, 229, 230–1
post-term use bans 282
quality controls 284–6
removal of clauses 314
restrictions 230–1, 263–5, 267–8, 302–3
royalties 286–9
specific clauses, objections to 218
sublicensing bans 267, 281–2
technical specifications 285
territorial restrictions 238, 240, 242–7, 268–9, 273–8
unenforceability 217–18
vertical *vs.* horizontal (old classification) 208–9, 210, 214, 226*n*, 254, 260
withdrawal 253–4, 265–6, 270, 287
see also **restriction of competition**
Lowe, Philip 149
loyalty rebates 79, 90, 161–2, 174–5
abusive/illegal 175–8
and IP rights 182–7
'average avoidable costs' test 185
'meeting competition' defence 186

Machlup, Fritz 152–3
margin squeezing 194–8
and IP rights 197–8
defined 195
linked with refusal to supply 195
rejected claims of 196
similarities with excessive pricing 195
marine transport 67–8, 313–14
'market opening' test 233, 234, 243–7
market power
and tying 136
dominant power's (ab)use of 93–5
measurement 211–12
regulation 33–6
market share 59–60, 62, 222
absence of restrictions 253–4
limitation 262–3
low 223–4, 229
market(s)
national *vs.* single 203
partitioning agreements 236–7
see also **aftermarkets; 'market opening' test; national markets; product markets; related markets**
medical treatment, methods 48
mergers 26–7
Microsoft 81–2, 83–5, 111–19, 311–12, 322–3
Commitment Decision 315
compulsory division 311
see also Table of Cases
Mischo, Advocate General 44–5, 122, 151
mixed bundling 128–9, 311–12
linked with rebates 181
of patented and unpatented goods 142, 288
monopoly/ies 36, 112–13
(alleged) advantages 15
de facto 45–6, 58–9, 61–4, 68–9, 85–6, 104–5
state-conferred 54
music catalogues 156–7

'naked restrictions' 182
national markets, detachment from single 203
'new product' rule 105, 108, 117–18
Nikpay, Ali 165*n*
'Nine No-Nos' 240–1, 240*n*, 251
no-challenge clauses 289–90
non-compete obligations 282–3
non-territorial provisions 279–90
'ancillary restraints' doctrine 279, 280
normal commercial practice, concept of 78

objective justification 77, 138–41, 180, 321, 322–3
absence, finding of 119
failure to prove 139
reduced transaction costs 140–1
standard of proof 139, 141
types of 139–40
OEMs (original equipment manufacturers) 182–3, 186
OFTEL 124–5
Oliver, Peter 165
Ordoliberalism 225–7, 234, 327

packaging materials 133, 167–8
Padilla, Jorge 153
passive sales, protection against 265
patent pools *see* **technology pools**
patent(s)
ambushes 4
essential, selection of 294–5
integrity of process, concerns for 289
licensing 235–6, 287
market power 6
patented goods, bundling with unpatented 142
portfolios, acquisition of 7–8
relevant, search for 295
'reverse' settlements 3–4
scope of protection 13
'thickets' 7–8
performance rights 168, 244–5
pharmaceutical industry 3–4, 76–7
commercial strategies 7

plant breeders' rights 242, 246–7
Posner, Richard A. 241*n*
postal services, cross-border 148–9, 191
predatory pricing 90, 161, 189–94
as abusive *per se* 189
cost analysis 193
intention to eliminate 189
less efficient competitors, impact on 193–4
methods of analysis 189–90
prospect of recoupment 190
pricing
cartels 301, 312–13
control of 60–1
exclusionary policies 161–87
geographical differentiation 148–9, 196–7
see also **Baumol-Willig rule; compulsory licensing; discriminatory pricing; excessive pricing; predatory pricing; unfair pricing**
primary line injury 164–5, 175
product formulation 293–4
product market(s)
distinguished from product 38–9
distinguished from technology market 208, 261
geographically separate 148–9
linked 166–7
methods of defintion 47–9, 207–8
narrowness 43–53
defence 45
primary 47–9, 85–8, 95, 97–8
secondary 46–7, 85–6, 88–9, 95–8, 109–11, 114, 154–5 *see also* **downstream**
separate 49, 51–3, 95–6
see also **relevant market; substitutability**
productive efficiency 14
proportionality principle 28, 80, 87, 152, 157, 159
purchase, acquisition of competitors by 78, 86–8, 220

Qualcomm 7
quality
competition on the basis of 190–1
controls 284–6
obligations 285
quantity rebates 163–4, 175–6
contrasted with loyalty rebates 176–8

rail services 52
raw materials, indispensable 105–6
rebates, conditional 174–87
and IP rights 181–7
exclusionary purpose 174–6
restriction of competition 177–80
standard of proof 180
typology 180
viewed from buyer's side 178–80
see also **loyalty rebates; quantity rebates**
refusal to supply 80–1, 89, 93–125, 310
'essential facility' doctrine 101–2, 104–7
'exceptional circumstances' test 98–9, 102–9
existing customers 93–4, 109–11
linked with margin squeezing 195
new customers 94, 99–100
Reischl, Advocate General 45
related markets 89–91
vertical relationship 89–90
relevant market 37–55
definition 37–8, 67, 69, 132–3, 207–8
economic criteria 53–4
geographic 53–5, 261
regulatory policy 41–2
separate assessment 166
tying of non-relevant product sales to 41–5
see also **product market; substitutability**
relevant product, definition 40–3
remedies 119–20, 307–17
alternative 323–4
behavioural 308–9, 309*n*
commitment decisions 315
compulsory licensing 309–10
information technology 311–12
limits 313
penalties 315–17
positive 308
prohibitive of futuree conduct 310
purpose 307–8
structural 308–9, 309*n*
research and development
block exemption 298–9
costs 151
joint ventures 214, 292–3, 298–9
restriction of competition 210, 211–12, 215, 224–31, 233–49
'ancillary restraints' doctrine 233, 234, 247–8, 279, 280
categorization 212
'freedom of action' doctrine 225–7, 227*n*, 229, 233, 234, 236, 238
judicial approach 233
'market opening' doctrine 233, 234, 243–7
more economic approach 233
non-territorial restraints 247–9
per se rules 322
policy change 238–41
'scope of the patent' doctrine 212, 234, 235–6, 247*n*
widening of scope 236–7
'reverse' settlements 3–4
royalties 286–9
and technology pools 296, 301, 302–3
calculation 288–9
collection 155–9
differing rates 168–9
duration 287

licence provisions 267
minimum, clause 270

'safe harbour' 204, 205–6
agreements/provisions lying outside 266–71
Schumpeter, Joseph 15
'scope of the patent' doctrine 233, 234, 235–6, 247*n*
adjustment of concept 239–40
'second tier' regulation 119–20
secondary line injury 164–5, 175–6
self-assessment *see* **licensing**
self-defence 79
separate markets 66–7
and IP rights 167–9
and price discrimination 166–9
SIEC (Significant Impediment of Effective Competition) test 47
SLC (Substantial Lessening of Competition) test 47
SMEs (small and medium-sized enterprises)
protective measures towards 27–9
sales restraints restricted to 240
solvent products 50–1, 65–6, 93–4
Soviet Union 14
spare parts, trade in 43–5, 49, 78–9, 95–6, 154, 313
'arbitrary' refusal to supply 96–7
SSOs (Standard Setting Organizations) 293
licensing out 296
obligations 295
standardization agreements 298–9
sublicensing, bans on 267, 281–2
subsidiary companies 220–1
substitutability 38–40
concept of 38–9
limits 40
tests for 39–40

technological integration 129–30, 138, 141
technology/ies 46–9, 55
'essential' 300–1
defined 301*n*
limitation of development 115–17
new products 105–6 *see also* **market openings**
'non-essential' 301–2
superiority in 62, 71, 78–9, 81–2
see also **computer products**
technology market (distinguished from product market) 208, 261
technology pools 210, 291–305
administrative personnel 303–4
anti-competitive concerns 300–2
de facto industrial standards 303
individual restraints 302–3
innovative/pro-competitive benefits 292
institutional framework 303–5
legal framework 298–9
legal sources 300
'non-essential' technologies 301–2
obligations 291–2
product formulation 293–4
technology transfer 131, 202
agreement guidelines 255–7, 258, 260–1, 274–5, 276, 280, 285–7, 300, 302–5, 326
block exemption 203–4, 205–7, 209–10, 217, 218, 255–66, 300, 326
disapplication 265–6
scope 257–8
withdrawal 265–6
promotion 277
telecommunicatons 10, 123–5, 154, 191–3, 196–7
telephone installations 45
television
listings 69, 85–6, 102–7
royalty collection 158
territorial provisions 273–8
field of use restrictions 278
levels of protection 273–4
protection against manufacture 275–6
sales restrictions 276
see also **licensing agreements**
territoriality 238–40
exclusive 242–7
exemptible 274–8
restricted to SMEs 240
see also **licensing agreements**
trade, benefits of IP rules for 12–13
see also **interstate trade**
trade marks
interference with functions 24
non-equivalence to non-branded goods 163
transaction costs, reduction 140–1
turnover
categorization by 222–3
fines calculated on basis of 315–16
tying 127–42, 285–6, 311–12
and coercion 136–7
as abusive 127–8
as illegal *per se* 131
as pro-competitive 285–6
block exemptions 286
case law 130–42
'commercial usage' defence 138–40
contractual 128
defined 127–8
efficiency defence 140–1
exacerbated by rebates 181
forms of 128–30
gift of tied product 137
harmfulness threshold 136
likelihood of foreclosure 137–8
objective justification 138–41

tying (*cont.*)
relationship with IP rights 130–1, 136, 142
'separate products' test 131–5
tied component, independent manufacturers of 132
see also **mixed bundling**; **technological integration**

Ullrich, Hanns 304–5
undertakings, independent 219–21
defined 219
unfair pricing 96–7, 98
and IP rights 150–9
unilateral effects 212
United States
antitrust law 147, 147*n*, 240–1, 252, 257, 304–5
competition policy 70–1, 251, 257, 321, 324–5
Fair Trade Commission 252
IP licensing 205
patent law 6
price regulation 147, 147*n*
treatment of tying 134, 141

Vallina, Roberto 157
Venit, James S. 77*n*, 80
Vinje, Thomas 106*n*

Waelbroeck, Michael 168
Whish, Richard 179

yardstick competition 147–9, 148*n*, 157